# RESTORATIVE JUSTICE: INTERNATIONAL PERSPECTIVES

ISBN 1-881798-07-0


Distributors:
For the U.S.A. and Canada:
Criminal Justice Press
P.O. Box 249
Monsey, NY 10952, USA
Telefax (+914) 362 8376

For all other countries:
Kugler Publications bv
P.O. Box 11188
1001 GD Amsterdam, The Netherlands
Telefax (+31.20) 638 0524

# Restorative Justice: International Perspectives

edited by

*Burt Galaway and Joe Hudson*

Criminal Justice Press, Monsey, NY, U.S.A.
Kugler Publications, Amsterdam, The Netherlands

# CONTENTS

# ACKNOWLEDGEMENTS

Heartfelt thanks to the many authors who have contributed original papers to this book. The articles provide a stimulating set of ideas for consideration, debate and discussion. We extend appreciation to Rich Allison of Criminal Justice Press for his encouragement and support of this project. Thanks also to Claudette Cormier, Faculty of Social Work, University of Manitoba, who worked long and hard to put the manuscript into a form that could be submitted to the publisher. And finally, we acknowledge with great appreciation the grant from the University of Manitoba Faculty of Social Work Endowment Fund that provided the financial support for the final preparation of the manuscript.

# CONTRIBUTORS

Bazemore, Gordon. Associate Professor. Florida Atlantic University, School of Public Administration, Fort Lauderdale, Florida, U.S.A.

Estrada-Hollenbeck, Mica. Graduate Student. Department of Psychology, Harvard University, Cambridge, Massachusetts, U.S.A.

Flaten, Caren L. Disability/Mental Health Coordinator. Rural Alaska Community Action Program, Anchorage, Alaska, U.S.A.

Griffiths, Curt Taylor. Professor. School of Criminology, Simon Fraser University, Burnaby, British Columbia, Canada.

Haley, John O. Professor. School of Law, University of Washington, Seattle, Washington, U.S.A.

Hamilton, Ron. Nuuchaanulth Nation, Port Alberni, British Columbia, Canada.

Harding, John. Chief Probation Officer. Inner London Probation Service, London, England.

Harland, Alan. Graduate Program Chair. Department of Criminal Justice, Temple University, Philadelphia, Pennsylvania, U.S.A.

Immarigeon, Russ. Director. Kinship Project, State Wide Youth Advocacy, Inc., Hillsdale, New York, U.S.A.

Jervis, Bernard. Manager. Community Corrections Office, Wellington, New Zealand.

Lee, Angela. Senior Research Adviser. Ministry of Justice, Wellington, New Zealand.

Leibrich, Julie. Research Fellow. Department of Justice, Wellington, New Zealand.

Marcus, Michel. Executive Director. Forum for Urban Safety in Europe, Paris, France.

McCold, Paul. Assistant Professor. Department of Sociology and Criminal Justice, Old Dominion University, Norfolk, Virginia, U.S.A.

McElrea, Frederick W.M. District Court Judge and Youth Court Judge, Auckland District Courts. Auckland, New Zealand.

Minor, Kevin I. Associate Professor. Department of Correctional Services, Eastern Kentucky University, Richmond, Kentucky, U.S.A.

Morrison, J. T. Graduate Student. College of Law Enforcement, Eastern Kentucky University, Richmond, Kentucky, U.S.A.

Netzig, Lutz. Social Worker/Social Scientist. TOA Program of WAAGE.

Nielsen, Marianne O. Assistant Professor. Department of Criminal Justice, Northern Arizona University, Flagstaff, Arizona, U.S.A.

Pranis, Kay. Restorative Justice Planner. Minnesota Department of Corrections, St. Paul, Minnesota, U.S.A.

Pratt, John. Senior Lecturer. Institute of Criminology, Victoria University, Wellington, New Zealand.

Retzinger, Suzanne M. Family Relations Department, Superior Court, Ventura, California, U.S.A.

Rössner, Dieter. Professor. Faculty of Law, Martin Luther University, Halle, Germany.

Salem, Richard A. President, Conflict Management Initiatives, Evanston, Illinois, U.S.A.

Scheff, Thomas J. Professor Emeritus. Department of Sociology, University of California, Santa Barbara, California, U.S.A.

Stuart, Barry. Judge of the Yukon Territorial Court. Yukon Territorial Court, Whitehorse, Yukon.

Trenczek, Thomas. Jurist, Criminologist and Board Member of WAAGE.

Umbreit, Mark S. Director, Center for Restorative Justice & Mediation, School of Social Work, University of Minnesota, Minneapolis, Minnesota, U.S.A.

Van Ness, Daniel W. "Lee", Triq il-Pedidalwett, High Ridge, St. Andrews, Malta.

Wagner, Andrea. Psychologist. School of Criminology, University of Cologne, Cologne, Germany.

Walter, Michael. Professor. School of Criminology, University of Cologne, Cologne, Germany.

Wemmers, Jo-Anne M. Research Officer. WODC, Research and Documentation Centre, Ministry of Justice, The Hague, The Netherlands.

Wynne, Jean. Coordinator. Leeds Mediation and Reparation Service. West Yorkshire Probation Service, Oxford Place, Leeds, England.

Wright, Martin. Visiting Research Fellow. University of Sussex, Brighton, Sussex, England.

Yazzie, Robert. Chief Justice of the Navajo Nation, Window Rock, Arizona, U.S.A.

Zion, James W. Solicitor to the Courts of the Navajo Nation, Window Rock, Arizona, U.S.A.

# INTRODUCTION

by

## Joe Hudson

and

## Burt Galaway

This book deals with the theory, research, and practice of restorative justice in the U.S., Canada, England and Wales, Australia, New Zealand, Japan, and Germany. Chapters by John Pratt, Robert Yazzie and James W. Zion, Barry Stuart, Marianne O. Nielsen, and Curt Taylor Griffiths and Ron Hamilton present detailed descriptions of Aboriginal restorative practices. These authors show that current restorative justice approaches mirror ancient ways of settling disputes. The chapters present restorative justice practices at different points in the justice system on the basis of referrals from prosecutors, judges, and probation and parole officials. Additionally, Richard A. Salem deals with dispute settlement between staff and inmates of a correctional institution, Michael Walter and Andrea Wagner present research on police strategies including restorative approaches to manage difficult situations, and Kay Pranis describes a statewide effort to implement restorative justice practices at all points within the justice systems and in local communities.

Restorative justice is often associated with victim and offender reconciliation programs (VORPs). The origins of these programs in North America are traced by Mark S. Umbreit and by Russ Immarigeon. The first VORP was established in Kitchener, Ontario, Canada in the early 1970s. Subsequently, the first American program was established in Elkhart, Indiana. Umbreit notes that over 175 programs are currently operating in the U.S. and Canada. Most VORPs work with both property offenders and their victims, but Caren L. Flaten describes the experiences of a VORP that works with juvenile offenders who have committed serious violent offenses and their victims. Immarigeon reviews the use of victim-offender reconciliation with adult inmates who have committed serious violent offenses. VORP programs have been established in many other countries including New Zealand, Australia, England and Germany. John O. Haley describes a restorative approach that is the primary way criminal disputes are handled in Japan. Most North American victim and offender mediation or reconciliation programs are small. For example, the four Canadian programs in the Umbreit study have from one to four staff. Jo-Anne M. Wemmers describes a program in the Netherlands; Jean Wynne describes a program in Leeds, U.K.; Lutz Netzig and Thomas Trenczek, as well as Dieter Rössner, provide information on several victim-offender mediation programs in Germany. These are all modest efforts, although the German legislation appears to allow for a more widespread application and the Leeds program has expanded throughout that probation district.

Both Pratt and Frederick W.M. McElrea describe the family group conference approach that is now universal in New Zealand; this approach has similarities to victim-offender mediation, with efforts directed to resolve disputes informally in a non-professional setting involving such key participants as both offenders and victims. Suzanne M. Retzinger and Thomas J. Scheff provide an analysis of the conferencing process based on observations of replications in Australia. McElrea proposes expanding the New Zealand family group conference to deal with adult offenders through a community conference process.

## ELEMENTS OF A RESTORATIVE JUSTICE APPROACH

Three elements are fundamental to any restorative justice definition and practice. First, crime is viewed primarily as a conflict between individuals that results in injuries to victims, communities, and the offenders themselves, and only secondarily as a violation against the state. Second, the aim of the criminal justice process should be to create peace in communities by reconciling the parties and repairing the injuries caused by the dispute. Third, the criminal justice process should facilitate active participation by victims, offenders, and their communities in order to find solutions to the conflict.

High value is placed on direct involvement by the relevant parties—victims, offenders and community members. All parties have responsibilities associated with participation in the dispute settlement process. Offenders are responsible for acknowledging the wrong done, making apology, expressing remorse, and being willing to compensate or make reparation. The responsibilities of victims are to accept the expressions of remorse made by the offender and to express a willingness to forgive. Community members participate by providing necessary support and encouragement to the parties to arrive at a settlement and provide opportunities to carry out the agreement. Martin Wright notes that restorative justice is based on the key principles of reparation and mediation. Netzig and Trenczek note that both these principles are critical; historically, reparation was incorporated in a process aimed at settling the dispute and reconciling the parties. Reparation, whether in material or symbolic forms, and victim and offender involvement in settling the dispute are key elements of a restorative justice approach. This personal involvement distinguishes the restorative justice approach. Haley argues that the state and its criminal justice system cannot stand in as a fictitious surrogate for real people who have been personally afflicted by a crime. The debts offenders owe are not to an abstract entity called "the state" but to their victims and actual communities.

The notion of direct participation by victims and offenders, rather than through the state as a surrogate, has been well-developed by the proponents of restorative justice. Less well-developed, however, is the idea of how the community, or more correctly the communities of victims and the offenders, can be active participants in the process. Paul McCold notes this deficiency and attempts to develop a role for the community. The matter is also addressed, although less directly, by Michel Marcus in examining conditions for creating peaceful communities; by Stuart, in his description of the involvement of Aboriginal communities in circle sentencing; and by McElrea, in his description of family group conferences and views about extending this practice to community conferences for adults. The involvement of the communities will require that restorative justice processes be decentralized—located in the neighborhoods of the victims and offenders—and that the processes be open and public. This may run counter to notions of privacy and confidentiality, especially in juvenile proceedings.

Another aspect of community participation, and one which is only implicit in these papers, is the likely deprofessionalization of the process. Empowering communities, as well as victims and offenders, may require placing the process in the hands of non-professional community members. By their very nature, professions remove power from others and concentrate it in their own alleged area of expertise. Marcus, for example, notes the tremendous increase in minor property crimes, suggests that the professionalized criminal justice system cannot effectively deal with these offenses, and examines the appropriate role for restorative justice in dealing with these at a local neighborhood level. McElrea sees the possibility for representatives from social agencies and law enforcement to participate with community residents in dealing with offenses in a restorative justice program. The importance of local community control is emphasized by McCold, who defines a local community as a social group of any size whose members reside in a specific locality, share government, and have a common cultural and historical heritage. These local communities are responsible for acting immediately to protect victims and offenders, holding offenders accountable, and insisting on active involvement of the interested parties in the resolution process. The importance of local participation in restorative justice programs is further emphasized by Griffiths and Hamilton and by Stuart in their examinations of justice in Northern Canada.

The idea of family and community involvement may also extend to families and communities sharing responsibility for the offense and for peacemaking. Pratt notes that in traditional Maori customs, kin and clan groups took responsibility for accepting punishment and paying compensation; this notion of collective responsibility was very foreign to the individual responsibility notion of the British. McElrea notes that in the family group conferences, families and extended kin may take responsibility for the behavior of their youthful offender and that this idea might also be extended to adults where responsibility for compensation might be made by a broader group. Yazzie and Zion note that family and clan members often make payment on a relative's behalf in the peacemaking processes of the Navajo. One of Haley's illustrations from Japan has family members of the offender approach the victims to make peace. Stuart describes the circle sentencing process as addressing influences within communities that contribute to crime, as well as the specific offense and victimization that brings the circle together.

## PROCESS OF RESTORATIVE JUSTICE

The chapters describe restorative justice programs that operate in different settings and in different ways; they all agree, however, on the central role played by the mediator or facilitator. How this role is played out, particularly in terms of relations between victims and offenders, differs from one setting to another. The neutrality of the mediator is seen as important by Flaten, while Yazzie and Zion report that Navajo community peacemakers are not expected to be neutral but to offer opinions on what should be done to settle the dispute. In this, they act more as guides or teachers than neutral mediators.

Umbreit, Bernard Jervis, Netzig and Trenczek, and John Harding present the case for formal mediator training; others, such as Marcus, raise the more fundamental question of whether we want a new profession of mediators or want to retain the informal character of mediation by relying largely on community volunteers. Is there danger of a new bureaucracy arising, composed of formally trained professionals who take over the process from victims, offenders, and local community representatives? What is appropriate training if volunteers from the community are to be relied upon to serve as mediators? Wynne reports on a project in England that provided two days of formal training for volunteers, and then matched them with experienced mediators to gain experience before being given their own cases. Other jurisdictions, such as the New Zealand neighborhood described by Jervis that runs a community supervisor service, rely on trained criminal justice professionals to carry out the mediation role. Harding notes, however, that the mediator role is time-consuming and will require extra financing for probation services to do more than a very limited amount of work.

Key operations carried out in restorative justice programs can be identified in three phases—the pre-mediation phase, the mediation phase and the follow-up phase. Most programs carry out similar tasks and activities within each phase.

## Pre-Mediation Phase

The restorative justice program must have procedures established for intake, and a set of activities to be carried out in preparing for mediation. Intake activities include collecting and recording information on cases assigned or referred to the program, and making decisions about program eligibility and admission. Many programs, such as those reported by Rössner in Germany and Stuart with Aboriginal persons in North America, have intake criteria requiring the offender to have admitted guilt and agreed to participate in meetings with the victim and other interested parties. Victim willingness to participate is almost always an eligibility condition.

Several of the chapters emphasize the importance of adequate preparation for mediation. Stuart refers to the critical nature of preparation for circle sentencing, and notes that investing more time and effort in the pre-hearing work with offenders, victims, families, and support groups will lead to more successful outcomes. The research reported by Flaten shows that preparation for mediation is the most important variable for a successful mediation. Key tasks involved in preparing for mediation or conferencing are contacting the parties; securing a willingness to participate; and agreeing on the date, time, and place to hold the meeting. Retzinger and Scheff emphasize the importance of the facilitator not delegating responsibility to others to prepare for conferences. Instead, they see the importance of facilitators convening their own conferences by telephoning each participant to invite them; this is the beginning of a bond or relationship between the facilitator and participants. These authors also emphasize the importance of holding conferences as soon as possible after the offense. At the same time, they argue for maximizing the number of participants in the sessions but fail to appreciate that maximizing participation may conflict with the timeliness of the meeting.

Mediators usually have discretion to decide which parties to contact first, and they exercise this discretion depending on the circumstances of each case. Most programs emphasize voluntary participation by both victims and offenders; this is often a criteria for program admission. The job of the facilitator is to clearly communicate the purpose of the planned meeting and the process to be followed to potential participants. Some facilitators engage in several meetings with victims and offenders to assist them in preparing questions, practicing responses, and providing more detailed information about the process. Chapters by Flaten and Umbreit describe the amount of preparation time and effort given by coordinators in mediation programs.

Several chapters emphasize the importance of the location for the mediation meeting. Flaten and Wynne emphasize the importance of participants choosing the setting for the meetings, giving particular attention to an assessment of the safety for each party. Participants must see the mediation setting as being safe. Stuart believes that this means holding meetings in settings that are familiar to participants, such as schools, churches, or community centers in the local neighborhood.

While victim and offender meetings are often seen as central to a restorative justice approach, many of the chapters describe programs that involve relatively little formal contact between the parties. Rössner reports research in Germany showing that many restorative programs fail to require personal contact between victims and offenders. Jervis notes that face-to-face negotiations are bypassed in New Zealand probation services if both parties agreed on the amount of reparation and the schedule. Netzig and Trenczek report that only approximately one-third of German victim-offender mediation cases involved face-to-face meetings; the other two-thirds involved no contact between the parties except through a mediator who carried out a form of shuttle negotiation. Jervis reports on research in New Zealand showing that face-to-face meetings between victims and offenders occurred in only 4% of court cases, largely because judges and probation officers underestimated the willingness of victims to meet their offenders.

## Mediation Phase

Practices vary, but mediation sessions usually involve ceremonies, welcomes, and introductions; clarification of the process to be followed and meeting guidelines; discussion by each of the parties ending in an agreement; and closing comments. The chapters dealing with restorative justice practices among indigenous peoples emphasize the importance of beginning the mediation sessions with prayers or other cultural ceremonies. Welcoming comments are then made by the mediator, followed by participant introductions and statements about why they are participating in the meeting. The mediator explains the process to be followed and the groundrules for the meeting. Each party is provided an opportunity to participate, discuss and ask questions. In many programs, victims are offered an opportunity to explain the personal impact of the offense and share their feelings about it. Offenders explain and apologize for their behavior; other parties such as family members and friends who are also participating in the meeting have opportunities to speak, ask questions, and provide information. The focus then turns to what the offender is prepared to do to restore victim losses. Victims respond to the offenders' proposal, and agreement is usually reached on how the losses will be restored and how the other concerns expressed by victims and other parties are to be addressed.

There are two other key outcomes, which Retzinger and Scheff call symbolic reparation. The first is that the offender clearly expresses genuine shame and remorse for his or her actions. The second is that victims take at least a first step toward forgiving the offender for the incident. These two outcomes are referred to as the core sequence, are seen as generating repair and restoration of the bond between victim and offender, and serve as the key toward reconciliation. The same points are made by Julie Leibrich when reporting on the results of a study of former offenders. She notes that some kind of shame was the most important reason that ex-offenders gave for going straight. Restorative justice programs must shame offenders by having victims tell of the effects of crime on them, as well as provide offenders with a way back from the shame and into acceptance. Mica Estrada-Hollenbeck notes that both elements are critical to successful mediation, and that no additional shaming is necessary beyond that which is experienced by the offender as a result of a victim's recounting the personal impact of the crime. Several of the authors, including Stuart, Umbreit and Flaten, report that mediation sessions take from one to two hours, on average. Time must be provided for victims to receive answers from offenders about why they committed the offense and their current feelings about it, for victims to tell offenders about the effects the offense had on them, for offenders to make apologies, for victims to accept apologies and consider forgiveness, and for victims and offenders to negotiate a reparation agreement.

## Follow-up Phase and Outcomes

Relatively little attention is given in these chapters to activities that are carried out following the mediation session. This may be due to the practice in some programs of having officials located in other agencies or programs handle follow-up responsibilities, leaving the facilitator or mediator strictly responsible for preparing and holding mediation sessions. Key activities involved in follow-up are monitoring the agreement with respect to the responsibilities being carried out, intervening as necessary to address issues as they arise, and making some final decision about ending the process. Flaten reports on research showing the importance of follow-up and the relative lack of attention given to this phase of the mediation process. She notes the importance of keeping victims informed about the offender's progress.

A variety of outcomes are suggested for restorative justice programs in these chapters, including those relating to the offender, victim, community, and formal justice system. Outcomes or objectives held for offenders in mediation programs include:
   · restoring or reintegrating the offender back into the community,
   · providing offenders with an understanding of the human impact of what they have done,
   · holding offenders accountable,
   · reducing future criminal behavior,

· giving offenders a sense of having been treated fairly, and
· increasing social competence.

Victim outcomes reported in these chapters include:
  · providing an opportunity for participation in the justice process,
  · receiving answers to their questions and a better understanding of why they were chosen to be victimized,
  · restoring the emotional and material losses to victims,
  · reducing their fears, and
  · giving them a sense of having been treated fairly.
For both parties the aim is to achieve a sense of closure and improve their ability to move on with their lives.

Increased citizen participation in victim- and -offender mediation programs is seen as leading to improved citizen understanding of crime and criminal justice, and to safer communities. Stuart, for example, notes that participants in sentencing circles often address the underlying contributors to crime in their communities. Outcomes of restorative justice programs for the criminal justice system include improving or enhancing the quality of justice as perceived by crime victims, reducing caseload pressures felt by the courts, and humanizing the justice system.

Little research is reported in these chapters on the extent to which these objectives are met. Umbreit reports research showing that victims are less likely to remain upset about the crime as a result of having participated in mediation meetings, and report less fear of being re-victimized by the same offender. Wynne reports low recidivism from two follow-up studies of offenders who took part in mediation sessions; however, no comparison groups were used and the likelihood of selection bias means that the results must be viewed with some caution. In short, while restorative justice programs strive to achieve a variety of outcomes, little rigorous evidence is available to support the extent to which these are actually achieved. Kevin I. Minor and J.T. Morrison make the important point that expectations for program outcomes should be kept realistic and modest to prevent a major disappointment if they are not met.

## SIGNIFICANT ISSUES

These chapters identify a number of issues associated with restorative justice practices. Among these are the extent to which restorative justice practices can be incorporated in the formal criminal justice system; the spread of social control; the extent to which programs operate fairly; and public support for restorative justice.

Should restorative justice programs be separate from or part of the criminal justice system? The essential question is whether the key concepts of restorative justice are so incompatible with the essentially retributive nature of the criminal justice system that criminal justice organizations cannot be expected to operate in a restorative manner. Pranis, however, suggests that restorative justice practices can be introduced into criminal justice, and she is working to expand restorative justice practices within the criminal justice system in Minnesota. Walter and Wagner describe a study of how police officers manage difficult situations, noting that many of these situations—although certainly not all—are managed in a restorative manner. Both McElrea and Pratt note that the family group conference approach in New Zealand has the potential for converting the entire youth justice system to a restorative approach. Family group conferences are supported by legislation and are uniformly used across the country to respond to juvenile offenders. Jervis describes a legislative policy framework in New Zealand that shows considerable promise for a restorative justice approach to adult offenders. There is legal provision and preference for reparation, a preference for mediation that is the process to arrive at a reparation amount, and the possibility of offenders making payment in services to victims if they do not have means. Despite the statutory framework, it is clear that the provisions are getting very limited use by the courts and probation officers. Gordon Bazemore outlines a detailed set of programmatic principles for implementing a restorative justice policy. He stresses, however, that to transform an agency from either a retributive or individual treatment paradigm to one of restorative justice necessarily involves getting staff involved in the process of making the transformation as they figure out how to implement a restorative justice approach within their own setting. The support must grow throughout the organization and cannot be imposed top-down.

Minor and Morrison note that efforts to incorporate restorative justice in the formal criminal justice system has the potential for cooptation, in which the offender is seen as offending against both the victim and the state. In turn, this can lead to additional punishments. Bringing a wide variety of participants into the restorative process and opening it to public view may have the effect of recharging the emotional atmosphere originally surrounding the offense. Minor and Morrison identify three options that could be pursued. First is the option of gradually substituting restorative justice programming for traditional criminal justice practices; this trend is likely to be strongly resisted by established agencies and criminal justice professionals. Further, as Pranis notes, the great risk in pursuing this option is that the existing system, with its overwhelming orientation to offenders, will be unable to shift to a truly victim- and offender-centered approach to resolving crime. The second option, identified by Minor and Morrison, is to allow restorative and traditional criminal justice programs to coexist independently of one another. This means that decisions would have to be made about cases that are appropriate for restorative justice programs and those that are more suitable for the more traditional justice system. Wright, however, identifies a number of problems in operating two systems side by side. He suggests a solution involving distinctions between mediation and reparation. The offender would be offered opportunities to make reparation within the formal justice system. An opportunity would then be offered to both victims and offenders to participate in mediation, which would be defined as the private aspect of the offense. The third option, also raised by Minor and Morrison, is to graft restorative justice onto established agencies in the justice system. They note that this may lead to undermining restorative justice by goal displacement, another form of cooptation by the criminal justice system, and may lead to more specialized and bureaucratized forms of restorative justice.

This issue of the manner and extent to which restorative justice practices can sit within the formal justice system is particularly significant with Aboriginal programming efforts. Pratt reports that in New Zealand there have been strong calls for a separate adult justice system for Aboriginal persons. He believes that New Zealand is at a crossroads with respect to integrating restorative practices in the formal justice system with adults; Yazzie and Zion, Griffiths and Hamilton, Stuart, and Nielsen all report that similar developments are taking place with Aboriginal persons in North America. As reported by Haley and McElrea, Japan and New Zealand are probably the only countries that have given a central place to a restorative approach within the formal system of justice. New Zealand has legislated restorative justice for young offenders, and Japan has historically placed restorative approaches in a central place in the administration of justice.

Proponents of reform in the criminal justice system have been concerned about the tendency of many reforms to extend the net of social control. This occurs when an innovative program designed to serve as an alternative to other interventions receives offenders who would have been given less or no actions against them in the formal system. Programs have attempted to avoid spreading the net of social control by setting clear admission criteria, applying admission criteria consistently and monitoring their application. Restorative justice, however, may require a rethinking of this concern. For example, is the victim of a home burglary by a first-time, naive offender any less deserving of an opportunity to participate in the system than the victim of a burglary carried out by a sophisticated, repeat offender? Should the process go forward even if the first-time burglar may experience sanctions that he or she would not normally have experienced in the formal system? Expanding the system of social control to ensure that reasonable actions are taken in regard to all offenders may not be undesirable. The key questions are what is reasonable, who decides, and what is the degree of formality or informality in the process. Rather than debating widening or narrowing the network, it may be more useful to debate which offenses should be dealt with by the state through the formal system of justice, which should be dealt with more informally by community processes, and how victims and offenders can be involved in the decisions as to what are reasonable requirements.

Research on implementation of the family group conference approach in the New Zealand youth justice system found that the net had been widened in the sense that many more youngsters were receiving sanctions, but that these were sanctions determined by the youngsters, their families, and the victims rather than the courts; further, the use of both formal court processes as well as incarceration was significantly decreased (Maxwell and Morris, 1995). Is expanding social control necessarily an undesirable thing, if it is informal with key decisions being made by the participants, including families, and when there is a concomitant reduction in both the more formal processes and the use of the more severe sanctions? The matter may hinge on the extent of control exercised by the state through formal organizations, compared to more informal social control exercised by families and neighborhoods.

Wright notes that a key issue is fairness of sentencing, or the extent to which proportionate penalties are imposed on offenders who have committed similar offenses. Victims may make different demands on offenders with similar offenses, and a system of individualized justice is likely to result. McElrea, however, offers several responses to this concern. He notes that courts have an oversight role in jurisdictions where restorative justice approaches are used extensively, as in New Zealand, and can guard against possibilities of major disparities based on sex or race. Further, the current system of justice is not uniformly applied, and there is always a balance struck between uniformity and flexibility. Griffiths and Hamilton make the same point about the importance of ensuring that the rights of victims are adequately protected and appropriate sanctions imposed. They caution against particular people within communities exercising considerable power over the restorative practices and compromising the administration of justice. Netzig and Trenczek emphasize the importance of protecting victims from being misused in the role of helping offenders within a restorative justice program. They argue for national standards for programs and, along with McElrea, suggest a role for the judiciary in overseeing restorative justice programs. Wright notes that defendants might also feel induced to plead guilty and participate in a restorative justice program when they may have had a valid defense against the charges. Prosecutors may overcharge defendants and then agree to reduce charges given the defendants' willingness to admit guilt and participate in a restorative justice program. The solution that Wright proposes is to offer participation in a mediation program only after the prosecutor has made a decision to charge.

The debate about fairness and proportional sentences or requirements may illustrate a potential incompatibility between a restorative and retributive justice approach. The concept of proportionality is essentially a retributive justice notion that comes into play when the state is imposing punishment to ensure that offenders who committed like offenses are handled the same way. If one rejects the notion of state-imposed punishment, a common theme among the restorative justice writers, then the matter of proportionality and fairness is less important than reconciliation and creating peace in neighborhoods, so long as victims and offenders believe they have been handled fairly even though the requirements and responses may be very different across a group of offenders who have committed similar offenses. Fairness is not uniformity but satisfaction. Several of the authors have addressed the need for safeguards for victims, but none have addressed the need for safeguards for offenders. Historically, one of the reasons for the development of the more formal criminal justice system was to protect offenders from the unmitigated vengeance of victims and their families; and, as the system developed, to secure some reasonable balance between the penalties the state could impose and the seriousness of the offense. Advocates of restorative justice will need to give some careful attention about how to avoid vigilantism. There is no assurance that all victims and communities are interested in reconciliation and peace; some may be interested in carefully nurturing and preserving anger and hatred that can be vented by overly harsh and cruel responses to offenders.

Will the public support movement toward a system based on the philosophy of restorative justice with emphasis on reconciliation and peace making? Public support will be essential if the political will is to be developed to make this transition. Umbreit found considerable support for restorative justice among victims and offenders who had participated in Canadian programs, as did Netzig and Trenczek in their study of a program for adult offenders in Hannover, Germany. Angela Lee's review of the research, as well as data collected from focus groups in New Zealand, finds considerable public support for reparation and victim-offender mediation so long as the victim agreed to participate. Daniel W. Van Ness reviewed United Nations documents and found significant support for the concept of restorative justice, noting that this support has been emerging over the past several years. In his concluding summary chapter, Alan Harland is optimistic about the future of restorative justice, but notes that proponents must overcome two challenges if the concept is to gain the political and public support necessary to flourish. The first is to reconcile differences among the supporters, and the second is to define and clarify the most essential aims and related mechanisms.

## REFERENCES

Maxwell, G. and A. Morris. (1995). "Deciding about Justice for Young People in New Zealand: The Involvement of Families, Victims and Culture." In: J. Hudson and B. Galaway (eds.), *Child Welfare in Canada: Research and Policy Implications.* Toronto, CAN: Thompson Educational Publishing.

# PART I
# THEORY FOR RESTORATIVE JUSTICE
# PRACTICE

# 1. RESTORATIVE JUSTICE AND INTERNATIONAL HUMAN RIGHTS

by

## Daniel W. Van Ness

**Abstract:** *The past 50 years have witnessed growing international concern for human rights, reflected in the development of human rights law and in a range of international standards and norms guiding criminal justice policymakers and practitioners. These standards and norms reflect various criminal justice theories that have risen and fallen over the past half-century. Restorative justice theory offers a conceptual framework that may reconcile apparently inconsistent criminal justice norms and standards. The apparent inconsistencies may simply reflect a paradigm shift from a legalistic understanding of crime to a model that recognizes the injuries to victims and communities as well. A review of the documents included in the* <u>Compendium of United Nations Standards and Norms in Crime Prevention and Criminal Justice</u> *finds significant support for restorative justice theory. The documents indicate that: (1) states must balance the interests of victims, offenders, and the public; (2) victims and offenders must have access to formal and informal dispute resolution mechanisms; (3) crime prevention requires comprehensive action by government and the community; (4) government's role in responding to particular crimes should be to provide impartial, formal judicial mechanisms for victims and offenders; and (5) the community's role must be to help victims and offenders reintegrate.*

The past 50 years have witnessed the development of international human rights law. The fundamental human rights of individuals has been a topic of discussion since the time of the Greeks and Romans (Forsythe, 1991) and several international conventions and treaties relating to slavery, trade unions, the protection of non-combatants during war, and the rights of minorities were negotiated in the late-nineteenth and early-twentieth centuries (Rodley, 1987). Prior to World War II, however, the subject of human rights was deemed a matter of national, not international, concern. The events preceding that war and the atrocities that took place during it acted as the catalyst for the internationalization of human rights. The Preamble to the Charter of the United Nations (U.N.), adopted in 1945, expressed a commitment "to reaffirm faith in fundamental human rights, in the dignity and worth of the human person, in the equal rights of men and women and of nations large and small." This was followed a few years later by the U.N. General Assembly's adoption of the Universal Declaration of Human Rights and then by a succession of documents on human rights, notably the International Covenant on Economic, Social and Cultural Rights and the International Covenant on Civil and Political Rights and its Optional Protocols.

Portions of each of these documents address the criminal justice system directly. In addition, U.N. bodies have developed a range of standards and norms related specifically to crime prevention and criminal justice. The *Compendium of United Nations Standards and Norms in Crime Prevention and Criminal Justice* (U.N., 1992) catalogues 39 separate conventions, model treaties, declarations, guiding principles, basic principles, codes of conduct, and standard minimum rules covering the topics of international cooperation; treatment of offenders; the judiciary and law enforcement; juvenile justice; protection of victims; capital punishment, torture, and other cruel, inhuman, or degrading punishments; and suppression of prostitution. In addition, it includes nine human rights declarations, conventions and principles that address various aspects of criminal justice practice.

## AUTHORITY OF U.N. STANDARDS AND NORMS

Not all these human rights documents can be considered international law in the sense that they impose legal obligations on states or give individuals access to international tribunals for redress. Nevertheless, all have considerable moral weight and international significance because they are products of international discussion and agreement. They fall into the following general categories, only the first of which is clearly international law.

(1) Covenants, conventions, and protocols are multilateral treaties and are accepted as binding international law for those countries that enter into them. Examples include: the International Covenant on

Economic, Social and Cultural Rights; the Convention for the Suppression of the Traffic in Persons and of the Exploitation of the Prostitution of Others; and the Second Optional Protocol to the International Covenant on Civil and Political Rights aiming at the abolition of the death penalty.

(2) General Assembly resolutions are recommendations. Over time these may become part of customary international law, and many international law scholars argue that this has in fact happened with the Universal Declaration of Human Rights (Rodley, 1987). Other examples of resolutions include the Basic Principles for the Treatment of Prisoners, and the Declaration of Basic Principles of Justice for Victims of Crime and Abuse of Power.

(3) U.N. Economic and Social Council (ECOSOC) resolutions are clearly not binding international law unless incorporated into domestic law. However, these do carry moral force, and by virtue of their acceptance and approval by the U.N. have "an international significance . . . superior by far to that enjoyed by international practices and standards which have not been so endorsed" (U.N., 1970). Member states are required to report periodically to the U.N. Secretary General on their compliance. Thus, these rules have an enhanced status, and member states have a political incentive to incorporate them into domestic law. Other ECOSOC resolutions include safeguards guaranteeing protection of the rights of those facing the death penalty, and the Standard Minimum Rules for the Administration of Juvenile Justice.

(4) Declarations of U.N. Congresses on the Prevention of Crime and the Treatment of Offenders are recommendations for national action as the member-states see fit. Examples include the Caracas Declaration, the Milan Plan of Action, and Guiding Principles for Crime Prevention and Criminal Justice in the Context of Development and a New International Economic Order.

Of course, a nation that incorporates the provisions of these documents into its domestic law has given them a legal authority independent of their status as international law. Those who drafted these standards and norms wanted them to be implemented. They were not prepared as an intellectual or academic exercise, but were intended to offer direction to governments on how to administer criminal justice. In fact, several of the documents are dedicated to addressing how other previously adopted standards and norms are to be implemented. These documents are intended to guide government officials responsible for developing and implementing criminal justice.

The standards and norms reflect various criminal justice theories that have risen and fallen over the past half-century, including the fall of the rehabilitative ideal in many Western countries and its replacement by desert theory, the influence of the victim rights movement, and the rising interest in mediation and conciliation in criminal justice.

For example, both the 1957 Standard Minimum Rules for the Treatment of Prisoners and the International Covenant on Civil and Political Rights, ratified by the U.N. General Assembly in 1966, state that the purpose of imprisonment is to rehabilitate the offender. These documents were developed during a time in which support for the rehabilitative ideal was high, and before widespread disillusionment with the perceived lack of success of such programs surfaced in North America during the late 1970s. On the other hand, the Body of Principles for the Protection of All Persons under Any Form of Detention or Imprisonment, approved by the U.N. General Assembly in 1988, says nothing about rehabilitation. Moreover, the 1985 Guiding Principles for Crime Prevention and Criminal Justice in the Context of Development and a New International Economic Order speaks of the need for "equivalent penalization of economic crimes and of conventional crimes of comparable gravity," which reflects a fundamental premise of the just deserts movement (Von Hirsch, 1993).

Victims of crime were not even mentioned in these documents until 1985, when the Declaration of Basic Principles of Justice for Victims of Crime and Abuse of Power was adopted by the U.N. General Assembly. Since that time, their interests have been noted in a number of documents such as the Basic Principles for the Treatment of Prisoners and the Standard Minimum Rules for Non-custodial Measures, both adopted in 1990. References to mediation and conciliation have also emerged of late, the result of experiences in North America and Europe with victim-offender mediation programs (Galaway and Hudson, 1990). The 1985 Guiding Principles for Crime Prevention and Criminal Justice calls for both unrestricted access to the legal system and the development of "more readily accessible methods of administering justice, such as mediation, arbitration and conciliation courts" (U.N., 1992, p.19). There are references to mediation as well in the Declaration of Basic Principles of Justice for Victims of Crime and Abuse of Power and in a subsequent resolution of the Economic and Social Council on implementation of that declaration.

It is not surprising—in fact, it is appropriate—that these documents should reflect changes in criminal justice theory and practice over time. As the Caracas Declaration noted, "[c]ontinuous efforts should be made to seek new approaches and to develop better techniques for crime prevention and the treatment of offenders..." (U.N. 1992, p.7). One would expect that international standards and norms would change with those new approaches and techniques. It is also not surprising that other fundamental concepts, such as the right of offenders to humane treatment and to respect for their dignity as human beings, have remained constant during this time of new theories and approaches. But the combination of change and constancy does present a challenge to officials who attempt to apply these standards and norms in their own countries, since these documents reflect a variety of criminal justice theories.

The Declaration on Implementation of Basic Principles of Justice for Victims of Crime, for example, notes the recent introduction of informal dispute resolution methods, such as mediation and conciliation, and calls on states to ensure that the "outcome is at least as beneficial for the victims as would have been the case if the formal system had been used" (U.N. 1992, p.213). But what did the drafters mean by "beneficial"? Formal and informal processes have different advantages and disadvantages, and different outcomes as well. What does it mean to ensure that the outcome of informal mechanisms is "at least as beneficial for the victims" as the formal system would have provided?

Another example is found in the Standard Minimum Rules for Non-custodial Measures provision that selection of a non-custodial measure be based on established criteria that consider the nature and gravity of the offense (seriousness), the personality and background of the offender (dangerousness), the purposes of sentencing, and the rights of victims (U.N., 1992). What victim rights are involved that would not already be addressed by considering the seriousness of the crime, the dangerousness of the offender and the purposes of sentencing? Further, the Basic Principles of Justice for Victims of Crime and Abuse of Power provides that "the views and concerns of victims [are] to be presented and considered at appropriate stages of the proceedings where their personal interests are affected, without prejudice to the accused..." (U.N., 1992, p.212). But when exactly are their personal interests affected, and may they speak only when their views benefit or are neutral to the defendant but not if they would prejudice the defendant in any way?

Some have argued that these difficulties arise because of the lack of

theoretical consistency that one finds in a series of documents negotiated over 50 years (Ashworth, 1983). But it is also possible that there
may not be such an inconsistency, that these are simply incomplete, not
contradictory, statements. In fact–they may reflect a paradigm shift from
a legalistic understanding of crime as an offense against the state to a
model that also recognizes injuries to victims and communities. If so, the
statements form a useful backdrop against which to consider a criminal
justice theory—restorative justice—that has emerged over the last decade. Restorative justice theory may offer a conceptual framework within
which to understand the criminal justice norms and standards that
have emerged from the U.N. over the last half century.

## RESTORATIVE JUSTICE THEORY

The modern concept of crime is legalistic; crime is considered an act
or omission that has previously been declared punishable by an authoritative governmental body. The social, psychological, physical or religious
factors surrounding such acts or omissions is of interest only in preventing the commission of similar crimes in the future, or in offering an accused offender avenues of defense against criminal charges. Furthermore, administration of modern criminal justice is the exclusive
responsibility of governments. Courts are established and maintained by
the government. With limited exceptions, prosecutions are brought in
the name of the government by an agency of the government. The overwhelming majority of criminal proceedings are initiated by public prosecution, even in nations that permit private prosecutions (Joutsen,
1987).

We are so accustomed to this way of thinking about crime that we
can forget that it is not how crime has always been viewed. In fact, the
notion of crime as lawbreaking is a relatively recent one that developed
during the rise of centralized governments in Europe during the Middle
Ages (Van Ness, 1990). Although legal systems prior to that time recognized that crime harmed community peace, they viewed it as primarily
an injury to the victim and the victim's family, and restitution was a key
means of repairing that injury and restoring community peace
(Wolfgang, 1965). The idea that the king was the victim of all breaches of
his peace took hold (Keeton, 1966), as kings discovered the power of the
legal fiction of the "king's peace" as a means of usurping the jurisdiction
of the courts of local rulers and of the Roman Catholic Church. The use

of victim restitution began to decline shortly after this development, giving way to fines and forfeiture laws (Schafer, 1977). Even so, private prosecution by the victim was the dominant method of starting criminal proceedings in England and the U.S. until the latter part of the nineteenth century (Hay and Snyder, 1989). The rise of professional police forces, public prosecution and professional correctional officials during the last century secured the concept that crime is a violation of the law in both national and international law (Steinberg, 1984).

Restorative justice theory was initially articulated by practitioners of victim-offender reconciliation/mediation, who drew from their observations of victim and offender satisfaction with mediated as opposed to adjudicated justice (Zehr, 1990; Van Ness, 1993; Umbreit, 1993; Galaway and Hudson, 1990; Wright, 1991). They harkened back to the older notion of crime and argued that while crime does involve lawbreaking, it more importantly causes injuries to victims, the community, and even offenders themselves and that these injuries have been largely neglected by the criminal justice system. The foundations of restorative justice theory may be summarized in the following propositions (Van Ness, 1993, p.259):

(1) Crime is primarily conflict between individuals resulting in injuries to victims, communities and the offenders themselves; only secondarily is it lawbreaking.

(2) The overarching aim of the criminal justice process should be to reconcile parties while repairing the injuries caused by crime.

(3) The criminal justice process should facilitate active participation by victims, offenders and their communities. It should not be dominated by the government to the exclusion of others.

Victims are those who have been harmed by the offender either directly or secondarily. All victims have the need to regain control over their own lives and the need for vindication. Being victimized is an experience of powerlessness--the victim was unable to prevent the crime from occurring. As a result, victims may need help in regaining an appropriate sense of power. Being victimized is also the experience of being wronged by another, which means that victims may also need official acknowledgement of the injustice and recompense. A community is harmed as its order, its common values, and the confidence of its members in its strength and safety are challenged and eroded. Offenders experience both contributing and resulting injuries. Contributing injuries are those that existed prior to the crime and that in some way may have prompted the criminal conduct of the offender. Resulting injuries are those caused by the crime itself or by its aftermath.

The most dramatic example of restorative justice has been victim-offender reconciliation or mediation programs. Victims and offenders meet together with the assistance of a trained mediator to begin to resolve the conflict and to construct their own approach to achieving justice. These programs enable the participants to resolve the conflict on their own, unlike the formal criminal justice system, which removes both the victim and offender from proactive roles. No specific outcome is imposed by the mediator; the goals are to empower participants, promote dialogue and encourage mutual problem-solving. Sometimes the victim and offender simply design an agreement to present to a judge or other supervising authority. On other occasions, this process produces more striking results as the victim and offender reach an emotional breakthrough, and repentance and forgiveness are offered and accepted (Umbreit, 1994).

Virtually every facet of the criminal justice system works to reduce victims, offenders and communities to passive participants. Defendants have few incentives to assume responsibility for their actions, and many incentives to remain passive while the government marshals its cases and their lawyers attempt to dismantle them. Victims are not parties of interest in criminal cases, but are citizen witnesses if needed by the prosecution. Thus, they have very limited control over what occurs and no responsibility to initiate particular phases of the process. Finally, there are few opportunities for direct participation by members of the community; they may be called as witnesses by the prosecution or defense, and in common-law countries they may participate as members of a jury.

Restorative justice theory places a much higher value on direct involvement by the parties. Victims are able to restore an element of control. Offenders are encouraged to assume responsibility as an important step in repairing the harm caused by the crime and in building a prosocial value system. Active community involvement strengthens the community itself and reinforces community values of respect and compassion for others. The role of government is substantially reduced from its current monopoly of the criminal justice process. Restorative justice demands a cooperative effort by the community and the government to create an environment in which victims and offenders may reconcile their conflicts and resolve their injuries. Victims and offenders are able to do this best when the government preserves order and the community promotes peace. The word "order" is sometimes used as though it were a synonym for public safety; we speak, for example, of the need for law and order as a means of ending crime in our streets. But safety is a broader concept that requires both peace and order. Peace is a cooperative dynamic fostered from within a community. It stems from the commitment of the community to respect the rights of its members and to help them resolve conflicts, as well as the commitment of community members to respect community interests even when those conflict with their individual stakes. These commitments lead communities and their members to address underlying social, economic and moral factors that may contribute to conflict within the community. Order, on the other hand, is imposed on the community and its members by government. It establishes external limits on behavior, and enforces those limits to minimize overt conflict and to control potentially chaotic factors. Like peace, a just order is important in establishing and preserving safety, and government has both the power and mandate to create such an order.

A series of figures will illustrate some of the features of restorative justice theory. Figure 1.1 illustrates how contemporary criminal justice focuses exclusively on the offender and the government. The government seeks to establish order by enacting laws and punishing those who vio-

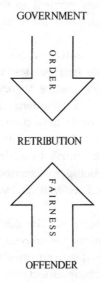

GOVERNMENT

ORDER

RETRIBUTION

FAIRNESS

OFFENDER

*Fig. 1.1.*

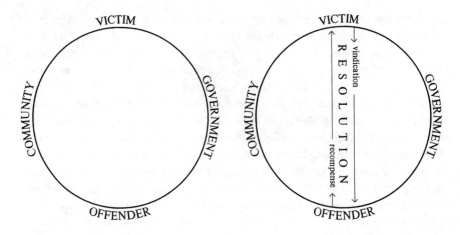

Fig. 1.2.                          Fig. 1.3.

late them. Because government's power is so great, due process safeguards have been developed over the centuries to ensure fairness in how
offenders are treated. One consequence is that the offender's posture is
defensive (and often passive), while the government plays the active role.
Criminal courts are arenas of battle in which the government is pitted
against offenders in a high-stakes contest to determine whether or not
the law has been violated, and, if so, what form of retribution should be
imposed.

Figure 1.2 illustrates how restorative justice theory returns to the ancient view that there are actually four parties: victim, offender, community and government. Restorative justice theory emphasizes that every
crime involves specific victims and offenders, and that the goal of the
criminal justice process should be to help them come to resolution (Figure 1.3). This response to crime is largely neglected by the criminal justice system and left to the civil courts to address. Resolution requires
that victims be vindicated by being exonerated from responsibility for
the injuries they have sustained as well as by receiving reparation for
those injuries.

But that is not all that is required. The offender must make recompense for there to be full resolution. Recompense and retribution are different. Retribution is defined as deserved punishment for evil done. The
definition underscores an important aspect of a society's response to offenders but it has two shortcomings. First, the active party, the pun-

isher, is the government; the offender is merely a passive recipient of punishment. Second, punishment that does not help repair the injuries caused by crime simply creates new injuries; now both the victim and the offender are injured. Recompense, on the other hand, is something given or done to make up for an injury. This underscores that the offender who caused the injury should be the active party, and that the purpose of punishment should be to repair as much as possible the injury caused by the crime.

Figure 1.3 deals with the micro response to crime. Figure 1.4 illustrates the macro response of crime prevention. It suggests the roles that restorative justice theory gives to the government and to the community in establishing safety. Safety is obtained in part through governmentally imposed order, but the community must also contribute by forming strong, stable, peaceful relationships among its members. This cooperative relationship between government and community is the basis for crime prevention. Combining Figures 1.3 and 1.4 reminds us of the need to consider both the micro and macro responses in conjunction with each other. The victim's and offender's need for resolution, and the government's and community's need for public safety, must be addressed in the same process (Figure 1.5). This dual thrust contrasts with the separation of civil and criminal law in most modern jurisdictions, a separation that can force either-or choices for victims and the government in deciding whether and how to proceed against the of-

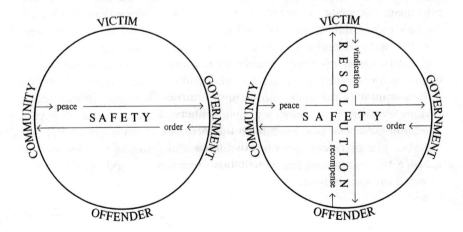

_Fig. 1.4._                          _Fig. 1.5._

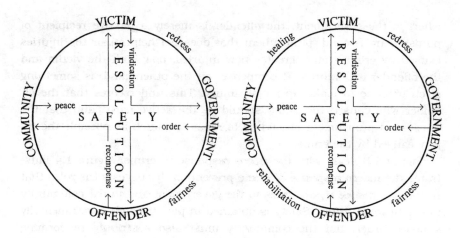

Fig. 1.6.                                      Fig. 1.7.

fender. Figure 1.6 shows the restorative justice goals that govern the relationships of government with individual victims and offenders. The government helps reestablish order by ensuring that reparation takes place. It facilitates redress to victims through restitution and compensation while ensuring that offenders are treated with fairness.

Figure 1.7 completes the circle by presenting a restorative justice perspective on the role of the community. The community seeks to restore peace between victims and offenders, and to reintegrate them fully into itself; the goals for victims can be expressed as healing and for offenders as rehabilitation. The circular construction of the figures suggest the dynamic and dependent relationships that are necessary among the parties under restorative justice theory. Peace without order is as incomplete as recompense without vindication; healing without redress is as inadequate as rehabilitation without fairness. A society cannot select certain features of the model and omit others; all are essential. That very comprehensiveness is a fundamental aspect of the paradigm shift of restorative justice theory. Restorative justice theory seeks to address and balance the rights and responsibilities of victims, offenders, communities and the government.

# RESTORATIVE JUSTICE AND INTERNATIONAL HUMAN RIGHTS

Does restorative justice theory offer a framework that could give conceptual consistency to international standards and norms in criminal justice? One might begin answering this question by reviewing U.N.-generated documents (1992) to identify underlying assumptions—either expressed or implied—concerning (a) the roles of victims, offenders, communities, and governments in the criminal justice process; (b) the strategies that should be pursued in crime prevention; and (c) the goal of the criminal justice process in resolving the conflict between the victim and the offender. This paper will consider 29 of the documents (see Appendix). The following paragraphs summarize what those documents might reveal when viewed through a restorative lens (Zehr, 1990). There is significant support for the following statements, which are certainly consistent with restorative justice theory (all citations are to U.N., 1992).

*(1) Balance: States must balance the interests of victims, offenders and the public.* Victims, offenders, the community and the state have distinct interests that must be respected (pp.112,116,119). The documents are directed to governments and emphasize the need to respect the interests of the other parties: the human rights of the offender (pp.242,250,251,268), the procedural and compensation rights of the victim (pp.211-213), and the safety interests of the community (pp.7-9,213,250-252). Several documents explicitly provide for the balance of these interests. For example, a fundamental aim of the Standard Minimum Rules for Non-custodial Measures is that governments "endeavour to ensure a proper balance between the rights of individual offenders, the rights of victims, and the concern of society for public safety and crime prevention" (p.116).

*(2) Resolution: Victims and offenders must have access to formal and informal dispute resolution mechanisms.* Formal mechanisms are the impartial judiciaries maintained by the government (pp.7,18,149–154,268-270); informal mechanisms are community-based mediation, arbitration and conciliation courts (pp.19-20,213). Victims must be able to gain access to these dispute resolution mechanisms, and they must be able to receive redress through them (pp.211-213). Further, these mechanisms should provide opportunities for offenders to pay restitution and to perform community service (pp.120,210), and they should generally eliminate any financial advantages to those who commit crimes (p.15).

*(3) Prevention: Crime prevention requires comprehensive action by government and the community.* The Caracas Declaration proclaimed that it was necessary "to review traditional crime prevention strategies based exclusively on legal criteria" (p.7). The documents reviewed suggest that the government and the community have unique roles in achieving public safety. The government provides order by: protecting its citizens (pp.45,213,243,250-252); creating orderly judicial and administrative proceedings to respond to accusations of criminal conduct (pp.7,18,149-154,213,268-270); clearly declaring what conduct is prohibited and what the penalties will be for violation of that prohibition (pp.7,19,244,251); cooperating with other states in addressing transnational crime (pp.4,21,42,240); establishing clear and equitable decision-making criteria (p.15); and providing for sectoral planning and coordination (pp.7,9,15). The community, however, must also be engaged in crime prevention, particularly in establishing social justice (pp.7-9), instilling prosocial values in its members (pp.7,37), and becoming actively involved in the criminal justice system (pp.19,124-125). Furthermore, the Universal Declaration on Human Rights notes that not only do individuals have rights *within* the community, but they have responsibilities *to* the community as well (p.244).

*(4) Law: Government's role in responding to particular crimes should be to provide impartial, formal judicial mechanisms for victims and offenders.* For victims, these mechanisms must provide: redress through restitution (pp.8,212-213); the opportunity to participate at various stages of the criminal process (p.212); specific procedural rights within that process (pp.211-212,262); and protection generally of their interests (p.213), and compensation when restitution is inadequate (pp.16,212-223). At the same time, the mechanisms must be fair to offenders by: establishing limits to the punishments they may be given (pp.242,250,260-262,268); providing orderly procedures through which guilt or innocence as well as penalties may be considered (pp.242,250-251); ensuring procedural rights during those proceedings (pp. 42-43, 81, 117-118, 122-123, 242-243, 250-251, 268-270); providing equitable treatment compared to other accused offenders (pp.15,46,95,112,117); and affording humane treatment during the offender's sentence (pp.111,250-251,268-270).

*(5) Reintegration: The community must help victims and offenders reintegrate.* Some victim injuries cannot be addressed or redressed

adequately through the criminal justice system (pp.124-125). Consequently, the community must assist victims by providing victim services (pp.27,211,212) and by offering vehicles for conciliation with the
offender (pp.19,212-213). The community also plays an important
role in the rehabilitation of the offender (pp.122-124) when it creates
an environment that will facilitate his or her reintegration when released (pp.99,100,120-122,250-251). This requires that contacts
with family, friends, and religious and assistance organizations be
maintained during incarceration (pp.99-100,269), and that education
and work opportunities be provided (pp.112,269). Conciliation with
the victim may also play an important part in the offender's rehabilitation (p.19). The significance of community participation in the
criminal justice system to assist reintegration is a fundamental reason for transferring foreign prisoners to the country of their national-
ity (pp.106,128).

## CONCLUSION AND IMPLICATIONS

Just as it is necessary to reconsider "traditional crime prevention
strategies based exclusively on legal criteria" (U.N., 1992, p.7), so it may
be necessary to reconsider criminal justice processes based exclusively
on the model of crime as an offense against government. Such a reconsideration is under way, as demonstrated in the inclusion of victims'
rights, for example, in recent criminal justice standards and norms
promulgated under the auspices of the U.N.

Restorative justice theory is an attempt to describe a criminal justice
process based on a model of crime as injury to victims, offenders and
communities. Such a model proposes particular roles for the community
and government in crime prevention and response. It also offers a
means of recognizing and balancing what may otherwise appear to be
competing interests among the victim, offender, community and government. A review of U.N. (1992) documents suggests that restorative justice theory may offer a means of synthesizing conceptually the norms
and standards that have emerged over the last half-century.

If so, future international standards and norms in criminal justice
may be expected to reflect the following 'new approaches':

(1) Current norms and standards emphasize individual rights. The
Universal Declaration of Human Rights alludes to responsibilities but
is quite vague on that topic. A restorative justice framework opens up
the possibility of considering responsibilities as well as rights.

(2) Efforts to deal with transnational crime will consider not only the need for governments to cooperate in preserving order, but how to structure offender recompense for the injuries of victims of those crimes.

(3) Discussion of regional dispute resolution mechanisms will not be limited to regional criminal courts, but will also include regional conciliation and mediation mechanisms as well.

(4) Attempts to retreat from individual human rights protection will be carefully scrutinized to ensure that they do not impede the fairness afforded offenders.

## REFERENCES

Ashworth, A. (1993). "Some Doubts About Restorative Justice." *Criminal Law Forum* 4:277-299.

Forsythe, D.P. (1991). *The Internationalization of Human Rights.* Lexington, MA: Lexington Books.

Galaway, B. and J. Hudson. (1990). *Criminal Justice, Restitution, and Reconciliation.* Monsey, NY: Criminal Justice Press.

Hay, D. and F. Snyder. (1989). "Using the Criminal Law, 1750-1850: Policing, Private Prosecution, and the State." In: D. Hay and F. Snyder (eds.), *Policing and Prosecution in Britain 1750-1850.* Oxford, UK: Clarendon Press.

Joutsen, M. (1987). "Listening to the Victim: The Victim's Role in European Criminal Justice Systems." *Wayne Law Review* 34:95-124.

Keeton, G.W. (1966). *The Norman Conquest and the Common Law.* New York, NY: Barnes & Noble.

Rodley, N. (1987). *The Treatment of Prisoners Under International Law.* Oxford, UK: Clarendon Press.

Schafer, S. (1977). *Victimology: The Victim and his Criminal.* Reston, VA: Reston Publishing.

Steinberg, A. (1984). "From Private Prosecution to Plea Bargaining: Criminal Prosecution, the District Attorney, and American Legal History." *Crime and Delinquency* 30(4):568-592.

Umbreit, M.S. (1994). *Victim Meets Offender: The Impact of Restorative Justice and Mediation.* Monsey, NY: Criminal Justice Press.

United Nations (1970). *Working Paper by the Secretariat, Fourth United Nations Congress on the Prevention of Crime and the Treatment of Offenders* (U.N. Doc. A/CONF 43/3). New York, NY: Author.

— (1992). *Compendium of United Nations Standards and Norms in Crime Prevention and Criminal Justice* (Sales No. E.92.IV.1). New York, NY: Author.

Van Ness, D.W. (1990). "Restorative Justice." In: B. Galaway and J. Hudson (eds.), *Criminal Justice, Restitution, and Reconciliation.* Monsey, NY: Criminal Justice Press.

— (1993). "New Wine in Old Wineskins: Four Challenges of Restorative Justice." *Criminal Law Forum* 4:251-276.

Von Hirsch, A. (1993). *Censure and Sanctions.* Oxford, UK: Clarendon Press.

Wolfgang, M.E. (1965). "Victim Compensation in Crimes of Personal Violence." *Minnesota Law Review* 50:223-241.

Wright, M. (1991). *Justice for Victims and Offenders.* Milton Keynes, UK: Open University Press.

Zehr, H. (1990). *Changing Lenses: A New Focus for Crime and Justice.* Scottdale, PA: Herald Press.

# Appendix: Human Rights Documents Reviewed for this Paper

The following is a list of the documents reviewed in this paper that were drawn from the 1992 *Compendium of United Nations Standards and Norms in Crime Prevention and Criminal Justice.* The level of approval each has received is noted.

## (1) Standards of General Application

- Declaration of the Fourth United Nations Congress on the Prevention of Crime and the Treatment of Offenders (endorsed by Economic and Social Council, 1971).
- Caracas Declaration (adopted by the Sixth U.N. Congress on the Prevention of Crime and the Treatment of Offenders, 1980; endorsed by the U.N. General Assembly, 1980).
- Milan Plan of Action (adopted by the Seventh U.N. Congress on the Prevention of Crime and the Treatment of Offenders, 1985; endorsed by the U.N. General Assembly, 1985).
- Guiding Principles for Crime Prevention and Criminal Justice in the Context of Development and a New International Economic Order (adopted by the Seventh U.N. Congress on the Prevention of Crime and the Treatment of Offenders, 1985; endorsed by the U.N. General Assembly, 1985).
- Recommendations on international cooperation for crime prevention and criminal justice in the context of development (adopted by the U.N. General Assembly, 1990).

## (2) International Cooperation

- Guidelines for the Prevention and Control of Organized Crime (adopted by the Eighth U.N. Congress on the Prevention of Crime and the Treatment of Offenders, 1990).
- Measures Against International Terrorism (adopted by the Eighth U.N. Congress on the Prevention of Crime and the Treatment of Offenders, 1990).

- Model Treaty on Extradition (adopted by the U.N. General Assembly, 1990).
- Model Treaty on Mutual Assistance in Criminal Matters (adopted by the U.N. General Assembly, 1990).
- Model Treaty on the Transfer of Proceedings in Criminal Matters (adopted by the U.N. General Assembly, 1990).
- Model Treaty for the Prevention of Crimes that Infringe on the Cultural Heritage of Peoples in the Form of Movable Property (recommended by the Eighth U.N. Congress on the Prevention of Crime and the Treatment of Offenders, 1990).

**(3) Treatment of Offenders**
- Standard Minimum Rules for the Treatment of Prisoners (adopted by the First U.N. Congress on the Prevention of Crime and the Treatment of Offenders, 1955; approved by the U.N. Economic and Social Council, 1957).
- Procedures for the Effective Implementation of the Standard Minimum Rules for the Treatment of Prisoners (approved by the U.N. Economic and Social Council, 1984).
- Model Agreement on the Transfer of Foreign Prisoners and Recommendations on the Treatment of Foreign Prisoners (adopted by the Seventh U.N. Congress on the Prevention of Crime and the Treatment of Offenders, 1985; welcomed by the U.N. General Assembly, 1985).
- Basic Principles for the Treatment of Prisoners (adopted by the U.N. General Assembly, 1990).
- United Nations Standard Minimum Rules for Non-Custodial Measures (the Tokyo Rules; adopted by the U.N. General Assembly, 1990).
- Model Treaty on the Transfer of Supervision of Offenders Conditionally Sentenced or Conditionally Released (adopted by the U.N. General Assembly, 1990).

**(4) Protection of Victims**
- Declaration of Basic Principles of Justice for Victims of Crime and Abuse of Power (adopted by the U.N. General Assembly, 1985).
- Implementation of the Declaration of Basic Principles of Justice for Victims of Crime and Abuse of Power (resolution of the U.N. Economic and Social Council, 1989).
- Victims of Crime and Abuse of Power (resolution of the U.N. Economic and Social Council, 1990).
- Protection of the Human Rights of Victims of Crime and Abuse of Power (resolution of the Eighth U.N. Congress on the Prevention of Crime and the Treatment of Offenders, 1995).

**(5) Human Rights**
- Universal Declaration of Human Rights (adopted and proclaimed by the U.N. General Assembly, 1948).

- International Covenant on Economic, Social and Cultural Rights (adopted and opened for signature, ratification and accession by the U.N. General Assembly, 1966; entry into force, 1976).
- International Covenant on Civil and Political Rights (adopted and opened for signature, ratification and accession by the U.N. General Assembly, 1966; entry into force, 1976).
- Optional Protocol to the International Covenant on Civil and Political Rights (adopted and opened for signature, ratification and accession by the U.N. General Assembly, 1966; entry into force, 1976).
- Second Optional Protocol to the International Covenant on Civil and Political Rights, aiming at the abolition of the death penalty (adopted and opened for signature, ratification and accession by the U.N. General Assembly, 1989).
- Convention against Torture and Other Cruel, Inhuman or Degrading Treatment or Punishment (adopted and opened for signature, ratification and accession by the U.N. General Assembly, 1984).
- Principles of Medical Ethics relevant to the Role of Health Personnel, particularly Physicians, in the Protection of Prisoners and Detainees against Torture and Other Cruel, Inhuman or Degrading Treatment or Punishment (adopted by the U.N. General Assembly, 1982).
- Body of Principles for the Protection of All Persons under Any Form of Detention or Imprisonment (approved by the U.N. General Assembly, 1988).

# 2. THREE PARADIGMS FOR JUVENILE JUSTICE

by

## Gordon Bazemore

**Abstract:** *Two limited and incomplete paradigms now define the parameters of the debate over the future of the juvenile justice system in the U.S. Neither the traditional individual treatment model nor the retributive justice model that has recently gained dominance over juvenile justice policy provides an adequate framework for preserving a distinct justice system for juveniles. A restorative paradigm offers an alternative value base, new goals and objectives, and new priorities for policy and practice. Both treatment and retributive intervention is one-dimensional and offender-driven. The restorative paradigm provides a three-dimensional focus on meeting the needs of victims, offenders, and communities and involving each in the justice process. Restorative justice will be implemented only through continual improvement of the local juvenile justice system's ability to engage all those affected by juvenile crime.*

Current juvenile justice policy discussions in the U.S. seem to contain a bit of something old, something new, something borrowed and something blue. Something old is the *parens patriae* philosophy that historically distinguished youths from adults in terms of maturity and culpability, and that authorized the state to provide treatment in the best interests of juveniles brought before the court. This treatment was to be provided according to medical model assumptions that delinquency is a symptom of underlying personal disturbance and interpersonal problems of the offender (Rothman, 1980). The medical model and the parens patriae philosophy form the core of the individual treatment paradigm.

A more criminalized or punitive juvenile court model (Feld, 1990, 1993) is something apparently new, although actually borrowed from the adult criminal justice system, the just deserts model (Von Hirsch,

1976; Schneider and Shram, 1983), and the "get-tough" ideological assault of the Reagan justice department on leniency in the juvenile court (Regnery, 1986; Manfredi and Rossum, 1989). The term "retributive justice" is used to describe a paradigm whose focal concerns include a primary emphasis on the value and priority of punishment, a lesser emphasis on rehabilitative goals, a central emphasis on desert as the primary rationale for decision making, and an expanded role for formal adversarial adjudicatory and dispositional processes (Feld, 1990; Bazemore and Umbreit, 1995; Zehr, 1990).

Something truly new and also "blue"—to use the word metaphorically to describe the horizon of juvenile justice—is the alternative paradigm that may emerge to guide the future. While this future may bring the formal abolition of the juvenile court (Feld, 1990), or simply expand the current system by leaving bad enough alone (Rosenberg, 1993), it may also offer hope for reinventing juvenile justice based on a very different vision and an alternative framework. A restorative justice paradigm could offer a new framework and provide a different lens for viewing youth crime and developing new responses to it (Zehr, 1990).

Thus far dialogue about the future of juvenile justice in the U.S. has been limited to debates about the need for more punishment, more treatment or new combinations of both. And although there has been a substantial amount of recent discussion and some new excitement about the potential of reparative programs and practices such as restitution, community service, and victim offender mediation (e.g., Schneider, 1985; Galaway and Hudson, 1990; Umbreit and Coates, 1993; Bazemore and Maloney, 1994), restorative justice has rarely been discussed in U.S. policy forums as a systemic framework for guiding juvenile justice reform (Bazemore and Washington, 1995; Pranis, 1995). This is in part because few attempts have been made to outline the components of a restorative juvenile justice paradigm as a practical alternative to both the treatment and retributive justice models. Restorative justice has been strong on vision and weak on the specifics of policy, management and implementation (Van Ness, 1993; Ashworth, 1993).

The current crisis facing U.S. juvenile justice is best understood as a conflict between two flawed and incompatible paradigms, both of which provide limited, one-dimensional responses to youth crime. This chapter will explore prospects for a restorative paradigm for the juvenile court, and consider implications for change in the juvenile justice mission.

## PARADIGMS, PARADIGM SHIFTS AND JUVENILE JUSTICE POLICY

A term stronger than "crisis" may be needed to characterize the current scene in most juvenile justice systems. In many states, these systems seem to be quickly unravelling or are being deliberately dismembered (Lemov, 1994; Juvenile Justice Update, 1995). In others, juvenile justice is under the most severe attack experienced since the founding of the juvenile court almost a century ago. Recent statutory changes in states such as Georgia, Oregon and Florida mandating fixed sentences in adult prisons for youth meeting minimum or no age requirements place further limits on the already restricted jurisdiction of the juvenile court. The most recent wave of statutory changes represent only the latest and most extreme round of assault on a court and system that has undergone more than a decade of structural, procedural, and ideological transformation (Feld, 1990, 1993; Walkover, 1984).

Some advocates of preserving the juvenile court have proposed efforts to reaffirm (McHardy, 1990) or revitalize (Krisberg and Austin, 1993) the individual treatment mission of juvenile justice. Although these arguments represent a commendable attempt to retain a rehabilitative emphasis in juvenile justice, some have suggested that this mission is no longer sufficient to sustain or regain public support (Feld, 1993; Bazemore, 1993). In fact, the speed at which states seem to be effectively dismantling their juvenile justice systems and limiting the discretion of traditional juvenile court decision makers reflects doubt about the viability of the treatment model, and suggests deep public disillusionment with the juvenile court. On the other hand, the new retributive justice approach is incompatible with the very rationale for a separate and distinct court and justice system for juveniles based on their special developmental status and a concern with rehabilitative objectives.

## Individual Treatment and Retributive Justice Paradigms

A paradigm is essentially a lens for viewing a problem and a framework for thinking about its solution (Zehr, 1990). Like any lens, a paradigm focuses our vision in a certain way while limiting or filtering out alternative viewpoints. Paradigms shape our understanding of reality and "...determine how we solve problems. They shape what we 'know' to be possible and impossible (and) form our common sense...things which fall outside the paradigm seem absurd" (Zehr, 1990, p.87). Paradigms also set priorities and provide guiding themes for justice systems. For more than a decade, the paradigms of individual treatment and retributive justice have set priorities for juvenile justice intervention and fixed the parameters of the policy debate about the juvenile court.

The juvenile court was founded as a quasi-welfare agency with a vague justice mandate; treatment was based on medical model assumptions about the causes of delinquency (Rothman, 1980; Platt, 1977). Based on these assumptions, delinquency is viewed as symptomatic of underlying disturbances, and the nature and seriousness of the offense are seen as less of an issue than providing therapeutic services aimed at correcting these presumed disturbances. The individual treatment paradigm, or what is known in Europe as the social welfare model, brought about a view of juvenile crime in which "...an offense is not taken at its face value, but as a sign of malfunctioning socialization. Intervention is trying to rectify the social deviance by a reaction suited to the personal problems and needs of the young offender" (Walgrave, 1993, p.3).

The individual treatment model has been both fairly and unfairly criticized as ineffective (Martinson, 1974; Lab and Whitehead, 1988) since coming under fire in the 1970s as part of a more general attack on rehabilitation (e.g., Martinson, 1974). It has also been depicted as stigmatizing, paternalistic, expensive, inequitable, and lacking in legal safeguards or standards for limiting duration and intensity (Lofquist, 1983; Pittman and Fleming, 1991; Walgrave, 1994). Treatment practices have changed since the 1970s, and few juvenile justice professionals today explicitly endorse the medical model (Palmer, 1992). Nonetheless, the assumption of the offender as a passive object in need of therapeutic and remedial services still dominates much of the rhetoric and day-to-day reality of juvenile justice intervention (Bazemore, 1991; Walgrave, 1994).

But while the effectiveness of the treatment paradigm in achieving rehabilitative goals is frequently questioned, other expectations have not been addressed at all. Specifically, the treatment mission fails to formally address the need to effectively sanction, or to denounce and provide meaningful consequences for, juvenile crime, and has failed to specify any role for juvenile justice in enhancing public safety. As a result, juvenile court decision makers have been ambivalent and inconsistent in carrying out the sanctioning function and responding to public safety needs (Rothman, 1980; Schneider, 1990; McAnany et al., 1984).

They have often disguised punishment as treatment (Rothman, 1980; Miller, 1991), confused sanctioning and public safety objectives, and tended to view sanctioning as an alternative to treatment rather than as a primary component of juvenile court intervention (Melton, 1989; Bazemore and Umbreit, 1995).

In the 1970s, as the *parens patriae* philosophy began to decline in influence, criticisms of treatment and widely documented inconsistencies in juvenile justice decision making brought numerous pressures on juvenile courts for reform. Application of the just deserts philosophy (von Hirsch, 1976; Schneider and Shram, 1983; Thompson and McAnany, 1984) was one attempt to bring rationality to the erratic decision making in the juvenile court, and to affirm the importance of the sanctioning function. Though intended to reduce arbitrary and excessive use of punishment, just deserts policies and practices as implemented resulted in an expansion of punishment. Adoption of mandatory and determinate sentencing guidelines, juvenile codes that deemphasized the role of rehabilitation and removed references to the needs of offenders, expanded prosecutorial powers, and, fewer restrictions on transfer to adult court (Feld, 1990) have led to increased incarceration and longer stays in residential and detention facilities, with no discernable impact on crime rates (Castellano, 1986; McAllair, 1993).

In addition, just deserts reforms sent several questionable messages to policymakers and the public. First, in giving new legitimacy to punishment for its own sake, retributive policies signaled to prosecutors and other decision makers that this was an appropriate and just response to delinquent behavior. Second, as some criminologists might have predicted (Christie, 1982; Wilkins, 1991), by equating sanctioning with punitive measures aimed solely at causing pain and discomfort to the offender, the legitimization of retributive punishment created an outcry for more severe punishments as it became apparent that existing levels were not achieving the desired effect. This helped to close off consideration of less harmful and less expensive forms of sanctioning that appeared weak and inadequate by comparison (Bazemore and Umbreit, 1995), helped to expand the use of incarceration and fueled what now appears to be an ever-increasing demand to transfer greater numbers of juveniles into the criminal justice system (Butts, 1994; Feld, 1990).

## Toward A New Paradigm

Juvenile justice professionals must respond to the conflicting demands of an increasingly dominant retributive justice paradigm and a weakened individual treatment mission. Punishment may satisfy the public need for retribution, but it may also have counter-deterrent and other negative side effects. Punishment creates problems of adjustment that encourage further delinquency (Link, 1987) by undermining self-restraint (Lepper, 1983), stigmatizing lawbreakers, weakening conventional community bonds by affecting job prospects and family relations (Sampson and Laub, 1993), and damaging conventional peer and adult relations (Zhang and Messner, 1994). Ironically, punishment may also encourage lawbreakers to focus on themselves rather than their victims, as they learn to take the punishment without taking responsibility for the offense (Wright, 1991). Increasing the severity of punishment may have little or no impact if decision makers have miscalculated the extent to which the offender experiences a sanction such as incarceration as punitive (Crouch, 1993). But it may, on the other hand, increase the probability of isolation and estrangement (Zhang and Messner, 1994) or even drive offenders to greater lengths in order to escape punishment (Wright, 1991).

Despite its inadequacy, punishment in the public mind is at least somewhat related to the offense. Treatment, on the other hand, appears to be related solely to the needs of the offender. For most citizens, juvenile justice treatment programs provide only benefits to offenders and ask for little or nothing in return. There is little in the message of the treatment response that attempts to communicate to an offender that he or she has harmed someone, should take action to repair damages or make amends, and must receive a consequence that is linked to the harm caused by the offense. Moreover, since treatment often requires little of lawbreakers beyond participating in counseling or remedial services, these interventions typically do little to reinforce conventional community values such as the work ethic.

But punishment and treatment are not the only options for juvenile justice. It is possible, for example, to envision a more empowering, effective and marketable rehabilitative agenda that is also consistent with a non-retributive approach to sanctioning (Bazemore and Maloney, 1994; Bazemore and Cruise, 1995). Such an agenda would emphasize the need for more structured pathways to community reintegration following the sanctioning process, and seek to increase acceptance of lawbreakers by improving their capacity to make meaningful contributions to the community (Braithwaite, 1994; Moore and O'Connell, 1994). Students of sanctioning have observed that there are effective ways to provide consequences for crime, and to respond to legitimate community needs in order to affirm positive values and send messages to offenders that they have harmed others and that criminal behavior is unacceptable (Braithwaite, 1989; Wilkins, 1991; Garland, 1990; Grasmick and Bursik, 1990). Expressive, non-punitive sanctions aimed at communicating value-based messages to offenders and the community should be more effective in regulating conduct. Further, such sanctions are more likely to promote community solidarity and peaceful dispute resolution than those based on vengeance and the intent to inflict pain (Griffiths and Belleau, 1993; Wilkins, 1991; Bazemore and Umbreit, 1995).

What the philosopher Thomas Kuhn called a paradigm shift occurs at a time of crisis brought on by the failure of the current paradigm to facilitate understanding of problems or provide guidance in formulating solutions and developing new options (Kuhn, 1962). Paradigm shifts inevitably bring about confusion, ambiguity, and disruption as old ways of thinking and doing business are put to the test, but the new paradigm can also unleash maximum creativity. In the early stages of a paradigm shift we are allowed to imagine dealing with problems without benefit of or hindrance from sacred institutions and commonsense philosophies. In responding to youth crime, for example, we may ask what solutions might be invented to assist youths in growing up to be law-abiding adults, to provide meaningful consequences for crime, and to help ensure public safety—if there were no probation units, no residential treatment programs, and no juvenile courts.

Reforms that move the system toward a new paradigm must address the content of intervention by providing a different understanding of youth crime and by promoting concrete alternatives to both individual treatment and retributive responses. Paradigm reform could also transform the context of intervention by changing the role of participants and potential participants in the justice process. Most justice professionals and many policymakers and citizens remain convinced that a separate and distinct juvenile justice system can more effectively respond to juvenile crime than criminal courts and adult corrections (Rosenberg, 1993; Bazemore, 1993); an encouraging sign that a new paradigm may be emerging is that many are beginning to ask new questions that challenge the content and context of both treatment and retributive intervention. Advocates of community policing have questioned whether efforts to increase arrests, enhance motorized patrol and reduce response time are effective in preventing crime (Sparrow *et al.*, 1990). In a similar vein, juvenile justice professionals and policymakers are beginning to conclude that: juvenile court sanctions send unclear or ambiguous messages to offenders; residential programs isolate offenders but do not protect the public, while community supervision strategies often provide little structure to the offender's day and do not effectively promote community safety; rehabilitation programs offer few opportunities to actively engage offenders in productive activity, and thus do not provide the linkage to community groups and institutions necessary to improve prospects for conventional adulthood; and victim and community needs are not addressed in the current juvenile justice enterprise. Support for a paradigm shift is based in part on recognition of the limits of choices offered by the retributive and treatment models, and the detachment of both from the real problems of offenders, victims, and communities (Christie, 1982).

## EXPLORING A NEW PARADIGM: RESTORATIVE JUVENILE JUSTICE

Restorative philosophy and practice is based on ancient concepts and practices (Schafer, 1970; Davis, 1992; Van Ness, 1993). The reemergence of interest grew out of several developments in the 1970s and 1980s, including the experience with reparative sanctions and processes such as restitution, victim-offender mediation (Hudson and Galaway, 1975; Schneider, 1985; Galaway and Hudson, 1990; Umbreit and Coates, 1993), the victims' movement, and the rise of interest in informal neighborhood justice and dispute resolution (Messmer and Otto, 1992). Restorative justice may also be viewed as one component of an overarching paradigm of public problem-solving and citizen participation known as communitarianism (Moore and O'Connell, 1994; Braithwaite and Pettit, 1990). A key element of this larger paradigm is an emphasis on mutual or collective responsibility for building stronger communities, which, in turn, builds upon the experience of the women's movement, of the peace and social justice movement (Pepinsky and Quinney, 1991; Harris, 1993), and of the community policing movement (Sparrow *et al.*, 1990). The restorative framework is also closely linked to emerging theoretical perspectives on the role of meaningful sanctioning, and the importance of citizen involvement in the response to crime and enforcement of community norms (Braithwaite, 1989, 1994; Wilkins, 1991; Adler, 1991).

The distinction between paradigms of justice is based primarily on answers to four general questions of content and context: What is the essence of crime, and what should be done about it? Who should the justice system serve, and how should its clients be involved in the justice process? How should the justice system address the basic needs of its clients and meet general societal expectations? What role should justice professionals play in fulfilling these functions vis à vis the roles of citizens, victims and offenders? Regarding the first question, restorative justice differs most clearly from retributive justice in its view of crime as more than simply lawbreaking or a violation of government authority. Rather, what is most significant about crime is the harm to victims and communities that is its result. A restorative justice response to crime places primary emphasis on repairing this harm and on healing the wound caused to the fabric of the community (Van Ness, 1993). Restorative justice is neither punitive nor lenient. Its objectives are reparation of harm done to victims, recognition by the offender of harm caused by the offense, and conciliation and reconciliation among victim, offender, and community.

The restorative justice focus on repairing harm and resolving conflict rather than punishing offenders has been thoroughly discussed elsewhere (Zehr, 1990; Galaway and Hudson, 1990; Wright, 1991; Davis, 1992; Van Ness, 1993). The remainder of this chapter, therefore, focuses on the additional three questions. First, while restorative justice is especially concerned with elevating the status of victims (Zehr, 1990; Umbreit, 1994), what is most unique about a restorative paradigm is its three-dimensional emphasis on victim, community and offender. It is thus important to operationalize this unique commitment to each of these clients and its implications for broadening the context of juvenile justice intervention. Second, how can a restorative paradigm carry out essential juvenile justice functions in response to basic public needs and expectations in a way that differs significantly from both the individual treatment and the retributive justice paradigms? Finally, what are the implications of restorative justice for the roles of staff and juvenile justice clients?

# THREE CUSTOMERS OF RESTORATIVE JUVENILE JUSTICE

Ultimately, as Wilkins (1991) asserts, "it is now generally accepted that the problem of crime cannot be simplified to the problem of the criminal" (p.312). Both punishment and treatment responses to crime are practically and conceptually incomplete (Byrne, 1989). Each takes a one-dimensional view of the offender and operates from a closed system logic (see also, Reiss, 1986) that limits the context of justice intervention by targeting only offenders for service and/or punishment, and that fails to include other parties in the response to crime. Victims can rarely count on reparation, assistance, or acknowledgement and typically do not participate in any meaningful way in the juvenile justice process. Community members are seldom asked for input or informed of their potentially vital role in meeting sanctioning, rehabilitation and public safety objectives. Both punishment and treatment interventions place offenders in a passive role—as the object of treatment or services on the one hand, and of punishment and surveillance on the other (Eglash, 1975). Few opportunities are provided for lawbreakers to actively make amends for their crimes or to practice productive behavior that might facilitate reconciliation, habilitation and reintegration. Neither treatment nor punishment are capable of involving and meeting the needs of offender, community, family and victim (McElrae, 1993; Walgrave, 1993). Restorative justice is based on the assumption that the response to crime cannot be effective without the joint involvement of victims, offenders and the community. It is based on the principle that justice is best served when each of these parties receive fair and balanced attention, are actively involved in the justice process and gain tangible benefits from their interactions with the juvenile justice system. Each party is viewed as a client or customer of justice intervention in a three-dimensional response to crime.

## Restoring Victims

The elevation of the victim's role in restorative justice and the focus on victim needs (Zehr, 1990; Umbreit, 1994) is based in part on a reaction to the current state of affairs, in which the quality and quantity of victim involvement is low and is driven by retributive rather than restorative priorities (Elias, 1993). The interests of prosecutors, judges, defense attorneys, and treatment program directors in winning cases, processing offenders, or securing clients generally take precedence over the needs and concerns of victims (Wright, 1991; Messmer and Otto, 1992). A restorative juvenile justice would devote attention to the needs of victims: to have their victimization acknowledged; to have their losses restored; to be allowed to participate in the justice process; and to be given a decision-making role within this process.

Two obstacles limit efforts to address the needs of victims and to involve them in a meaningful way as participants in the juvenile justice process. First, the failure to distinguish between a victim-centered and a victims' rights approach has resulted in a tendency to equate victim support with efforts to restrict offender rights. Victims' rights advocates have often pitted victim against offender and spearheaded political efforts to get tough with offenders through mandatory and determinate sentencing and other retributive policies (Fattah, 1993; McShane and Williams, 1992; Elias, 1993). Second, some juvenile justice professionals and youth advocates are philosophically opposed to the victim focus. From their perspective, youths are not accountable for their actions because they are themselves often victims of crime, including child abuse (Widom, 1991). From a restorative perspective, however, such victimization does not remove the need for offenders to be accountable to those they have harmed and to understand the consequences of their actions (Eglash, 1975). There are more practical obstacles to developing a victim focus in offender-driven juvenile justice systems, however. These include the fear and uneasiness even sympathetic staff may experience at the prospect of engaging citizens they perceive to be angry and vengeful, and the fact that responsibility for more intensive offender surveillance (Armstrong, 1991)—together with the influence of higher caseloads (Lemert, 1993)—has decreased the time community supervision staff have to attend to such responsibilities as victim notification, restitution, and victim services (Shapiro, 1990). Ultimately, in the absence of a new mission that gives priority to victims' needs and that values victim involvement, the victim as juvenile justice customer will compete unsuccessfully in agencies traditionally focused only on addressing youth and family needs.

## Restoring Offenders

The restorative justice paradigm also responds to the mutual powerlessness of victims and offenders in the current system, and under-

scores the need for communities to provide opportunities for offender repentance and forgiveness (Zehr, 1990; Van Ness, 1993). Such forgiveness would become the second step in a reintegrative shaming process
(Braithwaite, 1989). After reinforcing the offender's obligation to redress
harm to victims, and monitoring and facilitating reparation of harm,
members of the offender's community would then encourage and create
conditions to facilitate the offender's reentry into the community (Makkai
and Braithwaite, 1994; Zehr, 1990).

The new retributive juvenile justice emphasis offers little support for
this process, and one of the greatest obstacles to implementing a reintegrative response to offenders in juvenile justice systems has been the
logic of the treatment model itself. First, the singular focus on the psychological needs and social deficits of the offender limits the view of this
customer to that of object of remedial services or therapeutic intervention. In contrast, a restorative view depicts the offender as capable of actively making amends to victims and the community (Schneider, 1985).
Moreover, the three-dimensional focus of restorative justice demands
that the needs of offenders cannot be meaningfully addressed in isolation from the needs of victims and communities. Reintegrative strategies
that are insensitive to the impact of offenders on communities (Byrne,
1989), for example, ignore the obligation to the community as customer,
and thus also minimize the likelihood of offender reintegration. On the
other hand, juvenile justice budgets dominated by allocations for detention centers as the primary means of accomplishing public safety goals
restrict the amount of resources that can be devoted to meeting victim
needs or accomplishing reintegrative goals for offenders (Bazemore and
Schiff, 1995). Implicit in restorative justice philosophy is the assumption
that true rehabilitation is unlikely until the offender becomes aware of
the harm caused by his or her behavior to victims and makes an effort
to make amends (Eglash, 1975). Rehabilitation will also not occur without the active support and involvement of the community.

## Restoring Communities

Restorative justice responds to crime at the micro level by addressing
the harm that results when a specific offense is committed, through
sanctioning focused on victim reparation (Van Ness, 1993). At the macro
level, restorative justice addresses the need to build safer communities
in which most conflicts that lead to crime can be peacefully resolved

(Van Ness, 1993) and the cycle of violence broken (van Gelder, 1993). The juvenile justice system and the community should play collaborative and complementary roles in both micro and macro responses to crime, with juvenile justice and the rest of the criminal justice system assigned the responsibility for order, and the community the responsibility for restoring and maintaining peace (Van Ness, 1993; Zehr, 1990).

The retributive and treatment models have limited the scope of juvenile justice to offender-based intervention focused on marginally effective efforts to protect communities by incarcerating offenders, increasing community surveillance, or providing treatment to known offenders. Identifying the community as customer would also require that juvenile justice professionals begin to target community groups, as well as offenders and victims, for intervention and involvement in efforts to actively address community safety needs and reduce neighborhood fear. Braithwaite (1989,1994) notes the importance of active citizen participation in the social control process in low-crime societies; thus, a restorative juvenile justice would engage community groups in efforts to define and reinforce limits of tolerance against youth deviance, through shaming and reintegration processes. Citizens and community groups would be asked to play more active guardianship roles in a collaborative effort to build safer communities. Juvenile justice staff may also facilitate offender participation in community restoration by involving youths in efforts to rebuild communities, enhance community safety, or restore the environment (Bazemore and Schiff, 1995).

## SANCTIONING, PUBLIC SAFETY AND REHABILITATIVE FUNCTIONS

Traditionally, justice systems have been expected to address the need to sanction crime and offenders, enhance public safety, and rehabilitate offenders. In recent years, justice systems have also been asked, or required, to assume greater responsibility for helping to restore victim losses, although this need has received lowest priority in most justice systems (Elias, 1993; Galaway and Hudson, 1990). The promise of a restorative justice paradigm is a unique, balanced focus that addresses community expectations that juvenile justice systems attend to each of the three traditional needs, while giving new priority to restoring victims of crime. The restorative paradigm would address these needs in an integrated way that tends to merge—rather than compartmentalize—sanctioning, rehabilitative, public safety, and victim restoration interventions. It is important to identify the values underlying a restorative approach to each function and the performance objectives sought at the completion of intervention that, in turn, drive decisions about general policy and specific priorities for practice and programs. These values, outcomes, and programs most clearly differentiate a restorative response to each juvenile justice function from the response of the retributive and treatment paradigms.

## Accountability: The Sanctioning Function

A major priority of any justice system is to publicly denounce harmful behavior and to provide consequences for offenders. The treatment model does not address the sanctioning function; the retributive model gives priority to punishment through incarceration as the primary means of sanctioning offenders for violations against the state. Thus, success in juvenile court sanctioning seems to be measured by how much punishment is inflicted. The contrast among sanctioning values and assumptions, performance objectives, and priorities for practice in the restorative justice, retributive, and treatment paradigms is outlined in Table 2.1. Restorative justice values define accountability for crime as the obligation of offenders to make amends to victims rather than to receive punishment by the state. Performance objectives in restorative justice are driven by the needs of victims for material, physical, and emotional restoration and involvement, and, simultaneously, the need for offenders to understand the consequences of their actions and to actively make amends for the harm done. Sanctioning programs and practices that facilitate this restoration would be given priority over those focused on offender punishment or treatment. In addition, in contrast to the rule-driven, impersonal procedures of retributive justice focused on defining winners and losers and fixing blame (Zehr, 1990; Messmer and Otto, 1992), a restorative justice process relies heavily on informal sanctioning and resolution of underlying problems, conflict reduction through dialogue and mediation, and efforts to achieve mutually satisfactory agreements (Messmer and Otto, 1992; Bazemore and Umbreit, 1995).

Table 2.1. Sanctioning: retributive accountability, individual treatment and restorative accountability.

| | Retributive Justice | Individual Treatment | Restorative Justice |
|---|---|---|---|
| Values and Assumptions | Accountability is to the justice system and is defined as the offender taking punishment. | Sanctioning is irrelevant, incidental and generally inappropriate. Emphasis is on problems of the *offender*, not the *offense* or resulting harm. Accountability is the responsibility of the system to meet the offender's needs. | Accountability is to victims, and is defined as making amends to victims and the community. When an offense occurs, an obligation to victims incurs. Victims have the right to active involvement in the justice process. |
| Performance Objectives | Are offenders punished? Are punishments swift, certain, appropriately severe and fair? | Are youths' needs identified? Are youths referred to the appropriate treatment programs? How many complete these programs? | Are victims restored? Are victims involved? How much restitution is paid and how many community service hours are worked per amount ordered? Are victims satisfied? Are offenders made aware of harm due to their offense (and hopefully experience remorse)? How many reparative settlement agreements are negotiated and completed? How prompt is the completion of res-torative requirements? What is the *quality* of service work and of the overall process? |
| Priorities for Practice | Incarceration; electronic monitoring; required treatment; punitive fines and fees. | Programs that provide therapy and services; minimal emphasis on sanctions except to enforce treatment requirements. | Restitution; victim-offender mediation; victim-impact panels and awareness education; victim services; restorative community service; direct victim service or victim-driven service; restorative fines. |

## Restoration and Reintegration: The Rehabilitation Function

How would a restorative paradigm address offender rehabilitation? Thus far, the restorative justice literature (Galaway and Hudson, 1990; Zehr, 1990; Van Ness, 1993) has devoted primary attention to victim needs and the concern with restorative processes. Relatively little attention has been paid to offender rehabilitation. In part, this omission seems based on an attempt to circumscribe the role of the criminal justice system, minimize intrusive intervention and emphasize the primary role of developmental or socializing institutions in accomplishing habilitative/rehabilitative functions (Braithwaite, 1994; Polk, 1994). A restorative emphasis on rehabilitative and safety goals does not necessarily imply an increase in justice system control and intrusion or a denial of the role of developmental institutions. The customer focus of restorative justice is a facilitative one that seeks actively to engage communities, organizations, victims and offenders, rather than simply criminal justice agencies in meeting each justice need. Moreover, failure to explicitly address rehabilitation as part of a holistic restorative framework leaves a void that is likely to be filled by either a warmed-over medical model, or new get-tough approaches such as boot camps that attempt to merge rehabilitation with shock and punishment (Morash and Rucker, 1988; Bazemore, 1991).

The traditional individual treatment model would be replaced by a broader reintegrative agenda in a rehabilitative model influenced by restorative justice values and goals. One approach consistent with the core values of restorative justice gives priority to the goal of competency development, which requires that offenders "exit the system more capable of being productive and responsible in the community" (Maloney et al., 1988; Bazemore, 1991). Individual treatment has focused primarily on efforts to reduce or eradicate problem behaviors; a competency development approach to reintegration emphasizes the need for a broader concern with maturational development, especially by means of acquiring survival skills required for daily living. Table 2.2 compares retributive, treatment and restorative model approaches to the rehabilitative function.

Individual treatment based on medical model assumptions of offender deficit and incompetence emphasizes avoidance of negative influences, and acquisition of positive self-esteem and attitudes through participation in therapeutic and remedial services that tend to keep young

| | Individual Treatment | Retributive Justice | Restorative Justice |
|---|---|---|---|
| Values and Assumptions | Primary and initial focus on identifying deficits and developing ameliorative approaches to correct problems; delinquents defined as in need of services, assumed incompetent, disturbed, and incapable of productive, rational action without remedial therapeutic intervention; most offenders need individual treatment and benefit from therapeutic interventions. | Punishing the offender based on desert is first priority. Rehabilitative needs can be considered if they do not interfere with state's need to punish. | Primary and initial focus on identifying strengths and building on the positive; youths and families viewed as resources; youths assumed competent and having capacity for positive action; preventive and proactive; emphasis on change in community institutions and adult behavior; offenders learn best by doing; counseling and therapy needed on a limited basis as support for active engagement. |
| Performance Objectives | Do offenders avoid negative influence of designated people, places and activities? Do they follow rules of supervision (e.g., curfew, school attendance)? Do they attend and participate in treatment activities (e.g., counseling)? Have they completed all required treatment and are they terminated from supervision? Do they display improvements in attitude and self-concept? Are they psychologically adjusted? Have their family interactions improved? | No intermediate objectives for rehabilitation *per se*; reduced recidivism based on deterrence or threat of punishment. | Do youths begin new, positive relationships and positive behavior in conventional roles? Are offenders given the opportunities to practice and demonstrate competent, conventional behavior? Do youths show competency through completion of productive activities (service and/or work with community benefit? Are stigmatizing placements avoided? Is there a significant increase in measurable competencies (academic, social occupational, etc.)? Are there improvements in offender self-image and public image (community acceptance), and increased bonding? |
| Priorities for Practice | Group and family counseling; casework probation; drug therapy and drug education; recreational activities; remedial education. | None. | Work experience and employment; youths as drug educators/researchers; youths in new roles as recreational aides; youths develop cultural education projects; youths as mediators; recycling and community beautification projects; intergenerational service projects with the elderly; cross-age tutoring (juvenile offenders teach younger children); peer counseling; anger management decision-making skills training; cognitive restructuring; family living skills. |

offenders in the passive role of service recipient. In contrast, a reintegrative approach, based on competency-development assumptions that youths and their families are resources to themselves and others, seeks to actively engage youths in roles that allow them to practice being competent, gain valued skills and improve their community image. This approach measures success by increases in feelings of belongingness and usefulness, which strengthen bonds to conventional groups (Bazemore, 1991; Polk and Kobrin, 1972; Hirschi, 1969).

## Restoration and Community Protection: The Public Safety Function

Traditionally, juvenile justice professionals have been unable to articulate a clear role for the juvenile justice system in enhancing public safety. As a result, the system has often reacted to public demands for protection using the limited and expensive strategy of incarcerating individual offenders. A restorative paradigm would challenge juvenile justice managers to define community protection more holistically, just as community policing has moved from responding to crime incidents by arrests to a broader emphasis on preventative strategies. A restorative juvenile justice approach to protecting the community would thus have both an internal focus on strengthening controls in individual offenders and an external community focus. The macro focus on the community would emphasize both prevention and risk management, and would target adults and adult institutions as well as juvenile offenders for intervention (Lofquist, 1983; Pittman and Fleming, 1991). Juvenile justice staff would adopt a problem-oriented, rather than case-driven, outlook (Klein, 1988; Bazemore and Schiff, 1995) that moves beyond treatment and individual offender surveillance. Table 2.3 compares the three paradigms in their approach to the public safety function.

The individual treatment mission has not addressed public safety needs, and the emphasis on secure confinement in the retributive model confuses risk management and punishment objectives (Klein, 1993). A restorative model would give first priority to community and victim needs for safety and security, and would take whatever actions are necessary to minimize risk to citizens, including confinement of offenders who pose a threat to others. In most cases, however, safety and security will mean a focus on strengthening community supervision—and enhancing the community's role in supervision—for offenders on probation

*Table 2.3.* Public safety: individual treatment, retributive justice and restorative justice.

| | Individual Treatment | Retributive Justice | Restorative Justice |
|---|---|---|---|
| Values and Assumptions | Public safety is not part of the role of juvenile justice. | Public safety requires extensive investment in and use of locked facilities; in the community, intensive surveillance and monitoring are the best strategies to protect the public. Community-based risk management viewed as ineffective for most offenders. | Public safety is best achieved by collaborative efforts of justice systems and community groups to develop preventive capacity. Incarceration is a limited, expensive, and "last-resort" solution for most offenders; structuring the offender's time and providing a clear continuum of sanctions and incentives provide best approach. The public has a right to a safe and secure community. The community has a responsibility to actively promote healing and restoration. |
| Performance Objectives | None. | Are offenders incarcerated and detained? Is recidivism reduced through deterrence or threat of incarceration? | Is recidivism reduced—especially while offenders are under supervision in the community? Do citizens' feelings of safety and confidence in the juvenile justice system increase? Are community "guardians" created? Is preventive capacity of schools, families and community agencies improved? Is offender bonding and reintegration increased? Are community members directly involved? |
| Priorities for Practice | Residential treatment. | Extensive use of detention; incarceration; electronic monitoring and surveillance. Absence of intermediate consequences for violation of community supervision; little collaboration or effort to build community prevention; resources invested in facilities vs. community safety. | Intensive structuring of offender's time and opportunities for bonding through participation in productive activities involving conventional adults (e.g., work experiences, alternative service); clear policy options for consequences of non-compliance with supervision requirements and incentives for compliance; engage community "guardians" in the process; collaborate with community policing units; school prevention programs such as conflict resolution, mediation, and anger management; parent training and parent-child mediation; incarceration for offenders who represent risk to community safety with intensive aftercare; use of volunteer community members. |

and those exiting residential programs. A comprehensive, restorative approach to reducing the potential threat presented by offenders on community supervision would attempt to ensure that the offender's time is structured around productive activity (Maloney *et al.*, 1988). Intervention must also focus on strengthening the capacity of neighborhoods, community groups, and citizens to prevent delinquency, provide supervision and guardianship, and resolve conflict if the goal is to promote public safety and decrease feelings of fear and insecurity. Most importantly, public safety objectives in a restorative model cannot be pursued at the expense of rehabilitative and reparative sanctioning goals.

## Role of Juvenile Justice Professionals and System Customers

Current administrative protocols have evolved over time to support policies and practices consistent with either the treatment or the retributive paradigm. Juvenile justice managers wishing to implement a restorative justice model must address fundamental issues of management and organizational priorities that determine resource allocation, job descriptions, and performance measures (Umbreit and Carey, 1995; Bazemore and Washington, 1995). One of the first steps is a critical examination of traditional roles and responsibilities of staff, offender, victim and community in the justice process. The tasks of addressing sanctioning, public safety and rehabilitative goals are left to professionals in most juvenile justice systems. Neither the retributive justice framework nor the individual treatment mission has allowed policymakers to articulate meaningful, active roles for the community, victims and offenders in meeting juvenile justice needs. As Table 2.4 suggests, a restorative justice paradigm would change the context of intervention by articulating new roles for each customer/client in accomplishing sanctioning, rehabilitative and public safety functions. The new social ecology of intervention implied by a restorative approach (Bazemore and Schiff, 1995) would also require new roles for juvenile justice staff. Such new roles would move beyond the narrow focus on providing offender-directed services and surveillance to a primary emphasis on facilitating involvement of both the community and the victim.

In the sanctioning arena, for example, staff would not only monitor restitution and community service, but ensure that opportunities for earning funds and completing community service in a creative and pro-

*Table 2.4.* New roles for a restorative juvenile justice.

|  | Sanctioning through Accountability | Rehabilitation through Competency Development | Enhancing Public Safety |
|---|---|---|---|
| Offender | Actively work to restore loss to victims and community; must face victims or surrogate victims. | Actively involved as resource in service roles that improve quality of life in community, and provide new experiences, skills, and self-esteem as productive resource for positive action. | Become involved in constructive competency building and restorative activities in a balanced program; develop internal controls and new peer and organizational commitments. |
| Victim | Active involvement in all stages of the process; document psychological and emotional impact of crime; participate in mediation on a voluntary basis; help determine sanction for offender. | Provide input into the rehabilitative process; suggest community service options for offender. | Provide input regarding continuing safety concerns, fear, and needed controls on offenders; encourage protective support for other victims. |
| Community | Involved as mediators; develop community service and paid work opportunities for offenders with reparative obligations; assist victims and support offenders in completing obligations. | Develop new opportunities for youths to make productive contributions; build competency and a sense of belonging. | Provide "guardianship" of offenders, mentoring and input to juvenile justice systems regarding safety concerns; address underlying community problems that contribute to delinquency. |
| Juvenile Justice Professional | Facilitate mediation; ensure that restoration occurs (by providing ways for offenders to earn funds for restitution); develop creative/restorative community service options; engage community members in the process; educate community on its role. | Develop new roles for young offenders that allow them to practice and demonstrate competency; assess and build on youths' and community strengths; develop community partnerships. | Develop range of incentives and consequences to ensure offender compliance with supervision objectives; assist school and family in their efforts to control and maintain offenders in the community; develop prevention capacity of local organizations. |

ductive way are available. Staff would also work directly with victims to ensure that their needs are met and that they are given the opportunity to participate meaningfully in the justice process. Staff must also engage community groups, such as employers, to ensure that offenders are given opportunities for involvement in work, service and other positive roles. Finally, to enhance community safety, juvenile justice staff must collaborate with and assist other agencies and organizations as resources to aid in promoting more secure and stable neighborhoods. Juvenile justice professionals in such roles are preventive in that they attempt to change both individual and institutional conditions, such as the lack of positive roles for youths (Polk and Kobrin, 1972; Lofquist, 1983), that stifle positive youth development. Juvenile justice professionals adopting a restorative approach would attempt to strengthen the capacity of community socializing institutions—schools, places of work, civic organizations and churches—that are ultimately responsible for the conventional transition of youths into productive citizens.

## IMPLEMENTING RESTORATIVE JUSTICE

Restorative juvenile justice systems cannot be constructed overnight, and they cannot be achieved through mandates. The complexity of juvenile justice requires that reform efforts be carefully planned, deliberate, and include input from staff as well as all other stakeholders in the system and the community. Implementation should be viewed as a continuous process of strategic improvement in local juvenile justice that engages all those who are affected by juvenile crime. While the goals and values of the model are constant, there is no single *a priori* recipe for operationalizing restorative justice principles. Problems with the model will need to be resolved as they arise by communities, victims, offenders, and their families working with the juvenile justice system to develop appropriate policies based on restorative principles and values. Flaws in the model and as-yet-unanswered questions should be viewed in the context of the less-than-perfect resolution of problems of crime in the current retributive justice system.

The increased reliance on informal processes associated with restorative justice (Zehr, 1990; Umbreit, 1994), for example, seems difficult to envision in a system in which formal rules and procedures are in part intended to protect offenders from the abuses of unrestricted retribution. Proponents of restorative justice would counter that in most cases the current court process is itself often highly informal rather than adversarial (Hackler, 1991), and is based on negotiation and bargaining in the service of the retributive ends of the state (and the professional interests of attorneys) rather than the interests of fairness and due process. Several immediate concerns and cautions need to be addressed, however, by policymakers and administrators considering a restorative juvenile justice alternative.

## Cautions and Challenges to Implementation

Most juvenile justice systems, though influenced predominantly by retributive justice philosophy and the individual treatment mission, contain some elements of policy and practice that meet restorative objectives. Practices such as restitution, victim-offender mediation, and meaningful community service—as well as work experience, dispute resolution, and other practices aimed at meeting competency development and public safety goals—are the building blocks upon which further restorative practices can be developed.

Despite the strong potential of these programmatic interventions, as well as the positive public acceptance and promising evaluation findings from empirical studies of restitution and victim-offender mediation programs (Schneider, 1985, 1986; Butts and Snyder, 1991; Umbreit and Coates, 1993), there are dangers in a primary reliance on innovative programs and practices as the sole basis for reform. In recent years juvenile justice systems have been especially vulnerable to panacea solutions such as boot camps (Finckenauer, 1982), and to a program-driven approach to reform that fails to consider the fit between new programs and existing values, policies, and bureaucratic constraints of traditional justice agencies (McShane and Williams, 1992). Programmatic reform, even when based on coherent, theoretical principles, may lead to a dilution of even the most innovative practices to fit existing management protocols. Community service, for example, may quickly become marginalized or may be used as a punitive add-on rather than a primary sanction directed toward restorative ends (Bazemore and Maloney, 1994; Shapiro, 1990). Similarly, increased involvement in the justice process is of little benefit to victims if the system uses it only to aid in securing convictions or in increasing the length or severity of punishment (Elias, 1993).

An initial challenge that may limit consideration of the restorative agenda for juvenile justice is the inevitable question, does it work? Despite the remarkable lack of data on the effectiveness of current juvenile court interventions, and strong evidence of failure in some cases (Lab and Whitehead, 1988), the most frequently asked question about restorative justice is likely to be what impact the approaches can be expected to have on recidivism and other outcomes. At this stage, a more appropriate and far more important question than "does it work" is "will restorative justice be given a chance." Will it be implemented with integrity to the values and intervention goals discussed here, or repackaged to meet the objectives of retributive juvenile justice or the treatment paradigm (Van Ness, 1993)? Some of the performance objectives presented in this chapter, as well as some of the benchmarks of Zehr's (1990) restorative justice yardstick, can help to answer the question, "how will we know restorative justice when we see it?"

## Seeds of the New Paradigm

Although restorative justice as a paradigm has actually been more widely discussed in the context of the criminal justice system (Galaway and Hudson, 1990; Zehr, 1990), there is currently both a greater need and stronger prospects for implementation of the restorative model in juvenile justice. The need is a function of the current state of crisis and threat to preservation of a distinctive juvenile justice system. The stronger prospects are based on the greater precedent in the juvenile justice system for restorative practices and programs (Schneider, 1985, 1990; Umbreit and Coates, 1993), and an informal ethic generally more compatible with restorative values and process.

Much reform in juvenile justice continues to be crisis-driven and imposed on juvenile justice agencies and systems from the outside (Cohn, 1994; Schwartz et al., 1991); some juvenile justice managers, however, are joining others in state and local government who are attempting to restructure or reinvent their organizations and systems by choosing a more long-term, participatory, and broadly focused path to reform.

## CONCLUSIONS

The current dominance of the retributive model in juvenile justice, coupled with an increasingly punitive national climate, may make the vision of a restorative justice seem distant, even utopian (Walgrave, 1993).

Moreover, many problems facing juvenile justice managers today are symptoms of social-structural changes in the economy and of social policy failures (Wilson, 1987) that have produced a generation of neglected children that appears to be transforming a child welfare crisis into a juvenile justice crisis (Inciardi *et al.*, 1993). Problems such as family and neighborhood disintegration, increasing drug sales and use, and child abuse challenge these youths and their families and make crime an attractive option for many young people. The solution to these problems lies beyond the capacity of any court or justice system.

A primary distinguishing characteristic of a restorative juvenile justice is its emphasis on engaging communities in sanctioning and rehabilitation of offenders, restoring victims, and enhancing public safety. The magnitude of this challenge is exemplified by the fact that the disperse, transient and disconnected residential enclaves of the modern urban metroplex often bear little resemblance to any standard notion of community in which residents experience a sense of connectedness to others (Van Gelder, 1993). In such communities, the prospect that at-risk adolescents and young people will be able to develop bonds to conventional adults is even less likely. In Currie's (1994) view, if one were to design a prototypical criminogenic community, one could do no better than to look to current urban neighborhoods in the U.S. Such a community would:

- separate large numbers of people, especially the young, from the kind of work that could include them securely in community life;
- avoid providing new mechanisms of care and support for those uprooted, perhaps in the name of preserving incentives to work and paring government spending; and
- promote a culture of intense interpersonal competition and spur its citizens to a level of material consumption many could not lawfully sustain (Currie, 1994).

Addressing needs in such settings moves juvenile justice professionals out of the realm of criminal justice and into the arena of social justice. While restorative justice acknowledges the inevitable connection between these realms (Zehr, 1990; Pepinsky and Quinney, 1990), a restorative juvenile justice would not directly effect issues of racism, poverty, and oppression. By focusing on engaging communities in resolving the harm caused by crime and changing the lens through which crime is viewed, however, it could begin to model a collaborative process for solving these problems while engaging citizens directly in the response to youth crime and victimization. The challenge to juvenile justice professionals is to provide leadership by adopting new values and strategies that attempt to rebuild a sense of community.

What are the benefits for juvenile justice systems and state and local governments that wish to invest in the reform process implied by restorative justice? Those already involved in the process are becoming convinced that one advantage may be the preservation of the juvenile justice system itself (Bazemore, 1993). Juvenile justice agencies and systems that identify and engage their real customers in the effort to respond to youth crime—and that put forward clear, objective, performance outcomes based on offender competency, victim restoration, and public safety goals—are more likely to change their organizational image from one of tax liability to one of community asset. In the process, juvenile justice professionals may also help to empower victims, offenders and community members.

## REFERENCES

Adler, J. (1991). *The Urgings of Conscience: A Theory of Punishment.* Philadelphia, PA: Temple University Press.

Armstrong, T. (ed.) (1991). *Intensive Interventions with High-Risk Youths: Promising Approaches in Juvenile Probation and Parole.* Monsey, NY: Criminal Justice Press.

Ashworth, A. (1993). "Some Doubts About Restorative Justice." *Criminal Law Forum* 4(2):251-276.

Bazemore, G. (1991). "New Concepts and Alternative Practice in Community Supervision of Juvenile Offenders: Rediscovering Work Experience and Competency Development." *Journal of Crime and Justice* 14:27-35.

—(1993). "Abolish, Preserve or Restructure: A Case for the Balanced Approach". In: *The Juvenile Court: Dynamic, Dysfunctional or Dead?* Philadelphia, PA: Center for the Study of Youth Policy, School of Social Work, University of Pennsylvania.

—and P. Cruise (1995). "Reinventing Rehabilitation: Exploring a Competency Development Model for Juvenile Justice Intervention." *Perspectives* 19(4): forthcoming.

—and D. Maloney (1994). "Rehabilitating Community Service: Toward Restorative Service in a Balanced Justice System." *Federal Probation* 58(1):24-34.

—and M. Schiff (1995). "Community Restorative Justice: Toward a New Ecology for Community Corrections." *International Journal of Comparative & Applied Criminal Justice* (Winter):forthcoming.

—and M. Umbreit (1995). "Rethinking the Sanctioning Function in Juvenile Court: Retribution or Restorative Responses to Youth Crime." *Crime and Delinquency* 41(3):296-316.

—and C. Washington (1995). "Charting the Future of the Juvenile Justice System: Reinventing Mission and Management." *Spectrum, The Journal of State Government* 68(2):51-66.

Braithwaite, J. (1989). *Crime, Shame, and Reintegration.* New York, NY: Cambridge University Press.

—(1994). "Thinking Harder About Democratising Social Control." In: C. Alder and J. Wundersitz (eds.), *Family Conferencing and Juvenile Justice.* Canberra, AUS: Australian Institute of Criminology.

—and P. Pettit (1990). *Not Just Deserts: A Republican Theory of Criminal Justice.* Oxford, UK: Oxford University Press.

Byrne, J. M. (1989). "Reintegrating the Concept of Community into Community-Based Corrections." *Crime & Delinquency* 35(3):471-499.

Butts, J. (1994). *Offenders in Juvenile Court, 1992.* Washington, DC: Office of Juvenile Justice and Delinquency Prevention, U.S. Department of Justice.

—and H. Snyder (1991). *Restitution and Juvenile Recidivism.* Pittsburgh, PA: National Center for Juvenile Justice.

Castellano, T. (1986). "The Justice Model in the Juvenile Justice System: Washington State's Experience." *Law and Policy* 8:479-506.

Christie, N. (1982). *Limits to Pain.* Oxford, UK: Martin Robertson.

Cohn, A. (1994). "The Future of Juvenile Justice Administration: Evolution vs. Revolution." Paper presented at the 21st National Conference on Juvenile Justice, Boston, March.

Crouch, M. (1993). "Is Incarceration Really Worse? Analysis of Offenders' Preferences for Prison over Probation." *Justice Quarterly* 10:67-88.

Currie, E. (1994). *Reckoning: Drugs, the Cities, and the American Future.* New York, NY: Hill and Wang.

Davis, G. (1992). *Making Amends: Mediation and Reparation in Criminal Justice.* London, UK: Routledge.

Eglash, A. (1975). "Beyond Restitution: Creative Restitution." In: J. Hudson and B. Galaway (eds.), *Restitution in Criminal Justice.* Lexington, MA: Lexington Books.

Elias, R. (1993). *Victims Still: The Political Manipulation of Crime Victims.* Newbury Park, CA: Sage.

Fattah, E. (1993). "The New Victimology as Anti-Criminology: Some Critical Reflections on the Ideological Transformation of Victimology." Paper presented at the 11th International Congress on Criminology, Budapest, August.

Feld, B. (1990). "The Punitive Juvenile Court and the Quality of Procedural Justice: Disjunctions between Rhetoric and Reality." *Crime & Delinquency* 36:443-464.

—(1993). "The Criminal Court Alternative to Perpetuating Juvenile [In] Justice." In: *The Juvenile Court: Dynamic, Dysfunctional, Or Dead?* Philadelphia, PA: Center for the Study of Youth Policy, School of Social Work, University of Pennsylvania.

Finckenauer, J. (1982). *Scared Straight! and the Panacea Phenomena.*
Englewood Cliffs, NJ: Prentice-Hall.

Galaway, B. and J. Hudson (eds.). (1990). *Criminal Justice, Restitution, and Reconciliation.* Monsey, NY: Criminal Justice Press.

Garland, D. (1990). *Punishment and Modern Society: A Study in Social Theory.* Chicago, IL: University of Chicago Press.

Grasmick, H. and R. Bursik (1990). "Conscience, Significant Others, and Rational Choice: Extending the Deterrence Model." *Law and Society Review* 24(3):837-886.

Griffiths, C.T. and C. Belleau (1993). "Restoration, Reconciliation and Healing: The Revitalization of Culture and Tradition in Addressing Crime and Victimization in Aboriginal Communities." Paper presented at the 11th International Congress on Criminology, Budapest, August.

Hackler, J. (1991). *The Possible Overuse of Not Guilty Pleas in Juvenile Justice* (monograph). Edmonton, CAN: Centre for Criminological Research, University of Alberta.

Harris, K. (1991). "Moving into the New Millennium: A Feminist Perspective on Justice Reform." In: H. Pepinsky and R. Quinney (eds.), *Criminology as Peacemaking.* Bloomington, IN: Indiana University Press.

Hirschi, T. (1969). *The Causes of Delinquency.* Berkeley, CA: University of California Press.

Hudson, J. and B. Galaway (1975). *Restitution in Criminal Justice.* Lexington, MA: Lexington Books.

Inciardi J., R. Horowitz and A. Pottieger (1993). *Street Kids, Street Drugs, Street Crime: An Examination of Drug Use and Serious Delinquency in Miami.* Belmont, CA: Wadsworth.

Juvenile Justice Update (1995, February). Kingston, NJ: Civic Research Institute, Inc.

Klein, A. (1988). *Alternative Sentencing: A Practitioners Guide.* Cincinnati, OH: Anderson Publishing.

—(1993). Community Protection as an Intervention Paradigm in a Balanced Juvenile Justice System. Unpublished manuscript.

Krisberg, B. and J.F. Austin (1993). *Reinventing Juvenile Justice.* Newbury Park, CA: Sage.

Kuhn, T. (1962). *The Structure of Scientific Revolutions.* Chicago, IL: University of Chicago Press.

Lab, S.P. and J.T. Whitehead (1988). "An Analysis of Juvenile Correctional Treatment." *Crime and Delinquency* 34:60-83.

Lemert, E. (1993). "Visions of Social Control: Probation Considered." *Crime and Delinquency* 39(4):447-462.

Lemov, P. (1994). "The Assault on Juvenile Justice." *Governing* (Dec):26-31.

Lepper, M. (1983). "Social Control Processes, Attributions of Motivation and the Internalization of Social Values." In: E.T. Higgins, D.N. Ruble and W.W. Hartup (eds.), *Social Cognition and Social Development: A Sociocultural Perspective.* New York, NY: Cambridge University Press.

Link, B. (1987). "Understanding Labelling Effects in the Area of Mental Disorders: Assessment of the Effects of Expectations." *American Sociological Review* 47:456-478.

Lofquist, W.A. (1983). *Discovering the Meaning of Prevention: A Practical Approach to Positive Change.* Tucson, AZ: AYD Publications.

Makkai, T. and J. Braithwaite (1994). "Reintegrative Shaming and Compliance with Regulatory Standards." *Criminology* 32:361-385.

Maloney, D., D. Romig and T. Armstrong (1988). *Juvenile Probation: The Balanced Approach.* Reno, NV: National Council of Juvenile and Family Court Judges.

Manfredi, C.P. and R.A. Rossum (1989). "Historical Trends, Legislative Developments, and Professional Attitudes: Implications for Legislative Reforms and Juvenile Justice." *New Designs for Youth Development* 9:3-9.

Martinson, R. (1974). "What Works–Questions and Answers About Prison Reform." *Public Interest* 32:22-54.

McAllair, D. (1993). "Reaffirming Rehabilitation in Juvenile Justice." *Youth and Society* 25:104-125.

McAnany, P.D., D. Thompson and D. Fogel (1984). *Probation and Justice: Reconsideration of Mission.* Cambridge, MA: Oelgeschlager, Gunn & Hain.

McElrae, F.W.M. (1993). "A New Model of Justice." In: B.J. Brown (ed.), *The Youth Court in New Zealand: A New Model of Justice.* Auckland, NZ: Legal Research Foundation.

McHardy, L. (1990). "Looking at the Delinquency Problem from the Juvenile Court Bench." *International Review of Criminal Policy* 39/40:113-118.

McShane, M. and F. Williams (1992). "Radical Victimology: A Critique of the Concept of Victim in Traditional Victimology." *Crime and Delinquency* 38:258-271.

Melton, G. (1989). "Taking Gault Seriously: Toward a New Juvenile Court." *Nebraska Law Review* 68:146-181.

Messmer, H. and H. Otto (eds.). (1992). *Restorative Justice on Trial: Pitfalls and Potentials of Victim Offender Mediation.* International Research Perspectives. Norwell, MA: Kluwer Academic Publishers.

Miller, J. (1991). *Last One Over the Wall: The Massachusetts Experiment in Closing Reform Schools.* Columbus, OH: Ohio State University Press.

Moore, D. and T. O'Connell (1994). "Family Conferencing in Wagga Wagga: A Communitarian Model of Justice." In: C. Alder and J. Wundersitz (ed.), *Family Conferencing and Juvenile Justice.* Canberra, AUS: Australian Institute of Criminology.

Morash, M. and L. Rucker (1990). "A Critical Look at the Idea of Boot Camp as a Correctional Reform." *Crime and Delinquency* 36(2):204-222.

Palmer, T. (1992). *The Re-Emergence of Correctional Intervention.* Beverly Hills, CA: Sage.

Pepinsky, H.E. and R. Quinney (eds.) (1991). *Criminology as Peacemaking.* Bloomington, IN: Indiana University Press.

Pittman K. and W. Fleming (1991). "A New Vision: Promoting Youth Development." Testimony to House Select Committee on Children, Youth and Families. Washington, DC, September.

Platt, A. (1977). *The Child Savers: The Invention of Delinquency.* Chicago, IL: University of Chicago Press.

Polk, K. (1994). "Family Conferencing: Theoretical and Evaluative Questions." In: C. Alder and J. Wundersitz (eds.), *Family Conferencing and Juvenile Justice: The Way Forward or Misplaced Optimism.* Canberra, AUS: Australian Institute of Criminology.

—and S. Kobrin (1972). *Delinquency Prevention through Youth Development.* Washington, DC: Office of Youth Development.

Pranis, K. (1995). "Introduction to Restorative Justice." *Restorative Justice Newsletter* (March). St. Paul, MN: Minnesota Department of Corrections.

Regnery, A. (1985). "Getting Away with Murder: Why the Juvenile Justice System Needs an Overhaul." *Policy Review* 34:65-68.

Reiss, A. (1986). "Why are Communities Important in Understanding Crime?" In: A.J. Reiss and M. Tonry (eds.), *Communities and Crime.* Chicago, IL: University of Chicago Press.

Rosenberg, I. M. (1993). "Leaving Bad Enough Alone: A Response to Juvenile Court Abolitionists." In: *The Juvenile Court: Dynamic, Dysfunctional or Dead?* Philadelphia, PA: Center for the Study of Youth Policy, School of Social Work, University of Pennsylvania.

Rothman, D. (1980). *Conscience and Convenience: The Asylum and its Alternatives in Progressive America.* New York, NY: HarperCollins.

Sampson, R.J.and J.H. Laub (1993). *Crime in the Making: The Asylum and its Alternatives in Progressive America.* New York, NY: Harper-Collins.

Schafer, S. (1970). *Compensation and Restitution to Victims of Crime.* Montclair, NJ: Smith Patterson.

Schneider, A. (1985). *Guide to Juvenile Restitution.* Washington, DC: Office of Juvenile Justice and Delinquency Prevention, U.S. Department of Justice.

—(1986). "Restitution and Recidivism Rates of Juvenile Offendes: Results from Four Experimental Studies." *Criminology* 24(3):533-552.

—(1990). *Deterrence and Juvenile Crime: Results from a National Policy Experiment.* New York, NY: Springer-Verlag.

— and D. Schram (1983). *A Justice Philosophy for the Juvenile Court.* Seattle, WA: Urban Policy Research.

Schwartz, I., W. Barton and R. Orlando (1991). "Keeping Kids out of Secure Detention." *Public Welfare* 46(Spring):20-26.

Shapiro, C. (1990). "Is Restitution Legislation the Chameleon of the Victims' Movement?" In: B. Galaway and J. Hudson (eds.), *Criminal Justice, Restitution, and Reconciliation.* Monsey, NY: Criminal Justice Press.

Sparrow, M., M. Moore and D. Kennedy (1990). *Beyond 911: A New Era for Policing.* New York, NY: Basic Books.

Thompson, D. and P. McAnany (1984). "Punishment and Responsibility in Juvenile Court: Desert-Based Probation for Delinquents." In: P. McAnany, D. Thompson and D. Fogel (eds.), *Probation and Justice: Reconsideration of Mission.* Cambridge, MA: Oelgeschlager, Gunn & Hain.

Umbreit, M.S. (1994). *Victim Meets Offender: The Impact of Restorative Justice and Mediation.* Monsey, NY: Criminal Justice Press.

—and M. Carey (1995). "Restorative Justice: From Vision to Implementation." *Federal Probation* 59:47-54.

Umbreit, M.S. and R. Coates (1993). "Cross-Site Analysis of Victim-Offender Mediation in Four States." *Crime and Delinquency* 39:565-585.

Van Gelder, S. (1993). "The Ecology of Justice: Making Connections to Stop Crime." *In Context* 38:11-14.

Van Ness, D. (1993). "New Wine and Old Wineskins: Four Challenges of Restorative Justice." *Criminal Law Forum* 4(2):251-276.

Von Hirsch, A. (1976). *Doing Justice.* New York, NY: Hill & Wang.

Walgrave, L. (1993). "Beyond Retribution and Rehabilitation: Restoration as the Dominant Paradigm in Judicial Intervention against Juvenile Crime." Paper presented at the 11th International Congress on Criminology, Budapest, August.

—(1994). "Criminological Prevention in the City: For a Crime Prevention that is Really Criminological Prevention." Paper presented at the 49th International Conference of Criminology, Leuven, Belgium, May.

Walkover, A. (1984). "The Infancy Defense in the New Juvenile Court." *University of California at Los Angeles Law Review* 31:503-562.

Widom, C.S. (1991). "Child Victimization: Risk Factors for Delinquency." In: M.E. Colton and S. Gord (eds.), *Adolescent Stress: Causes and Consequences.* New York, NY: Aldine de Gruyter.

Wilkins, L. (1991). *Punishment, Crime and Market Forces.* Brookfield, VT: Dartmouth Publishing.

Wilson, J. (1987). *The Truly Disadvantaged.* Chicago, IL: University of Chicago Press.

Wright, M. (1991). *Justice for Victims and Offenders.* Buckingham, UK: Open University Press.

Zehr, H. (1990). *Changing Lenses: A New Focus for Crime and Justice.* Scottsdale, PA: Herald Press.

Zhang, L. and S.F. Messner (1994). "The Severity of Official Punishment for Delinquency and Change in Interpersonal Relations in Chinese Society." *Journal of Research in Crime and Delinquency* 31:416-433.

# 3. THE NEW ZEALAND YOUTH COURT: A MODEL FOR USE WITH ADULTS*

by

## Frederick W. M. McElrea

**Abstract:** *The New Zealand Youth Court is based on restorative justice principles in the sense that power is transferred from the state to the community. Family group conferences are used as a mechanism for producing a negotiated, community response; involvement of victims as key participants makes possible a healing process for both the offender and victim. The practices under the legislation reflect in part the introduction of Maori concepts into the system for responding to youthful offenders. With minor modifications, the same model can be extended to adult offenders, using the notion of community rather than family group conferences.*

The inadequacy of the usual theories of punishment, retribution, deterrence and reformation is at the heart of the present problem in criminal justice. There are a variety of views on the theory of punishment, but there is agreement that the criminal justice system is not working. Crime rates keep climbing and prison populations keep growing, at considerable expense in human and financial terms. The needs of neither offenders nor victims are satisfied. The existing theoretical bases of punishment seem bankrupt. The deterrent aspect of imprisonment is questionable, as evidenced by the failure of longer prison sentences to reduce serious crime; convictions for violent offending in New Zealand increased by 41% between 1985 and 1992, despite custodial sentences for violent crime increasing in length by 58% over the same period (New Zealand Department of Justice, 1993). Whether the courts are meting out just

---

*Earlier versions of this chapter have been published in the *Journal of Judicial Administration* (Australia) and *Public Sector*, published by the New Zealand Institute of Public Administration.

deserts satisfactorily from the public's point of view seems always to be the subject of challenge. Rehabilitation is bedeviled by lack of resources and a dearth of publicized success stories. But a much better model of justice is at hand. It is already at work in the Youth Court in New Zealand and has the potential to transform adult courts as well. The traditional objectives of sentencing are little more than attempts at rationalizing the status quo, whereas the Youth Court model requires a new way of thinking about criminal justice. Although the concept may seem new, it has its roots deep in the heritage of New Zealand.

## THE YOUTH COURT MODEL OF JUSTICE

There are three distinctive elements of the Youth Court model: transfer of power from the state to the community; family group conferences as a mechanism for producing a negotiated, community response; and involvement of victims as key participants making possible a healing process for both offender and victim. The principal structural features of the Youth Court are:

1. A division of function between the Family Court, which handles care and protection cases, and the Youth Court, which handles offending by young persons (those over age 14 but not over age 17).

2. A sharp separation between adjudication for liability and the disposition of admitted or proved offenses. The adversary system is maintained in full for the former, including the right to trial by jury of all indictable offenses, the appointment of a youth advocate in all cases, and the use of traditional rules concerning the onus and standard of proof (beyond reasonable doubt) and the admissibility of evidence.

3. For really serious offenses (purely indictable) the young person is dealt with in the adult court unless a Youth Court judge decides to allow him or her to remain in the Youth Court.

4. A diversion system operates to keep young persons away from the Youth Court. Both of the traditional means of obtaining a suspect's attendance before the court, arrest and summons, are carefully restricted. No arrest can be made unless it is necessary to prevent further offending, the absconding of the young person or interference with evidence or witnesses. Further, no summons can be issued without first referring the matter to a youth justice coordinator, who then convenes a family group conference (FGC). If the members of the FGC all agree, including the police officer present, the matter is han-

dled as decided by the FGC and will not go to court.

5. The FGC is attended by the young person, members of his or her family (in the wider sense), the victim, a youth advocate (if requested by the young person), a police officer (usually a member of the specialist Youth Aid division), a social worker (in certain cases only), and anyone else the family wishes to be there. This last category could include a representative of a community organization, *e.g.*, drug addiction agency or community work sponsor potentially helpful to the young person.

6. The youth justice coordinator (an employee of the Department of Social Welfare) arranges, attends and, in most cases, facilitates the meeting.

7. Where the young person has not been arrested, the FGC recommends whether the young person should be prosecuted, and, if not, how the matter should be dealt with, with a presumption in favor of diversion. All members of the FGC (including the young person) must agree as to the proposed diversionary program, and its implementation is essentially consensual. Where the young person has been arrested, the court must refer all matters not denied by the young person to an FGC, which recommends a disposition to the court. Occasionally, an FGC recommends a sanction to be imposed by the court. Usually it puts forward a plan of action, e.g., apology, reparation (in money or work for the victim), community work, curfew and/or undertaking to attend school, or not to associate with co-offenders. The plan is supervised by the persons nominated in the plan, with the court usually being asked to adjourn proceedings to allow the plan to be implemented.

8. The Youth Court nearly always accepts such plans, recognizing that the Children, Young Persons, and Their Families Act 1989 places the primary power of disposition with the FGC. In serious cases, however, the court can use a wide range of court-imposed sanctions, the most severe being three months' residence in a social welfare institution followed by six months' supervision. Alternatively, the court may convict and refer the young person to the District Court for sentence which can include imprisonment for up to three years.

9. Proceedings are usually withdrawn if the plan is carried out as agreed. If the plan breaks down the court can impose its own sanctions. Thus, the court acts as both a backstop (where FGC plans break down) and a filter (for patently unsatisfactory recommendations).

# Restorative Justice

There is much common ground between the New Zealand approach to youthful offenders and restorative justice. Van Ness (1989) enunciates three fundamental principles of restorative justice:

(1) Crime results in injuries to victims, communities and offenders; therefore the criminal justice process must repair those injuries.

(2) Not only the state, but also victims, offenders and communities, should be actively involved in the criminal justice system at the earliest point and to the greatest possible extent.

(3) The state is responsible for preserving order, and the community is responsible for establishing peace.

The New Zealand system is substantially a restorative model consistent with these principles. The idea of restorative justice did not originate in the writings of criminologists or of legal philosophers, nor in the many experiments in victim-offender mediation. Rather, it is to be found deeply embedded in a variety of ancient cultures. The Jubilee Policy Group of Cambridge refers to legal codes promulgated in Sumeria (2050 BC), Babylonia (1700 BC), Rome (449 BC) and Kent (the laws of Ethelbert, 600 AD) as concentrating on restitution, but not as an end in itself: "The commitment required by the criminal justice system was not only to address the wrong, but also to vindicate the victim, reconcile the parties, and re-establish community peace" (Burnside and Baker, 1992, p.10).

Zehr (1990) describes one essential theme of the Bible as *shalom*, a Hebrew word encapsulating God's vision for humankind. The term refers to a condition of "all rightness" in various dimensions. Biblical justice seeks to make things right, to restore shalom. "Offenses were understood to be wrongs against people and against shalom, and the justice process involved a process of settlement" (Zehr, 1990, p.141). Zehr contrasts the modern and biblical concepts of justice. In contrast to modern justice, biblical justice: searches for solutions; focuses on making right; aims to bring together; is based on need rather than deserts; focuses on the harm done; has a holistic context for individual responsibility; upholds the spirit of the law; and considers people, rather than the state, to be the victim.

In Canada, a submission of the Assembly of Manitoba Chiefs (1989) to a Canadian inquiry notes:

...the adversarial system is antithetical to the traditional approach of conflict resolution practised by aboriginal people. ... Aboriginal people believe that: a) victims' needs must be met to help them regain a sense of harmony and respect as a member of their families and community; b) offenders must accept responsibility for their actions not only for themselves, but for the hurt that they have brought to their families and community; c) offenders should remain in the community and take control of their own lives and that of those who have been hurt, and to assume responsibility in restoring the harmony of the community; and d) remedies for Indian offenders should include restitution and restoration with emphasis on healing and accountability, not punishment.

On one level it may seem obvious that the change from small- to large-scale communities, from rural to less personal urban environments, has worked against the retention of a more community-based system of control. However, because that change has also permitted the creation of new forms of community based on voluntary association rather than neighborhood or family, it cannot entirely account for the change. In any event, the transformation of the face of justice occurred long before modern urban society evolved. Most commentators point to the rise of the nation state; without a powerful state, justice necessarily resided with the local community. The Jubilee Policy Group (1992) suggests that the Norman invasion of England was the beginning of the change in Britain:

> William the Conqueror and his descendants had to struggle with the barons and other authorities for political power. They found the legal process a highly effective instrument in asserting their dominance over secular matters and, through their control of the courts, in increasing their political authority. To this end, William's son, Henry I, issued in 1116 the Leges Henrici, creating the idea of the 'King's Peace' and asserting royal jurisdiction over certain offenses by which it was deemed to be violated. These included arson, robbery, murder, false coinage, and crimes of violence. A violation of the King's Peace was an offence against his person, and thus the King became the primary victim in such offenses, taking the place of the victim before the law. The actual victim lost his position in the process, and the State and the offender were left as the sole concerned parties [pp.10-11].

A second consequence of the King's jurisdiction in the matter of offending was a movement away from restitution for the victim and towards fines payable to the state. Fines became a source of revenue and were consistent with the idea of paying a debt to society. This consequence reinforced the first consequence, *i.e.*, the displacement of the victim by the state as central protagonist in the dispute with the offender.

In present times, the central role of the state in modern society is being critically examined and (often) cut back. We should not assume that a restorative model is no longer possible or desirable.

## The Youth Court as a New Model of Justice

The New Zealand system of youth justice has parallels elsewhere but is quite distinctive in four respects:

1. No other system of justice replicates the FGC and its unique combination of participants.

2. Most mediation schemes involve the voluntary participation of both victim and offender.

3. The Youth Court legislation in New Zealand applies across the board, to all young persons, in all parts of the country.

4. It is the first time that a Western legal system has introduced a restorative model of justice by legislation.

But it is essentially the practice of youth justice as experienced by its practitioners that is restorative, rather than the legislation underlying that practice. The Act spells out objectives and principles to be applied in youth justice. These are partly restorative, but mostly reflect a narrower emphasis on strengthening relationships between a young person and his *whanau* (extended family), *hapu* (subtribe), and *iwi* (tribe), and enabling the family group to resolve youth offending. The partly restorative aspects of the act, however, should not be downplayed; the question of accountability is of particular interest.

The Act propounds the principle that young people committing offenses should be "held accountable, and encouraged to accept responsibility, for their behaviour" and should be "dealt with in a way that acknowledges their needs and that will give them the opportunity to develop in responsible, beneficial and socially acceptable ways." These provisions emphasize accountability and membership of a wider community; they are not soft or woolly concepts. Young people, even though they are often themselves victims, are encouraged to take responsibility for the consequences of their actions, and not to blame others or "the system". In this way they can start to take control of their own lives. The traditional court system has become too ritualized, too depersonalized, to hold offenders accountable. Pelikan (1993) has pointed out that mediation processes have an empathic and educative effect by way of an in-ner drama that has a socialising value for juveniles. In contrast, she says, the outer drama seen in the courtroom too often produces the op-posite effect, an inner withdrawal, the operation of defense mechanisms, a shunning of the deep-rooted acceptance of responsibility.

## PROSPECTS OF APPLYING THE YOUTH COURT MODEL TO ADULTS

Two of the three defining features of the Youth Court model, the transfer of power from the state to the community, and the central role of the victim in producing a healing process, are not limited in principle to young offenders. The needs of individuals and societies that a restora-tive model seeks to address are the needs of all people, not just those re-lating to young offenders. The real issue is whether and how the FGC could be adapted to adults. The starting point must be the meaning of family for young people and for adults.

### Families

The explicit objectives of the Children, Young Persons and their Fami-lies Act are very heavily family-oriented. It is natural that the emphasis should be on families when dealing with children and young persons, because families are their natural community, the source of their rela-tionships of dependence or interdependence, and the most likely basis of social control. Families in this context may have a narrow, nuclear con-notation, or an extended sense as in Polynesian culture. The control that is inherent within family relationships is based on complex needs, for acceptance, respect, love, food, shelter and warmth, companionship, role models, and the satisfaction of being a contributor. The mutuality of rights and obligations in the family context is an experienced fact and, in turn, a foundation for wider social relationships. Such notions strongly support the involvement of families in finding solutions to young people's offending. But what happens as the young person grows up, leaves home and becomes an adult?

The influence of families upon their members (and _vice versa_) does not cease at a given age. Seventeen, eighteen, and nineteen year olds, especially those who have left home, may be independent in some im-portant respects but are likely to continue to depend upon family in varying degrees to meet some of their emotional and social needs. Some family ties will change in character as young people mature. There may be less dependence or discipline, and more friendship and respect. As some family ties become less meaningful or are lost altogether, others may take their place as the individual marries, has children, gains sisters or brothers-in-law and so on. Very few people can be quite without family of any sort, and it would be wrong to shape a model of justice around those few. It follows that families are still likely to play an important role for most adults. In addition, there are other non-family-based relationships of respect, and other communities to which the offender belongs. These might be a substitute for, or a valuable supplement to, family relationships. Often there will be voluntary associations that have taken the place of family or former neighbor relationships. Needs for acceptance, self-affirmation, social involvement, friendship, fun and spiritual sustenance do not evaporate with adulthood or independence. They all require that we are in meaningful relationships with others.

## Community Group Conferences

An adult equivalent of an FGC would seek to tap the relationships of respect and influence that apply to the adult offender. Are there family members, a spouse or de facto partner, siblings, favorite cousin, even children, who are concerned for his or her well-being? Is there a cultural unit (*hapu, iwi,* or Pacific Island community) that might be prepared to support one of their own? Is there an employer, ex-employer, work mate, fellow football player, former teacher or school friend who can still provide meaning and support in a perhaps confused life? Even a non-voluntary association may be relevant. A periodic detention warden or community work supervisor who got on well with the offender in the past could be a valuable person in a time of need. The importance of an FGC is that it brings together several representatives of the community to which a young person relates so as to provide a negotiated, community response. The task with regard to adults is exactly the same: to get the relevant community to take responsibility for helping the offender to address the wrong he or she has done, to repair the damage and to affirm him or her in any remedial steps for the future. In the process the victim's needs are addressed, and the offender can be restored to a place of respect in the community.

All of the foregoing leads to the notion of a community group conference (CGC). A coordinator would invite the victim (and supporters, if desired), a police representative, family members if appropriate, and persons representing other significant relationships for the offender. Imagination and perseverance would be necessary skills in assembling a community group. If, despite skilled endeavor, no such persons can be found, there may be a place for voluntary associations (*e.g.*, a local church group, cultural association, or service organization) to fill the gap. Finally, an agency offering assistance to address a specific need (illiteracy, alcoholism, budgeting help) might appropriately be included in a CGC. If the crime has no victim, what then? This question also arises in youth justice. An FGC is still held, as it is where a victim is invited but declines to attend. Even with so-called victimless crimes, others may have been adversely affected. Therefore, there may still be the opportunity to confront the harmful nature of the offender's conduct in a personal way, and from that confrontation to build something positive in the offender's life.

An adult system following on the Youth Justice model would have diversionary mechanisms, in particular, restrictions on the arresting or summonsing of offenders, so that a CGC could consider alternatives to prosecution. If agreed by all members of the CGC (including the victim and the police), no prosecution would ensue and the matter would be dealt with as decided by the CGC. The police would need the power to arrest in some form, at least where it is necessary to prevent further offending, ensure the offender's attendance in court, or prevent interference with evidence. The police might argue for the right to arrest persistent offenders or those to be charged with serious offenses, for example, purely indictable offenses.

But it would be unwise to bypass the CGC process altogether for such offenders for two reasons. First, there is evidence that even serious offenses may be well-suited to victim-offender mediation. Thus, Marshall (1995) notes that among the various British programs for voluntary victim-offender mediation were cases of a more serious type, in particular, assaults (including sexual assaults). He continues:

> Reparation schemes in the experimental years were usually chary of accepting many such serious cases (and other agencies chary of referring them), partly because of worries that things might go wrong or get out of hand, partly because they usually need more preparation time than is available...Nevertheless, some schemes did deal with a considerable number of assaults and some very serious crimes, in-

cluding a manslaughter. Their experience with these was that, if the victim wanted to take part, they were just as likely to be successful as minor cases, and involved an even greater pay-off in terms of benefits for both victims and offenders. It was therefore recommended that each case should be considered on its merits, rather than having an arbitrary cut-off point in terms of seriousness from a legal perspective [p. 226].

Second, from the point of view of repeated offending, there may be a distinction between those who reoffend after experiencing CGCs, and those whose earlier offending was dealt with under the traditional system. There is no reason to exclude the latter from the full benefits of a new approach. Two of the studies surveyed by Marshall (1995) reported reduced offending (estimated at 10 to 20%) for adult, repeat offenders who met their victims.

For these two reasons it would be unwise to assume that serious cases or repeat offenders should be excluded from the CGC process. Where an arrest is made of a young person, the court must refer all admitted or proved offenses to an FGC. The same approach would have merit with adults. Of course, serious cases are still likely to result in a term of imprisonment, either as an agreed outcome of a CGC or because it is thought necessary by the court, but there will still be value in the CGC in terms of the restoration of the victim's rights and assistance to the court in sentencing. For the very serious offenses, such as rape, the victim may not be ready to face the offender for some time, even years, after the event. This should not be a reason to avoid a CGC. A representative of the victim would be entitled to attend on behalf of him or her and there should be an obligation on the offender to meet with the victim at some later point if and when the victim deems it appropriate.

## Accountability for Adults

One of the benefits of restorative justice is that it encourages people to accept responsibility for their behavior and its consequences for others. Is there any reason why a new Criminal Justice Act should not have as one of its guiding principles the proposition that those committing offenses should be "held accountable, and encouraged to accept responsibility, for their behavior" and to "develop in responsible, beneficial and socially acceptable ways"? There would be a greater acceptance of responsibility and fewer false denials if the offender attends a CGC. Some proponents of restorative justice criticize the adversary system for encouraging denials of responsibility: "Even if he is legally guilty, his attorney will likely tell him to plead 'not guilty' at some stage. In legal terms 'not guilty' is the way one says 'I want a trial' or 'I need more time'. All of this tends to obscure the experiential and moral reality of guilt and innocence" [Zehr, 1990, p. 67].

In the past, the law has concentrated on the dangers of convicting one innocent person and has so arranged the laws of evidence and procedure that this risk is reduced to a minimum. When a person could be hung for stealing, that sort of comment was entirely understandable, but now it is perhaps time to acknowledge each wrong trial result as an injustice. What does it do to the person who is in fact guilty to be found not guilty? And what does it do to the victim, to victim-offender and other relationships, and to the respect for justice in the community? The adversary model should not be dropped, nor the presumption of innocence abandoned, but it should not be assumed that there are no personal or social costs incurred when the guilty are declared not guilty. Society will support a system that encourages those who are guilty to admit their guilt and focus their attention on making right the wrong they have done.

The legal process too often fails to confront offenders with the reality of their offending. They do not experience the hurt and anger of the victim nor the understanding, forgiveness, and even support that can follow a genuine and personal expression of contrition. Any feelings of victimization on the offender's part are likely to be accentuated by punishment handed down in the name of a faceless state. Judges, lawyers and others in court all play their parts in a ritualized process or drama; it is hardly surprising that many defendants, their attention almost entirely on their own predicaments, shuffle through their lines with little more in mind than a desire to get off the stage as quickly as they can. A restorative model is the antithesis of this process.

## Equal Treatment

One concern expressed about the Youth Court model is that it is likely to produce different outcomes in like cases. If the essence of justice is treating like cases alike, how then can justice be done? Does too much depend on the attitude of the victim? The answer to this question has four parts. First, the Youth Court model applies the same law throughout the land. It is not a system for localized justice, despite its emphasis on the role of the community. It is important that the courts retain their overseeing role to guard against the possibility of oppressive custom or sexist or racist outcomes. Second, critical attention needs to be paid to the assumption that the existing system of justice does treat like cases alike. Sentences calculated according to two or three variables (*e.g.*, nature of the crime, seriousness of the case and previous convictions of the offender) might produce an appearance of equal treatment, but only at the expense of doing justice in individual cases. Uniformity and flexibility are competing elements of justice.

Third, the court retains the power to reject the recommendation of an FGC and impose a sentence itself. In fact, experience has shown that a high proportion of FGC plans are accepted by the courts. The residual power to reject a plan has not interfered with the reality of the transfer of responsibility to the community because judges have entered into the spirit of the Act. Nevertheless, the residual power to reject a plan, although little used, is a means of avoiding seriously disproportionate outcomes. The courts' intervention occurs much less frequently than might be expected, for a number of reasons: judges recognize that sentencing, even by courts, is not an exact science; FGC proposals are usually a very responsible and often imaginative response to the situation; the court is strongly influenced by both police and victim agreement to the plan; and youth justice coordinators can advise conferences that a particular plan is so excessively onerous or unduly lenient that it is unlikely to be accepted by the court.

Fourth, the effect on victims is, even under the old system, one of the matters taken into account, and to a certain extent offenders takes victims as they find them. Two drivers' carelessness cause accidents. One victim dies, and the other is not injured at all. One driver goes to prison and the other is fined. If this is acceptable, why should the victim's response not be a permitted consideration? A system that depersonalizes the victim's response or removes it from the equation in the name of uniformity does not produce justice for either victim or offender.

## Prospects of Acceptance by the Public

Is the concept of a CGC too novel to be accepted by a public thought to be in favor of a tougher approach taken to crime? At present the public is shown only two responses to crime, hard and soft. Deterrent and retributive approaches are associated with being hard on criminals, while reformation and rehabilitation are regarded as soft. Inevitably, if soft options do not work the call is for governments, the police and the courts to get tough on criminals. There seems to be no other course. But the Youth Court model is not soft. It is harder for an offender to confront his or her victim than to stand in court and accept punishment. FGC plans are generally quite strict, and can be enforced more readily than impersonal court orders. Acceptance is much more likely if the public can understand that there is a third option that is not soft but that uses community resources to find alternatives to purely punitive measures like imprisonment.

Is the public as vengeful as some seem to think? Those who have first-hand knowledge of victim-offender mediation report on the desire of both sides to take part in such processes, 60% of victims and nearly all offenders in the U.K. experience (Marshall, 1995), and also note the general absence of vindictiveness on the part of victims (Stewart, 1993). Nor is it new to involve the community in providing solutions. Neighborhood Watch programs and community policing are two manifestations of a clear trend in this direction. Indeed the New Zealand government has promoted a crime prevention action program, and the New Zealand Police have announced a five-year strategic plan, both of which are strongly community-based. In many ways, a CGC system would be a practical manifestation of thinking already well-developed in New Zealand.

The idea of negotiated, rather than imposed justice is also one that has parallels readily found in the 1990s. Alternative dispute resolution is a well-developed movement in New Zealand and elsewhere. Many judges are regularly raising the question of settlement of civil disputes in pretrial conferences. The Court of Appeal has encouraged parties to negotiate settlements of Treaty of Waitangi disputes. Major environmental issues are often resolved by a process of detailed negotiation among all interested parties. The high rate of agreement at FGCs is testimony to the ability of the parties to resolve most cases of youth offending. Instead of imposing a solution from the top through the power of the state, it may be better for the parties most directly affected to negotiate a solution, with the state retaining some degree of oversight.

## Likely Consequences of Applying Restorative Justice to Adults

One immediate consequence of the introduction of the new Youth Court model in New Zealand was a dramatic reduction in the number of young people appearing in court. Only 16 per 1,000 young people appeared in the Youth Court in 1990 compared with an average of 63 per 1,000 in the three calendar years immediately preceding the Act (Maxwell and Morris, 1992). Would a similar system for adults mean fewer courts and fewer prisons? The answer to this question should be yes. Criminal courts would still be needed for dealing with arrested persons, trying defended cases and overseeing the sentencing process of CGCs, but both the number of cases in court and the proportion of those where the court would be required to impose sentence would be likely to drop substantially. The proportion of custodial sentences is also likely to drop sharply, if the Youth Court experience is relevant. FGCs strive to find a community-based solution, and often produce a more imaginative and suitable plan than the courts could achieve. The knowledge that the victim has agreed to that plan has a palpable effect on the judge where an FGC has recommended something other than prison. Gone is the assumption that the state represents the victim in seeking a punitive sanction.

And what of the effect on the crime rate? Any answer would be very speculative, but, once again, the Youth Court experience may be relevant. There is no evidence of any overall increase in youth offending, despite the increase in adult offending over the same period. Robertson (1993) has shown that cleared offenses attributed to young people were stable or decreased throughout the period 1981-1991, while adult offending increased. But over the period 1990-1992, when police numbers were increasing, there was a slight increase in the rate of youth offending as measured by cleared offenses. The New Zealand Department of Justice (1994) released statistics showing that the number of prosecuted cases for defendants aged 17, 18 and 19 dropped by 27% over the five years from 1987 to 1992. This would tend to suggest that the new Youth Court is producing young adults less likely to be prosecuted in the adult courts. The meaning of the 1994 figures, however, is currently under debate. It would be a mistake to seek to justify a restorative justice system solely by prosecution or cleared offense statistics. It cannot be a cure for crime, which is part of our human predicament. There are other benefits, for victims and others involved, that cannot be measured in a statistical way.

The chief danger is that restorative justice will be seen as a means of saving expenditure on courts and prisons and will be adopted for fiscal reasons, without the recognition that the community requires financial resources if it is to take on this new role. Community groups serving youth are not receiving the funding that they deserve. It would be better not to make any change at all than to do so without proper funding. Otherwise, the obvious short-term savings will be taken (*e.g.*, by closing prisons), the community will be left struggling and unable to cope with the extra load, and when the system is seen to be foundering it will be discarded as unworkable. Other theories of punishment have had their turn, with substantial resources invested in their prescribed remedies. Restorative justice for adults should not be introduced unless there is the political will and the financial commitment to give it a serious trial. If implemented in a serious way, restorative justice has the potential to produce a system of criminal justice that the community would be proud to own.

## REFERENCES

Assembly of Manitoba Chiefs (1989). *Final Report to the Aboriginal Justice Inquiry.* Winnipeg, CAN: Author.

Burnside, J. and N. Baker (eds.) (1994). *Relational Justice: Repairing the Breach.* Winchester, UK: Waterside Press.

Jubilee Policy Group (1992). *Relational Justice: A New Approach to Penal Reform.* Cambridge, UK.

Marshall, T.F. (1995). "Restorative Justice on Trial in Britain." *Mediation Quarterly* 12(3):217-232.

Maxwell, G.M. and A. Morris (1992). "Youth Justice in New Zealand: A New Paradigm for Making Decisions about Children and Young People who Commit Offenses." *Commonwealth Judicial Journal* 9(4):24.

New Zealand Department of Justice. (1993). *Corrections Operations.* Wellington, NZ: Author.

—(1994). *Northern Law News* 17:2.

Pelikan, C. (1993). "Who Wants what Kind of Justice?" Paper presented at the 11th International Criminology Congress, Budapest, August.

Robertson, J. (1993). "The 'Tidal Wave' of Juvenile Offending." *Children* 11:8-10.

Stewart, T. (1993). "The Young Justice Co-Ordinator's Role: A Personal Perspective of the New Zealand Legislation in Action." In: B.J. Brown and F.W.M. McElrea (eds.), *The Youth Court in New Zealand: A New Model of Justice.* Auckland, NZ: Legal Research Foundation.

Van Ness, D.W. (1989). *Restorative Justice: Theory, Principles and Practice.* Washington, DC: Justice Fellowship.

Zehr, H. (1990). *Changing Lenses: A New Focus for Crime and Justice.* Scottdale, PA/Waterloo, Ont., CAN: Herald Press.

# 4. RESTORATIVE JUSTICE AND THE ROLE OF COMMUNITY

## by
## Paul McCold

**Abstract:** *There are many different levels of community; the community of standing in any given dispute will depend on factors such as the level of harm inflicted, the relationships of the disputants and the aggregation represented. Victim, offender, and community each have roles defined by their injury, corresponding needs, and responsibilities. Local communities have five general needs that arise from criminal conflict: a sense of justice, community empowerment in conflict resolution, reestablishment of peaceful relationships, a sense of safety and hopefulness, and concrete actions to prevent the recurrence of similar conflicts. The responsibilities of local communities are to act immediately to: protect victim and offender, hold offenders accountable and insist on active involvement of interested parties in the resolution process, provide resources for victim and offender to seek healing, provide public education and serve as a model for peaceful conflict resolution processes, and seek the systematic sources for recurring conflicts and encourage amelioration at their etiological source. There are no existing models of a full restorative justice system in operation, but the family group conference model being developed in New Zealand and Australia is helpful.*

The U.S. seems gripped by an addiction to the powerful drug of vengeance—the primary driving force behind current criminal justice policies. The pain and fear caused by crime results in ever-greater demands for punishment of offenders, as if there is no other way to stop the violence. "It is important to realize that blaming is fun. Anger is fun. Hatred is fun. And like any pleasurable activity, it is habit forming—you get hooked on it" (Peck, 1993, p.38). There never seems to be enough punishment to satisfy the craving, despite huge increases in prison populations. The escalating level of the "get-tough" rhetoric only fuels the public fear, which generates an ever-greater demand for punitiveness.

The U.S. is already the most punitive nation in the modern world, and still continues to construct more prisons in spite of the lack of any credible empirical evidence that punishment of any kind or amount reduces crime. The age-old myth that punishment can prevent violence (Pepinsky and Jesilow, 1985) rarely seems to be challenged. The American public's desire for vengeance is deeply ingrained in history (Newman, 1978). Only by renouncing the social values and institutions that promote the myth that violence can be overcome with punishment—evil with evil—and exposing the "myth of redemptive violence" (Wink, 1992) can Americans ever hope to escape the cycles of vengeance and violence (Mackey, 1990). Ultimately, the current system of criminal justice is in pursuit of safety and justice for our communities. But a punitive and vengeful approach to criminal conflict can only increase the level of violence that is already endemic to the culture (Pepinsky, 1991). "The cries for retribution throughout this land are cries for safety, for justice, and for relief from an unworkable criminal justice system. So long as we hear the cries for retribution, we know that we have not achieved justice. The community has been broken and has not been restored" (Mackey, 1990, p.15).

## RESTORATIVE JUSTICE

Restorative justice offers a different paradigm of crime and society's response to it, and is suggested as a replacement for our existing criminal justice system (Zehr and Umbreit, 1982; Weitekamp, 1992; Galaway, 1989). Restorative justice "...is a practice that contains the seeds for solving a new problem—the inadequacy of the criminal justice system itself, as it lurches from crisis to crisis, based as it is on an outdated philosophy of naked revenge" (Marshall, 1992, p.26). The paradigm shifts once the implications of the rejection of punishment as a response to conflict begin to emerge. This perspective grew out of work with crime victims and efforts to help victims find a sense of healing. "Forcing the perpetrator to suffer does not really alleviate the victim's distress, nor does degrading the wrongdoer erase the humiliation felt by the injured party" (Karmen, 1990, p.31).

Restorative justice views criminal conflict as an injury to personal relationships and the property of those involved (Christie, 1977). It replaces punishment of the offender as the basis for justice, with attempts to heal the injuries of all parties—victim, offender, and community—involved in criminal conflict. Rather than a violation of the rules of law, crime is a serious form of interpersonal conflict involving concrete harms (Zehr, 1990). Crime is only one type or level of interpersonal conflict; offensive and unhealthful acts affront the sensibilities and preferences of society, but these conflicts are social problems, annoyances, public health problems—not crime. Conflicts are the property of the victim, the offender and their local community. Victims are people who are directly injured by crime. The victim might not be a person, per se, in the case of property crime against businesses; the victim might also be the community, if community-owned property is damaged. Otherwise, the community has a direct interest in the conflict but is not the victim. "Crime is a violation of people and relationships" (Zehr, 1990). The community, family members of the victim and even family members of the offender are all secondary victims, and have needs directly related to the crime. This is much different from viewing crime as an offense against the state, the society or the community. Also, the offender is not the victim: while most offenders have previous histories of victimization, each of those have a corresponding offender and are not at issue regarding present responsibilities.

Crime victims have a variety of needs created by the harms they suffer in the course of the crime. The loss of control and orderliness experienced is often more damaging than any physical or material loss suffered. Victims need to bring meaning to the crime event in order to restore predictability and order in their lives. They need vindication that what happened to them was wrong and undeserved, and opportunities to express and have validated their anger and pain. Victims need to be restored to a sense of control and safety in their lives (Zehr, 1990). Crime victims also need their offender to understand the injury caused them, as well as their family and friends. If the offender can be made to appreciate the injury and to develop a sincere sense of lament, the victim can have the chance to heal emotionally from the harm and go on with his or her life. The act of holding offenders accountable for their actions goes a long way toward healing the victim, and is the beginning of healing for the offender as well. Offenders do not need to be punished; they need to be held accountable. Real accountability includes taking responsibility for the results of one's behavior. Offenders must be allowed and encouraged to help decide what will happen to make things right, what they can do to undo the harm they caused. Only by empowering offenders in this process can they learn to take responsibility—to begin to learn to become responsible. Restorative justice is very different from our current repressive and punitive system of justice (the obedience model).

Restorative justice approaches, in practice, have been limited to victim restitution programs, offender accountability and victim awareness programs, and victim-offender reconciliation programs. Karmen (1990) suggests there are at least four distinct political orientations supporting restorative schemes with divergent goals and clashing philosophies. These perspectives view reparation as: (1) a punishment oriented toward the offender (victim in line after the state); (2) a treatment mechanism for the rehabilitation of the offender (offenders need accountability); (3) a way to help victims (victims have a right to recompense); and (4) a vehicle for reconciliation of relationships.

The first criminal justice program providing a restorative approach to crime was victim restitution sentencing. This was based on the premise that offenders owe something to their victims, at the least, they should pay the victim for out-of-pocket financial expenses occurring as a result of their wrongful act. Restitution is not new, and its recent rediscovery has led to a plethora of programs implemented in diverse jurisdictions that seem to have received widespread public support. Why should justice systems require offenders to repair the damages their crime inflicted? Under what theory of punishment? As an added punitive deterrent, an additional fine imposed upon the offender would add little to the threat of a longer prison sentence. As rehabilitation, the offender might gain some insight to help change his or her behavior, although the concern is more for the offender than the victim. Likewise, under a retributive scheme, restitution can be justified to make the punishment better fit the crime, also directed at the offender. To combine the justice aspects due to victims and the therapeutic effects perceived for offenders requires an entirely different theoretical perspective, a restorative theory. No theory of punishment includes an equal place for crime victims' concerns. The current punitive system is renowned for adding additional injuries to crime victims. Restitution or community service under the existing justice system will necessarily be offender-focused, and, therefore, anti-victim-biased (Shapiro, 1990). "Even when courts order restitution, and the judgment thereby seems to favor the victim, restitution as a sentencing option still embodies, first and foremost, the penal and correctional interests of the state" (Karmen, 1990, p.282, citing Triebwasser, 1986).

There has been a flurry on the part of correctional authorities to implement programs stressing the importance of offenders (especially juveniles) understanding the consequences of their actions. The federal government, California, and Minnesota have taken legislative and administrative action to include victim awareness sensitivity training in their rehabilitation programs under the name of restorative justice (National Victim Center, 1994; California Youth Authority, 1994). Often, these programs include victim restitution and community service sentences in their package of restorative justice reforms, along with intermediate community-based surveillance and sanctioning systems (Bazemore and Maloney, 1994; McLagan, 1992; Van Ness, 1989, 1990; Van Ness et al., 1989). Yet, it seems self-evident that any restorative scheme implemented and operated by correctional institutions will also necessarily be offender-focused.

"Victim-offender reconciliation programs, usually run by nonprofit community groups, use negotiation and mediation to make the process of reparation therapeutic for both parties" (Karmen, 1990, p.285). These programs are based upon the premise that crimes are harms done by one person to another person, and that the resolution of justice must directly involve the parties to the crime. Like restitution, victim-offender reconciliation programs assume that offenders owe something to their victims and need to assume responsibility for them directly. The details of what is owed are worked out in an agreement between the victim and offender. A trained mediator helps the parties find a mutually satisfactory method of reparation and restitution. Early results from program evaluations demonstrate the success of this approach for victims, offenders and society (Umbreit, 1994). However, as examples of restorative justice principles in practice, victim-offender reconciliation programs are only part of a larger whole.

What structural processes does restorative justice propose to address the social inequities and values that contribute to the production of street crime? "The question becomes whether reconciliation programs and organizations can be more sensitive and responsive to the larger profile of conflict that envelops episodes of crime and delinquency" (Mika, 1992, p.563). Focusing too much attention on the process of saving individual victims and offenders may divert attention from the root causes that continuously produce a never-ending supply of victims and offenders. The answer to this astructural bias of restorative justice may reside in the least-explored leg of the three-legged stool-community. Delineating the role of the community in the restorative justice paradigm is essential to complete the theoretical structure. While individual citizens have been involved as volunteer mediators or service providers, the programs have all failed to include a strong role for the whole community in the process. "[L]aying out ways to operationalize the admirable notion of eliciting more active community involvement in the reconciliation process remains an elusive task" (Harris, 1989, p.35). Voluntary participation of individual citizens in the justice process is a valuable beginning.

> In a society with values emphasizing citizen participation in the affairs of state, increasing citizen participation does not require further justifications: it is a goal sufficient in its own right and does not need to be defended as leading to some more long term benefit. [Increased citizen participation will occur in two ways] (1) citizen victims, and (2) citizen negotiators, citizen volunteer case managers [Galaway, 1989, p.112].

Yet, the paradigm is nearly always expressed as equally including victim, offender and community. Surely, more is expected from the community than a commendable increase in citizen volunteer participation and the involvement of individual victims and offenders.

## INCLUSION OF COMMUNITY IN A RESTORATIVE JUSTICE PARADIGM

One of the foundational principles of restorative justice is the idea that the injury caused by crime is the property of the victim, the offender, and the local community. The conflict belongs to them, and they have a direct stake and interest in the resolution of the conflict. "The basic principles of restorative justice require a fundamental shift in the power related to who controls and owns crime in society—a shift from the state to the individual citizen and local communities" (Umbreit, 1994, p.162).

> The resolution and prevention of crime demands a positive effort on the part of society and assumption of responsibility by the community. Such responsibility is doubly evaded at present: by the community in leaving crime matters entirely in the hands of statutory agencies, and by the latter in considering that when a culprit has been adjudicated guilty and allotted a punishment that is the end of their responsibility [Marshall, 1992, p.25].

Effective crime control needs to be communized because most crimes of aggression are committed between persons living in the same community, and, thus, must be coped with by all the members involved and not by professionals who are outsiders (Mackey, 1981, citing Bianchi, 1978). Strong restorative justice programs are characterized by an environment that includes local community control (Mika, 1992).

It may be that part of the problem in addressing crime on a local level stems from a general lack of a sense of "community." The devastating social conditions in our inner cities are both a cause and a result of dysfunctional community (Stark, 1987).

Much of our trouble stems from killed neighborhoods or killed local communities. How can we then thrust towards neighbourhoods a task that presupposes they are highly alive? I have no really good arguments, only two weak ones. First, it is not quite that bad. The death is not complete. Secondly, one of the major ideas behind the formation of 'Conflicts as Property' is that it is neighborhood property. It is not private. It belongs to the system. It is intended as a vitaliser for neighbourhoods [Christie, 1977, p.12].

## Defining Community

The community cannot be specifically defined *a priori* within the restorative justice paradigm, as it depends upon the nature of the conflict. Restorative justice "concepts are directly relevant to the harms suffered in the course of everyday life and routine conflict, and where the event is not classified as a crime" (Peachey, 1992, p.552). The community with standing in any given conflict will be dependent upon a number of factors, including the level of harm inflicted, the relationship of the disputants, and the aggregation represented. There are many different levels of community, as there are different levels of dispute. Each offender and each victim are members of several communities and of informal organizations—personal communities such as family, friends, neighborhood and school organizations, and churches and community organizations. Offenders and victims are also members of a local community, a municipal subdivision, a metropolitan area, a state, and federal- and societal-level communities. Ultimately we are all members of the human community. Consider a dispute between young siblings. The boundary of the community whose interest is at stake is limited to the family. Should the conflict exist between married partners and the injury involved physical harm, the boundary of the interested community widens to include, at the least, other non-primary family members and associates. Where the conflict is between ambassadors from differing countries, the scope of the community at stake is on a much different scale.

How should the community be defined when the dispute involves normal, stranger crime (assault, robbery, theft, vandalism, etc.)—the type most often feared by the public? This is not to imply that domestic violence should not be considered a criminal conflict. Criminal harms are the province of the whole community, whether they involve intimates or strangers. Presumably it is the fear of stranger crime that produces the public demand for vengeance. The community with an interest could include the entire American public, since individual criminal conflicts contribute to the general fear of crime in society. If we wish to avoid "stealing the conflict" (Christie, 1977), it seems prudent to consider the minimal necessary boundary of community as that limited to parties with a direct stake (need and responsibility) in the specific conflict. "The resolution of conflict is the province of the entire community rather than the exclusive domain of specialized legal organizations. The conflict is not extracted from the community" (Cordella, 1991, p.42). The term local community is used to mean "a social group of any size whose members reside in a specific locality, share government, and have a common cultural and historical heritage" (Stein, 1979, p.272). There is also a personal level of community. This includes those individuals who know and are personally involved in the lives of the victim and/or the offender. The role of the local community, which is broader than that of the personal community, is the primary focus of this chapter.

Figure 4.1 suggests a useful framework provided by Mackey (1990). The victim, offender, and community each have roles defined by their injury and corresponding needs and by their responsibilities in relationship to a given conflict. There appears to be a direct relationship among injury, need and responsibility. Crime produces injuries that need to be repaired, and this need produces a responsibility to take affirmative action to seek satisfaction of these needs. But what are the injuries, needs and responsibilities of the local community?

## Community's Needs and Responsibilities

A frequently mentioned aspect of a community's needs is the desire for a feeling of safety. "Safety is the first consideration of the community. All decisions regarding the hurts that are crimes should be based on

|           | Injury | Need | Responsibility |
|-----------|--------|------|----------------|
| Victim    |        |      |                |
| Offender  |        |      |                |
| Community |        |      |                |
| Society   |        |      |                |

*Fig. 4.1.*

this consideration" (Mackey, 1990, p.60). Certainly, the community longs for a sense of justice. Like the victim, the local community suffers a loss of sense of safety, and requires reassurance that something is being done about it and that "steps are being taken to discourage its recurrence" (Zehr, 1990, pp.194-195).

Communities need to know there will be a firm and immediate response to violent crime—that such behavior will not be tolerated. Otherwise, fear and a sense of hopelessness begin to pervade a neighborhood, which can itself amplify criminal deviance (Stark, 1987) and adversely affect economic conditions, furthering more criminal deviance and fear (Reiss, 1986). "Maybe nothing could be done or nothing would be done. But neighbourhoods might find it intolerable that nothing happened" (Christie, 1977, p.10).

Communities not only have a need for concrete responses, they have an affirmative responsibility for providing them. This responsibility involves four concrete actions: (1) immediately protect the victim and others from further harm by the offender; (2) immediately protect the offender from vengeance; (3) set in motion the healing process of restorative justice; and (4) create those conditions most favorable to the complete restoration of both the victim and the offender (Criminal Justice Committee, 1989).

"Citizens and communities victimized by physical, emotional, or economic harm are justifiably angry and require a means to address the injustice that that anger represents" (Gehm, 1992, p.548). Communities need a mechanism to recover from the psychological injury caused to them by criminal conflict, a mechanism involving "rituals of forgiveness and release from anger" (Gehm, 1992, p.548). "Even if some past injustices never can be compensated for adequately, it can restore a sense of fairness to feel that everyone is trying" (Harris, 1989, p.40).

The ultimate aim should be to find a means by which institutional control and the imposition of official discipline can give way to community control, self-regulation and self-discipline—while still guaranteeing individual rights. [Community empowerment] involves encouraging communities to take responsibility for their own regulation. It makes communities accountable—and appears to strengthen them in the process [Moore, 1994, pp.4-5].

Part of the solution to peacemaking is the process itself. Empowering local communities to respond to their own conflicts meets the needs of the community to repair the psychological injury and anger of crime and helps to nurture the sense of community, thereby building responsible stewardship. Like the primary individual victim, the community has a need to bring meaning to crime and to develop an emotional understanding of the conflict. This requires a personalized understanding, rather than "an explanation of criminals as non-humans" (Christie, 1977, p.8).

The community needs to understand the human dimensions involved in criminal conflict. It needs to understand that most criminal harms are committed between persons known to each other, members of the local community. The community needs to understand crime as based on interpersonal conflicts, and needs an opportunity to reconcile victim with offender, and offender with the community. The community's injury is to *shalom*, right relationships, among members of the community. The damage is against peace, and requires a local effort to restore harmony in the community. There is a desperate need within our communities for "socially integrative interventions" (Messmer and Otto, 1992, p.1). A strategy of empowerment enables local communities to meet their need for peace, while empowering victims allows them to meet *their* needs for control and order. Empowering offenders allows them, in turn, to accept responsibility and become responsible. This much empowerment creates the potential for dynamic and innovative solutions to problems producing crime, including the capacity to challenge social norms themselves.

Both the offender and the community share responsibility for responding to criminal injuries; "both the offender and society have played some role in creating the problem, and both share responsibility for providing restitution" (Morris, 1994, p.5). If offenders are to be held accountable, and expected to behave responsibly, the community too must shoulder its responsibility to both the injury and its healing. Affirmative responsibilities of the local community include holding the offender accountable to the victim, and accepting responsibility for reparation offenders cannot meet.

The community has both the need for firm, integrative interventions to crime and the responsibility to provide such processes. Conflicts themselves are an important asset for communities (Prothrow-Stith, 1991). Every conflict represents an opportunity for reaffirming the importance of every member of the community to its overall health. Each conflict is an opportunity to demonstrate helpful problem-solving approaches, and to reaffirm the right of every member to be free of violence and secure in his or her possessions. Everyone who injures another should accept responsibility to repair those injuries. This should be the public lesson of a restorative response to crime.

The public educative function of the restorative justice process is the least often explicitly mentioned responsibility of the community. The responsibility for implementing peaceful problem-solving responses to general conflicts is therefore also the community's. Restorative justice advocates have always recognized the need to inspire non-punitive approaches to all conflicts in society, "to help victims and their families to realize both the futility and the counter-productiveness of retribution" (Mackey, 1981, p.52). One goal of restorative justice is community outreach, including "a community education component that emphasizes an alternative paradigm of justice, for the purposes of literacy in dispute resolution and peacemaking, grassroots ownership of local dispute resolution programs, volunteer recruitment and the like" (Mika, 1992, p.565).

One of the most consistently mentioned community needs is for a mechanism that can address and alter the existing social structures that are criminogenic—the root causes of criminal conflict. Primary prevention is the most widely discussed but the least implemented in practice. Yet, system reform is essentially and fundamentally imbedded within the restorative justice paradigm. "For punishment to seem fair, outcome and process need to relate to the original wrong. However, the societal context must also be viewed as fair, and this raises larger questions of social, economic, and political justice" (Zehr, 1990, p.210). Primary prevention responses also include changing values and attitudes that produce crime (e.g., sexism). "[T]he community also must examine its responsibility for the behaviors, must uncover the societal roots of sexual violence, understand them, and find ways to reduce the potential for such violence to occur" (Knopp, 1991, p.192).

But does society as a whole have a stake in the local restorative justice process? Is society an indirect or vicarious victim of local crime as a result of the fear and apprehension spread via the modern media? Society has a need to foster the capacity of local communities to control their own conflicts, and a responsibility to support that local capacity. Failure to empower local communities to restore right relationships has serious social costs that threaten a free society.

What is certain...is that societies that lack the capacity to exert community control over breaches of duty, and to exert community control to protect freedoms, will lose their freedom. This is so first because freedom can never be protected if encroachments on freedom cannot be sanctioned. Second, if citizens' persons and property cannot be secured by moralizing against criminals, then political demands for the repressive state will prevail. To the extent that moralizing social control collapses, a vacuum is created that will attract the most brutal, repressive and intrusive of police states [Braithwaite, 1989, p.186].

## COMPLETING THE RESTORATIVE JUSTICE PARADIGM

Local communities have five general needs that arise from criminal conflict: (1) a sense of justice; (2) community empowerment in conflict resolution; (3) re-establishment of peaceful relationships between conflicting individuals and their important social relationships; (4) a sense of safety and hopefulness; and (5) concrete actions to prevent the recurrence of similar conflicts. The responsibilities of local communities are to: (1) act immediately to protect victim and offender; (2) hold offenders accountable and insist on active involvement of interested parties in the resolution process; (3) provide the local resources for victim and offender to seek their healing; (4) provide public education and serve as a model for peaceful resolution processes; and (5) seek the systemic sources of recurring conflicts and encourage amelioration at their etiological source.

There are no existing models of a full restorative justice system in operation, but a number of promising approaches exists. Among these are the New Zealand model of family group conferences (Galaway et al., 1996; Morris and Maxwell, 1992; Morris et al., 1993; McElrea, 1994), and the Australian model of "community action conferences" (Moore, 1994; Braithwaite and Mugford, 1994).

Community Action Conferences...involve the perpetrator(s) of an offence and the victim(s) of that offence, together with the families and friends of victims and offenders. Each conference is coordinated by a police officer, whose role is to encourage participants to reach some collective agreement about how best to minimize the ongoing harm resulting from the offending behavior. Agreements usually involve some arrangements for appropriate restitution and reparation....The program has several aims. One is to give victims of offending behavior an opportunity to participate in the official response to that behavior. Another aim is to provide offenders with an opportunity to understand the consequences of their actions. Yet another is to involve the broader community of people who have been adversely affected by those actions. In practice, these three aims cannot be separated from one another. Involving a broader community of people encourages and supports the involvement of victims and both of these factors help young offenders to understand how far reaching the ramifications of their actions have been [Moore, 1994, p.5].

This approach to restorative justice practice involves local control of the process. The response by the community is inclusive of all primary and secondary victims, and the personal communities of victims and offenders. The local police are responsible for coordinating the process, but they do not control the outcome. Those community members with a direct stake in the outcome are empowered to provide concrete and socially relevant reparations and ameliorative solutions. The affirmation and acceptance of the victim and offender in their personal communities and in the local community as a whole is accomplished. Community members are restored to a sense of justice and peace, knowing that they themselves "did something about it." Local community resources are available to meet the needs of the victim and the offender, and a model of peaceful conflict resolution is played out in a public forum over and over for the whole community to learn.

The primary goal of restorative justice is the empowerment of victims, offenders and communities. Communities first must be empowered to control their own conflicts, the apparatus of criminal justice processes. The overwhelming majority of police, courts and jails operate at the municipal level of government. The criminal justice system is really not a separate entity from communities. The move toward community policing and community-level corrections should be further encouraged, and should come under local community control and involve local community citizens more directly. Grassroots community self-improvement programs need to be encouraged and strengthened (Sulton, 1990; McCoy, 1994).

One of the most consistently mentioned principles of restorative justice is that the process should provide the mechanism to question norms and alter existing social structures. While the possibility of structural reform is widely discussed, the programmatic considerations of this possibility are the least developed. How can the patterns of social maladies uncovered in the restorative justice process lead to larger social changes? Some of the maladies can be addressed by the community through such avenues as parenting education and alternative conflict resolution mechanisms. But how can any community alter economic conditions and social structures that contribute to crime? The resources required to alter structural inequities can only be met by larger political structures. Making our democratic political institutions more responsive to the needs of communities could provide a broader source for social justice more generally.

## REFERENCES

Bazemore, G. and D. Maloney (1994). "Rehabilitating Community Service: Toward Restorative Service Sanctions in a Balanced Justice System." *Federal Probation* 58(1):24-35.

Bianchi, H. (1978). "Returning Conflict to the Community: Alternative of Privatization." Buffalo, NY: U.S. Lecture Series, November.

Braithwaite, J. (1989). *Crime, Shame and Reintegration.* New York, NY: Cambridge University Press.

—and S. Mugford (1994). "Conditions of Successful Reintegration Ceremonies." *British Journal of Criminology* 34(2):139-171.

California Youth Authority (1994). "Impact of Crime on Victims Awareness Classes." Fact sheet. Paper presented at the annual conference of the American Society of Criminology, Miami, November.

Christie, N. (1977). "Conflict as Property." *British Journal of Criminology* 17(1):1-14.

Cordella, J.P. (1991). "Reconciliation and the Mutalist Model of Community." In: H. Pepinsky and R. Quinney (eds.), *Criminology as Peacemaking.* Bloomington, IN: Indiana University Press.

Criminal Justice Committee (1989). "One Application of Restorative Justice: A Restorative System of Criminal Justice." *Testimony on Restorative Justice.* Philadelphia Yearly Meeting, Religious Society of Friends, September.

Galaway, B. (1989). "Informal Justice: Mediation Between Offenders and Victims." In: P. Albrecht and O. Backes (eds.), *Crime Prevention and Intervention: Legal and Ethical Problems.* New York, NY: Walter de Gruyter.

—J. Hudson, G. Maxwell and A. Morris (1996). *Family Group Conferences: Research and Policy Implications*. Monsey, NY: Criminal Justice Press.

Gehm, J.R. (1992). "The Function of Forgiveness in the Criminal Justice System." In: H. Messmer and H.-U. Otto (eds.), *Restorative Justice on Trial*, pp.541-550. Dordrecht, NETH.: Kluwer Academic Publishers.

Harris, M.K. (1989). "Alternative Visions in the Context of Contemporary Realities." In: P. Arthur (ed.), *Justice: The Restorative Vision*. New Perspective on Crime and Justice, #7. Akron, PA: Mennonite Central Committee.

Karmen, A. (1990). *Crime Victims: An Introduction to Victimology*. 2nd edn. Belmont, CA: Wadsworth Publishing.

Knopp, F.H. (1991). "Community Solutions to Sexual Violence: Feminist/Abolitionist Perspectives." In: H. Pepinsky and R. Quinney (eds.), *Criminology as Peacemaking*. Bloomington, IN: Indiana University Press.

Mackey, V. (1981). "Punishment: In the Scripture and Tradition of Judaism, Christianity and Islam." Paper presented to the National Religious Leaders Consultation of Criminal Justice, Claremont, CA, September.

—(1990). *Restorative Justice: Toward Nonviolence*. Louisville, KY: Presbyterian Criminal Justice Program, Presbyterian Church (U.S.A.).

Marshall, T.F. (1992). "Restorative Justice on Trial in Britain." In: H. Messmer and H.-U. Otto (eds.), *Restorative Justice on Trial*, pp.15-28. Dordrecht, NETH.: Kluwer Academic Publishers.

McCoy, M.L. (ed.) (1994). *Confronting Violence in our Communities: A Guide for Involving Citizens in Public Dialogue and Problem Solving* (Study Circles Resource Centre). Pomfret, CT: Topsfield Foundation.

McElrea, F.W.M. (1994). "The Intent of the Children, Young Persons, and Their Families Act 1989—Restorative Justice?" Paper presented to the Youth Justice Conference of the New Zealand Youth Court Association, Auckland, February.

McLagan, J. (1992). *Report of the Ad Hoc Committee on Restorative Justice*. St. Paul, MN: Minnesota Department of Corrections.

Messmer, H.and H.-U. Otto (1992). "Restorative Justice: Steps on the Way Toward a Good Idea." In: H. Messmer and H.-U. Otto (eds.), *Restorative Justice on Trial*. Dordrecht, NETH.: Kluwer Academic Publishers.

Mika, H. (1992). "Mediation Interventions and Restorative Justice: Responding to the Astructural Bias." In: H. Messmer and H.-U. Otto (eds.), *Restorative Justice on Trial*, pp.525-539. Dordrecht, NETH.: Kluwer Academic Publishers.

Moore, D.B. (1994). "Pride, Shame and Empathy in Peer Relations: A Case Study with Implications for Theory and Practice in Education and Juvenile Justice." In: K. Oxenberry, K. Rigby, and P. Slee (eds.), *Children's Peer Relations*. Addeley, SA: University of South Australia.

Morris, A. and G.M. Maxwell (1992)."Juvenile Justice in New Zealand: A New Paradigm." *Australian and New Zealand Journal of Criminology* 26:72-90.

—G.M. Maxwell and J.P. Robertson (1993). "Giving Victims a Voice: A New Zealand Experiment." *Howard Journal of Criminal Justice* 32(4):304-321.

Morris, R. (1994). *A Practical Path to Transformative Justice.* Toronto, CAN: Rittenhouse.

National Victim Center (1994). "Crime Victims & Corrections." *Technical Assistance Bulletin* 4(4):1.

Newman, G. (1978). *The Punishment Response.* Philadelphia, PA: Lippincott.

Peachey, D.E. (1992). "Restitution, Reconciliation, Retribution: Identifying the Forms of Justice People Desire." In: H. Messmer and H.-U. Otto (eds.), *Restorative Justice on Trial,* pp.551-557. Dordrecht, NETH.: Kluwer Academic Publishers.

Peck, M.S. (1993). *Further Along the Road Less Travelled.* New York, NY: Simon & Schuster.

Pepinsky, H.E. (1991). *The Geometry of Violence and Democracy.* Bloomington, IN: Indiana University Press.

Pepinsky, H.W. and P. Jesilow (1985). *Myths that Cause Crime.* Cabin John, MD: Seven Locks.

Prothrow-Stith, D. (1991). *Deadly Consequences.* New York, NY: Harper Collins.

Reiss, A.J., Jr. (1986). "Why are Communities Important in Understanding Crime?" In: A.J. Reiss and M. Tonry (eds.), *Communities and Crime.* Chicago, IL: University of Chicago Press.

Shapiro, C. (1990). "Is Restitution Legislation the Chameleon of the Victims' Movement?" In: B. Galaway and J. Hudson (eds.), *Criminal Justice Restitution and Reconciliation.* Monsey, NY: Criminal Justice Press.

Stark, R. (1987). "Deviant Places: A Theory of the Ecology of Crime." *Criminology* 25:893-909.

Stein, J. (ed.) (1979). *Random House Dictionary of the English Language* (Revised Edition). New York, NY: Random House.

Sulton, A.T. (ed.) (1990). *Inner-City Crime Control: Can Community Institutions Contribute?* Washington, DC: Police Foundation.

Triebwasser, J. (1986). "Court Says You Can't Run from Restitution." *Law Enforcement News* June 28, pp.6-8.

Umbreit, M.S. (1994). *Victim Meets Offender: The Impact of Restorative Justice and Mediation.* Monsey, NY: Criminal Justice Press.

Van Ness, D.W. (1989). "Pursuing a Restorative Vision of Justice." In: P. Arthur (ed.), *Justice: The Restorative Vision* (New Perspectives on Crime and Justice, #7). Akron, PA: Mennonite Central Committee.

—(1990). "Restorative Justice." In: B. Galaway and J. Hudson (eds.), *Criminal Justice, Restitution and Reconciliation.* Monsey, NY: Criminal Justice Press.

—D. Carlson, Jr., T. Crawford and K. Strong (1989). *Restorative Justice Practice.* Washington, DC: Justice Fellowship.

Weitekamp, E. (1992). "Can Restitution Serve as a Reasonable Alternative to Imprisonment? An Assessment of the Situation in the USA." In: H. Messmer and H.-U. Otto (eds.), *Restorative Justice on Trial,* pp.81-103. Dordrecht, NETH.: Kluwer Academic Publishers.

Wink, W. (1992). *Engaging the Powers.* Minneapolis, MN: Augsburg Fortress.

Zehr, H. (1990). *Changing Lenses: A New Focus for Crime and Justice.* Scottsdale, PA: Herald Press.

—and M. Umbreit (1982). "Victim Offender Reconciliation: An Incarceration Substitute?" *Federal Probation* 46(4):63-68.

# 5. CREATING PEACEFUL COMMUNITIES

by

## Michel Marcus

**Abstract:** *Changing social and economic conditions are resulting in an increase of minor crimes and misdemeanors that is of concern to citizens but also largely beyond the control of a saturated, blind, and fractured criminal justice system. Reducing the sense of public insecurity can only result from an integrated community approach based on a policy of local development, concerted action involving community organizations, and the development of community regulation and social control mechanisms. Organizing a community-based reduction of insecurity is difficult because of social fragmentation within communities, stigmatization of high crime communities, and the relationship among residential turnover, community evolution, and crime. Four types of policies co-exist to support community-based crime regulation: community preservation via investment in the protection and support of the most stable communities, community control of troublemakers, damage reduction and redistribution focusing on vulnerable groups, and promotion of social cohesion to forestall the creation of an underclass.*

It is impossible to discuss reorganization of or changes to the criminal justice system or its alternatives without taking the socio-economic environment of states into account. Any crime deterrence policy is a reflection of social policies, modeled on economic evolutions, and must hinge on the strategic choices made in other sectors. Conversely, it is inconceivable to determine social policies without taking into account the criminal justice system's adaptability to new goals. This interpenetration of decision-making spheres calls for enhanced communication between those responsible for the various sectors as well as the constant creation of new professional methods.

Such mandatory reorganization poses dangers with regard to the

rights and freedoms of citizens. It can also give rise to financial inefficiency if determined solely at the centralized state and department levels. The development of cities and the urban phenomenon defines the
geographic framework for reorganization. The public increasingly addresses claims for social and cultural support, and demands for security
to the local elected representatives who are under pressure to broaden
areas of jurisdiction and intervention. This development marks the end
of the criminal justice system's monopoly over the social response to
petty crime. It forces us to use the new concept of urban security that
combines the spheres of prevention and retribution, and that leads to
strategies for reducing insecurity. The public's demand for security is
multi-faceted and oversteps the strict confines of the legal system and
the police. The social demand for security should be analyzed at the
neighborhood, street, and community levels, in order to aid in the production of a variety of institutional responses, such as those of the police
and the legal system. The possibilities for developing alternatives to the
criminal justice system ultimately rely on the condition of our societies.

The economic development of societies in Europe is distributed less
and less equally among the people. The social field is divided into three
increasingly distinct blocks. At one extreme is a group wielding economic power, in the center is a middle-class group of variable size depending on periods of recession or growth, and at the other extreme is a
burgeoning population trapped in poverty and exclusion. A portion of
this less-fortunate population has experienced unemployment for three
generations, but the ranks are increasingly swollen by new arrivals from
the middle-class who have been unable to adapt to economic restructur-
ing. The prospects for escaping poverty and exclusion are growing less
promising. Increased production and productivity in today's economic
sectors leads only to a reduction in the number of positions, and is coupled with new demands for professional qualifications that hinder the integration process. The public finance crisis threatens health and social
services safety nets and thus multiplies the handicaps.

Tensions are finding expression within cities and neighborhoods. Social bonds and values that make sense of the everyday cohabitation
rules among social groups face a grave threat. This vortex is aggravated
by racial tensions. Within Europe, migration from countries to the South
and East weighs heavily on the housing and labor markets. This new
labor force, by virtue of its under-qualification, is the subject of keen resentment from the natives of European countries. Violence rears its

head, and persecution motivated by racism and anti-Semitism becomes more frequent and brazen. The classical methods for integrating young people into our societies are undergoing a major crisis. The family has surrendered part of its role in educating children and has been weakened by dissolution into a single-parent model. Schools are seeking a new identity, inspired by the lack of opportunities for graduates, and more generally there is a profound questioning of the nature of the values that we may embody. All of this translates into a rejection of the political class, as well as a distrust of any collective action.

Over the past 20 years, all the countries of Europe have experienced an average 10% increase in criminality. This increase has occurred irrespective of economic growth and recession. Serious crime (traffic in arms and drugs, white-collar crime) has risen considerably, violent crime has remained relatively stable, and the sharpest rise has been in micro-criminality. Micro-criminality is comprised almost entirely of property crimes and has taken on a character of routine criminality, the cost of which is absorbed by insurance. Criminal justice systems have become mere insurance claim registries. Victims' services are kept to a minimum, police action is nonexistent, and recovery rates are very low. Because of the criminal justice system's practice of not prosecuting them, the enormous body of minor crimes comprises misdemeanors that have slipped into this category, as well as acts no longer perceived by the public as worthy of punishment. This grab-bag category touches very closely on the day-to-day lives of city dwellers. Many citizens are active perpetrators of these incivilities (transportation or telephone fraud, for instance), but they are also its resigned victims. Thus, a youth tears up a train seat under the reproachful gaze of travellers who nonetheless remain passive. This youth's behavior will ultimately nourish a discourse of insecurity among adults. Youths have become objects of fear. Adults are under the impression that young people act with impunity, and everyone has the perception that society's basic values are more seriously undermined by this incivility than by actual crime.

The development of these phenomena resulting from micro-criminality has engendered an institutional crisis and overflow. Was it this increase in micro-criminality that precipitated the crisis of our justice systems, or the reverse? This is a difficult question to answer. What we do know is that the crisis has become endemic and is translated by the accelerated development of the private criminal justice system. A review of most European criminal statistics reveals that on average, 30 of

100 offenses are reported to the police, action will be taken on half of these 30, and 5% of those will result in a conviction. The loss all down the line is considerable and justifies complaints about the public authorities' lack of response to criminal dealings that endanger the security of people and property.

## SATURATED, BLIND AND FRACTURE—ALL IS NOT WELL IN THE CRIMINAL JUSTICE SYSTEM

Criminal justice systems are saturated: no action is taken on the vast majority of complaints; prisons are more crowded than ever, with a significant recidivism rate; and non-custodial methods are at best completely marginal. The fiscal crisis endured by the public authorities prohibits significant expansion of the system's capacity. In France, to have one extra police officer on the streets seven additional positions must be created (bearing in mind working hours, holidays, and so on), and even the creation of 2,000 positions, which would represent a considerable budgetary effort, would have but a minuscule effect in terms of actual police presence. Even if possible, such an increase would not guarantee a reduction of insecurity. The effect of police presence largely depends on the tone of the historical and concrete relationship between the police and the people, and of the manner in which this presence makes itself felt. Police presence can provide temporary security, but numerous studies reveal that increased police presence in the public space can in fact increase the sense of insecurity. The reasons can be historical, such as in Spain and in Germany's new eastern lander where society's xenophobic and racist components are even more feared when in control of the forces of law and order, or methodological, such as in the case of motorized patrols, sirens, speed, and so on.

The criminal justice system, although by all appearances a unified model, is deeply divided between the actions taken with regard to petty and moderately serious crime, and that taken with regard to serious and more specialized criminality representing a more significant cost for society. The European states have improved their performance in the fight against serious and more specialized criminality. Financial means have been placed at the disposal of specialized crime prevention and retribution agencies, providing for the most sophisticated techniques and in-depth training. Specific procedures have been created, and regulation and punishment systems established. International cooperation reaches often remarkable heights. The situation is considerably different with regard to ordinary crime that has become an everyday event in cities. But it would be wrong to ignore what is often a close connection between micro-criminality and very serious crime. Phenomena such as international auto theft or the drug trade show the need for concerted action vis-à-vis both the locations where the crimes are committed and the circuits that provide financial backing.

Criminal codes cover a countless number of behaviors. However, this checking off of transgressions and the panoply of measures based on incarceration are inadequate for combatting micro-criminality. The retributive system intervenes randomly, without a coherent and stable policy. It is rendered passive, reduced to registering crime prior to delivering the receipt required for an insurance settlement. The material, especially computerized, means that must be invested are beyond the compass of public authorities. They are also liable to infringe on certain freedoms. There is an acceleration of the sense of impotency that judges and police officers have with regard to suppressing micro-crime, at the expense of the public interest, and of the recourse to highly retributive punishment (such as incarceration) for the tiny sample of offenders that chance has brought to the surface.

All European countries have modernized their criminal justice systems. But with what result? Modernization has meant progress in the fight against serious criminality, whose model is the forensic scientist rather than the beat cop, the higher court justice rather than the justice of the peace, and the prison sentence rather than the community service sentence. Modernization of the criminal justice systems benefits their retributive and penitentiary aspect. Productivity is increased; some sequences of the penitentiary system are privatized; new prisons are built. The result is a sharp rise in inmate population and a reduction of the meager amounts set aside for alternative processes, non-custodial sanctions, and social experiments. Lastly, modernization is of greater benefit to the organized victims (public or private) than to the mass of minor claimants and hidden victims.

In periods of social crisis, the criminal justice system acquires a new symbolic value—that of last resort—as if it were the final stage of the socialization process, following the family, the street, sports, and the schools, rather than a limited, *in extremis* response to situations that have not been settled by the other branches of officialdom. There is a crisis of legitimacy as regards criminal justice systems and other institutions—a crisis of values. However, the crisis is in response to the gap between legal standards and unwritten or social ones, between the seriousness scale enshrined in criminal codes and the public's perception of it, and between budget-breaking institutional priorities and city dwellers' priorities.

How do we answer those living in the neighborhoods when they say, "But everyone knows who the criminals are!"? What do we say to the offender who is known but not arrested, or arrested and released with a sense of impunity, or who finds him or herself the only one to be arrested among so many others? This crisis opens the floodgates to the development of private protection systems. The ability to privatize, symbolically or physically, the public space for personal or community use is not the preserve of the rich alone. A growling dog is all it takes for one individual to keep his fellow citizens from going confidently about their business. The disproportionate powers of dissuasion and control, owing to their cost, make privatizing the police one way of widening the gulf that separates the social strata in urban environments.

This catastrophic scenario develops from the scarcity of public services. It marks the end of the public space as circulation space, and the breakdown of the principle of equality before the law, of the universal right to security and of security as a public good. The impact of urban space fragmentation is policing for the middle class alone, private defense systems for the wealthy, and a shifting of crime to unprotected areas. Now widespread in Latin America, will the same scenario become entrenched in the collective European imagination? Wealthy and protected enclaves are to be found along the French Mediterranean and the Italian Riviera. In 1988, the European Council took cognizance of the growing influence of a private sector supplying protective equipment and guard personnel. In some countries, the number of private security guards has already eclipsed the number of public police. The question has now become one of how best to organize the partnership, while taking care to safeguard all the prerogatives of the public authority.

The shift to prevention from chaotic, unreliable and extremely costly retribution was only natural. Prevention is not a newcomer to the European intellectual scene. Developing a policy that would allow crime to be foreseen has always seemed an obvious idea. Why has this historically persistent idea not yet brought about such a policy? Researching the causes of criminality has absorbed a great deal of energy, at the expense of concrete crime deterrence proposals. Analyses abound with regard to what causes crime, but with the effect of dissolving criminality in the cauldron of social ills where nothing can be made out distinctly. Social policies have replaced a narrower approach to criminality and offenders. These policies, owing to their constant evolution, have encouraged imprecision in how they are applied, one of the most serious effects of which is that they have become irrelevant to the offenders. Social policies have fallen prey to increased financial costs not justified by the results achieved.

Preventive measures to deal with crime-ridden situations or places must be created but cannot be divorced from retribution; these two sectors—prevention and retribution—must become complementary. Crime is not exclusive to an individual, a private matter between him or her and divinity (religious or secularized in the person of the king) with the judge serving as intermediary. People have put down social and economic roots that nourish their behavior, including criminal behavior. Subsequently, it has become tempting to seek to put a halt to the commission of crime, thus minimizing the judicial intervention whose symbolism owes a great deal to the infrequency with which it is manifested. Prevention has attracted much deliberation. The rules of the game are quite clear; all those who do not benefit from prevention policies and their various provisions are dealt with by means of retribution. Improved prevention translates to less retribution.

Retribution is diluted to varying degrees, originating in both the internal and external factors of the criminal justice system. Judges must decide the thorny problem of sentencing in addition to deciding an individual's guilt or innocence. The system is wholly centered on incarceration, and its modernization consists of merely determining the stages for entry and exit. Helping someone find a job or a home, for example, becomes the *sine qua non* for the system to function properly. Those employed in the criminal justice system are thrown into the task of implementing structures that are intimately tied to prevention; it is a matter of forestalling incarceration or keeping the individual from reoffending once he or she has exited the criminal justice system.

The growth of the consumer society and the increasing complexity of social systems are multiplying the number of extremely varied retributive systems that have nothing in common other than the fact that they are non-custodial. The police and the courts are losing their monopoly over retribution. We have witnessed a certain blurring of the lines between professional practices, each sector borrowing from the other.

Thus, in the area of young offender facilities or law, the legal system has been prompted to assume a leadership role over all who work with young people. The police have overseen the establishment of prevention services in schools and the private sector, or have reorganized along community lines in order to maintain a constant dialogue with the public. The education sector is reintegrating punishment into the process of socializing young people. The drug phenomenon has had a great deal to do with bringing these practitioners closer together. They have all come to realize that their traditional efforts were no longer sufficient to solve the problem. Little by little, cooperative structures and regular meetings among professionals have been established, with a view to a gradual determination of the directions that should be taken. Intervention by the locally elected representatives has played a central role in so far as it has injected the pressure of public opinion into a debate previously reserved to professionals and activists. The policy of security has gained its legitimacy in the fusion of retribution and prevention.

## A POLICY FOR REDUCING INSECURITY

An insecurity reduction policy is defined by three objectives. First, such a policy must be based on multifaceted and comprehensive local development. Only under these conditions can it meet the needs of the individual. Petty crime and incivilities are indicative of a greater social malaise alienation vis-à-vis school, inadequate training, unsanitary housing, family violence, non-existent cultural tools, deplorable health conditions, a lack of organized recreation, and so on. Any intervention in one area, without taking the others into account, is doomed to failure. It is all well and good to renovate housing, but the renovation will need to be done over again very quickly unless you simultaneously consider the young people hanging around the front door. Forcing children back to school counts for nothing unless the pedagogical program content is transformed to take the child's cultural lag into account. Reconciling estranged spouses is pointless unless the question of shelter for the woman and her children is settled. Only a comprehensive development policy is capable of giving individuals back their dignity and allowing them to face their responsibilities. This policy is concentrated on poverty-stricken neighborhoods in Europe. The general context in these communities is the almost total lack of public services that the rest of a city's population enjoys. These neighborhoods have no public transportation; their mail delivery is very unreliable. This lack of services helps keep these populations under-developed, and accentuates their feeling of not being citizens like everyone else. Efforts to reintroduce services require careful consideration as to the nature of the service and how it should be adapted to a neighborhood's specific needs. It is imperative that this not lead to an introduction of summary, low-quality services.

Second, the policy for reducing insecurity arises through concerted action. Across Europe, local groups of partners are appearing at the municipal level. Their diversity is vast and justifies the use of the term "local coalitions". The administrative, financial and legal organization of the European states is extremely varied. The range between the image of the centralizing state and that of the federation or confederation is very broad. Despite this variety, local coalitions are gradually adopting the same way of operating. They involve the same partners: legal system, police, social workers, schools, public transportation, private sector and business people. Local coalitions' areas of investigation and action cover drug addicts to dropouts, even neighborhood development. The type of coalition is not necessarily unique, since a single city can have several coalitions. These coalitions can be decentralized at the neighborhood level. All the partners operate from a common understanding of the situation, mutually discussed objectives and results indicators. A local coordinator is appointed to animate local coalition(s). This is a new field, necessitating well-rounded training to enable the coordinator to share disparate professional views.

Third, the policy for reducing insecurity aims to develop community regulation mechanisms. These so-called community policies focus primarily on the development of the individual and his or her place within the community. Most community-based crime prevention efforts have sought to generate informal social control, i.e., to regulate crime without recourse to the law. In previous approaches, community social control was presumed to emerge from the development of home-grown community organizations, with active participation in the establishment of local organizations (social clubs, churches, political groups, and so on) on the part of those living there. These organizations were to obtain mutual aid at the community level (with the development of economic resources), and to serve as agencies for socializing young people, the latter a particularly important element for crime control. In the 1970s, this community development approach cleared the way to a more behavioral approach, with an emphasis on monitoring crime and disturbances.

A community identity is encouraged among residents to afford them the will and ability to exert control over criminal behavior in their neighborhood. A number of measures have been proposed, such as the creation of defensible space and better home security, residential clean-up and maintenance programs to combat vandalism and disorder, local tenant management initiatives, neighborhood watch projects, community-based policing, and direct tenant participation in residential management. Communities are organized with a view to empowering them to solve their own problems, including the control or regulation of internal predatory criminal behavior. Reducing insecurity (and creating a defensible space) means having people get to know one another and develop mutual trust, in order to create collective projects and representation and to foster debate. Mediation projects are explicit in this regard since they attempt to reduce insecurity by means of the debate between the protagonists. Successful experiences have shown that the feeling of danger against which we have to defend ourselves and the fact of seeing ourselves as potential victims can serve as pretexts for contact and the impetus for collective mobilization.

But why it is so difficult to organize a community-based reduction of insecurity? The initial problem is social fragmentation within the community. Crime-deterring activities are less common in heterogeneous, low-income, rental and poorly maintained neighborhoods with high turnover and crime rates, where residents have little personal influence over what happens. The obstacle is not anomie, but social fragmentation into small groups and cliques whose members are familiar with each other but disinclined to get to know those strangers, the other residents, who are seen as potentially dangerous. Mutual distrust and lack of confidence undermine organizational efforts, especially those requiring an exchange of information among and about the members. The residents can still see their neighbors and nearby friends as a source of mutual support, but these networks do not extend across the entire neighborhood.

The second problem is the stigmatizing of high-crime communities, an issue that has received little attention in community-based crime prevention theory and practice. At one time it was thought that a given neighborhood's high crime rate was the result of increased police vigilance in that area. But a deeper and internal stigmatization process can be detected within the community itself. As the reputation worsens, migration to and from a community becomes selective; those with personal resources, and who could have served as activists and representatives, tend to leave. Those with numerous personal problems, including a desperate need for housing, are the ones willing to move in.

The third problem is the relationship among residential turnover, community evolution and crime. Gaining informal social control over a high-crime community is dependent on keeping the majority of the community in place. Residents' satisfaction rises, the sense of territoriality is strengthened, and the turnover and break-in rates are reduced when the municipality develops a neighborhood's collective and private space, and creates better defensible space. Such an evolution creates favorable conditions for making tenants more organized and responsible, in spite of the increased poverty that sometimes occurs. This does not happen when a neighborhood is more or less abandoned by the financial backers of society, with a resulting high turnover rate. And the situation is even worse when the arrival of younger and more poverty-stricken residents precipitates the catastrophic departure of the former population.

The problem is not one of releasing a latent community spirit that housing design, deficient management, anomie or lack of community organization have prevented from being expressed. This supposed latent community often no longer exists, or exists only on a small scale. And if it does exist, it is at the very private level of neighborliness rather than of the neighborhood as a whole. Why has the sense of community been eroded in high-risk zones? The rising structural and long-term unemployment of youths and the spatial concentration of poverty undermine community bonds and citizens' ability to face disruptive behavior and victimization of residents. The poverty currently experienced by young people effects the formation of stable family systems. It produces men who have no personal ties and are vulnerable to the seduction of crime, and overburdened women who are no longer able to protect themselves from predators or their children from getting caught up in delinquency. In addition, the departure of the more stable members of these neighborhoods undermines community control even more, depriving the community of leaders and positive role models.

What is the outlook for community-based crime regulation today? Four types of policies co-exist. The first is community preservation via investment in the protection and support of the most stable communities, or portions of communities, in order to keep their living conditions from deteriorating as have so many others. The risk remains that the cost of such a strategy will be social balkanization and an increased marginalization of the excluded, if not reinforcement of racist and xenophobic trends.

The second policy is community control of troublemakers. If the younger poor must be excluded from stable communities, then perhaps they should be placed under the control of the community. The solution adopted by Chicago Housing Project officials for ridding some units of drug traffic, violence, and gang warfare meant police crackdowns, extensive searches,expulsion of unqualified occupants (mostly men), a curfew, protection of residents (mostly women) from predators, and a gang truce. Unfortunately, what often happens is that the will to get rid of troublemakers at any cost overrides civil liberties and rights. The war against drugs serves to justify the confiscation of goods without due process, injunctions and expulsions. Certain forms of community control are doubtless more acceptable than others. The primary goal must be containing and controlling the troublemakers in the name of respecting the freedoms of the other residents.

A third policy, damage reduction and redistribution, develops an approach focusing exclusively on the victim, with a view to protecting him or her and reducing the damage inflicted by crime. This can mean identifying vulnerable groups, single-mother families, for example, and developing a range of measures for sheltering them from predation and exploitation. It can also mean taking an interest in individuals who have been victimized in the past and letting them know that they are running a real risk of being victimized again. An approach centered on the people and places who bear a disproportionate amount of the suffering has not only the merit of being socially just (since it deals with the victims), but also represents an efficient use of the limited means available for crime prevention. It even results in a redistributive justice if, through the crime prevention effort, there is significant reduction of the risk run by those who are suffering the most, even at the price of a marginal increase of risk for the rest of society. This approach, however, is obviously of little help in responding to the perpetrator problem. Further, when one bears in mind the efforts taken to control domestic violence, it remains to be seen whether protecting the victim is enough to prevent the abuses of power that govern many relationships and create insecurity in cities.

Finally, policies are directed toward promoting social cohesion and forestalling the creation of an underclass. The breakdown of community-based insecurity reduction may be caused by a combination of structural trends and local policies that concentrate young unemployed men in one area and undermine the community's ability to control them. If so, then the solutions lie with social and economic policies. However, these policies will not eliminate the need to come up with ways to minimize, in spite of everything, the resulting insecurity and suffering, to protect the most vulnerable, and to rediscover common standards, a credible expression of disapproval, universal freedoms, and a coming together of individuals. This is the price that must be paid to bring an end to the balkanization of cities and the alienation of a rising number of young, and not so young, people with no resources and little to lose.

# 6. A THEORETICAL STUDY AND CRITIQUE OF RESTORATIVE JUSTICE

by

## Kevin I. Minor

and

## J. T. Morrison

**Abstract:** *This chapter approaches restorative justice from the perspectives of Emile Durkheim, Karl Marx and Michel Foucault—perspectives that have provided worthwhile bases for inquiry into the sociology of punishment. Restorative justice practices are compared and contrasted with more conventional sanctions, and a variety of issues are raised for restorative justice advocates to consider. These issues include: the questionability of satisfying community outrage through restorative practice; the need to address underlying contradictions that generate social conflict; the potentialities for cooptation, goal displacement, and net widening in restorative practice; and the need to overcome the alienation of community members from punishment processes brought about with the ascent of conventional sanctions.*

Restorative justice may be defined as a response to criminal behavior that seeks to restore losses suffered by crime victims and to facilitate peace and tranquillity among opposing parties (Galaway and Hudson, 1990). Active and cooperative participation of all parties (i.e., governmental officials, offenders, victims and other community members) is essential under restorative justice philosophy. Restorative justice is a combination of theory and practice; practices include programs such as restitution and victim-offender reconciliation. By contrast, the predominant response to criminal behavior today—what can be called traditional corrections—reflects an adversarial conception of justice and is characterized by retribution and utilitarianism. The aims of traditional sanctions (*e.g.*, incarceration) are to achieve vengeance, just deserts, deterrence, incapacitation, and/or rehabilitation by punishing offenders and placing them in treatment programs. Participation of victims and other community members is minimal. The state is almost exclusively responsible for directing actions toward offenders in an adversarial fashion.

Traditional corrections has undergone much theoretical scrutiny in sociological criminology (Christie, 1993; Foucault, 1979; Garland, 1990; Ignatieff, 1978; Michalowski, 1993; Rothman, 1971, 1980; Scull, 1977). This scholarship has enriched understanding of the development and operation of corrections in society. That restorative justice, as an alternative response to crime, has received far less theoretical attention is understandable since it is not yet as dominant in corrections as more conventional retributive and utilitarian themes. Nonetheless, as restorative justice evolves, it should be examined using the same theoretical frameworks that have already been applied to traditional corrections. It might be argued that since restorative justice is not as punitive as many reactions to crime, it should not (or cannot) be analyzed utilizing theories of punishment. However, both restorative justice practices and more punitive practices constitute legally condoned strategies for responding to crime and pursuing social control (Scimecca, 1991). These strategies are what theories of punishment, broadly construed, are meant to address. The purpose of this chapter is to examine restorative justice from the standpoint of major theoretical perspectives on punishment and corrections. The viewpoints to be considered include the Durkheimian, Marxist, and Foucauldian perspectives and follow Garland's (1990) scheme for distinguishing established approaches to punishment.

## THE DURKHEIMIAN PERSPECTIVE

Reciprocal interaction between social order (solidarity) and punishment is a key notion of Durkheim (1893, 1902). Durkheim envisioned certain moral values and norms, what he termed the collective conscience, as being more or less shared by members of a society and as representing the foundation for social order. Social order leads to punishment; the expressive or retributive aspect of punishment evidences itself from shared outrage emerging from an aggravation of the collective conscience. By contrast, the instrumental or utilitarian function of punishment strengthens and reaffirms the collective conscience. Punishment exacted contributes to and helps sustain the social order. Punishment is necessary to deter offending and preserve the collective conscience (Garland, 1990; Lynch *et al.*, 1993). Thus, Durkheim saw punishment as arising from violations of the collective conscience and as functioning to reaffirm that conscience.

Durkheim (1902) argued that punishment methods will generally become less harsh and intense as a society advances from simple (mechanical) to complex (organic) form. The collective conscience is likely to reflect strong religious sentiments in simple societies. Moral codes and norms assume a sacred quality, and infractions are interpreted as offenses against a sacred, supernatural entity. The result is that punishment is often harsh and physical in nature (e.g., flogging). In more complex, differentiated societies, the collective conscience is more secular in nature. Norm infractions are interpreted as offenses against such entities as humanity and property. Consequently, punishments become moderated and tend to revolve around imprisonment. Likewise, Durkheim (1893) posited that as societies become increasingly complex, repressive law will devolve and restitutive law will become more prevalent. Repressive law is tantamount to criminal law and is characterized by an emphasis on inflicting punishment. Restitutive law, designed to restore troubled social relations to a previous, untroubled state, is nonpunitive and exemplified by civil and constitutional law (Hunt, 1978; Milovanovic, 1994).

The growing popularity of restorative justice in modern society is partly consistent with Durkheim's thought. Although there is little evidence of a substantial decline in repressive law (Hunt, 1978), the proliferation of restorative justice practices can be taken as partial evidence of both an increase in restitutive law and a moderation of correctional methods. Durkheim, however, did not envision that restitutive law would entirely replace repressive law. Repressive law's emphasis on punishment, in Durkheim's view, accomplishes crucial purposes. It expresses emotional outrage and preserves the collective conscience.

It may appear unlikely, in the Durkheimian scheme of things, that restorative justice practices can adequately meet these purposes. Shared community outrage can be expressed through restorative justice practices, but such an expression is different from the expression achieved by punishment of offenders. Simply put, restorative justice is not a vengeful response to crime, and vengeful responses are perhaps the most blatant means of displaying emotional outrage. It is precisely this absence of vengefulness that can make restorative justice difficult for political officials to sell to constituents who demand a tough stance on crime. In effect, persons who view restorative justice as soft on crime and argue that it should not be used in response to criminal behavior— or should be used only with a very restricted range of petty offenses— are often arguing that restorative justice is not sufficiently vengeful to satisfy the sense of community outrage being experienced. The potential effect of this mindset can be to undermine community and political support for wide-scale implementation of restorative justice programs.

Lack of community support may stem from strong passions concerning criminal behavior, and positions grounded in strong passions are often exceedingly difficult to change. Interestingly, this criticism of restorative justice can be countered by drawing on the same Durkheimian ideas from which the criticism arises. Durkheim conceived punishment as being incapable of creating a moral order in society. Punishment can only express and sustain an established morality; a moral order is created through socialization and education. Punishment entails hostility, aggression and the infliction of harm (Evarts, 1990; Mead, 1918; Pepinsky, 1991) rather than education *per se*. On the other hand, restorative justice seems much better suited to moral education because it teaches communication, negotiation, compromise and related skills.

How, then, may a move away from punitive and toward restorative justice be enhanced? One way to do so is to realize that while punishment of offenders is driven by anger (from which vengeful motives derive), vengefulness is reinforced by punishment. The way we respond to offenders helps shape our emotions toward them (Garland, 1990). Garland, in his critique of Durkheim, suggests that our response to criminal behavior involves an array of contradictory and ambivalent emotions (*e.g.*, outrage, resentment, sympathy and compassion). We should recognize that punishment perpetuates itself; as long as punishment is our predominant response to lawbreaking, anger will be a predominant feeling toward offenders and anger will beget punishment. A restorative justice response might afford a different cycle of reinforcement, since less punitive or coercive programs may well mitigate hostile emotions.

An apparent contradiction arises if Durkheim is interpreted as predicting that restorative justice will be more acceptable to members of modern complex societies, where a secularized collective conscience prevails, than to members of simple societies. Restorative justice practices are prevalent in many simple societies. How can this be explained, given Durkheim's position on the relationship of the collective conscience to strong religious sentiments and the accompanying preference for harsh physical punishments in simple societies? It must be remembered that Durkheim saw the collective conscience of complex societies as being generally weaker than that of simple societies (Milovanovic, 1994); greater uniformity in life circumstances and a less extensive division of labor in simple societies translate into greater agreement on values and norms. An underlying assumption of restorative justice is that fairly strong interpersonal agreement on values and norms can be achieved. Theoretically, since such agreement is more prevalent in simple societies than in complex ones, restorative justice practices should be quite common in the former societies.

In sum, there is little in the Durkheimian perspective that insurmountably challenges the philosophy of restorative justice. At a most fundamental level, Durkheim viewed both law and responses to lawbreaking as reflecting a broad level of consensus on values and norms. Restorative justice can be seen as a way of building greater consensus upon an existing foundation of consensus.

## THE MARXIST PERSPECTIVE

Various Marxist perspectives on punishment have been forwarded. Rusche and Kirchheimer (1939) emphasize the role of economic factors in shaping responses to crime, especially labor market conditions and fiscal pressures faced by the state (Adamson, 1984; Scull, 1977). Genovese (1982) and Hay (1982) focus on the political and ideological forces that legitimate punishment and mould punishment's public image. Other writers combine and extend these ideas (Garland, 1985; Ignatieff, 1978; Michalowski, 1993). An overarching theme is that law and punishment operate within the confines of a society's dominant mode of economic production and concomitant political order. As such, law and punishment reflect social conflicts generated by contradictions and tensions inherent in the mode of production, and are generally biased in favor of groups possessing wealth and power. Marxists have criticized Durkheim's conception of the collective conscience. Marxists argue that agreements on values and norms, to the degree that agreements exist, are often illusory in that they emerge from dynamic and ongoing processes of political negotiation, compromise and ideological persuasion. What Garland (1990) terms the "ruling morality" or "dominant moral order" (p.52) (as a substitute for Durkheim's collective conscience) is ruling or dominant by virtue of having prevailed over competing moralities. Therefore, conflict underlies ostensible consensus. The function of punishment, from this standpoint, ceases to be preservation of the collective conscience and becomes instead preservation of the political and economic order that so strongly shapes the ruling morality.

Class antagonisms between the interests of labor and capital are a prime source of social conflict within a capitalist mode of production (Chambliss, 1988). It is only by addressing this and related contradictions inherent in capitalism that true and lasting progress can be made toward resolving conflict. Moreover, the primary responsibility for addressing social conflict and crime has increasingly shifted from the victim and local community to the centralized state (Hawkins and Alpert, 1989; Michalowski, 1985; Spitzer, 1979). Modern capitalism is characterized by a high degree of state control over deviance.

Advocates of restorative justice see crime as a type of social conflict and are concerned with restoring conflict to a state of peaceful social relations (Trenczek, 1990). The Marxist perspective also conceptualizes crime as conflict but views law and responses to lawbreaking as indicative of deeper, underlying conflict in society. Crime represents conflict, but conflict shapes law. To what pre-existing state of affairs do restorative justice practices seek to restore conflict? Logically, these practices can restore a given conflict to a peaceful, harmonious state only if such a state preceded conflict. Since the Marxist perspective does not imply prior existence of interpersonal peace and harmony, restorative justice practices may be of limited utility at best if they do not address the underlying contradictions that generate conflicts. At worst, the perspective implies that since consensus is illusory, efforts at promoting peace and harmony that do not address fundamental contradictions in the productive mode mainly serve the interests of advantaged groups who benefit from the illusion of consensus. From this standpoint, the functions achieved by traditional corrections are still achieved (albeit more subtly) by restorative practices. However, the educative effects of restorative justice, which are potentially capable of inducing morality in the Durkheimian perspective, become legitimating ideology. For instance, respect for private property relations is a message conveyed to property offenders in victim-offender reconciliation programs. Likewise, to require the offender to make restitution is to reinforce the principle of equity and the work ethic so central to private property relations. Such messages are particularly revealing when offenders come from less advantaged class backgrounds than victims.

To the extent that restorative practice fails to address fundamental contradictions, neither the inequitable distribution of resources typical of capitalist societies nor the social class disparities that pervade the spectrum of criminal justice will be abated by restorative programs. Restoration will entail restoration to the status quo. To illustrate, restitution can create heavy burdens for economically disadvantaged persons, many of whom are hard pressed to pay much of anything back to anyone. Restitution presents less of a burden when economically advantaged persons enter the criminal justice system. Moreover, even if wider-scale adoption of restitution programming does not ultimately culminate in restitution being disproportionately reserved for the economically well off, class inequities can surround the type of restitution performed. There is a qualitative difference between a middle- or higher-class person repaying a victim or community with money earned from a well-paying, respectable status job and a lower class, unemployed person performing menial labor in a community service project. Reconciliation programs pose similar difficulties, especially when offenders are from lower-class backgrounds than victims and/or program staff.

Scimecca (1991) makes an instructive distinction between conflict resolution and conflict settlement.

The distinction between *conflict resolution* and *conflict settlement* is that the former brings about an outcome that is self-supporting and stable because it solves the problem which produced the conflict, whereas the latter fosters an outcome which does not necessarily meet the needs of all concerned. A settlement of a conflict is accepted at the time because of the jurisdiction of a court, the superior bargaining power of the opposing party, or some coercive threat that has been exercised by the opposing party or by a third party [p.265].

Many restorative justice programs come closer to pursuing conflict settlement than conflict resolution objectives. Restorative justice advocates are aware of these issues, which helps explain why they are concerned over whether restorative justice programs should be separate from or part of the criminal justice system (Coates, 1990; Marshall, 1990; Volpe, 1991). From a Marxist perspective, a fundamental issue surrounding the incorporation of restorative justice and criminal justice is the potential for cooptation of the former, and there is some evidence that this potential has been actualized. Sessar (1990), for example, reports that in Germany the effect of victim participation in criminal justice is frequently to emotionalize the crime problem, thereby enhancing punishment rather than restitution. Under the existing adversarial philosophy, the criminal offends the impersonal entity of the state. When a restorative justice philosophy is added, the offender offends both the state and the victim. Thus, a subtle justification for additional punishment of the offender is created.

Ultimately, persons who favor wide-scale implementation of restorative justice programs have three choices. They may: (1) strive to gradually substitute restorative justice programs for traditional correctional practices; (2) allow restorative and traditional programs to coexist independently of one another; or (3) incorporate restorative practices into the extant repertoire of state-sponsored correctional interventions. Progress toward the first choice is bound to be hindered by resistance from the established political and correctional infrastructures. From a Marxist perspective, state control over deviance is an integral feature of modern capitalism and is not likely to be relinquished. The second choice implies that decisions must be made as to which cases are appropriate for restorative justice programming. Without drastic changes in public and political sentiments about the crime problem, restorative justice is likely to be used in only a fragmented fashion for the less serious offense categories. The third choice is appealing to those who believe that reforms can best be achieved at a grassroots level by grafting reforms onto established bureaucratic practices. However, encouraging restorative practices among agencies that are preoccupied with bureaucratic needs and interests can strongly undermine the intents of restorative justice. This variety of cooptation is commonly termed goal displacement.

Displacement of the intended goals of restorative programs is a salient concern given the bureaucratic nature of modern criminal justice systems. Traditional corrections operates within a highly bureaucratic framework; and the tendency to create, sustain, and sometimes expand agencies staffed by civil servants should caution restorative justice advocates. Emotion is jettisoned from vocational, bureaucratic duties as civil servants become specialized and professionalized. Echoing Max Weber, Garland (1990) observes "it is a characteristic of bureaucratic organizations that they operate in a passionless, routinized, matter-of-fact kind of way" (p.183). Yet, an understanding of offenders and victims as human beings, rather than as files or case numbers, seems essential to attaining genuine restorative justice. Compassion and understanding among victim, offender and other concerned parties are desirable outcomes of restorative practice, but these feelings may not be forthcoming in a setting that makes them subservient to bureaucratic priorities.

The Marxist perspective alerts us to a related consideration, specifically, the influences of fiscal factors on responses to crime. Community-based alternatives to incarceration restrain the costs of regulating criminals without completely relinquishing state control (Scull, 1977; Spitzer, 1993). Do crime control officials who support restorative justice policies do so because they find genuine merit in the restorative justice philosophy, or because they see these practices as fiscally sound maneuvers in an era of high crime, crowded prisons, and overburdened probation and parole agencies? Support for restorative justice can be expected to vary with fiscal climates to the degree that the latter motive overrides the former. Restorative programs may become part of the mentality that cheaper, but lesser, control is superior to no control at all, and the salutary aims of restorative justice will become secondary to fiscal and control objectives.

## THE FOUCAULDIAN PERSPECTIVE

Governmental power and control are central to Foucault's (1979) theorizing about punishment. For him, punishment and other state responses to crime are part of a diffuse and variegated network of power relations that, by virtue of being informed by knowledge of the objects of power, result in regulation and domination of those objects. Power depends on knowledge, and, when exercised, advances itself by deepening knowledge. The informed exercise of power against an object increases knowledge of the object, further facilitating power.

Foucault (1979) employs the term "discipline" to describe what has become the major governmental strategy of exerting power and control in modern societies. Discipline refers to a process of rendering people obedient to power and authority. In contrast to earlier capital and corporal punishments, which were directed at the deviant's body and meant to repress his or her behavior, discipline is a milder, gentler form of control that seeks to regulate behavior by transforming the mind and character. A main goal of disciplining deviants is to induce normality. The discipline and normalization process entails two fundamental phases. First, deviants must be assessed and classified in relation to some desired or normal standard of behavior. That is, knowledge must be gained about where the person's behavior is in relation to the standard. Second, the deviant is subjected to intervention meant to align his or her behavior with the standard. The intervention process deepens and re-fines knowledge, and establishes the stage for intervention modification should this prove necessary to attaining normality.

Foucault (1979) does not see the disciplinary process as restricted to governmental domains. The process increasingly permeates the various institutions of society (family, workplace, school, mental health, and so forth). All institutions use disciplinary techniques that are fundamentally alike, and it is common for deviants to be readily transferred from one disciplinary agency to another (from public school, to alternative school, to probation or another diversion agency, to prison or a mental hospital). Indeed, Foucault posits the existence of a carceral continuum, ranging from institutionalized methods of addressing comparatively mild deviations at one end, to methods of dealing with more severe deviations at the other end. At each point on the continuum, the concern is to identify and correct departures from normalcy.

> Prison continues, on those who are entrusted to it, a work begun elsewhere, which the whole of society pursues on each individual through innumerable mechanisms of discipline. By means of a carceral continuum, the authority that sentences infiltrates all those other authorities that supervise, transform, correct, improve. It might even be said that nothing really distinguishes them any more except the singularly "dangerous" character of the delinquents, the gravity of their departures from normal behaviour and the necessary solemnity of the ritual. But, in its function, the power to punish is not essentially different from that of curing or educating [Foucault, 1979:302-303].

Like Marx, Foucault sees the shift from corporal and capital punishments to milder disciplinary methods as coinciding with the development of capitalism. The proliferation of private property relations gave rise to the need for closer regulation of property crimes. Modern disciplinary punishments emerged to constitute a middle-ground between excess severity and no sanction at all, since corporal and capital punishments were perceived as excessively severe reactions to these crimes.

Foucault's perspective challenges the uniqueness of restorative justice philosophy and indicts its effects. Distinctions between restorative justice and traditional corrections (or, for that matter, distinctions between all modern forms of social regulation) become difficult to sustain. According to Foucault, political domination through discipline is the essence of any form of behavioral regulation. Restorative practices promote discipline and normality by teaching offenders how to communicate, compromise, empathize, repair wrongs and so forth. Foucault's ideas are therefore a reminder that despite whatever else restorative justice might be, it is still a way of exercising power and social control. Restorative programs increase knowledge of offenders and therefore enhance potential for exercising power over them. Restorative programs effectively provide greater power to normalize offenders.

It is important to contemplate the role of restorative justice practices in the expanding network of disciplinary state control described by Foucault. Restorative programs might be viewed as one of the merging points on the carceral continuum for both non-legal and legal types of social control. Closely linked to this issue is Volpe's (1991) point that restorative justice practices, like victim-offender mediation, can have the effect of widening the net of social control. Net-widening transpires when an innovative program, which is supposed to represent an alternative to more formalized and punitive intervention, receives offenders who would have had lesser or no further action taken against them if the innovative program had been unavailable. The innovative program is not used with the persons for whom it was designed, increasing numbers of persons are pulled into the criminal justice system and state control is extended over more citizens. This gives officials justification for allocating more funds and creating new agencies and programs. The process fuels itself because once such agencies and programs are created, they must be used. Also, persons who have been pulled into an innovative program due to net-widening can often anticipate stiffer sanctioning if they do not comply with program requirements. Ultimately, such practice derives its power and credibility from the threat of stiffer sanctions located on the carceral continuum. Hence, more and more persons may be subjected to escalating levels of state intervention.

One of the features of modern disciplinary punishments, identified by Foucault, is that these punishments tend to be hidden from public view, being administered in such low visibility contexts as probation offices, counselling agencies, halfway houses, prisons, and jails. The corporal and capital punishments of earlier times were often public affairs in which on-lookers could at least gain a vicarious sense of participation (Newman, 1985). Garland (1990) describes this removal of punishment from the public eye as having down-played and disguised the emotions surrounding punishment. Punishment has been transformed from an emotionally charged, public phenomenon into a prerogative of correctional bureaucrats who strive for rationalized management of punitive processes.

Movement toward restorative practice would help bring responses to crime back into the open, and, in so doing, would recharge the emotional dimension of punishment. Public spectacles like the mediation table, the neighborhood justice center, and offenders performing community service would replace public spectacles of the past, or what Foucault (1979) collectively labels "the spectacle of the scaffold" (p.32). Whereas older spectacles reaffirmed the power of the sovereign to repress, the newer spectacles would affirm the power of the state and its people to demand reparation for wrongs and reconciliation of conflicts. All this presumes the active participation of victims and community members in restorative justice programs. However, as punishment was removed from the public eye and rendered less emotionally compelling, community members grew alienated from punishment processes.

One must consider these historical trends and the many years of minimal community participation when considering ways to maximize community support and involvement. Community members are unlikely to assume responsibilities they are not accustomed to having if not convinced that it is in their best interests to do so. Furthermore, the more closely restorative justice programs are tied to the existing criminal justice apparatus, the greater the potential for community alienation from those programs. It was this apparatus that minimized community participation and de-emotionalized punishment in the first place. But the less closely restorative justice programs are tied to criminal justice, the stronger the barriers to their wide-scale implementation.

From Foucault's perspective, the underlying question becomes whether (and if so, how) to involve politically dominated citizens in a process of exerting political domination over offenders. But this question obscures a crucial point captured by Garland (1990) in a critique of Foucault. Regulation and control are not the only motives that guide reactions to criminal behavior. Similarly, oppressive domination is not the only outcome of such reactions. Benevolent and humanitarian motives also contribute, and some positive benefits transpire (e.g., acquisition of skills that will improve the quality of offenders' lives). The practices employed with offenders reflect divergent, sometimes contradictory motives, and outcomes are equally diverse. Neither motives nor outcomes are reducible to a singular construct.

Democratic freedoms imply the need for some kind of self-imposed or externalized regulation if civility is to exist. The alternative that usually comes to mind is a negative type of anarchy. Paradoxically, Foucault notes that the regulation needed to permit democracy also undermines its egalitarian principles. This is because regulation, by definition, implies superior-subordinate (regulator-regulated) relationships. A question, then, that returns us to Durkheim is, what type of moral values will serve as the regulatory underpinning for civil order? Concepts like compromise, reparation, and restoration present real alternatives to anger, retribution, and repression, despite the fact that both sets of concepts imply less than fully egalitarian social relations.

## CONCLUSIONS AND IMPLICATIONS

The Durkheimian perspective sensitizes us to the emotional and moral features of any response to crime, and, in this regard, there are important differences between restorative justice and traditional corrections. Because anger and force tend to beget anger and force, it is difficult to maintain the position that the moral and affective framework of traditional corrections is a constructive basis for crime control policy. Even though restorative justice may provide a more constructive basis, the Durkheimian perspective suggests that, in order to be more widely accepted and implemented, restorative justice programs will need to better mesh with public sentiments about crime and responses to it. Theoretically, restorative practice can help alter retributive sentiments. The implication is that restorative justice advocates should recognize and utilize the educative potential of their practice. Community emotions about crime are likely to heighten with the increased level of community participation necessitated by restorative programming. A backlash might transpire if the educative aspect of restorative justice practice has not successfully informed public opinion and curtailed retributive sentiments. The already strong calls for harsh punishment coming from community members could grow stronger, and restorative justice could eventuate in more rather than less punishment.

Counter to Durkheimian assumptions, evidence suggests a conflict interpretation rather than a consensus model of the origins of law and responses to lawbreaking (Akers, 1994). Researchers are endeavoring to explicate what type of conflict interpretation is most valid. Consistent with the Marxist perspective, much of this research indicates that a valid interpretation must attend to contradictions in social structure (Chambliss and Seidman, 1982; McGarrell and Castellano, 1991; Whitt, 1993). Consequently, restorative justice proponents should be wary of propagating images of consensus, lest their efforts provide ideological re-inforcement for highly unequal economic and power relations. To the de-gree that crime, law, and punishment are shaped by deep, underlying conflicts and contradictions, restorative justice practice should continu-ally strive to address conflicts and contradictions. When possible, re-storative practice should be creatively linked to structural reforms. Res-titution programs, for example, could operate as part of larger job creation initiatives designed to curtail economic inequality.

When attaching programs to criminal justice, proponents of restora-tive justice must actively preempt cooptation; otherwise, the integrity of these programs' intents may be compromised. It is questionable whether restorative justice programs should be justified (i.e., sold) primarily on the basis of fiscal merit. The programs are being accepted for a less than adequate reason if fiscal benefits are the primary consideration.

Foucault's perspective is a reminder that restorative justice is, at its crux, a coercive social control strategy that is not totally distinct from the less subtle forms of behavioral regulation it seeks to supplement or replace. Accordingly, it is important to recognize and counter the ten-dency of diversionary, subtle social control mechanisms to result in net-widening. When a program's admission criteria are developed and ap-plied, a guiding concern should be to avoid accepting cases that would have received lesser or no intervention in the program's absence; re-storative justice should generally be an alternative to more formalized punitive responses. The tendency for offender non-compliance with the requirements of restorative programs to result in stiffer sanctions can be countered. In part, this tendency results from the inclination to judge of-fender performance by preconceived norms for program operation and outcome. In rebuttal to Foucault, there is no *a priori* reason why restora-tive justice programs must strive to achieve a preconceived standard of normality. An instructive lesson from the symbolic interactionist tradi-tion is that norms can emerge from the process of interaction among program participants. Clearly, offenders are more likely to comply with norms they themselves have had some hand in creating. Expectations for program outcome should be kept realistic and rather modest. Modest and realistic expectations establish the stage for less disappointment and frustration when lofty outcomes are not forthcoming, and, in so do-ing, may quell the urge to employ stiffer sanctions.

Future theoretical inquiry could examine the linkages between re-storative justice and other criminological perspectives. For instance,

Braithwaite's (1989) reintegrative shaming perspective is consistent with the logic of restorative justice. This perspective stresses the importance of avoiding stigmatization and sustaining an atmosphere of interpersonal respect and interdependency when showing disapproval to law violators. Pepinsky's (1991) peacemaking model, which conceptualizes both crime and contemporary reactions to crime in terms of unresponsiveness, can be tied to restorative justice. Broadly defined, unresponsiveness is a kind of egocentrism, a cultural atmosphere of disregard for the effects one's actions have on other people. Moreover, unresponsiveness reproduces itself in that people who are treated in an unresponsive manner are likely to display unresponsive behavior toward others. The key to improving social control systems is to establish a cultural environment of responsiveness, wherein one's intentions and actions are "modified continually to accommodate the experience and feelings of those affected by one's actions" (Pepinsky, 1991, p.16).

As Durkheim realized, reactions to crime will always be guided by emotionally charged moral values; the crux of the matter is what values will explicitly serve as the guide. Advocates of restorative justice, reintegrative shaming and peacemaking appear to agree that responsive values should inform reactions to crime. The next step must be to confront the reality that responsive reactions to crime must be part of a wider system of social, political and economic justice premised on responsive values.

## REFERENCES

Adamson, C. (1984). "Toward a Marxian Penology: Captive Criminal Populations as Economic Threats and Resources." *Social Problems* 31:435-458.

Akers, R.L. (1994). *Criminological Theories: Introduction and Evaluation.* Los Angeles, CA: Roxbury.

Braithwaite, J. (1989). *Crime, Shame and Reintegration.* New York, NY: Cambridge University Press.

Chambliss, W.J. (1988). *Exploring Criminology.* New York, NY: Macmillan.

—and R. Seidman (1982). *Law, Order, and Power.* Reading, PA: Addison-Wesley.

Christie, N. (1993). *Crime Control as Industry: Towards Gulags Western Style?* New York, NY: Routledge.

Coates, R.B. (1990). "Victim-Offender Reconciliation Programs in North America: An Assessment." In: B. Galaway and J. Hudson (eds.), *Criminal Justice, Restitution, and Reconciliation.* Monsey, NY: Criminal Justice Press.

Durkheim, E. (1893). *The Division of Labor in Society.* Reprint. New York, NY: Free Press, 1964.

—(1902). "The Evolution of Punishment." In: S. Lukes and A. Scull (eds.), *Durkheim and the Law.* Reprint. Oxford, UK: Oxford University Press, 1983.

Evarts, W.R. (1990). "Compensation through Mediation: A Conceptual Framework." In: B. Galaway and J. Hudson (eds.), *Criminal Justice, Restitution, and Reconciliation.* Monsey, NY: Criminal Justice Press.

Foucault, M. (1979). *Discipline and Punish: The Birth of the Prison.* New York, NY: Vintage.

Galaway, B. and J. Hudson (eds.) (1990). *Criminal Justice, Restitution, and Reconciliation.* Monsey, NY: Criminal Justice Press.

Garland, D. (1985). *Punishment and Welfare: A History of Penal Strategies.* Aldershot, UK: Gower.

—(1990). *Punishment and Modern Society: A Study in Social Theory.* Chicago, IL: University of Chicago Press.

Genovese, E.D. (1982). "The Hegemonic Function of the Law." In: P. Beirne and R. Quinney (eds.), *Marxism and Law.* New York, NY: Wiley.

Hawkins, R. and G.P. Alpert (1989). *American Prison Systems: Punishment and Justice.* Englewood Cliffs, NJ: Prentice-Hall.

Hay, D. (1982). "Property, Authority and the Criminal Law." In: P. Beirne and R. Quinney (eds.), *Marxism and Law.* New York, NY: Wiley.

Hunt, A. (1978). *The Sociological Movement in Law.* Philadelphia, PA: Temple University Press.

Ignatieff, M. (1978). *A Just Measure of Pain: The Penitentiary in the Industrial Revolution.* New York, NY: Pantheon.

Lynch, M.J., G.R. Newman and W.B. Groves (1993). "Control Theory and Punishment: An Analysis of Control Theory as a Penal Philosophy." In: F. Adler and W.S. Laufer (eds.), *Advances in Criminological Theory, vol. 4. New Directions in Criminological Theory.* New Brunswick, NJ: Transaction.

Marshall, T.F. (1990). "Results of Research from British Experiments in Restorative Justice." In: B. Galaway and J. Hudson (eds.), *Criminal Justice, Restitution, and Reconciliation.* Monsey, NY: Criminal Justice Press.

McGarrell, E.F. and T.C. Castellano (1991). "An Integrative Conflict Model of the Criminal Law Formation Process." *Journal of Research in Crime and Delinquency* 28:174-196.

Mead, G.H. (1918). "The Psychology of Punitive Justice." *American Journal of Sociology* 23:577-602.

Michalowski, R.J. (1985). *Order, Law, and Crime: An Introduction to Criminology.* New York, NY: Random House.

—(1993). "The Contradictions of Corrections: An Inquiry into Nested Dilemmas." In: W.J. Chambliss and M.S. Zatz (eds.), *Making Law: The State, the Law, and Structural Contradictions.* Bloomington, IN: Indiana University Press.

Milovanovic, D. (1994). *A Primer in the Sociology of Law,* 2nd ed. Albany, NY: Harrow and Heston.

Newman, G. (1985). _The Punishment Response_. Albany, NY: Harrow and Heston.

Pepinsky, H.E. (1991). _The Geometry of Violence and Democracy_. Bloomington, IN: Indiana University Press.

Rothman, D.J. (1971). _The Discovery of the Asylum: Social Order and Disorder in the New Republic_. Boston, MA: Little, Brown.

—(1980). _Conscience and Convenience: The Asylum and its Alternatives in Progressive America_. Boston, MA: Little, Brown.

Rusche, G. and O. Kirchheimer (1939). _Punishment and Social Structure_. Reprint. New York, NY: Russell and Russell, 1968.

Scimecca, J.A. (1991). "Conflict Resolution and a Critique of Alternative Dispute Resolution." In: H.E. Pepinsky and R. Quinney (eds.), _Criminology as Peacemaking_. Bloomington, IN: Indiana University Press.

Scull, A.T. (1977). _Decarceration: Community Treatment and the Deviant —A Radical View_. Englewood Cliffs, NJ: Prentice-Hall.

Sessar, K. (1990). "Tertiary Victimization: A Case of the Politically Abused Crime Victims." In: B. Galaway and J. Hudson (eds.), _Criminal Justice, Restitution, and Reconciliation_. Monsey, NY: Criminal Justice Press.

Spitzer, S. (1979). "The Rationalization of Crime Control in Capitalist Society." _Contemporary Crises_ 3:187-206.

—(1993). "Toward a Marxian Theory of Deviance." In: F.P. Williams III and M.D. McShane (eds.), _Criminology Theory: Selected Classic Readings_. Cincinnati, OH: Anderson.

Trenczek, T. (1990). "A Review and Assessment of Victim-Offender Reconciliation Programming in West Germany." In: B. Galaway and J. Hudson (eds.), _Criminal Justice, Restitution, and Reconciliation_. Monsey, NY: Criminal Justice Press.

Volpe, M.R. (1991). "Mediation in the Criminal Justice System: Process, Promises, Problems." In: H.E. Pepinsky and R. Quinney (eds.), _Criminology as Peacemaking_. Bloomington, IN: Indiana University Press.

Whitt, J.A. (1993). "Toward a Class-Dialectical Model of Power: An Empirical Assessment of Three Competing Models of Political Power." In: W.J. Chambliss and M.S. Zatz (eds.), _Making Law: The State, the Law, and Structural Contradictions_. Bloomington, IN: Indiana University Press.

# PART II
# RESTORATIVE JUSTICE PRACTICE
# AMONG INDIGENOUS PEOPLES

# 7. COLONIZATION, POWER AND SILENCE: A HISTORY OF INDIGENOUS JUSTICE IN NEW ZEALAND SOCIETY

by

## John Pratt

**Abstract:** *Pre-colonial Maori concepts of justice involved restoring balance by compensating victims, promoting kinship responsibility, imposing corporal sanctions, using diffuse and uncertain sanctions, providing chiefs with considerable discretion, and instituting punishments of a public nature that involved the community. In the eyes of the British colonists, this system seemed to encourage disorder and crime, and was inconsistent with emerging European concepts of individual responsibility, demand for order and certainty in punishments, replacement of corporal punishments with imprisonment, and removal of punishment from public view. By the end of the nineteenth century, the Maori had been assimilated into the British way of life. But Maori practices are being restored, to some extent, in contemporary New Zealand practices regarding youthful offenders. Youthful offenders are most typically dealt with through family group conferences that involve meetings with the youth, his or her family, and victims to work out a satisfactory resolution to the offense. Using Maori concepts when responding to adult offenders is more problematic although pressure to reduce the use of imprisonment may result in greater acceptance of these practices.*

"...the chiefs first sat down to discuss [the *muru*] amongst themselves; and their deliberations ended in their being satisfied with destroying the village of Matowe...which had been the residence of Pomaree's son, whose death was the cause of all the late turbulent events" (Earle, 1966, p.185).

This meeting took place in early-nineteenth century pre-colonial New

Zealand; the local Maori community are discussing their right to plunder (i.e., *muru*) in compensation for the murder of the son of a chief, although it seems that there were some extenuating circumstances. The remedy was to burn down the entire village where the incident took place: "[the raiding party] contented themselves with this and a general plunder of whatever property their enemies possessed. They spared the lives [of the inhabitants] and the outrage was considered atoned for" (Earle, 1966, p.172). The process encapsulates a clear commitment to restorative justice. No courts and lawyers, but an informal setting where conflicts are resolved among family representatives. Nor did this example of restorative justice content itself with dealing only with trivial cases that might otherwise have been ignored while "business as usual" was being conducted in the courts.

In this indigenous justice system—although the idea of a system of justice is in itself a product of modernity and is not strictly applicable to justice in pre-modern societies—conflicts were not owned by individuals or state bodies, but were seen as effecting and involving the much wider extended families of victims and offenders. Indeed, the victim's "right to justice" could be handed down from one generation to another, and could be pursued against the wrongdoer and their next of kin or tribe. Hence the importance attached to dispute proceedings, which might last for days while a resolution was being negotiated. The justice system did not exist in isolation from the rest of society (as with the elitism and professional dominance to be found in the European model) but was completely integrated within it, rooted in the everyday experiences of Maori people. In Maori society, this was the way all conflicts were dealt with, from the most trivial to the most serious. It was a way of doing justice built on the belief that socially harmful behavior (*hara*), whether of a civil or criminal nature in Western terms, had been caused by an imbalance to the social equilibrium. Sanctions were provided for behavior that would be recognized as wrong in any European jurisdiction (for example, theft, rape, and murder). In addition, infringement of *tapu* (sacred areas) was rigorously sanctioned, lest the offended ancestors take revenge on those meant to police the tapu, as were civil matters (in Western terms), such as adultery (*puremu*) and trespass, and those of a religious nature such as sorcery.

Conflict resolution took the form of a hearing held on the *marae* (area in front of the communal meeting house, or *wharaenui*) or inside a special wharenui called the *wharerunanga*. Its purpose was to investigate the matter and attempt to restore the balance that had been disturbed, usually by redressing the harm done to the victim. The quantity of redress would be dependent on the degree of the offense: a form of compensation (*utu*) for some, with mediation to remove causes of tension. Other offenses, say, some breaches of tapu, would be seen as serious enough to warrant death. But the interests of the victim and his or her family or tribe were central to the administration of justice.

The right to inflict death or destroy a village, as in the opening example, grossly offends most Western cultural sensitivities; to many these forms of punishment have simply become unthinkable (Garland, 1990). But restorative justice has not. Restorative justice practices have almost become a taken-for-granted goal of criminal justice reformers and governments alike since Christie's (1976) account of conflict resolution among the Barotse people of Africa. Restorative justice is popular because it gives a more central role to victims, is not constrained by legal niceties, does not allow itself to be taken over by court professionals and may thus be a money saver.

This chapter will explore the manner of its disappearance from New Zealand society in the aftermath of formal British colonization in 1840: what happened to restorative justice in that space between its existence as a living form of dispute resolution practiced by the Maori, and its rebirth as a political and criminal justice issue in the current era. After examining the impact of colonization on Maori dispute resolution processes, some of the prospects and possibilities for reintegrating these into contemporary responses to juvenile and adult offenders will be given consideration.

## JUSTICE, PUNISHMENT AND COLONIZATION

The records of early British travellers to New Zealand give the impression that they found no legal form in existence in the country (Polack, 1838; Dieffenbach, 1843). Maori justice was referred to as consisting of quaint customs. To prevent such anarchy, British forms of justice and punishment were quickly introduced (Pratt, 1992). The first public building constructed in Wellington (now the capital city) was a replica of Pentonville prison, opened in London in 1840 and thought at the time to be the most modern building in Europe (Ignatieff, 1978). One of the most important reasons for these importations from Britain was a bid to assure New Zealand's European colonizers in the nineteenth century and beyond that they remained part of the Western cultural world at whatever distance they might be from it or however fragile their new society might be.

Thus the following comments on the opening of the first courthouse in Auckland (the then capital city) in 1842 summarize the cultural significance that systems of law and punishment carry with them.

> The court house is by no means an imposing structure, but it is not without some historical interest. In this unpretending building the advent of a new power in these islands was solemnly proclaimed. For a period of several years lawlessness had reigned supreme: every man had been a law unto himself, and the law of the strongest had prevailed; but the time had now arrived when the reign of justice was to be formally proclaimed: and, in this modest temple, its first and chief minister, for the first time, took his seat a fit personification of its purity: one well chosen to hold the balance even, and pre-eminently fitted to administer justice impartially between the native people and a still more powerful race. Trusted with all the powers of several courts at Westminster, the first Chief Justice opened the proceedings of the court. There was no display of pomp, or show of military power, yet the first act of the new tribunal spoke, trumpet-tongued throughout the land; and it was silently felt, by both races of its inhabitants, that a power had been established amongst them to which, henceforward, all would be compelled to bow [Swainson, 1859, p.57].

Commitment to the West, and Britain in particular, signified that alternative world views such as those of New Zealand's indigenous Maori people were not permissable. The way to nullify these views was not by force of arms and racial extermination, as had happened in the era of pre-modern colonization. Instead, the silencing of indigenous peoples was to be achieved in a way that appeared more humane and in line with the values of the Enlightenment. One of the justifications for colonization in the mid- to late-nineteenth century was to civilize the noble savages found in distant lands. Assimilation into the British way of life was to be the gift of civilization: "...it is ours to supply them with a system where the humblest may enjoy freedom from oppression and wrong equally with the greatest; where the light of religion and morality can penetrate into the darkest dwelling places. This is the real fulfilment of our duties..." (Earl of Carnavon, 1878, quoted by Eldridge, 1978, p.2). But this gift also meant that indigenous peoples would have to give up their own cultural identity and institutions and take on those of Britain.

The goal was to silence the civilization that had previously existed, not by slaughter and mass warfare, but by transforming its savage population into British subjects.

In New Zealand, formally colonized in 1840, the British imperial frontier was pushed to one of its farthest and most remote boundaries. Even so, the settlers were determined to recreate a Britain of the South Pacific. Thus the Canterbury Association wanted "to set an example of a colonial settlement in which, from the first, all the elements, including the very highest, of a good and right state of society shall find their proper place and their active operations" (Association for Forming the Settlement of Canterbury in New Zealand, 1848).

Later in the colonization, it was as if a new Great Britain (free of its social problems) was being established:

New Zealand is an integral part of Great Britain, an immense sea-joined Devonshire. An Englishman going thither goes among his countrymen, he has the same queen, the same laws and customs, the same language, the same social institutions and save that he is in a country where trees are evergreen, and where there is no winter, no opera, no aristocracy, no income tax, no paupers, no beggars, no cotton mills, he is, virtually, in a young England [Hursthouse, 1857, p.637].

Not only did the availability of land conjure up an idyllic setting but, Wakefield himself, in a letter of 1841, envisaged that "in all probability New Zealand will be the most Church of England country in the world". By the same token, the Canterbury Association wanted their settlement to be "a colony which would accord the Church a distinctive part in the social organisation, [and] which would reproduce the graduation of English society ...". Governor Grey claimed that the ideal of the Canterbury Association was a colonial settlement that would reproduce "an English county with the Cathedral city, its famous University, its Bishop, its endowed clergy, its ancient aristocracy and its yeoman farmers, its few necessary tradesmen, its sturdy and loyal labourers" (Purchas, 1903, p.32). And, of course, the promise of land had made New Zealand appear an arcadian paradise when advertised by the British emigration companies.

Not only were the same forces that shaped the format of modern penality present in New Zealand as in Britain, but specific ideas and initiatives were deliberately imported from Britain (irrespective of the differing nature of crime problems). One was the replica of Pentonville prison;

others included: the New Zealand Offences against the Person Act of 1867 (prescribing inter alia whipping for the offense of garrotting), following the English Offences Against the Person Act of 1866; and the Naval Training Schools Act of 1874, passed in the aftermath of a similar British initiative. The object of the last bill was to establish industrial schools for neglected and, in some cases, criminal children. Finally, the Probation of Offenders Act was introduced (the first in the world) in 1886, following a visit from the London representative of the Howard League who advocated such legislation.

Commitment to the British way of doing things denied legitimacy to the Maori way of justice and punishment. The latter operated according to very different principles from those emerging in Britain and Europe around the mid-nineteenth century. The individual responsibility of British penology contrasted with the kinship responsibility built into Maori beliefs about punishment. The blood and body sanctions prevalent in Maori society were beginning to disappear in Britain and to be replaced by imprisonment; sanctions could be diffuse and uncertain in Maori dispute resolution at a time when there was growing demand for order, certainty, and efficiency in British penology. The Chiefs had considerable discretion when, as Foucault (1978) has shown, the early-nineteenth century in Europe was the era of the penal code, prescribing an exactitude of punishments to be imposed. Punishments in Maori society were of a public nature, while in the West they were beginning to be removed from view altogether (Spierenburg, 1984). The most significant contrasts are summarized in Table 7.1.

## A HISTORY OF SILENCE

The onset of formal colonization in New Zealand and the importation of a British penal system meant that the Maori way of punishing would be submerged and silenced. This process took around 60 years (Pratt, 1992). There was some initial recognition of Maori penal practices, however, for reasons of population distribution, geography and Maori resistance. In 1846, this tolerance of Maori ways was restricted to intra-Maori crime. Subsequently, the spread of European settlement and increased levels of population, allied to pacification of the Maori in the aftermath of the 1860s land wars, led in 1867 to any such recognition being restricted to specific parts of the country. In 1893, when the assimilation process seemed complete, the very limited provision that still existed for

*Table 7.1.* Contrasts in justice and punishment in the mid-nineteenth century.

|  | **Maori** | **European** |
| --- | --- | --- |
| Criminal responsibility | kin | individual |
| Predominant modes of sanction | corporeal/compensatory | imprisonment/fine |
| Power to punish | chiefly discretion | determined by penal code and administered by judges |
| Place of punishment | public | increasingly private |
| Purpose of punishment | redress of the balance | deterrent; retributive toward individual offenders |
| Prosecutor | victim | state |

the Maori to deal with disputes "in their own way" was abolished altogether under the terms of the Magistrates Courts Act.

What helped to drive this process was cultural antipathy. The Maori system represented anarchy for Europeans. Any concessions to Maori penology meant that Maori wrongdoing would go unpunished and that lawlessness, which *muru* seemed to represent, would be the result. This in turn led to more fear and suspicion. The offender was punished in European criminal law; in Maori penology, the muru sanction secured compensation for victims and their kin from offenders and their kin. In European culture this seemed to involve nothing more than indiscriminate plunder. It was thus claimed that:

> the settler is exposed to daily provocation. His cattle for example stray from his paddock; he follows them to a neighbouring *Pa* (settlement), and is compelled to redeem them by an exorbitant payment. In the course of the altercation, a musket is perhaps pointed at him, or a tomahawk flourished over his head. On the other hand, should he try the experiment of driving Native cattle to the public pound for trespass on his cultivations, a strong party of Maori, with loaded muskets, breaks down the pound and rescues them. He has to main-

tain party fences without contribution from his Maori neighbour. Herds of native pigs break through his crops. The dogs of the *Pa* worry his sheep. To save his own farm he has to pay for the extermination of thistles on the neighbouring native land. Redress in the Courts of Law is not to be attained because it would be dangerous to the peace of the country to enforce the judgment. On the other hand, Natives freely avail themselves of their legal remedies against Europeans [Department of Maori Affairs, 1860a, p.5].

The imposition of sanctions in the Maori way was alarming for the settlers. Instead of restoring order, it seemed to lead only to further disorder.

Maori punishment practices thus seemed to be the antithesis of European trends. There was no commensurability, only uncertainty and inconsistency in the application of punishment. At the same time, in the aftermath of missionary influences, biblical frames of reference seemed to dominate Maori thought, in contrast to the more secular enlightenment values of Europeans (Porter, 1990). In the initial stages of colonization, the Maori had been sympathetic to the public features of the European system that still remained at this stage; these were, of course, in line with their own cultural beliefs. Outside of these elements, however, they found the system irreligious. Thus, in relation to "cases of adultery, seduction, drunkenness and swearing...at present there is practically no redress, which is, of course, incomprehensible to a savage" (Department of Maori Affairs, 1860b, p.112).

Even so, the *utu* principle still dominated their conceptual basis of punishment. Wrongdoing demanded compensation, commensurate to the quality of harm done, and payment had to be made to the victim. There was no place for the state in the punishment process, nor any concept of penal confinement. Indeed, in Wellington in 1843, after a chief had been convicted of theft, he is reported to have told the court that:

> as to any thing which could be done to him now, he was indifferent. He had been degraded by being handcuffed and kept in gaol and did not care for anything...then, on hearing the sentence [two month's imprisonment with hard labour] he loudly complained of the degradation of imprisonment and requested most earnestly to be killed with a tomahawk [*New Zealand Gazette and Wellington Spectator*, 1843, p.2].

In the early days of colonization, there were reports of cases from various parts of the country where sanctions against Maori defendants were not enforced or were subsequently nullified.

> ...on the establishment of British Government in New Zealand, petty thefts were of frequent occurrence in European settlements, but it was found difficult to apply the punishments usually inflicted by our law for such offences. Sons of powerful chiefs were every now and then the offenders, and their tribe would not submit to the indignity of their being imprisoned in a common jail, although they were always willing to give compensation [Shortland, 1852, p.241].

Similarly, Chief Te Heu Heu asked, "Why do you keep a prisoner for days and days awaiting his trial? If anyone commits a crime here I knock him on the head at once. Then, too, you put people in prison for such small things. Now, Judge, listen to me. If a man were to dare to take one of my wives or to take this (a beautiful hatchet made of greenstone and highly polished which he carried in his hand), I should kill him, of course, at once; but if he pilfers little things I take no notice" (Martin, 1884, p.59).

In 1862, it was reported that a Hawkes Bay Chief rescued one of his *hapu* (tribe) from the Clive lock-up, after he had been detained for theft (Despatches from Governor Sir George Grey, 1863). Long sentences of imprisonment might still be resisted. In the same year, after a case of attempted rape, the representatives of the local tribe would not surrender the Maori defendant but instead proposed a £50 fine and banishment, and offered to become responsible for his conduct in the future, a proposal the authorities accepted (Papers Relative to an Outrage Committed by a Maori at Mataure, 1863).

Even when, some years later, European sanctions seemed to have more acceptability amongst the Maori people as a whole and began to be seen by them as "the normal way" of punishing, the cultural significance of these sanctions was likely to carry a different weight for Maori recipients.

> ...a half-caste from Kawhia, who was sentenced to imprisonment for a short term, was set to work to cut up firewood for the court and offices. While he was employed at this work, it was ludicrous to observe the many procedures he resorted to, to hide his position from the Native passers-by. He would, as soon as he observed them, cease work and endeavour to make believe that he was simply there at his own will. At other times, when out for exercise, in charge of the constable, if he perceived any natives coming in the direction of the office, he

would run into the court-house lobby and conceal himself behind the door, in order to prevent them seeing him. It has often appeared to me that to fine a Native for theft means to punish some of his relatives, as the burden of paying the fine invariably devolves upon them, and the thief really suffers nothing. The above case clearly shows that the Natives consider it a disgrace to be imprisoned, but a fine is nothing [Department of Maori Affairs, 1876, p.7].

Although European sanctions might prevail, Maori culture meant that responsibility for fine payment could still be a shared one and that imprisonment carried particular shame. Prison completely destroyed the *mana* (esteem) of the convict.

Assimilation into the British way of life meant that Maori justice, like the rest of Maori cultural practices and institutions, came to be formally silenced. For the most part, by the end of the nineteenth century Maori penal practices existed only in outlying areas and continued to exist in this way until well into the twentieth century. From as late as the 1950s there are anecdotal accounts of members of one tribe having the right to destroy the property of a member of another in cases of domestic violence (Tauri, personal communication). So long as they drew no blood themselves, the matter was then considered closed, which a meal, prepared by the guilty party for his plunderers, was meant to symbolize. But other than this, particularly in the more heavily populated urban areas, Maori ways of justice were reduced to the status of a cultural memory or as a point of resistance to European dominance.

Overall, the Maori now seemed to be largely acquiescent to European sanctions. This is confirmed by an examination of Resident Magistrates' reports for the late-nineteenth century. In 1880, for example, four natives were charged with breach of the Dog Nuisance Act.

...although they expressed great indignation on being served with the summonses, which they tore in pieces as soon as they received them, they all appeared in court and upon conviction, paid a fine of 5 sh. and costs each, besides taking out collars for their dogs. They behaved so well that the Bench expressed surprise at their calm submission to the order of the court, this tax being so very distasteful to the Natives [Department of Maori Affairs, 1880:1].

The general picture seemed to be that "the Natives have shown every disposition to submit to the decisions of the court" (Department of Maori Affairs, 1880, p.6). In all the reports from the Resident Magistrates in this year there is only one reference to *muru* being considered, from Gisborne:

...a dispute which might have had serious consequences has arisen between the Aitonga-a-Mate and the Te Whanau-a-rua, the subject of the quarrel being the ownership of a piece of land. The former hapu, to assert their right, buried a child of rank upon it and on the counter-claimants threatening to disinter it, [the former] seized their arms and would have resented the outrage with death, had not the other desisted [Department of Maori Affairs, 1880, p.10].

Even so, the same magistrate was able to report that "the greatest Chief of Ngatiporou...was arrested on a warrant, and imprisoned for two months, without the slightest opposition from his people by whom he was surrounded" (Department of Maori Affairs, 1880, p.11).

By 1885 we find the magistrates reporting that "when cases do arise requiring the intervention of the authorities, [we], as a rule, meet with the greatest assistance and cooperation at the hands of the leading natives, and it is seldom indeed that [we] find any difficulty in effectively carrying out the law" (Department of Maori Affairs, 1885, p.3). Similarly:
...a remarkable charge of highway robbery was brought before me, seven natives being accused of taking by force from another Native a considerable sum of money...on the charge coming before the Supreme Court it was dismissed on a technical point...*The case is curious, as it shows how the law failed to punish what was regarded by Europeans and Natives as a serious offence an offence that would doubtless, if committed a few years ago, have caused bloodshed amongst Native people*" (italics added) [Department of Maori Affairs, 1880, p.5].

This acquiescence was repeated in relation to more general aspects of European culture. For example, "on the 13th August 1877 [council rooms were] opened [at Putiki Pa], and a number of European ladies and gentlemen attended by invitation from Mete Kingi, and partook of a most substantial luncheon, served up in true English style, with Maori young ladies, dressed in the height of fashion as waiters, under the supervision of Victoria Kemp" (Department of Maori Affairs, 1878, p.13). This was one report, among a range of others in the 1870s, drawing attention, for example, to plans for the introduction of private boarding schools for Maori and "partial adaptation of European dress and habitation".

By the 1890s we find a report that, through their manifest adaptation of European cultural practices, the Maori could now be seen more as good sports than a threat: "...the Natives seem to be remarkably sober; they take great interest in European sports, and were, I understand, successful in carrying off the prizes in the tug-of-war both at

Christchurch and Dunedin. I believe they display the utmost good humour on these occasions whether successful or otherwise" (Department of Maori Affairs, 1892, p.9). By 1900 it was claimed that "what better instance could be found of Maori adapting themselves to European manners than the brass band we have seen in our streets here for the last two or three weeks? Where these Natives came from there were very few Europeans, that was in the Waikato, but yet we found a most advanced state of civilization amongst them, a refined civilization of which no higher existed, the civilization of music" (New Zealand Parliamentary Debates, 1900, p.203).

The Maori themselves had not constituted a significant crime problem for much of this period. Resident Magistrates reports contained regular references to the law-abiding nature of the Maori. For example: "I have the honour to state that the Kaipara Natives have maintained their character for order, peace and a desire to conform to the Law in a manner worthy of imitation by their neighbours; as the very few cases between themselves have, hitherto, been settled without the necessity of appealing to Court" (Department of Maori Affairs, 1872, p.24).

This is reflected in the crime statistics of the time, displayed in Table 7.2. During this same period, the population balance changed from being roughly equal in 1860, to approximately 11:1 European to Maori by 1880, and 21:1 by 1910. Such crime figures must, of course, be treated with a great deal of caution. Clearly, until pacification was complete, Maori were only under the partial jurisdiction of the colonial authorities. A significant amount of Maori wrongdoing continued to have been dealt with in the Maori way and will thus not feature in the official statistics. However, taking this and population differences into account, Maori lawbreaking coming to official attention seems to have been a fairly insignificant problem, as the prison statistics displayed in Table 7.3 also confirm.

If the sole purpose of punishment was designed to ensure order and control offenders, then despite the inroads made to Maoridom itself, Maori penology was largely successful. This, though, is to ignore the consequences of the cultural values and meanings that a particular mode of punishment carries with it. The Maori punishment system, as seen through European eyes, only symbolized and encouraged disorder and crime. The _taua muru_, for example, seemed to resemble armed robbery; community participation in the punishment process represented anarchy. Colonial mentalities demanded the European system of

Table 7.2. Convictions in resident magistrates' and magistrates' courts.

|      | European | Maori |
|------|----------|-------|
| 1860 | 2,963    | 103   |
| 1870 | 11,990   | 114   |
| 1880 | 15,078   | 245   |
| 1890 | 13,885   | 243   |
| 1900 | 19,241   | 253   |
| 1910 | 32,435   | 455   |

(Source: Statistics of the Dominion of New Zealand, 1861-1911)

punishment, with its emphasis on individual responsibility, growing re-
moteness from the public and preference for non-corporeal sanctions.
The formal assimilation of the Maori into the British way of life was completed around the end of the nineteenth century. It would now be
against this yardstick that their conduct would be judged, regulated and
sanctioned, and by the array of government institutions such as the
modern penal complex. And it was only when put under this scrutiny
that Maori offending and imprisonment began to accelerate. In 1872, the
Maori constituted only 2.3% of distinct prisoners received; by 1902,
2.8%; by 1912, 3.1%; by 1934, 8.9%; and in 1995, around 50%.

## RESTORING RESTORATIVE JUSTICE?

For the Maori, the gift of civilization did not turn out to be all that it
was thought to be by their colonizers. Alongside this, disenchantment
with the formal gesellschaft process of law has been one of the striking
features of penal thought in New Zealand—and other Western societies—
over the last two decades. In New Zealand, this has coincided with a resurgence of interest in the rights and cultures of indigenous peoples.
One of the consequences of these two lines of development has been to
break the silence on Maori justice. A publication of the Department of
Social Welfare (1984) highlighted the need for a culturally appropriate
way of dealing with Maori juvenile offenders, by far the biggest consum-
ers of what was then a typical welfare-oriented juvenile justice system.
    More controversial is the work of Jackson (1988), whom the Depart-
ment of Justice commissioned to write a report on the place of the Maori

in the adult justice system and the causes of their over-representation. His response was to suggest that racial bias endemic in the system itself was one of the most significant influences, and that the proper place for the Maori should be out of the European system altogether. Jackson advised that the Maori be allowed to deal with conflicts that affected them in a way that was culturally appropriate. This meant a return to the principles of restorative justice that were embedded in the pre-colonial method of dispute resolution. It did not mean—a point neglected by many of Jackson's critics—a return to pre-1840 society. Whatever the fate of restorative justice, the solution arrived at in the introduction to this chapter could not happen today because, apart from anything else, Maori (and European for that matter) culture has changed in such a way as to make such a solution impossible in the 1990s. Obviously, the mode of justice in existence at any given time should reflect only existing values and norms, not those in existence over 150 years ago.

The responses to these possibilities in both juvenile and adult fields have been mixed. The Children, Young Persons and their Families Act of 1989 has revolutionized the way youth justice proceedings are managed in New Zealand. The act established the new Youth Court to replace the former Children and Young Persons Court, and created a new forum—the family group conference—aimed at providing a real alternative to court proceedings as a means of dealing with young people who have offended. The forum involves families in deciding what is the most appropriate response to a young person's offending (Maxwell and Morris, 1993, p.v). In this setting, presided over by social work representatives, the extended families of victim and offender meet and resolve the best way to put things right. This is usually achieved by way of such measures as an apology, restitution and/or community work. All but the most serious juvenile cases are now dealt with by this means.

> ...only 10 per cent of the juvenile offenders in our sample appeared in the Youth Court...only 5 per cent of the juveniles in our sample were subject to court orders and less than 2 per cent were subject to residential or custodial orders. At the same time, the young people are being held accountable for their offending through the imposition of sanctions. Families are participating in the processes of decision-making and are taking responsibility for their young people in most instances. Extended families are also becoming involved in the continuing care of their kin as an alternative to foster care and institutions. Greater acknowledgement is being given to the customs of different cultural groups and in some instances alternative methods of

Table 7.3. Number of prisoners committed to gaol.

|        | European | Maori |
| ------ | -------- | ----- |
| 1860   | 1,491    | 31    |
| 1870   | 3,428    | 52    |
| 1881*  | 4,502    | 159   |
| 1890   | 4,202    | 128   |
| 1900   | 4,477    | 130   |
| 1910   | 4,428    | 88    |

*This year has been selected because in 1880, 661 Maori were committed to gaol (a figure very much in excess of court convictions). It was an artificially inflated figure that year because of the large number of referrals to gaol, without trial, under emergency legislation.

(Source: Statistics of the Dominion of New Zealand, 1861-1911)

resolution through the use of traditional processes have been adopted. Victims are also involved to a greater extent than previously and than in other jurisdictions [Maxwell and Morris, 1993:191].

The new juvenile justice system of New Zealand represents a remarkable reintegration of Maori justice practices into ways of dealing with offenders.

The situation in the adult penal field is much more problematic. Historically, legislatures have always been more favorably disposed to the introduction of novel measures for dealing with juvenile rather than adult offenders (Platt, 1969). Thus, the publication of Jackson (1988) brought forth an outright rejection from the then Justice Minister. In part, this was in response to a demand by activists such as Jackson for a separate system of justice for the Maori, as opposed to any attempt to reintegrate some of its ideas and practices into the European system. A separate justice system would require full recognition of Maori sovereignty; it would be impossible to have a Maori justice system in a society dominated by European culture and power. Such separatist ideas have been condemned by Justice Ministers as representing a form of legal apartheid.

But progress has been made on this matter, although these have mainly been locally based initiatives, for example, marae-based hearings to deal with Maori child sex abusers, the introduction of enhanced police diversion procedures, and successful proposals put to the Parole Board to allow some Maori prisoners to be released into the safekeeping of their communities. There was also a notable case in 1989 where a Maori prisoner went on hunger strike, demanding that his case (discharging a loaded firearm with intent to endanger life) be heard on his *marae* rather than in the European court. There has been a marked lack of sympathy from the Maori for such ideas, preferring that Maori offenders be dealt with in the existing European system. Indeed, the elders in the above case refused to allow the prisoner's wishes (irrespective of how the Department of Justice might have reacted). Their decision has to be understood in the context of the way in which the offense endangered them, as *elders*, in addition to other people. Furthermore, the existing system serves a useful function for both Maori and Europeans; it allows modern bureaucracies to deal with conflicts on behalf of individuals and, where necessary, to simply take troublemakers out of society and into prison where they can be forgotten about.

Equally important is that the continued presence of the existing penal framework, for all its manifest failures and human and economic cost, is a signifier of cultural identity with the West and everything that that entails. As such, this particular aspect of Western culture helps to differentiate the Western way of life from that of the Islamic world or of indigenous societies. The Western way of doing things is regarded as natural; that to be found in other societies is then written off as backward or somehow less civilized. Hence, for example, the derogatory overtones that have become associated with Weber's (1954) depiction of *kadi* justice in Islamic society. For Westerners, it can appear to be founded on arbitrariness, religiosity and tyranny. In contrast, modern Western societies have penal codes that are secular and democratic. Thus, from the nineteenth century, as Rosen (1989) suggests, "as western jurisprudence shifted from a concern with natural law and its own romanticized projections of the natural justice of the folk to an emphasis on procedure, code and appellate hierarchy, the image of the qadi necessarily [and unfavourably] changed as well" (p.58-59). Equally, the public display of emotions that Islamic punishments can involve, for example, their corporeal nature and the involvement of the crowd, can seem barbaric to Western sentiments, where we have become used to order and decorum over such matters. In the Western way of punishing, it is most unlikely that there will be any infliction of bodily pain, and its delivery takes place, for the most part, out of the public gaze. We regard any departures from this standard (and in spite of all its failures) as uncivilized, unrestrained and allowing more primitive sentiments of vengeance to dictate the way we punish.

Punishment has come to be regulated and circumscribed by modern penal bureaucracies. Occasionally, community sentiments may be so powerful that private citizens decide to avenge themselves after particular incidents. But, by and large, this is avoided by the subsuming of public sentiments into Justice Department penal policies. The Western way of punishment, by its avoidance of these unsettling and foreign features, confirms how civilized its societies have become. Indeed, the apparent convergence of state interests and public passions that informs the Islamic penal code appears frightening to us in the West; here, we expect the state to organize and administer punishment divorced from any collegiance with the public. For the most part, the involvement of the latter, can only take place through indirect routes. This division between public and state interests means that we can voice our anger, or give rein to our curiosity, but only at a safe distance, which prevents other sensitivities prevalent in modern society from being disturbed.

Maori ways of justice and punishment, which do not involve imprisonment, will inevitably hold some interest in view of pressure on the New Zealand government to reduce the existing prison population (the rate of imprisonment at around 130 per 100,000 of population is among the highest in the Western world). It remains to be seen whether or not these ideas can outweigh new European initiatives based on more high-tech surveillance and containment in non-state funded facilities, and whether they can be reintegrated into the existing European adult penal system. In these respects, New Zealand is at something of a crossroads, unable to decide which route to follow. In the following case it chose both. In Auckland in 1993, a young Samoan man killed two Tongan children in a car accident and was charged by the police with causing death by dangerous driving. The Tongan family subsequently met with the Samoan and his family in a church. At the end of the day they announced that they had forgiven the Samoan and were reconciled. The Samoan himself emerged wearing a red sash, as a sign of his remorse. For the Tongan family, the matter was now closed. But not so for the criminal justice system, which subsequently sentenced the offender to five years' imprisonment. If this case confirms that the previous silence on this different way of resolving conflicts has been broken, it also shows the reluctance of the existing system to step aside in such matters. Justice had already been done to the satisfaction of those most closely involved; reconciliation had already been achieved but prison still ensued.

## REFERENCES

Association for Forming the Settlement of Canterbury in New Zealand (1848). *Prospectus.* London, UK: Author.

Christie, N. (1976). "Conflicts as Property." *British Journal of Criminology* 16:1-13.

*Despatches from Governor Sir George Grey* (1883). (Appendices to the *Journal of the House of Representatives* (AJHR), A to J, E). Wellington, NZ: Government Printer.

Department of Social Welfare (1984). *Daybreak.* Wellington, NZ: Author.

Dieffenbach, E. (1843). *Travels in New Zealand.* London, UK: John Murray.

Earle, A. (1966). *Narrative of a Residence in New Zealand.* Christchurch, NZ: Whitcombe and Tombs.

Eldridge, C. (1978). *Victorian Imperialism.* London, UK: Hodder and Stoughton.

Foucault, M. (1978). *Discipline and Punish.* London, UK: Allen Lane.

*Further Papers Relative to Native Affairs* (1860). (Appendices to the *Journal of the House of Representatives* (AJHR), A to J, E). Wellington, NZ: Government Printer.

Garland, D. (1990). *Punishment and Modern Society.* Oxford, UK: Oxford University Press.

Hursthouse, C. (1857). *New Zealand or Zealandia,* vol. 2. London, UK: Edward Stafford.

Ignatieff, M. (1978). *A Just Measure of Pain.* London, UK: Macmillan.

Jackson, M. (1988). *The Maori and the Criminal Justice System,* vol. 2. Wellington, NZ: Department of Justice.

Martin, M. (1884). *Our Maoris.* London, UK: London Society for Promoting Christian Knowledge.

Maxwell, G. and A. Morris (1993). *Families, Victims and Culture.* Wellington, NZ: Department of Social Welfare.

*New Zealand Gazette and Wellington Spectator* (1843). December 30, p.2.

*New Zealand Parliamentary Debates* (1900). Volume 115. Wellington, NZ: Government Printer.

*Papers Relating to an Outrage Committed by a Maori at Mataure* (1863). Wellington, NZ: Government Printer.

Polack, J. (1838). *New Zealand: A Narrative of Travels and Adventures.* London, UK: Richard Bentley.

Platt, A. (1969). *The Child Savers.* Chicago, IL: University of Chicago Press.

Porter, R. (1990). *The Enlightenment.* Basingstoke, UK: Macmillan.

Pratt, J. (1992). *Punishment in a Perfect Society.* Wellington, NZ: Victoria University Press.

Purchas, H. (1903). *Bishop Harper and the Canterbury Settlement.* Christchurch, NZ: Whitcombe and Tombs.

*Reports of the Waikato Committee* (1860). (AJHR, A to J, F). Wellington, NZ: Government Printer.

*Reports from Officers in Native Districts* (1876). (AJHR, A to J, F). Wellington, NZ: Government Printer.

—(1878). (AJHR, A to J, F). Wellington, NZ: Government Printer.

—(1880). (AJHR, A to J, F). Wellington, NZ: Government Printer.

—(1885). (AJHR, A to J, F). Wellington, NZ: Government Printer.

—(1892). (AJHR, A to J, F). Wellington, NZ: Government Printer.

Rosen, L. (1989). *Law as Culture in Islamic Society.* Cambridge, UK: Cambridge University Press.

Shortland, E. (1852). *The Southern Districts of New Zealand.* London, UK: Longmans.

Spierenburg, P. (1984). *The Spectacle of Suffering.* Cambridge, UK: Cambridge University Press.

*Statistics of the Dominion of New Zealand* (1861-1911). Wellington, NZ: Government Printer.

Swainson, W. (1859). *New Zealand and its Colonization.* London, UK: Smith, Gilder and Co.

Tauri, Juan. Personal communication.

Wakefield, E.J. (1868) (1973). *The Founders of Canterbury.* London, UK.

Weber, M. (1954). *Max Weber on Law in Economy and Society.* Cambridge, MA: Harvard University Press.

# 8. NAVAJO RESTORATIVE JUSTICE: THE LAW OF EQUALITY AND JUSTICE

by

## Robert Yazzie

and

## James W. Zion

**Abstract:** In 1982, the Navajo Nation established Navajo Peacemaker Courts, in which respected community leaders organize and preside over traditional Navajo process to resolve disputes that, in European traditions, might be considered criminal. Peacemaker court decisions are made by the participants because, consistent with Navajo concepts of freedom and individuality, one person cannot impose a decision upon another. If one person believes they've been wronged by another they will first make a demand for the perpetrator to put things right. If this is not successful, the wronged person may turn to a respected community leader to facilitate and organize a peacemaker process. The process is not confrontational, but involves family and clan members of victims and perpetrators talking through matters to arrive at a solution. The peacemaker has persuasive authority and draws on the traditions and stories of the culture to offer practical advice. The parties discuss the nature of the problem and work towards finding a resolution. The process ends in an action plan to solve the problem, often through reparation.

Judges of the Courts of the Navajo Nation have a conscious and consistent policy to return to traditional Navajo justice methods. The Navajo Nation covers more than 25,000 square miles of territory in the states of Arizona, New Mexico and Utah. Larger than nine states of the U.S., it has over 200,000 inhabitants. Navajos received their first Western-styled court system in 1892. The Navajo Court of Indian Offenses was an administrative and educational arm of the U.S. Bureau of Indian Affairs. The court used rules that were very similar to those utilized by American justices of the peace, and stated offenses that were very strange to Navajos. The rules of the court made it a crime to see a medicine man. They made it a crime to *be* a medicine man! They prohibited traditional domestic relations practices, including brideprice, polygamy, traditional probate and traditional divorce. Imposed land use practices where a male head of household received land permits for agriculture or grazing disrupted traditional land tenure. The Navajo Court of Indian Offenses enforced the requirement that Navajo children attend boarding school far from their homes. There, Navajos were stripped of their language, religion, and culture, and were isolated from their communities. The police model of law and adjudication aggravated rather than promoted healthy social values. More than 100 years of the police model of law fostered destruction of traditional Navajo legal institutions.

The family and clan are the core of Navajo justice; they are Navajo legal institutions. The dominant culture substituted police in the place of clan leaders and judges in the place of the people themselves. Policies such as the imposition of police and courts, individualistic land tenure, and disruption of a society with gender equality destroyed the effectiveness of Navajo families and clans as justice systems. The wage economy, destruction of a pastoral economy, and dislocation of people from their traditional land tenure fostered alcohol dependence, family violence, child abuse and neglect, and a host of social problems.

The Navajo Nation Council abolished the Navajo Court of Indian Offenses in 1958, and the Courts of the Navajo Nation came into existence on April 1, 1959. These courts are an organ of the Navajo Nation Government, created pursuant to the inherent authority of the Navajo Nation to establish a system of justice. They were created during the American termination era, when Indian affairs policy shifted from support of Indian nation government to open hostility toward the very existence of Indian nations as such. The Navajo Nation Council anticipated state takeovers of jurisdiction and sought to create a body that looked exactly like a state court. The council advocated training programs for judges so they could apply laws and rules familiar to most American lawyers. Former Navajo Court of Indian Offenses judges who were traditionalist were pushed out. White lawyer-advisors were hired to draft rules for the court, and in 1969 the *Navajo Law Reporter* began publication of case reports in English.

Did that satisfy the outsiders? Lawyers in the employ of the Navajo Nation touted the sophistication of the Navajo courts, and visitors arrived to take their own look. Their conclusion? The Navajos were getting it _wrong_! Navajo judges applied the alien rules from their own perspectives, sometimes substituting Navajo values but using the language of American law. Probate decisions recognized communal land ownership, disguising it as a trust of land or a grazing permit to be held by a relative for the benefit of children. Matrilineal land tenure for the benefit of families and clans were recognized by court decision. The traditional practice of the oral will, whereby a family elder could direct land use following death, became enshrined in Navajo Nation decisional law. When outsiders saw but could not understand such practices, they concluded that Navajo judges were stupid, ignorant or corrupt.

The Navajo Nation entered a period of conflict following the passage of the Indian Civil Rights Act in 1968. That federal statute imposed the U.S. Bill of Rights upon Indian nations without regard to cultural conflict or the inapplicability of Anglo-European versions of concepts such as due process or equal protection in Indian cultures. The judges of the Navajo courts asserted their authority to apply the Indian Civil Rights Act in independent judicial review of legislative and executive actions. The chairman of the Navajo Tribal Council responded through his white lawyer-advisor, who came up with a scheme for a court of appeal within the council. The council created a Supreme Judicial Council composed of a majority of council delegates and the chief justice, who could not vote. Funding for the Supreme Judicial Council terminated in 1982, and it was formally abolished in a court reorganization in 1985.

By 1981, many Navajos recognized that the new system was not working as it should. The chairman, members of the Navajo Nation Council Judiciary Committee, and judges called for the revival of traditional Navajo justice principles and methods. The first response to those calls was consciously to incorporate Navajo customs and usages in opinions that are written and published in English (Lowery, 1993). The judges who rendered the opinions looked to the _Bilagaanaa_ (white people, or the Anglo-European culture; the term Anglo is also popular in the Southwest) legal tradition to describe Navajo law. Sir Matthew Hale and Sir William Blackstone said that the English judges did nothing more than declare the customs of the English People in common law. Accordingly, the Navajo Nation judges call the use of Navajo customs, usages and traditions the Navajo common law. It is the law of preference. The difficulty was that while the Navajo judges declared Navajo values as rules of law in opinions, it was still a process of a powerful person (a judge) handing down decisions and rules from on high.

To carry the policy to its logical conclusions the courts had to identify the traditional institution that applied Navajo common law. That institution is *hozhooji naat'aanii*, which is rendered as peacemaking in English. The people who make up the institution are the traditional Navajo civil leaders, or *naat'aanii*, and disputants. In 1982, the Navajo Nation Judicial Conference, the judges sitting as a whole, created the Navajo Peacemaker Court. It is a court-annexed system of popular justice, whereby respected community leaders organize and preside over the traditional Navajo trial, *'ahwiniti* (where they talk about you), in the community in which the dispute arises (Zion, 1983; Bluehouse and Zion, 1993).

The policies that evolved during the period between 1981 and 1991 firmly established a preference for Navajo justice values, methods and procedures in the Navajo Nation courts. The Navajo Nation Council reconstituted the courts in the Judicial Reform Act of 1985, and the first justices of the Navajo Nation Supreme Court put their unique marks on the reformed system. In 1991, the Navajo Nation Judicial Conference adopted the Navajo Nation Code of Judicial Conduct. The judges wanted a code based on Navajo values; they did not want to repeat mistakes in adopting outside models wholesale. The Navajo Nation Code is based on principles of Navajo common law that outline the responsibilities of judges as public leaders, and that guide judges to actively respond to popular Navajo expectations (Tso, 1992). In 1992, the Navajo Nation Supreme Court adopted Rules for Domestic Violence Proceedings that incorporate Navajo common-law values. The rules provide for peacemaking of family violence cases, payment of restitution and use of peace bonds to reinstitutionalize the traditional practice of family members assuming responsibility for an offender. In 1994, the courts established a court access program for those who cannot afford a lawyer, based on the principle that the people should have free and easy access to their leaders, including judges. Other initiatives under study, including guardians *ad litem* for children and a gang suppression plan, actively utilize Navajo common-law principles.

The policy of the Courts of the Navajo Nation is clear: the courts operate using Navajo legal thinking, and court initiatives will reflect it. What is the foundation of that thinking? It is that law is not a process to punish or penalize people, but to teach them how to live a better life. It is a healing process that either restores good relationships among people or, if they do not have good relations to begin with, fosters and nourishes a healthy environment. This chapter describes some of the base values of Navajo legal thinking to show how Navajo justice fosters healing. Navajo common law is built on relationships and notions of how people should act within them. It is a mode of thinking that looks to the future in planning rather than to the past in punishment or penalties.

## WHAT IS "LAW"?

People think they know what the word "law" means, but when traditional Indian law or Navajo common law is spoken of, they are lost. They do not have the slightest notion of what we, as Indians, mean. For example, a group of business people from Farmington, NM, were unable to accept that traditional Navajo justice is not built on punishment or sanctions, and a visiting lawyer from Austria insisted that there must be some sort of table of penalties for traditional crimes. Law is something fundamental in Navajo legal thinking. It is absolute and has existed from the beginning of time. It is given by the Holy People from the time of beginning, and life comes from it (Yazzie, 1994). There is another way to describe the Navajo concept of law to better explain what it is to the Western English-speaking mind. The Navajo language is very precise. It conveys concepts that mean a great deal to the listener. Many Navajo words are action words that describe how something functions. For example, the Navajo word for a civil leader, *naat'aanii*, describes someone who speaks wisely and well. A lawyer or, *'agha'diit'aahii*, is someone who pushes out with words. He or she imposes decisions on others and is not a very nice person at all. Navajo words also convey feelings that carry deep connotations. One of the worst stereotypes about Indians is that they are stoic or do not have feelings. The Navajo language has words that tap deeply held feelings taught from childhood. Navajo elders say *hozhigo*, or do things in a good way, to their children. That is not an abstract exhortation to do good, but a very precise guide for human conduct.

We can look at law as norms that are applied by people who act in institutions. A norm is a sense of ought; it is a feeling. A norm shared by people as a group is a value, and systematic statements of values are moral principles. When people act out their shared values that is custom. The Navajo legal institution is the clan. Navajos trace their relations through their mothers, so that a Navajo is born of his mother's clan and born for his father's. The clan structure creates and reinforces reciprocal relationships among people. The ideal that guides the group and people in their relationships is *hozho*, which refers to the perfect state or that situation when everyone within the relationship functions well, and with respect, in relation to everyone and everything else.

Is force or coercion an element of the Navajo definition of law? Navajo common law is egalitarian and not the product of hierarchies of power. The state systems brought to the Americas from Europe rely upon the power and authority of the state. Elites chosen by the processes of the state (*i.e.*, police, lawyers, judges, jailers, and so forth) use force and coercion to make their systems work. This concept is alien to Navajo thought. Navajos believe in an almost absolute form of freedom or individualism that is very different from the western concept of the rights of the individual. The Navajo maxim is, "it's up to him". That means that every individual has freedom of choice and action, and that one Navajo does not tell another what to do. When someone invokes force against another in the form of demands upon spirit forces to coerce another, that is witchcraft. It invokes the death penalty under Navajo common law. The moral force of the group is used to persuade people to put the group's good above individual welfare. It is said say of a wrongdoer that "he acts as if he had no relatives".

Navajo common law is a system of shared feelings that are fostered in relationships. The values or shared feelings are conveyed in a strong, precise language. They are reinforced through teaching. How is it that people are trained or educated to respond to a values system? Each Navajo learns the values from infancy in traditional society. When a child first shows awareness of his or her surroundings by laughing, the relative who hears it must sponsor a "Baby's First Laugh" ceremony. It is an occasion where the baby first sees and recognizes the relatives who gather to celebrate the first laugh. It is a socialization process where a baby is taught the importance of relationships within the family. During the *kinaaldá* ceremony, a young woman who reaches puberty learns about the dignity of women as she becomes "Changing Woman", the principal (and female) deity of Navajo religion. The ceremony also reminds men of the dignity of women in a gender-equal society. There are other ceremonies that reinforce the basic pattern of Navajo life, which is grounded on the idea that people owe duties to their family and clan, as those bodies owe duties to individuals. The teachings are reinforced in Navajo creation scripture, songs, prayers and social gatherings. During winter, Navajos tell coyote stories that relate the foolishness or mistakes as a guide for human conduct. Many Navajo judges insist that children learn coyote stories because they are the law. Thus the Navajo belief system is strong, and is reinforced by socialization and the language itself.

## EGALITARIAN CONCEPTIONS OF DECISION-MAKING PROCESS

The process of law flows from conflict to judgment or a final decision. It is important to understand who makes the decision to resolve a conflict and how that decision is made. The very process of decision-making points to the healing component of Navajo justice. State systems use judges to make the decisions. The judges are selected on the basis of their education to hear the facts, apply the law and make wise decisions for others. This is alien to the Navajo concept of freedom and individuality, where one person cannot impose a decision on another. Instead, Navajos are their own judges in an egalitarian process.

What happens when there is a dispute? First, a person who claims to be injured or wronged by another will make a demand upon the perpetrator to put things right. The term for this is *nalyeeh*, which is a demand for compensation; it is also a demand to readjust the relationship so that the proper thing is done. In a simple situation such as theft, confrontation of the thief with a threat of public disclosure is usually sufficient. Women who are wronged by a sexual impropriety have the right to confront the offender in a public place to disclose the insult and demand compensation for it. In situations where individuals are unable to make a direct demand, or do not wish to do so, they will seek the help of relatives. There have been situations where young women herding sheep are sexually wronged; a relative of the woman will approach the man's relatives to talk out the situation and demand some sort of compensation or arrangement to mend it (Craig, 1995).

There are more formal dispute resolution methods to talk out disputes. A victim or a victim's relative will approach a *naat'aanii* to request his or her assistance in talking out a particular problem. A *naat'aanii* is a respected community leader, and often a basis for that respect is the very fact that a civil leader is also a clan leader. The *naat'aanii*-peacemaker will summon the interested parties for a group discussion of what to do. An important difference between state system adjudication and peacemaking is the identity of the participants and their role. Peacemaking is not a confrontation between two particular individuals who are immediately involved in the dispute, but a process that involves the family and clan relations of victims and perpetrators as active participants. They are involved because they have an interest in the matter; what affects their relative affects them. Relatives have an opinion about the nature of the dispute or what should be done to resolve it.

A *naat'aanii* will give notice to everyone affected and designate a place to talk out the problem. The process always begins with prayer, which is essential to the healing nature of peacemaking. Prayer is a process that summons supernatural help; the Holy People are called to participate directly. They are not summoned to be a witness, a custom that is reflected in the giving of the oath in courts. *Naat'aaniis* are called in to help the parties and to answer their demands for justice. The prayer is also an opportunity for the *naat'aanii* to focus the minds of the parties on a process that is conciliatory and healing, not confrontational and winner-take-all. Following prayer, the parties have an opportunity to lay out their grievances. There is venting, as in other mediation processes, where the victim has an opportunity to disclose not only the facts, but their impact. People have an opportunity to say how they feel about the event and make a strong demand that something be done about it. Relatives also have an opportunity to express their feelings and opinions about the dispute.

The person accused of a wrongful act also has an opportunity to speak. Human behavior is such that we often put forward excuses or justifications for our conduct. Many Navajo peacemaking cases involve alcohol abuse. A common psychological barrier where an individual is alcohol-dependent is denial. The person will say, "I don't have a drinking problem". In adjudication, a defendant accused of an alcohol-related crime will challenge the court to prove that he or she has an alcohol problem to be addressed in some sort of treatment program. Often, defendants referred to such programs do not wholeheartedly participate, using denial to fool themselves. Another barrier is minimalization, where someone excuses conduct by saying, "it's no big deal". We see this in domestic violence cases, where a batterer says, "It's no big deal for an Indian man to beat his wife". In some child sex abuse cases, perpetrators (falsely) claim that it is traditional to have sex with a stepchild or a young woman who has barely reached puberty. A third barrier is externalization, the excuse that the offense is someone else's fault. "It's her fault!" a batterer will say. "If she didn't nag me all the time I wouldn't have to beat her." Or, "It's her fault—if she would do what she is supposed to do, I wouldn't be forced to push her around." Another facet of externalization is excuses. "It's not my fault; I'm just a dependent alcoholic and I can't help myself." Many criminal defendants attempt to excuse their conduct by saying, "I was drunk". There is also a systemic excuse that is related to anomie (Greek for without law).

The police model inherited by the Navajo Nation has severe limitations. There are not enough police to patrol a rural nation that is larger than nine states. Limited police officers, who must prepare cases in a system where there is proof beyond a reasonable doubt and a defendant cannot be compelled to testify, limits the effectiveness of adjudication. The Navajo Nation also has an imposed social work model for child welfare which is overburdened. Accordingly, when the police or social work system is overburdened we sometimes hear the institutional excuse, "we can't do anything" .

How does peacemaking address these excuses; these barriers to solving problems? It confronts them directly. In peacemaking, the person who is the focus of the discussion gets to explain his or her excuses in full, without appearing before a judge to determine whether or not they are true. Instead, judges are the people who know the wrongdoer best— his or her spouse, parents, siblings, other relatives and neighbors. They are the reality check for excuses. In a case involving family violence, a young man related his excuses, exhibiting denial, minimalization and externalization. One of the people who listened was the young man's sister. She listened to his story and confronted him by saying, "you know very well you have a drinking problem". She then related the times she had seen him drunk and abusive. Having broken the barrier, she told her brother she loved him very much and was willing to help him if only he would admit his problems. He did. In another case, a young woman went to court to establish paternity for her child. The young man she said was the father denied it. The judge sent the case into peacemaking, where the parents and relatives of both were present. They immediately announced that the purpose of the meeting was to decide what to do with *their* grandchild. The families knew about the couple's relationship and the fact of paternity, so the case was quickly settled. The young man was not employed, so the families developed a plan whereby he would cut and haul firewood for the mother until he got a job. In peace-making, the people who know the facts directly or know the people in the process very well are the ones who develop the facts of the situation. They are not laid out for a judge to decide, but for the participants to discuss and know. The talking-out process of peacemaking is designed to clarify the situation and, where necessary, get to the root of the problem. Excuses do not prevail in a process that fosters full discussion to solve problems.

Peacemaking is a remedy for the "we can't do anything" excuse. Most cases in Navajo peacemaking are those brought directly by the people. For example, there was a situation where a couple broke up when their son reached adulthood. The man ran off with another woman, leaving his wife to make the mobile home payment. She had little education and no job. She got a low-paying job in a laundromat, but that was not sufficient to make the monthly payment. She went to the local legal aid program for a divorce to assure the payment, but was told that the program was overburdened and did not take divorce cases. The woman began going to her husband's place of work to demand money. Very soon, the receptionists and fellow employees made it known she was not welcome. One day, the woman confronted her husband in the parking lot and demanded the money for the mobile home payment. When he refused, she hit him. He got a domestic violence restraining order from the court, and the woman sought advice about what it meant and what she should do. She was advised to seek peacemaking. Within a few days, a peacemaking session was scheduled and the husband agreed to make the mobile home payment. The peacemaker set up a follow-up meeting to assure the agreement was carried out. In the meantime, the domestic violence case was dismissed.

The Navajo Nation child welfare program is overburdened with abuse and neglect cases. Accordingly, we see many applications for guardianships of children brought by grandmothers, aunts and other relatives of children. A guardianship is a form of private child welfare action in Navajo practice, and relatives seek court confirmation of arrangements to care for children. Often, relatives seek temporary guardianships to allow parents an opportunity to deal with personal problems or seek employment to create a stable household. In most state systems, child welfare cases are confrontational and challenge adults to explain why they are bad parents. Navajos use peacemaking for guardianship cases, and that forum allows relatives to discuss what is best for their children. Parents assert their excuses for the way they deal with their children, but the focus is genuinely upon the best interests of the child. There is no judge or social worker to make the determination of what is best for a child—the people most closely connected with the child make that decision. Direct access to swift justice within the community addresses the "we can't do anything" excuse, and the process utilizes readily available resources for problem solving. There is no need for a confirming medical statement in domestic violence cases, or for a home study in child welfare cases. The people who have a dispute treat it as a problem to be resolved within families, and take direct action on their own.

In peacemaking, a *naat'aanii* has persuasive authority. Peacemakers are chosen by local units of Navajo Nation government on the basis of their standing in the community and respect for their abilities. Peacemakers can be removed at any time should they lose respect. A peacemaker does not have the authority to make a decision for others or to impose a decision, but his or her power is not merely advisory. A *naat'aanii* has an opinion, and the process prompts him or her to express it. Given that peacemakers are chosen because of their wisdom and planning abilities, the process encourages them to act as guides and teachers. Their opinion will most likely have a strong impact on the decision of the group. The opinion is expressed in something called the lecture—an unfortunate rendering in English because the process is not an abstract exhortation about morality; it is a very practical and concrete process. The peacemaker knows all about the situation given that the parties and their relatives have an opportunity to vent, accuse, exhibit psychological barriers and engage in discussions to clarify things. He or she will then provide reality therapy and perform values clarification in a talk designed to guide the parties. The talk focuses on the nature of the problem and uses traditional precedent to guide a decision.

Navajos have a great deal of respect for tradition, and they recognize both a form of traditional case law and a corpus of legal principles. The case law can be in the form of what happened in the time of creation, *e.g.*, what First Man and First Woman, the Hero Twins or the Holy People did to address a similar problem. The case may involve Coyote or Horned Toad, and the foolishness of what Coyote did or the wisdom of Horned Toad to resolve a similar conflict. There are principles to be derived from ceremonial practice, songs, prayers or other expressions of

Navajo doctrine. The *naat'aanii* draws upon traditional teachings to propose a plan of action for the parties in order to resolve their dispute. Many peacemaking sessions are short, lasting only a few hours, but where emotions are particularly strong or it is difficult to break down the psychological barriers, peacemaking can last longer. The peacemaker may call a halt to the discussions to allow time for reflection and prepare for a resumption of talks on another day.

When the lecture is done, the parties return to a discussion of the nature of the problem and what needs to be done to resolve it. Planning is a major Navajo justice value that is sometimes ignored in state practice. *Nahat'a*, or planning process, is very practical. Non-Navajos sometimes mock traditional practice. For example, there are Navajos who look into the future using a crystal. A non-Navajo might ridicule that, but Navajos explain how it is done. When you hold a crystal in your hand, you see that it has many facets. You examine each closely, and upon a full examination of each side of the crystal you can see it as a whole. That describes *nahat'a*, where the parties closely examine each facet of the dispute to see it as a whole. The talking-out phase fully develops the facts so the parties can fully understand the nature of the problem that lies beneath the dispute. The lecture phase draws upon traditional wisdom for precedent and guidance. The prayer commits the parties to the process. Following full discussion, the parties themselves serve as the judges and make a decision about what to do. It is most often a practical plan whereby people commit themselves to a course of action.

Often, the action is in the form of *nalyeeh*, which also translates as restitution or reparation. Payments can be in the form of money to compensate for actual out-of-pocket loss. There are also payments in the form of horses, jewelry or other goods. The payment can be symbolic only and not compensate for actual loss. The focus is not upon adequate compensation, as in state tort or contracts doctrines, but upon a make-whole kind of remedy. The feelings and relationships of the parties are what is most important. For example, there are cases involving sexual misconduct where the victim demands symbolic compensation, often in the form of horses, cows or sheep. Can a price tag be placed on a rape? The act of delivering cattle as compensation is visible in a rural community. Members of that community will most likely know about the event, and the public act of delivering cattle or horses shows the woman's innocence. It reinforces her dignity and tells the community she was wronged.

Non-Navajo corporate parties have also participated in peacemaking, such as in a wrongful death-products liability case brought before the Navajo Nation courts in 1994. A child got scorched to death in a clothes dryer, and the child's parents brought a standard wrongful death manufacturer negligence suit. The corporate defendants were very nervous about the possible outcome before a Navajo jury. The child's parents were not so much concerned about getting money as they were with dealing with the emotional impact of their child's death. The parties went into peacemaking without their lawyers present, and they fully discussed the problem of what to do about the loss of the child. They addressed the parents' feelings about their loss and what the corporate defendants could and should do about it. The result was a monetary settlement that was within the range of usual rural Arizona state court verdicts. More importantly, the parties discussed what symbolic act the manufacturer and laundromat operator could take to assume responsibility for the death. Negotiated compensation can address the costs of actual loss, but it can also be an agreed resolution with only a symbolic payment. It addresses relationships.

Peacemaking also involves personal commitments to deal with underlying behavior. It can involve agreements to attend a ceremony. For example, the Honorable Irene Toledo of the Ramah District Court recognized that many violent assaults brought before her involved Vietnam veterans and other Navajos who returned from war. Upon examining the cases more closely, she recognized the presence of post-traumatic stress disorder from war. She also recognized that veteran parents were teaching their children violent behaviors. Navajos are familiar with war from many centuries of conflict with Spanish, Mexican and American invaders. There is a Navajo ceremony that addresses post-traumatic stress disorder, and it is quite effective in dealing with the memories of war. Judge Toledo urged some of the defendants to have the ceremony done, as well as to seek treatment through a Veterans Department hospital. Some replied, "I'm modern and I don't really believe in that tradition". The judge used peacemaking as a form of counseling for the defendants to urge them to have the ceremony performed. One veteran reported that while he "did not believe in it", he had the ceremony done and it worked.

Peacemaking is used to overcome psychological barriers and self-imposed impediments to personal responsibility. Parties in peacemaking will often agree to seek traditional ceremonies or modern counselling as part of the resolution of the dispute. When they do, they are fully committed to the process and they cooperate with traditional or modern treatment programs. One pilot project of the Navajo courts was the Minority Male Program. It was designed to offer diversion alternatives for persons charged with driving while intoxicated. Peacemaking proved successful in getting beneath the problem of drunk driving by motivating people to recognize that they indeed did have a drinking problem and should do something about it. Recidivism rates dropped for those who went through peacemaking.

Relationships and relatives are an important distinction that makes peacemaking unique. A person who agrees to pay *nalyeeh* may not have the personal wealth or means to do so. It is traditional for family and clan members to make the payment on their relative's behalf. The tradition is not simply that relatives assume obligations for others, although that is fundamental to Navajo society. When an individual commits a wrong against another, it shames the person's relatives—"He acts as if he had no relatives". The family will keep an eye on the offender to assure there will be no future transgressions. Where there is a particularly malicious or heinous act, community members will "kill with the eyes". That describes a practice where people keep a watch for an offender, and use social pressure to keep him in line with the community's expectations of proper behavior. We recognize this dynamic of Navajo custom for modern adjudication as well. Both the Rules for Domestic Violence Proceedings and the Navajo Nation Sentencing Policy include provisions to require offenders to get family member sureties for bonds to assure future good conduct. We call this the "traditional probation officer", where we recruit family members to assume supervisory obligations.

What makes peacemaking work? Peacemaking is based on relationships. It uses the deep emotions of respect, solidarity, self-examination, problem-solving and ties to the community. Navajo common law recognizes the individual and individual rights, but it differs from Western individualism in that the individual is put in his or her proper place within community relationships. Western legal thought speaks to "me" and "I", but the individual is viewed in the isolated context of individual rights. In Navajo legal thinking, an individual is a person within a community, it is impossible to function alone. They say that Navajos always go home: Navajos who have better potentials to earn a high income in a big city return home to a lesser-paying job because they cannot live outside Navajo society. Navajos responded to recent disclosures that the Navajo Nation has the lowest family and per capita incomes of all Indian nations of the U.S., and the highest poverty rate, by pointing out that their rural economies and lifestyles are a matter of choice. Yes, there is a great deal of poverty in the Navajo Nation and limited economic opportunities, but Navajos live as Navajos.

An important Navajo legal term is *k'e*, for which there is no corresponding word in English. *K'e* is the cement of Navajo law; it describes proper relationships, and underlies and fuels consensual justice. It is what allows a traditional justice system to operate without force or coercion. It allows people to be their own judges and to enforce binding judgments without jails or sheriffs.

Peacemaking agreements can be reduced to judgment and enforced as any other court judgment. In practice, the people prefer informal agreements and often do not seek court ratification of it in a formal judgment. Relationships and methods designed to build or reinforce them, supported by the strong emotional force of *k'e*, are the underpinnings of peacemaking. It is not a system of law that relies upon authority, force and coercion, but one that utilizes the strengths of people in communities.

## CORRECTIVE, RESTORATIVE AND DISTRIBUTIVE JUSTICE

Most state law methods are based on corrective justice. That is, the hierarchy of power attempts to maintain social control using state authority. The difficulty lies in abuses of authority, and people tend to resist being told what to do. They respond better when they buy into or accept a decision that they help make. Navajo justice methods are corrective in the sense that they attempt to get at causes that underlie disputes or wrongdoing. They address excuses such as denial, minimalization and externalization in practical ways in order to adjust the attitudes of wrongdoers. The methods educate offenders about the nature of their behaviors and how they impact others, and help people identify their place and role in society in order to reintegrate them into specific community roles. Navajo justice methods recognize the need to implement justice in a community context, because ultimately the community must solve its own problems. Navajo families, clans and communities were stripped of their long-standing responsibility for justice in adjudication and in the police and social work models. There are now more than 250 peacemakers in the Navajo Nation's 110 communities, and they accept that responsibility with a great deal of enthusiasm and energy. Navajo corrective justice can be immediate because it is carried out in communities. People expect an immediate resolution of their problems, and they do not want to wait on the schedules of judges and police officers.

Navajo corrective justice is actually restorative justice. It is not so much concerned about correction of the person as it is about restoring that person to good relations with others. This is an integrative process whereby the group as a whole examines relationships and mends a relationship gone wrong. Navajo justice uses practical methods to restore an offender to good standing within the group. Where the relationship does not exist in the first place (*e.g.*, as with dysfunctional families), peacemaking builds new relationships that hopefully will function in a healthy manner. Another way to describe the result of peacemaking is *hozho nahasdlii*. The phrase describes the result of "talking things out" and reaching a consensual conclusion. It says, "now that we have done these things and gone through this process, we are now returned to a state of *hozho*". The process determines the outcome, and is one of restored mutual and reciprocal relationships with a group functioning as a whole.

Another function of Navajo justice is known as distributive justice. Where there is an injury, the group identifies resources to address it. For example, when a Navajo is arrested and charged for an offense, relatives will collect money to post a money bond or buy a bail bond. When a family member is injured in an accident, others give financial support. It is a form of insurance, also known as *nalyeeh*. In peacemaking, there are practical discussions of the injured person's need and who has the resources to address it. Need is served with monetary, material and even emotional support. Distributive justice asks, "what do we have and how can we help?" It is based on reciprocal obligations founded in *k'e* for *hozho*.

Does peacemaking actually work? Is it romantic or practical? Does peacemaking speak to universals of human behavior or is it culture-specific to Navajos? The *Hozhooji Naat'aanii* (Peacemaker Division of the courts) staff report that recidivism rates among wrongdoers are only about 20%. There are reports of people telling of their personal satisfaction with peacemaking and how it has made a difference to their lives. Peacemaking does deal with homicides or murders (without using those classifications), and there are instances of deaths within family groups (and sometimes among strangers) where peacemaking is used to resolve the emotions and hardships that come in the wake of the killing of one person by another. The question of the kinds of cases handled is not as relevant as the result, restorative justice. Navajo cultural perspectives are unique. They are a product of the Navajo language and of the concepts it expresses. Navajo ceremonial practice and the norms, values and moral principles it maintains are perhaps unique to Navajos. However, we believe that we have identified human behavior that is universal and grounded in the norms of many cultures. We use psychological discourse and approaches to explain peacemaking so we can show the outside world what Navajos are doing. They are very practical, pragmatic and concrete in what they do.

## REFERENCES

Bluehouse, P., and J.W. Zion (1993). "Hozhooji Naat'aanii: The Navajo Justice and Harmony Ceremony." *Mediation Quarterly* 10(4):327.

Craig, V. (1995). Personal communication with the Chief Probation Officer, Courts of the Navajo Nation.

Lowery, D.L. (1993). "Developing a Tribal Common Law Jurisprudence: The Navajo Experience, 1969-1992." *American Indian Law Review* 18(2):379.

Tso, T. (1992). "Moral Principles, Traditions, and Fairness in the Navajo Nation Code of Judicial Conduct." *Judicature* 76(1):15.

Yazzie, R. (1994). "Life Comes From It: Navajo Justice Concepts." *New Mexico Law Review* 24(2):175.

Zion, J.W. (1983). "The Navajo Peacemaker Court: Deference to the Old and Accommodation to the New." *American Indian Law Review* 11:89.

# 9. SANCTIONING AND HEALING: RESTORATIVE JUSTICE IN CANADIAN ABORIGINAL COMMUNITIES

by

## Curt Taylor Griffiths

and

## Ron Hamilton

**Abstract:** *Many Aboriginal communities in Canada have developed restorative justice programs designed to address the needs of the offender, the victims of crime, and the community. Community-based, restorative justice programs provide a forum for sanctioning offenders while at the same time begin the healing process for victims, offenders and the community. Restorative justice programs adopt a holistic framework that expands the focus and response beyond the offense to include the offender's life situation, the needs of crime victims, the families of victims and offenders, and the larger community context. A review of several restorative justice programs operating in reserve settings and in an urban context highlights the success of these initiatives, as well as the factors that may undermine the efficacy of programs. Critical to the design and implementation of these programs is the need to: staff programs with emotionally healthy residents, give attention to the protection of vulnerable persons, provide for political intervention by power hierarchies, acknowledge that some offenders are too serious to be dealt with by restorative programs, consider the definition and role of elders, and encourage wide community consultation and participation.*

## ABORIGINAL PEOPLES AND THE ANGLO-CANADIAN JUSTICE SYSTEM

On December 4, 1993, a significant event was held in the gymnasium of an Aboriginal community situated on the west coast of Vancouver Island. The community held a traditional justice ceremony and potlatch (ceremonial feast), during which a man from the community who had sexually abused women in the community over a 35-year period faced his victims, their families, and invited witnesses. The event was made possible by one of the man's victims, the One Who Broke the Silence, who could no longer bear to return to the community, to see the offender, or to endure the pain of silence. The One Who Broke the Silence approached her eldest brother and the Speaker, and told them of her desire to resolve this long-standing crisis through a traditional justice ceremony rather than through the Anglo-Canadian justice system. Subsequently, three additional women publicly disclosed that they, too, had been sexually assaulted by the offender and that they would also participate in the ceremony. At the time of the ceremony, the age of the four victims ranged from late teens to mid-forties. All now had children, and three had married.

Three chairs were situated at one end of the gymnasium: one for the Speaker, one for the eldest brother of the One Who Broke the Silence and one for the offender. The victims, female elders and female relatives sat in the front row of a semi-circle. Behind them, in ever-widening semi-circles, sat witnesses from the village and from neighboring Aboriginal communities; witnesses play a very significant role in the culture of this particular Aboriginal nation. The proceedings were initiated by the Speaker, who detailed to the assembly both the reasons for the ceremony and the sequence of events that would occur during the ceremony. He then presented his cousin, the offender, to the assembly. The offender entered and took a seat between the Speaker and the eldest brother of the One Who Broke the Silence. It was the desire of the One Who Broke the Silence that the entire ceremony should be videotaped so as to provide a record for the community and for others.

The offender was a highly respected member of the community—a historian and a ritualist, singer, carver of masks, dancer, painter, and giver of names. He was also highly respected in the Aboriginal communities along the west coast of Vancouver Island. The offender then rose and spoke to the assembly, admitting his guilt for the offenses, describing in detail the crimes perpetrated upon the four victims, and relating

how, through intimidation of the victims and their families, he had managed to silence their pain and suffering for so many years. He then described his life and his descent into alcoholism. The offender acknowledged his responsibility for the crimes and for the physical and
emotional pain that he had inflicted upon the victims, both at the time of
the offenses and over the years since the incidents. Finally, the offender
begged for their forgiveness; not for them to forget, but, within the traditions and customs of the Nation, to forgive.

Following this, the offender approached each of the victims individually. Next to their feet stood a wash basin filled with water and, at the
side, a towel. In the culture of this Aboriginal nation, the feet of women
are washed during puberty ceremonies to signify their ascension to
womanhood. Because of the pain and anguish inflicted on them by the
offender, the four victims had, to this day, been denied their full womanhood. Now, in a symbolic gesture, the offender would wash the feet of
each of the victims, beginning with the One Who Broke the Silence. The
offender approached each of the victims individually, spoke to them and
apologized. The washing of the victim's feet followed. The washing began
the process of transformation for each of the women from sexual assault
victim to sexual assault survivor. The washing was the beginning of the
process of renewal, a process that would allow the women to live full
lives within the village. The washings took place before all of the assembled witnesses and in full view of the two video cameras.

When the feet of each of the victims had been washed, the water, basin and towel from each washing were taken from the gymnasium. Each
was carried by a man identified publicly by the Speaker as being respectable in the community. A fire had been built in the field adjacent to
the gymnasium. There, with the offender, the victims, their families, and
the witnesses looking on, the water, basin, and towel of each victim was
put into the fire. Following this, the One Who Broke the Silence approached the offender and removed from his face a mask. This mask,
which had been carved by the offender, symbolized the persona of the
offender at the time the offenses were committed and until the present
moment. Masks are among the most highly treasured possessions in
this Aboriginal culture and are normally used in dances to demonstrate
social status. The mask was taken by the One Who Broke the Silence
and placed, face up, on the fire. As the fire consumed the mask, a
prayer was chanted by the Speaker, accompanied by a rattle. The burning of the mask was the pivotal moment of the entire ceremony. It was at

this juncture that the ceremonial conversation involving the Speaker, the victims, and the offender ended and public conversation began. At this point, the victims became survivors and were spoken of as survivors of sexual abuse. The burning of the mask terminated the ceremonial formalities of the event. The nephew of the One Who Broke the Silence tended the fire until it was completely extinguished.

The offender, survivors, and witnesses then returned to the gymnasium, at which time the witnesses were asked to ratify the events that had occurred, offer their support to the survivors and speak to the offender. Prior to the ceremony, the Speaker had asked and encouraged persons to speak who would give strength and encouragement to the survivors and who had something positive to offer to the ceremony. For the next two hours, women from the village and from other communities came forward to speak—of the courage of the One Who Broke the Silence, of the courage of the other survivors who disclosed, of the pain they themselves had experiences as the victims of sexual assault, and of their support for the women and the community in the actions they had taken. One woman related her experience of being ostracized by her family and her band for breaking the silence in her community.

When all of the women who needed to speak were finished, a feast was held. The tables had been set up and arranged by the men in the community, who also cooked the food and served the assembly. Following the feast, the men in attendance were allowed to come forward and speak. One man after another came to the front and spoke to the assembly, offering words of support and encouragement to the survivors, acknowledging the courage of the One Who Broke the Silence and of the other three survivors, and speaking of the importance for communities to continue addressing the problems of sexual assault. One man who spoke was a from neighboring village and had been convicted of child sexual assault. This man shared his pain, his remorse, and his regret at not having participated in a traditional justice ceremony and not having had an opportunity to publicly disclose his offenses and apologize to his victims. The husband of the One Who Broke the Silence stood and spoke to the assembly, and then turned to tell the offender of the pain and anguish inflicted on his wife and of the anger that the husband harbored toward the offender. The husband then added that his grandmother always taught him to forgive others. He told the offender that while he will never forget, he does forgive. The final male to speak was the nephew of the offender, who admitted that he, too, was a sexual abuser of women.

This man introduced himself as the elected Chief of the tribe and as the younger brother of the One Who Broke the Silence. Importantly, his disclosure was unsolicited, completely spontaneous and a surprise to everyone in attendance.

The women and the men spoke of the ceremony as their justice system; rather than being an alternative to the Anglo-Canadian justice system, it was the Anglo-Canadian system that was the alternative. Many spoke of the need for Aboriginal communities to continue their traditions and culture, and to relate their frustrations and disappointments with the more formal criminal justice system. Many turned and spoke directly to the offender, who sat at the front of the assembly with the Speaker and the elder brother of the One Who Broke the Silence. They told him of their anger at what he had done to the women and to the community. They also spoke of forgiveness and a new beginning for him, the survivors, and the community. After the men had spoken, a potlatch was held. Blankets and gifts were given to the victims and their families, to elders, visiting Chiefs, persons who supported the victims, and to many of the other witnesses in attendance. Several days later, the man was sent to a six-month residential treatment program for Aboriginal sex offenders, with the costs assumed by the Chief and Council of the village.

This event was only one ceremony in a small village on Vancouver Island, unreported in the media and literally and figuratively miles away from the nearest courthouse, but it represented a very important step for the community. This traditional justice ceremony provided an opportunity for the victims of the sexual assaults to confront their abuser. It required the offender to fully disclose his crimes and to acknowledge full responsibility for his offenses to the victims, their families, and the assembled witnesses. The ceremony also was designed to provide the beginnings of healing in the community of the offender, his victims and their families. It provided an opportunity for forgiveness, but not for forgetting.

The ceremony was planned and carried out by the people in the community, without the assistance of the police, lawyers, the judiciary, or outside government. There was no government grant, no paid facilitators and no guidance from outside professionals. The traditional justice ceremony is illustrative of the increasing involvement of Aboriginal communities in responding to crime and trouble, and in creating forums for conflict resolution and restorative justice through which the needs of the victims, offenders, and community can be met. The ceremony is illustrative of the types of initiatives that Aboriginal communities are taking to reassert control over the administration of justice.

Aboriginal people are over-represented in the criminal justice system, from the arrest stage to incarceration in correctional institutions (Griffiths and Verdun-Jones, 1994). Information gathered by the Manitoba Aboriginal Justice Inquiry (Hamilton and Sinclair, 1991) revealed that while Aboriginal peoples comprise 6% of the total population in the province of Manitoba, more than 50% of the inmates in correctional institutions were Aboriginal. Further, in comparison with non-Aboriginal accused, Aboriginal persons were more likely to be denied bail, held in pre-trial detention, charged with multiple offenses, and awarded less time with their lawyer, and were twice as likely to be incarcerated upon conviction. Similar findings have been reported by commissions of inquiry in the provinces of Alberta (Cawsey, 1991) and Saskatchewan (Linn, 1992a, 1992b). Over-representation of Aboriginal peoples in the criminal justice system is due to "a mixture of discrimination on the part of the justice system and actual criminal behaviour on the part of Aboriginal people" (Hamilton and Sinclair, 1991, p.87).

The objectives and process of the traditional justice ceremony could not be more different than the adversarial Anglo-Canadian criminal justice system. The offender is held directly accountable to the victims of his or her crimes and is required to come before them, the community, and an assembly of witnesses to confess these crimes and to beg for forgiveness. This ceremony also provides an opportunity to begin the healing process for the victims, the offender and the community. The victims are supported at the ceremony by their families, community members and witnesses from neighboring tribes; the offender has the support of his or her family, who often travel to the community to be present at the event.

Westernized, adversarial systems of criminal justice center on winners and losers, and have retribution as their primary objective; traditional Aboriginal law and justice are based on a restorative model (Barkwell, 1991; Brodeur et al., 1991). The tenets of the Anglo-Canadian retributive model of law and justice and those of the Aboriginal restorative model of law and justice are outlined in Table 9.1.

Gossip, mockery, derision and shunning are among the more informal sanctions employed in traditional Aboriginal communities. Formal sanctions include song or drum duels (among the Inuit), banishment,

*Table 9.1.* Anglo-Canadian law and justice and aboriginal law and justice.

| Anglo-Canadian Law and Justice (Retributive Model) | Aboriginal Law and Justice (Restorative Model) |
|---|---|
| 1. Crime is a violation of the state. | Crime is a violation of one person by another. |
| 2. The focus is on establishing blame or guilt. | The focus is on problem solving and restoration of harmony. |
| 3. Justice is defined by intent and process. | Dialogue and process negotiation are normative. Restitution and reconciliation are used as a means of restoration. |
| 4. Community does not play a leading role. | The community acts as a facilitator in the restorative process. |
| 5. Action revolves around the offender. Accountability of the offender is put in terms of punishment. | The offender is impressed with his/ her action on the total order. |
| 6. Offenses are strictly legal and devoid of moral, social, political, and economic considerations. Past behavior is important. | The holistic context of an offense is taken into consideration, including the holistic context of amoral, social, economic, political and religious, and cosmic considerations. |
| 7. Social stigma of criminal behavior is almost unremovable. | Stigma of offenses is removable through conformity. |
| 8. Remorse, restitution and forgiveness are not important factors. | Remorse, repentance and forgiveness are important factors. |
| 9. Offenders play a passive role depending on proxy professionals. | Offenders take an active role in the restorative process. |

Source: Cawsey, R.A. (1991). *Task Force on the Criminal Justice System and Its Impact on the Indian and Metis People of Alberta*. Edmonton, CAN: Attorney General of Alberta and Solicitor General of Alberta.

various corporal punishments and, in rare instances, death. For Aboriginal peoples, the primary objectives of social control and the imposition of sanctions are resolution of the conflict, restoration of order and harmony in the group or community, and healing of the offender, victim, and community (Ross, 1992). In contrast, Western justice systems are primarily reactive in nature; they respond to crime by focusing primarily on the behavior of the individual offender and, in many cases, sanctioning offenders by removing them from the community, often for extended periods of time. The etiology of the criminal behavior is rarely addressed, and the needs and concerns of victims and communities are generally unmet. This has led to increasing concerns about the relevance of the Anglo-Canadian justice system for Aboriginal peoples.

## RESTORATIVE JUSTICE IN ABORIGINAL COMMUNITIES

Aboriginal communities in Canada have become increasing involved in developing community-based criminal justice services and programs designed to better address the specific needs of community residents, victims and offenders (Griffiths, 1989, 1990, 1992). This has included a number of programs centered on restorative justice. There has been a resurgence of traditional cultural practices for addressing issues of crime and justice in Canadian Aboriginal communities. These develop- ments are occurring against the larger political backdrop of the constitu- tional recognition of an inherent right to Aboriginal self-government, the assertion of control by Aboriginal bands and communities over all as- pects of community life, and the revitalization of Aboriginal communities and cultures.

Restorative justice initiatives have generally been developed within the larger context of the devolution of justice services to Aboriginal com- munities, and the creation of community-based justice services and pro- grams. Many community justice and restorative justice initiatives have involved a degree of collaboration between Aboriginal communities and representatives of the criminal justice system. These initiatives may be, but are not necessarily, premised on customary law and traditional practices. Most, however, do contain elements of traditional culture, in- volve community elders, and have a strong emphasis on healing, spiritu- ality, and responding to offenders in a holistic fashion by considering a wide range of issues beyond the specific criminal behavior. Several high- profile restorative justice programs have been initiated by Aboriginal communities in Canada.

## The Community Holistic Circle Healing Program, Hollow Water, Manitoba

This program was initiated in 1986 by the Hollow Water First Nation, an Ojibwa community in the province of Manitoba. Designed as a com- munity-based response to the high rates of sexual and family abuse that afflicted the community, it includes a 13-step process (described in Ta- ble 9.2). The Special Gathering in the Hollow Water program is a public event that shares many similarities with the traditional justice ceremony described at the beginning of this chapter. Traditional healing practices are used in an attempt to restore community, family, and individual peace and harmony. A healing contract is signed, and offenders apologize publicly to the victims and the community for the harm that has been done. The response is designed to consider the needs of all of the parties to the abuse—the victim, the offender and the community—and is directed beyond merely punishing the offender for a specific behavior (Lajeunesse, 1993). By early 1995, there were a substantial number of persons in the healing program, including 48 offenders, 83 relatives of offenders, 62 victims and 153 relatives of victims. Four offenders, 32 victims and 27 relatives of victims had completed the program. There had been only five offenders sentenced to jail. Only two offenders in the program have reoffended during the nine years the program has been in operation (Moon, 1995).

*Table 9.2.* The thirteen steps of the Hollow Water community holistic circle healing process.

---

(1) Disclosure → (2) Protecting the Victim/Child → (3) Confronting the Victimizer → (4) Assisting the Spouse → (5) Assisting the Family/Community → (6) Meeting of the Assessment Team/RCMP/Crown → (7) Victimizer Must Admit and Accept Responsibility → (8) Preparation of the Victimizer → (9) Preparation of the Victim → (10) Preparation of All the Family/ → (11) The Special Gathering → (12) Implementation of the Healing Contract → (13) The Cleansing Ceremony

---

## Canim Lake Indian Band Family Violence Program, Canim Lake, British Columbia

This community-based, band-controlled family violence program is designed for the management and treatment of adult and adolescent sex offenders, as well as for the victims of sexual abuse. One component of the program is the identification of sex offenders in the community who have not been detected by the police or otherwise subjected to sanctioning by the band or the criminal justice system. During an amnesty period, these individuals can contact the Family Violence Committee and acknowledge their responsibility for their offense(s), and can be placed in a treatment program without being subjected to criminal charges. The specific treatment interventions blend modern clinical techniques with traditional Aboriginal healing practices, and address the needs of the offender and the victim within a family and community context. To qualify for the treatment program, and as a condition of being diverted, the offender must sign a contract indicating a commitment to completing the program. The diversion status is revoked, and offenders are referred for formal prosecution by the external criminal justice system if they either reoffend or fail to complete the program.

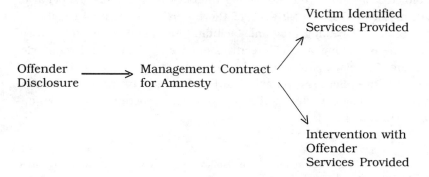

Victim Identified
Services Provided

Offender ⟶ Management Contract
Disclosure        for Amnesty

Intervention with
Offender
Services Provided

*Fig. 9.1.* The Canim Lake family violence program case process (simplified).

## Aboriginal Legal Services of Toronto Community Council Project

Development of restorative justice programs that incorporate elements of Aboriginal tradition and culture has occurred largely in rural and remote areas and most often on Aboriginal reserve lands. There are, however, large numbers of Aboriginal peoples who reside in urban centers across Canada, and the rate of Aboriginal migration to these centers continues to increase. With the exception of work by Griffiths and colleagues (1994, 1995) and by LaPrairie (1994a, 1994b), there has been little focus on the difficulties encountered by urban Aboriginal peoples, the nature and extent of their conflict with the criminal justice system, or the potential for developing alternative justice services and programs that might better address the needs of the urban Aboriginal community. This is due to a number of factors, including: (1) the lack of a land base; (2) the cultural and linguistic diversity of the urban Aboriginal community; (3) urban Aboriginal peoples' status as only one of many cultural and ethnic minorities; and (4) the lack of an established framework within which policy and programmatic initiatives relating to urban Aboriginal policing can be developed and implemented.

The Aboriginal Legal Services of the Toronto Community Council Project is one notable exception to the absence of programmatic initiatives by and for urban Aboriginal peoples. The underlying philosophy of this program is that the Aboriginal community is in the best position to respond to the needs of Aboriginal offenders, and that the deliberations of the council, which involve the direct participation of the offender, provide an opportunity to focus on the offender's needs and life circumstance rather than solely on the offense that has been committed. The council, comprised of Aboriginal volunteers, reaches decisions by consensus and has a number of dispositions available, including fines, payment of restitution to the victim, completion of a number of hours of community service, or referral to a treatment resource. The objective of the council is reintegration rather than punishment. An evaluation (Moyer and Axon, 1993) of the project identified a number of positive attributes, including: (1) design and control by the Aboriginal community; (2) an offender rather than an offense focus; (3) facilitation of offender access to urban programs and services; (4) a holistic orientation; and (5) a feeling among participants that their individual needs are met by the Community Council process. The success of the project indicates that it is possible to develop and apply the principles of restorative justice in urban areas with a diverse Aboriginal population.

## Restorative Justice and "Just" Communities: Lessons from South Island

In 1991, the First Nations of the South Island Tribal Council, situated on Vancouver Island, British Columbia, initiated the South Vancouver Island Justice Education Project. This project was designed as a collaborative effort between the outside justice system and the First Nations justice system. The program ceased operation two years later. The South Island Justice Education Project stands as the most notable failure of an Aboriginal-sponsored, restorative justice initiative in Canada. The factors that contributed to its demise are instructive. Among the objectives of the project were to improve the delivery of justice services to residents in the eight communities involved in the South Island Tribal Council, to involve the elder's council in the delivery of justice services, and to apply traditional Aboriginal practices in responding to offenders and addressing the needs of crime victims. These objectives were to be achieved through the use of various community-based alternatives, including diversion, dispute resolution and counselling. Funding was provided by the federal and provincial governments and by the provincial law foundation.

Following termination, a comprehensive review (Sheila Clark & Associates *et al.*, 1994) was conducted on all facets of the design and implementation of the project. The review included interviews with community residents and other key participants, and identified a number of strengths and weaknesses of the project. The identified strengths were the initial concept of devolving justice services to the community, the increased cultural awareness of community residents, the involvement of the elders, the recognition by communities of the need to begin the healing process and the increased attention to the justice needs of communities. These strengths, however, were far outweighed by the weaknesses of the project. These included: insufficient community consultation prior to implementation of the project; lack of credibility of the key participants; failure to address the specific needs of the communities; political unrest in the communities; family feuds within the communities; failure to meet the specific needs of victims and offenders; and inability to consider that not all community residents shared the same cultural values. Respondents indicated that politics had significantly compromised the project. Community residents and front-line personnel were excluded from initial discussions surrounding the project. Further, once the project was operational, there were instances in which members of the tribal council and some elders intervened and attempted to influence the case outcomes of family members who had been charged with offenses. Victims often felt pressured by project personnel not to pursue charges against offenders, and community residents perceived that individuals who were alleged to have committed serious offenses were, through family and political connections, able to be diverted into the program. These weaknesses provide critical insights into issues that must be considered by Aboriginal communities and outside funding agencies when community-based, restorative justice initiatives are proposed.

## CRITICAL ISSUES

The twin foundations of culture and community provide a potential basis for the development of community-based, restorative justice initiatives. The potential for utilizing restorative justice approaches in responding to crime and trouble in Aboriginal communities, however, must not obscure several critical issues that Aboriginal communities confront as they move to assume increasing control over the delivery of justice services. Attention must be given to the extent to which the community, its leadership, and others who would assume key roles at the local level are healed and healthy. Aboriginal communities across Canada have recognized the importance of healing in the process of community revitalization and the development of community-based justice programs. If such healing has not occurred, additional harm may be inflicted on the community and its residents. This is reflected in the experience of Hollow Water (Lajeunesse, 1993) in training residents to be self-awareness trainers.

> One of the key lessons we learned was that unless prospective trainers have themselves done a great deal of personal healing and growth work, and in particularly have already adequately dealt with addictions and abuse issues buried in their own past, they will not be able to effectively guide others through a process of self-transformation, and they may, in some cases, hinder the progress of others by denying or covering up issues they haven't dealt with themselves [p.A12].

Among the more significant and potentially divisive issues is ensuring that the rights of victims are protected within the community and that vulnerable persons, particularly women and female adolescents, are adequately protected. Aboriginal women have voiced concerns about the high rates of sexual and physical abuse in communities, and have questioned whether local justice initiatives provide adequate protection for violence and abuse victims and whether the sanctions imposed are appropriate. Peterson (1992) found that Aboriginal and Inuit women were concerned about the attitudes toward violence held by community residents and how this would impact the operation of community justice initiatives.

> There must also be an awareness of the fact that there can be differences that develop along generational lines and that older people may evidence a tolerance of violence against women that is no longer acceptable to younger women....While it is appropriate to explore alternatives for addressing issues of violence, such alternatives must not become a mechanism for excusing violent behaviour [p.75].

There are power hierarchies within Aboriginal communities that may either facilitate or hinder the development and success of restorative justice initiatives. Care must be taken to ensure that family and kinship networks and the community power hierarchy do not compromise the administration of justice. As in any community, there is a danger of a tyranny of the community in which certain individuals and groups of residents, particularly those who are members of vulnerable groups, find themselves at the mercy of those in positions of power and influence.

A notable attribute of the holistic healing circle program at Hollow Water and the family violence initiative undertaken by the Canim Lake Indian Band is that they have targeted offenders who have committed offenses involving sexual assault and violence. These offenses, which may have been committed over a lengthy period of time, have inflicted considerable pain and suffering on victims, their families and the community. Caution must be exercised in expecting or assuming that communities have the interest and/or expertise to respond, treat and control offenders convicted of acts involving violence and sexual assault. All communities have a threshold of offense severity beyond which the community may not want to assume responsibility. The specific threshold may vary across communities and depend upon the personal and community resources that individual communities can mobilize. The Canim Lake Family Violence Program has acknowledged that offenders who have committed offenses involving sexual assault and violence may require clinical intervention in addition to exposure to traditional healing practices. Both the Hollow Water and Canim Lake Indian Band programs include the option of referring offenders to the outside justice system. The majority of chiefs and councillors interviewed by the South Island Justice Education Project review team indicated that communities should be involved in the resolution of incidents involving less-serious offenses, but that those involving more serious transgressions should be handled by outside criminal justice agencies. Similarly, LaPrairie (1992) found that residents of Yukon communities supported offenders being sanctioned by the external justice system in cases involving serious offenses, in those where an individual continued to reoffend, and in those in which an individual did not abide by a community-imposed disposition. Griffiths and his colleagues (1995) reported similar views among residents of Eastern Arctic communities.

Aboriginal elders are often considered a cornerstone of community-based, restorative justice initiatives. However, the potential for elder involvement varies across Aboriginal communities, and, in many, it may be unrealistic to rely upon elders as a resource for addressing crime and trouble and as a basis for restorative justice initiatives. Field research has indicated that caution should be exercised in using the term "elder" and in the connotations attached to this term. A resident of a community in the Baffin Region (Eastern Arctic), Northwest Territories, commented:

> Elders and leaders are two very different things. I know some young people who are great leaders and I know some elders who are not. This elder concept is another white man's idea that suddenly the elders are the answer to all our problems. 'Get the elders. Talk to them.' Some of them might have some knowledge, but I know some young people who have knowledge as well. You have to be careful when you're using the word 'elder'. It's all very romantic, but is it practical?" [Griffiths et al., 1995, p.198].

In many communities, elders command the respect of residents and play a pivotal role in community life; in others, the authority and role of elders has been significantly altered by schools, government agencies, and elected chiefs and councils. In many communities, the elders have been replaced in leadership roles by younger, formally educated persons, a development that has further eroded their status. The experience of the South Island project highlighted the importance of the community consultation process, and of soliciting the views and concerns of average community residents in any deliberations and plans to create restorative justice programs. This includes representatives from all groups within the community, including persons from vulnerable groups, not just members of the hamlet council, tribal council or certain selected/appointed persons who represent the community. The absence of a community-wide consultation process contributed to the failure of the South Island project.

Canada's Aboriginal peoples are assuming greater control over the design and delivery of justice services at the community and reserve levels. This is part of a general movement toward self-government and the assertion of Aboriginal rights and sovereignty. It is also a consequence of the seemingly irreconcilable differences between the worldview held by Anglo-Canadians and Aboriginals, and the differing models reflected in the two systems of law and justice. Government-sponsored justice initiatives have been largely ineffectual in reducing the levels of conflict that Aboriginal people in Canada experience with the criminal justice system or in meeting the needs of Aboriginal victims, offenders, and communities. Criminal behavior is often only a symptom of deeper community and individual ills. Non-adversarial forums for responding to criminal behavior that provide for substantive community participation may be an effective way to respond to these ills. Aboriginal-controlled justice programs and services, premised on Aboriginal culture and traditional practices, hold great promise and can provide models that may be utilized by non-Aboriginal communities as the search for more effective criminal justice strategies intensifies.

## REFERENCES

Barkwell, L. (1991). "Early Law and Social Control among the Metis." In: S. Corrigan and L. Barkwell (eds.), *The Struggle for Recognition: Canadian Justice and the Metis Nation.* Winnipeg, CAN: Pemmican Publications.

Brodeur, J.-P., C. LaPrairie and R. McDonnell (1991). *Justice for the Cree: Final Report.* James Bay, CAN: Grand Council of the Crees.

Cawsey, R.A. (1991). *Justice on Trial* (Report of the Task Force on the Criminal Justice System and Its Impact on the Indian and Metis People of Alberta, vol 1. Main Report). Edmonton, CAN: Attorney General and Solicitor General of Alberta.

Griffiths, C.T. (1989). *The Community and Northern Justice.* Burnaby, CAN: Northern Justice Society, Simon Fraser University.

—(1990). *Preventing and Responding to Northern Crime.* Burnaby, CAN: Northern Justice Society, Simon Fraser University.

—(1992). *Self-Sufficiency in Northern Justice Issues.* Burnaby, CAN: Northern Justice Society, Simon Fraser University.

—and S.N. Verdun-Jones (1994). *Canadian Criminal Justice.* Toronto, CAN: Butterworths.

—D. Wood, E. Zellerer and G. Saville (1994). "Crime, Law and Justice Among Inuit in the Baffin Region, N.W.T., Canada: Preliminary Findings from a Multi-Year Study." In: K. Hazlehurst (ed.), *Legal Pluralism and the Colonial Legacy: Indigenous Experiences of Justice in Canada, Australia, and New Zealand.* Aldershot, UK: Avebury.

—D. Wood, E. Zellerer and G. Saville (1995). *Crime, Law, and Justice in the Baffin Region, N.W.T., Canada: Final Report.* Burnaby, CAN: Criminology Research Centre, Simon Fraser University.

Hamilton, A.C. and C.M. Sinclair (1991). *Report of the Aboriginal Justice Inquiry of Manitoba. The Justice System and Aboriginal People,* vol 1. Winnipeg, CAN: Queen's Printer.

LaPrairie, C. (1992). *Exploring the Boundaries of Justice.* Whitehorse and Ottawa, CAN: Department of Justice, Yukon Territory, First Nations of the Yukon Territory and Justice Canada.

—(1994a). *Seen But Not Heard: Native People in the Inner City. Report 1. The Inner City Sample, Social Strata and the Criminal Justice Sys-*

tem. Ottawa, CAN: Department of Justice.

—(1994b). *Seen But Not Heard: Native People in the Inner City. Report 2. City-by-City Differences—The Inner City and the Criminal Justice System.* Ottawa, CAN: Department of Justice.

Lajeunesse, T. (1993). *Community Holistic Circle Healing. Hollow Water First Nation.* Ottawa, CAN: Solicitor General of Canada.

Linn, P. (1992a). *Report of the Saskatchewan Indian Justice Review Committee.* Regina, CAN: Government of Saskatchewan.

—(1992b). *Report of the Saskatchewan Metis Justice Review Committee.* Regina, CAN: Government of Saskatchewan.

Moon, P. (1995). "Native Healing Helps Abusers." *The Globe and Mail,* April 8, pp.A1, A5.

Moyer, S. and L. Axon (1993). *An Implementation Evaluation of the Native Community Council Project of the Aboriginal Legal Services of Toronto.* Toronto, CAN: The Ministry of the Attorney General (Ontario) and Aboriginal Legal Services of Toronto.

Peterson, K.R. (1992). *The Justice House—Report of the Special Advisor on Gender Equality.* Yellowknife, CAN: Department of Justice, Government of the Northwest Territories.

Ross, R. (1992). *Dancing with a Ghost—Exploring Indian Reality.* Toronto, CAN: Octopus Publishing.

Sheila Clark & Associates, Valerie Lannon & Associates, Inc. & a.m. Research Services. (1994). *Building the Bridge. A Review of the South Vancouver Island Justice Education Project.* Victoria and Ottawa, CAB: British Columbia Ministry of the Attorney General, Department of Justice Canada and the Solicitor General of Canada.

# 10. CIRCLE SENTENCING: TURNING SWORDS INTO PLOUGHSHARES

by

## Barry Stuart

**Abstract:** *Circle sentencing, currently practiced in a large number of northern Canadian communities, involves community meetings to address both family and community circumstances that are the underlying causes of crime. The circles involve offenders, victims, the friends and families of each, and community members, and provide sentencing consultation to courts. Circle hearings are built on principles in mediation, Aboriginal peacemaking processes and consensus decision making. Criticism that circle sentencing takes too long fails to recognize the importance of investing time to accomplish the objectives of rebuilding relationships, devising rehabilitative plans and responding to victims' needs. Communities know better, and are prepared to invest the time and resources necessary for the circle hearing. Circle sentencing proceeds best in environments that are comfortable for resolving disputes and facilitating informal processes. Circle sentencing is inclusive, with everyone in the community welcome to participate. Its value goes beyond the impact on offenders and victims to include its influence on the community.*

In managing conflict, the use of the circle is not new; its principles, concepts and similar practices can be found in the history of most cultures. Processing conflict through circles enabled the parties, their families, and communities to participate in, and share the responsibility for finding solutions. Only in the last two centuries have we transferred primary responsibility for conflict from families and communities to professionals and the state. The formal justice system, a relatively new experiment in resolving conflict, is failing in part because it aspires to do too much. In so doing, it needlessly disempowers parties, families, and communities, and robs communities of an invaluable community building block; active involvement in constructively resolving conflict. This chapter draws on the collective experiences of northern communities with circle sentencing to illustrate how consensus and mediation principles expand participation in community issues, and empower both the parties immediately affected and the community to constructively work through conflict.

## DIFFERENT KINDS OF CIRCLES

There are many different circle processes. The differences arise chiefly from the purpose of the circle, who participates and the role of participants. Healing and talking circles focus on a particular concern common to all parties (men or women's healing circles, substance abuse groups), or are constituted to help someone with their healing journey (support groups for victims or for offenders). Such circles rarely involve justice professionals but may include professional treatment counsellors.

Community sentencing circles do not include lawyers or judges but depend upon lay justices of the peace, court workers and local police officers. Community court sentencing circles involve all the players found in court. These circles may be organized in one large circle, or split into an inner and outer circle. The inner circle is composed of the victim, the offender, supporters or members of their respective families, and justice professionals normally involved in court. The outer circle includes professionals who may be called upon for specific information and interested members of the community. Court circles, usually held in a courtroom, may simply include the counsel, judge, probation officer, treatment professionals, and family and friends of the offender and victim. There are many different structures used for a circle hearing. The process before, during and after a hearing has evolved uniquely in each community.

## Common Community Court Circle Procedures

Any offense can be sent to a circle. The process is substantially the same whether the circle involves serious or minor crimes. The more serious or complex the case, the longer and more demanding the circle process may be. However, single circles attempt to address the underlying causes of crime. Less serious crimes, such as under-age drinking, may take considerable time as the circle explores what can be done to prevent substance addiction by the young offender and by other young people within the community.

Some communities have established application procedures that impose significant tasks upon the offender to gain entry into the circle sentencing process. Prerequisites, common to all communities, include an acceptance of responsibility by the offender, a plea of guilty, a connection to the community, a desire for rehabilitation, concrete steps toward rehabilitation, and support within the community for the offender. The victim's input is a fundamental consideration in deciding whether a circle is appropriate. Acceptance into the circle is decided by a community justice committee or circle support group.

Work undertaken in preparation for a circle hearing profoundly affects the success of the hearing. Communities are increasingly investing more time and effort into pre-hearing work with the offender, the victim, families and support groups. Pre-hearing work that includes exchanging information, developing plans, and preparing all parties to participate reduces anxiety by the victim and offender over what might happen. Pre-circle preparation significantly reduces the length of hearings.

Some circles have been held in the court, but most are held in a community building such as a school, community center, church hall, or municipal or First Nation office. Location is important in generating a comfortable environment and in recognizing that the process belongs to the community. The attendance of elders, people with mediation skills and those with access to resources (teachers, health officials, business people) all enrich the process. While the circle is open to all, some communities assess the nature of the case to be heard and invite key people who can contribute to specific issues raised in the circle.

The circle hearing is built upon the principles of mediation, Aboriginal peacemaking and consensus decision making. Adversarial practices are replaced by practices common to a consensus process. This transition does not ignore the fundamental differences among participants, but seeks to move parties beyond positions to interests, to directly engage all affected parties, and to focus less on personalities or roles and more on the merits of issues advanced by all participants. There are many differences between the circle process built on consensus and mediation principles and the formal justice process built on adversarial principles. The most important differences in circle sentencing flow from empowering the offender, the victim and particularly the community to take primary responsibility for advancing their interests, to take ownership of the process, and to develop solutions incorporating their values, objectives, and resources. Employing consensus and mediation processes can never replace the need for formal justice processes, but it can improve the range of options for processing crime and for achieving the over-arching objectives of the justice system. Important differences arise from shifting to a consensus process. This shift introduces many new advantages, and requires a realignment in power and adjustments in the attitudes and roles of both community members and professionals.

## TIME TAKEN FOR CIRCLE HEARINGS

For some, a major downside of circle hearings is the time they take. With proper pre-hearing preparation, a circle sentence hearing will take from one to two hours. Without proper pre-hearing preparation, the case may often require two hearings; the first sometimes over two hours, the second significantly less.

An onerous backlog of cases in the formal justice system imposes greater emphasis on the quantity of cases processed than on the quality of problem solving in each case. In taking pride in accelerating the process, the justice system pays little regard to whether speed sacrifices other objectives.

Circle hearings do take longer than court hearings. Much of the time in circle hearings is taken up with ensuring that everyone is fully heard in working towards a consensus. The much broader spectrum of issues addressed in circles also extends hearing time. Rebuilding relationships, devising rehabilitative plans for offenders, responding to victim's needs, creating the comfort for all to participate, developing an overall consensus, sharing the pain and joy of healing, and identifying and redressing the underlying causes of similar crimes in the community all take time. For many Aboriginal people, the Western way of doing things quickly is offensive and demonstrates a lack of respect for the parties and the importance of their conflict.

Sentencing decisions profoundly affect the ability to achieve the over-arching objectives of the entire justice system, and more so than all other decisions in the justice system determine the future well-being of victims, offenders, and the community. Yet, priority in time, resources and training is accorded to trials.

Communities know better. They recognize the importance of sentencing, and invest time and resources before, during, and after the circle hearing. Communities appreciate that what happens in sentencing directly relates to their interests and well-being. Whether the extra time invested in circle sentencing is prudent depends on what participants aspire to achieve from sentencing hearings. For communities the extra time invested in circle sentencing is valuable since they directly benefit from: lowering recidivism rates; reconnecting offenders to communities; rebuilding broken relationships; addressing victims' needs; educating the community about specific and general problems within their neighborhood; generating community-based preventive measures; developing participatory skills; and building communities that can work together, revealing unrealistic public expectations about what a professional formal justice system can deliver, and revealing what the community can accomplish that the formal justice system cannot.

Three further points should be noted about the added costs caused by the additional time required by circle sentencing. First, consider current, intolerably high recidivism rates. If a community circle process significantly reduces recidivism, the resultant savings can more than offset extra processing costs in taking the extra time to get it right. Second, the benefits to overall community well-being must be assessed. Working collectively in the circle fosters a sense of belonging to a community and a feeling of having something valuable to contribute. The circle promotes involvement in advancing the overall well-being of the community by revealing the underlying causes of crime, which, in turn, generates community initiatives to redress adverse social conditions or respond to the healing needs of victims and offenders. Third, all community circle processes strive to be as dependent as possible on local resources and local people. Some communities have already moved to circles without lawyers, judges and other professionals. These community circles depend upon local justices of the peace, local people trained in mediation acting as keepers of the circle, the local police officer, the local court worker and a wide range of volunteers from the community. These community-based processes offer a less expensive method of processing many cases, and in a much shorter time span between offense and disposition. As communities gain more experience, as crown and police become more supportive, and as pre-hearing preparation improves, conclusions will be more readily reached in the circle and more cases will be completely directed out of the formal justice system during the pre-hearing stage.

## CREATING COMFORTABLE ENVIRONMENTS FOR RESOLVING DISPUTES

Community circle sentencing should be held in a room not associated in the public mind with the court. It is important for the community to choose the place for a circle hearing. The design of the courtroom serves a specific purpose. A raised dais for the judge, counsel tables placed in front of the real or imagined bar separating the players from the spectators, and the physical space arranged to highlight the roles of counsel and judge combine to reinforce the adversarial nature of the process and its domination by professionals. The physical setting of the courtroom frequently intimidates and effectively excludes public participation and ensures the judge's ability to dominate and control proceedings. A professional monopoly of the process is accentuated by the unique customs, practices, language, dress and culture of professional participants. Conversely, the place and procedures of community circle sentencing processes create a comfortable setting for community members and encourage their participation. The arrangement of chairs in a circle, without tables, goes a long way toward creating the impression and the fact that all participants equally share the responsibility to resolve issues raised in the circle. Many small details of the physical setting are important. For instance, something as innocuous as sharing the task of setting up and taking down the chairs in the circle contributes to informality and to a sense of shared responsibility among all participants for the process.

In the first circles, the judge primarily facilitated the circle hearing. Now some communities select one or two local people to act as keepers of the circle. They act as facilitators, ensuring respect for the teachings of the circle, mediating differences and guiding the circle towards a consensus. Empowering local people to host and run the circle is a critical step towards creating a comfortable participatory environment, affirming community responsibility, and ensuring that the values, customs, and concerns of the community influence the process. The keeper's knowledge of participants and *vice versa* both directly and indirectly assist in avoiding the tension that strangers introduce.

Opening the circle with a prayer introduces a spiritual awareness calling upon all participants to reach beyond their immediate emotions in seeking answers. The prayers offered by elders or others chosen by keepers of the circle are non-denominational. The joining of hands in prayer symbolically induces a sense of sharing, of a community formed by the circle. Most prayers, whether by Aboriginal or other members of the community, stress the interconnectedness of all things and of all people, instilling in each participant a sense of being an integral part of the community. An emphasis on interconnectedness suggests that the victim's, as well as the offender's, suffering is shared in part by everyone, that the disharmony and pain caused by crime affects the entire community, and that everyone shares the responsibility for finding solutions for the problems confronting victim, offender, and the community.

The keepers of the circle welcome everyone to the circle and then introduce themselves by explaining who they are, what they do, where they are from and why they are in the circle. The keeper then asks others, as the feather is passed around the circle, to similarly introduce themselves. Knowing who else is in the circle, what they do, and why they are in attendance removes the anxiety of guessing the identity and purpose of participants. During the introduction, many participants express concern for victims, offenders, and their families, and speak of their hope for the circle to find a way to heal all participants. Introductions help set the tone for the circle and begin to identify the pain, anger, and hope of different members.

Keepers discuss the teachings of the circle and explain the guidelines extracted from them. Questions from participants can generate changes or additions to the guidelines. Most guidelines are common to most communities. They include: speak from the heart, remain until the end in the circle, allow others to speak by speaking briefly, and respect others by not interrupting and by recognizing the value of their contribution. These guidelines reflect the essence of good mediation and consensus practices. The guidelines add sufficient structure to remove anxiety stemming from uncertainty, without denying the flexibility for the innovative problem solving that is essential to a consensus process. The teachings of the circle emphasize respect for all participants. Everyone must feel that their inputs and interests are respected. The final outcome must engender a sense in each participant that they have contributed.

The closing rituals include summarizing what has or has not been agreed, outlining next steps, thanking everyone for their participation, passing the feather for closing comments by all participants and joining in a closing prayer. The closing steps are particularly important to retain the constructive tone set by opening rituals and to solidify the progress towards peacemaking achieved in the circle. All these measures serve to locate the process within the community's control as much as possible, and foster a comfortable environment conducive to community participation.

## BROADENING PARTICIPATION

The circle sentencing process is inclusive, not exclusive. Everyone in the community has a stake in the outcome, and thereby a reason to participate. Although not all members may participate, it is important for them to know they can and are encouraged to do so. Most circumstances underlying crime flow out of families, out of communities. Circle participation fosters an appreciation of these circumstances and a broader range of public involvement in shaping plans to remove conditions causing crime.

### Offender Takes Responsibility

In court, head down and dressed for church, the offender listens to the Crown describe his or her character as deduced from the facts of the offense and a criminal record. Not a pretty picture, nor a complete one. The parts provided by defense counsel call on selected favorable aspects that present a positive, but equally incomplete, picture. Together the description of defense and Crown fail to adequately describe the offender's past or present circumstances, and reveal little of what offenders genuinely desire to do or can do to change their lives. In court, offenders usually decline when asked to speak. Those who do speak contribute too late to significantly alter the process or the result. Circles expect offenders to participate, to respond to what has been said by supporters, police, victims and their support group, and anyone in the circle. Offenders are not called upon solely to state what they wish to do, but why, how, and when. The circle wants to know how they feel about the crime, the victim, their life, their future and their community. Exposing one's feelings and private life in the Circle is not easy, but it can mark an important milestone in the offender's healing journey and in reconnecting to family, friends, and community. The salutary effects of participating directly can be significant.

> I never talked before. [I was] nervous as hell at first, didn't know how to get started, you know, but once started it felt good. It was me, standing up for me. They heard me, you know, listened to me. I had

to listen too. Court is not like that. I hardly ever listened too much, sorta tuned out, never said a word. That's what lawyers are for, eh. But in circle I had a say, I felt good, but knew I had to make it work. It was the toughest, yeah the hardest thing I ever did. No-one can say the circle is easy, they haven't been in it if they do. [The circle] made me feel like I could trust, had a chance to earn trust. [I] never believed others would really, you know, believe in me [Kwanlin Dun, offender, 1993].

Support group members help offenders prepare to take responsibility for their input, and step back sufficiently to ensure the offender does take responsibility. Being involved in the dialogue allows the offender to participate in a manner that presents a more revealing picture of his or her character, aspirations, abilities and true feelings. As stated by an offender from Kwanlin Dun (1992): "[The] thing about the circle is that bullshit don't carry you as far as it does in Court. If you try [in circle] you don't risk being judged just by the suits [judge and lawyers] but by everyone who really counts in your life. [You] must keep the teachings [of the circle], speaking from the heart must tell it all, no bullshit, cause the people in the community, they know what's bullshit."

## VICTIM'S INTERESTS

In the justice system, the victim's input has been significantly reduced since the state has replaced much of the role victims once played, and the focus has shifted from harm to the victim to violation of state laws. The state needs the victim's testimony to establish liability and the victim's pain to secure a punitive sanction. The formal system of justice can, and usually does, function with little regard for the victim's needs.

All communities encourage victim participation. Steps are taken to ensure the victim's interests are addressed if the victim decides not to participate. Communities develop support groups for victims and endeavor to ensure that the circle process responds to the needs of both victim and offender. If they do not wish to participate directly, victims can use a victim impact statement, rely on a spokesperson, or testify under oath in court in the usual manner. Victim participation immeasurably enhances the ability of the process to realize all circle objectives.

Achieving the objectives of the circle depends on more than perfunctory involvement of the victim. The input of victims can be instrumental in rehabilitating offenders, generating new initiatives to assist both offenders and victims, and providing an awareness of appropriate measures to redress the harm caused by crime. The ambitious objectives of the circle are more readily achievable when the victim fully participates. When the victim only partially participates, participates through others or fails to participate, the circle suffers, although not to the same extent as the court process, because others in the circle introduce the victim's concerns or speak of their own experiences as victims in similar offenses.

Victims suffer in carrying the anger, hostility and fear that crime often imposes in their life. The ability of victims to get on with their lives is severely handicapped when these destructive influences remain. The circle affords many victims an important step in unloading debilitating psychological injuries caused by crime. Participating in the circle enables some victims to begin to find answers to troubling questions about the crime and the offender, and to start the process of working through the anger, fear, and frustration. Many victims, disempowered by the crime and by the formal justice process, are empowered by participation in the circle:

> This is my third time [in the circle]. The first two times in Court was a joke, it had nothing to do with me, and did nothing for me. In fact, it hurt me, cause he [her husband] just didn't care, it didn't matter to him if he went to jail or not. He'd been there before, eh, so obviously he didn't learn anything cause we were back again. But this was different [being in the circle], it had to do with me. It was hard to speak, but when I got so much support, I did speak. This time, what happened involved me, it should have, eh. I mean, who was the crime done to, anyway? [Victim, Circle Sentencing, 1992].

## BUILDING CONNECTIONS TO AND WITHIN COMMUNITIES

Discussions within the circle alert the community to problems that need to be addressed. Often this awareness prompts offers of help. "After the circle...and what I heard then, I wanted to help. So I just kept stopping by, just to see how things were working out. [I] had some work to do, so [I] offered him a job to get some money into his jeans. Turned out good, he did good, real good. I know what it's like, so now I know what they're [family of offender] going through, I can help." (Kwanlin Dun, community member, 1993).

The value of circle sentencing derives not as much from its impact upon the offender, or upon the victim, but from its impact on the community. Helping others helps oneself. Participating makes one feel they belong. Being acknowledged and respected engenders respect and acknowledgement from others. Contributions to the circle are respected, built upon by others, and quickly become not the idea of the contributor but of the circle. Incorporating each input into building a consensus respects and immerses the contributor into the community of the circle. Living in the same place does not make a community. Sharing responsibility for resolving disputes in ways that enable people to contribute, respect, and learn from others connects people to their community and engenders a sense of belonging, a sense of community. By building participatory skills, affording people an opportunity to make a difference, and enabling them to share direct responsibility for resolving community conflict, the circle builds self-esteem and connection to the community. An inclusive consensus process run by and for people within a community is an essential community building block.

In some communities, fear of repercussions from speaking out in the circle can inhibit participation. This problem haunts all communities that have abrogated their responsibilities to professional peacekeepers. Regaining community responsibility must begin with the courage of some members to withstand criticism for speaking the truth. This is not an easy barrier to overcome. All communities must discover ways to help circle participants feel safe to speak from the heart.

The informal, personal involvement fostered by the circle causes professionals to reveal more than their professional persona. In so doing, their input and perspective gains new respect and credibility. Equally, they learn to understand and appreciate the values and concerns within the community. Participating in a circle consensus process can promote the understanding and acceptance necessary for them to serve as a vital resource within a community. A new police officer revealed a human side the community had not previously seen by demonstrating care and concern in the circle for the fate of a young offender he had arrested and charged. His participation in the circle—balanced, constructive, supportive, and human—forced the community to look through the uniform to find a person they could relate to and trust. Soon the officer and his family were welcomed by many into the community, into the lives and homes of people in the community who treated him less as a police officer and more as a trusted resource for the community. Unfortunately, this story lacks a happy ending. The police officer wanted to stay, the community wanted him to stay. But police officers in the Yukon are plucked from the community and transferred in accord with policies made outside the community and with little regard for the best interests of the community. Moving officers from town to town substantially undermines the often-proclaimed objective of community policing, and more than anything else handicaps the growth of local community-based justice initiatives.

## EXPANDING SCOPE OF ISSUES CONSIDERED

Most people affected by a crime, particularly victims and offenders, feel and see the crime in much broader terms than the narrow view imposed by the criminal justice system. The concerns, issues, fears and needs of most stakeholders in the conflict surrounding the crime are ignored or are only partially addressed within the justice process. Many stakeholders come to court expecting their issues to be resolved, but they leave with most issues unresolved. Issues unimportant to the justice system but crucial to the parties and community are excluded by the court, even though these issues are central to both the circumstances that provoked criminal activity and the circumstances that will govern future developments. Tragically, the court process may not only miss the opportunity a particular crime offers to do effective peacemaking work, but, by mishandling the conflict surrounding the crime, may escalate the conflict in a manner that can precipitate new, often more serious, crimes.

Neither the formal court process nor a community justice process can always resolve the larger conflict to remove pressures producing crime. Yet we could do much better by taking more time in the formal justice process to deal with the larger conflict, and by supporting community-based justice systems that possess a better understanding of the larger conflict and how to begin to diffuse it. The manner in which formal justice systems fail to respond to the conflicts that foster criminal behavior may be added to the popular list of factors causing crime.

Circle sentencing discussions may not always produce immediate resolutions of long-standing conflicts, but can prompt communities to implement or press for solutions to concerns revealed in the circle. By opening the process to probe the underlying causes of crime, and by exploring what is necessary to prevent further criminal activity, community justice systems redress the larger conflict. Circle sentencing begins to address the larger conflict by developing sentence plans encompassing the needs of both victim and offender, prompting other agencies to become actively engaged, and soliciting the willingness of offenders, victims, and their respective families and friends to become involved in finding solutions to the overriding problems causing tension and conflict.

Mediation prompted by circle hearings has been used after a circle ends to help resolve feuds between and within families to address long-standing unsettled scores, and reconcile disputes between victims and offenders. Support systems have been engaged to assist with parenting, sustain healing journeys, and to help victims and offenders in their struggle to move beyond the trauma of the crime and get their life back on track. Community members, appreciating for the first time in the circle the extent of assaults within a family, offer help to the offender to overcome alcohol abuse and anger, but accompany their help with a warning that no one will tolerate further abuse. Others within the circle become involved with the victim. Expanding the scope of the issues addressed improves the ability to redress the larger conflicts causing criminal activity. Engaging others in the community, in turn, enlarges the pool of remedial resources.

## CONCLUSION

While many communities reach out to take responsibility for conflict and crime within their midst, many voices cry for greater public investment in a professional justice system. Each year greater amounts of public funds are invested in professional justice resources, despite the well-documented failures of state justice agencies to redress crime within communities. Thus far, society has accepted reasons proffered by justice agencies for failure—namely they need more police, more courts, more jails, more professional resources of all kinds—and each year the public encourages the growth of formal justice systems by approving more resources. Community-based processes have been progressively marginalized by the burgeoning bureaucracies of state justice agencies. Justice budgets in many jurisdictions are growing at a faster rate than most other state investments in social and economic services. Many jurisdictions have reached the point of investing more in processing crime than in preventing it.

What now makes for exciting times is a recognition by increasing numbers of communities and justice professionals that a predominant reliance upon the state will not diminish crime; remove its underlying causes; build healthy, safe communities; re-establish family values and responsibilities; rebuild the lives of individuals who have fallen into crime; nor restore the lives of victims ravaged by crime. This mutual recognition has spawned a search for new partnerships between justice agencies and communities, and for opportunities for communities to assume responsibility for conflict. The courage of communities to get involved, and the wisdom of some in justice agencies to recognize the value of community involvement, has encouraged a shift away from an exclusive reliance on the professional justice system to resolve social ills that are far beyond its capacity, no matter how much the public invests in professional resources. The willingness of justice agencies to share responsibility with communities, their patience with the growing pains of community innovation, and their recognition of the ultimate advantage to all arising from community initiatives are all crucial to the development of strong community-based justice initiatives. Circles reveal the public's unrealistic expectations about what a professional formal justice system can deliver, and reveal what a community can accomplish that the formal justice system cannot.

Above all, circle sentencing is about community building. Its remedial potential will be principally felt in several years, when communities through circle sentencing become steeped in participatory skills and when a sense of responsibility for all community ills permeates beyond salaried professionals to volunteers, volunteers who know a healthy community depends on their input, not just on their tax dollars.

# 11. A COMPARISON OF DEVELOPMENTAL IDEOLOGIES: NAVAJO NATION PEACEMAKER COURTS AND CANADIAN NATIVE JUSTICE COMMITTEES

by

## Marianne O. Nielsen

**Abstract:** *Native-operated criminal justice services have developed in response to over-representation by Native peoples in the criminal justice systems of the U.S. and Canada. Most have been modifications of Euro-based programs, but new services are less likely to conform. Navajo Peacemaker Courts and Alberta Youth Justice Committees are associated with the courts of their respective countries. Peacemaker Courts are Navajo Nation courts that offer mediation in civil disputes. Youth Justice Committees are community-based sentencing advisory bodies for young offender courts. Although there are differences between the two programs, there are also important similarities, particularly with regard to developmental and operational ideologies, the latter based on the need to develop legitimacy with a number of constituencies. Differences arise out of the differing political statuses of Native peoples in the two countries. Peacemakers follow a healing paradigm of restorative justice because Native people in the U.S. have more sovereignty in establishing criminal justice services. The Youth Justice Committees follow a co-judging paradigm because of the lesser sovereignty of Canadian Native peoples. Indications are that a healing paradigm is their goal once they have established more legitimacy.*

Native Peoples are over-represented as offenders in the criminal justice systems of the U.S. and Canada. In both countries they constitute a minority of the general populations—0.8% and 3.6%, respectively (Utter,

1993; Frideres, 1993)—yet they are found in much larger proportions in correctional facilities. In the Canadian provinces and territories, Native inmates comprise anywhere from 2% to 88% of all admissions to provincial prisons, and 0% to 75% of all admissions to federal prisons (Frideres, 1993). In American correctional facilities they comprise only .02% of inmates in federal institutions, but can make up as much as 31% (Alaska), 25% (South Dakota), and 18% (Montana and North Dakota) of state correctional institutional populations (U.S. Department of Justice, 1993). American Indians make up much smaller proportions of the general population in these states: 15.6% in Alaska, 7.3% in South Dakota, 6% in Montana and 4.1% in North Dakota (Utter, 1993).

There is growing agreement in both countries that the Euro-based criminal justice system has been ineffective in dealing with Native Peoples. This recognition, as well as increased support for Native self-determination by the federal governments of both countries (McCoy, 1993) and the growing self-determination initiatives in Native communities, has contributed to the development of a wide variety of Native-run criminal justice services including police, tribal courts, courtworkers and legal aid, correctional institutions, and community corrections services. All of these operate as government-funded adjuncts to the Euro-based criminal justice system; most are modifications of Euro-based models, and none are completely independent of the federal governments of Canada or the U.S.

There has been a change in recent years in the nature and ideologies of new Native-operated criminal justice initiatives. They are still part of the justice systems, but are less likely to conform to Euro-based models of appropriate justice service roles and philosophies. Instead of meting out punishment, these initiatives try to heal or adjust the relationships among the participating parties (Zion and Yazzie, 1995). Among the new initiatives are the Peacemaker Courts of the Navajo Nation (Austin, 1993; Bluehouse and Zion, 1993; Lieder, 1993; Tso, 1992; Zion, 1983, 1995a, 1995b; Zion and McCabe, 1982; Zion and Yazzie, 1995; Yazzie, 1992, 1994) and the Youth Justice Committees in Alberta, CAN (John Howard Society of Alberta, 1994; Keenan, 1992; Mandamin, 1992; Nielsen, 1994a, 1994b; Sampson, 1992). This chapter examines the roles and ideologies of development and operation of these two initiatives. Similarities and differences in each area are noted and discussed in terms of the importance of establishing organizational legitimacy within the justice systems and Native communities of each country.

Data were gathered from in-depth interviews, observation and the existing literature.

## DESCRIPTION OF PROGRAM ROLES

The Navajo Peacemaker Courts and the Alberta Youth Justice Committees are both associated with the courts component of the justice
system in their respective countries. The specific roles these two initiatives play vary from community to community depending on the history,
socio-economic and political needs, and cultural demographics of the
communities. The Peacemaker Courts are one of five courts that operate
within the Navajo Nation (the others are district, family, small claims
and appellate). The Alberta Youth Justice Committees are Alberta gov-
ernment-sanctioned, community-based sentencing advisory bodies. Alberta Youth Justice Committees usually enter the justice process at the
courts stage, whereas Youth Justice Committees in other areas often enter at the pre-court diversion stage (John Howard Society of Alberta,
1994).

The Navajo Peacemakers, of which there are 241 located in 104 of the
110 chapters or semi-autonomous communities that make up the
Navajo Nation, are brought in by disputants to help them arrive at a harmonious settlement of a dispute. The disputants may be referred to the
peacemakers by the Navajo courts, the Navajo Nation service providers
(Police, Social Services and Behavioral Health, Indian Health Services),
or primarily by self-referral. Disputes may be based in land use, grazing
rights, and domestic conflict including child custody and family violence.
Criminal offenses, including sexual assault, have also been dealt with,
although most cases are civil disputes. The majority of disputants are
adult members of the Navajo Nation.

The peacemakers are respected members of the Navajo community,
both male and female, who are selected by their communities because
they have "demonstrated character, wisdom and the ability to make
good plans for community action" (Austin, 1993, p.10). They usually
have some relationship with the disputants so that they are not neutral
mediators. Peacemakers include medicine people, traders, lawyers, Native American church leaders and non-Indian clergy. They receive 16
hours of training and are supervised by the local judge (in cases where
the judge makes the referral and a court order is made). Peacemakers
assist disputing parties by encouraging them to talk through the disa-

greement, counselling or lecturing the parties based on Navajo spiritual narratives, helping the parties arrive at a solution to the problem, and assisting them to achieve consensus and harmony (Navajo Nation Judicial Branch, undated). Family and community members with an interest in the dispute are invited to attend, while some criminal justice system members are excluded (police in their official capacity are excluded, probation and parole officers are invited, and judges may or may not sit in). The results of the session may be enforceable by a court order if court referred. Administrative support is provided by the district court staff. In keeping with pragmatic Navajo values, peacemakers are paid a small fee by the disputants (Zion, 1983).

The Alberta Youth Justice Committees, of which there were 23 in operation and 22 in the formation stages as of August 1994, are composed of respected community members who represent the make-up of the community. In Native communities where there are status and non-status Indians, and Metis (individuals of half-Aboriginal, half-white descent), all three groups will be represented on the committee. In mixed Native and non-Native communities, both groups are represented. An important criterium for membership is caring about and wanting to help the young people in the community. Native Elders are heavily represented on the Committees. Currently most Youth Justice Committees are operating in Native communities, but the concept has lately been adopted by a number of non-Native communities.

The Youth Justice Committee members form sentencing panels whenever requested to do so by the court, and hold hearings to obtain information to make recommendations for appropriate sentences. The Youth Justice Committees serve primarily young offenders, although some assist adults and in some communities the committees occasionally bypass the courts (with the blessings of the court and the police) to deal directly with disputes. The Youth Justice Committees deal mainly with criminal offenses up to and including sexual assault; they have also assisted in domestic violence cases. Committee members may or may not receive training, depending on the wishes of the committee members. They are assisted by courtworkers from Native Counselling Services of Alberta and/or members of the Royal Canadian Mounted Police (RCMP), both of whom may give legal information on request, as well as assist with the administration of the program. The process followed during the hearing includes: allowing the offender to explain his or her actions; getting information from a wide variety of parties including parents, other family members, victims, the school, probation services, the police, and any other concerned individuals; trying to ascertain the underlying causes of the criminal behavior; counselling or lecturing the young person; and negotiating recommendations to make to the judge. Criminal justice personnel may or may not be invited to remain throughout the proceedings.

There are some important differences between the roles of the peacemakers and of the Youth Justice Committees. Peacemaker Courts handle primarily civil disputes, Youth Justice Committees handle primarily criminal offenses; Peacemaker Courts serve adults, Youth Justice Committees serve young people. The end products are also different. The Peacemaker Courts result in a process that will end a dispute between private citizens; the Youth Justice Committees result in a recommendation to a judge, who will decide on an appropriate punishment. There are also similarities in the roles: both initiatives are part of the court system, both use community members who care about the disputants/offenders, both involve family members of the disputants/offenders, both incorporate traditional Native practices into the justice system, both are less formal and adversarial than the Euro-based system, and both have healing as a goal. The origins of these differences and similarities can be traced to the operational and developmental ideologies of the initiatives.

## OPERATIONAL IDEOLOGIES

The ideologies underlying the operational processes show striking similarities. The terminology may be different but the principles are not. The operational principles underlying the Peacemaker Courts include: the equality of all participants; the need to talk things through; the invocation of spiritual powers to assist in the process; the need for informality; the guiding and persuasive role of Elders (*Naat'aanii*); the need to identify the underlying problems; the need to plan solutions; the origins of counselling and lectures in Navajo values; the need to establish consensus among participants; the need to re-establish and maintain solidarity (and obligations) in clan and other relationships; and the need to restore community, family, and individual well-being and harmony (Bluehouse and Zion, 1993; Yazzie, 1994). The operational principles underlying the Youth Justice Committees include: informality of proceedings; the court advisory role of community members; the need to establish a respectful setting; the need to identify underlying problems;

the need to let the offender have a say; the need to have the offender (and perhaps family members) take responsibility; the counselling role of committee members; the need to build consensus among participants; and the need to heal the offender, victim, and community (Nielsen, 1994b,1994c).

A comparison of the principles of the two initiatives points to a number of similarities: informality, the role of respected Native community members (Naat'aanii and Elders), the involvement of family, the identification of underlying problems, counselling or lecturing, and consensus building. A number of other principles are clearly related: talking things through and letting the offender have a say; restoring well-being, harmony, and healing; and re-establishing solidarity and expecting the offender to take responsibility. There are also differences such as the egalitarian, persuasive form of the Peacemaking Court compared to the more authoritarian, coercive form of the Youth Justice Committees; the guiding role of the Naat'aanii for the disputants compared to the sentencing court role of the Youth Justice Committee members; finding solutions compared to making recommendations to court; establishing a respectful setting compared to the invocation of spiritual powers; and the origins of counselling in Navajo values compared to the lack of stated origins for the counselling done by Youth Justice Committee members.

There are similarities, however, even in these differences. The Youth Justice Committee members see themselves as "helping the young person"; the phrase "putting them on the right path" is used frequently. The sentencing recommendations arrived at by the committee often address the underlying problems faced by youths and their families. The recommendations might be for the offender, and his or her family, to enroll in alcohol treatment, to spend time with an Elder in the bush to learn about cultural values, or to assist in the preparation of a spiritual ceremony but not to take part as that decision was left to the offender. The committee, because of its consensus-building ideology, relies on persuasion to reach agreement among the participants about the recommendations. But the coercive power of the court is never far away; the goal of the hearing is to make sentencing recommendations, and, if no agreement can be reached, the committee refers the case back to court.

There is also a coercive element to peacemaking but to a much lesser extent; if the disputants do not follow their contract, which is also a court order, they can be referred back to the district court. The Youth Justice Committee members, like the Naat'aanii, also lecture participants. The committee members, however, are more likely to place the lecture in a community context ("Think how scared the old people are when you drive like that!") or a personal context relating to their own experience. Native cultural values are often part of this, but not always and not always explicitly. In this way, the committee, like the *Naat'aanii*, communicate the values of the community.

The Youth Justice Committees place a great deal of emphasis on respect, for each of the participants and for the criminal justice system. One means of doing this is by using prayer at the beginning and end of the hearings. This suggests some similarity to the use of prayer in peacemaking, although in peacemaking the spiritual powers are seen as active participants in the process. Peacemakers also put a great deal of emphasis on respect, but in terms of *k'e*, a concept that incorporates love, solidarity, and obligation as well as respect (personal communication, James Zion).

These operational differences seem to arise from three sources: (1) the different cultural origins of the two programs, (2) the different niches they fill in the justice systems, and (3) the different ideological paradigms within which the initiatives operated. The first two points are self-explanatory; the third is not. Ross (1994a, 1994b) divided Canadian Aboriginal community justice projects into two paradigms: a healing paradigm and a co-judging paradigm. These paradigms articulate the same principles and have the same overall goals for the participants, but they follow different paths to achieving their goals. Ross (1994a) describes the co-judging paradigm as a "marriage between two systems" (p.248) in which Aboriginal peoples are granted roles within the Euro-based system. The healing paradigm, on the other hand, functions as an alternative to this system. The Youth Justice Committees are akin to the co-judging paradigm, and peacemakers are akin to the healing paradigm. The co-judging paradigm may need coercive force because it may not have as much legitimacy as the healing model in the eyes of the Native community or the criminal justice system. This argument becomes clearer in the investigation of the developmental ideologies that underlie the two initiatives.

## DEVELOPMENTAL IDEOLOGIES

The ideologies that were instrumental in the development of the Youth Justice Committees and the Peacemaker Courts are significantly similar. These developmental ideologies include three main principles:

(1) the ineffectiveness of the Euro-based adversarial courts in dealing with Native offenders, (2) the revitalization of traditional justice practices, and (3) the need for increased community control. The ineffectiveness of the Euro-based system was voiced in terms of the inappropriateness of an adversarial approach in handling Native offenders in both countries. In Canada, the number of young people involved in the criminal justice system was frequently mentioned, as was their lack of respect for the criminal justice system and the tendency of the Euro-based system to remove them from the community for purposes of incarceration or treatment (Nielsen, 1994b). Statistics on over-representation in adult and young offender correctional institutions were often used to back up these sentiments. This use of statistics was not as common in discussing the development of the Peacemaker Courts, perhaps because of the overwhelming number of other minority offenders in U.S. correctional institutions.

The differences in the court systems may also have had a part to play; in Canada, Native offenders are sentenced exclusively in Euro-based courts, whereas in the Navajo Nation they are sentenced by Navajo Nation courts as well as by the federal and state courts. The focus among the Navajo was on the adversarial nature of the current and past Navajo district courts, which are structured after the state courts, and the inappropriateness of this model for Navajo who still practice Navajo custom law and expect the criminal justice process to be a journey of healing, not of punishment (Tso, 1992). The current courts apply Navajo common law as their law of preference (Bluehouse and Zion, 1993), but are still structured on an adversarial model. The Peacemaker Courts, established in 1982, were seen as a remedy to this. This developmental principle calls into question the legitimacy of the Euro-based system in handling Native peoples, and suggests that Native-operated systems may have more legitimacy.

The second developmental principle is the revitalization of traditional justice practices. In both countries, the programs were spoken of as the evolution of justice practices that had been in existence since time immemorial. The Navajo Peacemakers were traced to clan Elders or peace leaders, *Naat'aanii*, who "arbitrated disputes, mediated quarrels, resolved family problems, and tried to correct wrongdoers" (Zion, 1983, p.106). Even during the operation of the Navajo Courts of Indian Offenses, judges might informally call on respected community members to mediate disputes over family matters or other everyday problems

(Zion, 1983). The Peacemaker Courts are supported by the other branches of the Navajo Nation Judicial Branch, because they are seen as a means to "give lasting legitimacy to the persistence of Navajo common law by bringing it into the court system" (Zion, 1983, p.92). Navajo history and society are dynamic. Thus, it is not surprising that the Peacemaker Courts are not static in their use of traditions. The Peacemaker Courts are based largely on traditional justice practices as recalled by Navajo Elders; research was also done by the Navajo Judicial Branch during the development phase. Zion (1983) notes that attention was paid to concepts taken from Quaker practices, as well as the practices of other Native American groups that traditionally used peacemakers (Zion, 1983).

The Youth Justice Committees were seen as an extension of the role of Elders in counselling young people and resolving disputes, and of the community in applying informal control measures against wrongdoers. The importance of restitution and healing as part of the process was also traced to traditional values and informal social control processes (Nielsen, 1994a, 1994c). The need for young people to learn more about their culture and beginnings was often seen as part of the young person's problem and was addressed, in some form, in the recommendations to the court. In both countries, legislation and government policies had been enacted in the past to destroy the cultures of Native peoples. Native peoples had developed a number of adaptive strategies that kept their cultures alive; today a major revitalization of Indian cultures is occurring. This revitalization is not limited to the reestablishment of cultural identities, but also includes the refashioning of Native-controlled institutions to reflect a selected blending of the old and the new (McCaskill, 1992). Youth Justice Committees and Peacemaker Courts can be described as manifestations of this refashioning of institutions.

The need for increased local community control—community ownership in Alberta and local empowerment among the Navajo—is the third developmental principle. Among the Navajo there are two important considerations: the right to choose traditional over Euro-based justice structures, and the need for more decentralization of power within the Navajo Nation to reflect traditional power structures. The right to choose justice structures (as well as educational, health, social service and other structures) is a matter of establishing sovereignty. Unlike Native groups in Canada, Native American groups have been recognized as domestic dependent nations (Lieder, 1993). The Navajo do not have complete autonomy but are working to reclaim much of what they have lost. They are also defending their sovereignty against states' attempts to regulate or police them (Lieder, 1993). The Navajo have used their sovereign power to establish their own social services, health care services, schools, police, correctional institutions and courts. The Peacemaker Courts were developed at the express wish of the Navajo Council, the governing body, to change the imposed Euro-based legal tradition and to "reinstitutionalize and legitimate traditional law and procedure" (Zion, 1995a, p.25). There has also been a push to return more power to the local chapters, in keeping with the traditional power structure. "Local decisions are the traditional Navajo way, in place of central control" (Yazzie, 1994, p.189). The dream of the peacemaker program administrators is to have the peacemakers administered at the local level, with the central office playing support roles such as providing training and aggregating information. The Peacemaker Courts are a movement towards both local empowerment and tribal sovereignty.

This political impetus differs from the situation in Canada, where the Youth Justice Committees were initiated at the local level with little or no assistance or even knowledge by band, province, or federal governments. The Young Offenders Act allows for the existence of the committees, which should receive provincial government designation but are operating without it to some extent, to no ill effect. Personnel at the Alberta Department of Justice are exasperated by this tendency of Youth Justice Committees to operate without government sanction and outside of established government guidelines, but believe that intervention in the situation is likely to do more harm than good.

The existing rights of Aboriginal people have been recognized by the Canadian Constitution (Section 35.1), but their sovereignty has not. Establishment of social institutions based on traditional practices, therefore, must still be approved by the Canadian federal government that has so far declined to allow the establishment of tribal courts (Macklem, 1992), except in the forms of justice of the peace courts (Morse, 1982). Other Native-operated justice initiatives have been allowed: police forces (the Dakota-Ojibwa in Manitoba and the Samson, Louis Bull and Siksika Bands in Alberta); minimum-security correctional institutions (Native Counselling Services of Alberta [NCSA] and the Kainai in Alberta); and parole and probation services (NCSA-run in Alberta). Native courtworkers appear in the Euro-based courts to provide Native suspects with information about legal terminology, processes and options.

Despite the important role played by Native courtworkers, there was still a need expressed at the community level for more direct community involvement in the court process, especially with young offenders. There was a strong sentiment that young offenders were the community's responsibility and did not benefit by being removed from the community, as was the common practice. Nor did the community benefit from losing its future potentially productive citizens. The provision of the Young Offenders' Act for Youth Justice Committees was struck on by community members and judicial personnel as a means of doing this. In the beginning, there was no intention for the committees to be part of the push for Aboriginal sovereignty, but there is a growing recognition among Native political organizations and community members that the committees have that potential. Some community members suggest that Youth Justice Committees have the potential to significantly replace the Euro-based criminal justice system in Native (and perhaps non-Native) communities. As with the Peacemaker Courts, and despite their avowed non-political status, the Youth Justice Committees may become part of the movement towards increasing Native political sovereignty.

## DISCUSSION

Survival, or the process of using and acquiring resources, is the most basic goal of any organization (Morgan, 1986). Respect and acknowledgement by the government and by Native communities that the group has the right to rule some niche within the justice system is instrumental for the organization to obtain further resources, including funding, clients and staff. Developing legitimacy is dependent on gaining recognition from other groups that the organization's structure, role, and areas of service are "proper, useful, and not in conflict" with other key actors and agencies (Ritti and Silver, 1986, p.28). If Peacemaker Courts and Youth Justice Committees are to survive and thrive, they must gain respect and acknowledgement from the justice system (especially the federal-government level of the system), the general non-Native public, and the Native community. The justice system provides the two initiatives with their legislated mandates, funding and clientele through referrals. The general public can influence the way the justice system distributes these resources. The Native community provides the two initiatives with clientele, staff and information. The Peacemakers and Youth Justice

Committees are dependent on these actors and must negotiate conformity to their wishes (Kotter, 1979).

The principles underlying the operational ideologies of the initiatives are necessary for establishing legitimacy with the Native communities, and, in the case of the peacemakers, the Navajo justice system. Positive responses to the traditional aspects of peacemakers or Youth Justice Committees cannot be assumed because of the degree of assimilation in both countries. Zion (1983) suggests that the Peacemaker Courts are acceptable to Native peoples for reasons that vary, depending on the degree of acculturation of the individual; he also mentions the need for funding to inform local chapters about peacemakers. Several respondents in Alberta mentioned the need to reassure local community leaders that the Youth Justice Committees were not usurping their powers. In both countries, mention was made of the need to inform community members about the goals and procedures of the initiatives.

With both initiatives, legitimation efforts during the developmental stages seemed to be aimed at the justice system and at the Native community, although the nature and strength of the efforts varied. In the case of the Youth Justice Committees, efforts were also aimed at the general public. Peacemaker courts did not need to put as high a priority on establishing legitimacy with the Euro-based, non-Native justice system as did the Youth Justice Committees. At one time, younger peacemakers suggested getting professional certification as well as recognition in the Tribal Code, but this was argued against by their older counterparts. An older peacemaker stated, "Peacemakers are recognized by the Holy People and do not need to have Earth Surface People [whites] tell us we're legitimate." Fear was expressed by respondents that policies and regulations would "tie us up" rather than allow peacemakers the freedom to interpret the Sacred Scriptures relevant to the case (personal communication, Phil Bluehouse). The peacemaker courts have very little contact with the non-Native system, since they receive their mandate and clientele from the Navajo Nation's justice system. It was not necessary to seek out members of the non-Native system to inform them about the ineffectiveness of the justice system in dealing with Navajo offenders, the resurgence in cultural revitalization and the need for sovereignty in providing justice services. Funding was slow in coming, however, and since its eventual source was located outside the Navajo Nation, the Bureau of Indian Affairs, this might be interpreted as a legitimacy problem with the non-Native system. Nor were legitimation efforts needed with members of the Navajo Nation justice system since the Judicial Branch was the originator of the initiative. Members of the branch were well aware of the three developmental principles and considered them legitimate. Other members of the Navajo justice system (police, legal services) were also supportive.

The Youth Justice Committees aimed most of their legitimation efforts at the Euro-based justice system, although the Native community and the general public also received attention. A number of conferences, sponsored by the RCMP and the NCSA, were held to convince criminal justice system and community members that the Youth Justice Committees were legitimate and useful. Converted members of the justice system were active in selling the Youth Justice Committees to dubious colleagues. Although the RCMP, NCSA and Department of Justice all implemented policies that instructed their staff to assist in the development of the committees, the cooperation of individual members of the system had to be ensured. It was not necessary to convince members of the Euro-based justice system, the Native community or the general public that the justice system was ineffective in dealing with juveniles; the justice system's lack of effectiveness has been and remains a major justice issue in Canada. The main legitimation issues in Alberta, with all three constituencies, was whether Native traditional practices were tough enough on young offenders and if Native peoples should be allowed to operate their own system. The support (and supervision) of the judges, the RCMP, the NCSA, and the Department of Justice served to defuse public concerns about traditional practices. The sovereignty issue remains and may worsen if the current tendency among some committees to operate outside of the justice system accelerates.

Most of the legitimation efforts of both initiatives have concentrated on the right to exist, as opposed to the form in which they have the right to exist. The issue of form may well be the most serious issue for the future. Peacemaking is not just another form of alternative dispute resolution (ADR) (Bluehouse and Zion, 1993). Navajos have been known to call it traditional dispute resolution and original dispute resolution (ODR) as a means of making the point that there are important differences in the systems and that one cannot be substituted for the other (Zion and Yazzie, 1995). The social arrangements in which the two systems originate are very different, as are the methods used (Zion and Yazzie, 1995). The superficial similarity to ADR has likely aided the Peacemaker Courts in gaining legitimacy outside of the Navajo Nation, but the similarity between ADR and ODR may leave the Peacemaker Courts vulnerable to pressures to conform to the standard model of ADR.

There is a tendency for organizations to receive pressures from other organizations to conform to the fashion of the time in proper organizational structures (Zucker, 1987). The Peacemaker Courts are well aware of these pressures. "Indian systems do not need instructions on empowerment, balancing disparities in bargaining positions, principles of ethics in mediation, or the kinds of disputes that mediation systems can or cannot handle. They do not need, and must not have, outsiders peering in to nod affirmance or indicate disapproval" (Austin, 1993, p.47). Not conforming to these pressures may have repercussions for survival. While the peacemakers may be able to use the principle of conforming to traditional practices to legitimate their structure, the peacemakers also exist under the umbrella of the Navajo Nation, which is an organization very susceptible to pressure from the Bureau of Indian Affairs. The Navajo Nation is also already bowing to pressures to conform its civil adjudication system to the Euro-system to make it more non-Native investor-friendly (Lieder, 1993). It is not unreasonable to imagine that someday pressures may also be aimed at the Peacemaker Courts to conform to ADR structures.

Similarly, the Alberta Department of Justice has developed guidelines for the development and operation of these committees (Nielsen, 1994c), but many communities find the guidelines inappropriate, onerous, even disrespectful, and therefore more or less ignore them. The Youth Justice Committees are individually unique; each is based on the needs and justice priorities of the community in which it is located. Because the committees have significant support from the judges, police, and other members of the criminal justice system (and possibly because of their lack of funding dependency on the Department of Justice), they can get away with their uniqueness, for now. Eventually, however, the Department of Justice may end its policy of tolerance, especially if some event with significant political repercussions occurs. This could lead to serious pressures to standardize the operations of the committees and have serious effects on their effective operation and legitimacy in Native communities.

Native Peoples have chosen two main models of restorative justice: a healing paradigm and a co-judging paradigm (Ross, 1994a). Communities that are concerned with gaining control over their legal systems seem more likely to choose a co-judging paradigm. Why should this be the case? This comparison between the Peacemaker Courts of the

Navajo Nation and the Youth Justice Committees of Alberta Canada suggests an answer. A lack of sovereignty means less legitimacy for new justice initiatives, in both their development and operation. There is still a deep-rooted paternalistic preconception within Euro-based society that Native-operated organizations are more likely to fail, are more inefficient and more poorly managed than non-Native-operated organizations (Nielsen and Redpath, 1994). Organizational legitimacy in a political reality where Native peoples do not have sovereignty is easier to obtain for Native-operated initiatives by designing an initiative that is directly supervised and supported by the Euro-based system. Once some degree of legitimacy is obtained, then expansion outside of the Euro-based system can occur, as is happening with the Youth Justice Committees. This expansion has every indication of following the healing paradigm that communities with more sovereignty and more legitimacy have chosen directly. This does not mean that Native-operated justice initiatives will some day achieve legitimacy and be able to comfortably settle into a niche within the justice systems of the U.S. and Canada. They can never achieve full sovereignty because of lingering paternalism and the tendency of organizations, Native and non-Native, to be pressured to conform to fashionable organizational structures. Achieving legitimacy will be an ongoing and possibly never-ending struggle for Native justice initiatives.

## REFERENCES

Austin, R.D. (1993). "Freedom, Responsibility and Duty: ADR and the Navajo Peacemaker Court." *Judges' Journal* 32:8-11, 47-48.

Bluehouse, P. (1995). Personal communication with the author.

—and J.W. Zion (1993). "Hozhooji Naat'aanii: The Navajo Justice and Harmony Ceremony." *Mediation Quarterly* 10:327-337.

Frideres, J.S. (1993). *Native Peoples in Canada: Contemporary Conflicts*, 4th ed. Scarborough, CAN: Prentice-Hall.

John Howard Society of Alberta (1994). "Toward the Establishment of Youth Justice Committees in Alberta." Unpublished manuscript.

Keenan, D. (1992). "Teslin Tlingit Justice Council." In: Royal Commission on Aboriginal Peoples (eds.), *Aboriginal Peoples and the Justice System*. Ottawa, CAN: Canada Communication Group.

Kotter, J.P. (1979). "Managing External Dependence." *Academy of Management Review* 41:87-92.

Lieder, M.D. (1993). "Navajo Dispute Resolution and Promissory Obligations: Continuity and Change in the Largest Native American Nation." *American Indian Law Review* 18:1-71.

Macklem, P. (1992). "Aboriginal Justice, the Distribution of Legislative Authority, and the Judicature Provisions of the Constitution Act, 1867." In: Royal Commission on Aboriginal Peoples (eds.), *Aboriginal Peoples and the Justice System*. Ottawa, CAN: Canada Communication Group.

Mandamin, L. (1992). "Aboriginal Justice Systems: Relationships." In: Royal Commission on Aboriginal Peoples (eds.), *Aboriginal Peoples and the Justice System*. Ottawa, CAN: Canada Communication Group.

McCaskill, D. (1992). "When Cultures Meet." In: R.A. Silverman and M.O. Nielsen (eds.), *Aboriginal Peoples and Canadian Criminal Justice*. Toronto, CAN: Butterworths.

McCoy, M.L. (1993). "When Cultures Clash: The Future of Tribal Courts." *Human Rights* 20:22-25.

Morgan, G. (1986). *Images of Organizations*. Beverly Hills, CA: Sage.

Morse, B.W. (1982). "A Unique Court: S.107 Indian Act Justices of the Peace." *Canadian Legal Aid Bulletin* 5:131-150.

Navajo Nation Judicial Branch (Undated). Various photocopied documents.

Nielsen, M.O. (1994a). "Informal Social Control: Contextualization for Aboriginal Community Youth Justice Committees." Paper presented at the meeting of the Law and Society Association, Phoenix, June.

—(1994b). "Native Canadian Sentencing Panels: A Preliminary Report." Paper presented at the annual meetings of the American Society of Criminology, Miami, November.

—(1994c). Youth Justice Committee: Guidelines for Development, First Draft. Unpublished manuscript.

—and L. Redpath (1994). "New Management and Aboriginal Organizations." Paper presented at the annual meeting of the Canadian Sociology and Anthropology Association, Calgary, June.

Ritti, R.R. and J.H. Silver (1986). "Early Processes of Institutionalization: The Dramaturgy of Exchange in Interorganizational Relations." *Administrative Science Quarterly* 31:25-42.

Ross, R. (1994a). "Duelling Paradigms? Western Criminal Justice Versus Aboriginal Community Healing." In: R. Gosse, J.Y. Henderson and R. Carter (eds.), *Continuing Poundmaker & Riel's Quest*. Saskatoon, CAN: Purich.

—(1994b). Managing the Merger: Justice-as-Healing in Aboriginal Communities. Unpublished manuscript.

Sampson, T. (1992). "South Vancouver Island Justice Education Project." In: Royal Commission on Aboriginal Peoples (eds.), *Aboriginal Peoples and the Justice System*. Ottawa, CAN: Canada Communication Group.

Tso, T. (1992). "Moral Principles, Traditions, and Fairness in the Navajo Nation Code of Judicial Conduct." *Judicature* 76:15-21.

U.S. Department of Justice (1993). *Sourcebook of Criminal Justice Statistics, 1992*. Washington, DC: U.S. Government Printing Office.

Utter, J. (1993). *American Indians: Answers to Today's Questions*. Lake Ann, MI: National Woodlands Publishing.

Yazzie, R. (1992). "Navajo Justice Experience—Yesterday and Today." In: Royal Commission on Aboriginal Peoples (eds.), *Aboriginal Peoples and the Justice System*. Ottawa, CAN: Canada Communication Group.

—(1994). "'Life Comes from It': Navajo Justice Concepts." *New Mexico Law Review* 24:175-190.

Zion, J.W. (1983). "The Navajo Peacemaker Court: Deference to the Old and Accommodation to the New." *American Indian Law Review* 11:89-109.

—(1995). Personal communication with the author.

—(1995a). "Law as Revolution in the Courts of the Navajo Nation." Paper presented at the Federal Bar Association Indian Law Conference, Albuquerque, April.

—(1995b). "Living Indian Justice: Navajo Peacemaking Today." Paper presented at the Alternative Dispute Resolution Conference, Vancouver, BC, CAN, February.

—and N.J. McCabe (1982). *Navajo Peacemaker Court Manual*. Window Rock, AZ: Navajo Nation Judicial Branch.

—and R. Yazzie (1995). "Indigenous Law in North America in the Wake of Conquest." Paper presented at the Prevencion de Conflictos y Solucion en Communidades Indiges Seminar, Cochabamba, Bolivia, March.

Zucker, L.G. (1987). "Institutional Theories of Organization." *Annual Review of Sociology* 13:443-464.

# PART III
# RESTORATIVE JUSTICE PRACTICE
# ISSUES

# 12. CAN MEDIATION BE AN ALTERNATIVE TO CRIMINAL JUSTICE?

by

## Martin Wright

**Abstract:** *Attempts have been made to resolve the intractable problems of criminal justice systems by involving the victim in the process, for example, through victim impact statements, but that adds yet another source of sentencing inconsistency. Many people, including victims, are attracted by moves towards adopting a new fundamental principle, restorative justice. But is there a danger that it will lead to pressure on victims to take part, infringe on defendants' right to due process or result in inconsistencies between outcomes? Can restorative justice operate effectively alongside the traditional system, or even replace it? As with the traditional system, there is no clear way of resolving all the competing requirements. It is better to think not of alternatives but of a continuum, and to work to move the center of gravity from the repressive towards the restorative.*

The criminal justice system is in trouble. Sentences are inconsistent and ineffective. The bafflement is expressed by an English judge who, after listing the principles of sentencing as punishment, retribution, deterrence, and reformation, doubts the effectiveness of deterrence by referring to the report of a nineteenth-century prison chaplain; of the 168 people the chaplain comforted while awaiting hanging, 160 had attended at least one public execution. He concludes that "We have never resolved the equation of punishment and retribution on one side and reformation on the other. I seriously doubt we ever will" (Wroath, 1995, p.38). Punishment undermines rehabilitation, reformative measures are not punitive and both leave out of account the social conditions in which the offender will have to live.

Recent attempts to square the circle have, paradoxically, added a fifth side to the square: the effect of the crime on the victim. Victim impact statements have not become popular in Britain, for reasons explained by Ashworth (1993): they will tend to influence courts towards more inconsistent, and probably more severe sentences, and could lead to a further ordeal for the victim if they were challenged by the defense. Despite this, the new national standards for the supervision of offenders in the community (U.K. Home Office, 1995b) require probation officers to include in their presentence reports a fourth-hand assessment of the effect on the victims, derived from the papers provided by the Crown Prosecution Service (CPS), which receives its information from the police, who obtain it from the victim. Victim Support has consistently argued that this is far too late; information should be made available to the CPS at the outset, and the training of all criminal justice personnel—from judges to court ushers—should include greater awareness of the effect of crime on victims (Reeves, 1994; Victim Support, 1995).

The Crown Court Witness Service has been established to support victims and other witnesses in England and Wales. Such services can be helpful to victims, act as a channel for the central collection of information on ways in which witnesses have been revictimized by the system, and prompt greater awareness of the victims' perspective. But while these services make the system more endurable, they have not changed its adversarial, retributive nature and hence the tough questioning to which victim/witnesses are liable to be subjected by defense lawyers. Other attempts to improve matters for victims include state compensation for certain victims of violence, and compensation (restitution) by the offender ordered by the court (Victim Support, 1993).

The emphasis in this chapter is on crimes with identifiable victims. Other offenses, such as environmental pollution where victims are not identified, are regarded as crimes against the community. Any discussion of victim-offender mediation must recognize that only a small proportion of recorded offenses are cleared up, and still more are not recorded. In England and Wales in 1993, for example, 1.3 million offenses were cleared up—24% of the 5.5 million recorded; the British Crime Survey estimated that crimes with victims totalled 18 million (U.K. Home Office, 1995a; Aye Maung, 1995).

More recently, several countries have seen movement towards adopting a new fundamental principle—restorative justice—which many people, including victims, find attractive (Zehr, 1990). This principle is based on two guiding premises: reparation, a response to crimes that focuses on making good the harm done; and mediation, an acknowledgement that the process, as well as the outcome, is important. Mediation can work well, as demonstrated by numerous case histories and research showing a high level of satisfaction among participants—a criterion not widely used for assessing the traditional system (Marshall and Merry, 1990; Umbreit, 1994). But when introduced in an adversarial and punitive system, mediation could lead to three problems: pressure on victims to take part, infringement of defendants' rights to due process and inconsistencies among outcomes.

Victim Support has suggested that victims "could feel under pressure to co-operate with the process, particularly if the alternative is that the offender will be prosecuted or imprisoned" (Victim Support, 1995, p.9). It has also been suggested that victims should be kept informed and consulted but not asked to make or influence decisions about the prosecution or punishment of the offender, because the state has rightly taken over responsibility for prosecuting offenders.

Secondly, the problem for defendants is the familiar one that the offer of diversion out of the system may induce some to plead guilty when they might have had a valid defense against the charges. If it is a question of mistaken identity, then clearly the case should go to trial. But there is a problem with the traditional system as well, because it is generally accepted that a substantial number of innocent accused persons, reckoning that they have little chance of acquittal, plead guilty (often to a lesser charge) "to get it over with" in the hope of getting a lighter sentence than if they had fought the case and lost. There is, however, another type of "not guilty" plea, wherein the defendant admits the act but claims justification. In such cases, where the two parties are likely to know each other, there could well be issues that would be better resolved through mediation than by a criminal trial.

The third concern is that different victims would make different demands on their offenders for similar offenses. Some might ask little or nothing of the offender so that one aim of criminal justice—proportionate denunciation of the seriousness of the offense—would not be achieved. It could be argued that offenders take a chance when they commit offenses (Will they be caught? Before which judge will they appear?), and the further chance of how much reparation their victim demands is just one more risk they take. There would, however, need to be a safeguard against victims who demand too much. As for the victim who asks too little, this could be dealt with through the conventional system. Whatever transpired between the victim and the offender could be regarded as a personal matter for them; the public interest would be represented separately by the courts. A separate question then arises as to the quantum: at present there is no logical basis for determining that a particular offense is worth a particular punishment. If, in addition, the court had to decide how much of the punishment to discount for a certain amount of reparation (in money, community service, or time spent in a rehabilitation program), courts' decisions would inevitably be even more subjective and inconsistent than they are already. This problem would be less serious if courts, as well as victims, imposed reparative measures; then the whole transaction would at least be carried out in the same currency.

Different methods have been tried to overcome these problems of operating in a mixed system, and particularly the question of voluntariness; the victim should not be under pressure, and the accused should not be offered an inducement to plead guilty when he or she may not be. In Northamptonshire, mediation is offered at the stage when police caution the offender; the question of mediation is raised with offender or victim only after the decision to caution is taken. In Leeds, similarly, most cases are referred after the decision to prosecute, provided that the defendant's lawyers have confirmed in writing that he or she will plead guilty and agrees to mediation (Wright, 1995). In Sandwell, West Midlands, the process is similar, and Victim Support is closely involved (Wright, in press). England does not have specific legislation on reparation and mediation.

In Germany, after victim-offender mediation for juveniles had become available almost everywhere, the following additions were made to the federal penal code (*Strafgesetzbuch*):

§46a.  **Victim/offender mediation, reparation**
If the offender:
1. through efforts to reach an agreement with the injured party (victim/offender mediation) has made good his action completely or very substantially, or seriously tried to do so, or
2. in a case where the reparation has demanded substantial personal contribution or self-denial, and the victim is completely or very substantially compensated,
the court can...mitigate the penalty or, if the offense carries a penalty of not more than one year's imprisonment or a fine of 360 day units [under the German day-fine system], refrain from imposing a penalty.

In §56, which relates to probation, a sentence is added:
In the decision the effort of the offender to make good the damage caused by the offense is to be taken into account.
§59a, on cautioning, is amended to read:
(2) The court can require the person cautioned:

1. To attempt to reach an agreement with the injured party or otherwise to make good the damage caused by the action,
2. to meet his maintenance obligations,
3. to contribute a sum of money to a charitable institution or to the state,
4. to undertake outpatient treatment or detoxification, or
5. to take driving instruction.

In this, no unreasonable demands shall be placed on the offender's ordinary life; also the requirements...shall not be out of proportion to the offense. [*Bundesgesetzblatt*, 1994; translated by the author].

In many places in Germany victim-offender mediation is operated by the branch of the probation service that provides presentence reports (*Gerichtshelfer*); the drawback of this is that the number of cases referred may depend on the workload and enthusiasm of individual officers. Elsewhere, mediation is operated by an independent service, as at Hannover, where *Die Waage* (the Scales) has been running as a demonstration project for three years. Cases are referred by the prosecutor or judge. The following case history shows how the service interacts with the criminal justice system.

The duty solicitor [attorney] referred a case to *Die Waage* in which a building worker had threatened to kill the Iranian owner of a fast-food kiosk with a metal pipe, terrifying him and making him fear escalation. The kiosk owner reported this to the police. Die Waage wrote to the accused, explaining the mediation process; he agreed to come and discuss it. He said that he had had a stressful time at work, and had "snapped" when the kiosk owner demanded payment of 70 Deutschmarks, which he maintained he had paid long ago. The victim gave his account: the debt had *not* been paid, and he had been told that the building worker had made racist remarks about him. He felt his tolerance in allowing credit had been abused. The victim would like his money back, but he also wanted to tell the accused that "you don't behave like that." A meeting was arranged; with the agreement of the accused it was held in the room behind the shop. The victim and the accused did not shake hands, but the victim offered tea. After some discussion, the accused said that he would apologize, and the victim said he was willing to accept that. The mediator led the discussion about the debt, the racist remarks and the threat to kill. The temperature was lower, and they could discuss it quite calmly. The accused had lost his job and had no money. The mediator explained that *Die Waage* has a fund that could pay the money, to be repaid when he found work. They shook hands, and on the way out the victim gave the accused some pears; the latter was very touched and accepted them. *Die Waage* gave a short report to the public prosecutor, who discontinued the case. [Netzig, 1994; summarized and translated by the author].

In another case, when referring the case the prosecutor indicated that he intended to impose a prosecutorial fine of 1,000 Deutschmarks for an assault on a woman. The victim originally wanted the accused to pay compensation of a month's wages, but after accepting that he was genuinely sorry and ashamed, she reduced her requirement to a further 1,000 Deutschmarks, and requested that instead of a fine the offender should pay the money to a women's shelter (see German Penal Code §59a [2] 3, above); this was done. The prosecutor makes known the intended penalty before the mediation takes place; thus, the victim is not under pressure. But in cases like this he or she may ask for less compensation, realizing that the offender could not pay the full amount as well as the fine.

A need is evidently felt for a public as well as a private component to the sanction; this also appears to be the case in England and Wales. Despite a law that compensation must be given priority over fines (Criminal Justice Act, 1982, section 67), courts continue to impose fines and thereby reduce the amount of compensation an offender can pay to a victim (Newburn, 1988). There are further variations of detail in the operation of victim-offender services in Britain (Shadbolt, 1994) and in the U.S. (Umbreit, 1994). In New Zealand and Australia, a new method—family group conferences—has been introduced for young offenders, in which both victim and offender are invited to attend, along with family or other supporters. The principles are not blame and punishment, but an acknowledgement by the offender of the effects of his or her action, and an action plan for the future (McElrea, 1994; Moore and O'Connell, 1994).

But do these initiatives expose victims either to the burden of decision making about the offender's future, or to intimidation by offenders who see mediation as a soft option? Mediation will need rethinking if victims are being exposed to serious risk. If not, victims will lose out if overprotectiveness prevents the development of a constructive new way of responding to crime. It is of course possible for mediation, like anything else, to fall short of the ideal; there have been examples from the U.K. (Davis, 1992) and New Zealand (Morris _et al._, 1993) of mediation services being operated in an offender-centered way. Bias towards the offender may occur, or seem to occur, when the mediation is run by the probation service or police rather than an independent agency. But the Victim Support contention that victims should not be required to make any decisions seems neither possible nor desirable. In many cases the victim has to decide whether to report the offense in the first place. Victim Support says (1995) that "it should never be suggested that victims have a personal choice whether to 'drop' or to 'press' charges against an offender, particularly one who is known to them, as this can make them vulnerable to intimidation" (p.11). Conversely, if the offense is likely to lead to a prison sentence and the victim wishes to stop the offender's violence but to continue in a relationship, the police and prosecutor should think carefully before charging the accused if another way of handling the situation, while protecting the victim, is available. In England and Wales, the Home Office has devised a formula in relation to the police decision of whether to caution an offender: "Efforts should be made to find out the victim's view of the offence, which may have a bearing on how serious the offence is judged to be. It should not, however, be regarded as conclusive" (U.K. Home Office, 1994, para. 7). In other words, the victim is listened to but the offender can truthfully be told that the victim did not make the decision. A similar method is used by mediation services that operate before the offender has been sentenced.

It appears that there is no clear cut-off point between decisions made by the victim and those made by officers of the criminal justice system. Between the clear extremes is a gray area in which the victim can influence the system and _vice versa_. Shadbolt (1994), as an outside observer of the British scene, sees the debate as purity versus pragmatism, which would also describe conflicting interests within the traditional system. The same applies to the relationship between mediation and sentencing. If the outcome of mediation is taken into account by the court, the prospective sentence could influence the mediation; if it is not, the offender could feel doubly punished.

As long as retributive and reparative methods run side-by-side, the solution may lie in separating them, with the state requiring reparation to the victim or the community, combined with punishment if that is still thought to be necessary and the communication between victim and offender a personal one independent of the system. But it may be unhelpful to try to insist on rigid divisions. This is understood in Japan. There, "the police invariably recommend a lenient disposition, if a suspect has shown sincere repentance about his or her alleged crime and the transgression against a social norm is not particularly serious" (Shikita, quoted by Haley, 1989, p.199-200). Further,

> ...the victim thus participates in the process. Restitution is ordinarily made and the victim has a voice in the authorities' decisions whether to report, to prosecute, or to sentence the offender...In this way the victims participate in the process but do not control it. Ultimately they must defer to the authorities' decision...The process gives the offender an incentive to make amends and the victim an opportunity to forgive. However, the victim does not assume the role of adversary or prosecutor, nor is he or she enabled to use the formal process vindictively for revenge [Haley, 1989, pp.200-201].

If there is pressure on the offender to offer restitution and the victim to accept it, this is evidently felt to be the pressure of social custom rather than of the criminal justice system; it enables the judges to impose shorter sentences, which some penal reformers believe is part of the reason for the relatively low crime rate in Japan.

It is interesting that moves towards bringing the victim into the process are in harmony with ancient traditions, from which younger Western countries may have something to learn. This is the case with neighborhood mediation (Wright, 1991), while the New Zealand family group conferences are influenced by the Maori "whanau [extended family] conferences" (McElrea, 1994, p.98). A consultation with First Nation Canadians also described the response to crime as a healing one, involving victims, offenders and community. Dealing with feelings can place the victim back in charge of his or her own life: "Being able to confront those who have hurt me and to take responsibility for my feelings is when my healing process began." Another interviewee considered that: "The process is helpful for offenders as well. We have traditional feasts which are used to complete this process of healing for victims and offenders. The legal system prolongs this process" (Krawll, 1994, pp.50, 51-52).

Clearly, no major change in Western countries is possible overnight, although the growing interest in restorative justice is encouraging. What should be the next steps towards introducing it? Two distinctions should be made: first, between mediation and reparation, and, second, between the private aspect of the offense (the emotional and tangible effects on the victim) and the public interest (the requirement that lawbreaking, when serious, should be publicly denounced). Mediation is always private (although the family group conferences in New Zealand and Australia bring in quite a number of those with an interest in the case); reparation is for both the victim, if he or she wants it, and the public, if the offense is serious enough. How would this be put into effect?

First, measures should be as voluntary as possible. Thus, offenders should be given the opportunity and incentive to offer reparation at any time after the offense. If the specific victim does not want to be involved, the offender should be able to make reparation to the community. The incentive would be the possibility of discontinuing the prosecution, or imposing a lower sentence. Once the offender had offered reparation, the possibility of mediation could be raised with both parties. This would not be part of the criminal justice process, but would be for the victim and offender to use in whatever constructive way they wished; it might, but need not, include discussion of the form and amount of any reparation offered. A further possibility is that some victims might want to help offenders achieve a more realistic understanding of the effects of their behavior, even though their own offenders have not been caught. For them, and for offenders whose victims do not want to take part, victim-offender groups offer another approach (Launay and Murray, 1989). This would represent the private aspect of the offense; it would be especially appropriate when victims and offenders knew each other, but would also work when they had been strangers.

The court would concern itself with the public interest, and would therefore take account officially of the reparation but not of the mediation. However, in another blurring of the dividing lines, it might consider that the public interest was well-served if the offender had given the victim the opportunity to express his or her feelings, and that therefore a mitigation of sentence would be justified. Where monetary compensation is to be paid, the German principle of a resocialization fund would have advantages for victims; such a fund will enable victims to be paid in full at once (and perhaps a percentage to be negotiated with other creditors), and offenders could pay in instalments. Offenders would be under moral pressure to do so, because if they did not the fund would be depleted and less able to help others in the future; further, by completing the payments offenders would help their reintegration into the community (Wright, 1988).

Sentencing would be simpler and more consistent if it were based entirely on the restorative principle (with containment only for reasons of public protection, not for punishment, and the use of non-custodial restraints such as disqualification unless detention was unavoidable). There would be a single quantum for the offense; if the victim demanded less for private reparation, more would be owed to the community in the court's order for public reparation. The victim would thus not be under pressure, because he or she could affect only the private/public distribution, not the total. There would still be questions about how much reparation a particular offense merited, and about the equivalence of reparation through money and community service. But the human rights implications are less serious when it is a question of how much good a person should be required to do, rather than how much pain he or she should be required to suffer.

At present, the closest we come to a restorative model is a hybrid one: some reparation can be made in places where a reparation and mediation service exists, but it is not clear whether or not courts mitigate the sentence on account of this. The problem with this model is that it attempts to introduce reparation and mediation in a way that is compatible with traditional criminal justice, such as proportionality of the sanction (though it marks a shift towards basing the proportionality more on harm than on criminal intent). This approach has been criticized (Davis et al., 1988) on the basis that reparation is used as a means of diverting offenders out of the system, and "deflecting or appeasing a retributive system" (p.129). Davis et al. (1988) stated that many reparation services were "interested primarily in diversion or mitigation", and offered victims "little beyond the possibility of serving the interests of 'their' offender" (p.129, italics in original). They argue that if reparation is accommodated within the present retributive system, it will be subordinated to efforts to mitigate punishment. Davis et al. (1988) make two suggestions: (1) reparation should be a voluntary process, a personal interaction between the victim and the offender that is separate from the courts and that therefore does not influence the sentence; and (2) the whole system should be reparative, both the victim-offender communication, if any, and the sentence of the court, to avoid the conflict between reparation and retribution. Zedner (1994) also questions whether mediation services can operate properly "in the shadow of the court" (p.237). She feels that reparation can fulfil the demands of punishment (except, presumably, the infliction of pain purely for the sake of retribution), but warns that "the attempt to accommodate reparative justice to the rationale of punishment so perverts its underlying rationale as to strip it of much of its original appeal, not least its commitment to repairing ruptured social bonds" (p.250).

In short, there is a danger that the ideal will be introduced in a way that does not focus through the new lens proposed by Zehr (1990). For example, suppose a victim, looking through a restorative lens, feels that the offender has made right a serious offense by an apology, reparation, or community service, and by a credible promise to behave better in the future. If the court says that this is not enough and also imposes punishment (with all its undesirable side effects), it is still looking through a retributive lens, in which the past harm by the offender is seen as having to be balanced by harm to the offender (Zehr, 1990, p.212). The new ideal would then have been subverted, to fit in with unregenerate punitive ways of thinking. The answer is probably that, yes, the transitional phase will be unsatisfactory. But, like Copernicus and Galileo, we shall have to spend some time getting other people to look through our telescope and verify our observations before they are persuaded. As with the traditional system, there is no clear way of resolving all the competing requirements, and restorative justice is not necessarily the last word. A future Newton or Einstein, studying human behavior, may find new ways of understanding the gravity and relativity of the harm that people inflict on each other. Meanwhile, in the move towards a system based on healing, it is better to think not of conflicting theories but of a continuum; for the time being, the best hope of progress is to work for a gradual shift from the repressive towards the restorative.

## REFERENCES

Ashworth, P. (1993). "Victim Impact Statements and Sentencing." *Criminal Law Review* 498-509.

Aye Maung, N. (1995). "The 1994 British Crime Survey." *Magistrate* (Mar):35.

*Bundesgesetzblatt* (1994) Part I, No. 76. Bonn, GER: Author.

Davis, G. (1992). *Making Amends: Mediation and Reparation in Criminal Justice.* London, UK: Routledge.

—J. Boucherat and D. Watson (1988). "Reparation in the Service of Diversion: The Subordination of a Good Idea." *Howard Journal* 27(2):127-134.

Haley, J. (1989). "Confession, Repentance and Absolution." In: M. Wright and B. Galaway (eds.), *Mediation and Criminal Justice: Victims, Offenders and Community.* London, UK: Sage.

Krawll, M.B. (1994). *Understanding the Role of Healing in Aboriginal Communities.* Ottawa, CAN: Solicitor General Canada.

Launay, G. and P. Murray (1989). "Victim/Offender Groups." In: M. Wright and B. Galaway (eds.), *Mediation and Criminal Justice: Victims, Offenders and Community.* London, UK: Sage.

Marshall, T. and S. Merry (1990). *Crime and Accountability: Victim-Offender Mediation in Practice.* London, UK: Her Majesty's Stationery Office.

McElrea, F. (1994). "Justice in the Community: The New Zealand Experience." In: J. Burnside and N. Baker (eds.), *Relational Justice: Repairing the Breach.* Winchester, UK: Waterside Press.

Moore, D.B. and T.A. O'Connell (1994). "Family Conferencing in Wagga Wagga: A Communitarian Model of Justice." In: C. Alder and J. Wundersitz (eds.), *Family Conferencing and Juvenile Justice.* Canberra, AUS: Australian Institute of Criminology.

Morris, A., G. Maxwell and J. Robertson (1993). "Giving Victims a Voice: A New Zealand Experiment." *Howard Journal* 32(4):304-321.

Netzig, L. (1994). *Täter-Opfer-Ausgleich—wie geht das? 15 Falldokumentationen (Victim-Offender Mediation: How Does it Work? 15 Case Histories).* Hannover, GER: Die Waage.

Newburn, T. (1988). *The Use and Enforcement of Compensation Orders in Magistrates' Courts.* London, UK: Her Majesty's Stationery Office.

Reeves, H. (1994). "Victims." *Criminal Bar Association Newsletter* (Sept):4-6.

Shadbolt, M. (1994). *An Investigation of Victim/Offender Mediation and Reparation Schemes in the United Kingdom* (Report to the Winston Churchill Memorial Trust). Henderson, NZ: Department of Justice, Community Corrections Division.

U.K. Home Office (1994). *The Cautioning of Offenders.* London, UK: Author.

—(1995a). *Criminal Justice: Key Statistics England and Wales.* Croydon, UK: Home Office Dissemination Unit, Research and Statistics Department.

—(1995b). *National Standards for the Supervision of Offenders in the Community.* London, UK: Author.

Umbreit, M. (1994). *Victim Meets Offender: The Impact of Restorative Justice and Mediation.* Monsey, NY: Criminal Justice Press.

Victim Support. (1993). *Compensating the Victim of Crime.* London, UK: Author.

—(1995). *The Rights of Victims of Crime: A Policy Paper.* London, UK: Author.

Wright, M. (1988). "Out of the Morass: A Rational Approach to Debt." *Probation Journal* 35(4):148.

—(1996). *Justice for Victims and Offenders: A Restorative Response to Crime.* 2nd ed. Winchester, UK: Waterside Press.

—(1995). "Victims, Mediation and Criminal Justice." *Criminal Law Review* (Mar):187-199.

—(in press). "Victims Meet Offenders in an English Urban Community." *International Journal of Comparative and Applied Criminal Justice* 19(2).

Wroath, J. (1995). "The Sentencing Dilemma." *Magistrate* (Mar):37-38.

Zedner, L. (1994). "Reparation and Retribution: Are They Reconcilable?" *Modern Law Review* 57(2):228-250.

Zehr, H. (1990). *Changing Lenses: A New Focus for Criminal Justice.* Scottdale, PA: Herald Press.

# 13. RESTORATIVE JUSTICE AS PARTICIPATION: THEORY, LAW, EXPERIENCE AND RESEARCH

by

**Lutz Netzig**

and

**Thomas Trenczek**

**Abstract:** *In modern industrial societies, citizens tend to delegate responsibility to anonymous institutions. Government and insurance companies, lawyers, and police are supposed to enforce the citizen's interests. Unfortunately, neither the criminal justice system nor traditional restitution schemes provide an active role for victims and offenders. This chapter reviews the development of program activities and restorative law in Germany, with focus on the leading victim-offender reconciliation program (VORP) for adult offenders, the nonprofit organization WAAGE ("scale") in Hannover. Case studies point out the dynamic of mediation, explain the specific role of the mediator and focus on the conflict-oriented approach of the program. An action research project that has been conducted from the beginning of VORP activity gives an unusual insight into and understanding of the perspectives of victims and offenders. Data are presented from 75 open-ended interviews conducted with participants from August 1992 through December 1994. The assessment of expectations and experiences focuses on the correlation of participation, satisfaction, justice and fairness.*

# SOCIETY, JUSTICE AND PARTICIPATION

## The Need for Justice and Participation

Justice is essential for both individuals and society. The most frequent cause of disruption, pain, and suffering is when situations and rules are perceived as being unjust. This is true of the relationship between nations and societies and also holds for the day-to-day contact between individuals. War, destruction, and personal catastrophes are based on the perception of injustice and unfairness. In contrast, when rules and relationships are perceived as fair and just, people and societies are able to develop and flourish. Further, conflicts are more likely to be solved in a manner that does not cause the destruction of the opponent, and that may lead to social peace if the social, political, and legal order is perceived as fair. But the critical question is, how are just relations established? How can rules be established that are considered to be just and fair and which prevent people behaving like wounded animals? What makes people and groups accept rules and regulations that prevent destructive conflict behavior?

Constructivism has taught about the subjectivity and the selectivity of perception. Human beings do not live in an objective world; rather, through observation, awareness, thinking, acting and communication they produce their own empirical reality (Watzlawick, 1978; Maturana and Varela, 1984; Richards and von Glaserfeld, 1987). Brains do not process sensory perception in the correct way. Instead, they assimilate perceptions according to certain transmitted or learned criteria that are significant for an individual biography. For each individual only the world he or she perceives exists, and this overlaps only partly with what others see. The order of social reality loses its appearance of objectivity. Social reality is composed of various aspects that are structured by a relevant personal priority. A person's specific individual interests, as well as the compatibility of personal experiences with existing knowledge, are particularly relevant for the definition of social situations. Thus, various realities are established by following different rules in the construction of personal truths.

Postmodern theories call this the transition of reality into a model of pluralistic constructions of life. Comprehensive blueprints of societal models, traditions, religions, political orders, and definitions of justice have lost their persuasiveness (Stierlin, 1992). Therefore, there is an increasing need for orientation in order to cope with growing uncertainty.

This is one reason why fundamentalism or systems that rely on brain-washing attract so many people. A participatory approach may offer a possible way out of the dilemma. People in today's Western hemisphere will accept only rules based on democratic consensus. Consensus, however, is inconceivable without the active participation of its addressees. Societies need to allow for the negotiation of rules and solutions in order to keep consensus alive. Negotiation processes are fundamental and vital in a democratic social reality because they are both the prerequisite for and the outcome of that part of social reality that is relevant to its individuals (Messmer, 1991). In modern industrial societies citizens have tended to delegate responsibility as far as most personal questions are concerned. People tend to pull back into their safe private spheres, losing the ability to deal with their differences and conflicts as a result of the trend toward individualization and isolation of interests. Governments, lawyers, the police and insurance companies are supposed to enforce citizens' interests. Conflicts are increasingly dealt with and settled by anonymous third parties. The consequences are fatal. If people lose the ability to cope with direct and interpersonal conflicts, intolerance and the potential for violence will grow.

But the opposite trend is evident in many social areas. Various levels of freedom have been created to make people more responsible. Large industrial groups, such as Sony, Chrysler and Ford, are shifting management techniques from a hierarchical mode toward a cooperative, team-oriented working process. Companies recognize that employees need to have more direct responsibility for outcome in order to maximize profits (Womack and Jones, 1990; Warnecke, 1992; Hammer and Champy, 1993). People in urban areas have begun to reorganize their communities. Neighborhood centers have been emerging that give citizens a say in the reorganization of social life. Furthermore, individuals need to be encouraged to exercise their own responsibility for conflict rather than to entrust the conflict to the care of professional services. Alternative dispute resolution is receiving more and more attention as the legal system comes up against its inherent limiting factors. The mediation of conflict is seen as one of the most promising means of dispute resolution in nearly every aspect of social life, including work, school, the family and divorce (Fisher and Ury, 1981). The importance of increasing community members' ability and capacity to manage their own conflicts is recognized.

## Criminal Justice Systems and Restitution

In the criminal justice system, victims and offenders are required to enact their roles as witnesses and defendants, but beyond that they remain passive. Once they have stated their immediate cases, the system steals their conflict and takes over (Christie, 1977). The system is very much concerned with reestablishing legal order, but fails to leave any room for the interpersonal resolution of conflict and the restoration of social peace. The same is true in many restitution proceedings. Definitions of restitution usually focus simply on the outcome, the concrete restitution agreement as a means of compensation for the victim. In practice, this is often reduced to the payment of a sum of money. Restitution is best characterized as an offender-oriented measure, with educational and penal functions (Galaway, 1987; Trenczek, 1995). The civil liability for damages takes on a penal character simply by virtue of the fact that the sentence is imposed and executed by the criminal justice system. Payment is enforced by the courts, and in the extreme case of a refusal, is enforced by revoking probation (Harland, 1982; Trenczek, 1995).

The significance of restitutive behavior in earlier legal systems has been pointed out time and again in the extensive American literature on restitution. But it is almost universally disregarded that in these legal cultures restitution was always incorporated into a process geared toward settlement and reconciliation (Pfohl, 1981; Fogel *et al.*, 1972; Jacob, 1970). Rituals of symbolic satisfaction and restitution were inextricably linked with the aim of settling the social disturbance and re-establishing the damaged communication and relationships between those involved in the conflict, thus restoring peace to the community. Compensation was not an end in itself, but simply an element within the framework of a wider solution to the conflict that mediation was designed to achieve. In contrast, social control in criminal law today is characterized by rituals of exclusion (Pfohl, 1981), to which any implemented restitutive elements are also subordinated. Both the criminal justice system and restitution schemes are clearly offender-oriented. In both concepts, the attention paid to the victim is purely functional, especially as he or she has to serve as a principal witness for the prosecution. The fact that the criminal act is often entangled in a complex interpersonal conflict structure is also ignored, which constitutes a major shortcoming in both of these ways of dealing with the problem (Fattah, 1992; Hanak *et al.*, 1989; Trenczek, 1992). As a result, the roles of victim and offender in both criminal and restitution proceedings do not provide for active participation (Trenczek, 1990).

Restitution programs occasionally employ mediation to determine the amount of restitution to be paid by the offender. Over and above that, mediation has no significant relevance in a conflict-resolving process. The shift may be from purely repressive to restorative sanctions, but restitution programs do not mediate in the victim-offender conflict; rather, they are involved in the negotiation of punishment. A repressive and pecuniary sanction like restitution has a certain innate appeal in today's world and, unlike reconciliation, has become dominant in criminal justice systems. Restorative justice goes beyond restitution and connotes a dynamic dimension, an interactive process of establishing justice and fairness. Its focus is on conflict resolution and the re-establishment of peace, and it is based on the voluntary and participatory nature of the conflict-resolving procedure. Therefore, mediation in particular is employed as a technique for increasing victim participation in the criminal justice process.

German Täter-Opfer-Ausgleich (TOA) programs are similar in approach and procedure to the North American victim-offender reconciliation programs (VORPs). They focus on the participation of both victim and offender, and emphasize the process of conflict resolution and reconciliation. Restitution for victims is seen as only one possible (symbolic) end in a conflict-resolving process that demonstrates that the damage done is made good. The German translation for reconciliation (Versöhnung, Aussöhnung) often has a strong religious connotation and has therefore been criticized as being an unrealistic goal for criminal justice purposes. Indeed, the North American VORPs do have strong historical and philosophical roots in the religious community, especially the Mennonite Church. But reconciliation actually has a broader, secular meaning, i.e., to resolve, settle, make consistent, or restore equity and equality. In this sense, reconciliation and conflict resolution are synonymous, and there is no other suitable translation in this context for the German word Ausgleich (literally, balancing out). For this reason, and because the acronym VORP has already been introduced into criminal justice terminology for participatory concepts and programs in which face-to-face encounters form an integral part, we will use reconciliation/VORP and Ausgleich/TOA interchangeably to describe the German concept of victim-offender mediation.

## The Law and Alternative Dispute Resolution

Dispute resolution is only possible within the confines of the law, which acts as an orientational and ordering framework. The law has to fulfil functions on several different levels. It represents a point of orientation for social behavior in its function as a normative mechanism for resolving conflicts, even if the ability of legal regulations to govern behavior tends to be overestimated. But norms will be violated without causing the norm itself to be invalidated as a result. Criminal law must serve as a means of orientation to guarantee basic principles of social behavior. Beyond that and preceding penalization both temporally and functionally, it must perform a regulatory and supervisory role by publicly monitoring particular norms thus ensuring their continuing and binding validity despite their violation. Force is an integral part of law—and of criminal law in particular—since it is the severest instrument of public social control (Frehsee, 1991; Rössner, 1992; Spittler, 1980).

Autonomous post-crime conflict resolution is dependent on the fact that enforcement measures are held in readiness although in the background, and can be activated to uphold the law and protect the weak. The conditions and demands of our way of life and of our social systems today appear to take out a currently relevant discourse of the validity of norms in concrete conflicts. The "heterogenization of value preferences" (Frehsee, 1991, p.56) in an open, pluralistic society has made a certain minimum level of consistent and binding norms indispensable for social contact. However, this must be distinguished from the question of whether public social control for purposes of reparation and conflict management respects the autonomy of the parties involved in both life and conflict contexts, and whether it can, if need be, permit them a degree of freedom to find their own consensus on alternative norms, without the law losing its function as an orientation yardstick for social action.

Criminal law makes it clear which legal interests are deemed worthy of particular protection, and who the victim and the offender are (Rössner, 1992). The results of victimological research, however, show that such definitions do not always live up to social reality. It is not always clear which person is the offender and which the victim. The emphasis on conflict rather than on a normative definition of criminality in TOA's mediatory approach provokes the question as to the legitimacy and scope of the prevailing definition of delinquency. There is no such thing as crime per se, but rather behavior that from a certain point on a continuum is defined as criminal.

## RESTORATIVE JUSTICE IN GERMANY

The TOA programs in Germany began with the aim of establishing a new aspect to the state's handling of criminal acts. The principle of *Wiedergutmachung* in German criminal law permits a perspective that contains the peacemaking aspect of the law. The German term Wiedergutmachung (literally "making good again", and best translated as "reparation" or "redress" in its deeper sense) is mentioned in several provisions in the criminal code (*e.g.*, sec. 46, 46a, 56b) and in the criminal procedure code (sec. 153a; [Trenczek, 1990]), and is a much wider concept than restitution and the compensation for damages or loss that occurs under civil law. The criminal law concept of Wiedergutmachung has both a material (damages) and a non-material and interactive component. Parties to the conflict are involved in making good the material and non-material consequences of the offense or injustice, and participation of both victim and offender is therefore required. The *Ausgleich* (balancing out, or reconciliation) between victim and offender must aim at overcoming the conflict, reaching an understanding, and deescalating the problem with a view to the future, thus making a contribution to a social and legal peace.

The concept of TOA has rapidly developed in the ten years that have passed since the first model projects in Germany. In the mid-1980s, pioneering work was carried out by a small circle of committed social workers and criminal justice officials as they experimented with TOA for crimes that had been carried out by young offenders under age 21 (Trenczek, 1990). TOA was judged favorably and considered to have been a success in studies carried out by independent research institutions (Schreckling *et al.*, 1992). In 1992, prominent German, Austrian, and Swiss criminal law lecturers called for changes in the administration of justice, and demanded that Wiedergutmachung be taken into greater consideration during criminal proceedings (Baumann *et al.*, 1992). In the same year, the first model projects for testing TOA were started in Hannover and Nuremberg with adult offenders and their victims. Again, in a matter of a few years, the projects were followed by changes in the law; in December 1994 TOA (in addition to Wiedergutmachung) was made an integral part of general criminal law. TOA is not only designated as a possible component in a probation order, or as a general basis for sentencing and grounds for mitigation, but sec. 46a of the Criminal Code also provides that TOA may constitute a sentence in its own right if other sanctions are dispensed with.

In order to coordinate the explosive development of TOA, especially in the juvenile delinquency sector, the Federal Ministry of Justice set up a Service Bureau as early as 1990. Experts offer practical advice and support for TOA projects throughout the country, publish a journal, and organize further training courses and conferences. The Service Bureau's most important job is planning and running a one-year on-the-job training course, which leads to a basic qualification for conflict counsellors in the TOA field (Netzig, 1993). The course has now firmly established itself and is a prerequisite for working as a professional mediator; approximately 350 social workers from juvenile probation services and nonprofit organizations have taken part. The number of projects practicing TOA in Germany has risen to over 200 within just a few years (Wandrey, 1994). Most of the participants have been organizations working with young people, but a similar boom for adult offenses can be expected now that the legal conditions have been finalized in the field of criminal law.

Such a rapid and complex development has its pitfalls. The outlines of TOA become blurred, there is a tendency to abuse or undermine the concept, and standards are called into question. Some District Attorneys' offices (*Staatsanwaltschaften*) try to put the projects out of existence by not referring cases. Some so-called TOA projects merely carry out the judiciary's restitution penalties and palm this off as TOA. Social workers confuse one-sided counselling with conflict resolution. If the attempt to establish a common base and common standards for structuring and running the great variety of TOA projects is unsuccessful, TOA will deteriorate into a travesty of itself, an insignificant didactic appendage to the criminal justice system—much to the disadvantage of the victims and offenders. Its emancipatory and empowering intentions, wherein its true value lies, would then burst like a bubble (Netzig, 1995a). To prevent this from happening, a group of experts has developed a manual that lays down standards for running TOA projects in Germany in a reputable manner (Kubach *et al.*, 1995). Its chief priorities include safeguarding the voluntary nature of an offer of TOA, training to ensure a high degree of specialization among mediators, networking among the projects, and keeping accountable statistics for monitoring the individual projects' success and aiding comparisons among them.

## WAAGE IN HANNOVER

The Verein für Konfliktschlichtung und Wiedergutmachung—WAAGE Hannover e.v. (Association for Conflict Mediation and Redress; WAAGE means scales) is a nonprofit organization founded in late 1990 that has been carrying out TOA within criminal law since the fall of 1992 (Netzig *et al.*, 1992). Victim and offender are given the opportunity to talk about the offense and its causes and consequences, and to negotiate a redress in the presence of an impartial mediator. A case's suitability for TOA does not in principle depend on the seriousness of the crime but on the acceptance of those involved. To gain the cooperation of the judiciary, however, the spectrum has been limited to cases involving moderately serious crimes such as theft and burglary, grievous bodily harm, damage to property, and fraud. In spite of this, mediation is carried out across the entire offense spectrum if either of the affected parties have initiated the contact to WAAGE themselves.

Despite the majority of juvenile programs in Germany (Trenczek, 1990), WAAGE does not focus strictly on diversion, although the aim is to have the case dismissed once the persons involved have resolved their conflict. Legal limits (sec. 153, 153a German Criminal Procedure Code) only permit the dismissal of misdemeanor offenses in adult proceedings (in contrast to juvenile cases, cf. sec. 45, 47 of the Juvenile Code, which also permits the dismissal of felony offenses). Thus, WAAGE also accepts cases where criminal justice proceedings may continue or where an additional (reduced) sanction may be imposed. WAAGE does not, however, accept any conditions imposed by the prosecution or the judiciary as regards the outcome of the mediation process. Once the parties have reached an agreement and fulfilled it, the case is returned to the referral source for a final decision. WAAGE manages a fund for victims, from which offenders without means may receive an interest-free loan in order to pay compensation to the injured party. The offenders then either pay the money back in instalments, or perform community or charity work.

WAAGE's central objective is to facilitate participation and conflict resolution. The initiation and facilitation of a controlled forum for settling and resolving conflicts is at the center of the idea of reconciliation. This reflects an interactive, conflict-oriented perspective on crime, a move away from one-sided partisanship toward an integrative approach that is sensitive to the needs and problems of both victims and offenders. With VORP, we are implementing specific communicative elements in the justice system. Victim and offender are given the chance to represent their own interests. VORP gives those involved the necessary freedom and space to enable them to cope with or make good both the emotional and material consequences of criminal acts, and thus actively participate in reducing and resolving conflicts.

The number of cases assigned to WAAGE by the District Attorney's Office fell far short of its initiators' expectations in the first 12 months of the project's operation. Department heads attributed their reticence to the need to keep down their workload. A great deal of effort was necessary to reduce their reservations, but the efforts bore fruit after a special TOA department was set up at the District Attorney's Office. Afterwards, both the quality and quantity of cases developed along the desired lines. Since the start of its TOA program in late 1992, WAAGE has completed 509 TOA cases involving 670 injured parties and 614 defendants. In 1994 the number of cases was 235, involving 313 victims and 282 offenders. WAAGE counts cases based on the number of judicial cases that have been filed, regardless of how many victims and offenders were involved on each occasion (e.g., two offenders with four victims equal one case). A total of 59 cases (in 1994, 41 cases) were proceedings in which both sides had been injured and in which both were accused of a crime. The most serious offenses being prosecuted in each case are:

|  | 10/92-12/94 | | 01/94-12/94 | |
|---|---|---|---|---|
| – Assault (Körperverletzung, sec. 233 StGB) | (199) | 39% | (96) | 41% |
| – Dangerous assault with weapons (gefährliche Körperverletzung, sec. 223 StGB) | (89) | 18% | (43) | 18% |
| – Malicious damage to property (Sachbeschädigung, sec. 303/304 StGB) | (52) | 10% | (24) | 10% |
| – Insulting behavior (Beleidigung, sec. 185 StGB) | (49) | 10% | (16) | 7% |
| – Unlawful compulsion (Nötigung, sec. 240 StGB) | (38) | 7% | (20) | 9% |
| – Threatening behavior (Bedrohung, sec. 241 StGB) | (30) | 6% | (8) | 3.5% |
| – Fraud (Betrug, sec. 263 StGB) | (17) | 3% | (10) | 4% |
| – Theft/Burglary (Diebstahl: sec. 243 StGB) | (14) | 3% | (8) | 3.5% |
| – Other | (21) | 4% | (10) | 4% |
| TOTAL | (509) | 100% | (235) | 100% |

Of the 509 (1994: 235) cases referred, 79 (1994: 42) were considered unsuitable for a TOA since the accused denied the charge. These cases were returned to the District Attorney's Office. Of the 430 (1994: 193) cases considered suitable in principle, 54%, or 232 (1994: 62%, or 120) were concluded. There was no reconciliation for 46%, or 195 (1994: 37%, or 73). Reasons for missing reconciliation were:

|  | 10/92-12/94 | | 01/94-12/94 | |
|---|---|---|---|---|
| – Offender could not be contacted: | (66) | 33% | (37) | 50% |
| – Offender refused to participate: | (43) | 21% | (8) | 11% |
| – Victim could not be contacted: | (7) | 4% | (5) | 7% |
| – Victim refused to participate: | (55) | 28% | (8) | 11% |
| – Mediation unsuccessful: | (27) | 14% | (15) | 21% |
| TOTAL | (198) | 100% | (73) | 100% |

WAAGE offers the injured party TOA only if the offender has indi-cated a readiness to participate. Most participants first learn about the possibility of a settlement out of court when they receive the WAAGE let-ter. One major problem has been difficulty contacting offenders who do not respond, or who return mail unopened. In the initial phase of the program approximately 25% to 30% of the parties turned down the offer, but in 1994 only eight victims and eight defendants refused to partici-pate. The reasons are varied. Some people do not want anything more to do with the matter and leave any further action in the hands of their lawyer. Some do not want to make the effort. Others would like the mat-ter to be decided in court by a judge. Sometimes the parties involved are so embittered from years of conflict that any attempt at reconciliation seems pointless. The most important element in terms of participation is that the affected parties can decide themselves whether they wish to take up TOA or not. Mediation is successful in nine out of ten cases if the victim and the offender are willing to attempt a settlement out of court. The manner in which cases are dealt with is determined by the needs and interests of the victims and offenders concerned. Many par-ticipants support the notion of a TOA, but reject a personal meeting with the other party out of fear, bitterness or plain idleness. Some injured parties are simply interested in the material aspect of the case. Face-to-face mediation took place in one third of the cases successfully dealt with; in about two-thirds of the cases mediation took place indirectly with the mediator, talking to each of the affected parties individually.

The most serious offense successfully dealt with was a case of an as-sault with weapons in which the injured party's nipple was split as a re-sult of a stab wound to the chest; the mediation resulted in damages of approximately $9,000 being paid to the victim. A particularly conflict-ridden situation was a case of indecent exposure, in which the female victim described to the offender in a session lasting nearly three hours the fear and anxiety she suffers as a result of his actions. The degree of difficulty in a mediation case is not dependent on the (normative) seriousness of the crime. Sometimes, offenses that appear relatively minor can conceal a serious underlying conflict. WAAGE has dealt with a large number of cases in which the victim and the offender knew each other before the offense occurred. The center has been able to settle both crimes involving domestic relations and disputes between neighbors and colleagues. The relationship between victim and offender has an influence on the way a TOA reconciliation develops and its chance of success; such cases generally prove to be particularly difficult and time-consuming.

The results of negotiations are varied. In some cases, a financial redress such as compensation for injury or damages has top priority. The victim and offender then negotiate the amount to be paid. The affected parties often agree on a symbolic gesture, for example, that the offender makes a donation to charity. Sometimes, after a successful settlement, they decide on a joint activity and go out for coffee or meet in the evening for a drink. In domestic cases, the affected parties are concerned with laying down rules for future behavior, such as a strict ban on any form of contact. With disputes among neighbors, the TOA usually ends in binding agreements that govern specific aspects of living next door to one another. WAAGE's mediators monitor compliance with the agreements, and payments are made through the association. The TOA has failed in only one case because the offender failed to keep his promise.

## EMPIRICAL ASSESSMENT OF RESTORATIVE JUSTICE

### Research Methods

Law-and-order policy considerations always address the success of TOA programs to justify their funding. But what does "success" mean? Should the focus be on criminal justice goals, or on the intrinsic aims of conflict resolution and VORP? Success for the criminal justice system is often expressed in recidivism statistics (Galaway, 1988). This standard reflects an overestimation of the influence of formal measures on whether a person will reoffend, aside from low selectivity (there are enough indications to show that legal measures are interchangeable in terms of the prevention of recidivism). Behavior toward the law is influenced less by a formal measure made at one point in time and more by personal biography, social chances, and the general social and cultural condition of a society (Galaway, 1988). Traditional measures have not been very successful using the yardstick of recidivism, the situation can hardly get worse by pursuing alternative methods of dealing with crime.

VORP is not yet a routine procedure, although the number of programs is growing. The number of cases is still small, and it is difficult to make a financial assessment of the costs and benefits of pursuing a VORP case. WAAGE Hanover has an annual budget of $130,000 that provides for two mediators and one part-time secretary. Mutual agreements between the affected parties may lead to a reduction in criminal, civil and appeal proceedings, but an efficiency evaluation of this kind is premature. Further, subjecting the program to a definition of success based on the criminal justice system is too limiting for an appropriate assessment of the conflict resolution approach. Participation is one of WAAGE's major goals; the views of the victims and the offenders are of great significance. Therefore, the affected parties have to be asked about their goals for mediation, and their experiences and criticism of TOA (Netzig, 1995b).

Face-to-face meetings by the parties is one step in facilitating conflict resolution, although the number of such encounters is low compared to the figures from juvenile TOA programs (Trenczek, 1990). However, it is important for the parties themselves to be able to decide which form of conflict resolution they wish to pursue. In cases where damage to property has been minor (and the emotional problems negligible), participants often find complex proceedings involving face-to-face contact unnecessary for settling financial compensation. Rates of mutual agreement and compliance with restitution obligations, the participants' satisfaction with the procedure and its results, and the change in attitudes toward the other party also stress different aspects of a definition of success. A program can only provide an opportunity for participation, and may not be able to prove if and to what extent reconciliation has occurred. Nonetheless, carefully undertaken evaluations that consistently take these restrictions into account can provide some indication as to whether VORP constitutes a practicable approach to crime. This kind of analysis of success is seldom undertaken to legitimate the criminal justice procedure.

The extensive surveys carried out by Umbreit (1990, 1991, 1992) are only partially applicable to the German situation due, for one, to the difference in legal systems. However, Umbreit's research methods and results would provide a good basis for a more in-depth survey of victims and offenders, adjusted to specific German circumstances. However, the academic research accompanying WAAGE's projects has placed its emphasis elsewhere. Mediation talks are emotionally charged situations. They are concerned with a criminal offense, material and non-material damage, injuries, and humiliation and anger. For the victims and offenders involved, mediation talks are usually accompanied by insecurity and anxiety. An abstractly standardized research approach would not be suitable in this case. In addition, the questions we are interested in suggest the need for an open and unstandardized method of questioning. We are not interested in a supposedly objective measurement of satisfaction, but rather in an evaluation of dimensions such as the major motivations, perceptions and assessments of the affected parties in connection with their attempts to resolve the conflict out of court at WAAGE. For this reason, the survey was carried out using qualitative, semi-structured interviews.

WAAGE is based on the concept of action research. The intention is to gradually and meaningfully improve what the project offers by constantly reflecting upon and reviewing practices. A survey of the views of victims and offenders plays an important role and has two functions. First, it helps to improve and optimize methods in practice, and, second, it aids the analysis of the mediation work. Shortly after each set of mediation talks, the mediators receive detailed feedback on the participants' views and points of criticism. In regular meetings and supervision sessions WAAGE's staff discuss the individual cases and air any problems that have been identified. Minutes are taken of the matters discussed at the meeting and their outcome, so that the learning and improvement process is documented in such a way that its progress can be clearly followed. The survey of parties is an aid to discovering the motives of victims and offenders, their interests and perceptions, and their evaluations and their attitudes. The survey is designed to enable those involved to explain what expectations they take with them into a mediation session, how they experience what happens, how well they think the mediator did his or her job, and which aspects played an important role in their subsequent satisfaction. Interviewing victims and offenders took place continually from October 1992 to February 1995; 75 qualitative interviews, lasting between 45 and 90 minutes, were carried out by staff of the Criminology Research Institute of Lower Saxony. The interviews were tape-recorded and transcribed.

# Findings

## Expectations and Motivation

Victims and offenders give a broad range of reasons for taking part in mediation talks. Trying to obtain a satisfactory solution to the incident is situated alongside a variety of hopes and aims regarding the outcome of TOA. The desire to settle the case out of court or the fear of negative alternatives also play a role in deciding on TOA. Often, the goals of the affected parties change while the reconciliation is in progress. Many victims, for example, initially say that they only have a material interest in the case, but as talks progress the non-material and emotional aspects of the case gain importance. Many victims participate in TOA because the crime has shaken, confused or frightened them. They want to ask the offender questions so that they can come to terms with what happened. They want to know what kind of person the offender is, why he or she committed the crime and what exactly happened as it occurred. Some victims, especially those who sustained injuries, only have a dim recollection of the event. Their fears escalate as their imaginations get the better of them and they feel threatened and traumatized by certain places or people's shadows. A face-to-face encounter with the offender can help these victims reduce their excessive anxiety. For other victims, it is more important to have one opportunity to tell the offender exactly what they think; to be able to get their anger, disgust, or grief off their chests; to let off steam; and to confront the offender with the consequences of his or her actions. The injured parties in neighborhood crimes often see an opportunity in TOA to finally put an end to the conflict, which has usually been going on for some time, and to put the dispute behind them. They want to clear up what happened in order to minimize the constant stress and threat to their environment and to avoid any further escalation of the conflict.

A victim of domestic crime illustrated the motives connected to their situation and their relationship to the offender:

> It would probably never have come out in court why he did it. It would have been established that he did it, that he broke my nose. Okay, whether it had been deliberately, or was an accident or had been done in self-defence, that could probably have been sorted out in court too. And after that they would have passed the sentence. Then I'd never have known why he did it! In the talks, as we both sat there, it came out a bit, why [...] Anyway now I know a couple of reasons for why it happened.

Many offenders take part because they want to make amends for what they have done. They hope to wipe the slate clean by means of material compensation. Pride and honor play an important role for male defendants. They want to take responsibility for the crimes they have committed. These offenders see an opportunity in TOA to show that they are fair and have the courage of their convictions, to admit to their mistakes, and to play an active part in minimizing the damage. The majority hope that settling the matter out of court and making good the damage caused will have a positive influence on the district attorney responsible for their case. First offenders want to avoid having a criminal record, and those with previous convictions hope to avoid a tough and/or expensive sentence. Further, many offenders also want the civil side of the case to be cleared up. They see an opportunity to settle the question of damages amicably and without an expensive court case. Offenders take part in TOA because they want to talk to the victim, explain their own behavior, apologize, ease their consciences and reduce feelings of guilt. Often, they express the wish that the victim will understand them and accept them as a person. Two offender comments illustrate reasons for participation:

· Well, it was important to me that he knew, I mean, the victim knew, that I wasn't a thug or anything. I wanted to prove to him that foreigners aren't all bad, there are nice ones too! I wanted to tell him that.

· This thing couldn't just be ignored. And so I said to myself, I've got the courage to say that it wasn't right what I did. [...] I'm a sportsman. I'm a fair man. And I say, when I'm in the wrong then I'll admit it. When I'm not in the wrong, then I won't.

## Participation and Satisfaction

During the course of mediation talks a surprising turnaround frequently occurs: financial demands take a back seat and non-material aspects gain in importance. Often both victims and offenders say that as a result of TOA they came to terms with what happened after getting to know the other party personally. Victims of violent conflicts in particular say that after initial scepticism, the mediation talks helped them to overcome the excessive fears resulting from the incident. They find that the open exchange of views at WAAGE aids in coming to terms with what happened. For many participants, the most important outcome of TOA is that the danger of further conflicts or a renewed escalation of the violence is diminished. They are able to overcome hate, anger and thoughts of revenge. The affected parties can now view the prospect of a possible chance meeting in the future without fear. This aspect of de-escalation is of great significance for incidents between neighbors colleagues, or relatives. Victims of crimes that occur within the family often see TOA as an opportunity to set clear and binding limits with the defendant, without destroying his or her life, ending the relationship, or drawing other members of the family into the conflict. A female victim of a nighttime assault commented:

> For me in the night that man was, if you like, the incarnation of fear, of danger. [...] What I've got out of [TOA] is that I'm glad that I got to know who [the offender] was, that I'm glad that I, sort of, heard it all from him, so that I know a little bit about what kind of a person he is, what kind of life he leads and that, really, he isn't violent. [...] I am really glad about that. [...] To see this phantom disappearing! Glad that the victim has the chance to have a good look at the offender. Just to see that he's only a human being as well and not some kind of monster! But also to have a protected space, to tell the defendant just what you think of him! [...] After he [the mediator] went out of the room, we had a bit of a chat [...] That was sort of important for me.

An offender in a case of assault with weapons commented:

> I now get on very well with the victim. I've thought about it: if it had come to a court case then it would have left a nasty taste in my mouth. Afterwards we had a meal here and then that was it. [...] As he said to me: He still would have been scared of me. Which I can understand. If you do things like I did there, I would have still been scared of whoever did it too. He isn't scared of me anymore, otherwise he wouldn't have gone for a meal with me. Anyway, I explained it again to him in the pub properly, how it was with me. And he could understand it as well.

Often, the non-material aspects stand out in the participants' statements concerning the outcome of TOA. The face-to-face encounter with the other party clearly has a value of its own for many participants. They were active in reducing the damage done and in negotiating the type of redress and amount of compensation, and could strongly identify with the result. TOA is a success from the point of view of those involved. For many people in our anonymous society, law and justice have deteriorated into abstract, empty phrases. In TOA, the affected parties experience that they too can decide what is just and fair. They themselves are responsible for sorting out the dispute and have the authority to do so. Their subjective criteria, views, and arguments are taken seriously and determine the outcome. The victims and offenders are able to identify with the result because they actively participate in settling the case and take part in negotiating any kind of redress.

The repayment behavior of those defendants who receive a loan from WAAGE's victim fund is remarkably good in view of their social circumstances, many are unemployed, in debt, and live off welfare support. Out of 34 loans totalling $26,000, payments are outstanding in only two cases, amounting to a total of $900. The offenders keep their word and pay off their debts, although they know that they cannot be legally forced to pay because they are classed as living below the subsistence level. Participation in TOA increases their sense of identification with the outcome. They are able to reduce the negative consequences of the offense without losing face and being humiliated. Sticking to the agreement becomes a question of pride and honor.

## TOWARDS A COMMUNITY JUSTICE APPROACH

A decision directly to involve victim and offender and to make participation easier, rather than focusing on punishment, does not mean that injurious behavior is accepted or discounted. Rather, it indicates a recognition of the limitations of the adversary process. The logical conclusion to the idea that criminal law is situated at the end of a long line of measures for social control is that formal measures should play a subsidiary role as a last resort. Therefore, conflict resolution must also be facilitated and initiated by the system itself. The current TOA/VORP model represents only one possible application. A community justice center that mediates in neighborhood disputes, as well as dealing with conflicts in the supposed tougher criminal cases, would be in keeping with the fact that there is no such thing as crime per se but rather behavior is defined as criminal. A community justice approach might be able to demonstrate that mediation and VORP, unlike a restitution order, is not an alternative sentence but constitutes a totally different approach to dealing with conflicts between people and represents an alternative way of thinking. Community justice forums need to provide means for the early expression and potential resolution of conflict. They need to provide support and participation to mediate in conflicts as they emerge, and before they become court statistics (Schonholtz, 1984). Victim-offender reconciliation is not a panacea but does constitute an attempt at implementing participation within the justice process.

# REFERENCES

Baumann, J., A. Brauneck, A. Borgstaller *et al.* (1992). *Alternativ-Entwurf Wiedergutmachung.* München, GER: Beck.

Christie, N. (1977). "Conflicts as Property." *British Journal of Criminology* 17.

Fattah, E. (1992). "Beyond Metaphysics: The Need for a New Paradigm." In: R. Lahti and K. Nuotio (eds.), *Criminal Law-Theory in Transition.* Helsinki, FIN: Finnish Lawyer's Publisher.

Fisher, R. and W. Ury (1981). *Getting to Yes.* Boston, MA: Houghton Mifflin.

Fogel, D., B. Galaway and J. Hudson (1972). "Restitution in Criminal Justice: A Minnesota Experiment." *Criminal Law Bulletin* 8:681-691.

Frehsee, D. (1991). "Täter-Opfer-Ausgleich aus rechtstheoretischer Perspektive." In: Bundesministerium der Justiz (ed.), *Täter-Opfer-Ausgleich Zwischenbilanz und Perspektiven.* Bonn, GER: Bonner Symposium.

Galaway, B. (1987). "Restitution as Innovation or Unfilled Promise?" *Federal Probation* 52:3-14.

Hammer, M. and J. Champy (1993). *Reengineering the Corporation.* New York, NY: HarperCollins.

Hanak, G., J. Stehr and H. Steinert (1989). *Ärgernisse und Lebenskatastrophen.* Bielefeld, GER: AJZ-Verlag.

Harland, A. (1982). "Monetary Remedies for the Victims of Crime: Assessing the Role of Criminal Courts." *University of California Los Angeles (UCLA) Law Review* 30:52-128.

Jacob, B.R. (1970). "Reparation or Restitution by the Criminal Offender to his Victim: Applicability of an Ancient Concept in the Modern Correctional Process." *Journal of Criminal Law, Criminology and Police Science* 61:152-167.

Kubach, T., L. Netzig, F. Petzold, M. Schadt and M. Wandrey (1995). "TOA-Standards." In: *Handbuch für die Praxis des Täter-Opfer-Ausgleichs.* Bonn, GER: Deutsche Bawaehrungshilfe e.v. (DBH)

Maturana, H.R. and F.J. Varela (1984). *Der Baum der Erkenntnis.* München, GER: Goldmann.

Messmer, H. (1991). "Zwischen Recht und Gerechtigkeit: Strukturen der Aushandlung einer Entscheidung im Rahmen von Diversionsverfahren." *Zeitschrift für Jugendrecht* 78:523-528.

Netzig, L. (1993). "Victim/Offender Mediator Training in Germany." *Mediation* 10(1).

—(1995a). "Von Segelbooten und Seifenblasen: Ein Essay über die rasante Entwicklung des Täter-Opfer-Ausgleichs und ihre Gefahren." In: T. Kubach, L. Netzig, F. Petzold, M. Schadt and M.

Wandrey (eds.), *TOA-Standards–Ein Handbuch für die Praxis des Täter-Opfer-Ausgleichs.* Bonn, GER: DBH.

—(1995b). *Täter-Opfer-Ausgleich aus der Sicht der Betroffenen.* Hannover, GER: WAAGE Hannover.

—F. Petzold and H. Pfeiffer (1992). *Projektkonzeption zum Modellversuch "Täter-Opfer-Ausgleich im allgemeinen Strafrecht."* Hannover, GER: WAAGE Hannover.

Pfohl, S. (1981). "Labeling Criminals." In: H.L. Ross (ed.), *Law and Deviance.* Beverly Hills, CA: Sage.

Rössner, D. (1992). "Autonomie und Zwang im System der Strafrechtsfolgen." In: G. Arzt, G. Fezer, U. Weber, E. Schluechter and D. Rössner (eds.), *Festschrift für Baumann.* Bielefeld, GER: Verlag Ernst and Werner Gieseking.

Richards, T. and E. von Glasenfeld (1987). "Die Kontrolle von Wahrnehmung und die Konstruktion von Realität." In: S.T. Schmidt (ed.), *Der Diskurs des radikalen Konstruktivismus.* Frankfurt, GER: Suhrkamp.

Schreckling, J. et al. (1992). *Bestandsaufnahme zur Praxis des Täter-Opfer-Ausgleichs in der Bundesrepublik Deutschland.* 3rd ed. Bonn, GER: Federal Ministry of Justice.

Shonholtz, R. (1994). "Neighborhood Justice Systems: Work, Structure, and Guiding Principles." *Mediation Quarterly* 5.

Spittler, G. (1980). "Streitregelung im Schatten des Leviathan." *Zeitschrift für Rechtssoziologie* 6:4.

Stierlin, H. (1992). "Entwürfe der Gerechtigkeit im Lichte der Systemischen Praxis." In: H.R. Fischer, A. Retzer and J. Schweitzer (eds.), *Das Ende der großen Entwürfe.* Frankfurt, GER: Suhrkamp.

Trenczek, T. (1990). "A Review and Assessment of Victim-Offender-Reconciliation Programming in West Germany." In: B. Galaway and J. Hudson (eds.), *Criminal Justice, Restitution, and Reconciliation.* Monsey, NY: Criminal Justice Press.

—(1992). "Towards a Reprivatisation of Social Control? An Assessment of Victim-Offender-Reconciliation." In: Centre d'Estudis Juridics i Formació Especialitzada (ed.), *El Derecho Penal y la Victima.* Barcelona, SP: Author.

—(1996). *Restitution Wiedergutmachung, Schadensersatz oder Strafe* (Restitution, Making Good, Compensation or Punishment?). Freiburg, GER: Nomos Verlag.

Umbreit, M.S. (1990). "The Meaning of Fairness to Burglary Victims." In: B. Galaway and J. Hudson (eds.), *Criminal Justice, Restitution and Reconciliation.* Monsey, NY: Criminal Justice Press.

Wandrey, M. (1994). "Praxisliste des TOA-Servicebüros." In: DBH-Servicebüro (ed.), Bonn, Ger. *TOA-Intern Rundbrief zur Praxis und Weiterentwicklung des Täter-Opfer-Ausgleichs.*

Warnecke, H.J. (1992). *Die fraktale Fabrik—Die Revolution der Unternehmenskultur.* Berlin, GER: Springer.

Watzlawick, P. (1978). *Wie wirklich ist die Wirklichkeit?* München, GER: Piper.

Womack, J.P. and D.T. Jones (1990). *The Machine that Changed the World.* NY: Rawson Associates.

# 14. WHITHER RESTORATIVE JUSTICE IN ENGLAND AND WALES? A PROBATION PERSPECTIVE

by

## John Harding

**Abstract:** *Public policy and correctional practice in England has moved in the direction of increased reliance on institutional provision. Concern is expressed about victims and help offered primarily through practical programs and emotional support to victims. In the 1980s a series of mediation and reparation schemes were developed by probation services, although the expertise gained from these projects has been largely lost because of discontinued funding. Recent national probation standards require probation officers to assess the impact of crime on victims using presentence reports, including an assessment of the offender's attitude and awareness of the consequence of the offense. The recent Home Office Victims Charter takes probation into a new arena by requiring that officers notify victims of parole consideration for any prisoner serving a life sentence. Reparative principles can be built into presentence recommendations in the form of compensation to individual victims or unpaid work for the benefit of the wider community. Probation must use these opportunities to consider the victim's perspective or risk playing an increasingly marginalized role.*

Any discussion about the place of restorative justice in the criminal justice process and outside it must be set in the context of the prevailing zeitgeist. Philips (1995), writing in the wake of a British citizen executed in the electric chair of a Georgia penitentiary, compares the American dilemma of rising crime rates and the authorities' failure to contain it with the British experience: "We too have a Government determined to replace liberal nostrums about criminal rehabilitation with containment and punishment. There are fears that the public has lost so much confidence in the criminal justice system that vengefulness might run rampant. There is indignation when criminals are portrayed as victims. There is confusion about what justice is" (p.23).

Three years previously the picture looked rather different. The U.K. Criminal Justice Act of 1991 came into effect, with the purpose of preventing and reducing crime and providing a more rational and coherent system for dealing with it. The central objectives of the act included:

- More consideration, support and respect for crime victims.
- The introduction of proportionality in sentencing, the greater the crime, the greater the degree of agency intervention.
- A reduction in the use of custody, especially for property offenses but with heightened penalties for violent offenders.
- The consolidation of community sentences as sentences in their own right and no longer as alternatives to custody.
- Effective communication and cooperation between all parts of the criminal justice system through the development of area and national criminal justice consultative committees, including representation by Victim Support Services.

The accepted shibboleths of the act were quickly distanced following the election of a new Conservative government in 1992. The new approach was best symbolized by Mr. Howard, the Home Secretary, who announced to a Conservative Party Conference in October 1993 that prison is effective in the sense that incapacitative sentences protect citizens from predatory crime. This statement stood in stark contrast to that of a predecessor, who framed the Criminal Justice Act of 1991 and said that prison was an expensive way of making bad people worse. New laws were subsequently passed in rapid succession, including the Criminal Justice Act of 1993 and the Criminal Justice and Public Order Bill of 1994, both of which served to strengthen law enforcement, the supposed deterrent effects of conviction and punishment, and the disabling impact of imprisonment. The prison population rose by 20% from 1992 to 1994. These increases are likely to be sustained with the introduction of the Criminal Justice and Public Order Act of 1994, which introduces: secure training centers for 12 to 14 year olds; increases in the maximum custodial sentences for young people aged 15 to 17; restricted the granting of bail; and new criminal offenses relating to demonstrators, squatters, and travellers.

The populist feeling that something must be done to quell the rising crime rate has led to an alliance between ministerial pronouncements and tabloid editorials stressing the need to empower and protect crime victims from the offender. The overriding mood of fear and anger in the public domain disregards the impact of any social and economic influences, such as the high rate of unemployment among offenders of all ages and a drive towards greater degrees of exclusion in the form of the extension of custodial powers for the courts. The debate over how to deal with crime has also engendered further questions about the extent, if any, to which victims should be entitled to influence decisions taken by the courts or the criminal justice services, and the nature of the recognition and support they should receive from society more generally (Faulkner, 1995).

The latest annual report published by the Home Office indicated commitment to helping victims of crime, and ensuring that their rights and interests are recognized and safeguarded (Home Office, 1995a). The Home Office has introduced new powers to allow courts to draw inferences from a defendant's silence. In addition, old-style committal proceedings are being abolished, thus obviating the need for witnesses to give information twice, and a new offense of witness intimidation has been created. National standards in relation to the supervision of offenders in the community, whether subject to community penalties or postrelease from prison, contain powerful messages for the U.K. Probation Service in terms of addressing victim's concerns and interests. In addition, the government can claim substantial assistance in the form of a national grant to Victim Support that provides practical help and emotional support to victims of crime. The grant is also being used to develop a service to help victims and witnesses attending the Crown Court. The Home Secretary, however, has evoked an angry reaction from the victim's lobby and a robust rebuttal from the Law Lords in an attempt to restrict the criminal compensation scheme with a cash-limited, tariff-driven proposal to prevent a doubling of the current £250 million bill to victims of violent crime by the turn of the century.

## DEVELOPMENT OF A PROBATION SERVICE PERSPECTIVE IN RELATION TO CRIME VICTIMS

The Probation Service has moved a long way from being seen as an agency primarily concerned with the rehabilitation of offenders, even though this perception is not necessarily shared by crime victims and the public at large. It is a service that is answerable to a variety of stakeholders including the Home Office, the courts, the Prison Service, and its partnered agencies, and less directly to the wider community. It is principally in the business of reducing offending behavior and protecting the public from further harm. The service is pledged to a holistic approach to offending and needs to articulate the victim dimension in its work. This realization first developed in a piecemeal fashion in the 1980s with probation staff taking a significant advisory role in the formation of a network of victim support schemes and helping establish victim-offender mediation and reparation schemes on a pretrial or post-conviction basis (Marshall and Merry, 1990; Harding, 1989).

The victim dimension in probation work has become a center-stage requirement through probation circulars from the Home Office, expectations contained in its three-year plan for 1995-1998 and national standards for the supervision of offenders in the community. The practical implications for the Probation Service of these policy initiatives cover a continuum of points of intervention, from the first probation contact with the offender in the shaping of presentence reports for the court through the delineation of a victim focus in supervision plans, to the consideration of the victim's interest prior to and on through the release of a prisoner on post-custodial forms of licence. National standards require probation officers writing presentence reports to assess the impact of the crime on the victim through reference to victim statements or other papers available from the Crown Prosecution Service (Home Office, 1995b). The officer is also expected to make an assessment of the offender's attitude towards the victim and the offense and his or her awareness of its consequences, drawing attention to any evidence of acceptance of responsibility, remorse, or guilt and any expressed desire to make amends. Finally, before compiling a proposal for the court, the officer is required to express a judgment on the offender's risk of reoffending and the risk of further harm to the public through the likelihood of either a violent or property crime.

Respondents to the British Crime Survey in 1992 indicated that half of those who were victimized were repeat victims and suffered 81% of all recorded crime. Four percent of the victims experienced four or more crimes in a year and accounted for nearly half of recorded crime (Home Office, 1992). Those most at risk of being repeatedly victimized are among the most vulnerable and disadvantaged members of the community. What are the implications of the research for work with offenders under supervision? First, probation staff need to ensure that the possibility of the offender victimizing the same victim on a repeat basis is explored as an integral part of supervisory work, just as the factors leading to offending are examined and confronted. This approach has become a common feature of work with offenders with respect to domestic violence, sex offending and racial harassment. It also needs to apply to work with burglars where there is a possibility of offenses being carried out on the same properties and with the same individuals. Offenders themselves, or their families, may well have been burglary victims. Skilled staff should examine the offender's own life experience in this respect and try to utilize it in heightening the individual's awareness of the victim's plight.

All the above approaches are secondary in the sense that the offender is not being confronted with the impact of the crime, either by the direct experience of his or her victim or by those of other victims who have suffered a related type of crime. In England and Wales, there have been a limited number of victim-offender mediation schemes that offer the possibility of holding the offender accountable for the crime and allowing some form of amends to be made. A Home Office study of a select number of such schemes in the 1980s showed high satisfaction rates in terms of victim-offender agreements (over 80%); outcomes in relation to reoffending for those participants who had face-to-face contact with their victims were positive if not statistically significant (Marshall and Merry, 1990). But there remains a key debate about the development, ownership and financing of mediation schemes.

Community service offers probation a further means of confronting the offender with the impact of crime, whether it be in crime prevention projects designed to clear up vandalized estates in the inner city or more direct work with the victims of crime through task groups that repair damage committed by burglars to victims' dwellings. Typically, community service projects in Inner London over the past few years have included renovating buildings damaged by crime, painting local youth clubs and community centers, improving and maintaining adventure playgrounds to give young people constructive activities, and participating in environmental projects to improve the appearance of the area. One community service unit has been working with the local victim support scheme and the police crime prevention officer to restore houses damaged by burglary. Community service offenders, led by a work supervisor, carry out essential repairs to a victim's house following a referral by the local victim support coordinator and a house security specification by the local police. Thirty-five victims have had their homes restored, and there is a waiting list of applications. No problems have been reported in supervising the offenders, and no difficulties have arisen between the offenders and the victims for whom they have worked. Part of the success lies in the probation officer visiting the crime victim before the repairs take place to listen to individuals' experiences of victimization and to allay any fears about the community service involvement. Ironically, such a program is costly in comparison to the more traditional types of community service group projects. However, it meets national standards terms of preventing crime, and benefitting the community and offenders (Johnson and Norman, 1995).

Probation and social services departments carry joint supervisory responsibility for offenders under age 18. The departments are enjoined, under national standards, to consider a range of methods in the approved supervision plan. Reparative work, including local environmental improvement and mediation projects with the victims of crime, is highlighted. The emphasis is on challenging the young offender, thereby leading to a greater sense of merited self-respect. The court should be informed in the presentence report if reparative work is proposed as part of the supervision order. There is no point in imposing mediation plans on offenders; they must be ready to change if the process is to have any lasting benefit. Equally, offenders cannot be forced to rethink their lives or take responsibility for their own behavior, they must be willing to work at it. Avril Wood, one of the most experienced mediators in the U.K., stresses that "...if courts imposed mediation, you would be revictimizing the victim. You can't impose a sentence on the victim" (Priestley, 1994).

## VICTIM INVOLVEMENT IN THE PRISONER'S RELEASE

The Home Office Victim's Charter (1990) requires the Probation Service to contact victims, or their relatives when possible, prior to the release of a life sentence prisoner and to take account of their feelings, wishes, or anxieties in the release planning process. The service is also expected to contact the victim or his or her family within two months of sentencing in cases involving serious sexual and other violent offenses. As with lifers, staff are required to notify such victims prior to release so that concerns can be properly expressed to the prison or Parole Board. The Victim's Charter requirement is an example of a major policy shift for probation, imposed from outside, for which probation staff were un-prepared in terms of practice and resourcing (Johnston, 1994). It takes probation into a new area of work that has the potential for a high public profile, especially if victims or their families feel their needs and rights have not been met. The lack of preparation relates, in part, to the loss of impetus by probation in direct work with offenders and their victims fol-lowing the Home Office sponsored mediation and reparation pilot projects in the mid-1980s; without further Home Office backing many of the skills developed in such programs were lost.

One probation area, West Yorkshire, was prepared for the Home Office Victim's Charter requirement through its continued funding of the Leeds Mediation and Reparation Unit. Staff with mediation skills were in a position to provide specialist services to victim's families prior to the release of their offenders from life sentences. In essence, the probation officer responsible for the post-sentence or pre-release planning of a prisoner returning to the service area refers the case to a mediation worker with the Leeds Unit so that he or she can start the process of consultation-giving with the victim's family.

Johnston (1994) found that victim's families were appreciative of in-formation about a prisoner's release because it helped them to plan ahead especially if the prisoner was released to the local area; it counter-acted disinformation spread by others; and it demonstrated that the au-thorities cared about the impact of decisions on victims. They also wel-comed the opportunity to express feelings to the mediator about the impact of the offense on family members. Following a session with the mediator, some of the interviewed victims or relatives sought further communication with the prisoner either directly or indirectly to find an-swers to unresolved issues. In one instance, a mother and daughter met the offender who made an arson attack on their house. Victims and of-fender were known to each other prior to the offense. The victim ac-cepted the apology, and the offender explained why their house was at-tacked. The victims felt reassured by the probation officer's release plan for the offender, and their concern about the offender returning to the local area was reduced. The process requires good communication among the home probation officer who will supervise the parolee, the mediator, and the victim's family. Such planning will involve careful risk assessment, motivational issues, and the willingness of all parties to meet and explore the process prior to the prisoner's release.

The West Yorkshire experience raises some fundamental issues for probation as to how contact with victims and their relatives are managed on a post-conviction, pre-release basis. Two approaches are recommended. The first is the West Yorkshire model, whereby a local mediation service, independent of mainstream probation but funded by it, acts as an honest broker between the probation officer responsible for planning aftercare of the prisoner and the victim's relatives. The second model is based on the contracting out of work by the probation authority with the victim's family to a voluntary agency offering mediation and support skills on a fee or grant basis. Currently, probation areas in England and Wales have the authority to use 5% of the total revenue expenditure to engage voluntary agencies in carrying out complementary tasks. Harris (1992), Nellis (1995) and others have argued that the probation officer of the future should engage not only with the statutory supervision of offenders but also with communities, victims, and potential victims. Harris suggests that it is no longer tenable to hold to the idea that the probation officer is solely identified with the behavior and needs of offenders, as crime hurts communities and offenders stand a good chance of becoming victims. Instead, probation must show a willingness to engage in issues of public concern and protection, not least in taking a fully responsible part in reducing victim's fears prior to the release of prisoners convicted of serious crimes against persons. Probation of the future could become increasingly marginalized without such a shift in practice and staff perceptions.

## SOME FURTHER FINAL ISSUES

In 1995, the Home Secretary issued a consultation document about punishment in the community (Home Office, 1995c). The main proposals are for:

- The introduction of a single integrated community sentence replacing and incorporating all the current orders available to adult courts.
- The matching of sentence elements to the three principals of punishment in the community: restriction of liberty, reparation and the prevention of reoffending.
- Increased discretion for the courts to determine the content of community sentences in individual cases, in particular, assessing the weight given to the three principals in the light of the offense and the likely response of the offender.

· The removal of the present requirement that offenders consent to community orders.

The reparative principal is envisaged as compensation to the individual victim or unpaid work for the benefit of the wider community. There is an expectation that the probation officer preparing a report would make an assessment of the suitability of reparative activity in every case where a report has been requested. Mediation between victim and offender was not mentioned, but if the proposal is carried through to legislation there is no barrier to the probation officer developing such a process as part of a supervision plan. The issue of consent is key: engaging the motivation of the offender is not just an issue of compliance with the terms and conditions of a court-based order, but a tangible sign of willingness to face up to the uncomfortable messages about offending behavior and the impact of the crime on victims and their relatives. The proposals may provide a welcome challenge to the Probation Service to consider the centrality of the reparative process in sentencing, but they do nothing to address the resources that would be required to restore the momentum of victim-offender mediation as an essential part of a supervision plan, nor do they address how such processes should be managed. The victim dimension in probation work has increased with government expectations and staff awareness, but the place of restorative justice and how it is managed rests uneasily under current arrangements.

Governmental priorities are directed towards an expansion of custodial plans for young and adult offenders alike. Such exclusive policies are only likely to confirm, rather than challenge delinquent identities leaving offenders to neutralize the impact of what they have done or minimize the gravity of their behavior. Ironically, when asked about appropriate penalties for offenders, victims of crime favor restitutional responses, particularly community service and the use of the compensation order. Hough and Mayhew (1985) found "...no support at all for the view that the courts are too soft for victims' liking. There is no substantial mismatch in terms of severity of sentences...." There seems to be a clear desire amongst victims that offenders should make some redress for the harm they have caused". Probation must seek every opportunity to amplify the victim perspective by seizing occasions to implant restorative justice as a central part of the overall supervisory process, and by playing back the significance of that reconciling process to policymakers, local communities, and other parties in the criminal justice system.

# REFERENCES

Faulkner, D. (1995). "The Criminal Justice Act of 1991: Policy, Legislation and Practice." In: D. Ward and M. Lacey (eds.), *Probation, Working for Justice*. London, UK: Whiting & Birch.

Harding, J. (1989). "Reconciling Mediation in Criminal Justice." In: M. Wright and B. Galaway (eds.), *Mediation and Criminal Justice*. London, UK: Sage.

Harris, R. (1992). *Crime, Criminal Justice and the Probation Service*. London, UK: Routledge.

Hough, M. and P. Mayhew (1985). *Taking Account of Crime: Key Findings from the 1984 British Crime Survey* (Home Office Research Study No. 86). London, UK: Her Majesty's Stationery Office.

Johnston, P. (1994). *Victims of Violence* (Cropwood Fellowship Paper). Cambridge, UK: Institute of Criminology.

—and A. Norman (1995). *Making Amends*. London, UK: Inner London Probation Service.

Marshall, T. and S. Merry (1990). *Crime and Accountability: Victim Offender Mediation in Practice*. London, UK: Her Majesty's Stationery Office.

Nellis, M. (1995). "Probation Values for the 1990s." *Howard Journal of Criminal Justice* 34(1):27-43.

Philips, M. (1995). "Justice for Victims." *The London Observer*, April 12, p.23.

Priestley, P. (1994). "Crime without Punishment." *Guardian Newspaper* (London), September 30.

U.K. Home Office (1990) *Victim's Charter*. London, UK: Her Majesty's Stationery Office.

—(1992). *British Crime Survey*. London, UK: Her Majesty's Stationery Office.

—(1995a). *Annual Report 1994/95*. London, UK: Her Majesty's Stationery Office.

—(1995b). *Strengthening Punishment in the Community* (Green Paper). London, UK: Her Majesty's Stationery Office.

# 15. HOW POLICE OFFICERS MANAGE DIFFICULT SITUATIONS: THE PREDOMINANCE OF SOOTHING AND SMOOTHING STRATEGIES

by

## Michael Walter

and

## Andrea Wagner

**Abstract:** *This study examines the management of 128 conflict situations by uniformed police in Bonn, GER. Data were obtained by means of participant observation and were categorized according to areas of conflict and conflict management strategies. Conflict situations were dealt with passively (cooling-off of the conflict, downgrading the conflict potential, and delegating the final resolution to other institutions) in more cases than active intervention by the police, even in situations such as domestic conflicts and conflicts involving physical attacks in which the parties expected active participation of the police. Further research should investigate the factors that influence strategies used by the police.*

Criminological research in the 1970s frequently viewed the police as an institution that declared socially disadvantaged groups to be criminal (labelling approach). Police sanctions were primarily aimed at marginals, in violation of the principle of equality before the law. Criminologists, in their studies of the police, have endeavored to reveal processes pertaining to the biased ascribing of criminal activity. The studies focused on proactive activities of the police to clarify conditions under which police officers developed the suspicion that a criminal offense had been committed (Feest and Blankenburg, 1972).

The present study assumed that the uniformed police can be understood as an agency responsible for the maintenance of public order rather than an agent of criminalization. Reactive behavior, which characterizes more than 90% of police activity relating to criminal prosecution, was accorded a greater priority than proactive behavior. The study focused on the strategies and techniques with which the police resolved reported conflicts.

The concept of privatization formed the theoretical background of the study. Two aspects were emphasized. One was the model of mediation. To what extent could the conflict resolutions be understood as a form of police mediation? Secondly, alternatives to criminalization and punishment were considered. Management strategies which are intended to maintain public order may show a tendency towards de-dramatization and also towards decriminalization. Under what conditions are offenses recorded (criminality ascribed) despite the de facto opportunity to privatize them?

The police have the power to designate an incident either as a private matter or as a public one. The term conflicts (Aubert, 1972) indicates incidents which have not yet been assigned to one of these categories by police officers. Conflicts frequently arise through a private individual being unable to cope with an incident and who subsequently requests the help of the police, using them as a remedial institution or social fire service (Hanak et al., 1989; Lehne, 1992). The call for help mainly concerns interpersonal problems between private individuals, who are often different from one another and who also differ with respect to the amount of power which they possess. The parties to the conflict often have antagonistic objectives. The resolution of the conflict by police officers is in the form of intervention or interaction with a third party (Bühl, 1972). This constellation has two implications for the nature and/or quality of the conflict resolution. Firstly, the police officers bring their official public and possibly even their personal interests into the situation, accompanied by their partly professional, partly individually tinted views and understanding of reality. They define the situation independent of the views of the parties to the conflict, although they are bound to a certain framework. Secondly, their solution does not encompass all matters in which the conflict is rooted. Police, primarily, focus on conflict moments which transformed the situation into a disturbance of public order, therefore triggering the intervention of the police. A resolution of the conflict by the police does not necessarily mean that the matter is concluded as far as the parties to the conflict are concerned. It merely leads to a termination of the disturbance of the peace and makes it appear that public order has been restored. The repertoire of possible modes of conflict resolution behavior ranges from the sovereign, authoritative type of intervention, through a more conciliatory type of intervention, to a passive attitude of restraint. The primary aim of the study was to determine the characteristics of police behavior inductively from the available data. This chapter, therefore, focuses on a description and analysis of the ways in which police officers deal with calls for help from private individuals.

## METHOD

Data was collected using a non-standardized participant observation method. Operations of the uniformed police of the city of Bonn were observed between May 15 and November 22, 1991. The operations were assigned by radio from an operations center. On rare occasions, less than 1%, they were performed on the initiative of the police officers themselves (routine checks). The operations were carried out with automobiles. They were performed by three different groups (usually of two male police officers each) in a regional area and from all three shifts. All observations were made by the same psychologist who, along with other observers, participated in the journeys. The psychologist made detailed records on tape that were later transcribed and made available for evaluation. The records were not made according to any particular predefined structure, but contained continuous descriptions, prefaced solely by the date of the observation, the shift, and the group concerned.

Figure 15.1 provides an overview of the total number of cases. A total of 397 assignments were recorded and transcribed. Only those cases which concerned conflicts to be resolved were of interest. The 113 cases in which a concrete punishable offense was to be prosecuted were filtered out as, were 13 operations which were carried out in order to prevent danger, and a miscellaneous category of 90 operations. These mainly concerned various police services and activities which could not be unambiguously assigned to one of the other groups of cases. This filtering out left 181 operations which concerned a social interpersonal conflict. But even this number was reduced. The police terminated the operation before actual police intervention took place in 48 cases. Of the remaining cases, no police operations took place in five, leaving 128 operations in which conflict-resolving intervention actually took place.

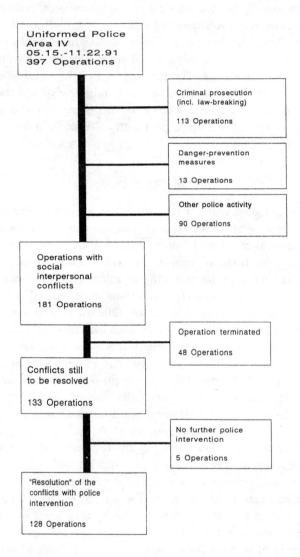

*Fig. 15.1.*

Two people participated in the conflict in the majority of cases (55). In about a quarter of the cases (32), there were three participants. Other persons, who could not be assigned to one of the conflicting parties but who were witnesses, were present in almost half the cases (59). The operations to resolve conflicts generally involved a person responsible for the conflict (offender) and an injured party (victim). In the majority of cases, the responsible party was present at the site of the incident (101). Sometimes he/she was contacted later (11). Even so, in 21 cases, no responsible party was present. The injured party was, in most cases, an individual natural person (96). In the remaining cases, legal persons or supra-individual institutions (department stores, etc.) constituted the injured party, most of which were represented by a natural person. Males dominated in the majority of cases, both as the injured party and as the person responsible for the injury. A man was the injured person in 55 cases, and in 94 of 122 cases in which the responsible party was known, the latter was also a man. Injury was caused by a woman in only 21 cases. A group of persons constituted the injured party in only four cases, and in seven cases, a group was the party responsible for the conflict. The operations center was informed by the injured party (40) or by someone representing the injured party (23) in half the cases. In the remaining cases, the police were generally unable to locate the informant.

Traffic conflicts comprised a total of 42 incidents, including road accidents, cases of unlawfully leaving the scene of an accident, and obstructing the flow of traffic. The road accidents usually involved only damage to property (24); only rarely was damage to persons involved (4). The leaving the scene of an accident cases were also related to road accidents. Of the latter, those involving damage to property only (7) could be differentiated from those involving damage to persons (1). An obstruction to traffic (six cases in total) consisted, for example, of an automobile parked in such a manner as to prevent another from driving away. A total of 26 incidents were domestic conflicts. Most of these concerned a disturbance of the peace in a house (18). The accusation that another inhabitant caused too much noise was usually an expression of an existing conflict situation between neighbors. Family disputes, either between husband and wife or between parents and children (4), were a second category of cases. The final category comprised cases in which an intruder had infringed a prohibition concerning entry to a particular premises (4). Property conflicts comprised a total of 54 incidents. Various types of theft, from shoplifting to break-ins (24), and damage to property (21) constituted the major part of the cases. A few cases of riding without a ticket (5) and of fraudulent behavior were also recorded. Conflicts with physical attacks (42) comprised incidents in which a person was physically injured (14), attacked (14), threatened (8), molested (3) or verbally attacked (3).

Some incidents were classified under more than one category because injury to persons and damage to property frequently appeared in combination. The 128 operations were in response to 164 conflicts that can be summarized as follows:

| | | |
|---|---|---|
| Traffic | (42) | 26% |
| Domestic | (26) | 16% |
| Property and material goods | (54) | 33% |
| Physical/personal | (42) | 26% |
| Total number | (164) | 100% |

# CONFLICT MANAGEMENT AND STRATEGIES

## Types of Strategies

A total of nine different strategies were defined, based on the descriptions of the different ways in which the police officers involved in the operation behaved. The primary objective was to abstract recurring actions inductively from the case material. Nine types of conflict management strategies were identified.

### 1. Gathering Information

Taking down the particulars of the parties involved and asking questions regarding what had happened provide an opportunity to defuse the situation, as well as to obtain information. The parties to the conflict are occupied and are able to let off steam. The procedure is drawn out even further by the examination of identification papers and by inspecting the objects and sites concerned. The parties to the conflict each speak with a different police officer and are, of necessity, separated from each other for a period of time. The cooling-off phase can be drawn out even further by means of further questioning.

## 2. De-Escalation by Soothing, Separating the Opponents and Physical Intervention

Varying types of soothing talk are frequently used in association with the separate questioning of the parties. The opponents are separated from one another and threatened with physical intervention, which threat is subsequently realized if necessary.

A slightly confused, elderly gentleman molested his wife in their mutual home, causing the woman to call for help. The police officers spoke to the man separately, and attempted to soothe him, at the same time threatening to take him to the station should his wife make another complaint. The officers soothed the woman, who was a nervous wreck, by assuring her that they would return if the molestation continued. When the police were called to the house not long after, they took the man with them to the police station.

## 3. Downgrading the Conflict in Order to Simplify Management

Plain events are easier to handle than complicated matters and, therefore, police officers are interested in reconstructing the events as simple ones removing potentially escalating moments.

After the police officers had finished interpreting and recording a rear-end collision, the injured party complained of a headache, which he postulated was caused by the accident. After the police officers had successfully pacified him, the original classification as an accident only involving damage to the bodywork could be retained.

## 4. Delegation of the Resolution of the Conflict to Other Agencies

The conflicting parties may be referred to other institutions, especially those responsible for matters of civil law. The police officers thereby deny that the problem has a public aspect to it, defining it solely as a private matter. The referral to another institution responsible for the matter is, at the same time, understood to be a service.

The interpretation of the events in the case of a road accident was clear to the police officers. One of the parties to the accident, however, was not satisfied with this. The police refused to record what had happened and remarked that the woman could contact the insurance company of the opposing party to the accident if she thought she had a right to claim for damages. The refusal to make a record of the accident was underlined with the threat that a precise recording of the accident would lead to the woman being fined.

## 5. Demonstration of a Superior Position by Behaving in an Authoritarian Manner

The police act as an embodiment of the authority of the State in order to induce one of the parties to the conflict to obey. Threatening with intervention and sanctions is characteristic of this, as is a demand that an order be obeyed within a certain time limit. This course of action also serves to prevent further work and to re-privatize the existing conflict, since the police officers assume that opposing parties will obey and that an escalation of the conflict will therefore be avoided.

Music played too loud in a restaurant constituted a nuisance to a neighbor; the police officers ordered the owner to ensure that the volume of the music was turned down by threatening to inspect the identification papers of the employees and the guests and to inform the governmental trade supervisory office if he did not do so.

## 6. Clarificatory Intervention by Acting as an Agent of Public Order by Means of Concrete Control and Safety Activities

The activities are forms of police control which may not be performed by others. The police activities concerned serve both to clearly define the situation and to supply remedial measures in the form of technical and practical intervention (Hanak *et al.*, 1989, pp.28-29).

## 7. Applying Sanctions

These strategies range from a simple informal verbal caution and admonition, through on-the-spot cautionary fines, to filing a complaint and criminal prosecution. The conflict is therefore resolved by sanctioning one or both of the parties involved. Reporting of an offense also means that the case must be passed on to the public prosecutor.

## 8. Bilateral Intervention

These are strategies that are to the advantage of one party to the conflict and to the disadvantage of the other party. According to the statement made by a prostitute, she was physically attacked by a client.

The man supposedly felt that he had not got what he had paid for. He refused to leave the brothel. The police officers banned him from entering the premises and took him into custody, thereby simultaneously protecting the prostitute from further attack.

## 9. Performance of Services

Police officers may resolve the conflict by providing services. Police officers helped a driver whose automobile was damaged by a maneuvering truck driver, without anyone noticing, to find the responsible party so that a claim for damages could be made.

## Use of Strategies

A total of 416 strategies was utilized in the 128 cases involving conflict management. The police used one strategy in 27 cases and two to four strategies in the majority of cases (72). Five to ten different strategies were applied in the remaining 29 cases. A mean of 2.37 strategies was used. The 416 strategies are distributed as:

| | | | |
|---|---|---|---|
| 1. | Gathering information | (77) | 19% |
| 2. | De-escalation | (59) | 14% |
| 3. | Downgrading | (35) | 8% |
| 4. | Delegation | (29) | 7% |
| 5. | Demonstration of authority | (32) | 8% |
| 6. | Clarificatory intervention | (57) | 14% |
| 7. | Sanctioning | (63) | 15% |
| 8. | Bilateral intervention | (37) | 9% |
| 9. | Performance of services | (27) | 6% |
| | Total | (416) | 100% |

The nine strategies were combined into four groups on a scale ranging from passive to active intervention. These four combined categories are:

1. Passive cooling-off (gathering information and de-escalation, 33% of strategies utilized).

2. Downgrading and delegating (downgrading and delegation, 16% of strategies utilized).

3. Demonstrative behavior (demonstration of authority and clarificatory intervention, 21% of strategies utilized).

4. Active intervention (bilateral intervention, sanctioning and performance of services, 31% of strategies utilized).

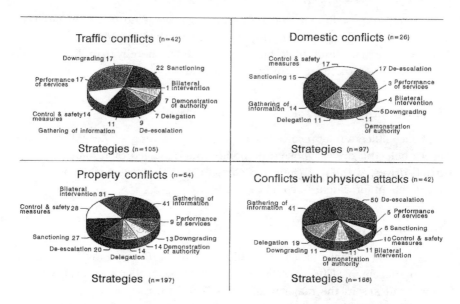

*Fig. 15.2.* Police conflict resolution strategies (number of classifications in relation to conflict category).

The passive strategies are in the majority. Within the active forms of intervention, the sanctioning procedures are prevalent, while the performance of services constitutes a relatively small proportion.

Figure 15.2 shows that the various strategies of the police are applied in differing degrees with respect to the four areas of conflict. One of the most striking observations is that more than half the strategies in the case of physical attacks consisted of typical cooling-off strategies, whereas the actual service portion remained very small. The police officers were especially concerned with reducing the drama of the situation. The distribution of the different strategies with respect to traffic conflicts was more balanced, and the service percentage was also greater. The relatively low percentage of sanctionings with respect to physical attacks, in comparison with traffic conflicts or property conflicts, is surprising. In the case of physical attacks, the police took the opportunity to allow the parties to let off steam and to reprivatize the conflict, an opportunity which would have been lost if sanctioning action had been taken.

Figure 15.3 shows the distribution of the passive-active intervention scale by the four areas of conflict. A distinction had to be made between

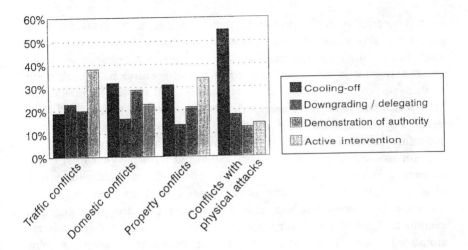

*Fig. 15.3.* Police conflict resolution strategies in relation to conflict categories (as percentages).

the management of pecuniary conflicts and those which were more concerned with the individual. Traffic problems and property conflicts are usually only related to money. With respect to the latter, the police intervened comparatively more frequently, were more active, and served the parties according to expectations. The situation was alleviated by relatively clear instructions as to how to proceed.

The situation was different with regard to domestic conflicts and conflicts where physical attacks were concerned. The parties were often left to sort their problems out themselves, although these incidents can have far-reaching significance for those concerned. The police were mainly concerned with restoring public order, placating the parties, and delegating management of the situation. They seldom performed any services themselves; passive strategies were more likely to be used than with the management of pecuniary conflicts.

## CONCLUSIONS

The police were confronted with circumstances containing elements of conflict in 34% of the situations encountered when answering calls for help. An analysis of the strategies employed in such conflict situations showed that, in the main, the conflicts were not actually resolved, but that strategies were employed which removed the public order aspect from the conflicts and reprivatized them. Among these strategies were cooling-off, de-escalating, downgrading, and delegating to other social institutions. Such passive resolutions are used for problem areas in which active intervention is expected or would seem to be logical, such as domestic conflicts and those involving personal physical attacks. The behavior of the police maybe experienced as a refusal to act. Active intervention occurred more frequently in road accidents and property or pecuniary conflicts. Even active forms of conflict resolution were not often of a mediatory nature, but were expressed as behavior which could be viewed as a form of sanctioning. The research was preliminary and consisted mainly of the creation of categories and of the recording of frequencies. The conditions determining different types of activity were not examined. Further studies must clarify when and on what grounds restorative justice is achieved and why the police frequently merely employ passive strategies.

## REFERENCES

Aubert, V. (1972). "Interessenkonflikt und Wertkonflikt: Zwei Typen des Konflikts und der Konfliktlösung." In W.L. Bühl (ed.), *Konflikt und Konfliktstrategie: Ansätze zu einer soziologischen Konflikttheorie*, pp.178-205. München, GER: Nymphenburger Verlagshandlung.

Bühl, W.L. (1972). "Einleitung: Entwicklungslinien der Konfliktsoziologie." In: W.L. Bühl (ed)., *Konflikt und Konfliktstrategie: Ansätze zu einer soziologischen Konflikttheorie*, pp.9-64. München, GER: Nymphenburger Verlagshandlung.

Feest, J. and E. Blankenburg (1972). *Die Definitionsmacht der Polizei: Strategien der Strafverfolgung und soziale Selektion*. Düsseldorf, GER: Universitätsverlag.

Feltes, T. (1988). "Polizeiliches Alltagshandeln. Konsequenzen für eine 'Neue Polizei' aus einer Analyse von Notrufen und Funkstreifeneinsatzanlässen in der Bundesrepublik Deutschland." In: G. Kaiser, H. Kury, and H. Albrecht (eds.), *Kriminologische Forschung der 80er Jahre: Projektberichte aus der Bundesrepublik Deutschland*, pp.125-156. Freiburg, GER: Eigenverlag Max-Plank-Institut für ausländisches und internationales Strafrecht.

Hanak, G., J. Stehr and H. Steinert (1989). *Ärgernisse und Lebenskatastrophen: Über den Alltäglichen Umgang mit Kriminalität*. Bielefeld, GER: AJZ Verlag.

Lehne, W. (1992). "Die Polizei Dienstleistungsbetrieb oder Institution staatlicher Herrschaftssicherung? Thesen zur Integration Zweier 'Polizeikonzepte'." *Kriminologisches Journal, Polizei-Politik*, 4. Beiheft, pp.34-45.

# 16. THE ROLE OF SHAME IN GOING STRAIGHT: A STUDY OF FORMER OFFENDERS*

## by

## Julie Leibrich

**Abstract:** A study of former offenders found that shame was a significant feature in decisions to go straight. It was the most commonly mentioned reason for going straight and the most commonly mentioned cost of offending. Three kinds of shame were evident: public humiliation, personal disgrace, and private remorse. Private remorse was the most influential and was triggered by an individual offending their personal morality—coming to think that their offending was wrong. There needs to be a strategic framework which simultaneously increases the costs of offending and benefits of desisting, and decreases the benefits of offending and costs of desisting. Restorative programs need to encourage offenders to evaluate a cost-benefit analysis of continuing to offend. Reintegrative shaming can be part of this process and is likely to be most effective when it results both in personal disgrace and private remorse. Offenders need support to go straight, and shaming which continues beyond their decision to go straight may impede them.

This chapter is based on the in-depth study of former offenders who examined the nature and process of going straight (Leibrich, 1993). Former offenders are experts on desistence from crime, but there are very few such studies, perhaps because of the practical and ethical difficulties of such research. The only three reported studies (Meisenhelder, 1977; Shover, 1985; Pinsonneault, 1985) revealed important information

*I thank my colleagues in the Department of Justice, Geoff Dunn, Mark Jacobs, Angela Lee, Vivienne Morrell and Ruth Wilkie, and also Judge Fred McElrea, for their valuable comments on this article.

about the process of going straight, but they looked solely at imprisoned male property offenders, used availability samples, and did not control for the amount of time since the last conviction. The present study looked at both men and women who had committed a variety of offences and whose last sentence was supervision (which puts a person under the supervision of a probation officer for between six months and two years). The sample was random and the time since the last conviction was approximately three years. The research was ethnographic and conducted from an atheoretical stance. The findings shed light on two of the current theories of desistance from crime, the rational choice theory and the theory of reintegrative shaming.

## THE STUDY

Forty-eight men and women from various ethnic backgrounds took part in the study. Two of the 50 people interviewed said that they were innocent of the offence for which they had received supervision and were excluded from this study. They were a random sample from one of four probation regions in New Zealand; the response rate was extremely high at 78%. The participants had moderately serious criminal histories, with an average of five convictions each, and represented a wide range of offences. Their average age was 32 at the time of the interview; only a third had formal educational qualifications and less than half were in paid employment. They were interviewed in their own homes for an average of two hours. In the first part of the interview, the person was encouraged to talk generally about their experiences; in the second part, they were asked a set of semi-structured questions. The interviews were audio-taped and transcribed verbatim. There was a systematic thematic analysis of the overall material as well as 12 case studies (Leibrich, 1993, 1994).

When the study began, a working definition of going straight was "not having offended since the last conviction". It soon became clear, however, that, to many participants, going straight meant being honest—not stealing, not ripping people off, and leading a responsible life. Only 25 of the 48 participants had totally stopped offending, yet almost all said they were going straight. This was because they perceived that their offending since the last conviction was less serious or less frequent.

The initial working definition was modified by the participants' perception of going straight. It became "not having committed the same or as serious an offence since the last conviction". Offence seriousness was defined according to Spier and his colleagues (1991). A total of 37 out of 48 people were classified as going straight, 25 said that they had not reoffended at all, and 12 had continued to offend to some extent but less seriously and, almost always, less frequently. An example of this included a person convicted of burglary, who no longer committed that offence but occasionally smoked cannabis. Eleven people were classified as not going straight because they were either still committing the offence for which they had been convicted or were now committing a more serious offence and had not been caught.

## REASONS FOR GOING STRAIGHT

Nearly everyone, 35 out of 37 people, said that they knew why they had given up crime. They gave an average of three reasons each, and there was a total of 22 distinct reasons, which were grouped into those which dissuaded people from crime and those which persuaded people to go straight.

### Dissuaders

Shame was the most commonly mentioned dissuader, described by a total of 19 people. There appeared to be three kinds of shame experienced: public humiliation, personal disgrace, and private remorse. Some people talked about more than one of these kinds of shame.

*Public humiliation* was the experience of having their behavior exposed in front of total strangers. Joseph, a Maori man in his thirties, convicted of assaulting his wife, felt utterly humiliated by his court appearance, because of the opportunity it gave for complete strangers to peer into his life:

> When I went in they read the charge out and it's an open court, you've got all the people in there and a lot of the ones that are in there, a lot just go in to sit and see what people get and what you're up for. And that was degrading for me too, you know.

Sasha, a Fijian woman in her twenties, convicted of shoplifting, also found the court experience harrowing:

> I cried. I couldn't help it... That's the worst bit, standing there in front, standing in the court room where these people are sort of look-

ing at you and staring at you... Yeah that was really horrible...I don't
think I'd ever want to go through what I went through that day... I'd
never do it again.

*Personal disgrace* was the experience of having their behavior exposed to people they either simply knew or loved and respected. This
disgrace was particularly painful when it also affected people close to
them. Sasha also experienced personal disgrace because she lost face
with her parents. Three years later, she still had to keep her offence se-
cret from her younger sisters. Rose, a European woman in her twenties,
convicted of drug offences, had been leading what she called a double
life for several years. Her court appearance finally exposed her:

> Five people went up on drug charges before me, including a good
> friend of mine, and ended up in jail, different drug, just cleaning up
> at the time. I went up after her, you know, and I was feeling really de-
> graded and sick. I knew the court registrar and I knew the Maori
> Warden and I'd met the court usher and I just felt like all these
> people knew what I'd been up to. And up until that stage I had man-
> aged to live a real double life between work and home. God knows
> how I managed to keep hold of my job..... Standing up in the court
> room I think was the most lowest point in my life and I didn't want to
> get any lower than that.

Similarly, Petelo, a Samoan man in his sixties, convicted of assault, explained through a translator the disgrace he had brought on the family
name:

> He says he was really ashamed, not only himself but the family name,
> you know. Sort of it's a collective sort of thing. I mean the shame not
> only falls on him but brothers, sisters. Maybe it's different from the
> Palagi (European) point of view because so many 'Turners' and so
> many 'Smiths' and things like that. But with the Samoans there's not
> very many (Petelo's surname), not many you've seen here. So once it's
> in the paper, all the Samoans know it's only me.

Grace, a European woman in her sixties, had a long history of shoplifting and had still not told her grown-up children about her several convictions. As she began to make new connections in her local community,
the prospect of personal disgrace was the strongest deterrent for going
straight:

> I really think I'd jump over the bridge if I took anything and got
> caught, I couldn't face people, I couldn't face the people that I am

friendly with at singing alone, you know... I'd be ashamed, you know, because I've got into a nice little clientele with the singers, and I would be very ashamed if anything should happen.

*Private remorse* was the experience of having offended one's own personal morality. This kind of shame seemed to be the most painful and most enduring in its effect. Some people used the interview as a kind of confessional. Maggi, a Tokelau Island woman in her thirties, had denied a fraud offence, even to her family, right up to the time of the interview, which she consciously used as an opportunity to confess:

I've been trying so hard to forget about it. And I said Oh no, it had to come out one day. I've got to tell *someone*. I think it's good telling you about it because I don't *know* you! And then I'll think back. Oh! I'm glad I told you! I'm *glad* I told someone. It's out in the open.

She described her extreme guilt and shame:

I've been carrying this heavy burden, you know, when I do remember it for a couple of days and then I feel so guilty I don't know. I don't know why I feel this way... Sometimes when I think about it, I think back and I remember what I did. I remember what I went through. And then I just burst into tears and I start shaking, my body starts shaking, my hands and you know.... I don't think anyone knows how sorry I am that I ever did it. Regret. You know I regret that I ever did what I did.

Samuel, a Rarotongan man in his twenties, convicted of theft, had an extremely strong sense of private remorse. His account of shame shows the distinctions between the different kinds of shame. He had never been able to talk about his offence to his girlfriend, Cheyanne, because he was worried that he would lose face with her. He decided to use the interview as a way of telling her about it. Fortunately, Cheyanne made him feel all right about things. In talking about his relief, he depicted the distinction between personal disgrace and private remorse:

It's relieved me quite a lot to talk about it. More than what I expected, actually. That's quite funny. Because Cheyanne started laughing about it and I felt good. I didn't feel as embarrassed as I did then. But still deep down inside, it is a big deal to me, something I was very concerned with. I know it's something that I will just never forget and will always be there with me.

Asked about how he felt about having a record, Samuel made the distinction between public humiliation and private remorse. He was not so concerned about the record of his conviction, as long as it was kept confidential. But "It's always going to be in here [pointing to his heart]. That record will always be there."

Other dissuaders mentioned by at least four people were worse penalties next time (11), distress due to time in a police cell (6), loss of children/partners/friend (6), too much anxiety from criminal activity (4), and ill-health (4).

## Persuaders

The development of self-respect was the most frequently mentioned persuader for going straight, and was described by a total of ten people. Self-respect is partly an absence of shame and relates more to overcoming personal disgrace and private remorse than public humiliation. One of the clearest accounts of the development of self respect was given by Rose, who had been so ashamed at her court appearance. By confronting her addiction, and leaving an abusive relationship, Rose finally realised her own worth and discovered a sense of self-respect, which persuaded her that going straight was worthwhile:

> Drugs cost me my life! Self esteem, self respect, honesty, trustworthiness, loyalty.... Loss of basically all the principles of life that keep a normal person together. By stopping, I got it all back, another chance to live, just being able to say who I am, to get, you know, I just got it all back, I just got given everything back. Slowly but surely. Freedom, a new way of life.

David, a Chinese man in his thirties, convicted of assault, talked about his sense of shame and worthlessness at the time of the offence. Gradually, through a new relationship and new job, he became increasingly convinced of his value and able to try new things:

> I realised that I was worth something... I learnt that I was a person and I had feelings that had to be cared for just like anybody else. And I learned that I was a lot more valuable than what I was portrayed to be.... I don't know, something just made me realise I'm a much more valuable person than I thought... I had to look deep inside myself to say well can I do this or can't I? Of course I can do it. If I don't give myself the opportunity I'll never know and I'll be saying if only I could, if only I could. I'm not going to be an if only.

Grace explained how good she felt about not shoplifting:

> I feel better about myself. I honestly do, there's no two ways about it, and it's a nice feeling. It's a nice feeling when you know, you know you're taking things and you're going to pay for them and doing the right way you know, it really is.

Page, a European man in his forties, with a history of serious property and assault crimes, had given up an opulent lifestyle to go straight. He made the point, very clearly, that he does not offend now because he has something he really values, "I've got everything to lose. I would lose my self-respect. I'd lose my job I suppose. And I'd lose the respect of a hell of a lot of people that've taken a hell of a long time to respect me."

Other persuaders mentioned by at least four people were wanting to meet family responsibilities (9), the birth of a child to themselves or their partner (9), reassessing what mattered in life to them (8), finding a partner (5), and finding faith in God (5).

## A Cost–Benefit Analysis of Going Straight

One set of questions asked all the participants about the costs and benefits of offending, and asked those who were going straight about the costs and benefits of going straight. Virtually everyone (35 of 36 people who were going straight and all of the 11 who were still offending) thought that there was at least one cost in offending. One offender was not asked about the costs and benefits of offending because of the circumstances of the crime. Shame was the most commonly mentioned cost, described by 17 of the 36 people going straight. Only two of the 11 people still offending mentioned shame as a cost; both of these were referring to earlier offending which they had since stopped (rape in one case and theft in the other). Other costs mentioned by at least four people were paying fines and court fees (6 going straight, 3 not), getting caught (6,0) having a record (0,6), loss of licence (3,1), and loss of friends (3,1).

About two-thirds of the participants (21 of 36 people going straight and eight of the 11 people still offending) identified at least one benefit of offending. Those mentioned by at least four people were getting goods and money (8 going straight, 4 not), meeting emotional needs (7,1), the thrill/buzz of stealing (5,1), the convenience of getting home (2,2), and the pleasure of a drug trip (3,1). The three people who were still offending, but who saw no benefit in it, were drunk drivers. Nearly all those going straight, 33 of 37, thought that there was at least one benefit to going straight. Feeling good about oneself, having a clear conscience, and being respected by others, all involve an absence of shame. Fourteen people mentioned at least one of these, which is quite consistent with what they said about developing a sense of self-respect as a persuader. Several people made the point that experiencing the benefits could be a slow process. Other benefits mentioned by at least four people were less hassle from the police (7), having a better life (6), and freedom (4). Four people were going straight, despite seeing no benefit in doing so. One of these had stopped because of serious illness; another in order to win a bet; and two were the same people who did not know why they had gone straight. Only 12 of 37 people going straight identified any costs in stopping offending. The only cost mentioned by at least four people was loss of goods and income.

It is possible to extend the economic model, and make a crude cost benefit analysis in which perceived benefits minus perceived costs equal either net gain or net loss. Looking at the 36 people going straight as a group, there was a perceived net loss in offending and perceived net gain in stopping. Almost everyone talked of the costs of offending, whereas a little over half said there were benefits. And over four-fifths of people said there were benefits, whereas only a third said there were costs for stopping offending. More people talked of the cost of offending and benefits of going straight, than of the benefits of offending and cost of going straight. Looking at the 11 people who were not going straight as a group, although all of them saw costs in offending, almost fourth-fifths also said that there were benefits.

## THE DECISION TO GO STRAIGHT

Most people decided to go straight and their decision seemed to have a rational basis, according to a simplistic summary of their cost-benefit analysis. This analysis, however, only looked at groups of people (rather than individuals) and did not look at the individual weight of any given cost or benefit. Moreover, this analysis is based on information gathered late in the process of change and could be a *post-hoc* rationalization. Only by looking at individuals in context does the essence of their experience become convincing. People's accounts of change were often rich and detailed. The metaphors they used to describe their experiences were powerful, and the emotional nature of some of the accounts quite moving (Leibrich, 1993).

People did seem to make an intuitive reckoning about whether offending was really worth it. Melanie, for instance, a European woman in her twenties convicted of shoplifting said "I saw that it wasn't worth carrying on". Similarly, Mark, a Maori man in his twenties convicted of theft, said "Just ended up winding down to not being worth it". Page, a European man in his thirties, with a mixture of offending said "There's more to me than go out there and commit a crime. I don't see the value in it. The spiritual value. I just can't see the value. It's not worth it". It is interesting that Jake, a European man in his thirties, convicted of burglary, and one of those not going straight, volunteered a similar argument about his decision to keep offending, "To go back again on what actually gets me to reoffend, I think I put the pros and cons. If the pros come up more that the actual cons then I will do it".

Some process of balance and action was one of the most common features of the individual accounts of change. Rarely did stopping offending just happen. Most people came to a clear and conscious decision not to offend again; almost like an act of will. The actual moment of decision was quite striking. People were clear about when they had made the decision and talked about that moment very vividly. These were turning-points in people's lives. The decision was the result of weighing up the worth of offending, and it was often triggered by a powerful emotional life event or by a sudden insight. People made the point that they changed when they were ready to change: that it was their decision. For some people, the first conviction caused immediate shame and shock. The process was usually slow and incremental for those with more than one conviction. The changes people described were gradual and often painful, and the extent of change sometimes partial. The main condition for deciding to go straight was the person having something of value that was too precious to risk losing, whether this was relationships, possessions, status, or a sense of self worth. Where the person had little of value in their life, there was little to lose by offending. The key to success lay in the degree of personal commitment to change and the extent to which their need for support was met.

One set of questions looked at people's commitment to staying straight. Two-thirds of the group, 22 of 33 people, said that nothing would make them offend again. Four people were not asked this question: in two cases because the persons had said they were not physically able to commit the offence again; in the other two because the persons had expressed such deep remorse about what had happened that to return to the issue in this way would have been too offensive. Most of the others described circumstances in which they felt they might need to offend again. Many people emphasised how hard it was to go straight. As Horris said, "You've got to have guts, man". Or Trintity, "Fuck! It was hard!". Despite saying that nothing would make them offend again, some people saw themselves as still at risk from addiction, poverty, the influence of old friends, or a destructive relationship.

Just over two-thirds of the group, 25 of 37 people, said that they knew how they had given up crime. They gave an average of two strategies out of a total of seven distinct strategies. Their strategies can be summarized as tackling personal problems and altering friendship networks. It was clear from their accounts that having reasons for going straight was not enough. They also needed a way of doing so, and this most commonly involved having some kind of support to deal with a problem (in several cases, addiction) and making new social networks. The need to replace old patterns with new ones (not simply to try to give up old patterns) was stressed in many accounts. It is best explained by Marcus, who turned his life around when several of his friends went to prison and he reached such a low point that he reached out for support. He began to get involved in a martial art, then got a job, and finally began to complete his education:

> It's like oil in a glass, you pour water into it and it slowly pushes the oil out. When something's going out, something's going in and I thought about this at that time and I thought well maybe replace it with water rather than oil.

Rose explains the importance of opportunities and the single-mindedness to take them:

> It was like somebody opened this big gate for me and I just kept going through these doors and they were closing behind me. It was not like I could go back. If I had consciously thought am I going to go back to my old way of life I would have started, you know, back tracking. Going back on those things. But I didn't. I just thought, you know, I like trying new things.

An experience of shame, including public humiliation and personal disgrace, were factors in people going straight, but on-going shaming or stigma was sometimes an obstacle in making that change. This could take various forms, a community simply knowing that someone had offended, the presence of a criminal record, or visible tattoos which people had acquired during the period of their offending. People were asked directly about one kind of stigma: criminal convictions. Most of the people going straight, 27 of 37, were concerned about having a conviction and saw it as a barrier to going straight. The main concern was that people knowing about their convictions stopped them getting a job. Some felt that people knowing they had a record made them the target of continued suspicion (for instance by the police or their local community). Mark explained how he felt picked on by his neighbors:

> Like any little thing happens and they're ringing the police on me. But I don't do it. Like the neighbor in that other house over there blamed me for being in their garage. The neighbor at the back blamed me for growing dope.

Four of the 11 people not going straight were concerned about having a conviction. These convictions were for crimes which they no longer committed. Most were not concerned, usually because it was no social disgrace for them. As Seamus, a European man in his twenties, convicted of drunk driving and theft said, "Na, well half the people I hang round with have got just as many convictions, not necessarily for the same thing. In the area I live in it's probably a way of life to some people".

## THE FREQUENCY OF SHAME IN THE ACCOUNTS OF CHANGE

Some kind of shame was the most striking feature of people's accounts of going straight. In talking about their reasons for going straight, a total of 24 of 37 people either mentioned shame as a dissuader or self respect as a persuader. In talking about costs and benefits, 17 people either mentioned shame as a cost of offending or mentioned feeling good about oneself, having a clear conscience, or being respected by others as a benefit of stopping. In total, 27 of 37 people mentioned the role of shame in their accounts of going straight. This leaves ten people who were going straight, but did not talk about shame. Five had been convicted solely for drunk driving and did not consider their behavior criminal at all. Three were young men who looked on their offending as hooning around until they settled down with a steady girlfriend. The remaining two were older long-term property offenders, who simply did not appear to be ashamed of their behavior. It was as if they had just got tired of offending.

The sample is too small to provide reliable predictive information about whether shame is related to certain features, such as sex, ethnicity, age or type of offending. The data suggests, however, that women may be more likely to experience shame. Possibly, shame is also related to cultural background and type of offence, but it does not seem to be related to age. Among the 37 people going straight, 13 of the 14 women but only 14 of the 23 men mentioned shame; nine of the 14 European, ten of the 15 Maori, seven of the 7 Pacific Islanders, and the one Chinese person mentioned shame. Looking at offence categories, 14 of the 18 convicted solely for theft, all four assault cases, one of five drink drive offenders, and seven of the nine mixed offenders, mentioned shame. The average age of those who mentioned shame was 32: the same as in the total group.

Private remorse was the most important kind of shame. It was provoked when offenders transgressed their own personal morality or sense of right and wrong. This became clear when people talked about their understanding of going straight, which to them meant being honest and not committing what they thought were serious offences. What they were really describing was selective offending, based on personal morality. Several people, for instance, had given up stealing when they came to think that it was wrong. Seamus, Toby, and Sarah had all given up stealing because they thought it was wrong, but they did not think that drunk driving was criminal as Sarah, a Maori woman in her forties, explains:

> I don't think that the driving (convictions) were like a criminal thing. I mean I was convicted but I, you know, like I don't think they're criminal things, you know. Like crime is like going out and stabbing somebody or breaking into something and things like that, but I was, you know...

Nick, Samuel and Jaydee had similarly stopped stealing because they thought that was wrong, but felt it was fine to smoke cannabis. Melanie made a clear moral distinction between acceptable and unacceptable theft. For example, she thought it was morally wrong to steal from individuals, but not from supermarkets. Kirk, a European man in his twenties, convicted of a mixture of offences, also had certain standards, "Yeah, let's put it this way, if there was something that was going to get stolen I didn't steal it from the likes of a friend. I have my morals". There were good examples of this kind of moral reasoning among all the 11 people classified as not going straight. There were various other reasons for continuing to offend, such as addiction, anger, and financial distress, but for the most part, these people said that they simply did not think that what they were doing was wrong.

None of the six drink drivers thought that drunk driving was a real crime. They talked about it with bravado and almost a kind of bonhomie. As Harry, a European man in his forties, said: "Get a bit of fire water in you, you're game as Ned Kelly, aren't you?" They continued to drink-drive mainly because they had decided that it was worthwhile— it was convenient, they liked driving, they were confident that they were good drivers even when drunk, and they viewed the risk of being caught and convicted as relatively small.

The two people convicted of assault who continued to get into fights both said that at times they just lost their temper and that alcohol was usually involved. But they also believed that they had to fight to keep their self respect. Patch, a European man in his thirties, would fight if someone else made a move on his lady friend. He said "Got to defend my pride". Mary-Jane, a Maori woman in her twenties, would fight if her ex's girlfriend taunted her and tried to embarrass her. "Saying nasty things to me in front of my kids really hurt me. So I just up and punched her". Both would have been more ashamed to *not* fight than to fight.

Similarly, neither of the two people who continued to be involved in drugs thought that drugs were wrong. One of the best examples of personal morality dictating selective offending came from Nga, a Maori woman in her thirties, who had stopped stealing (at least for herself), because she thought it was wrong.

> It just didn't feel right. I mean if I stole, stealing for myself was no good for me, but stealing for some other purpose was a good excuse for me to cheat them (i.e., the rich shopkeepers). Yeah. But it made me feel dirty every time I stole something and put it on, it made me feel dirty.

Instead, she had taken up drug-dealing, which Nga thought was a major shift in the right direction because she did not think marijuana was wrong. Indeed, she was quite convinced that it had considerable social value, "Marijuana doesn't kill you, it mellows you out, it doesn't cause fights, violence".

The three people who continued their theft reasoned that they simply needed to steal. All three also had some internal moral justification for when they did and did not steal, for instance, that the people they stole from were rich enough not to be hurt by it. To them, this made their stealing morally acceptable, and so there was no cause for shame. Jo was a European woman in her twenties, with convictions for assault, burglary, fraud, and drink driving. Although she said she was in less trouble than she used to be, she was frank about the fact that she still offended. Jo believed that most people offend in some way. Jake was also candid about his ongoing burglaries, and like Jo, believed that most people are engaged in some kind of crime. When asked if anything would stop him offending, he replied:

> I don't really think nothing would actually stop me offending, regardless of whether I was rich, poor, mediocre, married or whatever. I don't really think it would actually stop me. It may put a curb on it that's about it.

Personal morality is crucial in the process of going straight. Look at how clearly Marcus explained that connection:

> I'd think of stopping. I didn't really try. I didn't really try, I think, because I didn't see what was wrong in it, you know. I thought they're not going to miss it. It's only a book. Then other things, like if I burgled some place, they're making plenty of money, they're not going to miss it you know. I didn't feel the wrong in it then. I didn't think it was wrong.

The people who were not going straight, like those going straight, were asked how committed they were to their behavior. Nine of the 11 people not going straight said they did not see that there was anything that would stop them offending. This was largely because they really did not think that what they were doing was wrong. They found their own behavior acceptable.

## DISCUSSION

Former offenders, for the most part, came to a conscious decision to stop offending and had intuitively weighed up its costs and benefits. This supports the rational choice theory of desistance from crime which argues that, for property crime at least, individuals choose whether or not they will offend (Clarke and Cornish, 1985). The present study extends this concept to some other offences, such as assault, drugs and driving offences. This study also showed that, although the decision to go straight had an underlying rational basis, there was also an important affective and moral dimension to it, which determined how people perceived the costs and benefits. Several costs and benefits of offending and going straight related to emotional or spiritual experiences, and people were triggered to the decision by significant life events (such as death or separation) or by a sudden crucial insight. These were turning-points in people's lives. Overall, people chose to go straight when life began to have a better meaning for them, and when they began to have something of value that was too precious to risk losing. This could be material things or relationships or social status or a sense of integrity and self-respect. A recent reassessment of the Glueck longitudinal study has also identified the importance of turning points in the lives of offenders (Laub and Sampson, 1993).

Shame was the most commonly identified cost of offending and, conversely, feeling good about oneself was the most commonly identified benefit of going straight. Consistently, shame was the thing which most often dissuaded people from offending and the growth of self-respect was the thing which most often persuaded them to go straight. Seventy-three percent of people mentioned shame in their accounts of going straight. Shame can be one of the deterrents (or costs) of crime in a rational decision model of desistence (Grasmick and Bursik, 1989). The present research echoes some of Braithwaite's theory of reintegrative shaming (Braithwaite, 1989, 1993), but it also rings a slightly different note. The former offenders described three different kinds of shame: public humiliation, personal disgrace, and private remorse. Braithwaite's theory seems to be related to two of these: public humiliation and personal disgrace. He argues that the right kind of shaming leads offenders to desist from what he calls predatory crime and makes a crucial distinction between shaming which leads to excluding from society and shaming which leads to including into society: "the distinction is between shaming that leads to stigmatization—to outcasting, to confirmation of a deviant master status—versus shaming that is reintegrative, that shames while maintaining bonds of respect or love, that sharply terminates disapproval with forgiveness, instead of amplifying deviance by progressively casting the deviant out" (Braithwaite, 1989, p.12). Braithwaite's concept of shaming which leads to outcasting is consistent with public humiliation through the court process. It can also be seen in the descriptions of the obstacles created by having a record. This kind of stigma made it more difficult to experience the benefits of going straight, such as a job, a stable relationship, and being accepted into the community. Braithwaite's concept of shaming which leads to reintegration seems to be the same concept as personal disgrace. Several of the people in the present study who talked about having brought shame on their families, also talked about the families supporting them through that time.

Private remorse, the third kind of shame which emerged in the present study, is not obviously present in Braithwaite's theory. Recently, however, Grasmick has made the same distinction as in the present study between private remorse (his term is shame) and personal disgrace (his term is embarrassment): "Shame, or feelings of shame, are a self-imposed sanction that occurs when actors violate norms they have internalised. Shame can occur even if no one else is aware of the transgression. Embarrassment is a socially imposed sanction that occurs when actors violate the norms endorsed by people whose opinions they value" (Grasmick *et al.*, 1993, p.315). The present study suggests that shaming procedures, even if they reintegrate the offender into society, will not be effective unless the offender genuinely feels that what they did was wrong. Braithwaite's reintegrative shaming procedures may produce private remorse, but this link has yet to be clearly established. Establishing this link is a crucial step, because private remorse seems to be the most powerful form of shame.

Models of restorative justice may differ in the emphasis they place on (and the relationship between) restoring the victim versus restoring the offender; it is important, however, for any model to ensure that neither are harmed by the process. If the offender feels alienated after the restorative program (perhaps by feeling coerced into appearing to see things in a way in which he or she does not), then the offender may shift his personal morality still further from society's. Or, perversely, a shaming experience, which attempts to force shame on an offender who already feels private remorse, might be counter-productive, by traumatizing or alienating the person.

Several of these findings reflect earlier studies of former offenders. Pinsonneault, for instance, also found that people came to a decision to stop offending and claimed total responsibility for the autonomy of the decision. Events which gave meaning to life, such as being in love, having an interesting job, and satisfying family ties, provided an incentive for respecting the law (Pinsonneault, 1985; Cusson and Pinsonneault, 1986). Meisenhelder found that the threat of punishment in combination with the "pull of normality" was a major factor in going straight (Meisenhelder, 1977, 1982). The most influential factors were those which gave the individual a "meaningful bond to the conventional social order", such as a job, a home, a good personal relationship, and family responsibilities. He found that the stigma of having a record was destructive because the criminal's "social identity remains that of a criminal, while his personal identity is non-criminal" (1982, p.141). Shover found that offenders described what he called "a new perspective on self" in which they came to see themselves as wasting time, foolish, and not living life as they would like to. He also found that having a record could act as a counterproductive stigma (Shover, 1985).

Developing ways to stimulate private remorse about offending is likely to be one of the most effective components of any restorative model. It is not enough for people simply to be told that something is wrong, they actually have to think it is wrong if they are to offend their personal morality. It is offending oneself which seems to trigger personal remorse. And it is personal remorse which stops a person continuing to offend others. Restorative programs, therefore, need to challenge personal morality. A key part of this, given some of the moral reasoning heard in the present study, is to ensure that the victim is not simply a faceless person. The offender's idea that a victim is not really hurt by crime, must be challenged.

The fact that people weigh up the worth of offending, suggests a practical framework for restorative models of justice. A total strategy would increase the costs of offending and benefits of desisting, and decrease the benefits of offending and costs of desisting. A cost-benefit matrix shows this simply:

|  | Offending | | Desisting |
|---|---|---|---|
| **Costs** | ↑ Increase | | ↓ Decrease |
| **Benefits** | ↓ Decrease | | ↑ Increase |

The criminal justice challenge is to encourage and help people get over the metaphorical wall in this matrix. While they are still offending, it can be difficult to see over this wall to the benefits of going straight. But once they have crossed over, it is not the original costs of offending which keep them there, it is the benefits of being straight and the fear of new costs of reoffending (such as losing those benefits). This equation should be at the heart of the restorative process.

Decreasing the benefits of offending would involve dealing with some of the needs that the person met by offending. Increasing the costs of offending would involve producing the experience of shame, and making people feel that the penalties they feared would actually be exacted. Increasing the benefits of going straight would involve giving people access to some of the social rewards that they want to experience, such as jobs. Decreasing the costs of going straight is the least important part of the strategy, because most people did not see costs in going straight, once they were. Care needs to be taken when increasing the costs of offending, however, because these costs might in turn inhibit the benefits of going straight. This can be seen quite clearly with criminal records. Therefore, shaming needs to be time-limited. Purging records after people have been conviction free for a given time would increase the benefits of going straight by guaranteeing to remove one of the ongoing costs of offending. Going straight was usually a gradual process, involving a reduction in seriousness and frequency of offending. It may well take more than one experience of a restorative program before people internalize the need to be different. It may not be possible to make a person analyze the costs and benefits of offending, or to change their personal morality, but it is possible to give them information and feed-back which they can at least consider. Criminal justice policies will miss the mark if they are developed as though change was precise and orderly.

Going straight is related to personal values which are not necessarily in line with social pressures or the law. This study showed that offenders thought it was possible both to be going straight and to offend. Their selection of offending was determined by their individual sense of right and wrong. When people said they were straight but still offending, they did not generally think the offence they were committing was wrong. They did not think it was a real crime. By comparison, and more importantly, they had stopped committing offences that they thought were wrong. The finding that personal morality, rather than legal definition, determines the way we see ourselves is scarcely surprising. Eskridge has shown that 80% of New Zealand students define themselves as law-abiding citizens, although in the previous year 61% said they had smoked marijuana, 53% had driven while drunk, and 58% had stolen something worth less than $10. The findings were similar in American students (Eskridge, 1993). The only society in which crime is even likely to be reduced, is one in which its individual members genuinely concur with the legal definition of offending. Simply using external rituals of shame are unlikely to be effective when people have a different sense of right and wrong and no sense of belonging to the society which is trying to invoke shame. Most people needed support to go straight, either for solving problems or for making new social networks. Wanting to go straight may not be enough if people do not have the personal skill and circumstances in which to do so. When people internalized the need for change, they were committed to change. But if people are to be persuaded to give something up, they need to replace it with something they value at least as much. That may well be a sense of social belonging and personal integrity.

## REFERENCES

Braithwaite, J. (1989). *Crime, Shame and Reintegration.* Cambridge, UK: Cambridge University Press.

—(1993). "Shame and Modernity." *British Journal of Criminology* 33(1):1-18.

Clarke, R.V. and D.B. Cornish (1985). "Modelling Offender's Decision: A Framework for Research and Policy." In: M. Tonry and N. Morris (eds.), *Crime and Justice,* Vol. 6. Chicago, IL: University of Chicago Press.

Cusson, M. and P. Pinsonneault (1986). "The Decision to Give Up Crime." In: D.B. Cornish and R.V. Clarke (eds.), *The Reasoning Criminal: Rational Choice Perspectives on Offending.* New York, NY: Springer-Verlag.

Eskridge, C. (1993). "Self Report Deviance Amongst Students in America and New Zealand: A Cross Cultural Comparison." Paper presented at the Annual Meeting of the Western Society of Criminology, Monterey, CA, February

Grasmick, H.G. and R.J. Bursik (1989). "Conscience, Significant Others, and Rational Choice: Extending the Deterrence Model." *Law & Society Review* 24(3):835-861.

—B.S. Blackwell, R.J. Bursik Jr. and S. Mitchell (1993). "Changes in Perceived Threats of Shame, Embarrassment and Legal Sanctions for Interpersonal Violence, 1982-1992." *Violence and Victims* 8(4):313-325.

Laub, J.H. and J.R. Sampson (1993). "Turning Points in the Life Course: Why Change Matters to the Study of Crime." *Criminology* 31(3):301-325.

Leibrich, J. (1993). *Straight to the Point: Angles on Giving Up Crime.* Dunedin, NZ: Otago University Press.

—(1994). "Improving the Success Rate in Follow-Up Studies with Former Offenders." *Evaluation Review* 18(5):613-625.

Meisenhelder, T. (1977). "An Exploratory Study of Exiting From Criminal Careers." *Criminology* 15(3):319-334.

—(1982). "Becoming Normal: Certification as a Stage in Exiting from Crime." *Deviant Behaviour: An Interdisciplinary Journal* 3:137-153.

Pinsonneault, P. (1985). "L'Abandon de la Carriere Criminelle: Quelques Témoignages (Abandonment of the criminal career: some evidence)." *Criminologie Montréal* 18(2):85-116.

Shover, N. (1985). *Aging Criminals*. Beverly Hills, CA: Sage.

Spier, P., F. Luketina and S. Kettles (1991). *Changes in the Seriousness of Offending and in the Pattern of Sentencing: 1979-1988*. Wellington, NZ: Department of Justice.

# 17. FORGIVING IN THE FACE OF INJUSTICE: VICTIMS' AND PERPETRATORS' PERSPECTIVES*

by

## Mica Estrada-Hollenbeck

**Abstract:** *How are perpetrators' communications with victims important to the forgiveness process? Is communication primarily for victims, or are perpetrators also affected? Victims and perpetrators describe their perceptions of incidents when forgiveness did and did not occur. Researchers content-coded the micronarratives, assessed victims' and perpetrators' affect, analyzed the extent to which victims and perpetrators rated themselves and the other as contributors to the forgiveness process, and assessed victims' and perpetrators' ratings of relationship quality. The results indicate that forgiveness more heavily influences victims' emotions and assessments of relationship quality than the perpetrators'. Communication is important to victims' process of forgiveness, of moving from negative to neutral or positive feelings for the perpetrator, because communication provides an opportunity for perpetrators to express remorse and guilt, and to make amends. Communication enables perpetrators to gain knowledge of victims' forgiveness. Knowledge of forgiveness potentially influences perpetrators' cognitive representation of the conflict, their self-image, and the emotions, guilt, and anxiety associated with the incident. A context facilitating a forgiveness process, and potentially the restoration of justice, should include an opportunity for victims and perpetrators to communicate if both the victim and perpetrator desire to work towards forgiveness.*

*Gordon Allport Memorial Fund from the Psychology Department at Harvard University provided the funding for this research. Herbert C. Kelman, Ph.D., and Todd Heatherton, Ph.D., provided invaluable advice on the research project and William Weisberg offered helpful comments and suggestions on the draft.

When forgiveness is the response to injustice—occurring in the face of the injustice—is the perpetrator as involved as the victim in the forgiveness process? A man relayed his story of political imprisonment in South Africa that included the details of his experience of being tortured. He concluded his story by saying he had forgiven the torturer. By forgiving, he means that he no longer feels negatively towards the torturer, he no longer hates or desires revenge. He asserted, however, that in order for his community to be healed from this experience, and others like it, not only must he forgive the torturer, but the torturer must know that he is forgiven. Only in this way will justice be restored and harmony be able to flourish in their community. The presumption that the perpetrator should be as involved in forgiveness as the victim, is a basis for action. In South Africa, the action is to create a Truth and Reconciliation Commission in which those guilty of atrocities will come forward, confess their crimes, and, except in extreme cases, be pardoned by the government. The hope is that this judicial procedure will help victims to forgive, perpetrators to experience pardon, communities to experience reconciliation, and justice to be restored. There is much debate about enacting such a policy. Some feel that, after decades of abuse and millions of lives destroyed, "there can be no sufficient reparation or compensation for the destruction of family and community" (Duncan, 1994, p.4). Critics believe that perpetrators coming forward will tempt victims to take revenge and civil unrest will eventually occur. If victims want to forgive, it is safer to keep the perpetrators anonymous and leave the victims alone to negotiate their own forgiveness process.

People who want to forgive face the dilemma of how to promote forgiveness following unjust actions they do not condone. Alone, people do forgive in the face of injustice, sometimes without sufficient reparation and without seeking revenge (Flanigan, 1992). In many cultures, the judicial system supports this forgiveness process by setting up mechanisms for reconciliation and restoration of justice (Haley, 1988; Gibbs, 1963; Ury, 1990). Cultural and/or religious groups often play an integral role in facilitating forgiveness between their members. For instance, forgiveness is a central part of the informal dispute settlement methods of several communities in Africa (Gibbs, 1963; Ury, 1990). In the *Kpelle Moot*, an apology and the acceptance of an apology are central in the process of resolving disputes among community members (Gibbs, 1963). Likewise, among the Bushman, restoration of relationships occurs when "the perpetrator must ask forgiveness in front of the whole community"

(Ury, 1990, p.235). If the victim still feels angry, "the community holds a dance in a circle and they sing and ask the gods to remove the bitterness in [his] heart" (p.235). All these cases provide an opportunity for the perpetrators and the victims to confront one another.

Who experiences forgiveness? If forgiveness is defined as a victim's cognitive notation that he has changed from a negative to a neutral or positive feeling, then conceivably forgiveness occurs in the victim alone (Estrada, 1991; Estrada-Hollenbeck, 1994). The victim experiences the hurt, betrayal, bitterness, anger and vengeance, and so it is for him to let go of these feelings. When he does let go and is cognizant of this, the victim will say he has forgiven. There is evidence that a person can achieve forgiveness in the absence of, or in spite of, the perpetrator (Flanigan, 1992; Smedes, 1984; Casarjian, 1992). There are examples of victims forgiving people who have died and people with whom they have never interacted. In these cases, the victims no longer feel negatively towards the offending party and, therefore, forgive in the absence of the perpetrators. If forgiveness is purely an experience of the victim, how will communication with the perpetrator be important in the forgiveness process? Is communication primarily for the victim or is the perpetrator also affected?

## METHODOLOGY

Autobiographical narrative analysis is a methodology that enables the researcher to gain direct accounts of an individual's experiences with the phenomena being studied. Researchers developed and used this method to study phenomena which are hard to capture in the laboratory, such as divorce and romantic breakup (Harvey et al., 1988; Harvey et al., 1986; Vaughan, 1986), life changes (Heatherton and Nichols, 1994), criminal and antisocial activity (Katz, 1988), anger (Baumeister et al., 1990) guilt (Baumeister et al., 1994) and envy (Smith et al., 1994). Forgiveness is an appropriate subject to study using this method, since it is not easy to simulate significant life events that entail meaningful situations of forgiveness in a laboratory.

Micronarratives reflect each person's organization of reality, rather than valid objective phenomena. This is particularly relevant in a conflict situation in which an injustice has occurred. The two sides typically have very different versions of the history of their relationship. Determining that one rendition is more real or accurate than the other is irrelevant since each preserves her story with equal vigilance. Further, in many respects, it is impossible to determine the true history. Therefore, it is how a person cognitively organizes reality that is particularly useful, since it may affect how he or she feels and behaves.

Eighty-three subjects from Harvard University and the greater Cambridge, MA community signed up and were paid to participate in the micronarrative study. Their ages ranged from 18 to 40. Researchers randomly assigned these subjects to receive one of the following four tasks that varied by perspective (victim or perpetrator) and forgiveness outcome (occurred or did not occur).

Task 1. Please describe a meaningful life situation in which you wanted to forgive someone but did not.

Task 2. Please describe a meaningful life situation in which you wanted to be forgiven by someone but were not.

Task 3. Please describe a meaningful life situation in which you wanted to forgive someone and did.

Task 4. Please describe a meaningful life situation in which you wanted to be forgiven by someone and were.

When the subject arrived, researchers instructed him or her to write until he or she had completed the assigned task. Two independent judges read the narratives and issued dichotomous ratings for each of 17 items (please refer to Table 1 for a list of the items). Researchers instructed the judges to assess the presence of each item. The between-judge reliability was 0.54.

In addition, researchers gave all subjects two questionnaires. Firstly, the positive affect and negative affect schedule assessed affect (Watson et al., 1988). The second questionnaire asked for the subject's rating of important contributors to the forgiveness outcome and relationship assessments. To assess what factors were important contributors, subjects were asked:

There are many motivating factors and reasons why forgiveness occurs or does not occur. In the incident you described, how important were the following factors in determining whether forgiveness occurred or not?

Other person did something to make amends
Other person felt guilty
Other person said something to make amends
Other person desired to retain the relationship

Other person's emotional state
I desired to retain the relationship
I did something to make amends
I felt guilty
I said something to make amends
My emotional state

Researchers derived the list of factors from content-coding of micronarratives in a pilot study. Participants rated each item on a scale of 1 (not at all important) to 5 (extremely important). Subjects rated their relationship before the incident on a scale from 1 (stranger) to 7 (intimate relationship) and their current relationship, compared with their relationship prior to the incident, on a scale of 1 (much worse) to 7 (much better).

## RESULTS

The coding of the micronarratives provided a brief description of what was in the script of the stories told by each participant. Table 17.1 presents the proportion of narratives that contained each of these items when forgiveness *did not occur* from the perspective of the victims (Task 1) and the perpetrators (Task 2), and when forgiveness *did occur* from the perspective of the victims (Task 3) and the perpetrators (Task 4).

The content-coding reflects that the stories are similar for both the victims and the perpetrators. When forgiveness does not occur, both narratives explain that there was a history of problems, that the perpetrator did something that was not justified, that an apology was given, that the victim was justified, that the victim had a negative feeling, and that there was not a happy ending. However, relative to the perpetrators, the victims do not add as consistently that the perpetrator suffered too, that the perpetrator tried to make amends beyond the apology, or that the perpetrator sincerely felt guilty. The victims do add that the incident damaged the relationship and that the consequences were negative. The script of the story changed for both victims and perpetrators when forgiveness did occur. There is less discussion about long-term past events preceding the incident, and both describe the perpetrator's intentions as more justified. Still, victims and perpetrators refer to an apology but, in addition, both acknowledge that the perpetrator attempted to make amends and that he or she felt guilty. Victims and perpetrators still re-

Table 17.1. Results of content-coding.

| Item | Tasks | | | |
|---|---|---|---|---|
| | 1 | 2 | 3 | 4 |
| | % | % | % | % |
| Long-term past events preceding incident described | 64 | 52 | 52 | 42 |
| Perpetrator: | | | | |
| deliberately hurtful | 14 | 19 | 14 | 21 |
| response justified or justifiable | 14 | 38 | 14 | 37 |
| feels extreme negative emotion | 32 | 38 | 33 | 47 |
| experiences major suffering, distress or anxiety | 23 | 43 | 19 | 21 |
| apologizes | 45 | 48 | 48 | 47 |
| attempts to make amends | 45 | 62 | 62 | 63 |
| feels guilty | 36 | 62 | 57 | 63 |
| Victim: | | | | |
| response justified or justifiable | 77 | 81 | 86 | 84 |
| partial cause of incident | 23 | 33 | 29 | 47 |
| feels extreme negative emotion | 68 | 67 | 76 | 42 |
| experiences major suffering, distress, or anxiety | 36 | 43 | 57 | 21 |
| Forgiveness should take place to retain relationship | 50 | 43 | 67 | 63 |
| Conclusion: | | | | |
| damaged relationship | 86 | 67 | 38 | 68 |
| positive consequences | 27 | 14 | 52 | 53 |
| negative consequences | 64 | 48 | 33 | 26 |
| happy ending | 18 | 24 | 62 | 32 |

Note: Percentages represent the proportion of narratives codable on that dimension which were coded as having the specified features.

gard the victim's response as justified. Both agree that forgiveness should take place to retain the relationship. In the end, the victims and perpetrators agree that there are far more positive consequences and fewer negative consequences. The victims' scripts differ from the perpetrators', in that the victims still describe their own experiences of negative emotion and suffering more than the perpetrators. Interestingly, the victims do not describe the incident as damaging the relationship, whereas the perpetrators do. Victims and perpetrators are more similar in their accounts when forgiveness has occurred than when they have not forgiven. Yet overall, their scripts are quite similar.

The ratings of positive and negative affect were assessed. The results revealed that both victims and perpetrators were more negative and less positive when forgiveness had not occurred than when it had. However, contrast analysis confirmed that the differences were more pronounced for the victims than for the perpetrators, both for negative ($F(1.79)$= 5.965, p=0.01) and positive ($F(1.79)$=4.288, p<0.05) emotions.

Responses to the question regarding important contributors to forgiveness were factor analyzed using a varimax rotation. The analysis revealed two composite variables: *self-contribution* and *other contribution*. Self-contribution included subjects rating that what they did, said, felt, their own guilt and their own perception of the other's emotions were the main reasons why forgiveness did or did not occur. Other contributions included subjects rating that what the other did, said, felt, and the other's guilt and their own desire to maintain the relationship with the other, were the main reasons why forgiveness did or did not occur. These composite variables were then compared with the various perspectives and outcomes. Contrast analysis revealed that victims and perpetrators differ significantly in the extent to which each rates the other's importance in contributing towards forgiveness occurring or not occurring (see Table 17.2). This was not true for ratings of their own contribution towards forgiveness (see Table 17.3). The outcome—forgiveness occurring or not—had no effect on whom victims and perpetrators described as an important contributor towards that outcome.

The types of relationships existing prior to the offence between the victims and the perpetrators were not significantly different. However, the relationship following the offence was similar to the findings on effect. Both the victims and the perpetrators described their relationships as worse when forgiveness did not occur, than when forgiveness did oc-

*Table 17.2.* Other's contribution in forgiveness outcome table of means.

| | Outcome | |
| Perspective | No Forgiveness | Forgiveness |
| --- | --- | --- |
| Victim | 3.56 | 3.63 |
| Perpetrator | 2.64 | 2.85 |

($F(1, 79)$=5.77, p<0.05)

Table 17.3. Self-contribution in forgiveness outcome table of means.

| Perspective | Outcome No Forgiveness | Forgiveness |
|---|---|---|
| Victim | 3.27 | 3.10 |
| Perpetrator | 3.01 | 3.36 |

$(F(1, 79)=0.00, p<1.0)$

cur. This difference was more pronounced for victims than for perpetrators $(F(1, 79)=5.77, p<0.05)$.

## DISCUSSION

Victims' emotions are far more negative than perpetrators' emotions when forgiveness does not occur. Conversely, when forgiveness does occur, the victims feel significantly more positive than the perpetrators. The victims' assessments of the relationship quality follow a similar pattern; victims rate their relationships more negatively when there is no forgiveness and more positively when there is forgiveness, relative to the perpetrators. The narrative content-coding reflects a similar pattern. These findings demonstrate that victims' and perpetrators' emotional and perceptual experiences are not identical. The occurrence of forgiveness more heavily influences the victims' emotions and assessments of relationship quality than the perpetrators'.

The victim's narrative reflects more sensitivity towards the perpetrator when the victim experiences forgiveness. The victim learns, probably through interaction, that the perpetrator says, feels and/or does something that signifies that he or she felt guilty and made amends. The victim incorporates the perpetrator's reconciliatory actions into his or her narrative, reflecting a shift in his or her cognitive representation of the conflict. The analysis of other and self-contribution is further evidence that the victim perceives the perpetrator's contributions as important and equal to his or her own contribution. The victim shares the blame if he or she does not forgive, and shares the credit if he or she does forgive. There is little opportunity for the offender to reflect on remorse or guilt in a judicial system that does not allow for the perpetrator to communicate with the victim. This may have lasting consequences of hate, frustration, and hurt for the victim. A judicial system that allows the perpetrator to come forward, communicate guilt, and attempt to make amends could contribute to the victim's experience of forgiveness, facilitating the victim's experience of moving from negative to neutral or positive feelings for the perpetrator.

How will knowledge of the forgiveness affect the perpetrator? The narrative analysis indicates that both the victim and the perpetrator have a story to tell, which varies according to the outcome of the dispute. If the perpetrator does not know the outcome, for instance, if the victim never communicates that he or she has forgiven the perpetrator, then he or she will probably not experience changes in his or her story (cognitive representation of the conflict). He or she will continue to believe that the victim feels extreme negative emotions, is experiencing suffering, distress, or anxiety, and that there are few positive consequences from the episode. The results regarding the perpetrator's assessment of other and self-contribution suggest that the perpetrator views himself or herself as the primary contributor in the forgiveness process. It appears that the perpetrator carries the blame if the victim does not forgive, and takes most of the credit if the victim does forgive. Knowing that forgiveness has occurred, therefore, may have important implications for the perpetrator's self-image. The affect change is less dramatic for the perpetrator, but knowledge of forgiveness does affect the perpetrator's emotions such that he or she feels less negatively when he or she recalls situations in which the victim forgave, than when the victim did not forgive. This may relate to the perpetrator's description of experiencing more suffering, distress, or anxiety when the victim did not forgive in relation to when the victim did forgive. Perhaps the South-African man was correct in saying that the issue remains unresolved, and that justice is not truly restored as long as the perpetrator is oblivious of the victim's forgiveness process.

Peachey (1989) used the term restorative justice to describe the approach of "righting wrongs: restoring a situation or relationship as best one can following damage, injury, or other wrongdoing" (p.303). Similarly, Kim and Smith (1993) discuss forgiveness in terms of restoration of justice following a conflictual transgression: "...through what means should we restore justice in such cases? We could decide to forgive the wrongdoer or simply accept our unfortunate fate" (p.39). Alternatively, a person can take revenge. The results of this study suggest that forgiveness does contribute to improved relationships between the victim and the perpetrator, compared to when forgiveness does not occur. In this way, forgiveness is a contributor to the restoration of justice to the extent that it restores a neutral or positive relationship between the victim and perpetrator. This more positive relationship expresses itself in the victim's and perpetrator's stories regarding each other, their effect upon recalling interaction with the other, and the quality with which they regard their relationship.

The new constitution of South Africa contains a paragraph on National Unity and Reconciliation which reads:

> The adoption of this Constitution lays the secure foundation for the people of South Africa to transcend the divisions and strife of the past, which generated gross violations of human rights, the transgression of humanitarian principles in violent conflicts, and a legacy of hatred, fear, guilt and revenge.
>
> These can now be addressed on the basis that there is a need for understanding but not for vengeance, a need for reparation but not for retaliation, a need for *ubuntu* but not for victimization.

How can these goals be achieved? Will the Truth and Reconciliation Commission be the way to promote forgiveness and restore justice? This research suggests that a context which facilitates a forgiveness process should include an opportunity for the victim and perpetrator to communicate if both victim and perpetrator desire to work together towards forgiveness and to restore justice. In this way, the perpetrator has the opportunity to make amends, and the victim can share the release from negative emotions, guilt, and anxiety. Victim and perpetrator, in spite of the previous experience of injustice, can re-establish a relationship and contribute to the restoration of justice.

## REFERENCES

Baumeister, R., A. Stillwell and T. Heatherton (1994). "Guilt: An Interpersonal Approach." *Psychological Bulletin* 115(2):243-267.

Baumeister, R., A. Stillwell and S.R. Wotman (1990). "Victim and Perpetrator Accounts of Interpersonal Conflict: Autobiographical Narratives About Anger." *Journal of Personality and Social Psychology* 59:994-1005.

Casarjian, R. (1992). *Forgiveness: A Bold Choice for a Peaceful Heart.* New York, NY: Bantam.

Duncan, S. (1994). "National Unity and Reconciliation in the New South Africa." *Fellowship* 60(7-8):4.

Estrada, M. (1991). Forgiveness. Unpublished manuscript.

Estrada-Hollenbeck, M. (1994). "Understanding Forgiveness." *Interaction* 6(1):3-4.

Flanigan, B. (1992). _Forgiving the Unforgivable: Overcoming the Bitter Legacy of Intimate Wounds._ New York, NY: Macmillan.

Gibbs, J. (1963). "The Kpelle Moot: A Therapeutic Model for the Informal Settlement of Disputes." _Africa Journal of the International African Institute_ 33(1):1-11.

Haley, J. (1988). "Confession, Repentance, and Absolution." In: M. Wright and B. Galaway (eds.), _Mediation and Criminal Justice: Victims, Perpetrators and Community._ London, UK: Sage.

Harvey, J.H., R. Flanary and M. Morgan (1988). "Vivid Memories of Vivid Loves Gone By." _Journal of Social and Personal Relationships_ 3:359-373.

—A.L. Weber, K.S. Galvin, H.C. Huszit and N.N. Garnick (1986). "Attribution in the Termination of Close Relationships: A Special Focus on the Account." In: R. Gilmour and S. Duck (eds.), _The Emerging Field of Personal Relationships._ Hillsdale, NJ: Lawrence Erlbaum Associates.

Heatherton, T. and P. Nichols (1994). "Micronarrative Accounts of Successful and Unsuccessful Life Change Experiences." _Personality and Social Psychology Bulletin_ 20:664-675.

Katz, J. (1988). _Seduction of Crime: The Moral and Sensual Attractions of Doing Evil._ New York, NY: Basic Books.

Kim, S.H. and R.H. Smith (1993). "Revenge and Conflict Escalation." _Negotiation Journal_ 9:37-43.

Peachy, D.E. (1989). "What People Want From Mediation." In: D. Kressel and D.G. Pruitt (eds.), _Mediation Research._ San Francisco, CA: Jossey-Bass.

Smedes, L.B. (1984). _Forgive and Forget: Healing the Hurts We Don't Deserve._ New York, NY: Pocket Books.

Smith, R., W. Parrott, D. Ozer and A. Moniz (1994). "Subjective Injustice and Inferiority as Predictors of Hostile and Depressive Feelings of Envy." _Personality and Social Psychology Bulletin_ 20:705-711.

Ury, W.L. (1990). "Dispute Resolution Notes from the Kalahari." _Negotiation Journal_ 6(3):229-238.

Vaughan, D. (1986). _Uncoupling._ New York, NY: Oxford University Press.

Watson, D., L.A. Clark and A. Tellegen (1988). "Development and Validation of Brief Measures of Positive and Negative Affect: The PANAS Scale." _Journal of Personality and Social Psychology_ 54:1063-1070.

# 18. STRATEGY FOR COMMUNITY CONFERENCES: EMOTIONS AND SOCIAL BONDS

by

## Suzanne M. Retzinger

and

## Thomas J. Scheff

**Abstract:** *Community conferences are a new form for dealing with crime in Western societies. This procedure, which originated in New Zealand, diverts the offender away from the court into an alternative system that utilizes a meeting between victim, offender, and other interested parties to reach a settlement of the case. In Australia, conferences are being widely introduced for both juvenile and adult crimes and are also being used in educational settings for dealing with student offences. This chapter summarizes impediments to reconciliation between offender and victim in community conferences. The process of symbolic reparation is less understood than material reparation. There is a difference between aggressive emotions, such as anger and self-righteous indignation, which can be disruptive, and the expression of vulnerable emotions, such as shame, grief, and fear, which may be the key to reconciliation. Shame, in particular, is the master emotion which means the difference between conciliation and conflict; shame is related to the state of social bonds. Tactics can be used to overcome the impediments, leading to satisfaction on the victim's part, and reintegration on the part of the offender.*

These remarks are based primarily on the observation of nine community conferences in Canberra, Adelaide, and Campbelltown, AUS, in December 1994, but are also influenced by the published work of Braithwaite and his associates (1989, Brathwaite and Mugford, 1994; Moore, 1993), and conversations with Braithwaite, Terry O'Connell, John McDonald and Larry Sherman. We were strongly impressed by the power of the conference format. We consider it to be a justice machine. A movement, partially independent of what actually occurs during the formal conference, seems to be set in motion that tends toward justice and reconciliation.

Material and symbolic reparation processes occur side by side during community conferences. The process involving material reparation leads to the actual settlement: the undertakings agreed upon by the participants to compensate the victims and society for the offender's crimes. The settlement usually involves restitution or compensation for damage done, and some form of community service. The process of arriving at a settlement is entirely verbal, highly visible, and largely unambiguous; it provides the ostensible purpose for the meeting. Underlying the process of reaching a settlement is another, much less visible process of symbolic reparation. This process involves the social rituals of respect, courtesy, apology, and forgiveness, which seem to operate independently of the verbal agreements that are reached. Symbolic reparation depends on the emotional dynamics of the meeting and the state of the bonds between the participants. This chapter seeks to clarify the emotion process and the state of the bonds in community conferences, since they are much more ambiguous than the process of reaching verbal agreement. Awareness and negotiation of shame dynamics, in particular, are the keys to effective conferences.

The ideal outcome, from the point of view of symbolic reparation, is constituted by two steps: the offender first clearly expresses genuine shame and remorse over his or her actions. In response, the victim takes at least a first step towards forgiving the offender for the trespass. These two steps are the *core sequence*. The core sequence generates repair and restoration of the bond between victim and offender, after this bond had been severed by the offender's crime. The repair of this bond symbolizes a more extensive restoration that is to take place between the offender and the other participants, the police and the community. Even though the emotional exchange that constitutes the core sequence may be brief, perhaps only a few seconds, it is the key to reconciliation, victim satisfaction, and decreasing recidivism.

The core sequence also effects the material settlement. Emotional conciliation typically leads directly to a settlement that satisfies the participants, one that is neither too punitive nor too lenient, but seems more or less inevitable. Without the core sequence, the path towards settlement is strewn with impediments; whatever settlement is reached does not decrease the tension level in the room, and leaves the participants with a feeling of arbitrariness and dissatisfaction. Thus, it is crucially important to give symbolic reparation at least parity with material settlement. Unless this is done, conferences may turn out, in the long run, to be only marginally better than traditional court practices. Symbolic reparation is the vital element that differentiates conferences from all other forms of crime control.

The vital component of symbolic reparation, the core sequence, did not occur, however, during the formal part of the nine conferences we observed. Difficulty, tension, and arbitrariness were observed in reaching an agreement in all nine cases. However, in three of the nine cases, the vital movement from shame and remorse to forgiveness may have occurred immediately after the formal end of the conference. In two of the cases, the victims had conversations with the offenders, as they were awaiting forms to sign. In the third case, the facilitator, who saw the participants out of the building, reported that the victim had patted one of the offenders on the shoulder after he had made a tearful apology to her. These three instances suggest that it might be advantageous to build in delay after the formal end of the conference, such as the signing of a written agreement, which would allow the participants to finish their unfinished business of symbolic reparation. Built-in delay to the completion of the conference may turn out to be a significant part of the process of reparation, allowing oversight to the actions of the formal conference. The extraordinary complexity of the conference and the high levels of emotional tension make it likely that some such oversight will be necessary in a large number of cases, perhaps in the majority. In many cases, even a highly trained and skilful facilitator might find it difficult to overcome the impediments to symbolic reparation.

Symbolic reparation, unlike material settlement, depends entirely upon the play of emotions and social relationships during the conference. These dynamics are governed by two types of events. First, the management of shame, the master emotion, not only in the offender and supporters, but also in all the other participants, including the facilitator. Second, the degree of mutual identification and understanding which prevails: the state of the bond between the participants. The dynamics of social bonds are as important as shame, but the focus here is on shame dynamics. Since we treat bonds and emotions as equivalent, parallel phenomena, our proposals with regard to shame can easily be translated into bond language. The symbolic outcome of conferences depends upon the management of shame; symbolic reparation will occur to the extent that shame and related emotions are evoked and acknowledged by the participants. On the other hand, symbolic reparation will not occur to the extent that shame and related emotions are denied.

## SHAME AS THE MASTER EMOTION

Discussion of shame dynamics is difficult, because of limitations of the concept of shame in Western societies, where it is subject to extensive repression (Scheff, 1990; Retzinger, 1991; Scheff and Retzinger, 1991; Scheff, 1994). This repression is both caused by, and gives rise to, rampant individualism. These ideas are documented in Elias's magisterial study (1983) of the historical development of modern civilization. Elias used excerpts from European advice manuals over the last five hundred years to show the gradual but implacable repression of shame. The idea that one can be ashamed of being ashamed leads to the concept of continuous loops of shame, which is an explanation of the mechanism of repression.

One indicator of repression is the difference between the treatment of shame in the languages of modern and traditional societies. In European languages, and especially in English, the concept of shame is extremely narrow and negative. In the English language, shame has the meaning of disgrace and profound emotional pain. But in other European languages, there is both a shame of disgrace (as in the French *honte*) and a positive, everyday shame (as in the French *pudeur*), which refers to modesty, shyness, and (at least in classic Greek) awe. The possibility that there was once a positive shame in English is suggested by the word humility (because of its relation to humiliation), but humility has lost its relationship to shame in modern English.

The narrowness and negativeness of the concept of shame in modern societies is still more strongly suggested by comparison with the shame lexicon in the languages of traditional societies. The shame lexicon in Mandarin Chinese is much larger than those of modern societies (Shaver *et al.*, 1992). The Mandarin emotion lexicon also contains a large number of shame-anger combinations unknown in English. The shame lexicon is rich in traditional societies because its members are sensitive to social relationships, requiring awareness of shame and embarrassment, in contrast to the individualism of modern societies. The small and narrow lexicon of shame in Western languages, especially English, suggests that most forms of shame are being overlooked or avoided.

Recovering the positive facets of shame and the breadth of the shame concept from the maws of repression and silence is necessary if we are to understand shame dynamics. The positive aspects of shame have been explored by Lynd (1958), Tompkins (1963) and Schneider (1977). Lynd offers a representative statement, "The very fact that shame is an isolating experience also means that if one can find ways of sharing and communicating it, this communication can bring about particular closeness with others...." (1958, p.66). The idea expressed in this passage is crucially significant for community conferences; if the offender can come to the point of "sharing and communicating" shame, instead of hiding or denying it, the damage to the bond between the offender and the other participants may be repaired.

Recovering the actual breadth of the shame concept is also important for the conference process because shame is a Protean presence among all the participants. The offender stands publicly accused of wrongdoing and will be ashamed. The offender's supporters will be ashamed because of their relationship to him or her. The victim will be ashamed in the sense of feeling betrayed, violated, and/or impotent. The victim's supporters, in so far as they identify with him or her, will share this kind of shame. Disguised and denied shame inhibits the participants from repairing the bonds between them; it therefore blocks symbolic reparation. Retzinger (1991) has developed a systematic procedure for identifying shame, no matter how hidden or disguised, by reference to visual, verbal, and nonverbal cues. Members of modern societies require retraining in shame language, especially the language of gesture and innuendo, in order to become aware of shame in themselves and others.

We have drawn from the work of Lynd (1958), Tomkins (1963), Goffman (1967), Lewis (1971) and others to treat shame as a large family of emotions and affects (Scheff, 1990; Retzinger, 1991; Scheff and Retzinger, 1991; Scheff, 1994). Our definition includes the positive aspects of shame, what Schneider called "sense of shame", as well as embarrassment, humiliation, shyness, modesty, and feelings of discomfort, awkwardness, inadequacy, rejection, insecurity and lack of confidence. We give particular emphasis to loops or chains of shame and anger, as in Mandarin Chinese. The concept is much broader than the way shame is used in vernacular English, and recovers the broadness of the concept that is in use in traditional societies.

The most detailed treatment of shame in traditional societies can be found in a discussion of *whakamaa*, the conception of shame in Maori society (Metge, 1986). *Whakamaa* means shy, embarrassed, uncertain, inadequate, incapable, afraid, hurt, depressed, or ashamed (Metge, 1986). Only the inclusion of afraid (fear) differs from our usage. But the examples that Metge uses for afraid suggest not the emotion of fear (danger to life or limb), but social fear, that is, anticipation of shame. As in our usage, *whakamaa* concerns not only feelings, but also relationships. Maori usage also stresses the importance of acknowledging shame, and the disruptive consequences when shame is not acknowledged.

Because of repression of shame, community conferences conducted in modern societies may be more problematic in terms of emotions and relationships than those conducted in Maori and other tribal societies. Most traditional societies, like the Maoris, have a subtle and wide-ranging language of emotions and relationships which we in the West have lost. The understanding of shame in its positive, broad, and relational sense might be a crucial issue in the training of conference facilitators. How can a brief training significantly change the repression of shame and the individualism that has been inculcated by modern societies? The discussion of shame dynamics seeks to bring this issue into the open.

A theoretical issue of great importance for the operation of conferences is the difference between pathological and normal shame. Effective crime control requires normal (re-integrative) rather than pathological shame (Braithwaite, 1989). By paying close attention to the particular way shame is manifested, it is possible to distinguish, moment by moment, between the two forms of shame as they occur in social interaction. According to our theory, manifestations of normal shame, although unpleasant, are brief, as little as a few seconds. Shame, anger, and other related emotions which persist for many minutes are pathological. Shame is a highly reflexive emotion, which can give rise to long-lasting feedback loops of shame; one can be ashamed of being ashamed, and so on, around the loop, resulting in withdrawal or depression. Another loop is being angry that one is ashamed, and ashamed that one is angry, and so on around the loop. Furthermore, shame-anger loops can occur between, as well as within, participants. Indignation can be contagious, resulting in mutual and counter-indignation. Both individual and social emotional loops can last indefinitely. Persistent, relentless emotions, such as continuing embarrassment, indignation, resentment and hatred, are always pathological.

Shame plays a crucial role in normal cooperative relationships, as well as in conflict. Shame signals a threat to the social bond, and is therefore vital in establishing where one stands in a relationship. Similarly, pride signals a secure bond. Shame is the emotional cognate of a threatened or damage bond, just as threatened bonds are the source of shame. This equation allows shame language to be translated into relationship language, and *vice versa*. Goffman (1967) has argued that normal shame and embarrassment are an almost continuous part of all human contact; this is why the visible expression of shame by the offender looms so large in symbolic reparation. When we see signs of shame and embarrassment in others, we are able to recognize them as human beings like ourselves, no matter what the language, cultural setting, or context. Overcoming the public's narrow view of shame is the principal impediment to success for the conferences, and not far behind is training facilitators to be aware of and to manage shame.

## PATHS TO SYMBOLIC REPARATION: REFRAMING INDIGNATION AND ELICITING PAINFUL EMOTIONS

The offender needs to be in a state of perfect defencelessness, to use Moore's (1993) suggestive terminology, to clearly express genuine shame and remorse. Tavuchis (1991) makes a similar statement in his discussion of the effective apology. The offender needs to lay him or herself completely at the mercy of the victim, uncovering repressed emotions. This is a task of some magnitude since, in modern societies, states of perfect defencelessness are unusual even in private, much less at a public gathering. How is the offender to overcome the effects of repression in the presence of the participants whose own emotions are highly repressed? The principal paths may be reframing displays of moral indignation against the offender and eliciting a vivid expression of the painful emotions caused by the offender's crime, by at least one of the participants, usually a victim or a supporter of the victim (O'Connell, personal communication). These two paths are related; reframing aggressive emotions can lead to vivid expressions of painful emotions.

Moral indignation is a particular manifestation of shame and anger. The victim, especially, is likely to feel the shame of helplessness, impotence, betrayal, and/or violation caused by of the offence. However, this shame is not usually acknowledged, but masked by anger. Repetitive and relentless anger at the offender is an effective defence against feeling shame. It is unacknowledged shame that drives repetitive episodes of moral indignation. If this shame can be acknowledged (along with other hidden emotions such as grief and fear), anger and moral indignation directed towards the offender will be relatively short-lived and manageable.

Although other emotions are also important, moral indignation is emphasized, since this was the emotion we saw displayed most frequently and most intensely. There were two conferences which were exceptions. One was a drink-driving case. The overwhelming emotional movement in this conference was massive denial by the offender and his supporters. Rather than being too far from the other participants (isolated), this offender was too close (engulfed). The other exception was a case involving illegal use of an automobile. The crime was a technicality, since the offender had not known that the auto was stolen when she entered it. The predominate emotion at this conference was embarrassment, not by the offender and her mother, but by the facilitator, the arresting officer, and by us, the observers. Moral indignation against the offender(s) was the predominate emotion at the other seven conferences. It requires skill and sensitivity on the facilitator's part to recognize and rechannel this. Moral indignation is composed of shame and anger. The anger component is usually visible; in repetitive moral indignation, it is a mask for the underlying shame. Shame is carefully hidden, not only from others but also from oneself. The feelings of anger, violation, helplessness, and impotence that haunt victims are indications of hidden shame.

The shame component, the main emotional freight carried by indignation, is even hidden in dictionary definitions, which emphasize only anger. To find the shame component, we have to go to the root word, indignity, which means a humiliating insult to someone's self-respect. Labov and Fanshel (1977) hint at the key indicators of self-righteous indignation when they describe what they call "helpless anger" (shame-anger)˙in one of their subjects, Rhoda, directed towards her aunt, Editha: "...she [Rhoda] is so choked with emotion at the unreasonableness of Editha's behavior that she cannot begin to describe it accurately" (p.191). Labov and Fanshel continue in the same passage, attempting to describe the indicators of helpless anger, using terminology such as helpless exasperation and sarcastic exasperation. Rhoda's language, they say, implies that Editha's "violation of normal standards is so gross to the point of straining [her] verbal resources".

This description of "helpless anger" comes close to what we saw as self-righteous indignation at the conferences, particularly the term exasperation, and the idea that the helplessly angry person feels unable to describe the enormity of the other's trespass. The point is not that the subject feels unable, but that the trespass feels so overwhelming that it would defy description by anyone. The feeling that an emotion seems so unmanageable is a clue to the repression of the occluded emotions which drive the conscious ones. Use of the term sarcasm points towards a second dimension of indignation: the subject seems to feel that the enormity of the trespass is so obvious that the audience should (but does not) feel as strongly about it as he or she does. The sarcasm is directed not only at the offender, but also at the audience, who are not as angry about the offence as they should be. Repetitive indignation interferes both with the mutual identification (a secure bond) between victim and offender and between the victim and the rest of the participants. The participants are isolated from one another to the extent that indignation, a shame-anger loop, pervades a conference.

This analysis suggests a central point about the management of indignation. The expression of anger should be reframed so that the underlying emotions (shame, grief, fear) can surface and be discharged. Unless shame is acknowledged, expressions of indignation are likely to continue without relief (Scheff, 1990; Retzinger, 1991; Scheff and Retzinger, 1991; Scheff, 1994). The detection and reframing of moral indignation is a crucial component of effective conferences.

When moral indignation is repetitive and out of control, it is a defensive movement in two steps: denial of one's own shame, followed by projection of blame onto the offender. I am not dishonorable in any way, whereas the offender is entirely dishonorable. The participants must see themselves as being like the offender rather than unlike him or her, in order to identify with the offender (there but for the grace of God go I). Moral indignation interferes with the identification between participants. Uncontrolled repetitive moral indignation is the most important impediment to symbolic reparation and reintegration. To the extent that it is rechannelled, it can be instrumental in triggering the core sequence of reparation.

Shame/rage spirals can take a form other than moral indignation. Forms such as self-righteous rage (Horowitz, 1981) or narcissistic rage (Kohut, 1971) are not often seen at conferences. These other forms are likely to be more intense than indignation, and more likely to lead to verbal or physical assault. Unacknowledged shame in moral indignation is closer to the surface, and is more easily accessed by skillful questioning.

## Two Types of Moral Indignation

Moral indignation appeared in two forms, self-righteous indignation, the more flagrant form, and moral superiority, the more covert form. Self-righteous indignation was expressed most frequently and relentlessly by the victims, but also, in some cases, by the victim's supporters and even by the offenders' supporters, especially the offenders' parents. This emotion is expressed by what is said, but much more strongly, by how it is said, and in what context. For example, the victims in a fraud case in Canberra bombarded the offender with demands for the return of the money by one victim, and demands that the offender help protect the other victim's reputation. Not only the words, but also the manner of both victims conveyed their own self-righteousness and their feelings of betrayal by the offender, their distrust of him, and their feelings of helplessness and anger. The repetition of their demands, despite the responses of the offender, the crying of the offender's wife, and the attempts by the facilitator and the investigating officer to intervene, clearly signalled the victims' intense indignation. Labov and Fanshel (1977) have suggested that repetition of a request, especially if it disregards the other's responses, is at least challenging and, in many cases, actually insulting. Repetition implies disrespect in several ways: that the indignant person is not listening to the offender, or that the offender is not listening to the indignant person, or, more potently, that the offender is lying.

Self-righteous indignation was also expressed frequently and intensely in a break-in and theft case in Campbelltown. In this case, not only the victim, but also the parents of the offenders expressed indignation. The victim's flagrant indignation took the form of incredulity, not so much that the crime could have been perpetrated against her, but that the offenders were capable of such a deed. In the case of the parents, the incredulity was more that their children could be involved, that is, that the conference involved the parents. The parents in a Canberra shoplifting case also indirectly expressed incredulity that their son could be a thief. Most of their comments seemed to distance them from the offender, their son; they were hardly the kind of people to be spending time in a police station. Incredulity, hardly being able to believe what has happened, seems to be the chief visible cue to self-righteous indignation.

A second, more covert form of moral indignation occurs frequently, particularly by the police, in the form of lecturing the offender. The arresting officer in the cases we saw in Adelaide always gave some form of moral instruction to the offender. This tactic signals the moral superiority of the instructor to the offender, and therefore threatens the bond of mutual identification between them. In one case, even the facilitator joined the chorus: he gave the offenders a lengthy lecture on the nature of conscience. The lecture usually contains a threat as well, which also disrupts rather than builds the social bond. Threat implies that the offender is not responsible, but needs an external goad to make him or her behave. If mutual identification occurs, threat is unnecessary.

In Adelaide, the arresting officer always threatened the offenders with court. At first, the arresting officer in the break-in and theft case we observed in Adelaide was highly respectful towards the offender, and solicitous of his rights, both in the content and manner of what was said when she reported the nature of the offence. But later in the conference, perhaps because from her point of view the offender had not expressed shame and remorse clearly enough, she became very emotional, lecturing the offender on how stupid and silly it was to break the law, and on the certainty of strong punishment. At this point, her outburst showed self-righteous indignation, as well as moral superiority.

At the same conference, the victim of the break-in expressed moral indignation, and perhaps a sense of violation, by her repetitive discussion of the keys and locks of her house and the material goods that were stolen. The discussion of finding the stolen key, the problem of changing the locks, and the costs, went on for some time. It absorbed a significant proportion of the conference time, together with her discussion of the material losses. In this instance, and perhaps in several others, a skilled facilitator might have been able to interrupt the display of indignation, by interpreting it in terms of a sense of betrayal, helplessness, loss, and violation. In the fraud case, and in several others, it would have taken a great deal of skill and self-confidence on the part of the facilitator to be able to stem the torrent. It may be necessary to allow a preliminary outburst of indignation against the offender, but it is important that the facilitator be trained to detect repetitive waves of indignation, and be able to reframe them.

## The Hidden Shame Component in Indignation

Moral indignation of one of the victims in a case of school vandalism was so indirect as to be difficult to manage, even for a skillful facilitator. This instance illustrates the way in which shame that underlies indignation can be hidden from others and from oneself. The victim, "Fred Johnson", was a middle-aged teacher at the school that was vandalized. The vandalism was defamatory statements about the teachers spray-painted on the walls of the school. He was the principal victim: unlike the other teachers, each having only one defamation, Johnson had three:

Johnson is an old fogey.

Mr. Johnson sucks dick with Mr. Smith (another teacher).

Mr. Johnson is a bald-headed cocksucker.

The author of these defamations was unknown. The offender admitted to spray-painting only one statement, one which intimated a homosexual relationship between two students. Under repeated questioning, the offender indicated that he had no knowledge of the authors of the defamations against the teachers. The facilitator seemed somewhat puzzled by Mr. Johnson's presence at the conference, since she had understood he was to attend only if the principal could not be there to represent the school. Mr. Johnson explained that he decided to attend together with the principal because he also had some comments to make. Mr. Johnson first denied injury to himself. He explained that teaching as long as he had, "this kind of slander was water off a duck's back". He further denied injury by explaining, somewhat defiantly, that contrary to what students think, teachers stick together; one of his fellow teachers had phoned him about the defamations so that he would not be surprised by them.

Like his presence, there was a gratuitous element to these comments. They seemed somewhat unnecessary, and were carefully addressed to the air rather than to a particular person. Having denied injury, he then launched into an indirect verbal assault of the offender. He stated that when he counsels students, he tells them that such slander is cowardly. Johnson was insulting the offender, but only indirectly since he was calling him a coward only by implication. He repeated three more times this insinuation that students who resort to such actions are cowards, underhanded, have no guts. The offender's mother felt called upon to refute the charge of cowardice when it was her turn. She said that her son could not be a coward, because he plays rugby union!

Mr. Johnson's words and manner suggest a shame/rage spiral. He seems to have been humiliated by the defamations, but did not acknowledge this feeling to himself or others. For example, a statement such as "I was upset and offended by the graffiti" would be a step towards acknowledgment of shame. Instead, he denied injury, but made an indirect verbal assault on the offender. Rather than express his shame and anger, he attacked his putative attacker. His cycle of insult and counter-insult is counterproductive; it is the basis for all destructive and unending conflicts (Retzinger 1991; Scheff 1994).

The basic problem with indignation, a kind of impotent anger (shame/anger loop), is that, if it is repeated enough, it can damage the potential bond between the indignant participant and the offender. The torrent of criticism and disrespect gives rise to defensiveness on the part of the offender, the very opposite of the goal of symbolic reparation. This problem can be insidious, because the offender often displays cool from the beginning. This display, although it is a mask for shame, unfortunately triggers defensive anger in the participants, creating a vicious circle. The basic job of the facilitator is to ask questions which cut through the defensive stance of the participants. In this way, the conferences maintain a balance between the participants' anger at the offender and their respect for him or her, between shaming and reintegration. One way of contributing to this end would be to enlarge upon the formula used when separating the offense from the offender. Perhaps it is not enough to make this distinction abstractly. It might sometimes be necessary, if the air is thick with indignation, after condemning the offence, to ask the offender's supporters to name some of the offender's good traits. The facilitator could then summarize their positive comments, to bring the distinction between the bad offence and the good offender into high relief. This tactic would need to be handled with some skill and discretion to avoid antagonizing the victim's camp. Such initial support might make it possible for the offender to remain emotionally open in the face of moral indignation. Perhaps, if a space of this kind were created initially for the offender, he or she would become less defensive, whatever the participants' emotional responses.

# ENCOURAGING THE EXPRESSION OF PAINFUL EMOTIONS

Complementing the reframing of moral indignation is another tactic (O'Connell, personal communication, 1994). The offender may express genuine shame and remorse, even if he or she has defended him or herself against moral indignation. If one or more of the victims, or supporters of the victim, clearly express painful emotions (such as grief) that were caused by the offender's crime, the offender may be caught off guard and identify with that pain, even to the point that his or her defences are breached. Under these conditions, he or she will then show the shame and remorse that are necessary to generate the beginnings of forgiveness in the victim. An example was the victim who was highly indignant during the whole formal conference. However, when the offender offered her a tearful apology, she patted him on the shoulder, indicating identification and a step towards forgiveness. It is for this reason that O'Connell (personal communication, 1994) gives emotionality pride of place in the convening and facilitation of conferences. The chief focus of the facilitator in organizing and presiding should be setting the conditions that will allow painful emotions (such as grief and shame) to be felt, expressed, and shared by the victim, the offender, and other participants. However, O'Connell is referring to an emotionality that is primarily the painful emotions and not the aggressive ones, such as rage and anger. The goal of the facilitator is to encourage the former and to rechannel the latter. If aggressive emotions are interrupted and reframed, they may give rise to the expression of the painful emotions that are needed to trigger the core sequence. O'Connell's focus on emotionality and ours on shame gives rise to the following set of tactics that can be used to remove impediments to symbolic reparation.

1. *Have the facilitator convene his or her own conference.* He or she should personally telephone each of the participants beforehand, even if they have been invited by the victim or the offender. The facilitator needs to establish a preliminary bond with each of the participants prior to the conference. The personable facilitator can begin to connect with each participant, even by telephone. He or she can gather pertinent information that might not be included in the written documents, help to remove impediments to actually coming to the conference and maximally participating in it, or exclude those who might sabotage reparation. The initial telephone call may also give the facilitator preliminary information about the emotional openness of each of the participants. The most important

reason for the telephone call is to begin the process of bond formation that is necessary to ensure the success of a conference. Secure bonds are needed between at least some of the participants if the conference is to support the expression of painful emotions.

2. *Maximize the number of participants.* The reason for this tactic is directly related to emotionality. The larger the number of persons, the more likely that at least one of them will be emotionally open and able to express painful emotions, even in a tense situation. A large number also allows more possibilities for mutual identification, and for compensating for facilitator error. The expression of painful emotions caused by the offender's crime is usually the trigger for the core sequence of remorse and forgiveness. Large numbers of participants and telephone calls to each put a strain on the facilitator's time and patience. Unless the reasons are well understood, these two tactics will get short shrift.

3. *Question victims and their supporters on the very first feeling they had when they learned of the crime.* The first and other early feelings are likely to be painful emotions, such as grief, fear, and shame (in the form of helplessness and impotence). Usually, these first feelings are quickly covered up by anger and indignation. However, a skillful facilitator can help the victims find and acknowledge these early feelings, which will give them relief. Expression of these painful feelings can also have a profound effect on the offender, since they reveal the inner person of the victims: wounded, suffering beings like the offender. The importance of eliciting the victims' first feelings cannot be overstressed.

4. *Hold the conference as soon as possible after the offence.* Any substantial amount of delay will probably diminish the emotionality of the conference, or cause other problems. After a long delay, the conference will be an anticlimax, since the emotions involved will either have subsided or have been resolved. A delay of three months before one of the Adelaide conferences had destructive consequences. The case involved three offenders who had committed destructive acts against their school on two different occasions; on a subsequent occasion, one of the offenders had assaulted another of the offenders. The delay served to separate one of the offenders, the one who had committed the assault, from the other two. In the three-month interval before the conference, two of the offenders had made their peace with the school authorities; their families had worked out restitution with the school. This development only served to further isolate the offender who had not made restitution. The accolades which were given the two rehabilitated offenders served as de-

nunciations of the third offender. In re-integrating the two boys, the participants, except the facilitator, took on some of the characteristics of a lynch mob towards the third boy. Had the facilitator known of these developments, he would not have held a single conference, but had one conference for the two boys (or even cancelled it), and another one for the third boy. Unless the conferences are held in a timely fashion, they may be subverted by developments during the waiting period.

5. *Recognize that no intentional shaming is necessary.* The format of the community conference leads automatically to intense shame in the offender. At several of the conferences, when the offenders were asked why they did not bring their friends to the conference to support them, they answered that they did not want them to know. That is to say, they were already ashamed even before the conference began. Most people find the focusing of public attention on them embarrassing, even if caused by a good deed. Everyone will find the situation laden with shame when public attention arises out of a misdeed. Intentional shaming in the form of sustained moral indignation, or in any other guise, brings a gratuitous element into the conference, the piling of shame on top of the automatic shaming that is built into the format. This format is an automatic shaming machine. Since the automatic part is only implicit, it is less likely to arouse the offenders' defences. Shame can arise spontaneously from within the offender. But, in a format already heavy with shame, even small amounts of overt shaming are very likely to push the offender into a defensive stance, to the point that he or she will be unable to even feel, much less express, genuine shame and remorse.

6. *Ensure the specificity of consequences.* Attempts by participants to shame the offender by referring to conceivable, but indirect, consequences of the offence may be counter-productive. Examples are the use of videos of the results of car crashes, and members of the public as victims in a drink-driving case, evoking by the investigating officer of the losses to the public at large, from white collar crime in a fraud case, and calling of large-scale graffiti as copycat crimes by the principal in connection with the single graffiti of the offender in the graffiti case. These generalized consequences are apt to be shrugged off by the offender as completely unrelated to him, and in so doing, he mobilizes his defences. The consequences likely to have emotional effects on the offender are only those that are clearly and directly related to his own actions. This is the reason why victims are recruited from among the offender's supporters in drink-driving cases. The poor judgment that causes driving after

excessive drinking usually has other damaging consequences among those close to the offender. With encouragement from the facilitator, the offender's supporters are likely to air their emotions in a way that will bring home to the offender the destructiveness of his behavior. Poor judgment is a tactical concept, not a label to be used publicly. If the facilitator is to recruit victims from among the offender's supporters, he or she can use it in his or her own thinking to locate injuries caused by the offender's behavior to his own supporters. This idea is somewhat tricky, since it points to some kinds of offender behavior which may not be strictly illegal. For example, wife-beating is illegal, but verbal abuse is not, no matter how relentless and emotionally damaging.

7. *Drink-driving cases.* There is a large volume of these cases, and they are likely to be quite different from most other offences. A further difficulty is that most of the cases are a result of the detection of an illegal level of alcohol, so that there are no real victims due to the offence itself, and no direct possibility of restitution. The offender is usually an adult, rather than a juvenile, an adult who is adroit at denying responsibility for trespasses. Particularly important in these cases is knowledge of prior offences. Whether or not the offender has a drinking problem may be unclear from the first offence, but will become increasingly clear with each subsequent offence. People with drinking problems usually work out persuasive means of denial. They not only are able to persuade others of their innocence, but themselves as well. They are skilled at diverting blame from themselves to others, circumstances, the environment, anything that comes to hand.

A closely related problem is that the offender's supporters and, at times, even the victim's supporters and/or the facilitator, may collude with the offender's denial. In one case, the offender readily acknowledged that he had drunk a six-pack of beer, but insinuated that he or any other normal man could handle that amount of drink without interfering with his ability to drive. The implication being that drinking such a large amount was the norm, and therefore should not be illegal. As long as the offender is in denial, the likelihood of feeling shame and remorse is small. This is the reason for recruiting victims from among the offender's ostensible supporters. Anyone with a drinking problem is likely to insult and injure at least some of those close to him. By carefully questioning the supporters, a facilitator may often find at least one victim among them. The offender will be duly asked if he has a drinking problem. But the most powerful question is the one that is directed to-

wards the offender's supporters, "Has his drinking ever been a problem
for you?" This question may uncover a real victim at a conference for a
victimless crime. The encounter with this victim may yield a moment of
authentic shame and remorse from the offender.

8. *Multiple offenders and offences.* Conferences with more than one
offender and/or date of offence suggest the need for flexibility in following the question protocol that the facilitators have learned. This protocol,
which involves some four questions, is not intrusive when there is only
one offender and one offence. But at conferences with three offenders,
and in one case, three separate dates of offences, the procedure took on
a mechanical quality. Asking each offender four questions for each offence resulted in the facilitator monopolizing the floor, rather than spontaneous give-and-take among the participants. One way of avoiding this
dilemma would have been to ask the first offender each question only
once. Then, instead of repeating the question, the facilitator could have
asked each of the other offenders if they had anything to add. A second
issue concerning multiple offences involves the order in which the offences are taken up. The order was chronological at the conference involving multiple offences that we attended. But this ordering violated the
principle of emotionality, because the most emotionally laden offence
was not the first in time but the last (it involved an assault by one of the
offenders on the other). Allowing airing of this offence to occur last dis-
torted the discussion of the two prior offences, since the room was heavy
with tension between the assaulted boy and his assaulter. The discussion of this offence and the agreement reached partially resolved the
emotional tension between the two boys, but by this time it was too late
to have any effect on the discussions of the two earlier offences. A skilled
facilitator needs to foresee some of the emotional dynamics of each conference in order to ensure maximum effectiveness.

9. *Match silence with silence.* Many offenders, especially juveniles,
will offer minimal responses, rather than being full-fledged participants.
They manage a stance of cool, if not hostile, detachment. At an Adelaide
conference on theft, the offender, a large 16-year-old boy, gave minimal
responses throughout the conference. His posture was what is described
by the Maori as *whakamaa* response to public embarrassment, showing
the facilitator the top of his head by staring at his toes. However, near
the end of the conference, when it was time for him to apologize, he surprised us. Looking the victim right in the eye, he said the obligatory "I'm
sorry that I took your money". But he added, on his own, the additional

apology, "I shouldn't have taken advantage of you". His second apology was meaningful to all of us, because it was obvious that the victim was somewhat retarded. How can such additional responses be elicited when they are not forthcoming?

At times, skillful follow-up questions may elicit an additional response. But such questions will often be met with silence. Attentive silence on the part of the facilitator may work better than follow-up questions. Such silences require some self-confidence, and also, at times, quieting of other participants who want to rush in to fill the silence. Facilitator silence allows space for the offender, and may be less intrusive than probing questions.

10. *Build in an automatic delay after the completion of the conference.* If the participants only (no facilitators, police officers, or observers) are confined in a small space, conversation among them may lead to symbolic reparation, even if none occurred during the conference itself.

11. *Perform emotion exercises.* Another step may also be helpful in training facilitators. The present training sessions are oriented towards newcomers without experience of conferences. A second three-day training session for those who have had at least several months' experience as facilitators might now be in order. This second session could help the trainees make sense of the sessions they facilitated, their successes and failures. Unlike the initial session, it could be focused directly on emotions and relationships, since experiences at conferences would have prepared trainees to appreciate this approach. The second session could also be to lead directly into the arrangement of ongoing supervision; it might even be called a supervisory session.

One component of each of these advanced training sessions should be an exploration of the domain of emotions. Entering the realms of emotions can be problematic, because they are seldom discussed and little understood. Since most of us are embarrassed about emotions, one way to make the traverse is to begin with shared laughter, the kind that discharges embarrassment. Jokes work for some, but a more reliable method is to share with the class some humorous (that is, embarrassing) incidents from one's own life. This approach also allows the members of the class to identify with the teacher as a person like themselves. Without mutual identification in the class, learning is apt to be slow and tedious.

# CONCLUSION

The basic ideas and practices of community conferences radically contradict police culture and, indeed, the general culture of our societies in innumerable ways. Three days of training, or even a month, are not going to enable a trainee to throw off the beliefs and practices that have brought him or her to adulthood, and to a professional career, and enable him or her to interact in harmony with his or her colleagues. Some kind of continuing education will be necessary if the knowledge and attitudes fostered in training are not to be jettisoned later. The flow of events in conferences is rapid, complex, and often ambiguous. They tax the ingenuity and resourcefulness of even the most effective group worker. Thought needs to be given to the training and supervision of facilitators, and to provision for oversight.

Who should operate conferences? We have no recommendation as to whether police, social workers or mediators should fill the role of conference facilitators. However, whoever is chosen, it is important that the police be included in the early stages of planning the transition from court to conference, and that they are treated as an integral part of the new program. Since the police are the first to contact offenders, they have the power to help or hinder conferencing by their degree of cooperation. We also recommend that, whoever are chosen as facilitators, they be given specific training in recognizing and managing emotions, as indicated in #11 above. Conferences will begin to transform the dominant police and welfare culture, to the extent that police officers and other facilitators develop the understanding and skill needed for effective conferences. This transformation, together with community-building and empowerment in the control of crime, are the three great goals of the conferencing movement. For this reason, the development of training, supervision and oversight for facilitators contains a powerful force for changing our society in fundamental ways.

This chapter has outlined a strategy for maximizing the effectiveness of community conferences in the control of crime, and for training facilitators. These conferences are state-of-the-art among all current innovations for crime control. It is possible that the use of emotionality in generating mutual identification and secure social bonds may also have application to areas other than crime control. At the low end of the range of applications would be individual and family psychotherapy, and marriage counselling. The idea of the core sequence may be applied, not only in repairing the bonds between clients but also those between client and practitioner. This same idea may also be important in education for generating secure bonds between teacher and student and, therefore, more rapid and deeper learning. Finally, at the high end, the use of the conference format might be applied in mediation between groups, such as international disputes. The inclusion of techniques for encouraging the expression of vulnerable emotions and rechannelling aggressive ones might produce welcome innovations in conflict resolution.

## ACKNOWLEDGEMENTS

We gratefully acknowledge John Brathwaite's helpful comments.

## REFERENCES

Braithwaite, J. (1989). *Crime, Shame and Reintegration.* Cambridge, UK: Cambridge University Press.

—and S. Mugford (1994). "Conditions of Successful Reintegration Ceremonies." *British Journal of Criminology* 34:139-171.

Elias, N. (1983). *The Civilizing Process* (3rd edn). New York, NY: Vintage.

Goffman, E. (1967). *Interaction Ritual.* New York, NY: Anchor.

Horowitz, M. (1981). "Self-Righteous Rage and Attribution of Blame." *Archives of General Psychiatry* 38:1233-1238.

Kohut, H. (1971). *Thoughts on Narcissism and Narcissistic Rage. The Search for Self.* New York, NY: International University Press.

Labov, W. and D. Fanshel (1977). *Therapeutic Discourse.* New York, NY: Academic Press.

Lewis, H.B. (1971). *Shame and Guilt in Neurosis.* New York, NY: International Universities Press.

Lynd, H. (1958). *On Shame and the Search for Identity.* New York, NY: Harcourt.

Metge, J. (1986). *In and Out of Touch: Whakamaa in Cross Cultural Perspective.* Wellington, NZ: Victoria University Press.

Moore, D. (1993). "Shame, Forgiveness, and Juvenile Justice." *Criminal Justice Ethics.* Winter/Spring:3-25.

O'Connell, T. (1994). Personal communication. December.

Retzinger, S. (1991). *Violent Emotions.* Newbury Park, CA: Sage.

Scheff, T. (1990). *Microsociology.* Chicago, IL: University of Chicago Press.

—(1994). *Bloody Revenge.* Boulder, CO: Westview Press.

—and S. Retzinger (1991). *Emotions and Violence.* Lexington, MA: Lexington Books.

Schneider, C. (1977). *Shame, Exposure, and Privacy.* Boston, MA: Beacon Press.

Shaver, P.R., S. Wu and J.C. Schwartz (1992). "Cross-cultural Similarities and Differences in Emotions and Their Representation." In:
M.S. Clark (ed.), *Review of Personality and Social Psychology*, Vol.
13. Newbury Park, CA: Sage.

Tavuchis, N. (1991). *Mea Culpa: The Sociology of Apology and Reconciliation.* Stanford, CA: Stanford University Press.

Tomkins, S. (1963). *Affect, Imagery, Consciousness*, Vol. 2. New York,
NY: Springer.

# 19. PUBLIC ATTITUDES TOWARDS RESTORATIVE JUSTICE

## by

## Angela Lee

**Abstract:** *Considerable research has been undertaken to ascertain public attitudes towards reparation or restitution, but less to assess attitudes towards a process which uses both reparation and mediation. The public finds the idea of offenders paying restitution to victims attractive. There are limits to its use as an alternative to imprisonment, and the public favors the use of reparation or restitution for less serious offences and offenders. There appears to be considerable support for its use in relation to property offenders. The studies also indicated public acceptance of both reparation and victim-offender mediation with less serious offending and offenders. The focus group discussion research carried out in New Zealand indicated that there may be a level of support for using the process for a wider range of offences, provided the victim was happy for this to occur.*

It will be important to know how acceptable restorative justice is to the general public if restorative justice is to be introduced, or maintained, in any country, as a substantial part of the way to deal with crime. Governments are unlikely to support its development if the public find the concept unacceptable. This chapter summarizes the current state of knowledge about public attitudes towards restorative justice. The chapter focuses on research findings that have been published in the last decade and places special emphasis on work that has been undertaken in a recently completed focus group discussion study in New Zealand. The review concentrates on the views of the general public; research specifically on the views of victims of crime or justice officials has been excluded. However, the research on public attitudes will include members of the public who have been crime victims or who work in the justice system.

The public tends to think that the underlying causes of crime are social rather than individual. Unemployment, poverty, and lack of education are frequently cited as important causes, and improvements in
these areas promoted as solutions to crime (Canadian Sentencing Commission, 1987; Doble, 1987; Newport and Saad, 1992; Umbreit, 1994).
The public's attitude towards restorative justice will also be influenced
by their conception of criminals and their degree of knowledge about
crime and sentencing. The public's image of an offender tends to be that
of a violent offender who is often a recidivist (Brillon, 1988; Doob and
Roberts, 1988; Saladin et al., 1988; Thomson and Ragona, 1987). In the
light of this, it is not surprising that the public also overestimates the
amount of violent crime and recidivism (Doob and Roberts, 1988). People appear primarily to want the justice system to prevent crime and to
provide safety from offenders (Brillon, 1988; Doble, 1987), and imprisonment can appeal as being a way to achieve this goal (MRL Research
Group, 1995). The general desire for harsher sentencing, which has
been found by some public opinion polls (Doob and Roberts, 1988;
Innes, 1993; Roberts, 1992), may in part be a reflection of this need for
security. Research using more sophisticated methods, which provide
those surveyed with more information on the offender and the offence,
has tended to find less punitive attitudes (Lee, 1994; Roberts, 1992).

## WHAT IS RESTORATIVE JUSTICE?

According to Martin Wright (1991), the principles of restorative justice are support and reparation for the victim, with mediation being used
if necessary, reparation to the victim or the community, and co-opera-
tion in rehabilitation by the offender, with limited use of restrictions or
detention. Bringing "victims, offenders and the community together with
government in repairing injuries caused by crime" is how Daniel Van
Ness (1990, p.9) describes restorative justice. For Howard Zehr, it is "the
victim, the offender, and the community in a search for solutions which
promote repair, reconciliation, and reassurance" (1990, p.181), with the
outcome resulting in restoration rather than the imposition of pain.
Marshall suggests that justice should be "reparative or restorative, seeking to mend the harm that has been caused by an offence, in material,
psychological and relationship terms, while giving the parties involved
real responsibility and an opportunity for participation in all the decisions that are made affecting them" (1991, p.33).

# Reparation and Restitution

Two key themes of restorative justice are reparation or restitution to the victim, and victim-offender mediation or conciliation. In addition, the aim of reducing the use of custodial sanctions is often explicitly or implicitly associated with restorative justice. Reparation and restitution are usually in the form of financial restitution by the offender to the victim or, less frequently, the provision of services to the victim. The undertaking of some form of community service can also be regarded as a form of reparation.

Canadians appear to favor alternatives to imprisonment, such as probation, restitution, community service and fines, rather than spending money on building more prisons in order to overcome prison overcrowding. Also, when the public is asked about the most appropriate sentence for breaking and entering, there is support for offenders undertaking work which is beneficial to the community or the victim, or for offenders paying back the victim in some other way (Doob and Roberts, 1988). Later research has also found support for alternatives to incarceration for non-violent offenders, with the most popular alternative being properly supervised community service (Adams, 1990). A survey of citizens in Manitoba and Alberta found strong support for spending more money on education and rehabilitation, rather than building prisons, and for restitution rather than jail for a home burglary (Galaway, 1994a, 1994b).

Research in several U.S. states has shown support for the use of reparation. Just under three-quarters of a survey sample of Ohio residents indicated that victim compensation was acceptable as an alternative to imprisonment (Knowles, 1984), and a subsequent survey showed strong support for restitution as an alternative to custodial sanctions for juvenile offenders (Knowles, 1987). In Minnesota, Imho Bae (1991) found approval of restitution as an alternative to imprisonment for property offenders. This endorsement of restitution was confirmed by a later survey, which found that most people liked the idea of the offender paying compensation rather than receiving a short prison sentence for burglary (Umbreit, 1994). A survey in Illinois indicated acceptance of probation plus volunteer work as a sentence for burglary, with the level of acceptance increasing if all the property from the burglary was recovered (Thomson and Ragona, 1987). In Alabama, restitution is acceptable to the public, particularly when it is combined with strict probation, and there is also support for the use of community service (Doble and Klein, 1989). The proposition that non-violent offenders should be forced to work to earn money to pay restitution to their victims was endorsed by most respondents to a North Carolina survey (Hickman-Maslin Research, 1986). A study using focus group discussions in ten locations throughout America found that respondents favored the use of alternatives, including restitution and community service, and support for this increased after respondents were informed about the cost of incarceration; however, these alternatives were not seen as suitable for violent or repeat offenders, or for drug dealers (Doble, 1987).

Support for reparation is also evident in Britain. Results from the 1984 British Crime Survey indicated that most people approved of making some non-violent offenders pay compensation to their victims instead of going to prison, and also supported making some non-violent offenders do community service instead of going to prison (Hough and Mayhew, 1985). A 1986 public opinion poll found that three-quarters of respondents favored more convicted adult offenders being made to perform community service as an alternative to imprisonment (Morgan, 1986, cited in Wright, 1989).

The International Crime Surveys which were undertaken in 1989 and 1992 have confirmed the widespread acceptance of punishments with a reparative element. In most countries in the industrial world, community service was selected as the most suitable punishment for a recidivist burglar (Van Dijk, 1992). The New Zealand Department of Justice took part in the second International Crime Survey; community service was chosen as being more suitable for a recidivist burglar than a fine, prison, a suspended sentence, or any other sentence. Of the countries in the industrial world, New Zealand had the second highest level of support for this sentence (Van Dijk, 1992; Lee, 1994).

Galaway has undertaken two major investigations of public opinion towards reparation in New Zealand (Galaway, 1984; Galaway and Spier, 1992). Both studies used substantially the same methods and questions. Two random samples of 1,200 people drawn from the electoral rolls were presented with identical descriptions of property crimes, and were asked to indicate whether imprisonment or some other penalty would be appropriate. The alternative penalties consisted of a fine, probation, community service and periodic detention (community work in day custody). The list of alternative sanctions provided to respondents in one of the random samples (the experimental group) included reparation to the victim. The earlier study indicated that the public would be likely to accept a reduction in the use of imprisonment for property crimes if offenders had to pay reparation to their victims. However, the results of the later survey showed some moderating of the public's support for using reparation instead of imprisonment. An opinion poll undertaken by Listener/Heylen in 1994 (Lee, 1994), repeating questions which had been used in a 1985 survey, found a slight increase (from 79% to 83%) in the proportion of respondents agreeing with periodically detaining offenders to do community work of a public or charitable nature.

## Victim-Offender Mediation

A small number of studies have examined public acceptance of victim-offender mediation or reconciliation as a process for redressing the wrong done by an offender. A public opinion survey of 825 adults conducted in Minnesota assessed support for victim-offender mediation (Umbreit, 1994). The survey asked participants what their response would be to a program where the victim and the offender meet in the presence of a trained mediator, the offender learns how the offence affected the victim, and a plan for compensating the victim for losses is worked out. Just over half of those surveyed said that, if they had been the victim of a non-violent property crime committed by a juvenile or young adult, they would be very likely to participate in the program, and a further 31% said that they would be somewhat likely to participate. Galaway replicated this study in the provinces of Manitoba and Alberta in Canada with similar findings (Galaway, 1994a, 1994b). Results of 1985 and 1994 opinion polls in New Zealand indicated a reasonable level of acceptance of mediation linked to restitution (Lee, 1994). Just over half the respondents to the 1994 poll agreed that offenders should meet with their victims and, where possible, put things right; in 1985, only 41% favored this proposition.

In Hamburg, Germany a mail survey of a random sample of 1,799 people selected from the central residents' register was undertaken in 1984 and 1985 (Boers and Sessar, 1991). The survey assessed attitudes toward restitution in relation to various types of offences. Restitution instead of punishment was favored for most of the hypothetical criminal incidents. In 24% of the cases, the respondents said they would accept private settlement of the case (which included restitution or reconciliation) with or without a mediator and, in a further 18% of cases, there was acceptance of restitution or reconciliation mediated by an officially appointed person. Agreements on restitution initiated and supervised by the criminal justice system were acceptable in an additional 17% of cases. However, mediation and restitution or reconciliation was much more likely to be accepted in relation to minor crimes than more serious offending.

## FOCUS GROUP DISCUSSION STUDY

The New Zealand Department of Justice commissioned a research study to investigate public opinion towards restorative justice (MRL, 1995). Sixteen focus group discussions were held in four centers (three urban and one urban/rural) in October and November 1994. Participants were allocated to different groups according to their ethnic origin, gender and age, as set out in Table 19.1. Overall, the groups had a representative spread of income. A maximum of seven people participated in each group, which lasted approximately three-and-a-half to four hours. Groups with Maori participants were facilitated by Maori moderators living in the region.

*Table 19.1.* Composition of the 16 focus groups.

|        | Maori       | Non-Maori   |
|        | Age group   | Age group   |
|--------|-------------|-------------|
| Female | 17-24       | 17-24       |
|        | 25-44       | 25-44       |
|        | 45-60       | 45-60       |
|        | over 60     | over 60     |
| Male   | 17-24       | 17-24       |
|        | 25-44       | 25-44       |
|        | 45-60       | 45-60       |
|        | over 60     | over 60     |

The first part of the focus discussion was concerned with attitudes towards the current justice system, and what the participants thought the ideal justice system would be like. The discussion about the ideal justice system contained elements of restorative justice, such as more participation by the victim, including victim-offender meetings. However, this discussion was usually in the context of making the justice system more strict. The participants wanted the justice system to do somewhat contradictory things. They wanted to feel safe and secure through knowing that offenders were locked away, or were deterred from offending because of the threat of harsh sentencing; yet, at the same time, they wanted a fairer society and a focus on preventive and rehabilitative measures. After discussing the ideal justice system, participants were given a very brief description of the concepts of restorative justice and asked about their initial reaction. The groups were then given a fuller description of restorative justice. This description mentioned victim-offender meetings, the aim of putting things right, and points of difference between the current system and restorative justice. Finally, the participants were asked what they thought about specific aspects of restorative justice.

In general, participants expressed the view that restorative justice would be a move in the right direction, and would improve the current system, although there were reservations as to how restorative justice would work in practice. "...we are running out of alternatives. The prisons are full. The justice system is choking. The time is right" (Maori, male, 25 to 44 years). "Idea sounds excellent but the victim might not want to see offender. I think the community needs healing and so do offenders" (non-Maori, female, 17 to 24 years). Approval of restorative justice reflected the desire expressed by many participants for a society which is concerned about people, and emphasizes healing and caring. Female participants tended to accept the idea of restorative justice more readily than did male participants. Three of the Maori groups rejected the idea of restorative justice, because they perceived it as maintaining a European system of justice.

A number of benefits and concerns were raised during the discussion about restorative justice. All the participants perceived that it would change the position of the victim. The importance of victims' rights in any restorative process was constantly referred to by participants. Victims having more input into the outcome of a case, and being given an opportunity to express their feelings, were generally seen as positive aspects.

"I'm interested because you have got a meeting between two people with a mediator. It is vital each know and understand the process. Peace of mind for victim and also offender achieves something. Equality on both sides. Everyone has their say" (Maori, male, over 60 years).

"Under the present system, the victim has very little input. This is more balanced between the two. People get upset about the system at present time. I'm in favor of this more balanced approach" (non-Maori, male, 45 to 60 years).

There were some concerns about the victim meeting the offender. Participants questioned whether it would be reasonable to expect the victim to invest their time, energy, and resources in a system that they thought would assist the offender. "Depends on the victim, but if (the) offender (is) angry or hardened, then nothing really comes out of it, just frustration for the victim" (non-Maori, female, 17 to 24 years).

The participants considered that hearing about the impact of their behavior should have a rehabilitative effect on offenders. However, there was also concern that some offenders, particularly repeat offenders, might not be affected by the process and might also pretend to feel remorse in order to get a lighter sentence. Participants were apt to raise this concern if they viewed the causes of offending to be individual rather than social. "He would only be there because he was forced, or to get a more lenient sentence" (non-Maori, female, over 60 years). Timing was an issue raised by women participants in particular; they felt that the timing of the meeting should be decided by the victim. Reconciliation, which is a goal of restorative justice, involves the establishing or re-establishing of a positive relationship between the victim and offender (Zehr, 1990). The participants tended to get very concerned if this idea of victim and offender (re)establishing a relationship was included in the description of restorative justice. They either interpreted it as referring to a loving affiliation, and found it repugnant to suggest that the victim should establish such a relationship with an offender, or they thought that the use of the word relationship implied that restorative justice would only be used when the victim and offender knew each other.

The majority of participants indicated that all types of offences and offenders could be dealt with appropriately in a restorative system, as long as the victim freely wanted this to happen. "I feel if it is going to be part of our system, and if the victim requested it, I would say give it a go for all crimes. It's the victim's right to want to face that person" (non-Maori, female, over 60 years). When presented with a list of specific types of offences, property crimes were more frequently selected as being appropriate for restorative justice than crimes against the person or drug offences. From a list of possible mediators, the participants most frequently chose the independent moderator as the type of person they thought should facilitate victim-offender meetings.

Concerns about personal safety and the role of the state were also raised in the groups. The question of personal safety worried some participants, who feared that victims might be subjected to retribution from disgruntled offenders or their associates. Many participants did not want restorative justice to replace the present system. Non-Maori participants were particularly concerned that the State should retain an overview capacity to ensure fairness. There were also concerns about the potential costs to the taxpayer of adding another layer to the justice system. Despite the concerns raised within the groups, there was support for restorative justice programs being introduced on a trial basis, and being evaluated.

## CONCLUSION

Considerable research has been undertaken to ascertain public attitudes towards reparation or restitution, but less to assess attitudes towards a process which uses both reparation and mediation. The public finds the idea of offenders paying restitution to victims attractive. There are limits to its use as an alternative to imprisonment, and the public favors the use of reparation or restitution for less serious offences and offenders. There appears to be considerable support for its use in relation to property offenders. The studies also indicated public acceptance of use of reparation and victim-offender mediation with less serious offences and offenders. The focus group discussion research carried out in New Zealand indicated that there may be support for using the process for a wider range of offences, provided the victim was happy for this to occur. To be acceptable to the public restorative justice schemes will need both to hold offenders accountable for their actions, and to lead to what the public considers appropriate outcomes. The public will need to feel confident that the violent offender will not pose a threat to people's safety, and that the victim is satisfied with the outcome of the restorative process. If restorative justice can reconcile the public's desire for safety and rehabilitation, then it is likely to receive public support.

## REFERENCES

Adams, M. (1990). "Canadian Attitudes Toward Crime and Justice." *Focus on Corrections Research* 2(1):10-13.

Bae, I. (1991). "A Survey on Public Acceptance of Restitution as an Alternative to Incarceration for Property Offenders in Hennepin County,

Minnesota, USA." In: H. Messmer and H. Otto (eds.), *Restorative Justice on Trial: Pitfalls and Potentials of Victim-Offender Mediation.* Dordrecht, NETH: Kluwer Academic Publishers.

Boers, K. and K. Sessar (1991). "Do People Really Want Punishment? On the Relationship Between Acceptance of Restitution, Needs for Punishment, and Fear of Crime." In: K. Sessar and H. Kerner (eds.), *Development in Crime and Crime Control Research.* New York, NY: Springer-Verlag.

Brillon, Y. (1988). "Punitiveness, Status and Ideology in Three Canadian Provinces." In: N. Walker and M. Hough (eds.), *Public Attitudes to Sentencing: Surveys from Five Countries.* Aldershot, UK: Gower Publishing Company Limited.

Canadian Sentencing Commission (1987). *Sentencing Reform: A Canadian Approach.* Ottawa, CAN: Ministry of Supply and Services.

Doble, J. (1987). *Crime and Punishment: The Public's View.* New York, NY: The Public Agenda Foundation.

—and J. Klein (1989). *Punishing Criminals the Public's View: An Alabama Survey.* New York, NY: Edna McConnell Clark Foundation.

Doob, A.N. and J. Roberts (1988). "Public Punitiveness and Public Knowledge of the Facts: Some Canadian Surveys." In: N. Walker and M. Hough (eds.), *Public Attitudes to Sentencing: Surveys from Five Countries.* Aldershot, UK: Gower Publishing Company Limited.

Galaway, B. (1994a). "Manitoba Public Views about Restorative Justice." Winnipeg, CAN: Faculty of Social Work, University of Manitoba.

—(1994b). "Alberta Public Views about Restorative Justice." Winnipeg, CAN: Faculty of Social Work, University of Manitoba.

—(1984). *Public Acceptance of Restitution as an Alternative to Imprisonment for Property Offenders: A Survey* (Study Series No. 12). Wellington, NZ: Department of Justice.

—and P. Spier (1992) *Sentencing to Reparation: Implementation of the Criminal Justice Act 1985.* Wellington, NZ: Department of Justice.

Hickman-Maslin Research (1986). *Report prepared for North Carolina Centre on Crime and Punishment Based on a Survey of Registered Voters in the State of North Carolina.* Raleigh, NC: North Carolina Center on Crime and Punishment.

Hough, M. and P. Mayhew (1985). *Taking Account of Crime: Key Findings from the Second British Crime Survey* (Home Office Research Study No. 85). London, UK: Her Majesty's Stationery Office.

Innes, C.A. (1993). "Recent Public Opinion in the United States Toward Punishment and Corrections." *The Prison Journal* 73(2):220-236.

Knowles, J. (1984). *Ohio Citizen Attitudes Concerning Crime and Criminal Justice.* Columbus, OH: Office of Criminal Justice Services.

—(1987). *Ohio Citizen Attitudes Concerning Crime and Criminal Justice.* Columbus, OH: Office of Criminal Justice Services.

Lee, A. (1994). "Public Attitudes Towards Crime and Criminal Justice." *Criminal Justice Quarterly* 8:4-8.

Marshall, T. (1991). *Criminal Justice in the New Community: Bending to the Trends in Politics, Society, Economics and Ecology.* Paper presented at the British Criminology Conference, York.

MRL Research Group (1995). *Public Attitudes Towards Restorative Justice.* Wellington, NZ: Department of Justice.

Newport, F. and L. Saad (1992). *Economy Weighs Heavily on Minds of Americans.* Los Angeles, CA: Creators Syndicate.

Roberts, J.V. (1992). "Public Opinion, Crime, and Criminal Justice." In: M. Tomry and A. Reiss Jr. (eds.), *Beyond the Law: Crime in Complex Organizations.* Chicago, IL: University of Chicago Press.

Saladin, M., Z. Saper and L. Breen (1988). "Perceived Attractiveness and Attributions of Criminality: What is Beautiful is Not Criminal." *Canadian Journal of Criminology* 30:251-259.

Thomson, D.R. and A.J. Ragona (1987). "Popular Moderation Versus Governmental Authoritarianism: An Interactionist View of Public Sentiments Toward Criminal Sanctions." *Crime and Delinquency* 33(2):337-357.

Umbreit, M.S. (1994). *Victim Meets Offender: The Impact of Restorative Justice.* Monsey, NY: Criminal Justice Press.

Van Dijk, J.J.M. (1992). *Criminal Victimisation in the Industrial World.* The Hague, NETH: Directorate for Crime Prevention, Ministry of Justice.

Van Ness, D.W. (1990). "Restorative Justice." In: B. Galaway and J. Hudson (eds.) *Criminal Justice, Restitution, and Reconciliation.* Monsey, NY: Criminal Justice Press.

Walker, N., M. Hough and H. Lewis (1988). "Tolerance of Leniency and Severity in England and Wales." In: N. Walker and M. Hough (eds.), *Public Attitudes to Sentencing: Surveys from Five Countries.* Aldershot, UK: Gower Publishing Company Limited.

Wright, M. (1989). "What the Public Wants?" In: M. Wright and B. Galaway (eds.), *Mediation and Criminal Justice.* London, UK: Sage.

—(1991). *Justice for Victims and Offenders: A Restorative Response to Crime.* Milton Keynes, UK: Open University Press.

Zehr, H. (1990). *Changing Lenses: A New Focus for Crime and Justice.* Scottdale, PA: Herald Press.

# 20. CRIME PREVENTION THROUGH RESTORATIVE JUSTICE: LESSONS FROM JAPAN

by

## John O. Haley

**Abstract:** *Japan is the only industrialized country, other than Korea, in which crime rates during the past half century have declined. This may be because Japanese officials and culture reinforce values of confession, repentance, forgiveness, and leniency. When Japanese offenders confess, offenders or their families typically approach victims to make redress and seek forgiveness, and victims typically accept the offerings of redress and offer pardon, which is often communicated formally to prosecutors and courts. Japanese criminal justice officials are primarily concerned with controlling criminal behavior through the processes of confession, repentance and forgiveness, built on community mechanisms of social control. In the presence of confession and forgiveness, some prosecutors tend to divert most cases, and those that reach court are treated with leniency. The Japanese approach is not fully explained by cultural differences with Western societies; the values of confession, repentance, and forgiveness are also found in Western cultures. However, Western legal institutions tend to ignore these values and, instead, reinforce demands for retribution and revenge.*

Japan has been uniquely successful in dealing with crime during the past 40 years. It has managed not merely to contain criminal conduct, but also actually to reduce crime in nearly all categories. Japan's success in preventing crime is well-known. The number of major crimes per capita in Japan is significantly lower than in any other industrial country, except for Korea. In 1990, for example, only 1,324 major offences per 100,000 persons were reported in Japan, and a mere 912 in Korea, compared to 5,820 in the U.S., 8,630 in the U.K., 7,108 in Germany, and 6,169 in France (Ministry of Justice, 1992). More significant, however, is Japan's (and Korea's) achievement in reducing crime. As indicated in Table 20.1, Japan's crime rates for the most serious non-traffic offences (homicide, rape, arson, assault, and burglary) have steadily fallen during the postwar period.

*Table 20.1.* Reported cases of major crimes in Japan, 1955-1982.

|      | Homicide | Rape  | Arson | Assault | Robbery |
|------|----------|-------|-------|---------|---------|
| 1955 | 3,269    | 4,580 | 1,245 | 23,644  | 3,785   |
| 1956 | 2,862    | 8,567 | 993   | 28,397  | 3,434   |
| 1958 | 2,906    | 8,230 | 966   | 40,367  | 3,092   |
| 1960 | 2,844    | 8,080 | 969   | 38,445  | 2,983   |
| 1962 | 2,503    | 7,570 | 758   | 38,488  | 2,268   |
| 1964 | 2,501    | 8,384 | 772   | 45,238  | 1,968   |
| 1966 | 2,278    | 8,210 | 700   | 45,352  | 1,824   |
| 1968 | 2,297    | 7,725 | 666   | 42,002  | 1,280   |
| 1970 | 2,146    | 6,430 | 814   | 37,832  | 1,175   |
| 1972 | 2,188    | 5,484 | 799   | 32,314  | 984     |
| 1974 | 1,870    | 4,485 | 748   | 32,415  | 840     |
| 1976 | 2,113    | 3,394 | 876   | 26,368  | 939     |
| 1978 | 1,862    | 2,897 | 2,004 | 18,135  | 1,932   |
| 1980 | 1,684    | 2,610 | 2,014 | 15,301  | 2,208   |
| 1982 | 1,764    | 2,399 | 2,291 | 14,836  | 2,251   |
| 1984 | 1,762    | 1,926 | 1,980 | 13,615  | 2,188   |
| 1986 | 1,676    | 1,750 | 1,776 | 10,808  | 1,949   |
| 1988 | 1,441    | 1,741 | 1,629 | 10,004  | 1,771   |
| 1992 | 1,238    | 1,548 | 1,491 | 7,362   | 1,653   |
| 1992 | 1,227    | 1,504 | 1,418 | 6,773   | 2,189   |

Sources: Hōmusho (Ministry of Justice of Japan), *Hanzai Hakusho* (White paper on crime), 1988-1994. Tokyo. Ministry of Justice of Japan, *Summary of White Paper on Crime*, 1964-1992. Tokyo.

Some argue that Japan's record of crime reduction is a product of cultural factors, ranging from ethnic homogeneity to postwar prosperity (Suzuki, 1983). Such explanations are less persuasive when other societies with similar attributes but rising crime rates, such as Sweden (Stack, 1982), are compared, or considering that most crimes, especially the most violent crimes, even in Japan are committed within subcultures and between persons who are not strangers (Hōmusho, 1992). Profiles of crime do not support conventional cultural explanations.

Whatever merit cultural factors—from social cohesion or ethnic and cultural homogeneity to family stability or high rates of literacy and educational achievement—may have in determining Japan's relative lack of crime, unless these variables are conceded to have become increasingly stronger and more pervasive during the past 40 years, they do not explain the reduction of crime in postwar Japan. Not only is Japan different, but the Japanese must also be doing something different. That something is the focus of this chapter.

The Japanese experience demonstrates the effectiveness of a restorative model of criminal justice. Although the Japanese emphasis on a restorative approach can be explained as a product of Japanese culture, particularly its communitarian orientation, as well as the trial-and-error experience of Japanese criminal justice authorities (Haley, 1991), it is neither unique nor exclusive. Much that we and others actually do outside our formal criminal justice system is similar in both the approach and the results. What is exceptional about Japan is the centrality of a restorative approach in the formal system. Japanese authorities have discovered a set of responses that tend to work better than what all western industrial societies tend to do in their formal systems of criminal justice. The good news is that the Japanese approach not only works, but it can also be replicated and adapted to other cultures and formal systems of criminal justice.

The label restorative justice can be applied to any approach or program within a system of criminal justice that emphasizes the offender's personal accountability to those harmed and the community, in a process in which the victim and community participate directly in determining what the offender should do to make reparation and to allow reintegration. There is a precondition. The community must condemn the conduct. What has been done must be acknowledged as wrong, especially by those who surround the offender. A community that condones certain behavior cannot expect its criminalization to be effective. Everyday experience teaches that conduct condemned as wrongful by those whose approval counts is, in fact, generally prevented and controlled. Restorative justice builds on such disapproval to correct future behavior through the restoration or reintegration of remorseful offenders back into the community, maintaining or even enhancing the effectiveness of community control (Braithwaite, 1989; Zehr, 1990.) The aim is correction not punishment of the offender in a process that promotes and protects the interests of victims and the community. A group of

13- and 14-year-olds in Seattle asked to design a criminal justice program which they thought would work, came up with essentially the same approach. The offender should admit wrong-doing and demonstrate remorse and acceptance of responsibility for any injury caused by being willing to compensate the victim. In turn, the victim should participate in determining the appropriate compensation and, in return, be willing to pardon the offender. Finally, the justice system should respond to the offender in these circumstances with extreme leniency in penalty, coupled with efforts to ensure the offender can be reintegrated into a community (family, friends) who can provide effective support and control.

The first element of a restorative approach is offender accountability. This begins with acknowledgement by the offender of the wrong committed, with apology and remorse being expressed to the community and to those harmed by the wrong. Offender accountability also requires a willingness to compensate, or otherwise make reparation to, those harmed, and to take measures necessary to prevent future misconduct and reoccurring wrongs. The second, and equally crucial, element is a reciprocal acceptance of the offender's expression of remorse by those injured, and a willingness to allow the restoration of relationships between the accountable offender and the community; in other words, to pardon. There is greater hope of reform if the offender is reintegrated into the community and given the opportunity to regain self-respect and a sense of self-worth by means of correction. To effect both reparation and pardon, however, victim and community participation, perhaps with mediated confrontation, is necessary. The state and its law-enforcing representatives cannot stand in as a fictitious surrogate for real people who have been personally affected by the crime. The debts offenders owe are not to society in the abstract, but to victims and actual communities. In short, restorative justice is a process through which remorseful offenders accept responsibility for their misconduct to those injured and to the community that, in response, allows the reintegration of the offender into the community. The emphasis is on restoration: restoration of the offender in terms of his or her self-respect, restoration of the relationships between offender and victims, as well as restoration of both offender and victims within the community. It is not surprising that restorative justice is the prevalent pattern in most, if not all, social organizations, whether religious or secular, from families to other closely knit communities, in which there is a high degree of mutual interdependence, collective identity, and cooperation among their members. No contemporary criminal justice system in any industrial state is as restorative as the Japanese. The Japanese have institutionalized a process of confession, repentance, and absolution, in which, at every stage of the formal criminal justice process, offenders are diverted and restored to the community for corrective support (Haley, 1990, 1991, 1995).

## THE JAPANESE MODEL

The formal system of criminal justice in Japan is similar to most industrial democracies, reflecting the influence of continental European, particularly German, law and legal institutions with the addition of American-inspired constitutional protections (Appleton, 1949; Meyers, 1950; Nagashima, 1963; Dando, 1965; Koshi, 1970; Clifford, 1976; Castberg, 1990; Westermann and Burfeind, 1991; Thornton and Endo, 1992). It has few features unknown to the criminal justice systems of other industrial countries in the West. Each stage in the process, from the apprehension of offenders to the determination of guilt and application of punitive sanctions, is governed by substantive and procedural rules of special statutes, codes, and constitution common to other modern industrial states. Each stage also has the familiar roster of special players: police, prosecutors, defence attorneys, and judges.

At each stage of the formal system, however, Japanese criminal justice authorities routinely divert offenders back into the community. Japanese law enforcement statistics partly tell the story. In 1992, for example, the Japanese police cleared 636,290 non-traffic criminal offence cases out of a total of 1,742,366 reported non-traffic offences: a 36.5% clearance rate (Ministry of Justice, 1993). In so doing, they identified 284,908 suspects who could be subject to prosecution (Ministry of Justice, 1993). Of those suspects, whose cases were disposed of during 1992, the police arrested and referred less than 87,347 (approximately 25%) to public prosecutors, nearly 90% of whom were also subject to detention (jail) (Ministry of Justice, 1993). About 73% were released without further police process, but were apparently reported for prosecution, and an additional 2% were arrested but released (Ministry of Justice, 1993). Many other offenders are not reported to the procuracy at all, pursuant to Article 193 of the Code of Criminal Procedure, which gives the police discretion to close simple cases (*bizai shobun*). B.J. George cites statistics showing that, between 1975 and 1980, an average of

Table 20.2. Disposition of persons accused or convicted of non-traffic-related penal code offenses in Japan, 1985 and 1990.

| | 1985 | Total | Homicide | Arson | Rape | Assault Robbery |
|---|---|---|---|---|---|---|
| No. of persons reported to prosecutors as offenders | 374,162 | 2,252 | 1,162 | 2,120 | 8,962 | 2,120 |
| Percentage of suspended prosecutions | 34.6% | 5.8% | 15.5% | 19.4% | N/A | 6.9% |
| No. of persons prosecuted in ordinary trial proceedings | 36,653* | 945 | 491 | 421 | 155 | 313 |
| No. of persons convicted in ordinary trials (district courts, 1st instance) | 36,641* | 945 | 488 | 421 | 155 | 313 |
| No. of suspended executions of sentences (district courts) | 19,152* | 206 | 141 | 143 | 55 | 89 |
| No. of persons subject to executed sentences of imprisonment: | 15,249* | 770 | 267 | 212 | 68 | 247 |
| for 6 to 10 year terms | 661 | 340 | 50 | 12 | 0 | 26 |
| for 3 to 5 year terms | 2,861 | 236 | 37 | 84 | 0 | 189 |
| for 6-month to 1-year terms | 8,363 | 4 | 14 | 17 | 40 | 3 |

*Table 20.2.* Cont'd.

| | 1990 | Total | Homicide | Arson | Rape | Assault Robbery |
|---|---|---|---|---|---|---|
| No. of persons reported to prosecutors as offenders | 284,987 | 1,637 | 793 | 1,540 | 5,385 | 1,951 |
| Percentage of suspended prosecutions | 37.8% | 6.1% | 16.8% | 16.1% | N/A | 7.7% |
| No. of persons prosecuted in ordinary trial proceedings | 27,410* | 572 | 292 | 311 | 158 | 243 |
| No. of persons convicted in ordinary trials (district courts, 1st instance) | 27,405* | 571 | 292 | 311 | 158 | 243 |
| No. of suspended executions of sentences (district courts) | 15,612* | 123 | 102 | 115 | 60 | 81 |
| No. of persons subject to executed sentences of imprisonment: | 11,653* | 450 | 205 | 187 | 88 | 199 |
| for 6 to 10 year terms | 426 | 192 | 37 | 21 | 0 | 24 |
| for 3 to 5 year terms | 2,379 | 137 | 112 | 119 | 0 | 141 |
| for 6-month to 1-year terms | 6,272 | 0 | 11 | 14 | 53 | 1 |

*Includes traffic-related offenses.

Sources: Hōmusho (1981, 1986, 1991).
Saikō Saibansho (1981, 1986, 1991).

17.6% of non-traffic Criminal Code offences were disposed of in this manner, and notes that assaults, thefts, fraud, embezzlement, and gambling were the most common types of offence (George, 1984). One Japanese source suggests a higher estimate: the Tokyo Metropolitan District police fail to report about 40% of all referable cases (Shikita, 1982). Less than 25% of all cleared non-traffic criminal cases become subject to police arrest, referral to the prosecutor, and pretrial detention; at least an equal proportion of offenders are released without further process.

Public prosecutors in Japan generally prosecute only about 5% of all prosecutable cases in ordering criminal proceedings. They allow the majority (53% in 1992) to be adjudicated in uncontested summary proceedings (_rakushiki tetsuzuki_), based on documentary evidence in which the maximum penalty is currently 500,000 yen (or U.S. $5000 to $6250 at prevailing exchange rates), and most of which are criminal traffic offences. As indicated in Table 20.2, for example, in 1992, Japanese public prosecutors faced a total case-load of 2,220,515 alleged offenders, of which 360,482 were juveniles (ages 14 to 19) who were remanded to the appropriate family court. Of the remaining 1,860,033 adults, 1,177,582 (53%) were tried in summary proceedings and only 89,058 (slightly under 5%) were prosecuted as ordinary criminal trials (Ministry of Justice, 1993). Prosecution was suspended in 556,013 cases: nearly 30% of all prosecutable cases involving adult offenders (White Paper, 1990, p.61). The ratios of formal prosecution to summary proceedings vary significantly, depending upon the nature of the offence. Summary proceedings are not available for more serious offences for which a fine is not a statutory option. Consequently, no homicide cases are submitted to summary proceedings.

In all cases, prosecutors exercise discretionary authority to suspend prosecution of convictable offenders (Dando, 1970; George, 1984; Goodman, 1986; Foote, 1992). Prosecutors routinely suspend prosecution in 30 to 35% of all non-traffic Criminal Code offences (George, 1984). The ratios are not uniform, however. They vary with the crime committed. Prosecutors exercised this authority in 1992, for example, to suspend 45 of 1448 (3%) prosecutable homicide cases (Ministry of Justice, 1993). Fraud and extortion do not carry an optional fine as a statutory penalty and, thus, summary prosecution was not permitted in these cases; but prosecution was suspended in 24% of prosecutable fraud cases and in 16% of all prosecutable extortion cases.

Nearly all suspects reported by the police are convictable. For the police, as well as the prosecutors, to lose a case means a significant loss of face. Thus, police tend to continue the investigation until they are convinced that the suspect is guilty and conviction will result (Miyazawa, 1992). In 1992, for example, only 2.4% of all suspects were released due to insufficient evidence or similar grounds (White Paper, 1993, p.62). For similar reasons, those who are prosecuted are nearly always convicted. Conviction rates in Japan consistently hover around 99.5% (Saikō Saibansho, 1977). Of the total case-load of 1,230,034 defendants (including traffic-related offence) in 1992, only 91 were acquitted in formal non-summary trials in district courts (Ministry of Justice, 1993). Yet, the courts seem equally lenient. Few offenders are subject to more than a minor fine or prison term. In summary proceedings, as noted, the maximum penalty is about U.S. $5000. In practice, however, most offenders pay much less. Of the 1,150,696 defendants in summary proceedings concluded in 1992, only 6,017 (0.5%) were fined the maximum 500,000 yen. Eighty-seven percent were fined less than 100,000 yen and over 40% were fined less than 50,000 yen (U.S. $500 to $625) (Saikō Saibansho, 1993).

Very few convicted offenders serve more than one-year terms for crimes that carry a prison sentence. For example, in 1992, Japanese courts sentenced 47,684 persons to imprisonment. However, 60% (28,480) received suspended sentences, and more than two-thirds of those whose sentences were not suspended were subjected to prison terms of less than one year (Saikō Saibansho, 1993). Table 20.2 includes figures on Japanese sentencing patterns for serious offences. They show, for example, that in 1992 sentences were suspended for nearly 25% of those convicted of homicide, 34% for larceny, 26% for robbery, 37% for arson, and 13% for rape. Moreover, only about 45% of all imprisoned offenders actually serve a full term. More than 50% are paroled before the expiration of their sentences (Abe, 1963; Oyama, c. 1978). Thus, in 1992, of over 900,000 offenders identified by the police for having committed a non-traffic criminal offence, less than 20% (173,962) were prosecuted at all, and only 6% (54,336) in formal trial proceedings for which the penalty could be more than a fine. Nearly all of those prosecuted were convicted (99.99%), but less than half (40%) were imprisoned, only 4% received prison terms of five years or more, and about half of these will serve less than the maximum. In other words, less than 0.1% of all offenders in Japan actually spend five years or more in prison, and less than 2.5% are incarcerated at all. Criminal justice in Japan is extraordinarily lenient. Although identified as offenders by the police, many are never reported. Although convictable, large numbers are released by prosecutors without prosecution. Although prosecution is tantamount to conviction, the overwhelming majority of those convicted receive no more than a minor fine, or have their sentences suspended.

A variety of factors go into the decisions by police, prosecutors and judges on how to treat offenders: whether to report, prosecute, sentence, parole, or divert an offender out of the formal system and back into his or her community. These include considerations common to most criminal justice systems: the gravity of the offence, the circumstances and nature of the crime, and the age and prior record of the offender. Added to this matrix, however, are additional factors that appear to be missing elsewhere, at least in the West. The attitude of the offender in acknowledging guilt, expressing remorse, and compensating any victim, as well as the victims' and the community's responses in expressing willingness to pardon and to correct, are determinative elements in the decision of whether to report, prosecute, sentence, or parole the offender. Minoru Shikita describes the pattern with respect to the police:

> [T]he police, with the general accord of the chief public prosecutor of a district, need not refer all cases formally to the prosecution, but may report cases in consolidated form monthly, provided the offence are minor property offence, the suspects have shown repentance, restitution has been made, and victims forgive the suspects (1982, p.37).

Even in those cases referred to public prosecutors, Shikita notes that the police invariably recommend a lenient disposition if a suspect has shown sincere repentance about his or her alleged crime and the transgression against a social norm is not particularly serious (1982). That most suspects do confess to the police is beyond doubt. Walter Ames reports an estimate in Okayama prefecture that 95% of all suspects confess during police interrogation (1981). Others report similar percentages (Bayley, 1976). Similar considerations motivate prosecutors in deciding whether or not to divert the offender by suspending prosecution. The critical factors include the existence of a confession, sincere repentance by the suspect, and pardon by the victim (Parker, 1984). Japanese judges also uniformly confirm that the defendant's acknowledgment of guilt, sincerity in displaying remorse, evidenced in part by compensation of the victim, and the victim's forgiving response, are pivotal in their decisions on whether or not to suspend sentence. One senior Japanese judge is said to have refused to allow defendants to leave the courtroom, even after conviction and sentencing, until they have confessed and expressed remorse.

Typically, the suspect not only confesses, but through family and friends, also seeks letters from any victims addressed to the prosecutor or judge that acknowledge restitution and express the victim's sentiment that no further penalty need be imposed. So customary are such letters, that most Japanese attorneys have some sense of the amounts usually required. There is, however, no formal, institutionalized program for reparation and pardon. Japan does not have organized victim assistance organizations or either volunteer or government supported victim-offender mediation programs. The process of reparation and pardon operates informally as a social response to crime buttressed by widely shared values and expectations. As described by Professor Atsushi Yamaguchi:

> The lack of provisions for victim restitution does not mean that it has virtually no role to play in the Japanese criminal justice system. Rather, victim restitution is considered to be one of the crucial factors affecting the decisions of prosecutors, the criminal courts and the parole boards, not to mention the informal disposition by the police (1990, p.167).

Thus, both victims and the community participate in the process. Reparation is ordinarily made and the victim has a voice in the authorities' decisions regarding whether to report, prosecute, or sentence the offender. The experience of an American resident of Tokyo is illustrative. His summer house was burned down by a burglar, in a clumsy attempt to destroy any incriminating evidence. Once the suspect had been apprehended and charged, intermediaries arranged for the suspect's father to meet the American owner and offer to pay the entire amount of the damage. The American first insisted that this was not necessary because the house was insured. Only after the father prostrated himself, begging to pay some amount in compensation, with the intermediary explaining that some reparation was necessary as a matter of social custom, did the American relent and agree to accept money for the uninsured furniture and other personal belongings destroyed in the fire. In return, he wrote the necessary letter to the authorities explaining that compensation had been paid. In addition, whenever the American was asked to return to the community to assist the police and prosecutors in their continuing investigation, the young offender's father and mother insisted on meeting him at the train station to drive him the block or two to the police station, often waiting for several hours in the cold, not knowing which train he might be on. In this way, offenders and their families express their accountability and make reparation directly to victims, who are thereby enabled to participate in the process without controlling it. The possibility of diversion gives the offender an incentive to make amends and provides the victim with the opportunity and inclination to pardon. However, victims do not assume the role of adversary or prosecutor, nor are they able to use the formal process vindictively for revenge. Ultimately, they must defer to the authorities' decision. The burglar-arsonist, in the preceding account, was prosecuted, convicted, and served some time in prison.

Participating in the informal process of diversion are members of the families of both victim and offender, their friends, neighbors, fellow workers, employers, the members of their communities as supporters, intermediaries, and, equally important, agents of future control. The actions of the parents and neighbors, as well as of the intermediary in the case of the arsonist-thief, illustrate the extensive involvement of those closest to the offender, as well as any victim in the process of community disapproval, offender accountability, victim reparation, and offender restoration and control. Japanese criminal justice authorities, thus, rely heavily on community participation, both through formally-organized programs and informal family, firm, and neighborhood relationships. They count on community support for their efforts and, above all, the corrected offender. The latter is not just a matter of altruism. The family (grandparents, parents, siblings), as well as others related to an offender, must demonstrate their acceptance of responsibility for the offender and their willingness and ability to provide future control. This is obviously the most difficult feature of the Japanese model for others to emulate. The Japanese, however, teach us the need to foster greater community, including family, support to offenders who wish to reform.

The overriding aim of the Japanese system is to control crime. Consequently, its fundamental emphasis is correction. Determination of guilt is, of course, essential. Neither crime control nor correction results when innocent suspects are convicted. Law enforcement officials at all levels tend to share this objective, in what Shikita (1982) refers to as an integrated approach to criminal justice. Thus, their roles are not confined to the formal tasks of apprehending, prosecuting, and adjudicating. Once convinced that a suspect is an offender, their concern for evidentiary proof of guilt shifts to a concern over the suspect's attitude and prospects for rehabilitation and reintegration into society, including acceptance of authority. The authorities are not concerned with abstract notions of just deserts or of a debt to society to be satisfied by a penalty. They focus instead on the offender. Penalties may be imposed for deterrence, and offenders incarcerated to incapacitate, to prevent future criminal activity. However, they do not insist on imposing a penalty that fits a particular offence, or have special concern for equal treatment of different offenders for a like offence. Although the Criminal Code and related statutes provide more serious penalties for more serious crimes, and equal treatment of offenders is a constitutional norm, neither of these principles preludes the Japanese police, prosecutors, or judges from making the offender, the victim, and the community their principal concern and from adapting the penal system to serve a correctional goal.

Leniency is considered an appropriate response if the correctional process has begun. The sincerity of confession and remorse in turn becomes a significant factor in deciding whether correction is likely. Since confession and repentance provoke leniency, and most do confess, law enforcement authorities also generally expect offenders to confess and to behave with remorseful submission. For a suspect, whom the authorities believe to be guilty, not to confess, poses a dilemma. Either they have erred and the suspect is not guilty, or he is unrepentant, in denial, and therefore less correctable. In these circumstances, it is not surprising that police, prosecutors, and judges are tempted to induce or coerce an acknowledgement of guilt. The more convinced the authorities become that the suspect is guilty, the more likely they are to resort to harsh and abusive measures. Yet, there is also a mitigating incentive for them to re-examine more carefully the evidence of guilt before attempting to coerce the suspect.

Most studies of the criminal process in Japan note the evidentiary importance of confession, but seldom proceed further to analyze its implications or to note the victims' role in the process. A few depict the dark side. Futaba Igarashi, for instance, is among the best known critics of the use of confessions in the Japanese-criminal process. As an attorney, she has written extensively on the use of torture and threats by police interrogators to coerce confessions from suspects, especially in cases involving violent activities by political dissidents (Igarashi, 1977, 1980, 1984). Most English language studies of the Japanese police have been far more positive. They also focus on the evidentiary value of the confession, but they generally conclude that the Japanese not only share a propensity to confess, but also expect lenient treatment, explained to a large extent by child-rearing practices and other cultural phenomena (Bayley, 1976; Ames, 1981; Parker, 1984). Conceding the temptation of the police and procuracy to coerce confessions from seemingly unrepentant suspects, Bayley argues:

> Despite these factors in favor of pressing for a confession, most informed observers—lawyers, criminal reporters, law professors and prosecutors—contend that instances of abuse of persons in custody are rare. Celebrated cases have occurred but the incidence is small...(1976, p.152).

Bayley notes the strength of "the psychological compulsion to confess" and the "enormous moral authority" of the Japanese police (Bayley, 1976). "So," he concludes, "guilt is admitted in Japan for a variety of reasons: because it is a moral imperative, but also because it is a quid pro quo for leniency" (1976). Japanese tend to be more critical (Miyazawa, 1992).

No person in Japan is convicted solely by confession. Unlike the U.S., the U.K., and other common law jurisdictions, there is no guilty plea in civil law systems like Japan, to eliminate the need for a trial on guilt. In all cases, even summary proceedings, an evidentiary hearing is necessary to determine that a crime has been committed and the guilt of the accused (Dando, 1965). Moreover, because there is no jury or lay participation (as in Germany), the judges (in all criminal and civil trials except those for minor crimes and for civil claims a three judge panel is required) have a duty to clarify the evidence and, as the finder of fact, to be convinced of guilt and, thus, of the reliability of any confession (Dando, 1965). Prosecutorial and judicial scrutiny of collaborative evidence is not likely to be as vigorous if the accused has confessed and offers no defence. Nevertheless, such procedural protections may not be as important a control on accuracy as the concern of judges, police, and prosecutors over the sincerity of the confession and demonstrated remorse. The possibility of diversion itself provides a telling test of credibility. The less severe the penalty, and the greater the possibility of restoration, the less the incentive an offender has for false denial. With confession the process of correction can, therefore, begin.

Cultural explanations tend to be equally, albeit more subtly, ethnocentric, by quarantining the Japanese experience and denying its relevance outside Japan's peculiar cultural setting. There is no question that history and societal values underpin the pattern of confession, repentance, and absolution, in Japan. East Asian legal orders all place emphasis on confession. At least as early as the T'ang dynasty (AD 619-906), codified Chinese law provided for more lenient treatment to those who confessed. If the commission of the crime itself was unknown to the authorities, confession resulted in pardon (Johnson, 1979), and for all categories of crime, confession gained a reduction in penalty (Johnson, 1979). Similar patterns are observed in contemporary China (Cohen, 1968). Differentiated from evidence or proof of guilt (Shiga, 1974), confession was a means of insulating the officials from committing error, and of maintaining the legitimacy of their authority. Thus, the authorities pressed for confession and, in turn, regulations were imposed on torture and other means of coercion to protect the credibility of confessions as evidence. Hulsewe (1955) notes the existence of an edict restricting the use of torture to ensure the accuracy of coerced confessions from as early as AD 84. During the era of Mongol domination under the Yuan dynasty (AD 1280-1386), greater emphasis was placed on the victims' restitution and penalties were reduced (Ch'en, 1979). Apparently, in the succeeding Ming (AD 1368-1644) and Ch'ing (AD 1644-1912) dynasties, the severity of penal sanctions was restored, although compensation of the victim continued to be demanded as an additional penalty (Ch'en, 1979).

Societal values in Japan also encourage the use of confession, but, more importantly, they also permit a lenient response. Repentance and forgiveness is a pervasive theme evident throughout Japanese culture, from adaptations of Western fairy tales to conventional social behavior (Bayley, 1976). In this respect the West, not Japan, should be considered remarkable. The moral imperative of forgiveness as a response to repentance is surely as much a part of the Judeo-Christian heritage as the East Asian tradition, as evidenced in the Book of Jonah as well as the parable of the unforgiving servant (Matthew 18). However, whatever the reason, unlike Japan, Western societies have failed to develop constitutional props for implementing such moral commands. Instead, the legal institutions and processes of Western law both reflect and reinforce societal demands for retribution and revenge. This contrast between Japan and the West illustrates the failings of most cultural explanations. Most depict reality in static terms. They offer rationalizations for what exists and miss the critical contrasts between the reinforcement and disintegration of similar values in different societies.

There must also be community consensus that the crime does represent wrongful conduct. Japanese criminal justice authorities are acutely aware that their approach is not effective within gangs (*yakuza*) and other deviant communities. Therefore, they tolerate a degree of illegal behavior within such communities, so long as the general community is not affected. Consequently, there is close surveillance of gangs and gangster activity, but the police do not attempt to eliminate such organizations altogether. David Bayley suggests several reasons, including strictly interpreted laws against entrapment, and fears of potential police corruption. He includes a negotiated tolerance:

> Another explanation may be that there is a tacit agreement, sometimes renegotiated in face-to-face meetings, between police and yakuza that the police will turn a blind eye to certain forms of yakuza criminality as long as they will protect the public from the violence of their members, hangers-on, and street punks in general and do not import and sell drugs (Bayley, 1991, p.185).

In effect, the police and other law enforcement authorities in Japan appreciate the utter impossibility, short of a fully mobilized police state, of successfully eliminating crime as long as role models accept what others may define as deviant. The best that can be done is to tolerate a degree of criminal activity in exchange for control over their members and avoidance of what most authorities consider to be the illegal activities that pose the greatest dangers for the society as a whole.

## LESSONS LEARNED

Few Japanese or outside observers seem yet to recognize the implications of the Japanese experience. Typical is a study of Tokyo, undertaken by the Citizen's Crime Commission of Philadelphia (1975); the study identified two dozen differences between Japan and the U.S. that would account for significantly lower crime rates in Japan. Some were purely cultural: Japan's ethnic homogeneity, its insularity, the cohesion of the family unit, a sense of self-discipline, the influence of meditative religions, high literacy rates. Other explanations were more structural or institutional: the accommodation of unskilled workers in the work-force, a unified, national crime control system, and emphasis on counselling and mediation of disputes, police recruitment and training, the family court system. Nowhere, however, did the report mention how offenders or the victims of crime are actually treated within the system. Nor did it explain how crime in Japan has been reduced. Apparently, no statistics are kept by Japanese authorities on confessions or compensation, nor have Japanese criminologists displayed much interest in assessing the positive impact of confession and compensation on either offender or victim. Studies by the principal criminological research programs in Japan, such as the National Research Institute of Police Science, typically concentrate on the clarification of factors that contribute to criminal behavior, rather than rehabilitation. We can search their voluminous publications in vain for even a description of the informal process, much less its effects. Criminologists and criminal law specialists have also been preoccupied with Western approaches to the neglect of indigenous patterns. Haruo Abe, for example, excoriates judges for being too lenient (Abe, 1963). Others adopt Western concerns and approaches (Miyazawa, 1970, 1992). The Japanese, no less than their counterparts in the West, tend to view Japan's experience in static, cultural terms, seemingly buttressed by the somewhat smug belief that Japan's success is largely the product of a unique cultural identity.

Nevertheless, evidence continues to mount that the Japanese pattern—acknowledgment of guilt, expression of remorse, including direct negotiation with the victim for restitution and pardon as preconditions for lenient treatment, and sparing resort to long-term imprisonment—does contribute to a reduction in crime. The most recent empirical study of recidivism in relation to the disposition of offenders in Japan, confirms prior research (Haley, 1990; Kawada, c. 1978; Dando, 1970; George, 1984). Recidivism rates decrease in correspondence with the early diversion of offenders and their restoration to the community. Those who serve prison terms are considerably more likely to become repeat offenders. A growing amount of literature is emerging outside Japan on the importance of acknowledgment of guilt and restitution of victims to the psychological rehabilitation of offenders and attitudes of victims towards the offender and the criminal justice system. Studies by Elaine Walster, Ellen Berscheid, and G. William Walster (1967, 1970, 1973) seem especially noteworthy for evaluating the Japanese approach (Macauley and Walster, 1971). They and others (Sykes and Matza, 1957) have found that offenders attempt to relieve distress experienced after committing a crime involving harm to others by justification, derogating the victim, and denying responsibility, or restitution. Although decades of research on recidivism have yielded few conclusive findings (Maltz, 1984), studies that deal with even discrete facets of a restorative approach to criminal justice note similar results (Van Voorhis, 1985; Baxter *et al.*, 1993).

Limited intervention—for example, a few hours of victim-offender mediation—cannot be expected to have a significant effect on the offender (Marshall, 1995; Umbreit, 1995, 1994). There is, however, considerable empirical support for the notion that encouraging offender remorse, acceptance of the need for correction, and victim reparation, together with the prospect of being able to rejoin and participate as an accepted member of the community, do tend to reduce recidivism. An added benefit of the Japanese approach is that the emphasis on victim reparation and restoration reduces societal demands for revenge and retribution and, thus, facilitates efforts by law enforcement authorities to provide effective means for offender correction. As societal demands for punishment and retribution are reduced, the authorities are able to respond with greater leniency. The now abundant empirical evidence on victim participation in the legal process in the United States and Canada, indicates that victims who have some voice in the process are not only more satisfied with the process itself, but also, if negotiated restitution is attempted, may be less inclined to view whatever penalty imposed as inadequate (Goldstein, 1982; Haley, 1995; Umbreit, 1992, 1995). This would also explain why the Japanese are more tolerant of leniency and are more willing to accept whatever punishment the law prescribes. Hamilton and Sanders (1992) found that Japanese were considerably more likely to prefer a response to criminal behavior that tends to restore relationships, in comparison to the Americans who favored sanctions that tend to isolate and outcast offenders. It appears, therefore, that the Japanese approach contributes a process of positive reinforcement, in which correction is more likely both to succeed and to be a more socially acceptable and politically feasible objective.

Many of the most effective programs to correct or prevent behavior operate on similar principles. One of the most familiar, strikingly effective, and cost efficient, is Alcoholics Anonymous. Other examples include a variety of treatment programs for drug abuse as well as violence control that are premised on the patient's acknowledgement of the need for correction and submission. Closer to the Japanese model, and more thoroughly restorative, are initiatives in Canada designed to deal with offences in indigenous First Nation communities. By means of circle sentencing, the community, including those in authority, the victims and their supporters, as well as the families and friends of offenders, join together to deal with the offence, its causes, and the accountability of the offender (LaPrairie, 1994; Stuart, 1994). In New Zealand, a similar program of family group conferences is being used nationwide for all juvenile offenders, under the 1989 Children Young Persons and their Families Act (Brown, 1994; Braithwaite and Mugford, 1994).

The most noteworthy of all is the Australian family conferencing program, which was influenced by both the New Zealand example and John Braithwaite's theory of social control, a model explicitly based on Japan (Braithwaite, 1989; Braithwaite and Mugford, 1994). As in the case of Japan, the Australian program is managed by criminal justice authorities: the police. It expands more familiar North American victim-offender mediation efforts by including the widest feasible circle of those hurt by the offence, potentially anyone affected negatively, as well as the extended family and friends of the offender. The process proceeds in a manner that is otherwise nearly the same as victim-offender mediation, with a trained police officer as facilitator. Each participant relates how he or she was affected. The offender is thus confronted with the fullest possible accounts of the consequences of the act, but is also given the opportunity to explain and to express remorse. The family becomes an important source of disapproval as well as of restoration. The offender is not left as an outcast, but is enabled by the experience to begin to earn his or her way back into the community by accepting responsibility, including corrective future action, and making acceptable amends. These programs demonstrate that nearly all the most effective efforts to correct offenders reflect elements of the Japanese approach as a model of restorative justice, and that integration of these elements into a coherent system of criminal justice is possible.

The lessons of the Japanese experience are being learned. Whether directly related, as in the case of Australia, or simply coincidental, as in New Zealand, an increasing number of experimental programs, based on a restorative approach, are demonstrating the efficacy of the Japanese approach in very different cultural and institutional contexts. This is not to say that the Japanese criminal justice system can or should be fully replicated. What we have to learn from Japan is simpler and more basic: that restorative approaches are successful in correcting offenders, empowering and healing victims, and restoring the community. The Japanese experience thus provides insights for other industrial societies seeking to establish a more humane and just system of criminal justice, one free from the human and economic costs of overcrowded prisons, increasing crime, and victim alienation. The lesson learned is that restorative justice works.

## REFERENCES

Abe, H. (1963). "The Accused and Society: Therapeutic and Preventive Aspects of Criminal Justice in Japan." In: A. von Mehren (ed.), *Law in Japan: The Legal Order in a Changing Society*. Cambridge, MA: Harvard University Press.

Ames, W.L. (1981). *Police and Community in Japan*. Berkeley, CA: University of California Press.

Appleton, R.B. (1949). "Reforms in Japanese Criminal Procedure Under Allied Occupation." *Washington Law Review* 24(4):491-530.

Bayley, D.H. (1976). *Forces of Order: Police Behavior in Japan and the United States*. Berkeley, CA: University of California Press.

Baxter, B.L., P.H. Salzberg and J.E. Kleyn (1993). *The Effectiveness of Deferred Prosecution in Reducing DWI Recidivism: An Update*. (Technical Report 93-01). Seattle, WA: Alcohol and Drug Abuse Institute, University of Washington.

Braithwaite, J. (1989). *Crime, Shame and Reintegration*. Cambridge, UK: Cambridge University Press.

—and S. Mugford (1994). "Conditions of Successful Reintegration Ceremonies: Dealing with Juvenile Offenders." *British Journal of Criminology* 34(2):139-171.

Brown, M.J.A. (1994). "Empowering the Victim in the New Zealand Youth Justice Process." Address to the 8th International Symposium on Victimology, Adelaide, AUS.

Castberg, A.D. (1990). *Japanese Criminal Justice*. New York, NY: Praeger.

Citizen's Crime Commission of Philadelphia (1975). *Tokyo: One City Where Crime Doesn't Pay*. Philadelphia, PA: Author.

Ch'en, P.H. (1979). *Chinese Legal Tradition under the Mongols: The Code of 1291 as Reconstructed*. Princeton, NJ: Princeton University Press.

Cohen, J.A. (1968). *The Criminal Process in the People's Republic of China: An Introduction*. Cambridge, MA: Harvard University Press.

Dando, S. (1965). *Japanese Criminal Procedure*. South Hackensack, NJ: Fred B. Rothman (translated by B.J. George).

—(1970). "System of Discretionary Prosecution in Japan." *American Journal of Comparative Law* 18(2):518-531.

Foote, D.F. (1992). "The Benevolent Paternalism of Japanese Criminal Justice." *California Law Review* 80(2):317-390.

George, B.J. (1984). "Discretionary Authority of Public Prosecutors in Japan." *Law in Japan: An Annual* 17:42-72.

Goldstein, A.S. (1982). "Refining the Role of the Victim in Criminal Prosecution." *Mississippi Law Journal* 52(3):515-561.

Haley, J.O. (1990). "Confession, Repentance and Absolution." In: M. Wright and B. Galaway (eds.), *Mediation and Criminal Justice: Victims, Offenders, and Communities*. London, UK: Sage Publications.

—(1991). *Authority Without Power: Law and the Japanese Paradox*. London, UK: Oxford University Press.

—(1995). "Victim-Offender Mediation: Lessons from the Japanese Experience." *Mediation Quarterly* 12(3):233-248.

Hamilton, V.L. and J. Sanders (1992). *Everyday Justice: Responsibility and the Individual in Japan and the United States*. New Haven, CT: Yale University Press.

Hōmusho (Ministry of Justice of Japan) (1988-1994). *Hanzai Hakusho*, [annual] (White paper on crime). Tokyo, JAP: Author.

—(1983). *Hōmu Nenkan Shōwa 58 Nen* (Yearbook on Administration of Justice 1983). Tokyo, JAP: Author.

Hulsewe, A.F.P. (1955). *Remnants of the Han Code* (Vol. 1). Leiden, NETH: Brill.

Igarashi, F. (1977). "Daiyo Kangoku Mondai Ni Tsuite." (Concerning the Problem of Substitute Jails). *Jurisuto* 637:116-125.

—(1980). "Nase 'Keiji Ryuchijo' ga Hitsuyo Ka?" (Why are 'criminal detention centers' necessary?). *Jurisuto* 712:85-91.

—(1984). "Crime, Confession and Control in Contemporary Japan. *Law in Context* 2:1-30 (translated by G. McCormick).

Johnson, W. (1979). *The T'ang Code: General Principles* (Vol. 1). Princeton, NJ: Princeton University Press.

Kawada, K. (c. 1978). Suspension of Prosecution in Japan. Unpublished paper prepared for United Nations Asia and Far East Institute for the Prevention of Crime and Treatment of Offenders, Tokyo, JAP.

Keisatsu cho (National Police Agency) (1979). *Hanzai Tōkei Shōwa 54 Nen* (Crime Statistics, 1979). Tokyo: Author.

—(1985). *Keisatsu Hakusho Shōwa 60 Nen* (Police White Paper 1985). Tokyo: Author.

Koshi, G.M. (1970). *The Japanese Legal Advisor: Crimes and Punishments*. Rutland and Tokyo, JAP: Charles E. Tuttle.

LaPrairie, C. (1994). Altering Course: New Directions in Criminal Justice. Unpublished paper.

Macauley, S. and E. Walster (1971). "Legal Structures and Restoring Equity." *Journal of Social Issues* 27(2):17-95.

Maltz, M.D. (1984). *Recidivism*. New York, NY: Academic Press.

Marshall, T.F. (1995). "Restorative Justice on Trial in Britain." *Mediation Quarterly* 12(3):217-231.

Meyers, H. (1950). "Revisions of the Criminal Code of Japan During the Occupation." *Washington Law Review* 25(1):104-134.

Ministry of Justice of Japan (1964-1992). *Summary of White Paper on Crime* [annual]. Tokyo, JAP: Author.

Miyazawa, K. (ed.) (1970). *Hanzai to Higaisha: Nihon no Higaishagaku* (Crime and Victims: Study of Victims in Japan). Tokyo, JAP: Seibundo.

—(1992). *Policing in Japan: A Study on Making Crime.* Albany, NY: State University of New York Press.

Nagashima, A. (1963). "The Accused and Society: The Administration of Criminal Justice in Japan." In: A. von Mehren (ed.), *Law in Japan: The Legal Order in a Changing Society.* Cambridge, MA: Harvard University Press.

Oyama, K. (c. 1978). Criminal Justice in Japan. IV. Unpublished paper prepared for United Nation Asia and Far East Institute for the Prevention of Crime and Treatment of Offenders, Tokyo, JAP.

Parker, C.J. (1984). *The Japanese Police System Today: An American Perspective.* Tokyo, JAP: Kodansha International.

Saikō Saibansho Jimu Sōkyoku (Supreme Court of Japan General Secretariat) (1984) *Shōwa 59 Nen Shihō Tōkei Nenpō: 2 Keijihen* (1984 Judicial Statistics Annual Report: Vol. 2, Criminal Cases). Tokyo, JAP: Author.

Saikō Saibansho Sōkyoku (1993). *Heisei 4 Nen Shihō Tōkei Nenpō: 2 Keijihen* (1993 Judicial Statistics Annual Report, Vol. 2, Criminal Cases). Tokyo, JAP: Author.

Shiga, S. (1974). "Criminal Procedure in the Ch'ing Dynasty." In: *Memoirs of the Research Department of the Toyo Bunko.* Tokyo, JAP.

Shikita, M. (1982). "Integrated Approach to Effective Administration of Criminal and Juvenile Justice." In: *Criminal Justice in Asia: The Quest for an Integrated Approach.* Tokyo: United Nations Asian and Far Eastern Institute.

Stuart, B. (1994). "Sentencing Circles: Purpose and Impact." *National* 3(4):13-20.

Supreme Court of Japan (1977). *Outline of Criminal Justice in Japan.* Tokyo, JAP: Author.

Sykes, G.M. and D. Matza (1957). "Techniques of Neutralization: A Theory of Delinquency." *American Sociological Review* 22(6):664-670.

Thornton, R.Y. and K. Endo (1992). *Preventing Crime in America and Japan: A Comparative Study.* Armonk, NY and London, UK: M.E. Sharpe.

Umbreit, M.S. (1995). "The Development and Impact of Victim-Offender Mediation in the United States." *Mediation Quarterly* 12(3):263-276.

—(1994). *Victim Meets Offender: The Impact of Restorative Justice and Mediation.* Monsey, NY: Criminal Justice Press.

Van Voorhis, P. (1985). "Restitution Outcome and Probationers' Assessments of Restitution: The Effects of Moral Development." *Criminal Justice and Behavior* 12(3):259-286.

Walster, E. and E. Berscheid (1967). "When Does a Harm-Doer Compensate a Victim?" *Journal of Personality and Social Psychology* 6(4):4.35-4.41.

—E. Berscheid and G.W. Walster (1970). "The Exploited: Justice or Justification?" In: J.P. Macaulay and C. Berkowitz ( (eds.), *Altruism and Helping Behavior.* New York, NY: Academic Press.

—E. Berscheid and G.W. Walster (1973). "New Directions in Equity Research." *Journal of Personality and Social Psychology* 25(2):151-176.

Westermann, J.D. and J.W. Burfeind (1991). *Crime and Justice in Two Societies: Japan and the United States.* Pacific Grove, CA: Brooks/Cole.

Yamauchi, A. (1990). "Victim Restitution and the Japanese Criminal Justice System." In: V. Kusuda-Smith (ed.), *Crime Prevention and Control in the United States and Japan.* Dobbs Ferry, NY: Transnational Juris Publications.

Zehr, H. (1990). *Changing Lenses: A New Focus for Crime and Justice.* Scottsdale, PA: Herald Press.

# 21. RESTORATIVE JUSTICE THROUGH MEDIATION:

# THE IMPACT OF PROGRAMS IN FOUR

# CANADIAN PROVINCES

by

## Mark S. Umbreit

**Abstract:** *Data was collected from four Canadian victim-offender mediation programs, two serving primarily adult offenders and their victims and two serving primarily juvenile offenders and their victims. Post-program interviews were held with victims and offenders as well as with a comparison group of victims and offenders, who were referred to the programs but who chose not to participate; mediation sessions were observed and interviews were conducted with criminal justice officials. From 1991 through 1993, 4,445 offenders were referred to the programs, the majority of whom were adults. Thirty-nine percent of the referrals resulted in a face-to-face meeting with the victim and, when mediation occurred, 93% resulted in an agreement. Both victims and offenders who participated in mediation were significantly more likely to be satisfied (78% for victims and 74% for offenders) than those who were referred but did not participate. Ninety percent of both victims and offenders reported satisfaction with the terms of the mediated agreement. Eighty percent of both victims and offenders who participated in mediation reported that they had been treated fairly by the justice system; there is a significant difference between this group and those who did not participate in mediation. Victims who participated in mediation were significantly more likely than victims who did not participate in mediation to report that it was important for them to receive answers to questions from the offender, important for them to tell the offender the impact the event had had on them, important to receive an apology from the offender, and important to receive restitution from the offender. Offenders who participated in mediation were more likely than*

*those who did not participate to report that it was important to them to tell
the victim about what had happened, important to them to be able to
apologize to the victim, and important to them to negotiate a restitution
agreement with the victim. Victims who participated in mediation were
significantly less likely than those who did not to report fear of subsequently being revictimized by the same offender. The findings from this
Canadian study are strikingly similar to earlier reported findings from an
American study which used the same methodology and data elements.*

Mediation of criminal conflicts is a powerful expression of restorative
justice which emphasizes that crime is relational (not just against the
state), that the role of victims in the justice process should be elevated,
and that the focus of justice should be upon restoring emotional and
material losses left in the wake of crime, and upon building safer communities through active citizen participation (Zehr, 1990). High levels of
client satisfaction with the mediation process and outcome have consistently been found over the years in studies throughout North America
and Europe (Coates and Gehm, 1989; Collins, 1984; Dignan, 1990;
Fischer and Jeune, 1987; Galaway, 1988; Galaway and Hudson, 1990;
Gehm, 1990; Marshall and Merry, 1990; Perry *et al.*, 1987; Umbreit,
1989, 1991, 1993, 1994, 1995; Umbreit and Coates, 1993; Wright and
Galaway, 1989). Studies have found higher restitution completion rates
(Umbreit, 1994), reduced fear among victims (Umbreit and Coates,
1993; Umbreit, 1995), and reduced future criminal behavior (Butts and
Snyder, 1991; Schneider, 1986; Umbreit, 1994). Multi-site studies have
been completed in England (Marshall and Merry, 1990) and the U.S.
(Coates and Gehm, 1989; Umbreit, 1994). This chapter reports findings
from four victim-offender mediation programs in Canada.

Most victim-offender mediation programs employ a process of intake,
preparation for mediation, mediation, and follow up. Two of the programs (Winnipeg and Ottawa) refer to their clients as the accused, since
no formal admissions of guilt have occurred. Similarly, these two programs refer to complainants rather than to victims.

During the intake phase, case information is logged and the case is
assigned to a mediator. The preparation for the mediation phase involves
a considerable amount of work. The parties involved in the conflict will
be contacted separately and interviewed. In most victim-offender mediation programs, the mediator will call and then later meet separately with
the victim and the offender. In two of the programs in this study, however, the mediator had no prior contact with the parties. Staff in the

agency contact the parties by letter and most often interview them by phone. An in-person interview will occasionally be conducted when deemed appropriate. The mediation phase consists of the joint victim-offender meeting. The agenda usually focuses first on clarifying information about the alleged or actual criminal behavior, and on expressing concerns that one or both parties may have. The second part of the mediation session addresses the issues related to the impact that the conflict had on the parties, usually culminating in a discussion of the losses experienced by the victim and the potential for the offender to compensate the victim. This often results in the parties negotiating an agreement to restore losses incurred or to address other concerns. Mediation sessions tend to range in length from one to two hours. The follow-up phase consists of monitoring completion of any negotiated restitution that was agreed upon, intervening if additional issues arise or conflict develops between the parties, and scheduling follow-up joint meetings between the involved parties when appropriate, although this is not frequently done.

## METHODOLOGY

Community-based non-profit organizations, providing mediation services for referrals from the criminal justice system, were examined in Langley, British Columbia; Calgary, Alberta; Winnipeg, Manitoba; and Ottawa, Ontario. The programs in Langley, Calgary, and Winnipeg identify themselves as victim-offender mediation programs, whereas the program in Ottawa identifies itself as a criminal court mediation program. The four program sites are diverse in program design, community acceptance, caseload size, history, case management procedures, and impact on the criminal justice system; the diversity is summarized in Table 21.1. The programs in Winnipeg and Ottawa accept primarily adult cases. Both staff and community volunteers serve as mediators. Some programs also accept referrals from defence counsel, police, and either party involved in the incident. The Victim Offender Reconciliation Program in Langley and the Victim Young Offender Reconciliation Program in Calgary are more similar than the other two sites. The Victim Offender Mediation Program of Mediation Services in Winnipeg and the Criminal Pretrial Mediation Programme of The Dispute Resolution Centre for Ottawa-Carleton are also more similar to each other than to the Calgary and Langley sites.

*Table 21.1.* Program characteristics by site.

|                              | Calgary            | Langley            | Ottawa             | Winnipeg           |
| ---------------------------- | ------------------ | ------------------ | ------------------ | ------------------ |
| Program Start                | 1985               | 1982               | 1989               | 1979               |
| Organization Type            | Private Non-profit | Private Non-profit | Private Non-profit | Private Non-profit |
| Total Budget, 1991           | $69,025            | $55,000            | $55,000            | $105,290           |
| Total Budget, 1992           | $55,000            | $55,000            | $75,000            | $120,758           |
| Total Budget, 1993           | $55,000            | $55,000            | $85,000            | $122,000           |
| Staff (FTEs), 1991           | 1.7                | 2                  | 1                  | 4                  |
| Staff (FTEs), 1992           | 1.5                | 2                  | 1.6                | 4.6                |
| Staff (FTEs), 1993           | 1.5                | 2                  | 1.6                | 4.5                |
| # of Volunteer Mediators, 1991 | 0                | 30                 | 3                  | 50                 |
| # of Volunteer Mediators, 1992 | 0                | 30                 | 7                  | 55                 |
| # of Volunteer Mediators, 1993 | 1                | 25                 | 10                 | 55                 |
| Mediation Training Length    | 40 hrs.+ Apprentice-ship | 30 hrs. Class +3 Obser-vations | 3 Days + Apprentice-ship | 4.5 Days Apprentice-ship |
| Co-Mediators Routinely Used  | No                 | No                 | No                 | Yes                |
| Primary Referral Source      | Probation          | Probation          | Crown              | Crown              |
| Point of Case Referral       | Post-sentencing    | Pretrial/ Court Order | Postcharge/ Pretrial | Postcharge /Pre-plea/ Pretrial |
| Most Frequent Offence        | B & E              | Mischief           | Assault            | Assault            |

The Youth Advocacy and Mediation Services Program in Calgary was initiated in 1985 by the Calgary John Howard Society. This program assists victims better to understand their feelings about being victimized, and presents an opportunity to become more involved in the criminal justice system. The young people who choose to participate are given the opportunity to discuss the offence with the victim and decide upon a restitution agreement. From 1991 through 1993, 258 cases were referred to this victim-offender mediation program. The Victim Offender Reconciliation Program (VORP) in Langley, British Columbia, was initially developed in 1982 by the Langley Mennonite Fellowship and later became one of several programs of the Fraser Region Community Justice Initiatives, which was founded in 1985. The VORP is a community-based alternative that empowers participants to devise their own solutions in face-to-face encounters guided by trained community mediators. This program serves courts in both Langley and Surrey. From 1991 through 1993, a total of 851 cases was referred to the VORP. The Dispute Resolution Centre for Ottawa-Carleton was established in 1986 as a community based non-profit agency with the mandate to demonstrate and facilitate the practice of conflict resolution techniques within the community. The Centre works closely with crown attorneys. Mediation is conducted in selected cases after a charge has been laid by the police, but generally before the case has been set for trial. From 1991 through 1993, a total of 689 cases were referred to the Dispute Resolution Centre. The criminal court program of the Mediation Services in Winnipeg was established in 1979 as a victim-offender mediation project of the Mennonite Central Committee of Manitoba. In 1992, Mediation Services became independent of the Mennonite Central Committee, partly to establish a broader base of community support and involvement in the organization. The purpose of Mediation Services is to promote peace and restorative justice within the community by empowering people, through education and mediation, to resolve conflict using non-violent conflict resolution processes. From 1991 through 1993, a total of 2,647 cases were referred, representing the largest volume of case referrals to a single victim-offender mediation program in Canada.

Both quantitative and qualitative data were collected and analyzed. Phone interviews with victims and offenders were conducted two months following either the mediation session (experimental group) or the date that the prosecutor, court, or related agency, disposed of the case (comparison group). Twenty-four mediation sessions were observed. Interviews with court officials, program staff, and volunteer mediators, as well as reviews of records, were used to examine how the process of mediation with offenders and their victims was being applied, and to identify any public policy implications. Emphasis was placed upon understanding the application of the mediation process and the outcomes in differing programmatic and cultural settings. A total of 610 interviews were conducted with participants referred to mediation, involving 323 victims and 287 offenders. Fifty-nine percent of the victims were male, with an average age of 33 years; 86% were white. There were no significant differences between the mediation and no-mediation samples for victims. Eighty percent of offenders were male, with an average age of 24 years; 80% were white. Most offenders from the Ottawa and Winnipeg

Table 21.2. Program outcomes by site.

| | Calgary | Langley | Ottawa | Winnipeg | Combined |
|---|---|---|---|---|---|
| Case Referrals, 1991 | 40 | 317 | 178 | 725 | 1,260 |
| Case Referrals, 1992 | 79 | 349 | 200 | 963 | 1,591 |
| Case Referrals, 1993 | 139 | 185 | 311 | 959 | 1,594 |
| *Total Case Referrals, 1991-93* | *258* | *851* | *689* | *2,647* | *4,445* |
| Mediations, 1991 | 12 | 142 | 60 | 335 | 549 |
| Mediations, 1992 | 28 | 107 | 85 | 393 | 613 |
| Mediations, 1993 | 51 | 82 | 114 | 327 | 574 |
| *Total Mediations, 1991-1993* | *91* | *331* | *259* | *1,055* | *1,736* |
| Successfully Negotiated Agreements, 1991 | 11 (92%) | 141 (99%) | 53 (88%) | 299 (89%) | 504 (92%) |
| Successfully Negotiated Agreements, 1992 | 24 (86%) | 105 (98%) | 79 (93%) | 358 (91%) | 566 (92%) |
| Successfully Negotiated Agreements, 1993 | 48 (94%) | 81 (99%) | 111 (97%) | 290 (89%) | 530 (94%) |
| *Successfully Negotiated Agreements, 1991-1993* | *83 (91%)* | *327 (99%)* | *243 (94%)* | *947 (90%)* | *1,600 (93%)* |
| Proportion of Mediations to Case Referrals, 1991 | 33% | 45% | 34% | 46% | 44% |
| Proportion of Mediations to Case Referrals, 1992 | 36% | 31% | 43% | 41% | 39% |
| Proportion of Mediations to Case Referrals, 1993 | 37% | 44% | 37% | 34% | 36% |
| *Proportion of Mediations to Case Referrals, 1991-1993* | *35%* | *39%* | *38%* | *40%* | *39%* |

Table 21.3. Canadian cross-site program sub-samples.

| | Experimental Groups Participating in Mediation Samples | | Comparison Groups Referred but No-Mediation Samples | | Total Sample |
|---|---|---|---|---|---|
| | Victims | Offenders | Victims | Offenders | |
| Calgary Program | 7 | 7 | 2 | 5 | 21 |
| Langley Program | 42 | 41 | 37 | 42 | 162 |
| Ottawa Program | 42 | 16 | 22 | 12 | 92 |
| Winnipeg Program | 92 | 95 | 79 | 69 | 335 |
| TOTALS | 183 | 159 | 140 | 128 | 610 |

sites were adults. Aboriginals were the most frequent minority race for both victims and offenders. The most common offence referred was assault, followed by property crimes such as vandalism, theft, and burglary. The sub-samples within program sites are identified in Table 21.3.

## FINDINGS

The programs received 4,445 referrals during 1991 through 1993. Referrals were primarily adult cases. The Winnipeg program received a total of 2,647 cases during this three-year period. Langley had 851 cases referred, followed by the Ottawa-Carleton program with 689 referrals, and the Calgary program with 258. Nearly all referrals in Winnipeg and Ottawa were adult cases, while in Langley and Calgary most referrals were youth. Mediation sessions between the involved parties were held in 39% of the cases referred. Mediation rates were 35% in Calgary, 38% in Ottawa, 39% in Langley, and 40% in Winnipeg. Successfully negotiated agreements which were acceptable to both parties were reached in 93% of the cases that were mediated: 90% in Winnipeg, 91% in Calgary, 94% in Ottawa, and 99% in Langley.

Seventy-eight percent of victims and 74% of offenders who participated in the mediation reported satisfaction with the manner in which the justice system responded to their case, compared to 48% of victims and 53% of offenders who were referred but never participated in mediation (victims: $\chi^2 = 30.33$; 1 df; p = <0.005; offenders: $\chi^2 = 12.26$; 1 df; p = <0.005). Satisfaction with the outcome of the mediation session was reported by 89% of the victims and 91% of the offenders.

Table 21.4. Victim satisfaction with criminal justice system comparing mediated to non-mediated case.

| | Combined Sites* | | Calgary | | Langley | | Ottawa* | | Winnipeg* | |
|---|---|---|---|---|---|---|---|---|---|---|
| | Med. | Non-Med. | Med. | Non-Med. | Med. | Non-Med. | Med. | Non-Med. | Med. | Non-Med. |
| Satisfied (%) | 78.0 | 48.0 | 86.0 | 100. | 58.0 | 57.0 | 85.0 | 52.0 | 82.0 | 41.0 |
| Dissatisfied (%) | 22.0 | 52.0 | 14.0 | 0.0 | 42.0 | 43.0 | 15.0 | 48.0 | 18.0 | 59.0 |
| n= | 178 | 134 | 7 | 2 | 40 | 37 | 41 | 21 | 90 | 74 |

* Finding of significant difference between mediation and non-mediation samples (p = 0.05 or less).

Table 21.5. Offender satisfaction with criminal justice system comparing mediated to non-mediated cases.

| | Combined Sites* | | Calgary | | Langley | | Ottawa* | | Winnipeg* | |
|---|---|---|---|---|---|---|---|---|---|---|
| | Med. | Non-Med. | Med. | Non-Med. | Med. | Non-Med. | Med. | Non-Med. | Med. | Non-Med. |
| Satisfied (%) | 73.9 | 53.2 | 28.6 | 100.0 | 83.0 | 59.5 | 68.8 | 41.7 | 74.2 | 47.8 |
| Dissatisfied (%) | 26.1 | 46.8 | 71.4 | 0.0 | 17.0 | 40.5 | 31.2 | 58.3 | 25.8 | 52.2 |
| n=157 | 126 | 7 | 5 | 41 | 42 | 16 | 12 | 93 | 67 | |

* Finding of significant difference between samples (p = 0.05 or less).

Table 21.6. Victim satisfaction with outcome of mediation.

|            | Combined |      | Calgary |       | Langley |      | Ottawa |      | Winnipeg |      |
|------------|----------|------|---------|-------|---------|------|--------|------|----------|------|
| Satisfied    | (188) | 89%  | (7)  | 100% | (31) | 82%  | (39) | 93%  | (81) | 90%  |
| Dissatisfied | (19)  | 11%  | (0)  | —    | (7)  | 18%  | (3)  | 7%   | (9)  | 10%  |
| Totals       | (177) | 100% | (7)  | 100% | (38) | 100% | (42) | 100% | (90) | 100% |

Table 21.7. Offender satisfaction with outcome of mediation.

|            | Combined |      | Calgary |       | Langley |      | Ottawa |      | Winnipeg |      |
|------------|----------|------|---------|-------|---------|------|--------|------|----------|------|
| Satisfied    | (139) | 91%  | (7)  | 100% | (37) | 97%  | (14) | 93%  | (82) | 88%  |
| Dissatisfied | (13)  | 9%   | (0)  | —    | (1)  | 3%   | (1)  | 7%   | (11) | 12%  |
| Totals       | (152) | 100% | (7)  | 100% | (38) | 100% | (15) | 100% | (93) | 100% |

Perception of participating voluntarily in mediation was reported by 90% of victims and 83% of offenders at the combined sites; 91% of the victims and 93% of the offenders would participate in mediation again. Being fairly treated by the justice system was expressed by 80% of victims and 80% of offenders who participated in mediation, compared to 43% of victims and 56% of the offenders who were referred but who never participated in mediation (victims: $\chi^2$ = 43.59; 1 df; p = <0.005; offenders: $\chi^2$ = 12.17; 1 df; p = <0.005). The mediated agreement was viewed as fair by 92% of the victims and by 93% of offenders.

The importance of the victim receiving answers from the offender about what happened was more likely to be found among victims (87%) who participated in a mediation session with the offender, at the combined sites, than among victims (51%) who were referred but who never participated in mediation ($\chi^2$ = 50.19; 1 df; p = <0.005). The importance of the victim telling the offender the impact the event had upon him or her was more likely to be found among victims (89%) who participated in a mediation session with the offender, than among victims (51%) who were referred to mediation but who never participated in it ($\chi^2$ = 57.2; 1 df; p = <0.005). The importance of the victim receiving an apology from the offender was more likely to be found among victims (74%) who participated in a mediation session with the offender, than among victims (40%) who were referred but who never participated in mediation ($\chi^2$ = 36.49; 1 df; p = <0.005). The importance of the victim having been able to negotiate restitution with the offender was more likely to be found among victims (88%) who participated in a mediation session with the offender, than among victims (52%) who were referred but who never participated in mediation ($\chi^2$ = 51.52; 1 df; p = <0.005). The importance of the offender being able to tell the victim about what happened was more likely to be found among offenders (84%) who participated in a mediation session with the victim, than among offenders (68%) who were referred but who never participated in mediation ($\chi^2$ = 10.04; 1 df; p = <0.005). The importance of the offender having been able to negotiate a restitution settlement with the victim was more likely to be found among offenders (98%) who participated in a mediation session with the victim, than among offenders (77%) who were referred but who never participated in mediation ($\chi^2$ = 29.48; 1 df; p = <0.005). The importance of the offender apologizing to the victim was more likely to be found among offenders (78%) who participated in a mediation session with the victim, than offenders (67%) who were referred but who never participated in mediation ($\chi^2$ = 4.52; 1 df; p = <0.05).

An apology by the offender was more likely to have been seen among offenders (84%) who participated in a mediation session with the victim, than among offenders (30%) who were referred but who never participated in mediation ($\chi^2$ = 85.09; 1 df; p = <0.005). Fear of being revictimized by the same offender was less likely to be expressed among victims (11%) who participated in a mediation session with the offender, than among victims (31%) who were referred but who never participated in mediation ($\chi^2$ = 18.83; 1 df; p = <0.005). Remaining upset about the crime was less likely to be expressed by victims (53%) who participated in a mediation session with the offender, than among offenders (66%) who were referred but never participated in mediation ($\chi^2$ = 5.4; 1 df; p = <0.025).

The vast majority of criminal justice officials (n=45) (police constables, crown attorneys, defence attorneys, judges, probation officers) were supportive of mediating in appropriate criminal conflicts; they indicated an awareness that the major benefit provided by mediation was to address the emotional and informational needs facing the parties. Criminal justice officials at three of the four program sites indicated a high degree of satisfaction with the services provided by the local mediation program. They emphasized highly dedicated and committed program staff, competent and professional staff, and effective management and resolution of cases that are referred to the program.

Table 21.8. Victim's perception of fairness in justice system.

| Perceived: | Combined* | | Calgary | | Langley | | Ottawa* | | Winnipeg* | |
|---|---|---|---|---|---|---|---|---|---|---|
| | Med. | Non-Med. | Med. | Non-Med. | Med. | Non-Med. | Med. | Non-Med. | Med. | Non-Med. |
| Fair (%) | 79.9 | 42.7 | 42.9 | 50.0 | 63.2 | 48.6 | 87.8 | 42.1 | 86.4 | 39.7 |
| Unfair (%) | 20.1 | 57.3 | 57.1 | 50.0 | 36.8 | 51.4 | 12.2 | 57.9 | 13.6 | 60.3 |
| n= | 174 | | 124 | 7 | 2 | 38 | 35 | 41 | 19 | 88 68 |

\* Finding of significant difference between mediation and non-mediation samples ($p = 0.05$ or less).

Table 21.9. Offenders' perception of fairness in justice system.

| Perceived: | Combined* | | Calgary | | Langley | | Ottawa | | Winnipeg* | |
|---|---|---|---|---|---|---|---|---|---|---|
| | Med. | Non-Med. | Med. | Non-Med. | Med. | Non-Med. | Med. | Non-Med. | Med. | Non-Med. |
| Fair (%) | 80.1 | 56.2 | 57.1 | 100.0 | 81.0 | 69.2 | 68.8 | 47.0 | 83.3 | 47.0 |
| Unfair (%) | 19.9 | 43.8 | 42.9 | 0.0 | 19.0 | 30.8 | 31.2 | 53.0 | 16.7 | 53.0 |
| n= | 156 | | 121 | 7 | 5 | 37 | 39 | 16 | 11 | 96 66 |

\* Finding of significant difference between mediation and non-mediation samples ($p = 0.05$ or less).

## CONCLUSIONS

1. The findings relating to high levels of client satisfaction and perceptions of fairness with mediation in four Canadian Provinces are consistent with prior research in the U.S. which used a similar methodology, including common data elements and instruments (Umbreit, 1994; Umbreit and Coates, 1993). These similarities are summarized in Table 21.10. These findings were also consistent with a number of other studies conducted in the U.S. (Coates and Gehm, 1989; Galaway, 1988; Gehm, 1990; Umbreit, 1989, 1991) and in Europe (Dignan, 1990; Marshall and Merry, 1990; Messmer and Otto, 1992).

2. The quality of justice experienced by victims and offenders can be significantly enhanced by expanded use of mediation in criminal conflicts.

3. Mediation can provide an opportunity for victims to become actively involved in the process of holding the offender accountable, and of gaining a greater sense of closure.

*Table 21.10.* Comparison of Canadian and U.S. studies.

|  | Combined Canadian Victim-Offender Mediation Program Sites (4) | Combined American Victim-Offender Mediation Program Sites (4) |
|---|---|---|
| Victim satisfaction with mediation process | 78% | 79% |
| Offender satisfaction with mediation process | 74% | 87% |
| Victim satisfaction with mediation outcome | 89% | 90% |
| Offender satisfaction with mediation outcome | 91% | 91% |
| Victim perceptions of fairness in mediation | 80% | 83% |
| Offender perceptions of fairness in mediation | 80% | 89% |

# REFERENCES

Butts, J.A. and H.N. Snyder (1991). *Restitution and Juvenile Recidivism.* Pittsburgh, PA: National Center for Juvenile Justice.

Coates, R.B. and J. Gehm (1989). "An Empirical Assessment." In: M. Wright and B. Galaway (eds.), *Mediation and Criminal Justice.* London, UK: Sage Publications.

Collins, J.P. (1984). *Evaluation Report: Grande Prairie Reconciliation Project for Young Offenders.* Ottawa, CAN: Ministry of the Solicitor General of Canada, Consultation Centre (Prairies).

Dignan, J. (1990). *Repairing the Damage.* Sheffield, UK: Centre for Criminological and Legal Research, University of Sheffield.

Fischer, D.G. and R. Jeune (1987). "Juvenile Diversion: A Process Analysis." *Canadian Psychology* 28:60-70.

Galaway, B. (1988). "Crime Victim and Offender Mediation as a Social Work Strategy." *Social Service Review* 62:668-683.

—and J. Hudson (1990). *Criminal Justice, Restitution, and Reconciliation.* Monsey, NY: Criminal Justice Press.

Gehm, J. (1990). "Mediated Victim-Offender Restitution Agreements: An Exploratory Analysis of Factors Related to Victim Participation." In: B. Galaway and J. Hudson (eds.), *Criminal Justice, Restitution and Reconciliation.* Monsey, NY: Criminal Justice Press.

Marshall, T.F. and S. Merry (1990). *Crime and Accountability.* London, UK: Home Office.

Perry, L., T. Lajeunesse and A. Woods (1987). *Mediation Services: An Evaluation.* Manitoba, CAN: Research, Planning and Evaluation Office of the Attorney General.

Schneider, A.L. (1986). "Restitution and Recidivism Rates of Juvenile Offenders: Results From Four Experimental Studies." *Criminology* 24(3):533-552.

Umbreit, M.S. (1989). "Victims Seeking Fairness, Not Revenge: Toward Restorative Justice." *Federal Probation* 53(3):52-57.

—(1991). "Minnesota Mediation Center Gets Positive Results." *Corrections Today Journal* (August):194-197.

—(1993). "Juvenile Offenders Meet Their Victims: The Impact of Mediation in Albuquerque, New Mexico." *Family and Conciliation Courts Review* 31(1):90-100.

—(1994). *Victim Meets Offender: The Impact of Restorative Justice & Mediation.* Monsey, NY: Criminal Justice Press.

—(1995). *Mediating Interpersonal Conflicts: A Pathway to Peace.* West Concord, MN: CPI Publishing.

—and R.B. Coates (1993). "Cross-Site Analysis of Victim Offender Mediation in Four States." *Crime and Delinquency* 39(4):565-585.

Wright, M. and B. Galaway (1989). *Mediation and Criminal Justice.* London, UK: Sage.

Zehr, H. (1990). *Changing Lenses: A New Focus for Crime and Justice.* Scottsdale, PA: Herald Press.

# 22. VICTIM-OFFENDER MEDIATION: APPLICATION WITH SERIOUS OFFENSES COMMITTED BY JUVENILES

by

## Caren L. Flaten

**Abstract:** *The idea of using mediation as a tool to aid in the rehabilitation of juveniles has been explored since 1986 at a state agency that provides detention and residential services for youths in the juvenile justice system. A gruesome murder committed by a juvenile left two sisters searching for answers regarding the death of their mother, father, and aunt. This incident sparked realization that increased services were needed to provide for a more balanced system of justice and led to the mediation of serious offenses with juvenile offenders and their victims, in an attempt to provide a more restorative type of justice. This chapter describes seven serious offense mediations that were conducted with juveniles who had been convicted of murder, attempted murder, and burglary. The participants reported that the mediation was successful in terms of meeting goals of reconciliation, accountability, and closure. Careful preparation of participants and a time lag of about one year between offence/victimization and the mediation contributed to the success. These mediations resulted in an exchange of information, expression of emotions, and an increased understanding, rather than plans for restitution.*

This research was an in-depth study of the seven serious offense mediations that were undertaken in Anchorage, AK, to determine what factors contributed to their reported success. The mediations were all conducted with juveniles who were residing at McLaughlin Youth

Center, a state juvenile correction facility. The mediators reported that mediations had been successful in terms of meeting goals of reconciliation, accountability, and closure. The research was conducted to determine whether the mediation was considered successful by the participants and what variables contributed either to the success or lack of success of the mediation.

The process of victim-offender mediation appears to be effective for some, but not all, serious offense crimes. Bringing victims of serious crime together with their offender and a mediator is done in a relatively small number of cases because, according to Marshall and Merry (1993), it requires a lengthy period of preparation for both parties, and extensive coordination with other services in which the parties are likely to be involved. The success of all victim-offender mediations appears to lie in the personalizing of the crime (Hughes and Schneider, 1989).

Three questions were explored in the research:
1. Did the victim, offender, and mediator consider the mediation to be successful?
2. What variables contributed to the success of the mediation?
3. What variables contributed to the lack of success of the mediation?

The mediations were all co-facilitated by three mediators, with one assuming the lead role. The victim's advocate, offender's counsellor, and lead mediator participated in the mediations. The number of participants for each mediation ranged from four to ten, with an average of five per mediation. All the mediations, except one, took place at McLaughlin Youth Center. The seven serious offense mediations involved four crimes: victimization incidents including manslaughter, attempted murder, breaking and entering with attempted murder, and burglary. Preparations had been agreed to by all the participants prior to entering the mediation. The mediations followed the traditional victim-offender mediation model. They all began by the victim telling the offender how the crime had affected his or her life, which was then followed by the offender telling his or her story. Between one and two years following the mediation, efforts were made to interview all those who had participated. This was not possible in all cases, because some participants could not be located and one refused to be interviewed. The interview schedule included open and close-ended questions and was undertaken in personal interviews, in all cases except one. Information about those who participated in the mediations and those who were interviewed is summarized in Table 22.1.

*Table 22.1.* Participants in the seven mediations and participants interviewed.

|  | Number Participating in Mediation | Number Interviewed |
|---|---|---|
| Offenders | 7 | 4 |
| Victims | 11 | 7 |
| Victim's advocate | 4 | 4 |
| Offender's counsellor | 7 | 6 |
| Mediators | 7 | 6 |
| TOTALS | 36 | 27 |

# FINDINGS

## Manslaughter Case

This mediation involved a 16-year-old youth who shot and killed a 14-year-old youth. The crime occurred in the bedroom of the victim's home. Also in the room at the time of the murder was the victim's brother. The father, stepmother and two younger sisters were at home asleep for the night. The offender had been friends with the victim for many years, and was living with the victim's family due to difficulties experienced in his own home. The two families lived in the same neighborhood. The crime occurred at around 11:00 in the evening. When the offender arrived at the house after being out for the evening, he went to the bedroom that he shared with the two brothers and began playing a Russian Roulette type of game with a pistol. He reportedly pointed the gun at and pulled the trigger on himself first, with nothing happening. He then pointed it at the victim and shot him, which resulted in death. The younger brother witnessed the crime. The victim ran from the home and was apprehended a few hours later. He was charged with and convicted of manslaughter.

The mediation took place at the local victim advocacy office; participating were the victim's stepmother, brother, two younger sisters, and the offender. The mediation, which lasted about two hours, began surprisingly calmly. The participants were nervous, but everyone was polite and appeared ready to meet. The victims were given the chance to speak first, letting the offender know how the crime had affected their lives.

The father of the victim spoke first and was able to describe his feelings in a way that was non-threatening to the offender. According to one mediator, the tone of the meeting was set by his demeanor. All participants who were interviewed for this report stated the meeting was one of caring and of sharing grief for the victim. All reported the mediation to be successful in terms of meeting the needs of asking questions and gaining closure to the crime. The stepmother stated her motivation to participate was that she wanted to see the offender and tell him that she forgave him. This was very important to her, and was reiterated many times during the interview. She said things such as that she just wanted him to improve his life and become someone, that she still cared for him, and that her hope was he would grow old and be a good person. The victim said that the crime had hurt her so much because she had viewed the offender as a son, and stated that she had lost two sons. This had upset her greatly as she considered it a big loss in her life. She viewed the mediation as helpful because she was able to tell the offender that she loved him as a son, and most importantly was able to tell him that she did not hate him, and only wished for him to do good and succeed in life.

Prior to seeing the offender, the stepmother's two young daughters were afraid that he was going to come into the home and hurt them; they knew him, and could not understand what had happened. According to the mother, seeing him and listening to what he had to say during the mediation helped her daughters to understand and believe that he would not be coming to the home to hurt them. The evening of the mediation was the first night since the murder that the girls had been able to go to sleep without a night light on. Obtaining answers to questions about the crime and hearing the offender say he was sorry was helpful. The mother and son both stated that the mediation was helpful and that they would recommend it to other victims. The son said that he would have liked to meet with the offender alone, as he would have said or asked questions differently if his parents had not been present. He was not as convinced about the honesty of the offender, and felt that his life was much too easy in the youth correction facility. He thought that the mediation was very helpful to his family and to him in terms of sharing grief and asking questions, but said that he had additional questions regarding the crime which were not answered. All the participants felt strongly that the mediation process should be available to other victims of serious crimes.

This mediation took place approximately two years after the murder had been committed. All agreed that this was appropriate, as it gave the participants time to work on the many issues of anger, grief, and loss, and to become ready to accomplish goals of reconciliation and closure. All those interviewed stated that these goals had been obtained. Preparation for the mediation was the variable most often cited to have contributed to a positive mediation. Being able to ask questions and talking about feelings were the second most often cited variables. The type of preparation that helped the victims the most was talking about the crime with the victim's advocate, and receiving information about the mediation process. The mediators spent several months working with the participants, and believed that the preparation with both the offender and victim was the most important predictor for success. The offender had been involved in role-playing and individual counselling in an attempt to prepare him for the actual situation. The victims had been informed about the process through several meetings with the local victims' advocacy group and also staff at the institution.

The second mediation involved the same crime. This mediation occurred when the biological mother, who lived in New York State, heard about the success of the first mediation. She also desired information on and answers to this crime; she flew to Anchorage, and a mediation was arranged. The offender had been released, but was located and voluntarily agreed to participate in this mediation. Participating in the mediation were the victim's mother and the offender. The mother took total control of this mediation, which lasted about an hour and a half. She had prepared questions, was confrontational with the offender, and demanded many answers. She voiced her anger at the offender. The mediators felt that she was appropriate in her display of anger, but that she did not pose a physical threat to the offender. The seating arrangements of the participants and the setting provided for the safety of all present. The mediators reported that the mother had a clear agenda, which was to obtain answers to her prepared questions, and to let the offender know the damage he had done to her life. Although this mediation was more confrontational and less healing for the participants than the first, the mediators felt it was beneficial to the offender to hear and understand the pain and anger the victim was still experiencing. In addition, the victim was able to receive answers to some questions and also to express her feelings about the crime to the offender.

The victim had received information regarding the mediation process from her ex-husband, which was instrumental in her wanting to have a face-to-face meeting with the offender herself. Additionally, she had talked with a mediator about the process and what she hoped to accomplish. This preparation, although minimal, was cited as helping her achieve what she wanted from the mediation. Neither the victim nor the offender were interviewed for this mediation. Both the mediators stated that the mediation was successful in terms of meeting the needs of the victim, and reiterated that the victim had verbally stated that she was satisfied with the mediation. They said that the victim obtained answers to many of her questions and had stated that she regained some power and control over her life. After the mediation, however, the mother was instrumental in the offender being fired from his place of employment.

## Attempted Murder

This case involved a crime in which a 16-year-old male shot his friend's mother with a 12-gauge shotgun. The crime occurred around 4:00 p.m. The mother was seriously wounded in the chest and required extensive surgery and hospitalization. The offender and the victim's son had cut the phone line to the house, and were in the house waiting for the father/husband to come from work. They had planned to knock him out, rob him, steal his car, and drive out of the state. The mother received a call from her son's school informing her of his absence. She was concerned about this and so left work early to check on her son. She arrived home before her husband and went up the stairs calling for her son. The boys were not expecting her home and were very surprised to see her. They were hiding and were scared. They did not know what to do since she had arrived home first, they panicked and threatened her with the gun. When she saw the weapon, she attempted to talk the offender into giving it to her, and in the attempt, was shot in the chest. After being shot, she waited in the garage for her husband to come home. Her husband arrived home from work to find his wife bleeding, and the boys still in the house. After his mother had been shot, the son panicked, fled to his room and stayed there throughout the reminder of the incident. The offender was still in possession of the shotgun, and also had a stun gun. The father was able to get the shotgun and, in the attempt, was shot by the stun gun. During this fight, the victim was afraid that her husband would seriously injure the offender and so attempted to intervene in the fight. The police arrived and apprehended the offender. He was convicted of attempted murder in the first degree.

The mediation was conducted at McLaughlin Youth Center, lasted for approximately two hours, and involved the victim and offender. The victim was given the opportunity to speak first, letting the offender know how the crime had affected her life. Both participants stated that the mediation had started out tense and business-like, but had soon become emotional. The offender reported that it started out as a shock to him and that he felt numb. In addition, he stated that he was not sure what was going to happen, and so was scared. He reported that the mediation became very emotional for him. The victim reported the meeting to be compassionate as well as emotional, and used the term resolved to describe the end. The offender was then given the opportunity to address the victim. All participants reported the mediation to be successful in terms of meeting the need to ask questions and to gain closure to the crime.

The mediation occurred about 18 months after the crime. The victim felt this was a good time for the mediation to occur as it gave her time to come to terms with the crime and to be ready to address what had happened. She shared that her life had changed in many ways, such as requiring extensive counselling, suffering setbacks in her work and extreme sleep deprivation. She stated that, if the mediation had occurred earlier, she might not have been ready to meet with the offender in the positive way that she desired. All the participants were highly satisfied with the outcome, both immediately after the mediation and approximately a year later. The offender stated that the mediation affected him because he had had time to think about it and to realize the impact his crime had had on the victim. He felt very strongly that the mediation had helped him in his treatment process at the correction facility. The offender also stated that being forgiven and hearing the victim say that she did not hate him was beneficial in his treatment. The victim stated that the mediation changed her attitude towards the offender because he appeared regretful about how he had hurt her, and that she now felt at peace regarding the crime. She felt that the mediation was helpful to her, and was hopeful for the offender's future. She also felt enlightened, peaceful and hopeful.

The fourth mediation also involved this crime, and was with the husband. He reported being extremely thankful that he had been contacted and was included in a mediation. He felt he had been given adequate information regarding the process of the mediation. The mediation took place at McLaughlin Youth Center, and lasted about an hour. It was tense at the beginning, as a great deal of anger appeared to be present, but it was not out of control. As the meeting progressed, the anger and anxiety seemed to dissipate with an understanding being reached between the victim and the offender. The offender reported that he felt he understood what the victim wanted from him, and the victim reported that he saw the offender as a non-threatening person to his life when the mediation was over.

The offender thought the mediation was good. The victim stated that he still felt very strongly about the mediation, and could not praise it enough. He said, "The mediation saved my life, and I am so thankful I was able to participate". Preparation was cited by all the participants as being an important variable in the success of the mediation. Mentioned specifically was allowing sufficient time to pass and having the opportunity to express fear and anger prior to the mediation. The victim stated that, as a result of this mediation, he had an immediate release from the fear and hate he had been experiencing since the crime had occurred. He said that the mediation was a wonderful experience and that all the hatred that was driving him crazy had left as a result of it. In addition, he stated that the crime had affected his life emotionally, physically, and financially and, although the mediation did not cure all his problems, it went a long way in giving him the strength to address many of them.

## Breaking and Entering and Attempted Murder Case

Two males, aged 16 and 17, broke into a home, and shot and seriously wounded an adult male. The other occupants of the house, the victim's mother and two children, were not injured. The offenders were being pursued by the police. They had been involved in a crime spree and were attempting to avoid capture. The victim was upstairs reading when his son came into his room and told him someone had driven into the yard and had what appeared to be guns with them. The victim did not think this was possible and went to see who was there. As he was walking down the stairs, he saw the front door being forcibly kicked open. Offender A was wearing a ski mask. He entered the house, armed with a gun, and demanded the keys to the victim's vehicle. The idea was to switch vehicles in an attempt to avoid the police. While in the victim's house, the offender heard some noise upstairs. When he demanded the victim to bring the occupants down, the victim refused. A fight ensued, in which the victim attempted to wrestle the weapon away from the offender. The other youth (offender B) had circled around the house and entered from another entrance. Offender A yelled to his friend, "Shoot him, shoot him", which his friend did. The victim was shot in the side, which resulted in surgery and hospitalization. The offenders ran out of the house, hid the weapons, and walked to another house. They planned to ask the occupants for permission to use their phone in an attempt to get a friend to come and pick them up. The occupants of this house had been listening to the police on a scanner, and met the youths at the door at gun point. They held the youths until the police arrived. The offender in this case was charged and convicted of attempted murder. The injured victim got himself upstairs and directed his mother and two sons to lie in between some mattresses, as he was afraid that the youths might come back and start shooting.

The mediation with offender A lasted about one and a half hours and was reported to be surprisingly calm. The offender stated that he was nervous at the beginning but, after about 15 minutes, began to feel comfortable. The victim told the offender how the crime had affected his life. He was able to do this in a non-threatening manner, which set the tone for the remainder of the meeting. All the participants stated the meeting was open and honest. The victim described the meeting as open, honest and respectful. He stated that he felt there was some sincere regret and sorrow on behalf of the offender, which was helpful to him.

The victim then stated he had been contacted about 15 months after the crime occurred regarding the possibility of participating in the mediation. He felt that this was soon enough, stating that the timing of the mediation should be based on the rehabilitation progress of the offender. His motivation to participate in the mediation was to be helpful in the rehabilitation of the offender. The offender then stated he did not feel any pressure to participate in the mediation, but would have liked more information about the mediation process itself. He said he wanted to participate to let the victim know that the crime had not been directed at him personally, and that he wanted to tell him he was sorry.

The victim and offender were asked to rate the mediation with regard to how they felt about it approximately one year later. The victim stated that he felt the same positive level of satisfaction, and the offender then stated he would never forget what went on at the mediation. He further stated that the mediation was more helpful in his treatment process than all the other services he had participated in during the 30 months he had been in the correction facility. The offender shared that, while out on a weekend pass, he and his friends had contemplated burgling a house. He stated that he kept on seeing his victim's face in his mind, and could not break into the house. He further stated that this was a direct result of participating in the mediation. Talking to his victim face-to-face had provided him with the impetus to remember the hurt and pain he had inflicted, which prevented him from re-offending. Variables that contributed to the success of this mediation were the victim wanting to help in the offender's rehabilitation process, knowing about the mediation process, and preparation of both the victim and the offender.

All the participants were asked what they found most satisfying about the mediation experience. The victim was thankful for the opportunity to be able to let the youth know that he hoped he was changing for the better, and that he had had the opportunity to see him as a real person. The offender said that actually realizing he had hurt more than the victim, and hearing how he had affected the entire family, was very powerful to him. He also stated that he felt it was important to tell the victim that the crime was not personal and that he was sorry. The victim said he thought it had really helped for he and the offender to see each other as real persons and felt that, because of this, it might help the offender not to repeat offenses. He stated that he had already regained control over his life, but that the mediation had added to the feeling that he had handled the crime in the right way.

The sixth mediation was conducted with the victim and offender B, who had done the actual shooting. He was convicted of attempted murder in the first degree. The mediation lasted for about one hour, which all participants felt was an adequate amount of time. The session began tensely, with the victim sharing what had happened to him and his family as a result of the crime. Soon the mediation became a caring and emotional experience for all involved, as the victim was very forgiving to the offender, telling him to improve his life, and that he wished him well. The mediators reported the meeting to be so emotional and healing that, by the time it was over, there was not a dry eye in the room.

The participants were asked what they had found to be most satisfying about the mediation experience. The victim stated that letting the youth know he wanted him to change and providing the offender with the opportunity to see him as a real person was the most helpful. All the participants felt that preparation was crucial for a mediation to be successful. The mediators stated that it was important to make sure that the offender's level of empathy was such that the mediation would be beneficial. They also stated that it was helpful to explain to the offender the ways in which the mediation could help him. The victim reported the same responses to this mediation as he did to the previous one. He felt the offender was sorry for the crime and that the mediation had helped him to believe that the offender was making progress in his rehabilitation effort. All said that they would participate in the mediation experience again if given the opportunity, and would recommend it to other victims of serious crime.

## Uncharged Burglary Case

The victim's home had been burgled and a snow machine had been stolen. The victim, who believed the crime had been committed by a juvenile, desired to meet with a juvenile who had committed similar crimes. The staff at McLaughlin were aware that this particular offender had committed the crime but, when they asked him if he would agree to participate, he was told that he would not have to inform the victim that he was the actual person who had committed the crime. The offender, however, did let the victim know that it was he who had committed the offense. Participating in this mediation were the victim and the offender. Preparation was again cited as being the most important variable that contributed to the success of the mediation. The offender had participated in some role-playing activities and had been involved in intensive treatment for over a year prior to the mediation occurring. He was ready and willing to meet the victim.

When asked how they felt about the mediation after approximately one year had passed, the offender felt about the same, but the victim did not. The victim was dissatisfied that the restitution agreement had not been completed. He was unaware that the offender was still incarcerated, which prevented him from performing work for the victim. Additionally, the serious offense mediation did not have the sanction to authorize restitution agreements made between the victim and the offender, so that there was no enforcement procedure for this agreement. The victim stated that he wanted to ensure himself that the bad guy had been caught, and wanted to hear him admit that he had done the crime. He also stated that it was important for him to be able to vent his anger. The offender stated that it was important for him to be able to say he was sorry and to agree to do some restitution for the victim. The victim also felt that offenders should write papers on what they perceive went wrong in their lives, and how they got into their present situation. From this, he felt that society could better understand how to help them and others. He thought that mediations would be a good place to address this, as a possible agreement could be reached between the victim and offender. He said he thought that the offender was sorry about the crime he committed, but he was not positive about this. He felt strongly that the offender should be held accountable for what he had done, and said the mediation did not succeed in this venture as the offender had not followed through on his agreement with him. In addition, he stated that he still had some unanswered questions regarding the crime. The mediators felt the mediation was helpful to the offender, as it helped him realize he had committed a crime against a real person and not just an object. Also, both mediators and offender reported that realizing he had hurt an entire family was significant.

## DISCUSSION

The primary goal of this research was to determine whether serious offense mediations were perceived as being successful. Participants in six of the seven mediations viewed them as very successful. All the victims reported the mediation to be helpful to them in terms of closure. One victim said, "Can you imagine wanting to kill a 16 year-old kid?" "I was consumed with hate and rage and was worried what I would do when he got out." He stated that the mediation changed all that, and he was so thankful he had been able to participate. They all felt it was helpful in the process of accepting and understanding the crime as a past event. One victim reported having the first complete night's sleep since the crime had occurred, which he said was a direct result of the mediation. In another case, the victim stated that, after the mediation, her children were able to go to sleep without a night light for the first time since the crime. Many of the victims were concerned about the rehabilitation process, and stated that they felt it was important to tell the offender they wanted him to improve his life. Hearing the offenders say they were sorry and seeing them in person was very helpful to four of the victims. One victim reported that he had been living with such intense hate and fear that it was interfering with his daily functioning. After the mediation, however, not only did he not hate or fear the offender, but he also wished him well and offered to assist him in his re-habilitation process.

The offenders remarked that the mediation helped them to under-stand how they had affected more than just the individual they had physically harmed. One offender reported that it bothered him very much to know that an entire family was scared now because of him. He did not like the idea that he was viewed as a monster, and said that the mediation helped him realize how his crime had affected a wide range of people. Two of the offenders reported that actually seeing the victim made the victim very real to them. The power of the mediation was illus-trated by one of the offenders. His story about not being able to burgle a house because he kept on seeing the victim's face in his mind, speaks of the power and effectiveness of the crime being personalized as a result of the mediation. The offenders also stated that it was helpful to them to be able to tell the victims they were sorry and to explain that the crime was not personal.

All the victims felt strongly that the mediation process should be available to everyone who desires to participate, and that this informa-tion should be made available to other victims. One of the victims ex-pressed it best when she said, "My everlasting gratitude to the people who made the mediation possible, and for the intelligence, compassion and concern we were given...I wish more victims had this opportunity". All the participants in these mediations felt that all serious crimes were appropriate for mediation, depending on the willingness of the partici-pants and progression of treatment of the offender.

Preparation was the most important variable cited to contribute to the success of the mediation. The actual amount of preparation time was difficult to determine because of the many telephone conversations, counselling sessions, pre-mediation meetings, and the self-preparation completed by the participants. All the participants stated that they had undergone a great deal of preparation, which had involved many hours, taken place over many months, and had occurred in a variety of ways. In all the mediations, at least a year had passed since the crime had occurred, and many of the participants had been involved in some form of counselling, or had been in close contact with the victim's advocacy organization. All the participants felt that it was important to allow at least a year to pass before participating in the mediation. Having the opportunity to vent anger, sorrow, and other feelings, were variables cited as important in aiding in the success of the mediation. The offenders interviewed for this report felt strongly that the participation should be voluntary, and that a sufficient amount of treatment time should pass before a mediation could occur. The amount of treatment time necessary varies with each individual and can be determined by the mediators and the treatment team.

The mediators addressed issues of safety in terms of providing a safe location for the meeting. It is important for the victims to know that they are safe, which includes positioning of the participants. This should be addressed prior to the mediation. Some participants prefer to have a table or some type of barrier between them. All these issues should be addressed in the pre-mediation meetings, and be agreed upon by both victim and offender. One of the reasons why these mediations appeared to be so successful was that both the victim and the offender were given many choices for setting up and preparing for their mediations. Provision of a means of leaving the meeting in order to gain control of one's emotions was also identified as an important variable for ensuring the success of, and also feelings of safety and comfort during, the mediation. Participants need to be aware that they can get up and leave at any time, with the option of returning when they are ready.

Recommendations for improving the experience included allowing adequate time for debriefing following the mediation. These mediations were powerful and elicited varying emotions from all the participants, including the mediators. Debriefings were found to be necessary between the mediators. as well as with the victim and the offender in order to share thoughts and emotions. Making sure that the victim and offender both felt safe was a priority in all the mediations. Safety is an area that should always be addressed, with input from all the participants. Some of the participants would have liked a follow-up mediation or a way in which they could stay in touch with the further treatment progress of the offender. It was important for many of the victims to know how the offender was doing in treatment.

The mediations were helpful in the healing process of many of the participants, primarily because of the dialogue that occurred during the mediation. Serious offense mediations differ from property offense mediations, in that obtaining the traditional restitution agreement is not a primary goal. Facilitating dialogue between the participants to aid in the healing process appears to be a primary goal of serious offense mediation. The process is also emotional, healing, and beneficial to the offenders. Many of the mediators who were interviewed stated that they saw more emotions expressed by the offenders during the mediation than they had seen at any other time during treatment. These serious offense mediations were successful in all individuals who participated in them. Serious offense mediations require intensive preparation and a sensitivity to the special needs of the participants. The possibility of participating in mediation should be extended to a wide variety of victims and offenders.

## REFERENCES

Hughes, S.P. and A.L. Schneider (1989). "Victim-Offender Mediation: A Survey of Program Characteristics and Perceptions of Effectiveness." *Crime and Delinquency* 35(2):217-232.

Marshall, T.F. and S. Merry (1990). *Intermediate Outcome in Crime and Accountability: Victim Offender Mediation in Practice.* London, UK: Home Office.

# 23. SITUATION, ETHICAL GROUNDS AND CRIMINAL POLITICAL PERSPECTIVES OF VICTIM-OFFENDER RECONCILIATION IN THE COMMUNITY

## by
## Dieter Rössner

**Abstract:** *After World War II, criminal policy in Germany emphasized the reduction of repressive elements, and the system of imposing sanctions was oriented towards rehabilitation, including reducing the extent of imprisonment. For the past few years, constructive social alternatives have been considered in the field of ambulant sanctions. First is victim-offender reconciliation. In practice, compensation plays a considerable role, especially in criminal law relating to young offenders. Victim-offender reconciliation is mainly carried out by independent bodies of the youth welfare service and also by juvenile court assistance. Several projects have been started in the criminal justice system, and evaluation has shown good results. The majority of offences dealt with are bodily injury, theft, criminal damage, and, to some extent, robbery. The ethical explanation lies in the principle of self-responsible action and the principle that taking responsibility has priority over criminal constraint. Further, the victim's interests are taken far more into consideration, and conflict management gains importance. In 1992, a work group of German, Swiss and Austrian criminal law academics published a policy document (AE-WGM) that recommends introducing compensation into the system of legal consequences.*

*The German legislature has put this idea into practice under section 46 of the German Penal Code. This section provides that the judge may*

*decide to refrain from punishment in cases where a penalty of up to one
year is incurred and victim-offender reconciliation has taken place. The
public prosecutor may withdraw the charge on the same conditions. Victim-offender reconciliation has thereby become an integral part of the legal system of sanctions.*

## LEGAL FRAMEWORK FOR VICTIM-OFFENDER RECONCILIATION IN GERMANY

Twenty years ago, the goal of a modern system of sanctions in
Germany seemed to have been attained. Imprisonment for failure to pay
a fine, and the system of daily rated fines, had been established by
amendments to the criminal law. The priority of fines over imprisonment
was legally prescribed, the systems of disciplinary measures and probation were renewed, and caution with reservation of the right to punishment had been introduced. The reform was completed by the opportunity to sanction minor offences without conviction pursuant to Section
153a of the German Code of Criminal Procedure. These amendments
aimed at reducing, as far as possible, the harm caused by punishment,
by means of principles of proportionality and humanity. At that time, reform of the criminal system of sanctions was mainly regarded as being
complete; but it is now being questioned once again.

The dominance of treatment seen during the 1960s and 1970s is less
important, since no provable or general improvement has been seen. Research on sanctions is leading to the realization that criminal sanctions
are widely interchangeable with regard to their effectiveness, even from
the point of view of general prevention of crime. This disillusionment explains the growing interest in the search for constructive responses to
criminal offences (Schöch, 1992). Moreover, the victim and his or her interests and needs have increasingly become the focus of attention. Compensation for harm caused by the offence has come to the fore, as being
a positive response to criminal action (Rössner, 1992). Meanwhile, victim-offender reconciliation and compensation rank among the most
widely disputed proposals on reform in criminal policy. Despite its growing acceptance and legal applicability, victim-offender reconciliation is
still a marginal phenomenon when considering the whole system of
sanctions. Its application is generally recommended in studies, but the
real situation is different in practice.

There is a lack of systematically thought-out and problem-oriented integration of compensation into criminal law (Hering and Rössner, 1993). Within the framework of the German Code of Criminal Procedure, compensation is intended to be an alternative to formal sanctions (Section 380) or with regard to private criminal action (Sections 376 onwards). Conciliation proceedings prior to private criminal action are meant to settle criminal conflicts between victim and offender. In Section 153a (German Code of Criminal Procedure), the requirement to compensate is mentioned within the framework of informal dismissal of criminal proceedings regarding a minor offence. Compensation as an additional response accompanying sanctions is taken into account within the scope of suspension of sentence on probation (Sections 56 onwards, German Penal Code). When it comes to caution, with reservation of the right to punishment (Section 59, German Penal Code), the judge may dismiss the fine, subject to compensation for damage caused. Furthermore, voluntary offers of compensation and corresponding payments may serve as satisfaction. Reconciliation efforts should be considered in mitigation when fixing the penalty (Section 46 II, German Penal Code). The adhesion procedure, which was reformed in 1987 (Sections 403 onwards, German Code of Criminal Procedure), enables the verdict to be connected with a sentence for compensation of damages. Most of the rules are of little importance in practice. Fines are much more likely to be subject to condition rather than to compensation. The latter only applies in 1% of cases within Section 153a (German Code of Criminal Procedure), whereas there is a higher rate of suspension of sentences. Late in 1994, German legislature established a special regulation of compensation (Section 46a, German Penal Code) in general criminal law. It remains to be seen how the new regulations will influence legal practice, but major impacts are expected.

Compensation plays a more important role in criminal law relating to young offenders, because the first amendment of the Juvenile Court Law in 1990 (Section 45 II 2, Juvenile Court Law) explicitly emphasizes that efforts towards reconciliation are a reason for refraining from prosecution. Thus, the legal basis of projects dealing with victim-offender reconciliation has been strengthened. Victim-offender reconciliation is established as an independent legal consequence in two different sanctions of orders geared towards educative effects, and as disciplinary measures to punish the offender and to make it clear that injustice has been done (Sections 10 I 3 No. 7, 15 I No. 1). The victim-offender reconciliation system has been assessed positively in arguments concerning the new legal regulation. It reaches far beyond regulating damages, and provides the opportunity to reduce the mental strain on the victim and to restore confidence in the legal system. The offender is influenced in a positive manner by being confronted with the consequences of his or her actions, and by being forced to take responsibility for these actions. This kind of conflict management is much more suitable for the restoration of legal equilibrium, and for the effective prevention of recidivism, than any type of compulsion or suppression (Marks and Rössner, 1989; Rössner, 1990).

## RESTORATIVE LEGAL PRACTICE AND ITS EVALUATION

This evaluation is based on an assessment of all projects dealing with victim-offender reconciliation in Germany from 1985 until the end of 1990 (Bannenberg, 1993). It was compiled on the basis of the final reports on four extensive projects conducted among juveniles (Braunschweig, Cologne, Munich/Landshut, Reutlingen), as well as of a pilot project in Tübingen (Hering and Rössner, 1993). About 2,000 cases (approximately 350 of them adults) were covered.

Victim-offender reconciliation in projects in juvenile criminal law were carried out by the juvenile court assistance service, independent bodies, or an association set up to provide victim-offender reconciliation services. Victim-offender reconciliation among adults was only carried out by the court assistance service. Independent bodies for adult projects were not planned until 1991 and 1992. Victim-offender reconciliation work is conducted by social workers and social education workers, many of them from the offender's assistance service. Most of the projects were interested in restoring the legal equilibrium, as well as dismissing criminal proceedings after successful reconciliation. More importance was attached to the aim of preventing sanctions in youth projects than in adult projects. The public prosecutor's office referred most of the cases to the youth as well as to the adult projects. Far fewer cases were referred by the courts or by the juvenile court assistance service. A few cases were referred to the youth projects by the police. Admission criteria for most projects required a confession by the offender or clarified facts of the case, a real person as the victim, and voluntary willingness on the part of the victim and offender to attempt a reconciliation. Minor offences, which would have been dismissed, were excluded.

The study group included 439 cases from nine regular, not specially evaluated youth projects (compared to 1,257 cases in the four evaluated model projects); in addition, 155 cases from three regular adult projects were compared to 183 cases in the model project from Tübingen. Ineligible cases were not referred to the pilot projects or to Tübingen. For the remainder of the projects, 5% of youths referred and 9% of adults were not eligible. These cases were regularly returned without service. The rejection of cases was problematic, bearing in mind the small number of assignments. But it was clear that some admission criteria are required when selecting suitable cases for victim-offender reconciliation. A wide spectrum of cases was covered. In the youth projects, bodily harm had been inflicted on almost 55% of the victims (one-third of whom received long-term medical treatment, had to stay in hospital, or even sustained permanent physical damage). This rate was about 35% in the adult projects; a third of the victims suffering serious injuries. Among the most serious cases were attempted homicide, several cases of grievous bodily harm with serious consequences, and robbery and blackmail, accompanied by the use or threat of force. Financial damages were incurred in more than half these cases (55% in the youth and 51% in the adult projects). Damages of up to 500 DM were seen in the majority of cases; damages of above 1000 DM were incurred in about 35% of cases in the adult projects; this degree of damage occurred only occasionally among juvenile offenders. The compensation rate of financial damages was remarkable. Victim funds were only used in individual cases, and usually only up to an amount of 200 or 300 DM. Originally these funds were considered indispensable, but the persons involved quite often arranged some form of compensation that the offender could fulfill without difficulty. There were spontaneous payments, payments by installment, or manual work, to compensate for damages. Some offenders took up a holiday job to cover financial compensation. The obligations to pay were usually met satisfactorily by the offenders. Reconciliation failed in only a very few cases because of non-compliance with financial obligations.

A case example describes the importance of efforts to gain compensation for both victim and offender, and shows opportunities for sanctioning, by taking into account the compensation carried out:

> An 18-year-old had stabbed and wounded a 20-year-old, who had to stay in hospital for months. His lung was injured and the bodily harm inflicted upon him was considerable. The victim lost his job in addition to the injuries sustained. The offender gave himself up to the police and was taken into custody. The juvenile court assistance

service contacted the victim assistance service, which got in touch
with the victim. He was still in hospital and rejected personal contact
with the offender, due to the seriousness of the offence and its consequences; he had not yet come to terms with what he had suffered.
But he did not entirely preclude any future contact. The victim assistance service continued to keep in touch with the victim, and social
workers from the institution visited the offender in custody. The
offender initially disapproved of these efforts to provide compensation.
Later on, he was persuaded to get in touch with the victim. Again, the
offender was disappointed with the rejection attitude of the victim.
Following several mediation talks, the offender proved to be willing to
compensate for the damages; this was supported by counsels on both
sides. Defending counsel considered these efforts to be a clear indication of social adjustment, since the offender had expressed his desire
to return to school and to drop out of the skinhead scene. Furthermore, he had expressed his regret in a letter to the judge. He was
convicted of attempted homicide, given a suspended sentence and
placed on probation, due to the victim-offender reconciliation which
had taken place.

About 25% of the adults were women, which corresponds to the average for offenders. In the youth projects, the rate was 13%. Thus, girls
were slightly under-represented, and there was an even lower proportion
of girls (between 5% and 11%) in the model projects. About 40% of adult
offenders were between 21 and 30 years of age. Juvenile offenders of up
to 18 years committed about 60% of all offences, and young adults between 18 and 21 years about 40% (the only difference was in Cologne
where 41% was juveniles, 49% young adults and 9% adults). The proportion of foreigners stood at about 14% of all adult offenders and at
about 15% of all juveniles. This proportion shows an under-representa-
tion of foreigners, because they committed 25% of all offences at that
time. Juveniles were more likely to have committed previous offences
than adults (about 28% in Hamburg and 38% in Tübingen). Offences
committed by groups occurred in 50% of all cases of juvenile delinquents and in about 10% of adult cases. Most of the adult cases dealing
with offences against property were committed by married couples. The
typical offender taking part in a youth project was a German juvenile
aged between 14 and 17 years, who had a previous conviction (or was
known to the police following a diversion). Juvenile offenders were
equally as likely to act on their own as in a group. The classic offender in
adult projects was a German male aged between 21 and 30 years, without a criminal record, who was a lone operator.

Being an individual victim was an admission criterion, but several institutions were among those having suffered damage; 10% of juvenile and 18% of adult offences were against institutions. Several institutions were involved in offences of criminal damage, theft, embezzlement and fraud; these varied from small private shops, where the offender was known, to large institutions such as banks, shopping centers, cities or communities. These claimants accepted agreements regarding compensation or payment by installment with astonishing alacrity. The majority of victims were male: 68% in the youth projects and 65% in the adult. Victim and offender usually came from the same age group; just under 50% of victims of juvenile offences were under 21 years of age; the vast majority of victims of adult offences were between 17 and 40 years of age.

In adult projects, the victim and offender were known to each other in 57% of cases. Many offences had been preceded by serious, long-standing confrontations between partners or neighbors (54% in Tübingen and Hamburg, but only 5% in Düsseldorf, and 11% in Detmold). The victim and offender knew each other in about 31% of juvenile offences. Cases in the adult projects dealing with long-standing confrontations, such as relationships and neighborhood conflicts which escalated into an indictment, were often referred to the court assistance service in an attempt to achieve reconciliation. These cases were not usually suitable for victim-offender reconciliation, since the opinions of the conflicting parties had become entrenched to such an extent that no solution to the problem was possible.

There was a willingness to attempt reconciliation among both victims and offenders. Ninety-three percent of juveniles and 89% of adult offenders agreed to an attempt at reconciliation. The percentage of victims was 80% for victims of young offenders and 89% for victims of adult offenders. Peaceful settlement and compensation for financial or immaterial damage had top priority for victims, but there was a variety of motives for their efforts. Many victims of adult offenders did not want to close their eyes to the fact that the offenders were trying to compensate for the damage they had caused. The wish to see the offender convicted played a minor part. The victims quite often reported the offender, or the offence, to the police to make it clear to the offender that they were not willing to accept such behavior. There was a need to confront the offender with the consequences of his or her illegal deeds. The victims expected the offenders to take responsibility for and to regret their behavior, and to settle a conflict. Victims of juvenile offenders wanted to overcome their fear and to be able to deal with similar situations quite calmly. To improve their chances during criminal proceedings was an incentive for many offenders, and, in addition, there was the desire finally to settle the matter. They regretted the offence, and often, especially juvenile offenders, attempted an agreement even before an organized reconciliation.

Reconciliation was achieved in 75% of cases in both the juvenile and adult projects. Mediation involving personal contact between victim and offender in the presence of a mediator took place in 62% of all successful youth project cases; all other reconciliation was based on mediation without personal contact. In adult projects the reverse was true; reconciliation-based mediation occurred in 28% of cases, while in 70% reconciliation was achieved without any personal contact. An example of a successful adult victim-offender reconciliation was a 23-year-old who had pulled another man from his wheelchair and kicked him, while under the influence of alcohol. In the end, the compensation was satisfactory, and the charge was dismissed following efforts towards reconciliation and compensation for immaterial damage. About 25% of compensation cases failed, more than 75% of these coming to an end at an early stage, due to a lack of willingness to agree to reconciliation. Only about 5% of these cases failed because of non-compliance with the arrangements by the offender. In the other cases, no agreement could be reached during the negotiations, since the claims were regarded as being excessive, or the lawyers rejected the agreements. For example:

> Reconciliation after a bicycle accident initially failed due to the lack of willingness on the part of the offender, although the claimant had tried to bring about reconciliation. In the end, different opinions regarding the extent of compensation for damages were the decisive factors in the failure to achieve reconciliation. The proceedings resulted in a sentence. The juvenile was ordered to work 24 hours in the community.

The charge was dismissed following successful victim-offender reconciliation in 82% of all juvenile court proceedings; in about 77% without any further requirements. For the remainder, requirements and directives were imposed on the juvenile offenders following successful victim-offender reconciliation. Thirty-six percent of juveniles were convicted when reconciliation failed.

# AUTONOMY AND COERCION IN PENAL SOCIAL CONTROL

The operation of the criminal law system has experienced a change that requires fundamental redefinition. The decisive characteristics today are no longer dominated by punishment, *i.e.*, repressive coercion with retribution (as a necessary) evil, but rather the state establishment of the extent of penal social control. The state and the interests of both victim and community unequivocally and formally determine the area of control for infringements of elementary rights (Rechtsgüter) which have socially harmful consequences. This framework for control in a constitutional state is a necessary formal program; the state reaction, however, is not. The means of control extend from a renunciation of reaction (tolerance), informal (small) sanctions, to repressive punishment and preventive (disciplinary) measures.

There is a gradation between formal and informal criminal law; at the level of criminalization, norm-coercion and norm-validity of criminal law inevitably require the formal drawing of boundaries. If this fundamental need for coercion is fulfilled at the level of legal processing, the informal means of reinstating the legal equilibrium (Rechtsfrieden) take on considerable significance. Above all, autonomous and socially constructive forms are often far superior to formal punishment. The voluntary taking over of responsibility, even formally against the victim and community, is preferable to the compulsive, repressive imposition of responsibility. Autonomous and socially constructive conflict resolution is the primary goal in the whole framework of penal control. The dialectic relation between autonomy and coercion can be shown by way of the example of reparation in criminal law.

In criminal theory, responsibility and autonomy are the basis of every legitimation of criminal law. Penal responsibility is based on an autonomous decision concerning the criminal facts of the case. In consequence, autonomous acceptance of responsibility and reparation should represent material principles in coping with the criminal act, even after the act (*e.g.*, even withdrawal from the attempt and active repentance). The acceptance of responsibility and offender-victim compensation fulfill the goal of punishment through norm elucidation, victim rehabilitation and social constructiveness, so that repressive imposition of responsibility that points in the same direction becomes superfluous (Rössner, 1992a). In criminal law policy, autonomous means to the reinstatement of legal equilibrium (Rechtsfrieden) further repress punishment (or sentencing).

The functioning of the total system, however, depends on a lasting, residual coercion. The legal consequences themselves are only at the court's disposal. There is a sobering aspect in the relation between autonomy and coercion. The more penal control contains autonomous elements and the less faith it puts in repression, the stronger it is, in the final instance, dependent on institutional compulsion. In the ethics of criminal law, there is a tendency for the principle of reprisal to be substituted by constructive reaction to the principle of responsibility for the wrong committed (Rössner, 1992). The establishment of compensation as an autonomous means towards the reinstatement of legal equilibrium can be represented graphically as:

| Renunciation | Compensation | Punishment | Disciplinary |
| of reaction | as acceptance | as imposition | measures as |
| in case of | of responsibility | of | prevention |
| social tolerance | | responsibility | of danger |

A team of German, Swiss and Austrian criminal law academics have formulated an alternative draft regarding compensation (AE-WGM). The AE-WGM (Baumann, 1992) is the first attempt to lend legal shape to the principles of dealing with the offence in a more socially constructive way. These regulations can be considered as both the focal point of the present discussion and the basis of reform (Rössner, 1992; Schöch, 1992). According to the AE-WGM, compensation should be introduced into the system of legal consequences pursuant to Sections 38 onwards (German Penal Code). The global purpose of criminal law is "restoration of legal equilibrium", and compensation certainly contributes to reconciliation between victim and offender. The definition of compensation in AE-WGM is oriented towards the criminal purpose; it aims at the voluntary reconciliation of legal consequences: complete compensation for damages as well as mediation talks, an apology or a gift. Symbolic compensation is possible in the form of community work in cases of a lack of financial damage, victims being unwilling to accept any reconciliation, or an offence against the general public. This provides for equal treatment of offenders. Payments can be made to insurance companies. The proposed solution applies to all offences laid down in the German Penal Code, even though it focuses on minor or less serious crimes and offences against persons. The leading principles are voluntary compliance with the criminal standards and successful compensation of the victim's interests. Compensation payments must be completed before the opening of the trial if they are to be relevant to sanctions.

Compensation results in no punishment in cases in which imprisonment cannot exceed one year. The public verdict of guilty is added to completed payments of compensation. Punishment is only considered in exceptional circumstances if it is essential to have an effect on the offender or on the general public. Compulsory mitigation of sentence is considered beyond bounds in the case of major offences or when greater importance is placed on preventive reasons. Reconciliation of legal consequences is strengthened by the opportunity to suspend imprisonment. Legal consequences that give more priority to the taking of responsibility on the part of the offender than to punishment require procedures to develop the autonomous means and assistance to organize compensation for victims and offenders who seek help. Instructions should be given to victim and accused concerning opportunities for compensation and their right to participate in the compensation procedure. Essential tools for achieving compensation are purpose-oriented authority to interrupt the proceedings in the event of the appropriate efforts being made, intervention of extra-judicial arbitration bodies, and judicial compensation proceedings within interlocutory proceedings in the relevant court. Different ways of completing the proceedings range from dismissing the charge pursuant to a verdict of guilty and refraining from punishment, to integrating compensation proceedings into the order opening the trial and convicting in the case of compulsory mitigation of sentence.

The two fundamental sections of the AE-WGM are worded as follows, these definitions very clearly showing the underlying principles:

## SECTION 1

## Compensation

(1) Reconciliation is to make good the damages in terms of voluntary service by the offender. It serves to restore the legal equilibrium. Reconciliation shall mainly be carried out for the benefit of the victim; in the event of this being impossible, being unlikely to be fulfilled, or being insufficient in itself, reconciliation to the public (symbolic reconciliation) is to be taken into consideration.

(2) Voluntary service is also covered by the offender fulfilling the obligation he has assumed during the judicial or extra-judicial compensation proceedings.

# SECTION 2

## Reconciliation services

(1) The following reconciliation services are mentioned by name:

1. compensation for damages to the victim;
2. compensation for damages to a third party, especially insurance companies, upon whom the claim has developed;
3. further material services, such as payments to charitable institutions;
4. gifts to the victim or immaterial services, such as an apology or a reconciliation talk;
5. work performed, especially charitable services.

A combination of these different reconciliation services may be performed.

(2) Neither shall the victim nor the offender be burdened in an unfair or intolerable way by the reconciliation services.

In 1994, the legislator adopted this fundamental idea to a lesser extent by introducing Section 46a into the German Penal Code:

# SECTION 46 a

## Victim-offender-reconciliation; compensation

If the offender

1. has compensated or seriously attempted to compensate fully or to a large extent for the crime he has committed by endeavoring to enter into a reconciliation; or
2. has fully or to a large extent compensated for the damages in cases of compensation requiring considerable personal effort or some form of sacrifice, the court may mitigate the sentence pursuant to Section 49 I, or refrain from punishment in cases where the imprisonment is up to one year or a fine of up to three hundred daily rates is incurred.

## REFERENCES

Bannenberg, B. (1993). *Wiedergutmachung in der Strafrechtspraxis. Eine empirisch-kriminologische Untersuchung von Täter-Opfer-Projekten in der Bundesrepublik Deutschland.* Bonn, GER.

Baumann, J. (1992). _Arbeitskreis Deutscher, Schweizerischer und Österreichischer Strafrechtslehrer: Alternativ-Entwurf Wiedergutmachung (AE-WGM)._ München, GER.

Hering, R.D. and D. Rössner (eds.) (1993). _Täter-Opfer-Ausgleich im allgemeinen Strafrecht: Theorie und Praxis konstruktiver Tatverarbeitung: Grundlagen, Modelle, Resultate und Perspektiven._ Bonn, GER.

Marks, E. and D. Rössner (1989). _Täter-Opfer-Ausgleich. Vom zwischenmenschlichen Weg zur Wiederherstellung des Rechtsfriedens._ Bonn, GER.

Rössner, D. (1990). "Täter-Opfer-Ausgleich und Kriminalitätsverhütung." In: Frank and Harrer (eds.), _Der Sachverständige im Strafrecht: Kriminalitätsverhütung._ Heidelberg, GER.

—(1992). "Strafrechtsfolgen ohne Übelszufügung?" _NStZ,_ 409-415.

—(1992a). _Autonomie und Zwang im System der Strafrechtsfolgen._ In: Festschrift für J. Baumann zum 70. Geburtstag. Bielefeld, (pp. 269-279).

Schöch, H. (1992). _Empfehlen sich Änderungen und Ergänzungen bei den strafrechtlichen Sanktionen ohne Freiheitsentzug?_ Gutachten C zum 59. Deutschen Juristentag in Hannover. München, GER.

# 24. DEVELOPING REPARATION PLANS THROUGH VICTIM-OFFENDER MEDIATION BY NEW ZEALAND PROBATION OFFICERS

by

## Bernard Jervis

**Abstract:** *The New Zealand Criminal Justice Act of 1985 introduced the sentence of reparation, thus allowing compensation to be paid to victims of offenses. At first reparation was only applied to property offenses. This was amended in 1987 to allow reparation in cases where the victim suffered emotional harm. These provisions, together with the provision for payment of part or all of a fine to crime victims who suffered physical or emotional harm as the result of a criminal act, created, in law, an expectation that offenders should pay compensation to their victims. A further amendment to the Criminal Justice Act in 1993 allows a court imposing a sentence to take into account any offer of compensation, whether financial or by means of the performance of any work or service made by or on behalf of the offender to the victim. The Criminal Justice Act of 1985 was clearly in favor of reparation as a sentencing option, but research undertaken in 1989 showed that reparation was poorly used. There has been some increase in the use of reparation ordered without a reparation report. Victim-offender mediation is very rare, as is reparation in the form of service to victims.*

Research on the implementation of the Criminal Justice Act of 1985 with regard to reparation was undertaken in 1991 (Galaway and Spier, 1992). The report concluded that it was not clear why reparation was receiving limited use as a sentence by the courts. Possible reasons for this were that reparation is perceived as inappropriate because victims do not have tangible losses, judges and other criminal justice officials have philosophical and theoretical difficulties with reparation as a sentence, reparation is perceived as difficult to administer and preference is therefore given to other sentences, and procedures may not be in place for courts to systematically consider reparation when sentencing offenders.

There are, however, significant developments in the legislation of New Zealand that affect victims of offenses. These include amendments to the Summary Proceedings Act of 1957, which specifies the rules governing the kinds of questions that may be asked of victims of rape or sexual violation. The Act also allows for the court to be cleared while the evidence of victims is being heard. The Domestic Protection Act of 1982 creates a series of court orders which provide protection for people being abused by violent partners. The Criminal Justice Act of 1985, with amendments in 1987, contains provisions governing reparation and the part or whole payment of a fine to the victim. A further amendment in 1993 allows the court to take into account any offer of compensation, whether financial or by means of the performance of any work or service made by or on behalf of the offender to the victim. The Victims of Offenses Act of 1987 contains a series of measures designed to protect the victim, especially in the court. The Evidence Amendment Act of 1989 permits the use of videotaped evidence and closed-circuit television for child sexual abuse victims. There is also a series of regulations which specify the way videotapes should be made and stored, and who should be allowed access to them. The Children, Young Persons and their Families Act of 1989 creates the family group conference and specifies the victim's role in the conference. The Accident Rehabilitation and Compensation Insurance Act of 1992 allows for some compensation to victims of physical abuse and sexual abuse. New Zealand has taken initiatives to secure greater victim participation in the criminal justice system. The focus of this chapter is on the sentence of reparation and the use of mediation processes. The extent to which the problems and difficulties identified in the Galaway and Spier report are being addressed is examined.

## REPARATION AND THE CRIMINAL JUSTICE ACT OF 1985

The principal section of the Act concerned with reparation simply states that any court may sentence an offender to make reparation where the court is satisfied that any person suffered any emotional harm or any loss or damage to property. The clause including emotional harm was a 1987 amendment. The court can impose reparation in two ways. First, if it is satisfied as to the value of the loss or damage to property, and the maximum amount the offender will be required to pay does not exceed NZ$500, the sentence can be imposed without further inquiry. Second, the court may adjourn the proceedings and order a probation officer to prepare a report for the court, which canvasses the nature of the emotional harm, the value of the loss or damage to property, the means of the offender, the nature and extent of the offender's existing financial obligations, the maximum amount that the offender is likely to be able to pay, and the frequency and amount of any payments that should be required if payment is to be made by installments. Any probation officer required to prepare a reparation report must attempt to seek an agreement between the offender and the person who suffered the emotional harm or the loss or damage to property on the amount of reparation that the offender should be required to pay. If an agreement is reached, the probation officer reports the terms of the agreement to the court. Where agreement is not reached, the probation officer reports to the court that, with respect to emotional harm, the matter is unresolved. With regard to any loss or damage to property, the probation officer can either determine the value of the loss or damage on the evidence available, and report the value so determined to the court, or report that the matter is unresolved. The court can direct that reparation be paid at some future date or by instalments. A court may award, as compensation to the victim, any portion of a fine that the court thinks just for any offence arising out of any act that occasioned physical or emotional harm. This is qualified by the court being of the opinion that the act that caused the harm to the victim was unprovoked, and caused physical or emotional harm to the victim.

Departmental guidelines for probation officers on how this work is to be done were circulated in 1985. Reparation was to be considered a sentence of first resort that provides for the restoration of quantifiable property losses to victims by the offenders involved, and further provides opportunities for offenders and victims to negotiate the amount of reparation payable. Specific objectives were: (1) to increase the number of offenders sentenced by the courts to pay reparation; (2) to increase the level of reparation paid by offenders to victims; (3) to increase opportunities for offender awareness of the consequences of offending; and (4) to increase the number of cases where reconciliation was reached between offenders and victims. Emphasis was placed on the needs of victims by making reparation a sentence of first resort. It was considered desirable that there should be some procedure whereby the offender and victim could negotiate the value of the loss or damage and the amount payable as reparation, where the amount of reparation was in dispute.

The Department's guidelines for this work were clear and precise. All possible options for negotiation between the offender and the victim were covered. The probation officer was required to explain to both the victim and the offender that the court had the final decision in the matter, and may determine the value of the loss or damage and the amount payable as reparation. Where there was more than one offender, the probation officer was to inform the victim that each convicted offender may only be liable for a proportion of the value of the loss or damage. If the victim wanted to negotiate reparation, the probation officer was to ascertain whether the victim wanted to meet the offender, and directly negotiate the amount of reparation, and whether the offender wanted to meet the victim. If both parties agreed to meet, the probation officer was required to present all relevant documents and, if necessary, verify the loss by quote, assessment, or evaluation. A neutral site was to be used for the negotiation meeting. The probation officer's role was that of a mediator. Face-to-face negotiation could be bypassed if, during arrangements for negotiation, the probation officer concluded that both parties were agreeable to a specified amount of reparation payable, the conditions of payment, and neither party wanted to meet the other. When neither the victim nor the offender wanted to meet the other, but wanted to negotiate reparation through the probation officer, then the probation officer was required to consult with the victim and offender and explain to each of them the other person's position. Both parties were to be provided with the same relevant information. Where agreement was reached, the probation officer was to write down the details and seek confirmation from both parties. The probation officer was then to present these details as a report to the court. Copies of the report were to be provided to both the victim and the offender. When the court ordered reparation a copy of the court's order was provided to the victim.

The Department's guidelines for probation officers to negotiate reparation agreements between victims and offenders set out four functions for the probation officer. First, it was the responsibility of the probation officer to develop and maintain an interest in and commitment to the interaction. Second, it was the probation officer's job to monitor and improve communication between the parties. Third, the probation officer was to be aware of the process. This would include remaining sensitive to what was going on, separating factual issues from emotional ones, offering observations about the discussion between the victim and the offender to reinforce open communication, and confronting one or both parties if it was noticed that they were undermining the process or seemed insincere. The fourth function of the probation officer was to regulate the interaction. The probation officer's role is to act as a referee, encouraging or discouraging expression, and avoiding monopolization by either side. The probation officer has to keep the discussion to relevant points.

In 1987, the Criminal Justice Act was amended to allow reparation for emotional harm. The new legislation only identified emotional harm as an element for which reparation may be made. Galaway and Spier (1992), however, found that about 60% of probation officers interviewed perceived the process of addressing reparation for emotional harm as different from the process for property loss and damage. At the same time, just over 50% of the judges interviewed perceived a difference between the emotional harm report and the property loss and damage report. Galaway and Spier found that emotional harm reports had been used primarily to assess the extent of the emotional harm to the victim, to assist the victim in finding resolutions for this harm, and to secure victims' views regarding sentencing for transmission to the judges. The report concluded that rarely did emotional harm reports deal centrally with the matter of reparation from the offender for damages resulting from the emotional harm. The Justice Department was again clear in promoting policy guidelines for this work. The guidelines were similar to those issued in 1985, but additional operational objectives included assisting an offender and the victim(s) to reach agreement over the amount that the offender be required to pay by way of reparation. Further, the Victims of Offenses Act of 1987 was introduced, which outlined a set of principles governing persons dealing with victims. Victims were to be treated with courtesy, compassion, and respect for their personal dignity and privacy. The Act also introduced victim impact statements that were to be prepared for the courts and consideration of victims' needs in the setting of bail conditions.

Probation officers had to operate more carefully with victims than previously. The Department's guidelines stated that the victim should be contacted and advised of reparation for emotional harm, the role of the probation officer, the possible content of the reparation report, who can have access to the report, and the sentence of reparation. Should the victim wish to be interviewed, the probation officer should, during the interview, seek to determine the nature of the emotional harm suffered. If appropriate, the probation officer should ask the victim about a meeting with the offender. The probation officer was required to mediate between the victim and offender to reach an agreement on the amount the offender should be required to pay by way of reparation. A meeting between the parties was considered a possible and appropriate way of achieving this. Where either or both parties refused to meet or, having met, could not reach an agreement, the probation officer was to report this to the court. Other administrative guidelines included providing a neutral place for any interviews if the victim did not wish to be interviewed at Justice Department offices or in their own home. Home visits to the victim were considered inappropriate for contacting the victim in the first instance, unless the victim had invited the probation officer. Probation officers preparing reparation reports should not prepare any other pre-sentence report on the offender, thus providing some perceived equality of interest when interviewing victims and offenders. Where there are multiple offenders, one probation officer should prepare all the reparation reports, and thus only one officer is in contact with the victim. If there is an immediate need for personal or social support for a victim, the probation officer should undertake to provide this support until such time that an appropriate referral can take place. Should further time be required to work with a victim, the probation officer should request a further remand to enable them fully to canvass the nature of the emotional harm, especially if this is pertinent to sentencing.

## USE OF REPARATION

The Galaway and Spier (1992) report published in 1992 identified eight key areas for examination, following the finding of the report that reparation was seldom used: (1) Judges noted that the lack of offender means limited their ability to use the sentence, and that it raised victims expectations unrealistically; (2) enforcement was unpredictable or inadequate; (3) other problems noted were the lack of feedback to the courts, that the sentence lacked teeth, and was not a quick way to compensate victims; (4) judges were concerned that there were limits on their ability to combine reparation with other sentences, and that it was not appropriate for social welfare benefit frauds; (5) probation officers mentioned the problem of obtaining an accurate statement of means from offenders, as well as an accurate statement of losses from victims, the need for a longer remand period, especially when mediation is being used, and difficulty in arriving at agreements with victims, which are realistic for an offender; (6) probation officers also cited problems with the lack of adequate training for this work, and ambivalence as to whether reparation work was a legitimate part of probation work; (7) a survey of victims suggested that judges and probation officers may be underestimating the willingness of victims to meet their offenders; and, finally, (8) problems in relation to insurance companies.

A survey conducted in 1992 (Jervis, 1992) found that reparation reports represented 8% of all pre-sentence information provided to the courts. Face-to-face meetings between victim and offender occurred in only 4% of cases. Both parties were contacted by telephone in only 9% of reparation cases. Both parties were interviewed separately in 12% of reparation cases. One party was interviewed, and the other party telephoned, in 75% of reparation cases, with the offender being interviewed and the victim telephoned. No agreement was reached in 18% of reparation reports prepared for the courts. The court endorsed 69% of agreements reached between both parties. Reparation alone was the sentence in 6% of cases. Reparation was imposed with a term of imprisonment in 4% of cases. Reparation was imposed with periodic detention in 66% of cases. Reparation was imposed with other community-based sentences and monetary penalties in 24% of cases. Insurance companies were not classified as victims in seven of 39 probation districts in New Zealand. This survey confirmed findings from the Galaway and Spier research. In substance, the sentence was little used, and mediation conducted through face-to-face meetings between victims and offenders was a rarity. The probation officer acted in most cases as an intermediary between the victim and the offender, with communication with the victim mainly by telephone.

In 1995, a sample of judges and probation officers in the greater Wellington area, senior departmental officials, and management and community representatives were interviewed. In addition, current statistical. information held by the Justice Department and the 1994 Annual Report were reviewed. All reparation reports, pre-sentence reports and court disposition lists for November 1994, prepared by the three probation districts in the greater Wellington area, were also reviewed. The percentage of court orders resulting in reparation being used in the disposition of all cases was 17% in 1991 and 1992, with a slight decrease to 16.8% in 1993. An amendment to the Criminal Justice Act in 1993 increased from NZ$250 to NZ$500 the amount of reparation a court could impose without further inquiry. Thus, the court did not need to request a report from a probation officer, seeking agreement between the offender and the victim, if the amount of reparation to be ordered was NZ$500 or less. By November 1994, the number and percentage of orders resulting in reparation in all court dispositions had risen to 30%. Orders of under NZ$500 made up 75% of all orders. The amount ordered in this category represented 13.7% of the total reparation ordered in that month. A high number of orders resulting in reparation are therefore made without further inquiry, although the amount ordered makes up a relatively small proportion of all reparation ordered. In 1993, a total of 8,167 orders for reparation were made. In 1994, the total orders made as of December 1st were 12,850. This represents an increase of 57.3% on orders made compared to the previous year. This increase could be attributed to the legislation which raised the level of reparation that could be imposed without further inquiry. This is in contrast to the limited use made of reparation sentence in connection with reports made available to the courts by probation officers. The statistical data show that the number of reports requested by the courts when making orders for reparation has remained at 8% for the last three years.

Data for the period 1991 to 1994 show a trend of increasing amounts of reparation ordered. In 1991, NZ$10.3 million was ordered, with NZ$4.6 million being paid to victims. By 1994, the amount ordered had risen to NZ$13 million, with NZ$6.5 million being paid to victims. Comparing the amount ordered and the amount paid in any single year is complicated by time payment arrangements, enforcement action, and reparation not due for payment until later years. The Annual Report for 1994 shows a total of NZ$24.5 million still being unpaid to victims since the introduction of the reparation sentence. At December 1st, 1994, NZ$2.6 million of the total amount ordered that year had not been collected. But had it in fact been collected, some of it could not have been paid to the victims, as the victims' details were missing from the files. This was similar to 1993, when NZ$2 million was ordered but not collected and, had it been collected, could not have been paid to the victims as victims' details were missing. NZ$300,000 collected in 1993 was not paid to victims due to missing victim details; in 1994 this amount was NZ$400,000. This suggests a breakdown in the court process if victim details are not being obtained or are lost when reparation is ordered. The number of cases in which victim-offender mediation takes place is insignificant. Probation officers report that this is due to a lack of training and resources. There is no national training policy for this work, and it remains the responsibility of regional and district managers to provide training. The quality of this training is uneven and unclear. The offender remains the central focus for probation officers.

Comments from judges show a general attempt to address reparation in all cases. The means of the offender, however, may make the ordering of reparation unrealistic and impractical in some cases. The offender also remains the central focus for judges. The question of compensation being considered in other than monetary terms brought differing responses from judges. The general idea that work or service could be used to compensate the victim was, in principle, acceptable. Legislation in 1993 allowed this to occur. No statistical information is available to indicate what use is made of payment of compensation in the form of work or service to the victim. The impression is that this amendment to the legislation is neither well-known nor well-used. There are cultural factors to consider in New Zealand society. The Maori people are not the dominant culture, but there are traditional customs of reconciliation that are used following conflict or disharmony among people, families, and tribes. The Justice Department has encouraged the acknowledgement of traditional customs in matters being brought before the courts. There is general acceptance on this point by all officials interviewed. But a Court of Appeal ruling states that this does not obviate the court's responsibility to sentence. The concern of Maori community representatives goes beyond the offender, to include other members of the family if the offender is sentenced to a term of imprisonment or some other sanction of the court. Traditional reconciliation processes were regarded by community representatives as a healing process for the larger family or tribe. In these terms, traditional customs are more readily understood within the concept of restorative justice. The degree to which reparation is presently used by the courts requires an understanding of the present criminal justice system. Reparation is problematical within a retributive justice system. The present legislation does not provide an adequate process to place the victim more centrally in sentencing decisions. Reparation runs the risk of being used as an addition, to satisfy the growing concern that the needs of victims be heard in the criminal justice system. The fact that most reparation orders are made without any further inquiry, that most inquiries with victims undertaken by probation officers are made by telephone, and that payment of reparation is made in only 50% of all cases, serves only to reinforce the difficulties of this sentence.

## REPARATION IN THE CONTEXT OF A RESTORATIVE JUSTICE MODEL

The question of whether reparation is more readily understood in a restorative justice paradigm poses the dilemma of addressing reparation in the present model, in which it is only one of the sentencing options within a range of options that may be understood in restorative terms, or against a new model which presently does not exist, but in which reparation is the only sentencing option that would fit such a paradigm. The extent to which a restorative justice system could be considered requires a fundamental mind-shift in public perceptions of how conflicts should be resolved. A restorative justice paradigm differs significantly from the present operational framework. Restorative justice seeks to redefine crime, not so much as breaking the law, but as an injury or wrong done to another person or persons. Thereby, the victim and offender become central in the process, with the state and legal professionals becoming facilitators by supporting a system which aims at offender accountability, full participation of both victim and offender, and making good, or putting right the wrong. The primary goal of the criminal justice system in this framework is to restore the victim, the community, and the offender, to a state of wholeness as much as possible. In order to restore wholeness, the offender must accept responsibility for the harm done and must take action to repair that harm. The community must ensure an environment which supports the process of reconciliation for both the victim and the offender, while holding the offender accountable and, the government must ensure community safety and protection of individual rights in the process of reconciliation and restoration.

The Justice Department's policy on reparation concluded that reparation is an attempt to meld criminal and civil proceedings by doing justice to offender, community, and victim. The hope is that, by achieving greater justice for victims, the perceived need for other forms of sentence will diminish. The Justice Department believed that public confidence and satisfaction with the criminal justice system would be encouraged with a sentencing option that allowed the needs of victims to be met against the interests of offenders. To this degree, reparation can be seen in a restorative justice model, or at least recognized in restorative justice language. The limited degree to which it is being used in practice may suggest that it is the application that is problematical. A possible reason for this may be that it is only one sentencing option in a much wider set of penalties that can be imposed by the courts. There is no research available that measures the effectiveness of increased victim involvement in the criminal justice system, or whether these changes can be considered restorative. There are sentences of community service and periodic detention available to the courts that provide ways for offenders to contribute to the community they have offended against. Community service allows offenders to work with community organizations, thus providing the opportunity to be reintegrated into their community, make amends to the community, and learn work skills. It does not involve victims in any way, nor does the victim have any right of recourse. Victims will not receive any direct benefit from work carried out by offenders performing community service. Periodic detention work can be carried out for the same range of organizations, but this is not on a voluntary basis (community service requires the consent of the offender). The offenders sentenced to periodic detention are in custody and are required to perform this work. Again, the victim has no active involvement.

## CONCLUSIONS

Senior departmental officials reported that the poor use of reparation, based on the provision of reparation reports by probation officers rather than the disposition of reparation of all court sentencing, was due to amended legislation, increasing the level of reparation to be paid before a report from a probation officer could be requested. Other reasons given were that violent offenses precluded consideration of reparation and questions surrounding compensation in financial terms for emotional harm. It was generally believed that reparation did not have a high profile, that it was not encouraged politically or by the department, that probation officers did not see it as important, that it was not seen as a stand-alone sentence, and that it was not retributive. There was a general perception held by managers and probation officers that differing practices and views held by judges led them to believe that the judiciary was not victim focused. Judges reported, in contrast, a genuine desire to use reparation in all appropriate cases. Reparation has been ordered more significantly since 1993, but this has usually been in cases under NZ$500 which do not require any further inquiries of the victims concerned.

District managers and probation officers cited lack of training and resourcing as the major factors leading to the poor use of reparation. There was ambivalence among probation officers on the appropriateness of probation officers doing this work. However, general satisfaction was expressed by judges with reports prepared by probation officers. Victim-offender mediation was reported favorably by most managers, probation officers and judges, although it was not unanimously agreed that probation officers are best suited to do this work. There was unanimous agreement that victim-offender mediation was a specialized skill, and that successful work could only be achieved by persons operating with those skills. This point is important in considering any possible restorative justice model that adopts some form of mediation process. Victim-offender mediation is not significantly used by probation officers and, although there is no departmental training policy on this work, clear and precise departmental guidelines do exist to allow such work to be undertaken. Notwithstanding the limited use made of the reparation sentence in the New Zealand criminal justice system, the opportunity exists for victim involvement and victim offender mediation. The legislation and departmental guidelines are clear.

Examination of the Justice Department's stated objectives for the reparation sentence, first set in 1985, show the degree to which each objective has been met. The first objective was to increase the number of offenders sentenced by the courts to pay reparation. The number of offenders sentenced to pay reparation has increased significantly in the last two years, but this does not indicate what is considered a satisfactory level. If reparation should be considered in all cases, the objective has not been met. The second objective was to increase the level of reparation paid by offenders to victims. The amount paid to victims shows a general trend towards increasing. Again, no desirable level of payment was set and, therefore, it is only possible to say that the amounts of payments are increasing, but that the overall amounts being left unpaid to victims are high. The third objective was to increase opportunities for offender awareness of the consequences of offending, and the fourth was to increase the number of cases where reconciliation was reached between offenders and victims. Both these objectives center on some form of mediation process occurring. This work has not been successful, and is little used.

The New Zealand legislation and departmental policy statements on reparation use restorative language to describe this work. This suggests an intent not only to use reparation wherever possible, but also to be focused on the victim. In practice, that does not appear to be in place. Judges, probation officers and departmental managers are attempting to put into practice a process that cannot fully be successful because the legislation is trying to reconcile two diametrically opposed criminal justice systems. The present situation appears to be an 'addition' that cannot succeed. This was agreed by senior departmental officials and some judges, to the point where it was felt the Justice Department needed to re-visit the philosophy and intent of the legislation governing reparation, and identify its non-use. The sentence could lose credibility if not addressed. It was generally agreed that, if reparation is to be more widely used, much wider public awareness of the sentence should be promoted and addressed within the context of a restorative justice paradigm. Some judges believe this should be seen as a community system set up within a community environment that will support such a criminal justice system. One judge proposed a definition of restorative justice in which the state ceases to be the central focus of the process; that the criminal justice system and the court process be victim-centered, with the objective of a negotiated outcome that achieves healing for all parties. These responses suggest the need for debate on the ways in which any community should address questions of harmful actions to others. Placing the focus on the victim may not in itself resolve the conflict, and there may be other ways of meeting the needs of victims. The outcome, however, should be one where both victim and offender believe that they have been dealt with fairly.

## REFERENCES

Galaway, B. and P Spier (1992). *Sentencing to Reparation: Implementation of the Criminal Justice Act 1985*. Wellington, NZ: Department of Justice.

Jervis, B. (1992). "Use of Reparation Survey." In: *Report on Victim Related Policy and Practice in the United States and Canada*. Wellington, NZ: New Zealand Department of Justice.

# 25. RESTITUTION AND CONFLICT RESOLUTION IN THE NETHERLANDS

## by
## J.M. Wemmers

**Abstract:** *The Netherlands financial restitution has come to dominate restorative justice by pushing conflict resolution to the background. There are possibilities for restitution in both criminal and civil law. An experiment with creative restitution combined elements from criminal and civil law; defendants and their victims were given the opportunity to negotiate a mutually suitable solution to their conflict. The parties did not meet directly; instead, negotiations were carried out by lawyers representing either of the two parties. Of 163 cases, 58 resulted in an agreement between parties. In two-thirds of these cases, the parties agreed on a financial settlement. The remaining cases involved a behavioral contract or personal services for the victim. Restorative justice must guard the interests of both the victim and the offender if it is to mean more than just financial restitution.*

Since the 1970s, there has been growing interest in The Netherlands in the needs of crime victims. The early roots of this movement were in the resocialization or rehabilitation perspective. Rehabilitation involves changing the behavior of the offender, mental state, or values, in such a way that he or she ceases committing criminal acts. This ideology had dominated the criminal justice system in The Netherlands since the second world war (Winkel, 1990; Van Dijk, 1982). During the 1960s, probation and other after-care workers grew increasingly interested in victims of crime, but the interest was not always directed at victims' needs. The victim-offender meeting, for example, was viewed by some psychiatrists as particularly beneficial for the therapy of the offender (Van Dijk, 1982). By the early 1970s, conflict resolution and restitution were gaining attention as alternatives to imprisonment within this ideology (Steinmetz,

1990; Van Dijk, 1982). The first victim assistance project in The Nether-lands was set up in 1975 by a Humanitas probation and after-care or-ganization. This first project aimed at helping victims cope with the material and immaterial aftermath of victimization; conflict resolution formed an important method in this process (Ruyter, 1977; Steinmetz, 1990). By the late 1970s, this movement took another turn, leaving the rehabilitation of the offender and moving towards the needs of the vic-tim. Conflict resolution left the stage, while restitution gained impor-tance within Dutch victim policy. Recently, however, efforts have been made to put conflict resolution back in the picture. In this chapter, an experiment with creative restitution is outlined and the results of the evaluation are presented.

## POSSIBILITIES FOR RESTITUTION

Guidelines for the police and the public prosecution regarding the treatment of victims of crime have been in effect in The Netherlands since 1986. Three committees played a central role in the development of these guidelines. In 1981, the Committee on Victims of Violent Sex Crimes developed the notion of secondary victimization, and sought to avoid secondary victimization by improving the treatment of victims by law enforcement authorities (Werkgroep Aangifte Sexuele Gewelds-misdrijven, 1981). The Committee on Judicial Policy and Victims ex-amined how the position of victims could be improved within the frame-work of the existing criminal justice system. In 1985, the committee published its report which contained a number of recommendations, in-cluding restitution. Restitution was considered to have a pedagogical value for offenders by confronting offenders with the consequences of their offence. The payment of restitution allows offenders to repair the damages, and this constructive act can have a positive effect on their self-worth (Werkgroep Justitieel Beleid en Slachtoffer, 1985). In 1986, the recommendations of the Committee on Victims of Violent Sex Crimes and the Committee on Judicial Policy and Victims were introduced as guidelines for the public prosecution and police (Richtlijn Openbaar Ministerie en Politie, 1986). Originally, the guidelines applied only to vic-tims of serious violent and sex crimes but, in 1987, they were expanded to include all victims of felonies. The guidelines focus on the correct treatment of victims. This includes the referral of needy victims to vic-tim-assistance schemes, victim notification, and restitution. Police and the public prosecution have a duty to consider the victim's wish for restitution and, where possible, to attempt to arrange the payment of restitution by the offender.

In 1988, the Committee Legal Provisions Victims in the Criminal Justice Process (Commissie Wettelijke Voorzieningen Slachtoffers in het Strafproces, 1988) published a report which contained a number of recommendations regarding changes to the existing criminal justice procedure, to expand the existing possibilities for restitution. The pedagogical value of restitution, which had been used previously by the Committee on Judicial Policy and Victims, was one of the arguments put forward by the committee. In April 1995, the recommendations made by the committee were introduced as new guidelines for police and public prosecutors, and as new legislation to expand the possibilities for restitution within the criminal trial. Both the police and the prosecution are required to attempt to arrange restitution at the earliest possible stage of the criminal justice process. The guidelines are no longer limited to victims of felonies, but apply to all victims of crime.

The guidelines apply to victims within the criminal justice procedure. There are several possibilities for victims to obtain restitution both prior to and during a criminal trial. Prior to the criminal trial, restitution can be arranged with the assistance of the police or the public prosecutor. This possibility is usually reserved for straightforward cases involving material damages. The public prosecutor may dismiss the case or may choose to impose a transaction in combination with restitution. However, like a fine, a transaction is imposed by the public prosecution rather than the court. Both a transaction and a dismissal mean that the case will not be brought before the court, provided the offender fulfils the requirements imposed by the public prosecutor. The next level is the criminal trial. The introduction of new legislation in April 1995 has expanded the possibilities for victims to obtain restitution within the criminal trial. Until that time, there were two possibilities for restitution within the trial setting. The first was for the judge to combine restitution with a conditional sentence. Restitution is then designated as a special condition, which must be met in order to avoid the conditional sentence. The amount of money granted by the judge for restitution is not limited by a maximum. The public prosecution is responsible for executing the sentence. The other option was the civil party model. The basis for the civil party model has its roots in civil law. The victim may be added to the trial as a civil party. The criminal judge then considers the victim's claim and has the authority to grant or deny the victim's claim. If granted, the victim has a legal order verifying the right to restitution. However, in line with civil law, it is entirely up to the victim to enforce payment by the offender. The civil party model has serious limitations. The amount of restitution that a victim can claim is limited to a maximum of 1,500 guilders for felonies and 600 guilders for misdemeanors. This is intended to keep the victim's claim simple. The focus of the trial must remain on the criminal offence, and not on the civil damages of the victim. Another obstacle for many victims is that they, or their legal representative, must be present at the trial in order for their claim to be considered by the judge. The civil party model is of limited use to victims.

With the introduction of new legislation in 1995, judges may still order restitution in combination with a conditional sentence, but the civil party model has undergone several important changes. The quantitative limits of 1,500 guilders for felonies and 600 guilders for misdemeanors have been dropped. However, in their place, qualitative criteria have been introduced. The case must remain simple and clear cut. Simple means that the victim may not bring witnesses or experts to the trial to support the claim. The claim must stand on its own and, therefore, only straightforward cases will be considered within the criminal trial. The focus of the trial continues to be the criminal offence and not the civil claim. Victims who want to claim immaterial damages may find themselves unable to make use of this possibility. The victim, however, can split the claim into two parts: a simple and a complicated one. The simple claim can be handled during the criminal trial. The victim must take the complicated part of the case to a civil court. The victim no longer has to be present at the trial in order to make the claim, but it is entirely up to the victim to enforce payment by the offender (Wet Terwee, 1993). The new legislation also introduces restitution orders as a new sanction. Restitution may be ordered alone or together with an existing sanction. There are no limits on the amount of restitution that can be ordered, and the prosecution is responsible for its execution. As with fines, failure by the offender to pay restitution may result in a custodial sentence. In this way, the public prosecutor can pressure the offender to pay. When the offender has carried out the custodial sentence in lieu of payment, responsibility to pay restitution to the victim is absolved.

The possibilities for victims to obtain restitution within the criminal justice procedure all focus on monetary compensation for material damages suffered as a result of the crime. Restitution aims at confronting offenders with consequences of their offence, but takes a rather narrow approach to the kinds of consequences suffered by victims. Offenders are not confronted directly with the victim or with the pain and psychological damages suffered by the victim. Restitution within criminal law is relatively easier, usually takes less time, and is often less expensive than civil law. In civil law, a victim must be represented by a lawyer, has to pay court fees, and runs the risk of being obliged by the judge to pay the costs of the other party. However, civil law has certain advantages to criminal law. One of the most important advantages is the variety of ways in which compensation can be asked for and be awarded. Compensation can consist of an amount of money to be paid by the offender, but it can also include an obligation on the part of the offender to do certain things. Furthermore, the judge can forbid the offender to do certain things, such as to contact the victim or to enter the street where the victim lives. Such variety allows parties directly to address the problem at hand and seek a solution suited to their particular situation. A second advantage of civil law is that the victim has the initiative, and is not dependent on the decision of the public prosecutor about the criminal case. A third advantage is that there are no limits to the claim a victim can make; however, while victims are not bound by maximum awards or other restrictions, there is no guarantee that the offender will adhere to the judge's orders. It is the responsibility of the victim to take action in order secure compensation from the offender. Still, the flexibility of civil law makes it an attractive option for some victims. Many women (*e.g.*, victims of rape and incest) make use of the possibilities of civil law. They ask for large awards for immaterial damages and ask the judge for a restraining order.

## AN EXPERIMENT WITH CREATIVE RESTITUTION

In 1989, Humanitas, a Dutch probation and after-care service, presented a proposal to the Ministry of Justice, based on creative restitution. Restitution had formed an important part of the ministerial guidelines since 1987; the project was presented as a way to advance the use of restitution and re-introduced conflict resolution into victim care. The philosophy behind the project was abolitionist. Criminal justice was viewed as an ultimum remedium; a last resort, which should only be used when all other possibilities have been exhausted. The aim of the project was to allow offenders and victims to find a mutually suitable solution to the conflict between them, thus making further action by the criminal justice system redundant. The project made use of civil law. Parties would arrange a settlement which would be recorded by the courts. Parties had a considerable amount of freedom regarding the contents of the agreements. They could agree to a financial settlement, an apology, or the agreement could involve some sort of action on the part of the offender, provided both parties agreed. The project arranged for offenders to work through a temporary employment agency in order to repay the victim.

The organizers had made arrangements with the office of the public prosecutor in the City of Amsterdam. The office agreed that employees in the project could select cases which the public prosecutor had decided to try, but in which a summons had not yet been served. If a settlement was reached, then the public prosecutor would dismiss the case. If the parties could not come to an agreement, then the case would be placed back into the system, and the defendant would receive a summons. Humanitas requested financial support from the Ministry. This support was granted on condition that the project be evaluated; the Research and Documentation Center of the Ministry of Justice agreed to carry out the evaluation (Wemmers and Van Hecke, 1992). The project ran for 12 months and retained three full-time employees. These employees selected cases for the project at random. Once a dossier was selected, any other open cases involving the defendant were also drawn. There were no limits on the types of offenses, although the selected cases were originally intended for the police court judge: a judge who decides in cases where the maximum possible penalty is six months' imprisonment. The offenders were always 18 years of age or older and had committed a fairly serious offence. Both individual victims as well as organizations, such as department stores or the national telephone company, could be included in the project.

The project workers were responsible for the first contact with defendants and victims. The defendants were sent a letter informing them about the project and the fact that their case had been selected. They were also told that the public prosecutor had decided to serve them with a summons, but if they reached a settlement with the victim(s), their case would be dismissed. Defendants were then contacted by the project workers and asked if they were interested in the possibility of reaching an agreement. If the defendant responded positively, then the victim was approached and asked the same question. Both parties were provided with legal representation if they did not already have a lawyer. The project had a pool of lawyers who were committed to the goal of the project and had agreed to participate. Neither victims nor suspects were required to pay legal fees. Subsidy for the project provided for these costs. Negotiations were conducted by the lawyers for the two parties; the victims and the accused did not meet. Once an agreement had been reached, the lawyers would write up the settlement, which the victim and the defendant would sign. This was a legal document that the victim could use in civil law. In cases involving more than one victim, the defendant only had to reach an agreement with one victim in order for the case to be considered successful. When a settlement was not reached, the case was sent back to the office of the public prosecutor, where it would re-enter the criminal justice system. All traces of the project were removed from the files, so that the authorities could not see that the cases had undergone a failed attempt at conflict resolution, and be influenced by this. A successful case means that the victim has a legal agreement in hand. The defendant has yet to carry out his or her part of the deal. These cases were immediately dismissed by the public prosecutor; if the defendant failed to follow through with the agreement, the victim would be forced to take civil action. The organizers of the project formed a guarantee fund; when a defendant failed to follow through with a financial settlement, and the victim was an individual, the fund would take over the agreement. The victim would be compensated by the fund and the fund would have a civil agreement, which it could use against the defendant in court.

## The Results of the Evaluation

The evaluation was directed at two questions: does the project lead to settlements between parties; and, under what conditions do parties fail to reach an agreement? Both quantitative and qualitative data were collected. A total of 163 cases, 183 defendants and 192 victims, were included in the project during the research period; 83% involved only one offence. Thirty-three percent of the offenses were assaults, 48% property crimes, 15% vandalism, and 4% were other offenses. In 40% there was a relationship (*e.g.*, ex-spouse; acquaintance; family members) between the victim and the defendant. Eighty-seven percent of the defendants were men and half were younger than 33 years of age. A little more than half the group was of Dutch ethnic origin, one-quarter was Surinamese, and the rest were of various ethnic backgrounds. In all, 68% of the defendants were unemployed. Almost two-thirds had previous convictions, and 37% had no prior convictions. In addition, 75% of the defendants had had previous contact with the public prosecutor. Most of the victims were individual owners of small stores; 30% represented large organizations. Half the individual victims and small store owners were younger than 33 years of age. Among the 122 individuals, 63% were male. Seventy percent of the women and 57% of the men were victims of assault. The largest group of offenses was theft; 91% of the larger organizations and 50% small store owners were victims of this type of offence.

The procedure can be broken down into three phases: approaching the defendants; approaching the victims; and negotiations. Sixty-three percent (120) of the 183 defendants expressed an interest in reaching a settlement with the victim. Of the 63 defendants who dropped out of the project in the first phase, 29 responded negatively to the introductory letter, 33 said no after meeting with the project workers, and one died prior to any contact with the project workers. Factors associated with non-participation include recidivism, the type of offence, and whether the victim is an individual or an organization. Defendants without prior convictions were more likely to participate in the project than those with prior convictions. Defendants were less likely to participate when the offence concerned a theft. In contrast, defendants were especially likely to participate when the offence was an assault. They were less likely to participate when the victim was an organization than when the victim was an individual. Some felt that they were not (wholly) responsible for the offence, and saw participating in the project as an admission of guilt. A not unimportant factor affecting the participation of defendants in the project was the advice of the lawyers. Many defendants did not make a decision regarding participation until after they had spoken with a lawyer. The participating lawyers had expressed their commitment to the goals of the project, but their advice was often based on strategic arguments rather than on ideological grounds. For example, lawyers would advise defendants not to participate because, having examined their dossier, they thought that they could get a better deal for the defendant in the criminal justice system. In other cases, lawyers would foresee that the defendant would receive a custodial sentence in the criminal justice system and, therefore, advised their client to take part in the project.

The 120 defendants who made it through the first phase of the project represented 107 cases involving 119 victims. Ninety-five of the victims expressed an interest in reaching a settlement. Eight of the remaining victims responded negatively to the introductory letter and 16 said no after meeting with a project worker. Reasons for non-participation given by victims included that the offence was so serious it belonged in the criminal justice system, or that they had not retained any material damage as a result of the offence. Eighty percent of the victims responded positively to the project. Both parties were particularly likely to participate in the project when they knew each other. Victims of domestic violence often thought that the defendant would not have to go before a judge. Some of these victims also said that they had participated because they knew that the defendant wanted them to do so.

The case of one of the 95 victims who agreed to negotiate the case was sent back to the office of the public prosecutor prior to negotiations; thus, 94 victims actually entered the negotiation phase of the project. This resulted in 90 cases of negotiation involving 99 defendants. Fifty-eight of the 90 cases resulted in a settlement, and in 35 cases the parties were unable to reach an agreement. The overlap in these numbers is due to the fact that three cases involved both failed and successful negotiations. In all, 64 defendants signed agreements with 58 victims. Among the unsuccessful cases were 36 victims and 35 defendants.

Factors affecting the success of the negotiations included the amount of damages claimed by the victim, recidivism, the type of offence, and the attitudes of the parties involved. The larger the amount of damages claimed by the victim, the smaller the chance that the negotiations would be successful. Defendants who did not have any prior convictions were more likely to reach an agreement with the victim. Although cases involving assault were more likely to enter into negotiations, these cases were less likely than other types of offenses to result in a settlement. Negotiations had a good chance of ending in success when the offence was vandalism. The negotiations had a good chance of success when the parties were flexible and willing to make concessions.

The 58 settlements included several different types of agreements. In two-thirds of the cases, the parties agreed on a financial settlement. This included two cases in which the parties agreed to both a financial settlement and a behavioral contract. In one case, the defendant worked for a temporary employment agency to earn money to repay the victim. The amount of restitution agreed upon varied from 30 guilders to 4,500 guilders, and averaged 587 guilders. Both material and immaterial damage, such as pain and suffering, could be included in a settlement, and ten settlements included restitution for immaterial damage. In six cases, the victims settled for less than the actual amount of material damage they had suffered. Three settlements involved the defendant working for the victim. In all three of these cases, the victim was a large organization. Eight agreements involved the defendant agreeing to refrain from a particular action. Five of these eight agreements included a penalty if the defendant breached the agreement. If the agreement was breached, the victim was to report the offence to the police, and the defendant would automatically owe the victim a set sum of money, varying from 50 to 500 guilders. Six agreements required no action from the defendant; the parties simply agreed that the case was settled. In two cases, the settlement involved the defendant apologizing to the victim.

Once a settlement was reached, the case was dismissed by the public prosecutor. Settlements involving restitution or work were followed up by the project workers. Unfortunately, information regarding the success rate for the other types of agreements (*e.g.*, behavioral contracts in cases of domestic violence) is not available. In all, 39 financial and three work agreements were made. Of these 42 agreements, 34 were successfully completed by the defendants; 29 went according to the agreement while, in five cases, the defendants paid later than was agreed but eventually did pay the sum in full. Eight victims had not received any payment from the defendant at the time the study was closed. The project had access to a guarantee fund in order to help victims whose defendant had not followed through. Of the eight victims whose defendants did not meet the agreement, two were large organizations and the fund was only open to individual victims. Ten months after the experiment ended, two of these six victims had received payment from the fund.

## DISCUSSION

Restitution has received attention from both judicial authorities and policy-makers. Possibilities for restitution within the criminal justice system exist, and authorities are encouraged to use them. But the focus must remain on the criminal offence; as a result, only clear cut material damages can be included in the criminal justice procedure. This allows little room for creative problem-solving. Civil law does provide parties with a wide range of tools from which to chose, but civil law is costly and places a large responsibility on the victim. The experiment described in this chapter used civil and criminal law. It used civil procedures in criminal cases. The results show that negotiations between parties can lead to a mutually suitable solution to the conflict between them. Parties were able to reach an agreement in 36% of cases. In most cases, the parties agreed to a financial settlement. The high number of financial agreements suggests that financial restitution offers a suitable solution to many conflicts. Nevertheless, some cases used alternative solutions. Examples of this are cases where the defendant agreed to refrain from a particular action, or offered the victim a formal apology. For these cases, the concept of restitution used in the criminal justice system is too narrow.

The highest drop-out rate was in securing consent from the defendants. While 66% of the defendants agreed to participate in the project, 80% of the victims who were approached by the project workers agreed to enter into negotiations with the defendant. Based on this information, it is not possible to conclude that victims are more interested in restoration than defendants; the two groups are not independent. However, research on restitution shows that victims are often interested in restitution, and that restitution in the criminal justice system is relatively uncommon. A recent study on the implementation of the 1987 victim guidelines revealed that, among victims who retained damages as a result of the offence, 86% were interested in restitution, but that less than 20% of these victims were actually assisted by police and the public prosecutor in obtaining restitution from the offender (Wemmers, 1994). This finding may explain the strong interest in the project among victims. Yet, research by Gehm (1990) on North American victim-offender reconciliation programs (VORPs) found that the victims were particularly likely to refuse to participate in negotiations. He reports that 53% of cases never reached a meeting because the victim declined. One important difference between this project and VORPs is that the parties do not meet directly. Similarly, when police and the public prosecution assist in arranging settlements, victims and offenders do not come into direct contact with one another. Perhaps direct confrontation with the offender is an obstacle for victims. Factors affecting the success of the negotiations between parties include the perceived gains and losses derived from an out-of-court solution and the problem. This is especially true of defendants who, advised by their lawyers, weighed the potential outcome of a trial and were motivated to avoid a conviction. For victims, participation offers the possibility of obtaining a restitution which they may not otherwise have obtained. The factors associated with successful negotiations suggest that the process is based on rational calculations rather than on ideological arguments, such as a sense of duty, to make restitution to the victim.

Most restitution programs specify goals in terms of offender benefits (Hudson and Galaway, 1990). According to Hudson and Galaway, an important offender benefit is a reduction in the intrusiveness of the justice system. However, the benefits for offenders must not be translated into disadvantages for victims. There must be a balance between the interests of both parties. Despite the high degree of interest in the project among victims, the project is rather offender-oriented and contains several disadvantages for victims. One disadvantage is that, by approaching the defendant first, the project may inadvertently pressure victims to participate. This is a particularly important concern in cases where the defendant knows the victim, such as in domestic violence. A second problem is the absence of any safeguards for the victim. The cases were dismissed automatically once an agreement was reached. Civil law gives victims a large amount of responsibility. If the defendant breaches the agreement, it is up to the victim to take action. Such action may be costly and the victim, unfamiliar with the legal system, may be unable to cope with such a burden. While the project offered a guarantee fund, the fund was only available to a select group of victims, and was slow to provide relief. In cases where the agreement did not include financial compensation, but required a particular action on the part of the defendant, the victim had no safeguards at all. A third problem is the fact that, in cases involving more than one victim, the defendant only had to sign a contract with one of the victims for the case to be dismissed. This overlooks the interests of the other victims in the case, and leaves them without any opportunities for restitution.

While restorative justice may be beneficial to both the victim and the offender, it must be sensitive to the interests of both parties and employ safeguards to protect their interests. In the present project, this could be realized by making a few modifications. By combining the agreement with a conditional sanction, the victim could rely on the public prosecution to help enforce the agreement. This procedure is already being followed in protective mediation (Wauchope, 1994), where it has proven to be quite successful. It puts the victim in a better position, making enforcement the responsibility of the criminal justice authorities rather than of the victim. The threat of a possible sanction could motivate the defendant to follow through with the agreement. A second improvement concerns cases where more than one victim is involved. If the defendant makes an agreement with only one victim, and more victims are involved, the case should be re-entered into the criminal justice system, rather than be dismissed. The judge can bear in mind the fact that an agreement has been reached, while considering the other offenses. Thirdly, victims rather than defendants should have the first choice with regard to participation. This is particularly important in cases in which the victim and defendant are known to each other. In this way, defendants are not given an opportunity to pressure the victim into participation. With regard to the defendants, only those cases in which the defendant has clearly admitted responsibility for the offence should be included in the project. It is possible that the present design pressures innocent people into negotiations in order to avoid the threat of a conviction. The project could be further improved by replacing the lawyers with another type of mediator. Marshall (1990) suggests that mediation programs should have strong links with victim assistance schemes and probation services. In his view, such links could provide any necessary after-care. Experts from these two organizations could conduct the negotiations instead of lawyers. This could reduce the tendency among lawyers to base participation on a rational calculation of potential inputs and outcomes, and return the attention to restoration.

With the evolution of the victims' movement, restorative justice has been reduced to restitution for material damages. For the future, if restorative justice is to mean more than restitution and conflict resolution is to make a reappearance, then it must address both the position of the defendant and the victim. This can be done by combining elements from civil and criminal law. Despite its shortcomings, the experiment presented in this paper provides one example of how elements from civil and criminal law can be combined in restorative justice. Conflict resolution provides a viable alternative to sanctioning and allows parties to reach a mutually suitable solution to their conflict. However, it must be done with caution.

## REFERENCES

Commissie Wettelijke Voorzieningen Slachtoffers in het Strafproces (1988). *Wettelijke Voorzieningen Slachtoffers in het Strafproces.* The Hague, NETH: SDU Uitgeverij.

Gehm, J. (1990). "Mediated Victim-Offender Restitution Agreements: An Exploratory Analysis of Factors Related to Victim Participation." In: B. Galaway and J. Hudson (eds.), *Criminal Justice, Restitution and Reconciliation.* Monsey, NY: Willow Tree Press Inc.

Hudson, J. and B. Galaway (1990). "Restitution Program Models with Adult Offenders." In: B. Galaway and J. Hudson (eds.), *Criminal Justice, Restitution and Reconciliation.* Monsey, NY: Willow Tree Press Inc.

Marshall, T.F. (1990). "Results of Research from British Experiments in Restorative Justice." In: B. Galaway and J. Hudson (eds.), *Criminal Justice, Restitution and Reconciliation.* Monsey, NY: Willow Tree Press Inc.

Ruyter, L. (1977). *Project Gedupeerden van Misdrijven te Hoorn: Verslag November 1976–September 1977.* Amsterdam, NETH: Humanitas, Projectgroep Delinquentie en Samenleving.

Steinmetz, C.H.D. (1990). *Hulp aan Slachtoffers van Ernstige Misdrijven: Effecten van Slachtofferhulp en Primaire Opvang.* Wetenschappelijk Onderzoek- en Documentatiecentrum, Onderzoek en Beleid, 98. Arnhem, NETH: Gouda Quint bv.

Van Dijk, J.J.M. (1982). "De Positie van het Slachtoffer in het Strafproces: Achtergronden en Perspectieven." *Justitiële Verkenningen* 6:10-20.

Wauchope, M. (1994). *Protective Mediation: A New Approach to the Victim-Offender Relationship.* Paper presented at the Eighth International Symposium on Victimology, Adelaide, AUS, August.

Wemmers, J.M. (1994). *Slachtofferonderzoek Wet en Richtlijn Terwee: Onderzoek pre Terwee.* The Hague, NETH: Wetenschappelijk Onderzoek- en Documentatiecentrum, Ministerie van Justitie.

—and T. Van Hecke (1992). *Strafrechtelijke Dading.* Wetenschappelijk Onderzoek- en Documentatiecentrum, K23. The Hague, NETH: Ministerie van Justitie.

Werkgroep Aangifte Sexuele Geweldsmisdrijven (1981). *Rapport van de Werkgroep Aangifte Sexuele Geweldsmisdrijven.* The Hague, NETH: Ministeries van Justitie en Binnenlandse Zaken.

Werkgroep Justitieel Beleid en Slachtoffer (1985). *Eindrapport van de Werkgroep Justitieel Beleid en Slachtoffer.* The Hague, NETH: Ministerie van Justitie.

Wet Terwee (1993). "Wet van 23 December 1992 tot Aanvulling van het Wetboek van Strafrecht, het Wetboek van Strafvordering, de Wet Voorlopige Regeling Schadefonds Geweldsmisdrijven en Andere Wetten met Voorzieningen ten Behoeve van Slachtoffers van Strafbare Feiten." *Staatsblad* 29. The Hague, NETH: SDU Uitgeverij.

Winkel, F.W. (1990). *Slachtofferhulp: Verkenning en Sociaal-Psychologische Analyse.* Amsterdam, NETH: Swets & Zeitlinger.

# 26. LEEDS MEDIATION AND REPARATION SERVICE: TEN YEARS' EXPERIENCE WITH VICTIM-OFFENDER MEDIATION

by

## Jean Wynne

**Abstract:** *The Leeds Mediation Service has completed ten years of victim-offender mediation involving both juvenile and adult offenders and their victims. Participation must be voluntary on the part of both offender and victim, and may occur at any phase in the criminal justice process. Referrals come from a wide variety of sources, including victims and offenders themselves. The service is funded by the probation agency, but operates at arms' length from probation. Mediators are trained community people, and most are paid on a sessional basis. Mediation may result in an agreement for reparation or service to community or victim, but more often in an apology or no further action required; victims seem more interested in the fact that the offender is willing to meet, take responsibility for the offence, and extend an apology than receiving reparation. About 48% of referrals result in mediation; all types of offenses are considered. The majority of the offenders are young, with 61% being between the ages 13 and 22. Most of the offenders are male, 42% of the victims are male and 29% female; 8% are joint in the case of households, and 21% of the victims are corporate victims. There is no difference between men and women in terms of the likelihood that they will agree to participate in mediation. Follow-up studies indicate a lower recidivism rate for offenders who have completed mediation, although this may be a selected artifact as the program is careful to ensure that both victims and offenders are volunteers.*

The Leeds Reparation Project began in May 1985 as one of four government-funded pilot projects. The aim was:

> ...to test whether mediation/reparation was a valid way of working with high tariff offenders and whether it was possible to reduce the number of offenders in this group receiving custodial sentences. The objective was to work with 240 such offenders and their victims within the two-year period (Leeds Reparation Project Report, 1987, p.5).

The emphasis during the trial project was on offenders and victims meeting to negotiate some form of reparation. The form of reparation was to be made known to the court at the time of sentence and to be taken into account when sentence was passed. The two-year trial period seemed to show that mediation and reparation was of value in changing stereotypical attitudes and helping victims, but had only a small effect on actually diverting offenders from custody (Marshall and Merry, 1990).

The research indicated that the attitudes of victims who took part in mediation were less punitive towards offenders than those who did not. Victims who participated were more likely than those who did not to feel that they had obtained justice, through the imposition of a community-based penalty on the offender. The victims also appeared to understand and appreciate that any reparation carried out was voluntary. This may have been a surprise to those interested in the idea of reparation as a sentence. Certainly, the early thinking about reparation was that it could be a formal sentence in the same way as probation or a community service order. The idea was that, by carrying out reparation for the victim, the offender would have helped to pay off his or her debt to both victim and society. In this way, high-tariff offenders could be diverted from custody without the victims feeling that they had not received justice (U.K. Home Office, 1984). There was a loss of interest, however, by the Home Office after the trial period (Davis, 1987). The West Yorkshire Probation Service recognized the value of the work being done with victims and offenders for reasons other than diversion from custody, and took over funding of the Leeds scheme. Two specialist local coordinators were appointed to provide day-to-day management and to develop the scheme, with the assistance of a management consultant. The project title was changed to Leeds Mediation and Reparation Service (LMRS) to reflect the fact that it was no longer a pilot scheme.

The experimental project had been targeted at high-tariff adult offenders likely to receive a custodial sentence in the Crown Court. The limitations of targeting certain offenders meant that neither victims nor offenders were being offered equal opportunities. Only those victims whose offenders were referred to LMRS had the opportunity to pursue mediation. These were the victims of serious offenses and, mostly, repeat offenders. At that time, probation officers would refer the offender to the scheme during the preparation of a social enquiry report for the Crown Court. Clearly, there were many more victims, including those of first-time offenders and less serious offenses, who may have wanted to take part in mediation. Some victims may also have wanted to refer themselves to the scheme but, at that time, the appropriate administrative procedures were not in place to allow this. Once freed from the limitations of the research project, procedures and practice could be changed to fit the new aims and philosophy of offering mediation equally to victims and offenders. This meant that victims could also be referred, as well as offenders under the age of 18. It also meant that less serious offenses, which are normally dealt with in the lower courts, could be considered for mediation as well as offenses, such as sexual assaults and domestic violence, which had not been considered appropriate under the original pilot project specifications.

The assessment procedures were also changed so that victims and offenders were assessed on similar criteria. Originally the project assessed offenders on the basis of the genuineness of their remorse and their desire to put things right. There are difficulties in assessing genuineness. This criterion was dropped in favor of willingness to take part in mediation. Willingness is relatively easy to assess and applies equally to victims and offenders. The other criteria were safety and an admission of guilt on the part of the offender. From 1988 onwards, all types of offenses involving a victim were considered for assessment, and the referral could be made at any stage of the criminal justice process, rather than solely at the pre-court stage. This meant that offenders who had been sentenced could now be referred, and that victims who wanted mediation post-sentence could be accommodated. It also meant that young offenders who had received a caution instead of being sent to court could be referred. The aim was to provide a service of voluntary mediation for victims and offenders to use as would best benefit them. The definition of mediation as used by LMRS is "a process of communication which allows victims to express their needs and feelings and offenders to accept and act on their responsibilities".

## PHILOSOPHY AND PRINCIPLES

The philosophy and principles on which the service is currently operated are that mediation and reparation are based on a philosophy of
restoration rather than retribution...A successful resolution of the
conflict leaves all parties feeling that something has been gained
rather than that one party has lost. Applying conflict resolution principles to the criminal justice system means resolving some of the
effects of the offence for all parties (Quill and Wynne, 1993, p.6)

Thus, it is important to acknowledge that crime has deleterious
effects on everyone involved. The victims are left with feelings of loss and
powerlessness because they have no control over what happened to
them. They have a strong sense of loss, whether this relates to actual
possessions or their feelings of security in their home or neighborhood.
Offenders have to face a criminal justice process with degrading and
stigmatizing rituals, which often results in a denial process necessary
for coping with being an offender. Their families may suffer enormously
through the shame, stigmatization and sometimes financial effects of
paying fines, or lost income through serving a prison sentence. The local
community is often affected in cases of localized robbery, burglary, or
car theft. Neighbors are usually aware of what has happened and feel
fear as a consequence. The normal criminal justice process is limited in
its capacity to deal with this personal aftermath of crime. Victims can be
helped by the counselling and practical help provided by victim support
services, but these do not involve the offenders. Offenders receive assistance from their social worker or probation officer but, until recently,
these did not have the brief or time to contact victims. For many crimes,
some form of independent, neutral contact between victims and offenders can be enormously helpful in resolving some of the effects of the
crime.

Mediation can help victims in several ways:

1. It offers a choice. Victims have no choice about an offence occurring.
   Mediation offers them an opportunity to take part in the subsequent
   process and they can choose the level of involvement appropriate to
   them, whether this be an exchange of feelings via the mediator or a
   face-to-face meeting with the offender.
2. It offers accurate up-to-date information on the progress of the case.
3. It offers an acknowledgement of the hurt suffered by the victim, and
   acceptance of responsibility for that hurt by the offender.

4. It offers the possibility of some form of reparation.

5. It can help reduce fear of being re-victimized.

The victim has a choice as to when the mediation work takes place. For some victims, it is important that the work takes place before sentence, so that they have a voice in court. Other victims may feel strongly that they want to test out the offenders' sincerity; for these victims, it is important that the work takes place after the sentence, whether that sentence is served in the community or in prison. It is made clear to offenders that they will be expected to continue post-sentence and that the victim can choose the timing. Offenders may also be extremely nervous about participating and, at the start, cannot contemplate facing up to their victim. Given time, they may build up confidence, through a mediator, to enable them to achieve the appropriate level of mediation for their victim.

Mediation can help offenders by:

1. Aiding them to accept full responsibility for their behavior, however painful.

2. Enabling them to offer reparation in some way.

3. Enabling them to offer an apology.

4. Enabling them to put the offence behind them and make a fresh start.

5. Raising their self-esteem.

6. Helping reintegration into the community, which is particularly important in cases where the victims live in the same neighborhood.

What is important in practice is that mediators share the philosophy and values which underpin mediation. According to Marshall (1989), the values of openness, self-determination, collaboration, flexibility, non-discrimination, and non-violence are fundamental to the promotion of human rights. Openness and honesty are necessary for the success of the mediation process. If the facts of a case are in dispute, mediation may be difficult and unsafe. If the victim wants to meet the offender, knowing that the facts are in dispute, it may still be appropriate to go ahead, as long as there are no physical or emotional safety issues. Self-determination means that mediation must always be voluntary on both sides. It would be quite easy for a skilled mediator to push either victim or offender into taking the process beyond the level at which they feel comfortable, but the result would be dissatisfaction or eventual non-compliance with the process. The mediator's role is to encourage and enable victims and offenders to use the service in the way most satisfactory for themselves. This means resisting any temptation to bring about face-to-face meetings which would not be of use. LMRS has moved away from assessing success in terms of the number of face-to-face meetings achieved, to assessing participants' satisfaction with the process. Mediation principles mean treating people with equal respect. This is not to deny guilt on the part of offenders, but rather an acceptance of that guilt and of the offenders' wish to repair harm where possible. Non-discriminatory practice is essential if participants are to gain from the experience. Mediators strive to ensure that they are not discriminating against either side on any grounds, but, to achieve this non-discriminatory practice they have to be aware of power imbalances on the grounds of ethnicity, gender, age or any of the other areas of possible discrimination.

## STAFFING

From 1987 to 1991, the service had two full-time coordinators and one full-time clerical officer. A senior probation officer provided support and supervision and had responsibility for the scheme, although not in a full-time role. A third coordinator's post was established in 1992 to assist in continuing development in the Leeds area. This new post also enabled the half-time release of one of the experienced coordinators, in order to help establish mediation in one of the other five divisions of the West Yorkshire Probation Area. This development work is still continuing. In 1995, each of the five divisions had a mediation and reparation service, but the two newest schemes require support from the longer established schemes as they build up experience. LMRS has, since inception, had the benefit of an interagency committee. Advisory Committees have a key role in the support and development of mediation across the West Yorkshire Probation Area. Each committee consists of representatives from courts, sentencers, crown prosecution service, victim support services, police, and probation. LMRS' committee meets on a quarterly basis and provides invaluable support. The chair of LMRS' committee sits on the West Yorkshire Probation Committee, facilitating access to the highest levels of management.

The mediation work itself is mainly carried out by a team of volunteer and sessionally paid mediators. Currently, there are 17 mediators, although they are at different stages of training and experience. Some of the mediators have been with the service for between eight and nine years. There has never been a shortage of people wanting to train, and the service has never had to advertise for trainee mediators. People usually find out about the work of the service through the local volunteer bureau or through training as a probation volunteer. After an initial interview with a coordinator, the prospective volunteer is invited to attend the fortnightly mediators' meetings. These meetings are a mixture of business, training sessions and case discussions, and provide important peer group support for the mediators. The training sessions provide a rolling program, covering subjects such as the courts, probation, the criminal justice process, report writing, mediation skills, listening skills, working with juveniles, handling violence and aggression, non-discriminatory practice, and mediating specific offenses such as deception, domestic violence, and sexual assaults.

The basic training course is now held on a West Yorkshire-wide basis several times a year, because of the sheer number of mediators to be trained for the five services. The course covers two days and involves the prospective mediator in role-playing assessment procedures, indirect mediation interviews, and face-to-face meetings between victim and offender. The role plays are based on actual cases, and the trainees are expected to play them from the three different perspectives of mediator, victim, and offender. An essential part of the training course is the attitudes and values exercise, which helps mediators to realise their own values and how these fit in with the values of mediation. After completing the two-day course, new mediators apply formally and, at that point, police checks are carried out to find out whether the applicant has been convicted of any criminal offence. A police record does not necessarily bar the applicant from becoming a mediator, if the offenses were relatively minor and the applicant can show that he or she has since changed lifestyle. Any applicant with convictions for abuse against children would not be considered. Once the police checks and references are found to be satisfactory, the senior probation officer formally interviews applicants, during which time they are advised whether or not they are to be accredited as a mediator. Once accredited, trainee mediators accompany experienced mediators, until sufficiently experienced to mediate their own cases. All the mediators, including the trainees, receive individual support and supervision from a coordinator on a regular basis.

# THE MEDIATION PROCESS

Referrals are accepted from social workers, probation officers, police, victim support services, solicitors, courts, citizens advice bureaux, and individual victims and offenders. Either party can be referred or can refer themselves, usually by telephone. The coordinator collects information about the current whereabouts of both victim and offender, details of the offence, and whether compensation has been requested. The coordinator will discuss the suitability of the case with the referrer, and some cases are not accepted. Usually this is because of adverse safety issues. If the case is pre-court, the coordinator needs to know whether a police or crown prosecution service decision has been made about sending the offender to court and, if so, whether he or she is pleading guilty to the charge. If the case is at an early stage, and a plea has not been entered, the coordinator will write to the defendant's lawyer to check whether the defendant is admitting to the offence as charged, rather than admitting to a lesser charge or denying the offence entirely. Until this point is clear, the mediator will not usually make contact with the victim. Similarly, if the police or Crown Prosecution Service are considering administering a caution, rather than taking a young person to court, LMRS will not contact the victim until the decision has been made.

When the referral is accepted, the coordinator collects as much information about the offence as possible and then allocates the case to a mediator. The mediator is told whom it is appropriate to contact and what other information may need to be collected on first contact with one of the parties. The mediator will usually send a letter making an appointment to see the offender or victim. There are various arguments to support visiting either the victim or the offender first, but LMRS does not have a policy on who should be visited first. In practice, it may be that first contact is made with whoever is available. Some mediators feel strongly that they need to check out the offender's willingness before contacting the victim, in order to prevent re-victimization. Others feel that they prefer to contact the victim first, so that the victim does not feel that the mediator is putting the offender first. In cases where the victim has been referred, the victim is usually seen first, and it may take some time before the offender is seen. With victim referrals, the offender's details are not known and have to be traced through either the police, social services, or probation records. The difficulty with a victim referral is often that the offender has not been identified and charged.

At the first visit, the mediator provides information about the service and assesses whether the victim or offender is willing to take part in mediation. Their safety during the process is also assessed. Things to consider include the likelihood of violence, power imbalances between victim and offender, proximity of victim and offender in the community, the type of offence, whether others are involved, and fears of retribution. Other things to be assessed include the victim or offender's state of mind and physical abilities. There is no point in taking the case any further if the participant is emotionally unstable or, as occasionally happens with elderly victims, completely confused about the visit. The physical condition of victims and offenders is also important. Mediation may be helpful to those suffering from illness, but should not be pursued if it will put the victim or offender at risk. After the first round of visits, the mediator revisits both parties to exchange information, with their permission. During this second visit, the mediator will usually challenge the offender about the effect of the offence on the victim. Often the information is somewhat of a shock to the offender, and the mediator has to talk him or her through this quite painful stage. If the offender has a probation officer or social worker, the coordinator will inform them of how the victim feels, and of any difficulties the offender may have in receiving this information. The coordinator will also highlight any differences between the offender's account of what happened and the victim's.

Sometimes victims have a specific request for reparation, such as a sum of money to compensate them for their loss, or for a specific piece of work to be undertaken by the offender. However, the reparation required by the victim, in serious cases, is often at a more personal level than financial compensation or practical work. It is important for victims to know that their offenders accept responsibility for their behavior and its outcome. They want to know that offenders are aware of the physical and mental pain they have caused. The most requested reparation often seems to be assurance from offenders that they will change their behavior and not put someone else through this pain. In some cases, financial reparation of even relatively small amounts can be important to victims, and has to be negotiated. The smallest amount given to a victim so far is £5, whereas the largest amount negotiated was for £25,000 in a case of theft from an employer. In this latter case, the reparation agreement was put to the Court and endorsed by it. It was agreed by the Court that the reparation agreement also settled the civil case. Reparation is required in 35% of mediated cases; a breakdown of the different types of reparation requested is shown in Table 26.1. The reparation re-

Table 26.1. Type of reparation requested by victim.

| | | |
|---|---|---|
| Letter of apology | (43) | 44% |
| Personal apology | (12) | 12% |
| Financial | (11) | 11% |
| Financial and apology | (6) | 6% |
| Restitution | (1) | 1% |
| Letter and restitution | (2) | 2% |
| Practical work for victim | (9) | 9% |
| Practical work for third party | (1) | 1% |
| Compensation order with amount negotiated by service | (5) | 5% |
| Promise of future behavior | (6) | 6% |
| Other | (02) | 2% |
| Total | (98) | 100% |

quested by victims may be concrete items, such as financial compensation and practical work or, more personally, an acknowledgement of the effects of the offence through an apology or a promise by the offender to behave better in future.

The indirect mediation phase involves the mediator in the delicate and sensitive work of passing information between victims and offenders. At this stage, if safety factors allow, the mediator will ask both parties if they would like to meet face-to-face. Sometimes both parties ask for a face-to-face meeting, but the mediator, after discussion with the coordinator, will refuse because of safety considerations. For example, cases involving deception are not, in general, brought to a face-to-face meeting, to avoid revictimization of the victim. Usually deception cases involve a victim who is lonely and vulnerable and who placed a mistaken trust in the offender. There is a risk that the situation will be replayed by bringing them together again. With domestic violence, the violent partner may want a face-to-face meeting with the ex-partner to re-establish control. The mediator must be aware of power imbalances and protection issues, and not allow mediation to be used for this purpose. Indirect mediation allows both sides to explain their position safely without any risk of further violence.

The mediator will arrange a meeting if the criteria of willingness, safety, and admission of guilt are all fulfilled. At this stage, a second mediator is enlisted to help with the case and manage the meeting. A neutral venue is booked, at a time suitable to both sides, usually in a church hall, community center, or the office. Usually, each mediator picks up one of the parties and drives them to the meeting place. This allows for preparation time during the journey. Often the participants are very nervous and need reassurance. They may need to work out what they are going to say and be reminded of the things they were concerned about previously. The meeting attempts to follow the standard mediation format of introductions and ground rules, uninterrupted time, exchange of information, and negotiation, followed by possible agreement. This is the ideal. Most meetings do not follow that format exactly, and the mediator has to be skilled and confident enough to allow variations from the format. Some meetings do not end in agreement and the mediator must not force the parties to agree to something they do not want. It may be more comfortable for the mediator if a tidy ending is achieved, but the meeting must be about what the victim and offender want to achieve. At the close of the meeting, the case mediator sums up, and the second mediator notes any points of agreement. All present sign their names to these points. If the case is pre-court, they are given a copy of the agreement and asked if the court can be made aware of this agreement. If the case is post-sentence, they are simply given a copy for their own records. Where the offender is a young person who has been referred by a multi-agency panel, the victim and offender are made aware that the agreement, and a report of the meeting, will be sent to the panel for information.

Following the meeting, or indirect mediation, the mediator reports back to the coordinator who prepares the court or panel report and informs the referrer of the outcome. The mediation report contains a statement of the offender's attitude towards the victim and the offence, and any offer of reparation. It states how the victim is feeling about what happened and whether the offender can do anything to put things right. If the parties have made an agreement on financial reparation, this is put to the court and may be endorsed as a formal compensation order by the court. The mediator supervises practical work reparation. Over the past ten years, however, there has been less emphasis on practical reparation for a number of reasons. The offender may be given a sentence of community service, and fitting in extra reparation work could be difficult. Most victims do not want the offender anywhere near their own household. They may request reparation for a third party, but this can be difficult to arrange and supervise. Practical reparation is very costly in terms of mediator time. Finally, mediators are selected for their personal qualities, not for their ability to supervise practical work, and not all are able or choose to do this. If a different type of reparation has been agreed, such as voluntary financial compensation, the mediator will arrange to collect this and personally deliver it to the victim. A total of 48% of referrals go to either direct or indirect mediation.

## TYPES OF OFFENSES

LMRS assesses referrals for all types of crime which involve named victims. These offenses include arson, assault, burglary, deception, car theft, theft from employer, robbery, kidnapping, wounding with intent, sexual assaults, and domestic violence. Table 26.2 gives a breakdown of the type of offence, and the number mediated. There is no clear correlation between offence type and the likelihood of mediation. Some offence types result in just over half being mediated, and others in slightly under half. All three manslaughter cases were mediated, whereas only one out of six sexual assaults resulted in mediation. Some offenses, such as fraud against a government department, are not usually considered suitable for mediation. Even here, there are exceptions, as for example, where the offender worked in such a department and caused emotional damage to staff through her actions. Offenses such as football hooliganism, being drunk and disorderly, or affray, are not usually considered suitable for mediation, as it is difficult to identify a specific victim.

It is important not to have any preconceptions about what constitutes suitable cases; experience has shown that the perception of the victim and offender is a better indicator of suitability than that of the mediator or coordinator. For example, shoplifting from a branch of a chain of newsagents shops may not appear to be suitable; yet, when the mediator visited the manager of the shop, she found that there was a high level of distress among the staff. So much had been stolen recently that the staff felt under suspicion themselves. Similarly, theft from supermarkets may initially appear unsuitable, yet the Leeds scheme has had several very successful mediations between the store security officer and the offender. Explanations about the effect of shoplifting on the general public made a surprising impression on the offenders. Other cases, where stereotypical attitudes may prevent referral, are those involving elderly victims. Fears about upsetting elderly victims could prevent mediation from being offered, yet elderly people are very often extremely resilient and more able to cope than younger people. The mediators use their judgement as to whether it is suitable to offer mediation, but only

Table 26.2. Mediation by offence type.

|                                      | Mediation (n=281)* | | No Mediation (n=307)* | |
|--------------------------------------|------|------|------|------|
| Arson                                | (7)  | 70%  | (3)  | 30%  |
| Assaults                             | (46) | 38%  | (76) | 62%  |
| Burglary                             | (91) | 49%  | (95) | 51%  |
| Criminal damage                      | (24) | 57%  | (18) | 43%  |
| Fraud                                | (0)  | 0%   | (1)  | 100% |
| Manslaughter                         | (3)  | 100% | (0)  | 0%   |
| Receiving                            | (0)  | 0%   | (2)  | 100% |
| Robbery                              | (22) | 44%  | (28) | 56%  |
| Sexual assaults                      | (1)  | 17%  | (5)  | 83%  |
| Theft                                | (62) | 55%  | (51) | 45%  |
| Taking care without owners consent   | (13) | 54%  | (11) | 46%  |
| Other                                | (12) | 41%  | (17) | 59%  |

*Closed cases 1988 through 1992.

after visiting the elderly person to assess their willingness and safety in the mediation process.

Rape cases are considered, but extreme care is taken with these and other cases involving sexual assaults. No case of rape has yet resulted in a face-to-face meeting; very few cases have been referred or accepted. Probation officers working with the offender are careful about any request for mediation coming from the offender, and need convincing about the sincerity of the request. There is a consensus of opinion among probation and mediation staff that the request for mediation in rape cases should really come from the victim. Ideally, the victim could refer herself or be referred by a victim agency, if she felt that contact with the offender would be helpful to get questions answered or to challenge the offender about his behavior. In such a case, the timing would be right for the victim and she would not feel that the offender was seeking her out; rather, it would be her seeking him out.

## VICTIMS AND OFFENDERS

Each year the service accepts approximately 200 referrals for assessment. The majority of cases start with the offender being referred, usually by the probation officer for adult offenders or the police for young offenders. Considerably more victims may be offered the service, as many

Table 26.3. Age of offender when referred to mediation for cases closed 1988 to 1992.

| | | |
|---|---|---|
| 11-13 | (23) | 5% |
| 14-17 | (174) | 33% |
| 18-21 | (145) | 28% |
| 22-25 | (85) | 16% |
| 26-29 | (34) | 7% |
| 30-39 | (42) | 8% |
| 40-70 | (19) | 4% |
| | | |
| Total | 522 | 100% |

offenders have more than one victim. The majority of offenders referred to mediation are relatively young, with 61% being between 13 and 22 years. Table 26.3 shows the offenders' age at referral. LMRS has not routinely collected details of victims' ages, because it can be insensitive to ask for such details. Offenders' ethnicity is obtained by asking offenders how they categorize themselves. Usually this information is collected by probation officers at the report stage. Of those referred to mediation, 3% described themselves as black. These offenders included 2% who classified themselves as Afro-Caribbean, and 0.7% who classified themselves as Asian. A Home Office survey of offenders on probation in West Yorkshire showed that 3.5% were black and 1.8% were Asian. Victims' ethnicity is not routinely collected as, just as with age, it is considered insensitive to ask victims how they would categorize themselves ethnically when visiting them following an offence.

The majority of victims and offenders offered mediation are male; 92% of offenders and 42% of victims are male. Only 8% of offenders and 29% of victims are female; 21% of victims are organizational or corporate victims, and 8% are joint victims. Table 26.4 gives a breakdown of gender of victims and offenders. One of the stereotypes, often portrayed in the media, is that mediation involves a male offender and a female victim, suggesting that women are more likely than men to take part. Table 26.5 illustrates that this is not the case. At LMRS, almost equal numbers of men and women victims participate.

# RECONVICTION RESEARCH

The most frequently asked question by criminal justice agency personnel is "does mediation help to stop offenders re-offending?" So far

*Table 26.4.* Gender of victims and offenders for cases closed 1988 to 1992.

| Victims' Gender | Offenders' Gender | | | | | |
|---|---|---|---|---|---|---|
| | Female | | Male | | Totals | |
| Female | (16) | 3% | (126) | 26% | (142) | 29% |
| Male | (10) | 2% | (193) | 40% | (203) | 42% |
| Both (joint victims) | | | (41) | 8% | (41) | 8% |
| Corporate | (13) | 3% | ( 89) | 18% | (102) | 21% |
| Column Totals | (39) | 8% | (449) | 92% | (488) | 100% |

*Table 26.5.* Mediation participation by gender of victim for cases closed 1988 to 1992.

| | Mediation (n=280) | | No Mediation (n=282) | |
|---|---|---|---|---|
| Female | (73) | 44% | (93) | 56% |
| Male | (105) | 46% | (124) | 54% |
| Joint | (36) | 69% | (16) | 31% |
| Corporate | (66) | 57% | (49) | 43% |

LMRS has carried out two follow-up studies of offenders who took part in mediation. In 1988, the service examined the criminal records of all offenders who met their victims during the two-year trial period 1985-1987. Ninety offenders were involved, of whom 87% had a previous criminal record; 25% of these were persistent offenders who had five or more convictions. The research showed that 75% had no further convictions after one year, and 68% no further convictions after two years. A second follow-up study was carried out in 1992 and looked at those offenders who took part in mediation during 1989. Those who received a prison sentence of longer than one year for the mediated offence were excluded from the study, as they would not have had much time to re-offend and be processed. The results of the second study showed that, of the 69 offenders who took part in either indirect or direct mediation, 68% had previous convictions and 30% were persistent offenders. Young offenders who had no previous convictions were excluded from this research, as it was assumed that they were just starting out on their offending career. This assumption was wrong, as ten of the 11 first-time offenders had not re-offended over two years later. Of the 69 who were examined, 78% had no further convictions after one year, and 58% had no further convictions after two years. In comparison, "70% of prisoners currently released from prison are reconvicted within two years. For juveniles the rates have exceeded 80%" (West Yorkshire Probation Service, 1994).

## THE FUTURE

The West Yorkshire Probation Service has five mediation and reparation schemes covering the entire area. The policy on mediation and reparation was formulated in 1993, and the five services all follow this policy, to provide the same quality of service. Training for mediators is now on an area-wide basis, and several courses are provided each year. The most recent estimate suggests that about 80 mediators are registered (including prospective as well as trained mediators). LMRS has ten years' experience of mediation, but the newer services are at different stages of development. There is a need for all five services to operate consistently in order best to practice standards in line with both local and national experience and recommendations. How this can be achieved is one of several development issues for the management.

LMRS has always paid its mediators since inception, and the staff believe that this is one of the main reasons why LMRS has become known as a center of excellence for victim-offender mediation work. The positive outcomes of paying experienced mediators are that they stay with the service, are committed to training and developing practice, are more accountable to the management, and can be expected to take a variety of cases and work in a more directed manner than if they were volunteers. At a time of cash limits and budget cuts for probation services, however, the expansion of mediation services is difficult to envisage unless volunteer mediators are used. One way round this problem is to train probation officers to undertake mediation. However, there is a consensus of opinion that mediation should not be carried out by someone with another interest in the case. Should probation services fund mediation services at all? It may fit better with the philosophy of neutrality for mediation services to be fully independent of offender agencies. LMRS staff considered this issue some time ago, but felt that neutrality could be maintained by having neutral premises, a multi-agency advisory committee, and the use of specialist mediation staff.

# REFERENCES

Davis, G., J. Boucherct, D, Watson and A. Thatcher (1987). *A Preliminary Study of Victim and Offender Mediation and Reparation Schemes in England and Wales* (Research and Planning Unit, Paper No. 42). London, UK: Home Office.

Leeds Reparation Project (1987). *Report of Experimental Period: 1 May 1985-30th April 1987*. Leeds, UK: West Yorkshire Probation Service.

Marshall, T. (1989). "Values and Principles in Mediation: A Firm View of Practice Standards." In: *Mediation*, Vol. 6, No. 1, December 1989. Beconsfield: The Forum for Initiatives in Reparation and Mediation (now Mediation U.K.).

—and S. Merry (1990). *Crime and Accountability: Victim and Offender Mediation in Practice*. London, UK: Her Majesty's Stationery Office.

Quill, D. and J. Wynne (1993). *Victim & Offender Mediation Handbook*. Leeds, UK: Save the Children Fund and West Yorkshire Probation Service.

U.K. Home Office (1986). *Reparation: A Discussion Document*. London, UK: Her Majesty's Stationery Office.

West Yorkshire Probation Service (1994). *Crime, Criminals and the Criminal Justice System: Facts and Figures*. Wakefield.

# 27. PRISON-BASED VICTIM-OFFENDER RECONCILIATION PROGRAMS

by

## Russ Immarigeon

**Abstract:** *Twenty years after the first victim-offender reconciliation meeting, victim-offender meetings are increasingly being held in prisons. This chapter describes victim-offender reconciliation programs at five sites in Canada, the U.K., and the U.S. These programs have slightly different objectives from community-based victim-offender mediation programs; they emphasize sharing information and healing rather than restitution. They differ from one another in several ways, including continuity, objectives, and origins. This chapter identifies operational issues and reviews relevant evaluation research. Several recommendations are made to support further prison use of victim-offender meetings.*

Just over 20 years ago, the first victim-offender reconciliation meeting was held in Kitchener, Ontario, CAN (Peachey, 1989). Several years later, a victim-offender meeting was held in Elkhart, IN (Umbreit, 1985). Subsequently, the concept of victim-offender reconciliation has gained widespread and worldwide acceptance. In the U.S. and Canada, the number of programs has increased from 32 in 1985 to approximately 115 in 1993 (Immarigeon, 1994). Victim-offender reconciliation programs (VORPs) have experienced change and disagreement with regard to their philosophical base, and a broadening of the base of support. Many felt that VORPs should be operated mainly by religiously affiliated groups (Immarigeon, 1984), but official state agencies, including courts and probation, have come forward to advocate and implement their use. Some saw victim-offender reconciliation as an offender-oriented program that essentially used victims for purposes not necessarily in the interests of victims. But victim groups have become increasingly interested in victim-offender reconciliation, in part because they see that it serves the victim's needs as well as the offender's. Finally, people disagree over the philosophical or theoretical basis for VORPs. Some suggest that this form of restorative justice includes a role for punishment, while others express the anti-punishment nature of restorative justice, placing the emphasis on healing, repairing, or improving understanding of the relationship between victims and offenders. Victim-offender reconciliation has been used in prison settings. This chapter will define prison-based victim-offender reconciliation, provide brief overviews of five programs, and identify issues involved with starting and implementing such programs.

## PRISON-BASED VICTIM-OFFENDER RECONCILIATION

Prison-based victim-offender reconciliation meetings are voluntary meetings held between victims and offenders in a penal setting. The format for victim-offender reconciliation includes face-to-face meetings mediated by a trained community volunteer, with the objective centered on accountability and healing. Prison meetings, like community-based reconciliation programs, hope to make a constructive connection between victims and offenders. The major difference between community-based and prison-based victim-offender meetings is that prison meetings are not generally designed to reach agreements on restitution or community service. Rather, they focus on reparative aspects, and explicitly exclude such offender benefits as early release and parole considerations. Prison-based VORPs also often include more detailed and expansive coverage of victim issues. It is common, for instance, to find that these programs counsel offenders on the impact of crime on victims, prior to the victim-offender meeting. Victims are often asked to speak explicitly about their victimization.

These programs can be categorized along several dimensions. Do they involve the actual or surrogate victims of offenders participating in the program? More use surrogate victims, but the use of actual victims is still common. What purpose do they serve? Are they based on a restorative justice philosophy? Are they anti-punishment? Does the healing function, or the ability to make a personal connection between the victims and offenders, capture the main purpose of the program, or is it geared toward other objectives, such as instructing offenders on the consequences of crime to victims (victim sensitivity) or developing a sense of personal responsibility to improve job preparedness skills? There is a tendency to merge several functions into prison-based VORP programs. The purest model of a victim-offender reconciliation meeting is a meeting that is created for the victim and offender involved in a single criminal event, at the prison where the offender is incarcerated. Several such meetings have been held in New York State. Each of these meetings was for the explicit purpose of addressing needs expressed by the victim and the offender. None of these meetings explicitly served other functions, such as to explore restorative justice, to improve the criminal justice system, or even to make offenders accountable. These meetings were victim-initiated and were held to meet the desire and need of the victim to meet the person who committed the crime, to learn more about what happened when the crime occurred, and to bring closure to an episode that had been nagging at the victim's emotions for many years.

No surveys have assessed victim support, or lack of support, for meeting with the person(s) who victimized them; books have described victims who have met with the persons who had killed members of their families, to offer them forgiveness (Jaegger, 1983; Swift, 1994). Surveys have been completed with prisoners and have found strong support for the concept of victim-offender reconciliation. In New York State, a prisoner, as part of fulfilling requirements for a master's degree, surveyed 180 offenders incarcerated at a maximum-security prison, who had committed crimes against an identifiable person (Bitel, 1991). More than half these inmates were interested in meeting either the specific victim(s) of their crime(s) or a surrogate victim.

> Thirty-two percent of offenders (wishing to meet their victims) said that the most important thing that they would get out of meeting their victims would be 'their own peace of mind' or 'to be forgiven'; 28% said that it would help the victim see their side of the story; 12% said that they would use the opportunity to apologize to the victim; 6% stated that mediation would help break down stereotypes that victims hold about offenders; 5% said it would enable them to identify with victims and the process of victimization; 3% thought that it would improve their chance of early release at the parole board; while 5% did not know what they would get out of mediation, and 7% believed that they would not get anything out of a meeting with their victim (Bitel, 1991).

The Victim-Offender Reconciliation Program at Graterford, PA, surveyed prisoners on their attitudes toward crime victims, motivation for program participation, and expectations. "The reasons they cited for the commission of crimes were many and varied and did not reflect a tendency to deny personal responsibility by the offender. The reasons given for participation in the VORP and the individual goals for the group were constructive, consistent with the VORP concepts and indicated pre-seminar feelings of remorse and a need to express these deep-felt sentiments of concern for victims. No one appeared to take their involvement lightly" (Hall, 1993).

Finally, the Peace Studies/ATV Program at the Augusta Correctional Center in Craigsville, VA, distributed a survey on victim-offender issues to its board members and core group classes. The number of survey respondents is not known, but the survey found that 60% felt they had not been held accountable by the criminal justice system. The men overwhelmingly believed that it was important to tell victims and families of victims why they committed crimes; 90% felt that victim-offender meetings would help them; 98% thought they would help victims; 70% thought victim-offender meetings would be harder for victims; 20% thought they would be harder for offenders; 95% cared greatly what victims thought of them; 30% thought that lack of concern for victims and their families was the most important thing missing from the criminal justice system; 30% thought it was lack of help for offenders; 25% said the system did not ensure that the offender put things right; and 15% felt that victims were too rarely paid back for their pain, suffering and losses (personal communication from Michael Self, 1995).

## PROGRAMS

Jail and prison-based VORPs have emerged through individually planned efforts. In Canada, the Face to Face program was established in several jurisdictions, but this is the only single-model program that has been replicated in several places. Programs in the U.K. and U.S. have emerged from the efforts of either interested persons or agencies. It is not unusual to find programs operating with only the slightest knowledge of or connection with other VORP practitioners and experiences. Nine programs have been identified that offer, or have offered, victim-offender reconciliation services: the Restorative Justice Project in Madison, WI, U.S.; Genesee Justice in Batavia, NY, U.S.; the Victim/Offender Workshop in Ossining, NY, U.S.; Victims and Offenders in Conciliation in Rochester, Kent, U.K.; the Victim/Offender Reconciliation Group in Vacaville, CA, U.S.; Face to Face in Newfoundland and Saskatchewan, CAN; the Victim-Offender Reconciliation Program in Graterford, PA, U.S.; the Pre-Release Mediation Program in Cambridge, Ont. CAN; and the Victim-Offender Mediation Pilot Project in Langley, B.C., CAN (Immarigeon, 1994). Programs have been started by a criminal defense agency, county jail staff, prison staff, a victims' rights group, policy reform groups, and prisoners. Some have meetings between offenders and their actual victims, and some use surrogate victims. Programs can be distinguished by whether they have victim sensitivity training and/or employment training. The programs in Rochester, Madison, Batavia, Graterford, and Langley will be described in this chapter. Two involve meetings between offenders and their actual victims; the other three involve surrogate victims.

In 1981, Doug Call, a former divinity student and County Attorney for the Genesee County Department of Social Services, was elected county sheriff. He promised to reduce jail overcrowding through community alternatives, rather than by constructing new cells. Call and his staff worked closely with local judges, prosecutors, probation officers, and defense attorneys to establish community service, restitution, intensive supervision, and other victim services. Staff at the Genesee County Jail have expanded these initiatives to include victim-offender reconciliation, victim impact statements, and pre-sentence victim conferences. A typical Genesee Justice case involved a woman's four-year-old son who was sodomized by a member of her extended family. The Victim Assistance Program helped her through the criminal justice process, by addressing her needs as they became clear to her. Several victim-offender reconciliation meetings were set up after trial. "These meetings", she says, "have been the only contact between my husband, myself, and the offender. Although the emotional issues have not been resolved in our case, the contact was necessary to gain better understanding of both positions". Relatively few of Genesee County's victim-offender reconciliation meetings are held at the local jail. Moreover, these cases frequently divert offenders from imprisonment and often shorten stays in confinement. The Genesee program has not shied away from addressing consequences that emerge from serious and violent offending. No less important is the extent to which the program has gained the support of a broad coalition of court, law enforcement, and other criminal justice and social service agencies. The staff claim that differences between mediating non-violent and violent cases are less than one might expect; the key issue is remorse for the wrong that was committed.

The Reverend Peter Taylor, Chaplain at the Rochester Youth Custody Centre, Kent, England, a closed institution for approximately 350 young males aged from 16 to 21 years, was routinely asked, "What you do is good for offenders, but what about victims?" In March 1983, Taylor wrote to the local Victim Support Scheme staff, asking if they would like to participate in a program at the facility that would bring together burglars and burglary victims. The purpose of this program would be to help victims and offenders understand each other as people. He gained the approval of prison authorities to proceed with a victim-offender discussion group as a pilot program of three meetings. In April and May 1983, Taylor held meetings between interested parties, who suggested that police, as well as facilitators, be present, that no video be taken, and that only offenders having committed burglary, theft, or deception be admitted. The initial meeting consisted of four offenders, a like number of surrogate victims, two victim support volunteers, a facilitator, and the prison psychologist, who was to evaluate the scheme's impact. One victim was asked to share her feelings and thoughts, and other victims and offenders also did so. Topics discussed included the relationship of burglary to violence, offender moral codes, burglary prevention, offender motivation, deterrence, and offender perceptions of victims. Offenders gave reasons for their crimes, rather than expressing regret. The victims started to see that there was more to these young men than their criminal behavior. The second meeting, also held in the chapel, discussed whether property owners should have guns for protection (all parties agreed they should not), and then a role play unfolded in which victims and offenders agreed to a reparation agreement and sentence recommendation for the court. The final session offered an opportunity for more unrestrained sharing of victim and offender views. Both victims and offenders reported feeling that they had had no voice in the courtroom. Community service orders were viewed as impersonal, achieving little.

In January 1984, a new group of six victims and six offenders gathered for three sessions every month. Victim support and police representatives attended, and the sessions were videotaped. "In the role play exercises", prison psychologist Launay reports, "victims and offenders are given an outline description of a hypothetical case of burglary with details of the offender and victim. They are then asked to role play a pre-sentencing mediation situation of the VORP type with one of the organizers acting the role of the mediator. In the first instance, the victim is asked to play the role of the victim and the offender the role of the offender. The participants most skilled at role playing are also given the chance to reverse the roles and get the feeling of being in the other person's shoes." These hypothetical exercises revealed a range of attitudes toward mediation and reparation. "While some victims were happy to make a purely financial agreement with offenders", Launay says, "other victims demanded a convincing expression of regret and/or some form of guarantee that the offenders would not offend again" (Launay, 1987).

The Restorative Justice Project in Madison, WI, started in February 1984 after Dave Cook, project coordinator, heard about victim-offender reconciliation at a conference in Chicago. Cook spoke with his supervisor, who granted permission to try a few cases. VORP staff arranged and facilitated the VORP meeting, assisted in developing victim-offender contracts for restitution, and prepared a report of the VORP meeting for the correctional and parole authorities. VORP staff also monitored fulfilment of victim-offender contracts and were available to facilitate follow-up victim-offender meetings if problems arose. Over time, restitution agreements have diminished in importance, with victim-offender meetings focusing more on reconciling relationships and addressing feelings resulting from criminal activity and victimization. Initially, the program was structured to serve as an alternative to incarceration. Victim-offender agreements allowed offenders to use their participation to argue for an early release. The program started focusing on apology and forgiveness after an early case failed to gain early release for an offender. Between 1985 and 1989, the number of mediators with the project grew from three to 24. All cases involved adult felons with burglary and assault histories. The project handles approximately 25 cases a year. Offenders are eligible for the program if there is more than two months before their next parole hearing, they do not have an extensive prior record, there is an identifiable victim, and they are in minimum-security custody. Some meetings have been held in a maximum-security prison, and have also been held in community settings, such as probation offices, victims' homes, churches, or restaurants, because offenders are often released from prison before the full case acceptance process has been played out (Cook, 1989).

The Victim-Offender Reconciliation Program at the Graterford State Correctional Facility in Pennsylvania is a three-phase, volunteer-driven effort to make the criminal justice system function more usefully for victims and offenders alike. The program aspires to assist the prison by promoting good public relations, by supporting prison efforts to increase offender accountability, and by providing carefully designed, properly administered, cost-free programs. The program started in April 1992 and serves men with sentences for serious offenses, including murder. The first two phases operate as a weekly seminar, designed to help offenders understand the effects of crime on victims and the importance of taking responsibility for their actions. Videos, exercises, and discussion are used; victim advocates are possibly invited as guest speakers and resource people.

The goals of the first phase are to enable inmates to create a support group that encourages them to take personal responsibility for their crimes, enables inmates to learn the consequences of victimization, helps prisoners and victim advocates see crime in a restorative justice context, assists victim advocates to constructively interact with offenders, and allows participants to acknowledge one another. "Phase one was a successful period of awareness of the crime's impact and emotional sensitivity and growth", project evaluators reported in March 1993. "While recognizing the pain of revisiting one's crime and the difficulty of sharing personal feelings, often never before disclosed, the men felt the process was a powerful one whose value outweighed its difficulties for them. Group solidarity served to support the participants as evidenced by greater willingness for self-disclosure and mutual respect and the preservation of confidentiality" (Hall, 1993). The second phase of the program followed alternate weekly tracks when offenders met with surrogate crime victims and when they worked on writing letters to their own victims and survivors. The goals of this phase were to create a safe and supportive environment where victims and offenders could speak with one another respectfully, to enable victims and offenders to express how they experienced crime, to allow victims to describe the consequences of crime and criminal justice processing on their lives, to support offender-to-victim apology letter writing, to provide an opportunity for victims to express forgiveness, and for offenders to accept accountability for their actions, and to develop an understanding that restorative justice puts people and the harms they experience at the center of things.

In the last stage of the program, apology letters were given to Victim Assistance Program staff participating in the project. They contacted victims and survivors to let them know that such letters were available if they chose to receive and read them.

In Langley, British Columbia, a six-month pilot project explored the feasibility of victim-offender mediation with violent offenders and the victims and their families. Project staff worked with offenders incarcerated at a federal penitentiary in Canada for offenses such as armed robbery, rape, serial rape, and murder (when offenders were related to the victims). Mediation meetings were held with multiple victims in each case. A reviewer of the pilot project interviewed four offenders and 13 victims involved in the project. A major finding was that success should not be measured too narrowly by actual victim-offender meetings. A variety of factors, including geographical distance between the parties and a lack of readiness on the part of one party or the other, can delay or postpone a meeting. "Nonetheless", the evaluation notes, "highly significant results can occur for both victims and offenders who start the process but may not complete it" (Roberts and Jani, 1992). Both parties were impressed that someone cared about their case. Often they found communication with the victims or offenders powerful, difficult, or exhilarating. Initially, many parties were apprehensive about the situations a meeting might create. Meetings frequently released powerful emotions, however, giving the parties feelings of resolution.

## OPERATIONAL ISSUES

None of the evaluations of prison-based victim-offender reconciliation have been particularly rigorous, but they are informative and raise operational issues for practitioners wishing to establish a program, and for evaluators who want to design a more detailed research plan. VORPs and related meetings have occurred at the request of victims, offenders, and even of legal service providers. Most jurisdictions do not have a protocol for establishing such programs, and so it is initially necessary to set up meetings with key officials. Bureaucratic resistance or official suspicion is likely; thus, it is necessary to allay questions concerning motivation and related matters. Meetings with these officials will also expedite access to the prison. Prison administrators may create barriers. One prison, for instance, would not allow videotaping of meetings with the program's own equipment; the prison official wanted the program to rent facility equipment and pay overtime to the prison officer assigned to monitor the program. Prison administrators can also stop a program in its tracks, and have done so in at least one institution.

Program philosophies differ, and these differences do not necessarily fall along clear-cut lines. A California program recently reported that "we hold the view that the offender, not society, is responsible for his offense and that crime is a moral habit created entirely by personal choice. The only requisite for membership in the program is that the offender be able to freely admit his complete culpability for his crime. This is key. Crime is not a sociological aberration, it is a sin" (Rodrigues, 1990). Others might disagree. Admitting culpability is a reasonable prerequisite for program participation, because without it there is little likelihood of having a meaningful conversation or dialogue between victims and offenders. But is crime a sin? Are crimes committed solely because of personal choice? Offenders, and victims for that matter, may accept personal responsibility as an important factor for discussion, but they view crime more broadly. Specificity in program purpose is helpful to attract participants, but it can also discourage participation. Moreover, descriptions that represent the positions of program organizers more than those of victims and offenders are at risk of creating a process that is more valuable to them than to the victims or offenders. "A statement of principles", one observer notes, "situates the program on a philosophical map. It is a statement of identity. It reminds people participating in the program who they are and what values govern the operation and it tells the public, government, and clients what kinds of services and qualities to expect" (Sawatsky, 1988). But generalized references to terms such as accountability can lead programs to follow a route that neither organizers nor participants wish to see it travel. In particular, programs run the risk of being controlled by officials, or of becoming punitive rather than reparative.

Prison-based VORPs overlap with, and are frequently dominated by, victim-offender workshops that are more about encouraging sensitivity toward and understanding of victims and offenders. Perhaps it is a thin line between the two initiatives, but distinctions are probably wise, if only for the sake of clarity. Several examples of such victim-offender workshops can be found at Sing Sing in Ossining, NY, and at the Augusta Correctional center in Craigsville, VA. The Victim/Offender Workshop at Sing Sing emerged from meetings between prisoners and a Quaker Worship Group:

The V/O Workshops offer a forum between offenders and surrogate victims of crime, or their family members in the case of homicide. The groups are loosely facilitated by two volunteer psychologists. We have

secured funds to pay for the victims' transportation to the prison and
we provide a simple lunch. Prior to victims coming to the prison, the
offenders undergo a period of readiness to help them understand victims' issues and to orient them about what to expect. These meetings
have proved to be very successful and transforming for both victims
and offenders. Offenders are encouraged to accept responsibility for
their actions and to become sensitive to crime from the victims' perspective, particularly the domino effects set into motion following
crime. Meanwhile, victims are offered insight into crime which may
help them to protect themselves from future victimization and to learn
the reality of what prison does and does not achieve. Often, it allows
victims for the first time to feel that they are getting a chance to participate in the criminal justice system rather than being used by it.
Both groups report that often for the first time they are able to see the
humanity in the other. The aim of these workshops is to create a safe
space for healing and growth. We believe that the combination of
therapy and job skills training will address the moral and economic
deficits that play a large role in crime. Ultimately, it is our hope that
the restorative justice program will reduce recidivism and serve as a
bridge back to the community (M. Bitel, personal communication,
1991).

Like other programs, the Peace Studies/ATV program at Craigsville is
a three-phase process:

the initial phase of the program focuses on providing prisoners with
an intellectual grounding in the methods, history and practice of
peacemaking and non-violent approaches to conflict resolution. The
courses are theoretical in nature and practical in application. The
skills that Gandhi, King and history's other proven peacemakers used
in their struggles for justice can be used by all of us, whether individually in our personal lives or collectively in our public lives. The
second phase will focus on a victim/offender workshop, the third
phase will involve job training in a high-tech workshop environment.
Enrolment in one aspect is contingent on enrolment in the others. All
are seen as equally important (Peace Studies/ ATV, 1994).

Key elements in the program include intellectual grounding in non-
violent conflict resolution; a focus on the social conditions that contribute to crime; increased participation by crime victims in the criminal
justice process; the opportunity for prisoners to acknowledge the consequences of crime for victims; self-improvement through prisoner participation in organizing, planning, and implementing corrective solutions;
and the importance of job skills in an increasingly competitive economy.

# CONCLUSIONS

Evaluation research demonstrates that victim-offender meetings are positive. A 1988 evaluation of the Face to Face program at the Headingly Correctional Institution in Manitoba found that victims achieved greater understanding of offenders' backgrounds; victims discovered that offenders were also human beings; victims' emotions were released and fears subsided while they obtained peace of mind; victims' stereotypes of offenders were challenged in some ways; forgiveness and reconciliation were evident where victims, through dialogue, developed compassion toward offenders and empathy for their social conditions; offenders learned how victims felt; offenders' stereotypes of victims were rarely challenged, because offenders reported that they rarely gave any thought to victims in the first place; offenders received insight into the need to reorder lifestyle priorities; and offenders accepted a reparative approach (Sawatsky, 1988).

Prison-based victim-offender reconciliation is a powerful and practical method of healing some of the harms done by violent as well as non-violent crime. Hundreds of victim-offender reconciliation meetings have occurred without negative consequences. In fact, these meetings have been heralded by victims and offenders alike as a successful forum, in which victims gain an important measure of control over events they did not fully understand, and offenders learn what their offending has done to their victims. Nonetheless, the future of prison-based victim-offender reconciliation is unclear. Individual, once-off meetings, such as those held in New York State, are not likely to occur often. In part, this is because prisons are conservatively run, and the changes in daily routine required to bring about one of these meetings are unlikely to occur. In addition, in the U.S., penal practices are increasingly being challenged by politicians, law and order citizen groups, and budget constraints, for providing too many benefits to offenders in custody.

On-going programming may also be a victim of these repressive times. Community-based initiatives have been able to establish themselves in many locations, but restrictions on prisoner programming will most likely reduce the number of voluntary efforts, as well as state-funded ones. There is evidence that prisoner-organized efforts will increasingly focus on victim-offender reconciliation. In prisons where such programs have taken place, there are waiting lists of prisoners who want to participate but cannot, due to time, space, and other limitations. But prisoner-organized efforts have also been focusing, not unreasonably, on developing job skills for offenders who are likely to confront a difficult and demanding market economy when they are released from prison. Many of the programs which established prison-based victim-offender reconciliation are no longer operating, and it is too risky to forecast the longevity of those programs that currently provide these services. Nevertheless, the idea, and so far the practice, of prison-based victim-offender reconciliation, is positive; given the right set of circumstances, it is likely to be used more widely in the future.

Several approaches may improve the chances of further applications of victim-offender reconciliation in prison settings. Firstly, wardens and superintendents, as well as corrections commissioners, should receive more information on prison-based victim-offender reconciliation. These individuals are important to the program development process because, in the hierarchies typical of corrections departments, decisions are usually made from the top down. Support from one of these parties is crucial to the successful establishment of such a program. Further, some wardens, superintendents, and commissioners are supportive of new initiatives. Secondly, more attention should be paid to the philosophical and theoretical foundations of prison-based VORPs. What is the role of punishment, if any, within restorative justice programs? Thirdly, more research on these programs is necessary. More descriptive details are needed. Assessments should be made of programs that allow offenders to meet their actual victims, rather than surrogate victims. Adequate information is needed on matters such as who participates, the criminal history background of participating offenders, and the outcomes of these meetings. Also, it would be illuminating to learn more about the impact of these programs on the subsequent behavior and perceptions of participating victims and offenders. It would be unfortunate if the history and influence of these programs were lost in hard-to-locate documents, or in the failure to receive a well-conceived and properly designed evaluation.

## REFERENCES

Bitel, M.D. (1991). *"A Study of the Attitudes of Incarcerated Men Toward Victim-Offender Reconciliation and Reparation Schemes."* Masters Degree Thesis, State University of New York, New Paltz, NY.

—(1991). Personal communication.

Cook, D. (1989). *Victim-Offender Reconciliation Project at the Legal*

*Assistance to Institutionalized Persons Program (LAIP): The First Four Years.* Madison, WI: LAIP.

Hall, J. (1993). *Final Report: The Victim-Offender Reconciliation Program: The State Correctional Institution at Graterford, PA, May-December 1992.* Akron, PA: U.S. Office on Crime and Justice, Mennonite Central Committee.

Immarigeon, R. (1984). "VORP and the Criminal Justice System: Conflict and Challenge." *VORP Network News* 3(4):4,7-9.

—(1993). "Victim-Offender Reconciliation in a Penal Setting." *Corrections Compendium* 18(8):5-7.

—(1994). *Reconciliation Between Victims and Imprisoned Offenders: Program Models and Issues.* Akron, PA: U.S. Office on Crime and Justice, Mennonite Central Committee.

Jaegger, M. (1983). *The Lost Child.* Grand Rapids, MI: Zondervan Publishing House.

Launey, G. (1987). "Victim Offender Conciliation." In: B. McGurk, D. Thornton and M. Williams (eds.), *Applying Psychology to Imprisonment: Theory and Practice.* London, UK: Her Majesty's Stationery Office.

Peace Studies/ATV. (1994). *Program Information Handbook.* Craigsville, VA: Augusta Correctional Center.

Peachey, D. (1989). "The Kitchener Experiment." In: M. Wright and B. Galaway (eds.), *Mediation and Criminal Justice: Victims, Offenders and Community.* London, UK: Sage Publications, Inc.

Roberts, T. and S. Jani (1992). *Evaluation of the Victim Offender Mediation Pilot Project: Final Report.* Victoria, BC: University of Victoria Institute for Dispute Resolution.

Rodrigues, J.E. (1990). "Victim-Offender Mediation Inside the Walls." *Victim-Offender Mediation* (Spring).

Sawatsky, L. (1988). "Face to Face: An Evaluation." Winnipeg, CAN: University of Manitoba.

Self, M. (1995). Personal communication.

Swift, J. (1994). *A Cry for Justice: A Mother's Journey to Confront the Killer of her Children.* Boca Raton, FL: Cool Hand Communications, Inc.

Umbreit, M. (1985). *Crime and Reconciliation: Creative Options for Victims and Offenders.* Nashville, TN: Abingdon Press.

# 28. DESIGNING A REFORMATORY CONFLICT MANAGEMENT AND DISPUTE RESOLUTION SYSTEM THROUGH MEDIATION

by
## Richard A. Salem

**Abstract:** *A lengthy intervention by an outside mediator at a maximum-security reformatory mitigated racial violence, heightened racial understanding among all the parties, contributed to better management practices at the institution, and led to the development of conflict prevention and conflict management structures, which were still in use some 20 years later. The administration and staff initially resisted coming to the table, but they ultimately concurred in mediation ground rules that enabled them to engage in extensive joint problem-solving negotiations with inmates. While it may not be practical to attempt to replicate this mediation, the communications techniques that (1) created a listening environment, (2) humanized the conflict, and (3) led to collaborative problem solving in this case can be used to manage conflicts in correction settings elsewhere.*

In August 1973, a mediator from the Community Relations Service (CRS), U.S. Department of Justice, called to offer assistance to the Minnesota Commissioner of Corrections in response to widely publicized race riots at the State Reformatory for Men at St. Cloud. The Commissioner, known for his interest in innovative programs, was enthusiastic about the possibilities of mediation. He instructed his Deputy to meet with the mediator and reformatory Superintendent promptly.

But the meeting never took place. The Superintendent had his own plan for dealing with the violence, that did not include negotiating with inmates. He believed that custody officers could bring the situation under control if the reformatory was divided into "mini-prisons". As a consequence, inmates of color—now largely concentrated by race—would be permanently dispersed throughout the general population, and the entire inmate body would never come together again. The plan had been drafted and only awaited funding for additional staff, training and construction. The Deputy Commissioner, who was struggling with a serious alcohol problem, lent his support to the Superintendent's plan, even though it undercut both the mediator and the interests of the Commissioner.

Restorative justice addresses relationships between victims and perpetrators in a community setting. The community at St. Cloud was a closed society of administrators, staff and young men confined for serious violent crimes. This chapter describes the circumstances that led to mediation at St. Cloud, the long path to the table and the mediation process. The type of interpersonal communications engendered in the mediation process can be used today to minimize unnecessary conflicts, and to provide administrators, custody staff, and inmates with improved skills to respond to the myriad of conflicts which are inevitable in any correction setting.

## PARTIES TO MEDIATION

St. Cloud was a largely neglected institution in a state system that was nationally recognized for pioneering community-based corrections. Innovative community programs were so successful that only the state's most serious offenders were remanded to maximum-security institutions. By 1974, St. Cloud's population stood at 450 males in their late teens and twenties, most of whom were confined for serious crimes of violence. The reformatory reflected the increased racial diversity of urban areas. About 20% of its residents were people of color, twice the percentage of the state's population. There were 60 African-American inmates, most of whom came from the Twin Cities of Minneapolis and St. Paul, some 75 miles away; 30 Native-American inmates, most of whom had grown up on reservations; and eight Mexican-American inmates. The administrators were concerned about the increase in verbal and physical racial confrontations. They tried both to ease racial tensions and to meet the needs of inmates of color by permitting them to form ethnic culture groups as counterparts to the Alcoholics Anonymous, Jaycees, and other clubs that primarily served the white population. Culture groups were permitted to meet weekly with staff sponsors and advisors from outside the institution, ostensibly to discuss matters pertaining to their ethnicity, to maintain an office and library, to appoint an inmate coordinator, and to take off work to observe two ethnic holidays each year.

African-American inmates, organized as the Black Brotherhood Culture and Development Organization (BBCDO), pointed to the disproportionately large number of disciplinary actions against them as evidence of discrimination. The custody staff contended that more African-American inmates were sentenced to the disciplinary cell house, because they precipitated more incidents by flaunting the rules, taunting the staff and fighting. African-American inmates typically self-segregated during meals, recreation and evening activities. They often responded aggressively when they perceived discrimination. BBCDO members feared that they would be isolated in the general population if the mini-prison plan was implemented. Native-American inmates were organized to build a support system for members of their group who were struggling to survive in the reformatory environment. Many of them lived in the honor cell block, which provided special privileges for the well-behaved. The Native-American leadership rejected invitations to enter alliances with African-American groups, and would not be drawn into black-white confrontations. Mexican-American inmates were allied with the Native-American population. They were soft spoken as a group, and accepted the limits to their power and influence dictated by their small numbers. Among their few requests had been salsa in the canteen, and a ceramics shop where they could install a kiln which had been donated to them. The administration had promised them space for a crafts shop, but the designated room was preempted for another use and the promise went unfilled.

White inmates lacked organization or group cohesion. Their concerns centered on dining room conditions, visiting regulations and the physical comforts that could make reformatory life more bearable. Identifiable groups committed to racist activity were among the cliques formed in the white inmate population. The culture groups improved life for their members, but they irritated white inmates, who both envied and felt intimated by the sense of community and esprit they were witnessing among inmates of color. Creative white inmates from the general population soon requested, and were granted, permission to form German-American and Italian-American culture groups. The German-American group was disbanded after administrators determined that it was formed as a base for racial harassment and was fomenting violence. The Italian-American culture group survived after troublemakers had been purged from its midst. Most of the 25 members of the Italian-American culture group had Anglo-Saxon names; several had blond hair, but contended that their Italian heritage was on their mother's side. The primary activity at their weekly meetings was Italian language and culture lessons given by a mini-skirted student from the University of Minnesota prison legal assistance program. White inmates charged discrimination when their request to form a Scottish-American culture group was rejected by incredulous administrators.

The racial mix of inmates presented new challenges to the all-white administration and a staff of 300, drawn largely from the white population in rural Stearns County where St. Cloud was situated. All but six of the 130 custody staff were white. Administrators and staff also were frustrated by budget restrictions created by the increased flow of funds to community-based programs. Most of the custody staff were educated locally, and took entry level jobs at the reformatory. A major source of staff frustration was poor communications. There were few staff meetings, little formal communication at shift changes, vague policy guidelines, no up-to-date policy manual, minimal orientation for new staff, and no in-service training. Important information travelled through the grapevine; inmates often found out first. Some custody officers managed their jobs well, but others floundered in the cultural chasm between the races. These officers felt threatened and baited by the loud banter and aggressive behavior of African-American inmates, mistrusted the Native-American leadership's request for inmate-to-inmate counselling, and reacted with suspicion to the Mexican-American inmates' request for bottles of hot sauce. The new inmate dynamics, combined with the increasing presence within the reformatory of the Minnesota Ombudsman for Corrections, university law professors and students, inmate advocates, and the media, left the custody staff feeling that they had lost power to the confined population. Although unionized, custody officers were among the lowest paid civil servants in the state. Their job security was threatened by reports of the long-term proposal to merge St. Cloud with the men's prison at Stillwater; other jobs were not readily available in their community. They coped but, for many, the reformatory was a prison of another kind.

St. Cloud's administrators were increasingly troubled and frustrated by racial violence. They were confident, however, that the mini-prison plan, which would segregate inmates by reformatory job or school assignments, would solve the problem. Dining and recreation would be carried out in shifts, and clubs and other activities would be organized within cell houses. The Deputy Commissioner had included mini prisons in his annual work plan, and the Commissioner incorporated it into the Department's budget for the coming year. St. Cloud's administrators wanted no outside intervention. They were holding a finger in the dike until funding came through for the mini-prison plan, which they believed would restore order. The Commissioner of Corrections, preoccupied with his innovative programs, delegated responsibility for St. Cloud to the Deputy Commissioner who had decided to cast his lot with the Superintendent.

## ENTRY AND ASSESSMENT

After the riot at St. Cloud in August 1973, the mediator offered to dispatch a team to the reformatory to assess conditions and make recommendations. At first, the Deputy accepted the offer, but later phoned to say that the Superintendent had the situation in hand. The mediator learned in a follow-up call to the Commissioner that he had not been appraised of CRS' offer. He asked the mediator to meet with the Ombudsman for Corrections, who was investigating the riot, as was a legislative committee. The Ombudsman supported a mediation intervention, but there was no follow-up by the Department of Corrections. In December 1973, the Deputy again contacted the mediator, this time asking if he could arrange a 40-hour sensitivity training workshop, in anticipation of a reorganization into mini prisons at St. Cloud. Members of a CRS planning team spent two days meeting with administrators, staff and inmates. They heard numerous complaints about both racial problems and general operations. African-American and white inmates each felt the other was receiving preferential treatment; each group felt physically threatened by the other. Rumors abounded about the mini-prison plan. Union members were angry because they were not being consulted about the reorganization. Inmates of color perceived it as a blatant effort to disperse them and put them at physical risk in the white population. The CRS team advised the Superintendent that training would not be effective in the present climate. The Superintendent responded that he had just learned that funding for the mini prison would be delayed, and he had decided to postpone training.

The suicide of a Native-American inmate while in isolation—the first suicide in memory at St. Cloud—angered the Native-Indian population, and prompted another call to CRS from the Deputy. But he did not respond to CRS' renewed offer to conduct a pre-mediation assessment. That call finally came on a Friday afternoon in early April 1974. More than 100 inmates had been involved in a racial fight. The Deputy Commissioner wanted to know how soon CRS could begin mediation. The mediator and two other members of an assessment team found the situation far more serious than the Deputy had indicated. The riot led to the entire population being placed in lock-up, confined to their cells for 24 hours a day. The Superintendent had hastily assembled his own administration-staff task force, which he called a "mediation team". Its members said that high tension and threats of violence required that the lock-up should continue. A corrections specialist on the CRS team expressed concern at the length of the lock-up, now in its eighth day, but the Superintendent's team said it had no choice. The CRS team then commenced a series of meetings with the parties.

Administrators had little to say beyond the report of its task force. Union leaders were as unhappy with management as they were with the inmates. While they did not trust mediation, they agreed to come to the table if talks began. They would not be excluded from the process. Meetings with leaders of the five inmate groups reflected their fear of violence, and the pain and frustration that was being inflicted by the lock-up. All but the Black Brotherhood Culture and Development Organization pleaded for the lock-up to end. They pledged to work at preventing violence and were attracted to mediation, excited by the prospect of sitting across the table from the Superintendent. Members of BBCDO viewed the mediator as the administration's lackey, and treated him with hostility and distrust; for weeks afterwards their newsletter headlined the mediator as the "White Devil". They refused to discuss issues, insisting that there would be no mediation. They had given their demands to the Superintendent and wanted St. Cloud to remain in lock-up until those demands were met. As the mediator was leaving, one of their leaders yelled out, "If we come to the table, there are going to be bright lights and television cameras in the room". This told the mediator that the issue was not whether BBCDO would come to mediation, but whether the press would be there. Despite their anger and distrust,

African-American inmates, like all the others, found it difficult to resist (1) being out of their cells for sustained periods, and (2) sitting across the table from "The Man". By good fortune, the mediator had met an outside advisor to BBCDO a year earlier in Minneapolis on another matter, and was able to use that relationship to promote mediation, making it easy for BBCDO to save face while changing its mind. The advisor came to St. Cloud to meet with the African-American inmates, and emerged from the cell block several hours later with a revised list of demands that included the firing of the Director of Custody and discarding the mini-prison plan.

"BBCDO told me to make it clear", the adviser reported, "that this is not a negotiating agenda. It is a list of non-negotiable demands". That statement had a familiar ring. "Non-negotiable demands" often precede negotiations in volatile community conflicts. Such demands cannot be taken lightly, but they tend to dissipate when underlying issues are tabled and addressed.

Interactions with the confined population convinced the CRS team that the lock-up had become counter-productive. To continue it would further escalate tension. The Superintendent asked CRS to share these perceptions with his mediation team the following morning. When the CRS team entered the meeting room, the Superintendent's team was pouring over reformatory floor plans, which were spread across a table. They were devising a way to move the inmate body directly from their cells into a modified mini prison, insisting that tension was too high to end the lock-up. "We've had enough", said one, "We don't want them together again". Yes, there would be problems, but the team felt it could work, even without the additional staff, training and physical changes they had originally agreed were imperative. When the Superintendent said he supported the proposal, the mediator accepted the decision, but said mediation could not proceed at this juncture. He would consider returning, if asked, after the reorganization was complete. A concerned Deputy then intervened and struck a deal. The reorganization would not be implemented until mediation ended. The lock-up would end promptly.

It would take another crisis two weeks, however, before it was clear that mediation would proceed. Planning for mediation by inmates and their outside advisors was underway in late April, when the staff and inmates learned in a memo from the Associate Superintendent titled "The Group Plan" that, effective immediately, the confined population would eat and take their recreation in shifts related to their jobs and school assignments. The custody staff was incensed; it had received no notice that there would be a change in work schedules. The inmate groups and their advisors were furious. They told the mediator that they had been betrayed. The mediator felt victimized as well. But the Superintendent contended that the Group Plan did not violate his agreement with the mediator, since it did not entail housing transfers. Then the inmates discovered a confidential staff memorandum, indicating that construction would soon begin on a wall which would subdivide the cafeteria.

The Deputy Commissioner did not return the mediator's calls. The Commissioner, however, did, and asked what he could do to salvage the situation; he said he was unaware of the latest developments, but pledged drastic action. The mediator insisted that the Commissioner should express his concern directly to the outside advisors. A meeting was convened the following morning. The Commissioner heard it directly from the inmate's advocates and promised prompt action. "What if I replaced the Deputy Commissioner, the Superintendent and his Associate?", a visibly shaken Commissioner asked the mediator after the meeting. "Would that send out a signal that I want to straighten out the place?" "You might start with the Deputy", the mediator replied. "Let his replacement decide about the others." Within the week, the Deputy Commissioner was reassigned and was subsequently placed on extended sick leave. He was replaced by an Acting Deputy whose first order of business was to stop all moves toward the reorganization, and pledge, at meetings with the inmates and their advisors, that the mini-prison plan would be on the mediation agenda. The Acting Deputy said he would participate in the mediation on behalf of the Commissioner. No other personnel changes were necessary.

## PLANNING FOR MEDIATION

It was necessary to decide who would represent the parties at the mediation, how they would be selected, how to develop an agenda for negotiations. Ground rules were needed as well. Representation was dictated in part by the need for the small Mexican-American delegation to have two places at the table, and for the BBCDO to have the six seats they insisted were necessary for internal political reasons. The Native-American and Italian-American culture groups each agreed to four. Those 16 would be matched by a like number from the general inmate population; four to be selected from each of the four regular cell blocks in elections conducted by the Ombudsman. A total of 16 inmate delegates could be at the table at one time; the others would observe. Administration and staff could also have 16 seats, which was more than they needed or used. Cell-house elections were conducted by the Ombudsman with considerable fanfare and no problems. Leadership skills of inmates surfaced as candidates stepped forward, made brief election presentations to their peers and lobbied for votes. Procedures were set at a meeting of the 32 inmate negotiators, to enable them to develop an agenda. Each group would prepare its own list and when they were complete, the entire team would come together to decide on the final agenda. The inmates wanted time at night for their groups to meet, and they wanted access to St. Cloud policy statements and the mini-prison plan. They rejected an opportunity to designate a chair for their team, saying trust levels were too low; they asked the mediator to coordinate their work during his bi-weekly trips to the reformatory.

The process that followed was painfully slow. Custody officers were reluctant to grant inmates time out of their cells for planning. Apprehensive inmate groups became competitive and refused to share their draft agendas. Administrators were accused of lying when they said that an updated policy manual did not exist. A few members of the negotiating teams were remanded for disciplinary reasons. The parole of the most influential BBCDO leader set off a power struggle within the group. Outside advisors found it difficult to provide timely assistance. Law students, facing final examinations, withdrew from the scene. Inmates, enjoying their new-found status, were in no hurry to end the process. In late May, the draft agenda of the white population representatives was shared at a meeting of the entire 32-member inmate negotiating team. They had done their job well, addressing virtually all phases of institutional life. Their product stimulated the others to complete their lists. The task was finished a month later and, with the inmates' consent, the mediator compiled the final document. Only the mock Italian-American culture group was unable to come up with a culture-related agenda; its members were learning why their claim to status as culture group was not being taken seriously by anybody else. The staff and administration chose to add nothing to the agenda. The Superintendent was concerned that "racial tensions" were not listed. The mediator assured him that they would be addressed.

The agenda belonged to the parties, but the mediator was given authority to order the issues. They predictably fell into several categories. Some appeared to be easily resolvable (*e.g.*, the delay in inspecting and delivering books and magazines left for inmates by visitors). Others needed detailed discussion and research, and would be referred to working groups (*e.g.*, censorship guidelines for the inmate newspaper). Some agenda items would require additional information (*e.g.*, a racial breakdown of disciplinary actions), and others were beyond the control of the parties (*e.g.*, funding to increase inmate wages), but were subject to an agreement-in-principle (if the Commissioner would agree to seek funding from the Legislature). Complaints that appeared easily resolvable (*e.g.*, advancing wages to new inmates, so that they could have canteen money during their first month at St. Cloud) were placed at the top of the agenda, so that the parties could experience early progress. More important issues (*e.g.*, ground rules for culture group activities), and more difficult ones (*e.g.*, establishment of an inmate-staff advisory committee), followed. Issues that appeared intractable (*e.g.*, a Native-American "reservation" within St. Cloud) were placed at the bottom of the list, in the event that an impasse precipitated a breakdown in talks. It could be anticipated that crises would arise during mediation (*e.g.*, permitting law students prompt access to inmates), and it would be necessary to add an item to the agenda and deal with it promptly when it arose.

The ground rules, needed to maintain decorum as well as to build confidence in the process, allowed any party to bring outside resource people to the table as necessary. For the administration, this meant a lawyer familiar with recent court decisions on inmate rights; for the inmate parties, it meant that their outside support groups could be present, and they could bring in a psychiatrist to argue their case against behavior modification practices in the disciplinary cell house. The mediator was able to bring in the director of the canteen at a nearby Veterans Administration hospital, to work with the group examining St. Cloud canteen complaints. The director of the St. Cloud city human rights commission was permitted to observe, and the Ombudsman and law students could actively participate. The Ombudsman was further assigned the role of investigating inmate complaints of staff harassment in connection with participating in mediation. Protocols not agreed to beforehand became the first order of business at the table. It was agreed at the outset, for example, that there would be no media coverage, but at the insistence of inmate parties, it was agreed that the proceedings could be tape recorded. This was a cumbersome procedure that was soon abandoned.

## MEDIATION

The inmate parties came to the table well-prepared with articulate and logical presentations. Custody staff and administration listened carefully and provided clear responses. The inmates soon began to understand why the complexities of the government bureaucracy and union contracts precluded prompt action on some seemingly simple matters. Administrators quickly agreed to relax censorship of mail and reading matter, and assured the inspection and delivery of visitors' parcels within 24 hours of receipt. They insisted on retaining authority to censor the inmate newspaper, but acknowledged that clear guidelines were lacking and agreed to draft them with the editors. A shortage of visiting space led to an extension of visiting hours by 30 minutes a day until spring, when courtyard visits could be resumed. Administrators agreed to seek funding for an expanded visiting area.

Mediation humanized conflict at St. Cloud. Custody staff had banned the possession of hot sauce because they viewed it as a weapon to blind a person. They heard a compelling presentation on the importance of salsa in Mexican-American diets. Inmates also pointed out that there was no prohibition against cigarette lighter fluid or pressurized cans of lacquer used in the hobby shop; the officers yielded and salsa was made available in the canteen. Staff acknowledged inmate complaints of hair getting into the food, but said they did not know how to deal with it, short of mandating haircuts for the servers. At that point, the inmate who had presented the issue quietly took a hair net out of his pocket and tossed in on the table. "Would you wear that?", a surprised officer asked. Without uttering a word, the inmate took the net out of its plastic wrapping and put it on his head "That occurred to us", said the officer, "but we were afraid to ask". The problem was solved. Administrators agreed to seek funds for higher inmate wages, but nobody supported the Italian-American culture group's bid to incorporate a sick leave and vacation policy into the St. Cloud work program. "It was the only new idea we could come up with", the leader of the group later confided to the mediator.

On occasion, tempers flared. An abusive inmate remark to an officer led to a walkout at one session. The inmate apologized and it did not happen again. But a union representative told the mediator that the guards were distressed at the administration's soft stand, and planned to call more caucuses to take firmer positions. African-American inmates charged that their negotiators were being harassed, and BBCDO refused to come to the table when their key leaders were in D House. But the talks continued, usually for three days every other week.

Progress at the table was noted by an inmate's report on mediation in the inmate newspaper. He said, "Mediation...is a slow and sometimes questioning thing...but there are some competent people on both sides of the table...They are starting to acknowledge us as people, which is something kind of new around here...we are in the middle of an evolutional change; we are turning into people".

The goodwill built during the opening rounds held the parties in good stead when they came to the more difficult issues raised by the culture groups. Culture group meeting times had been reduced by 30 minutes, to three hours a week, due to a lack of money for overtime pay. The inmates asked the Superintendent to change the work shift by an hour in order to avoid the need for overtime. Union members objected, pointing out a clause in their contract which precluded a change of working hours solely to avoid overtime pay. But it was agreed to restore 15 minutes, until 8:45 pm, provided the inmates took responsibility for getting back to their cells in time for the 9:00 pm head count. BBCDO and its advisors brought in an expert to challenge the behavior modification system used to reward inmates in the disciplinary unit. The administration made few concessions, but everyone at the table gained a better insight into the painful choices imposed on inmates when they had to decide whether to use D House honor points to call their mothers, take a shower, or obtain an earlier release date from the unit. Everyone agreed with BBCDO's contention that there was racial discrimination in the disciplinary process. The Ombudsman was commissioned to conduct a case review, but no individual violations were cited. Further discussion resulted in the Superintendent agreeing to have an African-American custody officer, who was respected by the inmates, investigate all disciplinary actions for signs of racism. He would also investigate complaints of discrimination. In addition, the administration agreed to seek funding for race relations training for all staff and give culture groups an opportunity to meet with new hirees during their orientation period.

Many outside advisors were present for the heated and lengthy discussions about the mini-prison proposal. Not only would ethnic concentrations of inmates be dispersed into the general population, but also culture groups and other institution-wide group activities would be terminated. The culture groups said they would be isolated from their own members. The Native-American inmates pressed for their own cell house. BBCDO proposed an open house in which anyone could reside. The administration insisted upon unit programming, but made a critical concession:

> "As the result of these discussions, the importance of culture groups has been brought home", the Superintendent said. "If we do move into the mini-prison plan, the culture groups can continue meeting across cell house lines." The Minneapolis Tribune later reported that "whites who in the past have sometimes said so-called 'culture groups' received preferential treatment...said that the culture groups are important for other races to preserve their heritage".

In late September, the agenda turned to the inmate request for an Inmate-Staff Advisory Council. Discussion of the issue was conducted over six days. The administration backed down from its opposition to the plan, and proposed a separate Council for each cell house. The culture groups called the proposal divisive and said that they would not participate. After a long caucus, the administration agreed to a single Council, but reserved the right to abolish it later. Two days were spent working out details for the selection of Council members. The agreement included a strong statement recognizing that racial minorities at St. Cloud had needs for special representation. In addition to inmate representation from the culture groups and the general population of the four regular cell houses, administrators agreed to have one inmate on the Council who would represent the interests of the disciplinary unit inmates. Only delegates from the Italian-American culture group objected to this outcome. They had no representation. When challenged to provide a rationale for special consideration, they acknowledged that there was none, and voluntarily withdrew from mediation.

The final week was among the most difficult. The Native-American culture group made a cogent plea for an inmate-to-inmate counselling program, one in which designated inmates could leave their cells, under supervision, whenever they were called upon by a member of their group who was having an emotional crisis. The union opposed the plan because it would encroach on staff jobs. Inmate negotiators were unaware that the Superintendent had promised the union that he would not yield on this issue.

Arguing that "only a brother can counsel an inmate", an angry Native-American leader insisted that, "if inmate counselling had been available, we could have prevented that suicide from occurring". The administration stood fast without addressing the merits of the proposal. "We cannot have staff taking orders from inmates", the Superintendent insisted. "Decisions on counselling must be remain with staff." The door was shut. "This is the only issue we really cared about", the Native-American leader declared. "And it is the only one where you refuse to come up with a single alternative." The Native-American delegates walked out of mediation and their Mexican-American allies joined them.

Interest in mediation waned before the agenda was completed. Inmate terms at St. Cloud averaged 400 days, and by October some half of the original 32 negotiators had been released, transferred or, in one case, had escaped from the reformatory. The eight-member Mexican-American contingent had been reduced to three. Only one of the original six BBCDO leaders was in the institution. The Native-American and Mexican-American inmates refused to attend the signing ceremony. The following week they expressed their anger with a peaceful sit-down demonstration. The entire group was remanded to the disciplinary unit.

The signed agreement reflected some six months of effort by the people who lived and worked at St. Cloud, both to solve their most pressing problems and to design structures to prevent them from recurring. Several enforcement mechanisms were built into the agreement. First, any matters unresolved during mediation, and concerns about the enforcement of the agreement, would be considered by the Inmate-Staff Advisory Council. If that did not resolve the matter, the Ombudsman's office would review the grievance and report its findings. In addition, the Commissioner of Corrections agreed to include components of the agreement in the Management-by-Objectives (MBO) work plan for high-level staff. Achievement of MBO goals was a criterion for merit pay increases.

Eighteen months later, the mediator met separately with the Superintendent, his Associate, the head of the Native-American Culture Group, the Ombudsman, and some other mediation participants, at the State Capital during a national corrections conference. All talked positively about mediation and its aftermath. There had been no serious racial violence at St. Cloud since the conclusion of mediation. This the administrators attributed to the new mini-prison concept, as well as to mediation. The Inmate-Staff Council was functioning. There were fewer complaints about the disciplinary system, and fewer complaints of discrimination. The leader of the Native-American culture group, soon to be paroled, noted an improved understanding of cultural differences by inmates and staff.

## EPILOGUE

Some 15 years later, the mediator returned to St. Cloud to see whether there were visible signs of the mediation agreement. There had been virtually a complete turnover of inmates. The Superintendent had remained on the job and was now about a year away from retirement. "Yes", he noted, "many of the things in the old agreement are still in place". The culture groups were functioning within a modified mini-prison plan. The canteen committee was still in place and the increased visiting hours were retained, although the space for visitations had been increased. All staff received human relations training and new employees received this at the Academy, as part of their orientation; the agreement to permit inmates to meet with new staff never got off the ground. Nor were funds ever made available for a test kitchen. Inmate servers no longer wore hair nets, but they no longer had long hair. All disciplinary actions continued to be reviewed for signs of discrimination; the reviewing lieutenant was the same African-American officer who undertook the task immediately after mediation. He said that his reviews at times resulted in decisions favoring inmates. The racial disparities in disciplinary actions had been substantially reduced. His perception echoed that of the new Ombudsman: there was racism at St. Cloud, but it was both less severe and more subtle than it was in the mid 1970s.

The Inmate-Staff Advisory Council was meeting on the day of the mediator's visit. That day's agenda included a canteen financial report, planning for a large barbecue funded from the inmate welfare fund, complaints of night shift guards shining flash lights into the eyes of sleeping inmates, a request to replace faulty shower heads, and a request to use money from the inmate fund for sports equipment. There was also a complaint that the dress code, which precluded inmates from wearing symbols of youth gangs, needed clarification. "Why can't we keep 'washed' blue denim jackets if they are sent to us from outside", an inmate asked. "Is that a gang symbol?" The officer chairing the meeting promised to find out, and agreed that inmates had a right to know. He said he would try to obtain a copy of the list of contraband clothes and accessories for the next meeting.

Why did the Superintendent keep the components of the agreement in place, the mediator asked, especially since he was so vehement in his opposition to mediation?

"Was I?", the Superintendent asked "I don't remember that. We keep those things in place because they work for us."

# 29. A STATE INITIATIVE TOWARD RESTORATIVE JUSTICE: THE MINNESOTA EXPERIENCE

by

## Kay Pranis

**Abstract:** *The Minnesota Department of Corrections has created a full-time position to promote and support movement toward a restorative justice approach to the problem of crime. This reform initiative is based on voluntary participation. Strategies for gaining adherents include training, networking interested professionals to one another, and provision of technical assistance at a local level. The efforts of the initiative have resulted in widespread interest among corrections professionals and pockets of interest among other criminal justice professionals. Greater community involvement is a key element in restorative justice; thus, education efforts have extended beyond the criminal justice system. Challenges for achieving the vision of restorative justice include a system oriented toward punishment, staff feeling overwhelmed, opposition from some victims groups, the risk that the approach will not be applied uniformly and will thus benefit only some groups, and implementation that fails to reflect underlying restorative justice values.*

The American criminal justice system is in a state of crisis. The public is frightened and angry. Practitioners are weary and frustrated. Criminal justice policy is driven more by anecdote than by systematic information. Costs of current policies are not sustainable over long periods of time. Victims are often revictimized in the process. This widespread sense of dissatisfaction has given rise to a fundamental rethinking of the criminal justice system, and the formulation of an alternative approach to criminal justice, called restorative justice. Concerned individuals have been working to develop the theory and practice of restorative justice for over a decade, but these efforts have left the mainstream of criminal justice practice largely unaffected. The potential for restorative practices to transform criminal justice can only be realized if the practices move from the periphery to the mainstream. A state-wide attempt to achieve that shift is under way in Minnesota. In November, 1993, the Minnesota Department of Corrections (DOC) established a full-time position to promote restorative justice and to assist jurisdictions interested in implementing restorative approaches. Support by the state corrections agency has taken discussions of restorative justice from the periphery to the center across the State of Minnesota. The discussion in Minnesota has moved beyond corrections and court staff to involve victim service providers, law enforcement, educators, citizens, clergy, and policymakers at both state and local levels.

The purpose of this chapter is to identify the core values of the restorative justice framework being promoted in Minnesota, to specify the guiding principles that underlie efforts to secure the greater use of restorative values across the state, and to describe actual experience in this endeavor. There has been no blueprint to describe the path of the Minnesota initiative, but there is a clear set of principles identifying what the state means by the term restorative justice, and the way in which the state corrections agency encourages greater use of those principles in criminal justice practice.

## CORE VALUES, GUIDELINES AND PRINCIPLES

The core values of the restorative framework can be contrasted with the fundamental assumptions of the predominant retributive criminal justice model, as characterized by the following beliefs (Pranis, 1993):

| Assumption of the Retributive Justice Model | Assumptions of the Restorative Justice Model |
| --- | --- |
| 1. Crime is defined as an act against the state. A crime is a violation of a law, an abstract concept. | 1. Crime is defined as an act against another person and the community. Crime is an injury which violates personal and community harmony. |
| 2. The offender is accountable to the state for the crime. As a result, the state and the offender are in an adversarial relationship. The | 2. The offender is accountable to the victim and the community. The state has the responsibility to ensure that the offender is held |

tremendous power of the state in this relationship makes it necessary to protect the offender through a system of rights.

accountable to the victim and community and that the process of accountability is fair.

3. The threat of punishment deters crime and the execution of punishment changes behavior.

3. Offenders may experience suffering in the process of taking responsibility and repairing harm, but not as the primary means to impact their behavior.

4. Accountability is equated to suffering. If offenders have been punished, made to suffer, they have been held accountable. The outcomes of the system are measured by how much punishment was inflicted.

4. Accountability is defined as taking responsibility for behaviors and taking action to repair harm resulting from those behaviors. The outcomes of the system are measured by how much reparation was achieved.

5. Victims are peripheral to the process of responding to and resolving the criminal incident.

5. Victims and community have a key role to play in the process of resolving the crime.

6. The offender is defined by deficits and the victim is defined by material and psychological losses.

6. Offenders are defined by their behavior and by the capacity to take responsibility for their actions and take action to make reparation. Victims are defined by the losses and by the capacity to participate in the process of recovering losses and to begin healing.

7. Crime is entirely the result of individual choices with individual responsibility.

7. Crime has both individual and social dimensions. Offenders are accountable for their individual choices and communities are accountable for supporting victims, making it possible for offenders to make reparation, and for addressing the conditions which contribute to crime.

| 8. The criminal justice system plays a major role in controlling the level of crime. | 8. The criminal justice system can respond to crime and help repair the harm done, but can have only marginal impact on the level of crime. Crime control is a shared responsibility of the individual, the community and the state and is most effectively achieved through prevention efforts which increase social connections to conventional community members, increase individual competencies, and build the capacity of neighborhood institutions to meet the needs of residents. |

Restorative justice is not a program or a specific set of programs; it is a way of thinking about how to approach the problem of responding to crime, and a set of values that guide decisions on policy, programs, and practice. Restorative justice is based on a redefinition of crime as injury to the victim and community, rather than an affront to the power of the state. The primary purpose of the criminal justice system in the restorative model is to repair the harm done by the crime to whatever degree possible. Victim involvement is essential to define the harm done by the crime and to identify how the harm might be repaired. A comprehensive restorative response to crime begins to engage the community as a resource for reintegration of victims and offenders, and as a resource for monitoring and enforcing community standards of behavior. A restorative response to crime is a community-building response.

## BENCHMARKS FOR PROGRESS

The philosophical foundation guided the development of a set of benchmarks for assessing the level of restorative interventions existing in a system, and the direction for working toward a more restorative system. Most systems, although largely retributive, operate with some restorative components. The benchmarks for identifying the current level of restorative practice and opportunity for improvement are the extent of:

1. services available for victims;
2. victim opportunity for involvement and input;
3. offender opportunity and encouragement to take responsibility;

4. offender involvement in repair of the harm;
5. efforts to increase offender competency;
6. active involvement of community members in decision making and implementation; and
7. the use of processes which build connections among community members.

Efforts by a state agency to stimulate change toward the restorative paradigm present particular challenges. The restorative justice framework calls for inclusion of all stakeholders, especially victims and community members, in designing and implementing local practice. It is an empowerment model which must clearly be grounded in grassroots commitment at a local level. State agencies are not typically oriented toward grassroots participation. Corrections agencies are generally very hierarchal organizations. Restorative justice is based on participatory decision making, from individual cases to system design. The state is challenged to provide leadership while not usurping local power, just as local jurisdictions are challenged to operate without usurping individual power. The state must model the values of restorative justice in its process by providing vision and encouragement, but avoiding specific directives. There is an inherent tension between the desire by stakeholders for details of implementation to understand the framework, and the need for the state to leave details of implementation to local stakeholders. Corrections practitioners often became impatient with philosophy and just want to be told what to do. The question of 'how to' was turned back to the practitioners, asking them to apply the principles and to identify practices which fit these principles. Feedback from corrections practitioners became the basis for providing multiple examples of restorative practice, but the state initiative has resisted developing a detailed plan for a restorative system, because that might supplant the development of a local plan based on local needs and resources.

The shift represented by restorative justice is part of a larger shift in social institutions, from power-based structures and practices to relationship-based structures and practices. Community-based policing, for example, is based on building community relationships and using proactive problem solving, instead of brute force responses designed to demonstrate power over others. The field of social services is struggling to shift from a deficit model, in which a beneficent outside power rescues an individual or a community from weaknesses, to a capacity building model, in which individuals or communities rescue themselves, based on their own strengths and relationships in the community. The total quality management transformation in business and industry is fundamentally a shift from motivating workers, based on fear and power over them, to motivating workers, based on relationships and an opportunity to shape their own work lives. In the legal field, the movement toward greater use of alternative dispute resolution processes rather than courts, represents a similar shift from reliance upon the power and authority of the abstract law to reliance upon human relationships and interaction to reach agreement. All these processes give more power to those most directly involved, and decrease reliance on fear of consequences as the primary mechanism of achieving the desired behavior.

Several principles have guided the DOC's efforts to gain greater commitment to restorative justice values around the state:

1. Special outreach efforts to victim groups are important because victims have historically been left out of the criminal justice process, and many are skeptical that an initiative of the state bureaucracy for offenders can genuinely have victim interests at its center. An unwavering commitment to involve victims, despite obstacles which may be encountered, is critical to ensure that the outcomes are genuinely restorative.

2. Restorative justice must not be mandated by state government.

3. The work of operationalizing the principles of restorative justice must be done at a local level and must involve all stakeholders.

4. The appropriate role of the state is to articulate the vision, disseminate information, provide support and technical assistance to jurisdictions, implement pilot programs within its direct service operations, and monitor outcomes.

5. The process of implementing restorative approaches must model the principles themselves; victims must have a voice, and the community must be involved.

6. A clear understanding by practitioners of the philosophical underpinnings of the approach is essential to ensure that changes are substantive and not merely cosmetic.

7. Every criminal justice professional has opportunities within his or her span of control on the job to make changes toward a more restorative vision, even without major system change.

8. There are natural allies both inside and outside criminal justice who can bring depth and credibility to the advocacy of a restorative approach.

9. Energy is most effectively expended by working with those who are interested in trying restorative approaches. Results will convince skeptics more readily than direct persuasion; very few resources in the Minnesota initiative have been expended in trying to convert non-believers.

10. There is no single road map or blueprint for building a restorative system.

11. A feedback loop between the state effort and local efforts is very important.

12. Answers are not available to all the questions raised by the principles of restorative justice. The process of searching for answers should involve dialogue with all who have an interest in the question.

13. Be prepared to make mistakes.

## PUTTING THE PRINCIPLES INTO PRACTICE

The work of promoting and supporting the use of restorative practices in criminal justice in Minnesota is carried out across multiple systems. Corrections in the community is delivered through three different structures, each with different relationships to the DOC. Some probation and supervised release agents are employees of the DOC. The majority, however, are county employees and are not under the direct supervision of the DOC. In addition, the restorative justice initiative works actively with the police, judges, prosecutors, and defense lawyers. Progress toward a restorative approach requires engaging voluntary participation and interest. The state initiative has involved all levels of government (state, county, city) and multiple sectors of the community (schools, civic organizations, faith communities). The initiative efforts have been widely distributed and have been guided more by opportunity than by detailed action plans. The initiative attempts to build the capacity at all levels to think about criminal justice issues from a restorative perspective. Education about restorative justice is the primary strategy. Secondary strategies include linking people with common interests and complementary strengths, and engaging community leaders in discussions about creating safe communities. The initiative also provides support for systems attempting to implement specific restorative practices. Strategies for technical support include providing feedback on proposals, identifying expert resources for additional feedback, providing forums for collegial interaction, and maintaining a resource library.

Changes were evident at the end of the first year of the initiative. Most community-based corrections practitioners in Minnesota have been introduced to the restorative justice framework and many of them are exploring ways to implement the concepts of restorative justice in their daily work. Several innovative new community-based programs have been designed, based on the principles of restorative justice. Several jurisdictions have begun to engage the broader community in the discussion of restorative justice. Knowledge of restorative justice has been incorporated as an expectation in the hiring and promotion process for some positions in the Department of Corrections (DOC). The DOC Academy, for all new correctional officers and field service agents, includes a session on restorative justice.

Change is also apparent outside corrections. The Lt. Governor has identified restorative justice as an area of interest, and has convened a group of legislators to discuss the topic. Restorative justice has been included as a topic in a law enforcement training and at a major conference for law enforcement professionals. Restorative justice was included in training for new judges in Hennepin County. Department of Education officials have expressed an interest in linking the work on restorative justice with initiatives on violence prevention and service learning. Several newspaper articles have appeared. Three case examples illustrate the activities of the initiative in work with DOC employees, non-DOC corrections employees, and professionals outside corrections.

The DOC district supervisor of field services in Bemidji, MN, and the regional supervisor of Sentencing to Service, a DOC offender work crew program, requested assistance in the development of a new community-based program built on restorative justice principles. The restorative justice planner provided consultation to the team of supervisors for designing the new program, discussed the concept of the new program with national experts to get feedback on the viability of the approach, found theoretical work which supported key components of the program, and assisted in writing a grant for a pilot project. Staff in the Bemidji office began a broad community education effort, and made arrangements for the restorative justice planner to speak to the advisory board of the Sentencing to Service program and the county anti-violence committee, which included representatives from schools, human services, victim services, the clergy, courts, and local policymakers. The restorative justice planner was the main speaker at the annual campus community breakfast at the local state university. A lengthy article in the local newspaper extended the education beyond those attending the breakfast. By speaking to local groups, the restorative justice planner was able to provide legitimacy for the new initiatives and helped to build support for those efforts. The supervisors had been requested by the judges to develop an assessment process to determine the level of restorative practice in the thirteen counties of the judicial district. The restorative justice planner is working with them to draft an assessment tool. Information was also provided to the state university staff concerning local and national resources for the creation of a campus/community mediation program.

Court services in Carver and Scott counties are under the leadership of one director, who is not under supervision of the Department of Corrections. The director has organized advisory groups in both counties. The director arranged for the restorative justice planner to provide a presentation to each advisory group. Then, under the sponsorship of the advisory groups, a three-hour seminar for 125 key community leaders and criminal justice system professionals was held. The restorative justice planner provided assistance in planning the seminar, recruiting a national keynote speaker, and coordinating the program. The seminar provided education about restorative justice and enlisted support among key community leaders. The restorative justice planner conducted training with the corrections staff of the two counties, and helped them to identify current practice that is restorative and opportunities for expansion of restorative practice. A minister, who attended the community seminar, requested assistance in organizing a training for clergy and was provided with a program format, speakers, a video, and handouts for that training. Articles and draft papers have been provided to staff in Carver and Scott counties to support new program development in a restorative framework. The restorative justice planner contacted the school liaison officer at the Carver County Sheriff's Department and the director of the Carver Scott Coop Center, an alternative education institution, to encourage the development of a pilot project using family group conferencing. Subsequently, the school liaison officer and a probation agent from court services attended a three-day training on conferencing. The restorative justice planner will be providing support to them as they implement a pilot project involving the school, law enforcement, and court services. The restorative justice initiative is working with staff from the

Coop Center and the State Department of Education to explore further ways to integrate service learning and community service as a part of community accountability for juvenile offenders.

The work of the DOC's restorative justice initiative is not confined to corrections or to court personnel. Links with law enforcement have been forged through collaboration with the Bureau of Criminal Apprehension (BCA). There are clear parallels between the philosophy of community-oriented policing and the restorative justice framework. One of the responsibilities of the BCA is state-wide training for police. The restorative justice planner first networked with a BCA staff, who is also a member of a victims' advisory council. Material about restorative justice was shared and common agendas discussed. The staff member then shared this information with the staff responsible for organizing training on school violence for law enforcement, and with school personnel who designed the training around the restorative justice framework. In addition to incorporating a presentation on restorative justice, she encouraged speakers on other topics to read background material and make connections to restorative justice in their presentations. The director of the training unit at BCA attended the training and became familiar with the restorative justice framework. Information about family group conferencing was shared. The training unit staff were linked with others in the field who were interested in exploring this model. The training unit staff were also identified as key people in advancing restorative justice, and were invited to participate in a think tank originally convened by the Wilder Foundation. BCA staff have involved the restorative justice initiative in the cosponsorship and planning of the annual conference of the Minnesota Association of Women Police. The first day of that conference focused on restorative justice.

Most of the activities of the restorative justice planner are in the areas of identifying the most likely allies, providing them with information, linking interested persons with one another, maintaining a high level of enthusiasm, and providing support and encouragement for taking risks with new ideas. That process leaves room for individual professionals and community members to exercise their own creativity and power in working for change. Many practitioners and many community members want to act in a more restorative way, but have lacked a clearly articulated vision and permission to pursue that vision. One of the most gratifying aspects of the effort in Minnesota is the rejuvenation of career probation agents, at a time when corrections professionals are generally under siege.

## CHALLENGES AND OBSTACLES TO RESTORATIVE REFORM

The DOC supports the restorative philosophy, but policy in Minnesota, as in the entire nation, is moving in the opposite direction. Prison populations are growing rapidly, and the cost of that expansion threatens the availability of resources to work with victims and offenders in the community. Increasing dependence on incarceration may paralyze the system, making change even more difficult. Practitioners are frequently so overloaded that it is difficult for them to think about questions of underlying values or philosophy. There is also a great risk that the existing system, with its overwhelming orientation to offenders, will be unable to shift to a more victim-centered approach for resolving crime. The habits of the system are strong. Even in jurisdictions committed to shifting to restorative justice, corrections practitioners frequently forget to involve victim representatives in their planning at the beginning. Victims groups in Minnesota vary in their reaction to restorative justice. Some see potential for a much better system for victims; some are watching and withholding judgment; some are adamantly opposed, believing that in the process of implementation distortions of the philosophy will result in practices which are harmful to victims. They fear that the system will use victims to rehabilitate offenders, or that the court will order restorative activities without asking victims what they want. Even if asked, they fear that victims may not feel free to express their real feelings. There is a risk that a restorative approach might be unevenly applied, benefitting some racial or ethnic groups, but not others. Such an outcome would be exactly the opposite of the intention of the restorative justice initiative. Overseeing by the state is important to minimize the likelihood of biased results. The greatest risks involve implementation which fails to be true to the values underlying restorative justice. It is crucial that the values be clearly understood and frequently articulated, in order to guard against the dangers of straying from them in practice.

The restorative justice effort in Minnesota has gained momentum and has the potential to reshape the criminal justice system in the state. The approach is widely accepted in the corrections community; the initiative must now focus on other links in the system: prosecutors, defense lawyers, and judges. Research is needed to identify ways for the community to be more involved in both system decision making and working with victims and offenders. Engagement of the community in affirming and maintaining community standards is central to the success of restorative approach within the criminal justice system. A more systematic manner of victim involvement must be devised at both the state and the local level. As new practices are developed, the initiative needs to help develop tasks for measurement, assessment and evaluation.

## REFERENCES

Pranis, K. (1993). "Restorative Justice: Back to the Future in Criminal Justice." Working paper, Minnesota Citizens Council on Crime and Justice, Minneapolis, MN.

# 30. TOWARDS A RESTORATIVE JUSTICE FUTURE

## by
## Alan Harland

**Abstract:** *Whether restorative justice will in the future occupy more than its currently marginal role will depend significantly on the ability of its proponents to market it effectively to policymakers with authority to risk innovation in the administration of justice. This chapter outlines the likely concerns to which a marketing strategy of this type must be responsive, ranging from the clarification of goals and principles to the specification of processes and expected outcomes. It raises specific questions that restorative justice advocates may anticipate in each of these areas, suggests the need for a glossary of central terms and a compatibility index/ inventory that assesses each component of the criminal justice system on the degree to which it incorporates or departs from restorative justice ideals.*

The future of the restorative justice movement can be considered on several different fronts. First, one can proceed at a normative level, by asking which of the various principles and practices set out by the contributors to this book ought to play a significant role in shaping the future of criminal justice. What are the most central and most consistently touted ingredients of the restorative justice approach? A second level is more pragmatic in focus, asking what challenges must be met by its advocates in order to ensure that restorative justice might play such a role. Attention here shifts to the drawbacks and obstacles that must be addressed if it is to assume more than its current, very marginal, place in the administration of criminal justice. The third way involves predicting what its impact in all likelihood will be, in light of answers to the first two levels of inquiry.

One relatively recent development that might influence the future is the growth in attention in criminal justice to the need for a system-wide assessment, systematic policy and program planning as a way of escaping the frustrating failure of band-aid remedies and fragmented, crisis-oriented, responses to the many chronic problems, such as prison crowding, reoffence rates, burgeoning costs, and so forth (Harland 1991). In the U.S., for example, concerned criminal justice, political, and community leaders in a growing number of jurisdictions are working within teams, such as county and state, to coordinate committees to define and respond systematically to the most pressing problems confronting their criminal justice systems as a whole (McGarry and Carter, 1993). Such groups provide an unusually receptive forum for advocates of change to make the best arguments for their particular cause.

A useful way of gauging the future of restorative justice might be for proponents to imagine themselves with an opportunity to make their best case in a dialogue with a policy development and planning group. In preparation, it would be essential to crystallize answers to the most likely questions that the open, but often skeptical, participants in such a forum might raise. Policy development and planning groups are likely to demand clarification on several issues, before being persuaded that restorative justice ideas might be worth exploration and trial. The future of restorative justice depends to a large degree on the ability of its proponents to rise to the challenge, and to provide answers and present them as succinctly and convincingly as possible.

Dialogue in the hypothetical forum will probably consist of variants upon the general theme of "What are you trying to sell us, and why should we buy it?" Key actors must first be sure that they are defining the problem in similar ways before a collaborative change agenda can be agreed upon. As representatives of the status quo, they might ask whether (Covey 1989):

a. they are not doing the right things—a leadership problem of prioritizing the wrong goals; and/or

b. they are not doing things right—a management problem of inefficiency, ineffectiveness, and/or unfairness in process and outcomes.

Whether the ensuing dialogue concerns differences in goals and goal-priorities or in processes and outcomes, proponents of restorative justice still face at least two types of challenge. The first is to reconcile apparent differences within the ranks of its supporters. The second is to define and clarify the most essential aims and related mechanisms, beginning with restoration itself, but including others such as reconciliation, reparation to the community, mediation, circle sentencing, and so on. There often appears to be a broader consensus about the importance of these concepts than about their precise meaning.

## QUESTIONS ABOUT GOALS AND PRINCIPLES

## Crime Control

As an example of the consistency issue, Van Ness (this volume) states that "the overarching aim of the criminal justice process should be to reconcile parties while repairing injuries caused by crime". From Bazemore (this volume), however, we read that "restorative justice has as its primary objective reparation of harm done to victims...", but elsewhere that it "would give first priority to community and victim needs for safety and security and would take whatever actions are necessary to minimize risk to citizens, including confinement of offenders who pose a threat to others". Obviously, focus on public safety and risk management goals is less likely to encounter opposition than the others, although questions might surface about the role of general deterrence to this end, given the uncertainty that Immarigeon (this volume) notes in the role of punishment in a restorative justice system. Restorative justice may have something new to add by way of innovative processes for achieving public safety, such as Stuart's (this volume) description of the community-based preventive measures that can be generated via the Circle Sentencing process and the lessons from Japan in Haley's (this volume) chapter. Its centrality, as a goal, however, will be the reassurance sought by forum members.

## Reparation to Victims

Although unlikely to provoke little argument as a goal, *per se*, the difficulty for restorative justice advocates is overcoming doubts that reparation to victims can or should take priority over the more traditional mindsets of criminal justice practitioners. This will be especially true for prosecutors and judges, who see themselves as standard-bearers in a moral crusade to ensure the infliction of appropriately harsh measures of retributively required pain and suffering, or as the true public defenders, whose primary concern it is to protect society from recidivistic offenders through rehabilitation, incapacitation, and specific deterrence, and similarly inclined other individuals in the general population through general deterrence. Despite the prominence given to criticizing retribution in the restorative justice literature, many criminal justice professionals are like members of the public whose interest in retribution may be far less than often assumed (Gottfredson *et al.*, 1988), and may be satisfied *de facto* in many cases by dispositions that are reasonably designed to meet reparative and public safety concerns. If so, perceptions of conflict between restorative justice and utilitarian crime reduction priorities may be more problematic that between reparation and retribution.

Reparation also illustrates the importance of definitional clarity to the success of the hypothetical dialogue. The hurdle here is probably less intractable than the priorities issue, and stems from the widespread tacit acceptance of a very limited, out-of-pocket financial-loss notion of reparation in criminal courts. Extending it to include more adequate attention to the emotional injuries of victims, emphasized so emphatically by Netzig and Trenczek [wiedergutmachung] and others throughout this volume, seems less likely to raise objections at the level of principle than in terms of the practicalities of mediation and other methods of assessing quantum, and dealing with the limited financial and other resources of many offenders (Harland and Rosen, 1990).

## Reparation to the Community

When this is the issue, as opposed to individual victims, advocates face more fundamental challenges. If the restorative justice wisdom is to be widely accepted—viewing crime as an injury to personal relationships requiring a focus on direct victims, rather than as an offence against the state or society—participants in the test-marketing forum may be somewhat curious about being asked simultaneously to embrace what may seem to them equally abstract notions of harm-to community, and community-as-victim. The term "community" lends itself to a variety of defining criteria, ranging from geographic boundaries, to membership of a family, professional, or social group (Taylor, 1995). The term "harm is" probably susceptible to even more diverse interpretations (Feinberg, 1984). Other questions that advocates of this formulation might face include: does this mean that you would abolish the difference between criminal and civil liability? Or that you would decriminalize so-called victimless crimes such as drug use/possession and prostitution?

One of the advantages of the focus on direct victims' injuries is the linkage limitation (between injury and repair) it imposes on justice authorities to justify their sanctioning choices. Care must be exercised that the potential ambiguity of ideas such as harm and reparation to the community does not sabotage reparative intentions, by serving as an excuse to continue the same old poorly rationalized and vaguely calibrated doses of punishment that criminal justice decision-makers have become accustomed to dispense in the name of exacting what is due to other abstractions, such as society and the state. If holding offenders accountable for harm to an amorphous community is interpreted as just another way of making offenders pay retributively, rather than reparatively, it is likely to become as meaningless or as widely abused and corrupted to repressive ends as the notion of paying one's debt to society has been in the past (Bedau, 1977). A prime example might be the co-optation of community service sentences as an addition to the system's punishment arsenal, as simply another way of making offenders pay in the sense of making them suffer via involuntary penal servitude for their crimes. Similar concerns might be voiced about the risk of piling on offenders an array of costs, fees, and fines, designed to generate revenues to support a retributive *status quo*, but rationalized as reparative obligations to the system.

## Reconciliation

This is probably among the least intuitively marketable parts of the restorative justice goals package. Perhaps, due to its close identity with domestic assaults and divorce law, advocates may anticipate probable skepticism and misunderstanding about its broader significance and applicability in criminal cases. Advocates must be well prepared to define the concept and to answer inevitable questions about, for example, its meaning in stranger crimes, and crimes of violence, such as rape, to dispel notions that reconciliation is only something that makes sense in the minor types of dispute between neighbors and family members that so frequently appear in victim-offender reconciliation program newsletters and other accounts of mediation programs. Can some offenses be so serious as to foreclose the possibility entirely, perhaps taking offenders outside the community irrevocably? And how does reconciliation apply to offenders who do not acknowledge guilt, much less express remorse?

# Restoration

The very notion of restoration is a multi-faceted concept, and one that is essential to communicate well to key stakeholders whose buy-in will be central to shaping the future of restorative justice. Particular care must be devoted to the fullest development of this entry in the *glossary of central terms* that its advocates would do well to prepare. The potential for misperceptions and opposition, due to the complexity of the reparative elements of restoration as they apply to victims and the community, pales in comparison to the idea of restoring offenders. Unless well-explained, restoration as it relates to *offenders* is likely to engender skepticism, if not hostile derision, from some quarters. The danger is especially present if its ideological foes can dismiss it as being soft on crime, or suffering from similar political and popular impediments to change, including:

- It is simply the same old unsuccessful liberal reintegration and rehabilitation approach to coddling criminals.
- It is not tough enough on crime, as evidenced by its:
    - advocacy of a caring posture towards offenders;
    - focus on social justice, prevention, and institutional causes and collective responsibility for crime, diverting attention from where it belongs—blaming and punishing offenders;
    - unwillingness to condemn offenders along with their criminal behavior;
    - undermining the moral and practical legitimacy of retributive policies (are Von Hirsch [1976] and other retributivists totally wrong?); and
    - identity with various radical and/or fringe elements, such as religious do-gooders, peace-and-love types, feminists, indigenous peoples' rights groups, their politically correct academic supporters, and so forth.

The irony here is that some features of restorative justice that should be its strongest and most refreshing selling points can become easy targets for these kinds of attacks. The often mindless nature of such reactions should not be taken as an excuse to underestimate their potentially devastating political impact, and the corresponding need to craft thoughtful and compelling pre-emptive counterpoints. The value of a more balanced approach might seem to be self-evidently desirable in almost any undertaking. Such an assumption, however, would be a serious tactical error in a political climate in which anything seen as remotely pro-offender is suspect, however ludicrously, of being automatically anti-victim. The logical and empirical arguments in support of a caring approach to offenders must be constantly rehearsed and carefully packaged if they are to compete with the more familiar triumvirate of disinterested indignation, intolerance, and disgust (Hart, 1959), and the politics of exclusion and divisiveness that more typically seem to fuel criminal justice and other governmental policy debates in recent years. Finally, the perception that it is not the business of the criminal justice system to try to right the underlying social and cultural wrongs that maintain and encourage the existence of a stable and visible class of criminals is both deeply ingrained and a convenient excuse for its abject failure to reduce crime (Reiman, 1995). Thus, different references throughout this book to the importance of community responsibility, and of direct involvement in responding to both the needs of parties affected by the instant offence, and the broader underlying causes that might minimize the probability of its reoccurrence, must also be made as concrete as possible, whether by powerful illustration or by other means. Otherwise, this exciting aspect of the restorative justice case will remain vulnerable to facile diversionary contrasts with the American ethos of rugged individualism and antipathy towards almost any idea that can be tarred with the brush of socialistic sentiment.

## Additional Questions

Additional questions are likely to emerge along a variety of other goal-related dimensions, including:

### Equity

The high value placed on the individualized disposition of cases, and upon the flexibility of processes such as Circle Sentencing and different forms of victim-offender mediation, raises the issue of standards and other mechanisms by which undue disparity and discrimination may be avoided, and the principles of equity upheld in a restorative justice scheme. Similar questions should be anticipated over inequities potentially stemming from victims' exercise of veto power over offenders' access to mediated dispositions, as well as over the potential for discrimination on economic grounds because of the importance ascribed to financial restitution in decisions to resolve cases informally.

## Costs

Any policy group in a position to implement change in the administration of criminal justice is likely to ask whether it is congruent with cost-containment goals and related efficiency concerns. Responses to cost questions will depend on the particular process or practice being discussed. Care must be taken, however, to avoid selling restorative justice as a cheaper option. Although it is reasonable and important to document any likely savings attributable to, say, its diversionary effect on prosecution and correctional caseloads, McCold, Stuart, and Wright, respectively (this volume) point out that restorative justice will not be a complete alternative to more traditional and formal processes. Consequently, questions remain as to when and how it should replace or supplement existing arrangements, and at what potential cost savings or increase. At a minimum, some measure of credibility may be bought by a proactive accounting and heightened justification of aspects of the new approach that are most likely to *increase* demands of time and resources, such as the need cited by Pranis (this volume) for extensive training of mediation personnel, and the appointment of other specialized restorative justice personnel.

## Public and Professional Satisfaction

As with costs, concerns about "how is it likely to be received by the public, my staff, my peers?" are never far from our minds in any public policy dialogue. On this issue, whether as a prelude to measurement or to developing strategies to optimize results, advocates of restorative justice must be careful to distinguish between ways in which it is likely to be perceived by victims and other participants, versus those not directly involved, whose opinions are shaped by the popular media, education, and so forth. Early anticipation and documentation of areas that may be less readily understood and/or supported, provides important information about ways in which restorative justice advocates might strengthen their positions, via better communication strategies and/or modifications to the particular policy or practice involved. Of immediate concern, for example, might be the apparent unwillingness of the majority of victims to participate in mediation in the programs evaluated by Umbreit and others (this volume), and the relatively low level of support for mediation among the broader public noted by Lee.

## Fear of Crime

With the exception of isolated examples, such as certain victim programs and community policing, both of which are compatible with the principles of restorative justice, reducing fear of crime is rarely even mentioned among the traditional system's goals. Consequently, to the extent that it is featured as an important benefit of restorative justice processes, proponents have a potentially important marketing edge and at least a couple of natural allies. Proponents would do well to draw more pointedly on the extensive fear-of-crime literature (Baumer, 1978; Gomme, 1986) to emphasize the significance attached by experts in the area to this goal, as an important aim, independent of reducing crime itself. In addition, although the mechanisms for reducing fear among victims who participate, say, in mediation sessions, are intuitively obvious and, to some extent, empirically demonstrated by Umbreit (this volume), the case has not been made nearly so clearly as to how and why fear and its destructive consequences might also be reduced in the broader community. Reductions among actual victims cannot alone offset the determined efforts of politicians and the media to excite and fan the fears of the public as a whole.

## QUESTIONS ABOUT PROCESS AND OUTCOMES

One of the values of this book is the range of options that the contributors describe for putting restorative justice principles into practice. In addition to variations on victim-offender mediation, such as the Family Group Conference and Täter-Opfer-Ausgleich projects in Germany, the reader is exposed to intriguing innovations, such as Circle Sentencing, which in some ways resembles a group-dynamic version of sentence planning programs that are growing out of the sentencing advocacy movement in the U.S. and Canada (Yeager, 1992). It also includes examples of applications at different stages of the criminal justice process, ranging from the familiar pretrial diversion victim-offender mediations, to post-sentencing stages (Flaten [this volume]), including prison (Immarigeon [this volume]) and parole (Harding [this volume]). Expanding the range of options, however, complicates the dialogue with the policymakers responsible for making choices, and increases the information needed to support their decisions.

Advocates articulating their vision of restorative justice must be prepared to address roles and responsibilities of government, victims, offenders, community participants, and practitioners at all stages of the criminal process. What parts need the most urgent reform initially, being most seriously out of line with restorative justice ideals? They will need to be armed with a compatibility index or inventory that assesses each component of the system on the degree to which it incorporates and departs from those ideals. Most elements of the criminal justice enterprise incorporate at least some of these, and identifying them should aid in forging alliances that may help to establish the necessary foothold being sought. In addition to community policing and programs for victims and sentencing advocacy, for example, victims committees formed by correctional organizations such as the American Probation and Parole Association and the American Corrections Association, are beginning to expand their constituencies' awareness of restorative justice issues. Other prospective sources of support and assistance include areas such as dispute resolution and school discipline. One of the potentially more important kindred developments that only appears to have drawn little attention among restorative justice proponents, is the growing body of scholarship and related applications emerging under the heading of therapeutic jurisprudence (Wexler, 1990), that share an emphasis on the importance of process in improving criminal justice and, more extensively, mental health outcomes.

Proponents may expect to field specific questions about the best practice between and within available options: an unenviable task until more detailed descriptive and empirical evaluation evidence is generated. Does mediation become the modal approach for disposing of cases? What kind? What if the offender contests responsibility, or is not remorseful, or the victim refuses? What if the offender appears to need clinical diagnosis and intervention? What about victim safety? Offender due process rights? How is the idea of community involvement operationalized? What residual place is there for traditional criminal justice practitioners and practices? What role remains for prisons, jails, sentencing guidelines, mandatory sentencing, risk/needs instruments, and so forth? And, most critically, what evidence is there that any of the advocated changes will improve upon existing approaches, in terms of crime control, cost reduction, or any of the other major effectiveness, efficiency, and fairness concerns? In particular, if we are to learn from the mistakes of the past, studies explaining failures and problems among attempts to implement restorative justice innovations are just as important as those documenting successes.

# CONCLUSIONS

This sampling of the types of issues that might be anticipated from the participants of the hypothetical test forum does not imply that many of them have not been raised or answered well by the various contributors to this volume. The book is long and broad in its coverage, and its international scope is particularly impressive. What it documents so well, however, is a complex concept and related array of operational possibilities, some controversial, and most still to be rigorously evaluated. Together, they offer markedly different ways of thinking about and doing the business of criminal justice. Broad acceptance of the offer seems unlikely without a strategic plan for organizing and communicating its terms as systematically, concisely, and persuasively as possible to policymakers with the authority to influence change on this scale.

Absenting an official Restorative Justice Society or other obvious candidate from orchestrating such an effort, the chances are remote of any wholesale shift from a criminal justice system that draws much of its strength from the helplessness and dependency it encourages among victims, offenders, and the general public [We'll handle the crime problem for you], to one that seeks to empower them, through greatly expanded roles, responsibilities and levels of participation. Conversely, haphazard changes in the name of restorative justice, without a consistent, information-driven policy framework, are at high risk of being co-opted to ulterior ends. Witness, for example, the popularity of community service sentencing for predominantly retributive purposes, and the law-and-order support for encouraging sentencing opinions in victim impact statements, in the hope that they will lead to harsher punishment of offenders. Left to this pattern of development, rather than challenging the existing system at its core, restorative justice proponents may succeed only in making it more enduring, by making it more endurable.

Two of the ingredients identified by McElrea (this volume) as important to the future of restorative justice are political will and financial resources. Both are in very short supply at the moment. Neither is likely to be forthcoming unless policymakers are systematically engaged in the kind of dialogue outlined here. Their general questions can be summarized straightforwardly as:

What exactly is restorative justice, and in what ways does it most significantly improve upon what we do now?

– In terms of goals and principles?
– In terms of processes and outcomes?
Its future depends to a large degree on the ability of proponents to help come up with equally straightforward answers from the wealth of information in books such as this.

## REFERENCES

Baumer, T. (1978). "Research on the Fear of Crime in the United States." *Victimology* 3:254-274.
Bedau, H. (1977). "Concessions to Retribution in Punishment." In: J. Cederblom and W. Blizek (eds.), *Justice and Punishment.* Cambridge, MA: Ballinger Publishing Co.
Covey, S. (1989). *The Seven Habits of Highly Effective People.* New York, NY: Simon and Schuster.
Feinberg, J. (1984). *Harm to Others: The Moral Limits of the Criminal Law.* New York, NY: Oxford University Press.
Gomme, I. (1986). "Fear of Crime Among Canadians: A Multivariate Analysis." *Journal of Criminal Justice* 14:249-258.
Gottfredson, S., B. Warner and R. Taylor (1988). "Conflict and Consensus about Criminal Justice in Maryland.: In: N. Walker and M. Hough (eds.), *Public Attitudes to Sentencing.* Brookfield, VT: Gower Publishing Co.
Harland, A. (ed.) (1995). *Choosing Correctional Options That Work?: Defining the Demand and Assessing the Supply.* Thousand Oaks, CA: Sage Publications.
Harland, A. (1991). "Jail Crowding and the Process of Criminal Justice Policy Making." *Prison Journal* 71(1):77-92.
Harland, A. and C. Rosen (1990). "Impediments to the Recovery of Restitution by Crime Victims." *Violence and Victims* 5(2):127-140.
Hart, H.L.A. (1959). "Immorality and Treason." *The Listener* (July 30):162-163.
McGarry, P. and M. Carter (eds.) (1993). *The Intermediate Sanctions Handbook: Experiences and Tools for Policymakers.* Washington, DC: Center for Effective Public Policy.
Reiman, J. (1995). *The Rich Get Richer and the Poor Get Prison.* Needham Heights, MA: Allyn and Bacon.
Taylor, R. (1995). "The Impact of Crime on Communities. *Annals* 539: 28-45.
Von Hirsch, A. (1976). *Doing Justice: The Choice of Punishments.* New York, NY: Hill and Wang.
Wexler, D. (ed.) (1990). *Therapeutic Jurisprudence: The Law as a Therapeutic Agent.* Durham, NC: Carolina Press.
Yeager, M. (1992). "Client Specific Planning: A Status Report." *Criminal Justice Abstracts* (Sept):537-549.